# GOETHE AND ZELTER: MUSICAL DIALOGUES

*For Seóirse*

# Goethe and Zelter: Musical Dialogues

LORRAINE BYRNE BODLEY
*National University of Ireland Maynooth*

LONDON AND NEW YORK

First published 2009 by Ashgate Publishing

2 Park Square, Milton Park, Abingdon, Oxon OX14 4RN
711 Third Avenue, New York, NY 10017, USA

*Routledge is an imprint of the Taylor & Francis Group, an informa business*

First issued in paperback 2016

Copyright © Lorraine Byrne Bodley 2009

Lorraine Byrne Bodley has asserted her right under the Copyright, Designs and Patents Act, 1988, to be identified as the author of this work.

All rights reserved. No part of this book may be reprinted or reproduced or utilised in any form or by any electronic, mechanical, or other means, now known or hereafter invented, including photocopying and recording, or in any information storage or retrieval system, without permission in writing from the publishers.

Notice:
Product or corporate names may be trademarks or registered trademarks, and are used only for identification and explanation without intent to infringe.

**British Library Cataloguing in Publication Data**
Bodley, Lorraine Byrne, 1968–
  Goethe and Zelter : musical dialogues
   1. Goethe, Johann Wolfgang von, 1749–1832 – Correspondence 2. Zelter, Carl Friedrich, 1758–1832 – Correspondence 3. Authors, German – 19th century – Correspondence 4. Composers – Germany – Correspondence 5. Music – Germany – 19th century – History and criticism
   I. Title
   831.6

**Library of Congress Cataloging-in-Publication Data**
Bodley, Lorraine Byrne, 1968–
  Goethe and Zelter : musical dialogues / Lorraine Byrne Bodley.
     p. cm.
  Includes bibliographical references and index.
  ISBN 978-0-7546-5520-6 (hardcover : alk. paper)
   1. Goethe, Johann Wolfgang von, 1749–1832–Correspondence. 2. Zelter, Carl Friedrich, 1758–1832–Correspondence. 3.

ML423.G65B63 2008
780.92'243–dc22
[B]

2008050802

ISBN 978-0-7546-5520-6 (hbk)
ISBN 978-1-138-25928-7 (pbk)

# Contents

*Preface* — vii
*Acknowledgements* — ix
*List of Abbreviations* — xiii
*List of Music Examples* — xvii

A Musical Odyssey: Thirty-Five Years of Correspondence between Goethe and Zelter — 1

Section I   Early Years' Correspondence 1796–1814 — 29

Section II   Middle Years' Correspondence 1815–1825 — 179

Section III   Later Years' Correspondence 1826–1832 — 343

*Appendix* — 555
*Bibliography* — 557
*Index* — 569

# Preface

Cold print can be a harsh medium in which to bare all the faults of subjective letters written in the midst of busy active lives. Nuances in the handwriting or in the positioning of postscripts are all lost in the printing; irregularities in Zelter's punctuation, abbreviations and colloquial phrases are to some extent ironed out. Zelter used his literary abilities to further his cause but never laid claim to be a writer. The immediacy and urgency of his letters sometimes did not allow for constructional considerations: he dashed them off and in excitement or annoyance would sometimes make hasty judgements and criticisms that were reconsidered later. Goethe was a professional and disciplined writer whose letters show his ease with and command of words. Being able to consider his reactions and emotions allowed him a greater ease of expression. The character of both letter-writers and their varied sense of style were among the considerations which I had to take account in making this translation.

Anyone engaged in translation, and who has thought about it, knows that a grammatically correct or almost literal translation of any interesting text could well be unfaithful to it. Every good translation is an interpretation of the original text and will thereby contain critical commentary. A good translation must be, at the same time, close and free. The quest for precision is analogous to the quest for certainty and both should be viewed with caution by the translator. I do not suggest that linguistic precision in writing and translation is not something to strive for, but rather that it should not be placed higher than the advancement of the subject.

One may relatively easily find lexical meanings for the words, but it is overridingly important to find the tuning fork that can give the note and pitch of the overall music of the letters. Without some sense of the tenor of the voices, it is impossible to establish the translator's right-of-way into the letters. I was therefore lucky to hear this enabling note straight away, a familiar voice, one that has accompanied me since my years as a doctoral student at University College Dublin, where I developed not only an understanding of Goethe's language, but a fondness for the music and fortitude that characterizes his poetry. Consequently when I came to the task of translating these letters, I found the voice of these letters attractively direct even though the narrative method of letters can, at times, be oblique. Similarly Zelter's deep sense of irony and colloquial German was on my ear from conversations with German friends in Berlin. What I loved in translating this correspondence was a feeling of living in the presence of an understanding that assumes you share an awareness of the perilous nature of life and are yet capable of seeing it steadily and, when necessary, sternly. There is an undeluded quality about Goethe and Zelter's sense of the world which gives these letters immense emotional credibility and allows both men to make general observations about musical life which are grounded in experience. These letters have the cadence and force of earned wisdom, and their cogency and verity is marked, too, by the self-consciousness of two artists convinced that they must labour in their endeavours to produce work of lasting value.

Goethe and Zelter's lives embraced an extraordinary period in music history. In Goethe's first year of life Bach dictated on his deathbed the chorale prelude for organ, *Vor deinen Thron tret ich hiermit* (Before thy throne I now appear, BWV 668a), a work often played after the unfinished fourteenth fugue to conclude performances of the *Art of Fugue* and in the final year of Goethe's life, Berlioz was busy revising the *Symphonie Fantastique* in Italy. In order to translate the complete musical correspondence that these lives embraced, omissions had to be made: with reluctance I passed over engaging philosophical and literary debates, which show Zelter as a man of gusto and quick apprehensions, and omitted closing salutations which capture the tenor of an extraordinary friendship. Such sacrifices had to be omitted in order to unveil through music solidarities that are democratic and a discipline that is traditional and solitary – as many an artistic discipline sooner or later becomes, once it has been seriously embraced.

Goethe's engagement with music as a discipline has been called into question not only by scholars but also by the poet himself. Continually in the letters he bemoans the limitations of his musical experience in Weimar, the silence of his piano after his beloved Mendelssohn leaves. In the summer of 1807 (after the death of Anna Amalia) he laments: 'I am, unfortunately, so cut off from music and although we sometimes have really good voices, the little bits of operetta here and there are not enough. And so it seems as if all sound, all song in me has disappeared, and with it all my musical imagination.' For too long scholars have taken such statements at face value without contextualizing them against the broad backdrop of musical experience in Goethe's life: the amelioration of music at the Weimar theatre, whose programme was a macrocosm of contemporary operatic developments, during Goethe's years as artistic director (1791–1817); his delighted reconnaissance of local excellence: Carl Friedrich Abel, Johann Friedrich Armand von Uffenbach and Johann Adam Hiller in Goethe's early years to musicians in Zelter's circle, most notably Felix Mendelssohn, but also Spontini.

Lea Mendelssohn, when she visited the poet in 1822, recognized the potency of Goethe's engagement with music: an opinion Zelter reinforced when he read the preface to Goethe's translation of Diderot's *Neveu de Rameau* and declared 'it really hurt to realize that you know more about the art of music than I do'. While one could write this off as Zelter's veneration of the poet, the truth of Zelter's judgment became evident to me in the translation of the theoretical discussions about music where Zelter's languages buckles as he endeavours to hold in his own in the famous *Molldebatte*, the debate about the nature of the minor mode. Here Goethe shows himself as a writer of unparalleled scope, one who possessed a commanding sense of music in outline and a delicate capacity for eliciting fully-fledged meaning by brooding upon details. By contrast Zelter writes as a practical musician, and though his words buckle and break, there is a definite, unapologetic drive in his letters, a rallying cry that celebrates music for being on the side of life, continuity of effort and enlargement of the spirit.

# Acknowledgements

During the writing of this book there were times when I felt my role as editor was to be the intermediary through whom the suggestions and ideas of many people were channelled; whatever richness or insights this book contains is evidence of the generosity of so many scholars, librarians and friends on both sides of the Atlantic. My thanks are due to Professor Timothy Watkins at the Department of Music, Rhodes College, who invited me to give a lecture at the international Sing-Akademie conference in November 2003 and to Professor Christoph Wolff for his encouragement and warm reception of my paper on that occasion. I was very honoured to be offered the opportunity by Professor Jeremy Adler and Professor Martin Swales of the English Goethe Society to give a guest lecture on this correspondence in King's College London in 2002. I owe both scholars a great deal for their interest in my work and graciousness in publishing my paper in the *Publications of the English Goethe Society*. The substance of these pages was constantly illuminated and invigorated by the example of many fine scholars and dear friends: my greatest debt is to the eminent Schubertian, Professor Susan Youens (J.W. Van Gorkom Professor of Music, University of Notre Dame), whose seminal books continue to shape our understanding of Schubert and nineteenth-century song. For her encouraging belief in the need for this translation and generous endorsement of my work, I am profoundly grateful. Professor Nicholas Boyle (Schroeder Professor of German and President of Magdalene College, Cambridge) occupies a unique place in Goethe scholarship and without his work no one can venture into the study of Goethe, even less into writing about him. My decision to undertake a translation of these letters had his support for which I am immensely grateful. I remember with special pleasure my time as postdoctoral fellow at Trinity College Dublin where I was lucky to enjoy discussions with Professor Moray Mc Gowan (Chair of Germanic Studies and Head of School of Modern Languages) and time worrying about word choices with Professor Jürgen Barkhoff (Registrar of Trinity College Dublin): I warmly salute both men and thank them for their solidarity and example. I am sincerely grateful to a triumvirate of dear friends: Dr Claus Canisius, for his penetrating suggestion of the word 'dialogues' in the title and for his ongoing personal interest – as unfailing as it is unobtrusive – which acts as an inspiration and a stimulus; Professor Harry White (Professor of Music, University College Dublin) who has long been a premier guiding voice in musicology, and to whom I am profoundly grateful for his unwavering support of my research; and the eminent Graham Johnson, whose fine recordings of Zelter's Lieder serve the composer's legacy quite marvellously. Last but by no means least, my warmest thanks to Professor Gerard Gillen: during his time as Professor of Music at the

National University of Ireland Maynooth most of this book was written. Qualities I greatly admire in Zelter – a noble integrity, warmth of personality and lasting contribution to musical life – I find embodied in Gerard two centuries later.

This book required extensive archival research which was facilitated by many helpful librarians. Thanks to the perseverance of the Interlibrary loan staff at Trinity College Dublin and the National University of Ireland, Maynooth, I was able to conduct much of my preliminary research from Dublin and prepare thoroughly for my research trips to Germany. Dr Helmut Hell at the Preußischer Staatsbibliothek in Berlin was always ready to share the holdings of the rich collection of Zelter's manuscripts. Likewise the kindness of the curators at the Goethe and Schiller Archive in Weimar and Klassik Stiftung Weimar (Weimar Cultural Foundation) made exploring the extensive correspondence of Goethe and Zelter one of the most pleasurable research experiences I have had. It is a pleasure to record a depth of thanks to Olaf Molansky at Klassik Siftung Weimar who helped me to track down the cover image of Zelter, and to Karin Ellermann (Goethe- und Schiller Archiv, Weimar) who located and supplied the images for Zelter's musical citations. In addition to such research I must pay tribute to former scholars who have produced editions of these letters, most notably the seminal work of Hans-Günter Ottenberg, Sabine Schäfer and Edith Zehm, whose three volumes *Briefwechsel mit Zelter* in *Goethe Sämtliche Werke nach Epochen seines Schaffens* (Munich: Hanser Verlag, 1985–98) were of invaluable importance. My translation is made always in the knowledge of a considerable debt to these fine scholars for their sterling scholarship and inspiring example.

I warmly acknowledge a deep depth of gratitude to the Irish Research Council for the Humanities and Social Sciences, the organization that provided financial support for this project through a Government of Ireland Post-Doctoral Scholarship. This award allowed me to complete three books while beginning work on this research project. I am especially grateful to the National University of Ireland and to the Publications Committee at the National University of Ireland Maynooth whose support and encouragement of this book proved crucial to its preparation and progress: without their generous publication grants a critical edition of the complete musical correspondence would not have been possible.

Via Ashgate, I benefited greatly from Lorraine Slipper's editorial pencil on the first draft and Emily Ruskell's tact and intelligence in editing the second draft. I am most grateful to them and to Tom Norton, whose generosity with his time and meticulous attention to detail produced a fine index. Particular thanks are due to Ashgate's Music Editor, Heidi Bishop, who graciously guided me through the editorial process on a project that she cordially accepted as taking far longer than anticipated. My third book with Ashgate has given me the same joy as the previous two.

One person in particular has gone out of his way to make this endeavour a pleasure and has greatly enriched my knowledge and my life by his generosity; without his help, the quality of this translation would be greatly diminished. To him, Dr Dan Farrelly, my deepest thanks. Heartfelt thanks to my husband, Seóirse

Bodley, for his advice and help stretching back over many books. He shared every thought, hope and dilemma as I wrote, countered my uncertainties, and was always there for me: *l'amor che move il sole e l'altre stelle.* My final thanks are reserved for my lovely daughter, Bláthnaid, whose affection and receptiveness to everything around her brings immense joy.

Lorraine Byrne Bodley<br>
Dublin, September 2008

# List of Abbreviations

**I Periodicals**

| | |
|---|---|
| *AMZ* | *Allgemeine Musikalische Zeitung* |
| *GJb* | *Goethe Jahrbuch* |
| *GR* | *Germanic Review* |
| *GQ* | *German Quarterly* |
| *JALZ* | *Jenaische Allgemeine Literatur-Zeitung* |
| *JbSK* | *Jahrbuch der Sammlung Kippenberg* |
| *JbDSG* | *Jahrbuch der Deutschen Schillergesellschaft* |
| *ML* | *Music and Letters* |
| *MQ* | *The Music Quarterly* |
| *MR* | *The Music Review* |
| *NCM* | *Nineteenth Century Music* |
| *PEGS* | *Publications of the English Goethe Society* |
| *PMLA* | *Journal of the Modern Language Association of America* |
| *SchGG* | *Schriften der Goethe-Gesellschaft* |

**II Editions**

| | |
|---|---|
| *ADB* | *Allgemeine Deutsche Bibliographie* (56 vols, Leipzig: Duncker and Humblot, 1875–1912). |
| *Goethe HB* | *Goethe Handbuch*, (eds) Bernd Witte, Theo Buck, Hans-Dietrich Dahnke, Regine Otto and Peter Schmidt (4 vols, Stuttgart and Weimar: Metzler Verlag, 1996–99). |
| *Gespräche* | *Goethes Gespräche. Eine Sammlung zeitgenössischer Berichte aus seinem Umgang. Auf Grund der Ausgabe und des Nachlasses von F. Freiherrn von Biedermann.* Completed and edited by Wolfgang Herwig (4 vols, Zürich and Stuttgart: Artemis Verlag, 1965). |
| *GZ* | Goethe's Letters to Zelter. In *J.W. von Goethe. Sämtliche Werke nach Epochen seines Schaffens. Münchner Ausgabe*, vols 20.1, 20.2 and 20.3 *(Briefwechsel zwischen Goethe und Zelter in den Jahren 1799 bis 1832)*, (eds) Hans-Günter Ottenberg and Edith Zehm in collaboration with Anita Golz, Jürgen Gruß, Wolfgang Ritschel and Sabine Schäfer. |

| | |
|---|---|
| HA | Goethes Werke. Hamburger Ausgabe, (ed.) Erich Trunz (14 vols, Hamburg: C.H.Beck, reprint 1994). |
| MA | J.W. von Goethe. Sämtliche Werke nach Epochen seines Schaffens. Münchner Ausgabe, (eds) Karl Richter, Herbert G. Göpfert, Norbert Miller, Gerhard Sauder, Edith Zehm et al. (21 vols, Munich: Carl Hanser Verlag, 1985–98). |
| Reisebriefe (1862) | Reisebriefe von Felix Mendelssohn Bartholdy aus den Jahren 180 bis 1832, (ed.) Paul Mendelssohn Bartholdy, 3rd edn (Leipzig, 1862, reprint Bonn, 1947). |
| SNA | Schillers Werke. Nationalausgabe, edited in collaboration with the Goethe and Schiller Archive, Weimar, and the Schiller National Museum, Marbach (Weimar, 1943ff). |
| WA | Goethes Werke. Weimarer Ausgabe, (eds) Gustav von Loeper, Erich Schmidt, Hermann Grimm et al. on the instructions of the Grand Duchess Sophie von Sachsen-Weimar-Eisenach (143 vols, Weimar: Hermann Böhlau, 1887–1919; reprint Munich, 1987). |
| ZG | Zelter's Letters to Goethe. In J.W. von Goethe. Sämtliche Werke nach Epochen seines Schaffens. Münchner Ausgabe, vols 20.1, 20.2 and 20.3 (Briefwechsel zwischen Goethe und Zelter in den Jahren 1799 bis 1832), (eds Hans-Günter Ottenberg and Edith Zehm in collaboration with Anita Golz, Jürgen Gruß, Wolfgang Ritschel and Sabine Schäfer. |

**III Texts**

| | |
|---|---|
| Blumner | Martin Blumner, Geschichte der Sing-Akademie zu Berlin (Berlin: Horn & Raasch, 1891). |
| Bohnenkamp | Anne Bohnenkamp, '… das Hauptgeschäft nicht außer Augen lassend'. Die Paralipomena zu Goethes 'Faust' (Frankfurt am Main and Leipzig: Insel Verlag, 1994). |
| Eckermann | Johann Peter Eckermann, Gespräche mit Goethe (Leipzig: Brockhaus, 1836–48; Stuttgart: Reclam, reprint 1998). |
| GM | Karl Mendelssohn Bartholdy, Goethe und Mendelssohn (Leipzig: Hirzel Verlag, 1872). |
| Keudell | Elise von Keudell, Goethe als Benutzer der Weimarer Bibliothek. Ein Verzeichnis der von ihm entliehenen Werke (Weimar: H. Böhlau, 1931, reprint 1982). |
| KuA | Goethe, Über Kunst und Altertum, vol. 1 (Stuttgart, 1812–32; reprint Bern, 1970). |
| Mendelssohn Briefe | Rudolf Elvers (ed.), Felix Mendelssohn Bartholdy. Briefe (Frankfurt am Main: Fischer, 1984). |

| | |
|---|---|
| *MGG* | *Die Musik in Geschichte und Gegenwart. Allgemeine Enzyklopaedie der Musik. Unter Mitarbeit zahlreicher Musikforscher (...)*, (ed.) Friedrich Blume vols 1–17 (Kassel, Basel: Bärenreiter Verlag, 1949–86; reprint Munich: Deutscher Taschenbuch Verlag, 1989). |
| *RA* | *Briefe an Goethe. Gesamtausgabe in Regestform*, (ed.) Karl-Heinz Hahn (Weimar: Regestausgabe, 1980ff). |
| Ruppert | *Goethes Bibliothek. Katalog*, (ed.) Hans Ruppert (Weimar: Goethe Sammlung der Kunst, Literatur und Naturwissenschaft, 1958, reprint Leipzig 1978) |
| Schünemann | Georg Schünemann, *Carl Friedrich Zelter der Begründer der Preußischen Musikpflege* (Berlin: Hesse, 1932). |
| Zelters Königsberger Briefe | Joseph Müller-Blattau, 'Karl Friedrich Zelters Königsberger Briefe 1809' in *Altpreußischen Forschungen* 12 (1935): 256–76. |

## IV Archives

| | |
|---|---|
| GMD | Goethe-Museum Düsseldorf. Anton-und-Katharina Kippenberg-Stiftung. |
| GSA | Goethe-und Schiller-Archiv Weimar. |
| SBB PK | Staatsbibliothek zu Berlin. Preussischer Kulturbesitz. |

# List of Music Examples

| | | |
|---|---|---|
| 1 | Letter no. 95, ZG, Berlin, 6 April to 7 May 1808, Scottish hornpipe, *GSA* 28/1015, s.62. | 111 |
| 2 | Letter no. 252, ZG, Berlin, 11 January 1819, 'Klaggesang', *GSA* 28/1017, s.172. | 250 |
| 3a | Letter no. 258, ZG, Vienna, 20 July to 9 August 1819. Waiter's call, *GSA* 28/1017, s.178. | 257 |
| 3b | Letter no. 258, ZG, Vienna, 20 July to 9 August 1819. Waiter's response, *GSA* 28/1017, s.178. | 257 |
| 4 | Letter no. 333, ZG, Berlin, 12 April 1825, Zelter's sketch of the orchestral pit, *GSA* 28/1020, s.249. | 327 |
| 5a | Letter no. 460, ZG, Berlin, 14 May 1829, Zelter's sketch for the formation of triads, *GSA* 28/1024, s.381. | 432 |
| 5b | Letter no. 460, ZG, Berlin, 14 May 1829, Zelter's example of perfect and imperfect cadences, *GSA* 28/1024, s.381. | 433 |
| 5c | Letter no. 460, ZG, Berlin, 14 May 1829, Zelter's example of consecutive fifths in ascending triads, *GSA* 28/1024, s.381. | 433 |
| 5d | Letter no. 460, ZG, Berlin, 14 May 1829, Zelter's sequence of dominant–tonic chords (leading to a full close in F major), *GSA* 28/1024, s.381. | 433 |
| 6 | Letter no. 559, Berlin, 28 to 30 August 1831, Canon by Zelter, *GSA* 28/1026, s.481. | 521 |

# A Musical Odyssey: Thirty-Five Years of Correspondence between Goethe and Zelter

*Lorraine Byrne Bodley*

**A Veil of Silence: Reception History of the Goethe–Zelter Letters**

Goethe's letters to Zelter provide us with an almost embarrassingly rich testimonial to the intensity and variety of his intellectual life. Yet his critics have not made use of them. His biographers cite them only to illustrate his state of mind at a given moment, or to make an incidental point about his thinking on one or another matter. His exegetes have for the most part ignored the letters, arguing that one should either develop a working relationship with the whole body of letters or leave them alone. The first editor of these letters, Goethe's secretary, Friedrich Wilhelm Riemer, was of this opinion when he published the complete edition of the letters just two years after Goethe's death.[1] When this first edition of the letters appeared between 1833 and 1834 several of the artists' contemporaries were, for better or worse, against the boldness and buoyancy of Zelter's words,[2] and the musical conservatism of both its writers has since been criticized.[3]

---

[1] Johann Wolfgang von Goethe, *Briefwechsel zwischen Goethe und Zelter in den Jahren 1796 bis 1832*, ed. Friedrich Wilhelm Riemer (6 vols, Berlin, Hermann Böhlau, 1833–34).

[2] See, for example the private letters of Henriette (Hinni) Mendelssohn (née Meyer) to her daughter-in-law, Rosamund Mendelssohn, Berlin, 9 November 1833; Fanny Hensel (née Mendelssohn) to her brother, Felix Mendelssohn Bartholdy, 1 December 1833; Charlotte Stieglitz to Baron Stieglitz, Berlin 20 December 1833; Fanny Hensel to her brother, Felix Mendelssohn Bartholdy, Berlin, 27 November 1834. For positive reception see the private letters of Wilhelm Neumann to Karl August Varnhagen von Ense, Berlin 31 December 1833; Karl Ludwig von Knebel to Friedrich Wilhelm Riemer, Jena, 25 January 1834; Carl Gustav Carus to August Carl Graf von Bose, Dresden, 9 April 1834 and, on balance, Friedrich von Müller to Carl August Böttinger, Weimar, 23 September 1834. All letters are contained in the Münchner Ausgabe, 20.2, pp. 1673–80. Hereafter referred to as *MA*.

[3] See, for example: W.J. Wasiliewski, *Goethes Verhältnis zur Musik* (Leipzig: Sammlung musikalischer Vorträge, 1880); Wilhelm Bode, *Goethe und die Tonkunst*, (2 vols, Berlin: E.S. Mittler und Sohn, 1912); Hermann J Abert, *Goethe und die Musik* (Stuttgart: J. Engelhorns Nachf., 1922); Edgar Istel, 'Goethe and Music', *MQ*, 14 (1928): 216–54; Romain Rolland, 'Goethe's Interest in Music', *MQ*, 17 (1931): 157–94 and also

When considering the reception of the Goethe–Zelter letters in recent years, two publications stand out: Bettina Hey'l's study of literature discussed in the Goethe–Zelter letters[4] and the *Münchner Ausgabe* edition of the letters[5] alongside the correspondence of Goethe and Schiller. The editorial team for this edition, led by Hans-Günter Ottenberg, Sabine Schäfer and Edith Zehm, took for granted the letters' integrity and distinction as a correspondence and gathered together related documents in a detailed lengthy postlude to show the basis of this integrity and distinction. While Zehm assumed that these letters preserved the historical and imaginative world of both writers, this treatment has still not changed the way in which the correspondence is viewed, nor has it initiated a new era – or new terms – of appreciation. One reason for this neglect in musicology is that these letters have never been published in English. A.D. Coleridge's nineteenth-century translation *Goethe's Letters to Zelter* presents a selection of excerpts from 250 of the 900 letters;[6] Jeffrey Pulver's article 'Beethoven in the Goethe–Zelter letters'[7]

---

'Goethe the Musician' in Dagobert D. Runes (ed.), *Goethe Symposium* (New York: Roerich Museum Press, 1932): 3–17; Emil Voigt, 'War Goethe musikalisch?', *Musik*, 23 (1931): 321–7; Ferdinand Küchler, *Goethes Musikverständnis* (Leipzig, 1935); Friedrich Blume, *Goethe und die Musik* (Kassel: Bärenreiter Verlag, 1948); M. Heller, 'Goethe and Music', *GQ*, 22 (1949): 205–208; Louise Levin, 'Goethe and Music', *Contemporary Review*, 176 (1949): 225–30; M.H. Nathan, 'Goethe was musical', *Musical Opinion* (London, Nov. 1949); John Greenhill, 'Goethe's attitude towards music and contemporary composers', *Australian Goethe Society Proceedings* (1950); Guido Kisch, 'Music in Goethe's Life', *Monatshefte für deutschen Unterricht*, 42 (1950): 243–51; Hans Pleß, 'Goethe und die Musik', *Musikerziehung*, 3 (1950): 70–76; Anne-Marie M. Sauerlander, 'Goethe's Relation to Music' in J. Alan Pfeffer (ed.), *Essays on German Language and Literature in Honour of Theodore B. Hewitt* (Buffalo: The University of Buffalo Studies, 1952), pp. 39–55; W.C.R. Hicks, 'Was Goethe Musical?', *PEGS*, 27 (1958): 73–139; Susan Sonnet, 'Goethe and Music' in *Soundings: Collections of the University Library* (California: University of Santa Barbara, 1970), pp. 30–33; John L. Miller, 'Goethe and Music' in *Seminar: A Journal of Germanic Studies*, 8 (1972): 42–54; David Dalton, 'Goethe and the Composers of his Time', *MR*, 34 (1973):157–74; Meredith McClain, 'Goethe and Music: Nur wer die Sehnsucht kennt' (Texas: Texas Tech. Press, 1984), pp. 201–77; Ernst-Jürgen Dreyer, *Goethes Tonwissenschaft* (Berlin, Frankfurt am Main & Vienna: Ullstein, 1985); H. Zeman, 'Goethe und die Musik, Prologomena zu einem großen Thema' in *Wort und Ton im europäischen Raum. Gedenkschrift für Robert Schollum* (Vienna: Böhlau Verlag, 1989), pp. 109–14; Elmar Budde, 'Goethe und die Musik' in *Goethe Spuren. Ein Lese-Buch zum Konzertprojekt* (Göttingen: Wallstein Verlag, 1998), pp. 15–35.

[4] Bettina Hey'l, *Der Briefwechsel zwischen Goethe und Zelter. Lebenskunst und literarisches Projekt* (Tübingen: Niemayer Verlag, 1996).

[5] Hans-Günter Ottenberg, Sabine Schäfer and Edith Zehm (eds), *Briefwechsel mit Zelter* vols 20.1; 20.2 and 20.3 in Karl Richter (ed.) *Goethe Sämtliche Werke nach Epochen seines Schaffens*. Münchner Ausgabe (20 vols, München: Hanser Verlag, 1985–98).

[6] A.D. Coleridge, *Goethe's Letters to Zelter* (London: George Bell & Sons, 1887).

[7] Jeffrey Pulver, 'Beethoven in the Goethe-Zelter Correspondence', *ML* 17 (1936): 124–30.

is the only secondary source available in English, and there has never been a book published in English – or in German – which concentrates solely on the musical dialogues of these letters.

The three volumes of this correspondence do essentially rest upon this musical foundation. Flouted as this foundation has been and continues to be, it is this critical reception which will, ironically enough, make them attractive to cultural historians. This book is not intended as a panacea for musicological ills but is geared to effect what Seamus Heaney once called 'The Redress of Poetry'.[8] Heaney's idea of redress finds its roots in Simone Weil's book, *Gravity and Grace*,[9] which observes that if we know how something is unbalanced, we add weight to the lighter side of the scale. So what are the roots of this lack of equilibrium in critics' response to the Goethe–Zelter letters? And what counterweights need to be hung in the scale of their reception?

## Goethe and Musical Modernity

The pervasive image of Goethe as a musically conservative poet[10] has, without question, engendered the scholarly neglect of Goethe's correspondence with Zelter, which is one of the few areas in Goethe philology that has been left unexplored. It has also influenced the portrayal of Goethe's musical historicism as an excessive veneration of past musical styles, rather than the desire to challenge contemporary norms in art by asserting the validity of the art of a plurality of peoples and periods. The new perceptions of historical processes which emphasized modernity and granted little role to any reference to the past, and thereby engendered an increasingly teleological perspective on music history, portrayed Schubertian song as an evolutionary development, an improvement on Goethe's aesthetic theories

---

[8] Seamus Heaney, *The Redress of Poetry*, Oxford Lectures (London: Faber and Faber, 1995).

[9] Simone Weil, *Gravity and Grace* (Oxford and New York: Routledge Classics, 1992).

[10] See, for example: Wasiliewski, *Goethes Verhältnis zur Musik*; Bode, *Goethe und die Tonkunst*; Abert, *Goethe und die Musik*; Istel, 'Goethe and Music': 216–54; Rolland, 'Goethe's Interest in Music': 157–94 and also 'Goethe the Musician', pp. 3–17; Voigt, 'War Goethe musikalisch?': 321–7; Küchler, *Goethes Musikverständnis*; Blume, *Goethe und die Musik*; Heller, 'Goethe and Music': 205–208; Levin, 'Goethe and Music': 225–30; Nathan, 'Goethe was musical'; Greenhill, 'Goethe's attitude towards music and contemporary composers': 18–26; Kisch, 'Music in Goethe's Life': 243–51; Pleß, 'Goethe und die Musik': 70–76; Sauerlander, 'Goethe's Relation to Music', pp. 39–55; Hicks, 'Was Goethe Musical?': 73–139; Sonnet, 'Goethe and Music', pp. 30–33; Miller, 'Goethe and Music': 42–54; Dalton, 'Goethe and the Composers of his Time': 157–74; McClain, 'Goethe and Music: *Nur wer die Sehnsucht kennt*', pp. 201–77; Dreyer, *Goethes Tonwissenschaft*; Zeman, 'Goethe und die Musik, Prologomena zu einem großen Thema', pp. 109–14; Budde, 'Goethe und die Musik', pp. 15–35.

of song. And it is only in recent years that scholars have begun to chart the more complex contours of pre-Schubertian song.[11]

## Reconsidering Goethe's 'rejection' of Schubert

The neglect of the Goethe–Zelter letters in musicology has been influenced by the impression of a hapless relationship between Schubert and Goethe. The image of 'Poor Schubert', partly born of the Romantic idea of the 'unrecognized artistic genius, the artist who valiantly struggles for acceptance and yet is explicitly ignored by the world until after his death',[12] thus set in antithesis with the canonical artist and titanic personality of Goethe, has contributed to misconceptions about the relationship between Goethe and Schubert.[13] Goethe's 'rejection' of Schubert's first book of songs was claimed to have been influenced by Zelter, to whom Goethe supposedly sent the songs for advice. Such arguments are clearly unfounded: in the 891 letters exchanged between these artists there is no mention of Schubert Lieder; on the contrary, the letters prove the dispatch was never sent to Zelter, nor was he in Weimar during the period in which Schubert's first songbook arrived. In their

---

[11] See, for example, the seminal work of Otto Biba, 'Goethe in the Vienna Music Scene of his Era' in Lorraine Byrne (ed.), *Goethe: Musical Poet, Musical Catalyst* (Dublin: Carysfort Press, 2004), pp. 7–40 or the pioneering recording by Graham Johnson, *Songs by Schubert's Friends and Contemporaries* (London: The Hyperion Schubert Edition, 2004), CDJ33051/3.

[12] Christopher Gibbs, '"Poor Schubert": images and legends of the composer' in Christopher Gibbs (ed.) *The Cambridge Companion to Schubert* (Cambridge, 1997), pp. 36–55.

[13] See, for example: O. Linke in 'Schubert und Goethe', *Neue MusikZeitung*, 12 (1891); R. Boehmer-Aachen, 'Goethe und Schubert' in *Rheinische Musik -und Theaterzeitung*, 14 (1913): 486–89; Konrad Volker, 'Schubert und Goethe', *Die Musik*, 14 (1915): 129; M. v. Leinburg, 'Schubert und Goethe' (Munich: Propyläen Ausgabe, 1928); M. Zeiner, 'Goethe und Schubert', *Die Quelle*, 79 (1929): 105; Romain Rolland, 'Goethe's Interest in Music': 177 and 190; P. Riesenfeld, 'Goethe und Schubert', *Signale für die musikalische Welt*, 90 (1932): 267; Konrad Huschke, 'Schubert und Goethe', *Musica*, 7 (1953): 580–81; Alexander Witeschnik, 'Goethe und Schubert: Die Geschichte einer einseitigen Liebe', *Jahrbuch des Wiener-Goethe Vereins*, 67 (1963): 78–85; Joseph Müller-Blattau, 'Franz Schubert, der Sänger Goethes' in Joseph Müller-Blattau, *Goethe und die Meister der Musik* (Stuttgart: Klett, 1969), pp. 62–80; Dalton, 'Goethe and the Composers of his Time': 157–74; Ronald Taylor, Goethe-Schubert and the Art of Song' in Volker Dürr and Géza v. Molnār (eds), *Versuche zu Goethe*: *Festschrift für Erich Heller* (Heidelberg: Lothar Stiehm Verlag, 1976), pp. 141–9; Frederick W. Sternfield, *Goethe and Music*: *A List of Parodies and Goethe's Relationship to Music: A List of References* (New York: The New York Public Library, 1979), introduction, p. vii.

portrayal of a 'neglected Schubert',[14] scholars have overlooked the significance of Goethe's acknowledgement of Schubert's second dedication in his diary as early as 1825: 'Sendung von Schubert aus Wien, von meinen Liedern Kompositionen' (A parcel of my song compositions from Schubert of Vienna).[15] Johann Nepomuk Hummel, Weimar's most eminent musician at the time, and Felix Mendelssohn, friend and musical advisor to Goethe, did not discover Schubert until 1827.[16] Whether Goethe's failure to respond to Schubert in a personal letter of thanks was linked to his reticence in encouraging the younger generation of Romantic literary artists[17] or coloured by the sad reality that Goethe and Schubert never met,[18] one will never know. What is clear, however, from Metternich's new censorship laws, which were tightened up as a result of the Congress of Vienna, is that Schubert could not have published his op. 19 Lieder in Vienna – with the dedication to Goethe on the title page of this volume – without the poet's written permission.[19] At some point – perhaps the same day as Goethe acknowledged receipt of these songs in his diary – a written missive must have been sent to Vienna to allow these songs to be published with a dedication to the poet. The presumed loss of this letter[20] coupled with the legend of Schubert's neglect and Goethe's 'Olympian aloofness [and] blindness to new writers of talent'[21] have fuelled misconceptions surrounding Goethe's 'neglect' of 'Poor Schubert'.

---

[14] Gibbs traces this image of Schubert in musicology in: '"Poor Schubert": images and legends of the composer', pp. 46–8. A good example is the review of Newman Flower's book, *Franz Schubert: The Man and his Circle*, in *New York Times*, 25 November 1928, cited in Robert Winter, 'Whose Schubert?', *NCM*, vol. 17/1 (1993), p. 97.

[15] *Goethes Werke. Weimarer Ausgabe*, (eds) Gustav von Loeper, Erich Schmidt, Hermann Grimm et al. (Weimar: Hermann Böhlau, 1887–1912), III/10, 16 June 1825, pp. 68–9. Hereafter referred to as *WA*.

[16] R. Larry Todd, *Mendelssohn: A Life in Music* (Oxford: Oxford University Press, 2003), p. 72.

[17] Examples include the works of Wachenroder (*Herzensergießungen*), E.T.A. Hoffmann, Bretano and Kleist (*Das Kätchen von Heilbronn*). For an example of Goethe's polemical broadsides against Romanticism, see Johann Peter Eckermann, *Gespräche mit Goethe* (Stuttgart: Reclam, reprint 1998), 2 April 1829, p. 343. Hereafter referred to as Eckermann.

[18] On 16 June 1825, the same day as Franz Schubert's letter and manuscript containing the op. 19 settings arrived, Lea Mendelssohn sent an exemplar of Mendelssohn's newly published Piano Quartet no. 3 in B minor from Berlin, for which she had already requested permission to dedicate to Goethe. Goethe wrote to Mendelssohn, thanking him for the dedication of the Quartet, which Mendelssohn had played for him on his third visit to the poet in Weimar. See Karl Mendelssohn Bartholdy (ed.), *Goethe und Mendelssohn* (Leipzig: Hirzel Verlag, 1872), p. 50. Hereafter referred to as *GM*.

[19] Biba, 'Goethe in the Vienna Music Scene of his Era', p. 27.

[20] Ibid.

[21] Lesley Sharpe (ed.), *The Cambridge Companion to Goethe* (Cambridge: Cambridge University Press, 2002), introduction, p. 2.

## Like Breath on Glass: Reception of Goethe's Music Theatre

A third reason for the musicological neglect of this correspondence is encountered in *Germanistik* which has wilfully ignored Goethe's works of music theatre. The value Goethe placed on his musico-dramatic writings and the positive reception of these works during his lifetime challenges Hugo von Hofmannsthal's designation of Goethe's music theatre as 'Nebenwerke', works of secondary importance in the poet's creative canon. Yet the ripples from the stone which Hofmannsthal cast in 1913 spread through Goethe scholarship in Germany and beyond, where the works have been outside the canon of research almost up to the present day, as a cursory glance at the commentary on these works in the *Münchner Ausgabe* will affirm. In recent years this lacuna in Goethe reception has been addressed in the seminal work of such scholars as Benedikt Holtbernd,[22] Markus Waldura,[23] Thomas Frantzke,[24] and by the publication of Goethe's musico-dramatic works by Metzler Verlag in 2004. In the context of this scholarly tableau Tina Hartmann's mighty argosy of scholarship, *Goethes Musiktheater*,[25] is an important milestone in understanding Goethe's contribution to the rise of German national theatre.

## Constructing a Legend and the Culture of Weimar's Musical Refinement

This current revision of Goethe's musicality in contemporary musicological discourse is fettered by the mythologization of Goethe. Although the image of Goethe in the popular imagination is a matter quite different from the scholarly reception of Goethe's musical and literary works, the two worlds do cross over since any seriously revised perception of the poet is difficult to establish when the spectre of an unmusical poet keeps re-emerging in contemporary Goethean culture.[26] Twenty years before the Goethe–Zelter correspondence began, Goethe had already become an icon of German cultural gravitas, the founding figure of a national cultural heritage, and the enterprise of marketing and merchandising this

---

[22] Benedikt Holtbernd, *Die dramaturgischen Funktionen der Musik in den Schauspielen Goethes* (Frankfurt am Main: Lang, 1992).

[23] Markus Waldura, 'Der Zauberflöte Zweyter Theil. Konzeption einer nicht musikalischen und sozielen Formen', *Archiv für Musikwissenschaft*, 50 (1993): 259–90; 'Die Singpsiele', in Bernd Witte, Theo Buck, Hans-Dietrich Dahnke, Regine Otto and Peter Schmidt (eds), *Goethe Handbuch*, (4 vols, Stuttgart and Weimar: Metzler Verlag, 1996–99), vol. 2, pp. 192–3; hereafter referred to as *Goethe HB*.

[24] Thomas Frantzke, *Goethes Schauspiele mit Gesang und Singspiele 1773–1782* (Frankfurt a.M., Berlin, Bern, New York, Paris, Vienna: Lang, 1998).

[25] Tina Hartmann, *Goethes Musiktheater* (Tübingen: Max Niemeyer Verlag, 2004).

[26] See, for example, Knut-Olaf Haustein, *'Da schwebt hervor Musik mit Engelsschwingen': Goethes Dichtungen in der Musik* (Weimar: quartus-Verlag, 2005), Chapter 1, 'Wie musikalisch war Goethe', p. 24f.

great national poet had already been ushered in, in the *Intelligenz Blatt* of Bertuch's *Journal des Luxus und der Moden* (Journal of Luxury and Fashion, which ran from 1786 to 1827).[27] Yet the complexities of Goethe, his life's work and reception, are reduced the moment he is transformed into the signifier of a myth. Bottled up in this way he becomes a lifeless icon and the message in the bottle is a profoundly conservative one, more akin to the nationalistic tradition of Wilhelmine Germany than to Weimar in the early 1800s or the serious scholarship of the cultural foundation, *Stiftung Klassik Weimar* (Weimar Classics Foundation), which has recently begun to unwrap Goethe's Weimar and consider the process involved in producing various myths surrounding the poet, Goethe. While Henke, Kord and Richter's valuable study, *Unwrapping Goethe's Weimar*,[28] does not unravel the mystery of Weimar's musical past, an earlier voluminous lexicon, *Goethes Weimar*, by Effi Biedrzynksi[29] places countless evocative details into the hands of prospective cultural studies scholars and allows the reader to infer the crucial role that music played in the life of Weimar – a position recently acknowledged by the Weimar Classics Foundation and Institute for Musicology at the Liszt Hochschule which have begun to unveil the music of Weimar Classicism.[30]

## Unfolding Goethe's Engagement with Music

This quest for what was forgotten, concealed, revised or transformed lies behind my translation of *Goethe and Zelter: Musical Dialogues*. In this correspondence

---

[27] Friedrich Justin Bertuch and Georg Melchior Kraus (eds), *Journal der Moden*, vol. 1 (Gotha: Ettingersche Buchhandlung, 1786); Friedrich Justin Bertuch and Georg Melchior Kraus (eds) (ed. Carl Bertruch from 1807–12), *Journal des Luxus und der Moden*, vols 2–27 (Weimar: Industrie-Comptoir, 1787–1812); Carl Bertuch (ed.) (ed. Heinrich Döring from 1815), *Journal für Luxus, Mode und Gegenstände der Kunst*, vols 28–30 (Weimar: Industrie-Comptoir, 1813–15); Heinrich Döring (ed.) (ed. Stephan Schütz from 1825), *Journal für Literatur, Kunst, Luxus und Mode* vols 31-41 (Weimar: Industrie-Comptoir, 1816–1826); Stephan Schütz (ed.), *Journal für Literatur, Kunst und geselliges Leben* vol. 42 (Weimar: Industrie-Comptoir, 1827); Friedrich Justin Bertuch and Georg Melchior Kraus (eds), *Journal des Luxus und der Moden*. Abridged Edition (ed.) Werner Schmidt. 4 vols Rpt. (Hanau: Müller and Kiepenheuer, 1967–70).

[28] Burkhard Henke, Susanne Kord and Simon Richter (eds), *Unwrapping Goethe's Weimar: Essays in Cultural Studies and Local Knowledge* (Rochester, NY: Camden House, 2000).

[29] Effi Biedrzynski, *Goethes Weimar: Das Lexikon der Personen und Schauplätze*, 3rd edn (Zurich: Artemis and Winkler, 1994).

[30] Detlef Altenburg (General Editor), *Musik und Theater*, 5 vols. to date (Weimar: Studio Verlag, 2005–). See especially: Detlef Altenburg and Beate Schmidt, *Musik und Theater um 1800* (*Musik und Theater*, vol. 1); Thomas Radecke, *Theatermusik- Musiktheater. Shakespeare-Dramen aud deutschen Bühnen um 1800* (*Musik und Theater*, vol. 2) and Beate Schmidt, *Musik in Goethes Faust* (*Musik und Theater*, vol. 5).

Goethe's critical facility in contemplating music contradicts the common perception that the poet blindly accepted Zelter's musical opinions – a conjecture even contradicted by Zelter who admits to Goethe in the correspondence, 'you are the only person I know, whose musical judgment offers unique insight and value.' Although Goethe had been seeking a musical advisor early in the correspondence, Zelter swiftly recognized how the high voltage of Goethe's early talent embraced a rich array of musical experience including a detailed practical knowledge of contemporary music theatre. The only dependency which arises in the letters, therefore, is not a musical dependency, but a human dependency which first manifests itself after Schiller's death in 1805, where Goethe begins to write more frequently to Zelter, who forms an audience for the poet to whom he can speak comfortably and at length. So, too, Zelter's need for Goethe is evident upon the death of Zelter's second wife, intensified by the loss of three children and augmented by his abiding recognition that his friendship with Goethe greatly enhances his intellectual and musical life. While it may lie beyond the scope of this introduction to detail exhaustively the intensity and intimacy of Goethe's engagement with the musical life of his times, a brief glance at some of the main musical themes of this correspondence might countervail the critical reception of these letters.

### An Unended Quest: Goethe's Musicological Studies

Although questions of music theory had preoccupied Goethe from an early age,[31] it was not until his early years of correspondence with Zelter that Goethe's first formal papers on music began with a critical translation of Diderot's *Neveu de Rameau*.[32] What is most significant about Goethe's translation is that its annotations, which make up almost a third of the text, contain some important comments on music and music history and allow us to consider the poet's understanding of the art of music in the light of the eighteenth-century French debates between Rameau and Rousseau. In contrast to the concept espoused by the French Enlightenment, where music acquires intellectual responsibility by painting concrete images, Goethe argued that music reached beyond the senses to the intellect and imagination. Goethe had first criticized Diderot's concept of musical mimesis in a translation and discussion of the philosopher's *Essai sur la peinture* (1795). This belief is evident in Goethe's letters to Zelter where the poet's preference for suggestion rather than naturalism in programme music is apparent.[33] In his response to Zelter's

---

[31] In his diary, *Ephemerides*, Goethe had transcribed an excerpt from Hiller's journal, *Wöchentlich Nachtrichten, die Musik betreffend*, on the art of musical declamation and in the *Italian Journal* there are passages on the aesthetics of musical tempi WA I/32, p. 287.

[32] GZ 19 June 1805. *Rameaus Neffe: Ein Dialog von Denis Diderot* trans. J.W. v Goethe (Frankfurt a.M.: Insel Verlag, reprint 1996).

[33] GZ 9 November 1829.

Cantata, 'Johanna Sebus', Goethe draws a comparison between the musical and visual arts, yet in music he departs from the principles of imitation: 'It is a kind of symbolism for the ear, where the subject, in so far as it is in motion, or not in motion, is neither imitated nor painted, but produced in the imagination, in a way that is quite peculiar, and impossible to grasp, in so far as the thing described and the describer appear to stand in scarcely any relation to one another.'[34] For Goethe the visual symbol is at once effective and elusive; the musical symbol, by contrast, is emancipated from its original source and merely triggers the imagination.[35] The central purpose of art lies in the creation of *Stimmung*, an individual artistic voice, yet the domain of music hovers between thought and phenomena, spirit and matter. It is not representative of the particular, but expresses objects and emotions in the abstract, in their essential nature, and enables us to share them in this quintessence.

Although Goethe's letters to Zelter make no further reference to Rameau, his research on the French composer awakened his interest in such other theorists as the acoustician Ernst Chladni and the scientist Ernst Meyer,[36] and he was versed in the main musicological writings of his day. While reading Chladni's 1802 Theory of Acoustics,[37] Goethe made extensive notes, *Über die Nachteile der Stimmung in ganz reinen Quinten und Quarten nach Chladni*, on the problem of tuning and equal temperament.[38] He owned copies of and read Johann Mattheson's monumental folio *Der Vollkommene Capellmeister*,[39] Johann Josef Fux's 1725 counterpoint treatise, *Gradus ad Parnassum*,[40] and also Marpurg's *Abhandlung von der Fuge*,[41] which is largely based on *The Art of Fugue*, Bach's practical 'treatise'; so, too, Kirnberger's *Die Kunst des reinen Satzes in der Musik* (1771)[42] appealed to Goethe because the theoretician focuses on both principles and practical examples. Goethe's interest in Kirnberger's theoretical writing reveals his alliance with the progressive musical ideas which developed in Berlin scholarship. The breadth of Goethe's knowledge of and intimate familiarity with the music literature both of his day and of the past

---

[34] GZ 6 March 1810.

[35] GZ 2 May 1820.

[36] GZ 31 January 1803.

[37] Ernst Florens Friedrich Chladni, *Die Akustik* (Leipzig: Breitkopf und Härtel, 1803).

[38] *Über die Nachteile der Stimmung in ganz reinen Quinten und Quarten nach Chladni*, WA II/13, p. 461.

[39] Johann Mattheson, *Der vollkommene Capellmeister* (Hamburg: Christian Herold, 1739); *GZ* 4 January 1819. See Zelter's response on 2 June 1819.

[40] Johann Josef Fux, *Gradus ad Parnassum* (Vienna: Joannis Petri van Ghelen, 1725), *Steps to Parnassus*, translated by Alfred Mann (New York: Norton, 1943).

[41] Friedrich Wilhelm Marpurg, *Abhandlung von der Fuge* (Berlin, A. Haude and J.C. Spener, 1753; facsimile, Hildesheim. and New York: Georg Olms, 1970).

[42] Johann Philipp Kirnberger, *Die Kunst des reinen Satzes in der Musik* (Berlin: C.F. Voss, 1771–79; Facs. Rpr. Hildesheim: Georg Olms, 1968).

reveals his willingness to absorb new insights in his reception of music, as elements of enrichment and reorientation. The overall development of Goethe's theoretical knowledge reflects his immense curiosity and openness toward change; his power of integration is evident in his treatise on acoustics, which reveals the influence of Rameau's harmonic theory and counters contemporary idealist interpretations. Goethe's desire to collaborate on a theory of acoustics was partly realized in the daily conversations he had with Zelter in Carlsbad, July 1810. These discussions on music theory, music history and the human ear, which he carefully recorded in his diary,[43] informed the synoptical table of his *Tonlehre*. Goethe sketched the first draft of his musical mosaic on 28 July 1810. Following further discussions with Zelter in Teplitz in August 1810 he revised this fragmentary table and then set it aside until 1826, where he encloses it in the correspondence for the composer's consideration.[44] Goethe's enclosure of this table in his correspondence with Zelter is significant, for the *Tonlehre* addresses the artist and not the theoretician.[45]

The fragmentary table which Goethe sent to Zelter summarizes the poet's belief in the primacy of the ear in musical perception, and the primacy of the human voice in performance. Countering the idealist and Romantic interpretations of Schlosser, who saw a confrontation rather than a harmony between man and nature and believed the minor mode expressed an ethical will to emancipate man from nature, Goethe ingeniously reinterpreted Schlosser's notion of a *Tonmonade* to suit his own theory of polarities. In his *Theory of Sound* he reaffirms his conviction of the equality of the minor and major modes as poles of a fundamental duality in human nature.[46] He questions the *Empfindsamkeit* association of the minor mode with melancholy, and instead relates musical polarity to the duality in human nature. For Goethe, the major mode was an expression of all that is objective and connects the soul to the outer world, and the minor tonality is the mode of introspection and concentration. The instinct that leads Goethe from naturalism to abstraction in the *Tonlehre* is countered by an equally powerful aversion to Romantic subjectivity, which he recognized as being fundamentally akin to pure mathematics: both were human constructs without natural bases. In contrast to the works of Descartes, Leibniz, Rameau and Euler, where mathematics becomes fused with the emerging

---

[43] 15, 18, 28 and 29 July, *WA* III/4, pp. 140 and 143; 8, 16, 17, 20, 22 and 23 August 1810, *WA* III/ 4, pp. 146–7 and 148–9.

[44] GZ 9 September 1826.

[45] For Goethe's explanation of the *Tonlehre*, see also Goethe's letter to Christian Heinrich Schlosser, 6 February 1815, *WA* IV/25, p. 187. A very engaging comparative analysis of Goethe's *Tonlehre* with medieval music classifications of *musica mundane*, *musica humana* and *musica instrumentalis* is found in Claus Canisius, *Goethe und die Musik* (Munich: Piper-Verlag, 1998) and Claus Canisius, 'Goethes Tonlehre. Ergebnis seines lebenslangen Nachdenkens über Musik und Wissenschaft' in Andreas Ballstaedt, Ulrike Kienzle and Adolf Nowak (eds), *Musik in Goethes Werk. Goethes Werk in der Musik* (Schliengen: Edition Argus, 2003), pp. 114–21.

[46] Ibid.

science of physical acoustics, in the *Tonlehre* music is not perceived as being imitative of a mathematical or verbal paradigm. Goethe's metaphor for music was different: of all the arts, music was the furthest removed from nature and most highly structured according to abstract principles.

## An Eye for Innovation: Goethe's Engagement with Contemporary Music Theory

One of the most interesting aspects of Goethe's communication with Zelter is his interest in music as an acoustic phenomenon and his discussion of major and minor tonalities. The status of the minor chords and keys was a central issue between Rameau, Rousseau and the encyclopedists, and their debate is developed in the Goethe–Zelter letters. That Goethe was the leader in this discussion, and not reliant on Zelter's opinion, is evident as early as 1808. When Goethe asked Zelter why composers were inclined towards the minor mode, Zelter revealed his knowledge of Rameau's music theory, outlining the natural origin of the major triad in the overtone series and showing the minor chord as being derivative.[47] Goethe, who was working on the *Farbenlehre* at that time, replied with a line-by-line refutation of the derivation of the minor from the major.[48] If the minor chord could not be derived by dividing a vibrating string, Goethe deduced that this disqualified the argument. If the historical practice of music showed a development which culminated, as he thought, in the parity of major and minor modes, the modes had to be rooted in the sound-producing body (*corps sonore*), not in the accidental auditory mechanism of man. Goethe agreed that the evolution of compositional practice was not accidental: if composers had treated the minor chord as a consonance, though it is not contained in the overtones or the vibrating string, it must be naturally harmonious and cannot be a dissonance.[49] While similar convictions sent Rameau out to nature, Goethe referred back to man himself and he concluded the 1808 debate with the famous postscript, where he characteristically referred back to the musician's ear to clinch his argument: 'For what is a string and all mechanical division of it in comparison with the ear of the musician?'[50] Zelter's conciliatory response brought the debate to a halt. When Goethe reopened the discussion a year before his death,[51] this time it is Zelter who agrees with Goethe's musical opinion.[52] Goethe's creative thinking is evident in his combination of intense interest in the debate with highly critical thinking; a readiness to question established suppositions. Out of these theories Goethe created a musical world:

---

[47] GZ 20 April 1808; ZG 6 April to 7 May 1808.
[48] GZ 22 June 1808.
[49] ZG 15 May 1808.
[50] GZ 22 June 1808.
[51] GZ 31 March 1831.
[52] ZG 14 April 1831.

not the real world in which Zelter practised as a musician, but his own nets in which he tried to catch the real world.

## Goethe's Ear: Awakenings to a New Reality

Goethe's independent reflections upon music, as exemplified by the major-key/minor-key controversy with Zelter or by his draft of a system of acoustics, derive not least from his opinion that the sensual effect which music exercised upon his imaginative faculty was more important than preconceived aesthetic dogma. For Goethe, theory was the critical penetration of sensual perception, of what is audible as music. The primary encounter was of paramount importance to Goethe, followed by knowledge through reflection. Thus Goethe gave priority to listening to music. To Friederike Helene Unger Goethe named three qualities which characterized his listening to music: his conviction regarding the unique affective power of music, the frame of mind in which he listened to music, and listening, as far as possible, 'unreservedly' and 'repeatedly'.[53] Goethe placed great emphasis on repeated listening, not merely because of the importance of increased familiarization, but rather because, in the phase of actually coming to grips with the music – described by Goethe as a reflective process (*nachdenken*) – repeated critical listening provided him with several chances to check his first impressions and deepen them. Goethe's personal experience of this phenomenon is evident in his attendance at three performances of *Il Seraglio* before forming a critical impression of the work.[54] And in conversation with Johann Christian Lobe about developments in contemporary song, Goethe did not blindly accept the theoretical explanations Lobe offered, but asked the Weimar court musician to demonstrate his ideas on the piano before Goethe would accept them.[55] In a similar fashion he urged the 22-year-old Mendelssohn to play him pieces in chronological order and explain what each composer had done in order to further the art.[56] And in a letter to Zelter on 4 January 1819 Goethe records a series of instructional recitals in Berka where Schütz played to him every day for three to four hours at his request 'in historical sequence selections from Sebastian Bach to Beethoven, including C.P.E. Bach, Handel, Mozart, Haydn, Dussek too, and other similar composers'.[57]

---

[53] Goethe to Friederike Helene Unger, 13 June 1796; the full letter is given at the beginning of this correspondence.

[54] *Goethe Briefe*, 1 in Erich Trunz (ed) *Goethes Werke Hamburger Ausgabe* (14 vols, Hamburg: C.H.Beck, reprint 1994), Letter no. 393, *An Kayser*, 22 December, 1785, p. 493. Herafter referred to as *HA*.

[55] Hedwig Walwei-Wiegelmann, *Goethes Gedanken über Musik* (Frankfurt a.M.: Insel Verlag, 1985), pp. 143–4.

[56] GZ 3 June 1830.

[57] GZ 4 January 1819.

In his accounts of these recitals, Goethe's response to the music of J.S. Bach stands in complete contrast to the sociable aspect of music-making and performance. Lying down with his eyes shut in the Juno room of his *Frauenplan* house – in a state of heightened experience – Goethe listened attentively to Schütz's interpretations of Bach's preludes and fugues. This took place in November 1818.[58] Even before this significant encounter he acclaimed Fräulein Hügel's performance of Bach in 1815, many years before Mendelssohn's Berlin performance of the *St Matthew Passion* in 1829 heralded the revival which brought Bach's music to the attention of the public at large. The significance of Goethe's encounter with the music of Bach is apparent in a letter to Zelter in 1827, where he again records the private recitals in Berka. He recalls how he felt lifted out of the world: and experienced the moral power of music, its benediction, and describes how his entire attention was directed at the transacoustic background of the music.[59] Listening to Schütz's performance, Goethe experienced the very essence of Bach's music, its inner coherence and timelessness. When Goethe speaks of eternal harmony, he is, of course, alluding to the classical idea of a numerically structured cosmic harmony, which he believed to have witnessed upon hearing Bach's music. He describes Bach's instrumental music as resounding metaphysics, as the revelation of *musica mundana*, which gave him a sense of inwardly participating in the cosmic order. Within the framework of Goethe's *Tonlehre*, enclosed in a letter to Zelter on 6 September 1826,[60] the music of Bach would be classified in terms of numerical laws. In this way it contrasts with the anthropocentric, organic dimension of music, whose medium is the human voice, and with which Goethe ultimately had greater affinity.

**A New Mimesis: Goethe's Representation of Musical Reality**

As with his scientific studies, Goethe's portrayal as an *Augenmensch* is complementary to his musicality, for he often translated the effect music had upon him into pictorial terms. Various pictorial interpretations show how Goethe sought to capture the gestures of music pictorially, in a way which altogether matched the basic nature of music. During his visit in 1830, Mendelssohn reports that upon hearing the beginning of Bach's Overture in D Major, Goethe visualized a Baroque feast in tableau form.[61] While scholars have interpreted this form of criticism as a lack of technical ability, Goethe's method of approach is embedded in the universality of interdisciplinary thinking. His form of musical appreciation revealed relationships which a more narrow subject-specific approach might

---

[58] GZ 4 January 1819.
[59] GZ 17 July 1827, enclosure *MA* 20.1, p. 1021; see also *ZG* 9 June 1827.
[60] Walwei-Wiegelmann, *Goethes Gedanken über Musik*, pp. 214–20.
[61] Felix Mendelssohn to Zelter, 22 June 1830, Walwei-Wiegelmann, *Goethes Gedanken über Musik*, p. 183.

possibly have left unexamined. An example of this is his manner of thinking in analogies, which he drew between music, architecture and colour, and which transcended the limits of the individual arts. Goethe considered Leonardo's *Last Supper* to be the first fugue in the visual arts[62] and it is reasonable to assume Goethe was predisposed to synaesthesia. In his letters to Zelter Goethe openly acknowledged this visual orientation and he took cognizance of this when listening to music. Unlike Carl Philipp Emanuel Bach, who saw the gestures of music-making as a positive contribution to the communication process, Goethe held them to be a disturbing secondary phenomenon, which could divert attention from the unreserved reception of music if they were not in harmony with the music performed. With chamber music the communication between players enhanced the performance, but in opera the orchestral players should be hidden, for their gestures interfered with the musical drama.[63]

Goethe regarded not the eye but rather the ear as the sense organ, which permits the most direct access to the individual's innermost being. When Goethe found himself incapable of making more than a partial pictorial transformation of a quartet by Mendelssohn, whom he greatly esteemed, he described how it remained 'in den Ohren hängen'.[64] It remained on his ear until he had time to assimilate it. Conversely, when Mendelssohn played through the first movement of Beethoven's Fifth Symphony during his 1830 visit, Goethe remarked, 'That does not move one at all, it only causes astonishment.'[65] Goethe's verbal inadequacy in the face of Beethoven's Fifth is not an example of the poet's musical conservatism, as is usually claimed. Like Zelter, Goethe recognized Beethoven's brilliance as a composer and admired him with awe.[66] Beethoven's music had a diffuse emotional effect upon Goethe: some of it remained beyond rational grasp and was therefore incomprehensible. Interestingly, for Zelter, such incomprehensibility was part of its appeal and in his letter to Goethe on 6 April 1831, he considers, 'This is the advantage we derive from genius: it offends and reconciles, it wounds and heals; one must go along with it.'[67] Yet musical enjoyment, which Goethe described to Zelter as a balanced relationship between 'Sinnlichkeit und Verstand' (sensuality and intellect), was, for him, tantamount to 'Faßlichkeit' (intelligibility). By not

---

[62] GZ 31 December 1817.

[63] Goethe had implemented this idea in Lauchstädttheater: *GZ* 31 August 1802. See also *ZG* 12 August to 1 October 1819 and 12 April 1823.

[64] Eckermann, 12 January 1827, p. 206.

[65] GM, p. 36.

[66] ZG 14 September 1812.

[67] ZG 6 April 1831. It is, however, surprising that Zelter does not record the Berlin premieres of Beethoven's *Fidelio* in 1815 or the Ninth Symphony in November 1826. The latter can, perhaps, be exclaimed because there are fewer letters written by Zelter at the end of 1826 due to the relocation of the Sing-Akademie. His letter dated 'End of October 1826 to January 1827' reveals his preoccupation with Goethe's queries about his Theory of Sound.

being accessible to the intellect, Beethoven's instrumental music embodied the Daemonic for Goethe, the amoral world force which he had always inwardly rejected and once defined for Eckermann as that 'which cannot be accounted for by understanding and reason'.[68] While Goethe clearly recognized the emotional significance of music, he was deeply critical of the Romantic perception of music as self-expression, or the expression of the artist's emotions. While Beethoven was far removed from such doctrines of self-expression, and continually revised and clarified his musical ideas, Goethe believed the indirect influence of his tempestuous personality and the attempts to emulate him led to a decline in music brought about by expressionist theories of music.

**Goethe's Musicality Reclaimed**

To borrow Emerson's words, Goethe 'lived more fully and consciously on several levels than most other men'[69] and his catholic taste embraced music from early Byzantine chant to the motets of Palestrina, Morales and Allegri[70] from the music of Bach[71] and Handel[72] to contemporary works by Mozart,[73] Hummel, Beethoven, Schubert and Mendelssohn. Nowhere in these letters can you hear the drumbeats of obsession associated with Goethe's celebration of strophic song. Instead his susceptibility to the music of poetry, the physicality of his aural response as well as the fastidiousness of its discriminations, his poet's intelligence exercising itself in the activity of listening are evident in his discussions on song setting. While this compulsive Goethean music is clearly heard in Zelter's settings and there is a rightness in the pulse and movement of the best of these settings, a drumbeat that will not be denied, Goethe did not demand a rigid adherence to the musical metrics of poetry. 'I feel at once that your compositions are identical with my songs; the music, like the gas which is pumped into the balloon, merely raises

---

[68] Eckermann, 2 March 1831, (Stuttgart 1998), p. 486.

[69] Ralph Waldo Emerson, 'Goethe, or the Writer' (1850). In *Representative Men: Seven Lectures* (New York and Toronto: Random House Publishing Group, reprint 2004), p. 244.

[70] Goethe, *Italienische Reise*, 1 March 1788, *HA* 11, p. 542; 14 March 1788, p. 528; 22 March 1788, p. 530.

[71] GZ 4 January 1819 and GZ April 1827.

[72] GZ 24 April 1824, GZ 28 April 1824; Goethe to Friedrich Rochlitz, 2 April 1824, *WA* IV/38, pp. 100–101. Eckermann, 14 April 1824 (Stuttgart, 1998), p. 118.

[73] Eckermann, 11 March 1828, p. 687; 11 October 1828, p. 305; 6 December 1829, p. 387; 14 February 1831, p. 465 and 11 March 1832, p. 788. See also Goethe's conversation with Johann Christian Lobe in November 1821, *Goethes Gespräche. Eine Sammlung zeitgenössischer Berichte aus seinem Umgang auf Grund der Ausgabe und des Nachlasses von F. Freiherrn von Biedermann*. Completed and edited by Wolfgang Herwig (4 vols, Zürich and Stuttgart: Artemis Verlag, 1965), p. 190. Hereafter referred to as *Gespräche*.

them up,' he writes to Zelter in 1820. 'With other composers I must first see how they have understood the song and what they have made out of it.'[74] Although he was glad on one hand to identify in Weimar – rather than Berlin – the origins of Zelter's song tradition, Goethe was open to shaking that tradition up, reviving it and retuning it to other musical registers. Perhaps one of the most extraordinary examples of his willingness to learn is evident in his private audiences with the 22-year-old Mendelssohn[75] who most likely introduced him to Schubert's *Erlkönig* and unquestionably opened him to contemporary musical developments. 'Who can understand any kind of occurrence if he is not thoroughly acquainted with its development down to the present time?',[76] the octogenarian writes to Zelter, and he describes himself as 'passionately active, aspiring and keen to learn' from the musicians Zelter sends him.[77]

**In Pursuit of Zelter**

In a letter to Zelter in 1801, Goethe criticized the 'poor picture' of a person bequeathed to us by those necrologists:

> who, immediately after one's death, carefully balance the good and bad as perceived and applauded by the majority. They touch up his so-called virtues and vices with hypocritical righteousness, and thereby are worse than death in destroying a personality, which can be imagined only in the living union of those opposing qualities.[78]

In Zelter's case the opposite has been enacted by musicologists who have bequeathed to us the portrait of a blunt Zelter, who is falsely blamed for Goethe's persistence in espousing eighteenth-century concepts of musical aesthetics and ignoring such composers as Schubert and Berlioz. This image of the composer can obviously be linked to canon formation and to former detractors of pre-Schubertian song, as also to the complex trajectory of Mendelssohn reception, but it fails to recognize the self-divisions in Zelter. A stonemason who strove to study music, a born activist who was also a silence-seeking lyric composer, a self-made musician whose inability to produce anything of lasting value caused him much private pain, a cultural administrator and committeeman who did not really believe in democracy in the arts, Zelter embodied many contradictions. Lea Mendelssohn

---

[74] GZ 11 May 1820.
[75] GZ 21 June 1827.
[76] GZ 3 June 1830.
[77] Ibid. Goethe's willingness to learn from Felix – even as a small boy – is echoed in the Mendelssohn documents. See *GM*, p. 36.
[78] GZ 29 May 1801.

recognized these self-divisions in Zelter just months after her children commenced lessons with the composer:

> [...] he weaves so much spirit, taste, meaning, humour, even genius into his discourses everywhere, that I often regret not having jotted down the best of it. In his case the belief of the ancients, that man has two souls, seems to be true, for I cannot deny that the same man who charms us with the inspiration of an artist, touching seriousness of thought, and jokes à la Jean Paul, can also be downright insipid and prosaic.[79]

A mixture of Polonius and Tiresias, of bore and of bard, Zelter was more prepared than most to admit his contradictions. Enjoined by his calling to live fully and truly, Zelter gave full rein to what was passionate in his sensibility and sceptical in his intelligence; he could be majestic in public and mocking in private, tactical and obstinate, down-to-earth and elevated. Yet these were symptoms not of an absence of coherence but of an appetite for abundance; in fact, the coherence lay in his determination to live fully, and the honesty of perception and expression that this determination compelled turned him not only into the first Professor of Music in Germany but also into a great observer and reporter of his musical world and its inhabitants.

## Zelter and the Shape of Early nineteenth-century Music History

Zelter's active engagement in the musical life of Berlin and his discussion of concerts attended provides an important chronicle of concert life in Berlin at the beginning of the nineteenth century.[80] Zelter's descriptions of performances by the Berlin court opera reveal the court's choice of carnival for the main performance season; its penchant for mythological subjects;[81] its tendency towards action-packed scenes with emphasis on the visual spectacle rather than on the psychological impact of the drama;[82] as well as its inclusion of ballet.[83] While Zelter's letters record Gaspare Spontini's popularity and opposition in Berlin, they also mark the directorship at the Königliches Opernhaus of Count von Brühl and Wilhelm von Redern, who expanded the repertory to include the works of

---

[79] Letter of 14 July 1819, Lea to Henriette von Pereira Anstein. Quoted in Todd, *Mendelssohn: A Life in Music*, p. 44.

[80] See for example: ZG 27 August 1818; ZG 7 June 1820; ZG 21 July 1820; ZG 16 December 1825; ZG 26 January 1830; ZG 11-12 April 1830; ZG 26 October 1830; 1 November 1830; ZG 27 October 1831.

[81] Reichardt's setting of *Tod des Herkules*: ZG 13 April 1802.

[82] Winter's setting of *Die Zauberflöte II*: ZG 10 August 1803. See also ZG 29 October to 2 November 1830.

[83] ZG 14 April 1831.

more German composers including the world premiere of Weber's *Der Freischütz* (1821), successful performances of Weber's *Euryanthe* (1825[84] and 1827[85]) and the Berlin premiere of Spohr's *Faust* (1829).[86] As Zelter shared Goethe's love of the human voice, his letters celebrate performances by the most popular and successful divas of his day:[87] the attractive voice and technical skill of Henriette Sontag;[88] the imposing presence and rich flawless voice of Berlin's *prima donna assoluta*, Anna Milder-Hauptmann;[89] and the vocal prowess of Wilhelmine Schröder-Devrient which was matched by an innate dramatic skill.[90] In addition to marking the meteoric ascent of the diva in nineteenth-century concert life, Zelter's letters record such extraordinary performances as the first performance of Bach's *St Matthew Passion* for over a hundred years, conducted by Felix Mendelssohn in the Sing-Akademie, attended by the king and his retinue and counting the leading Prussian theologian Schleiermacher, the German philosopher Georg Wilhlem Friedrich Hegel, Heinrich Heine, Rahel von Varnhagen and Spontini among its audience.[91] An equally colourful record of the first setting of Goethe's *Faust*, composed by a crown prince and rehearsed by a royal cast, is contained within this correspondence.[92] In addition, Zelter's letters to Goethe highlight the cultural and musical problems of his age from the rise of a German national music theatre to the introduction of metronome markings,[93] from the question of authorship in Mozart's *Requiem*[94] to the beginnings of musical biography[95] and the rising debates about the nature of musical virtuosity.[96]

Like Goethe, Zelter criticized the virtuoso cult of individualism, which degrades the musical work to a mere vehicle for the demonstration of technical and artistic dexterity and so works against the listener's purely musically-oriented interest. At first Zelter complains bitterly about the general acclaim of Paganini's concerts of his violin concerti, his empty showmanship and the eccentricity of his playing, yet his openness to change is evident when he hears him perform publicly and acclaims in his performance and compositions a balance of musical content

---

[84] ZG 24 to 26 December 1825.
[85] ZG 5 September to 13 October 1827.
[86] ZG 13 to 16 November 1829.
[87] ZG 14 April 1831.
[88] ZG 28 October 1827; ZG 11 April 1830; ZG 10 May 1830.
[89] ZG 13 September 1812.
[90] ZG 2 February 1831.
[91] ZG 9 March 1829. See also ZG 17 April 1829.
[92] ZG 31 March 1816.
[93] ZG 10 May 1831.
[94] ZG 16 June 1827.
[95] ZG 1 to 9 July 1803; GZ 28 July 1803; ZG 12 to 22(?) March 1829; ZG 21 to 23 February 1830.
[96] ZG Good Friday, 1829; ZG 1 May 1829; ZG 14 May 1829; GZ 17 May 1829; GZ 9 November 1829; GZ 9 June 1831.

and profound knowledge of violin technique.[97] In a similar fashion he praises the clarity and precision of Moscheles's piano playing and the Classical balance of his compositional style,[98] and acclaims the clarity, evenness and delicacy of tone in performances by the Weimar Kapellmeister Hummel.[99] When Goethe envies the musical experience of Moeser's Quartet evenings in Berlin,[100] Zelter – aware of the poet's musical isolation – imagines Goethe in his audience[101] and gives many musicians letters of introduction to him.

**Imagining Mendelssohn's Childhood and Artistic Identity**

One of the most important introductions was to his pupil Felix Mendelssohn, whose early development is recorded in these letters. From the beginning Zelter was very conscious of Felix's extraordinary ability. His first mention of his young protégé to Goethe on 20 August 1821 acclaims Felix's talent and already augurs his departure.[102] He introduces Felix to Goethe in the winter of 1821/22 and after the visit his letters chronicle Mendelssohn's development. He describes 'his astounding piano playing';[103] and he recounts Mendelssohn's 'admirable industry'[104] without any trace of jealousy, admitting, 'Even if I fail to produce anything much myself, I keep my students focused.'[105] Zelter's praise may also have been augmented in the light of the publication and international reception of Felix's op. 1, where he was acclaimed as a second Mozart in Leipzig[106] and as a composer of genius in Paris.[107] It may also have been influenced by the composition of the second Piano Quartet op. 2, written in 1823, published and dedicated to Zelter the following year. It is no coincidence that the most substantial chamber work of 1823, revealing the formal and expressive influence of Beethoven, was dedicated to Zelter, whose relationship to the composer is generally misunderstood. In a letter to Goethe on 11 March 1823, Zelter acclaims the modernity of the work and

---

[97] See, for example, ZG 17 April 1829; 1 to 5 May 1829; 14 May 1829. See also GZ 17 May 1829; 9 November 1829; 9 to 13 June 1831.
[98] ZG 27 November 1824.
[99] ZG 30 April 1821; 22 to 23 May 1826; 25 to 27 May 1826; 5 to 8 March 1828; 16 to 17 January 1832.
[100] GZ 9 November 1829; ZG 17 November 1829.
[101] ZG 14 April 1831.
[102] ZG 9 March 1829. See also ZG 10 May 1830 and ZG 2 November 1830.
[103] ZG 11 March 1823.
[104] ZG 10 December 1824.
[105] ZG 17 March 1822.
[106] *AMZ* 26 (1824), columns 181–4.
[107] Henriette Mendelssohn to Lea Mendelssohn, 11 February 1824; see Peter Ward Jones, *Catalogue of the Mendelssohn Papers in the Bodleian Library, Oxford*, III (Tutzing: Hans Schneider, 1989), pp. 269–70.

considered it 'even better than the one he performed in Weimar'.[108] His generosity as a teacher again comes through in his appraisal of Felix's fourth opera, *Die beiden Neffen*, or *Der Onkel aus Boston* (*The Two Nephews*, or *The Uncle from Boston*), as that of a master.[109] He recognizes the sterling quality of his writing[110] and when he hears Felix's double piano concerto, he recognizes his individuality becoming more and more apparent[111] and avows to Goethe, 'I do everything I can to encourage him, as he drives himself on to experiment in the various new and more conventional forms.'[112]

Although the evidence of these letters verify Zelter's continual encouragement, and Larry Todd's brilliant book, *Mendelssohn's Musical Education: A Study and Edition of his Exercises in Composition*, generously extols Zelter's merit as a teacher of composition, it was difficult, at first, to dispel doubts as to what Zelter could have given Mendelssohn during these formative years. What could Zelter have given a student capable of composing the Sextet in D for piano and strings (op. 110) at the age of 15, or the Octet in E flat Major (op. 20) written a year later? A clue to the answer is found in the compositional notebooks in the *Preussischer Staatsbibliothek* in Berlin. While the fugal subjects in these early notebooks lack the musical impetus immediately visible in a fugal subject by Bach – and were most likely given by Zelter – it is clear that Zelter aimed to nurture Felix's musical intuition. The conversations recorded on Felix's first visit to Goethe confirm Zelter's understanding that this is something an individual has to find within himself. From Mendelssohn's early works, completed under Zelter's guidance, it is clear this Felix pursued composition with the idea of conquest, not of territory perhaps but of imagination – an awakening which would allow him to repossess his musical territory with new conviction.

Negative reception histories of Mendelssohn and Zelter go together hand in glove and when considering Mendelssohn's early development, we must re-evaluate the musicological image of his venerable teacher, Zelter, whose fidelity to his vocation and fulfilment of its public demands were steady and characteristically vigorous. There has been a sustained effort to criticize Zelter's compositional oeuvre when we should have honoured much else: his acuity as a critic and writer on music; his record as an active witness and committed participant in those times of important musical change; his wisdom and acuity as a teacher. While it lies beyond the scope of this preface to re-evaluate Zelter's relationship with Mendelssohn, let us briefly consider one aspect, namely contemporary reports of Zelter's possessiveness regarding his student, of which there is no evidence in these letters.

---

[108] ZG 11 March 1823.
[109] ZG 8 February 1824.
[110] ZG 11 March 1823.
[111] ZG 26 December 1824.
[112] ZG 6 June 1826.

Felix's lessons with Zelter commenced in 1819 and continued for approximately eight years. For A.B. Marx, who only completed a few figured bass exercises with him, Zelter was an uninspiring teacher, and he compared Zelter's teaching of Mendelssohn to observing a fish swim and then imagining he had somehow instructed the fish to swim. Marx's opinion contrasts with Abraham's appraisal, where he claimed that Felix's 'musical existence and direction would have been entirely different without Zelter'; an opinion which was shared by Felix, who praised his teacher for raising him 'not according to rigid, constructing theorems, but in true freedom, that is in the knowledge of proper boundaries'.[113] When Felix's formal lessons with Zelter were discontinued in 1827, Eduard Devrient's portrayal of an angry Zelter, who believed that Felix had 'learned everything from him and not yet outgrown his guidance'[114] does not hold any weight in these letters. From his first mention of Felix to Goethe, Zelter recognizes Felix would outgrow him, and throughout the correspondence we find Zelter mirroring Abraham's reasons that 'Felix's genius was [...] self-existent'. Moscheles believed that few, other than Zelter and Berger, truly recognized the youth's genius. A good example of Zelter's ability to pave Mendelssohn's path is found in the musical forms and dedications of his first publication. While the piano quartet played to Mendelssohn's strengths as a pianist and violinist, it also ingeniously avoided immediate comparisons with his musical forefathers. So, too, the dedication of op. 1 to Prince Radziwill, an important patron of the arts, and to Goethe (op. 3) announced Mendelssohn's significance as a composer. But beyond such sound musical guidance and unwavering encouragement, Zelter's greatest gift to his young protégé was, undoubtedly, the introduction he gave him to Goethe, who was one of the most generous presences of Mendelsohn's early years.

Between the ages of 12 and 21, Mendelssohn stayed in Goethe's home on four separate occasions, three of which are recorded in these letters.[115] According to Abraham, Goethe's warm reception of his son 'ennobled' Felix's youth.[116] More than this, Zelter's introduction of Felix to Goethe in November 1821 acted as a catalyst, channelling Mendelssohn's energies and talents in new directions. Buoyed by Goethe's comparisons with Mozart on the first Weimar visit from 2 to 19 November 1821, Mendelssohn was inspired to work in larger instrumental

---

[113] Todd, *Mendelssohn: A Life in Music*, p. 43.

[114] Eduard Devrient, *Meine Erinnerungen an Felix Mendelssohn-Bartholdy und seine Briefe an mich* (Leipzig: J.J. Weber, 1869); Eng. trans., Natalia MacFarren, *My Recollections of Felix-Mendelssohn-Bartholdy and his Letters to Me* (London: Richard Bentley: 1869; repr. New York: Vienna House, 1972), pp. 32–3.

[115] All four visits are recounted in *GM*. For a detailed reading of these visits and of Mendelssohn's relationship with Goethe in general, see Lorraine Byrne Bodley, 'Mendelssohn as portrayed in the Goethe–Zelter Correspondence'. In Nicole Grimes and Jacqueline Waeber (eds), *Mendelssohn in the Long Nineteenth Century* (in preparation).

[116] Abraham to Goethe, 26 November 1821 in Max Friedländer, 'Briefe an Goethe von Felix Mendelssohn', *GJb* 12 (1891): 111.

forms, and the subsequent publication of his piano quartet op. 1 in 1823 marked his entrance as a composer into the public domain. Felix's dedication of the B minor Piano Quartet on his third visit to Goethe in May 1825 is also highly significant, for it heralds a new phase in Mendelssohn's compositional development. The dedication of the Piano Quartet no. 3 to Goethe may have been inspired by the poet's comparison of the composer with Mozart, one of the few composers to have written in this genre.[117] Goethe's enthusiastic response to this dedication is evident in the letter he wrote to Felix, thanking him and praising the quartet as 'the graceful embodiment of that beautiful rich, energetic soul which so astonished me when you first made me acquainted with it'.[118]

As accounts of these early visits show, Goethe knew that Felix needed a tremendous amount of support to flourish: good teachers, attentive parents, ample opportunities for performance and display, access to avenues for publicity provided by the poet, who had set up a sequence of hurdles, acknowledged in the musical sphere, over which Felix had the opportunity to bound. All these steps are in place on the very first visit to Goethe, whose immediate identification with Felix was anchored in the high voltage of his early talent. Like Mendelssohn, Goethe had surpassed his local masters by early adolescence; and at an early age had moved to the European centres of artistry where he accomplished his art with obvious supremacy. The extraordinary friendship, which subsequently developed between the 12-year-old Mendelssohn and 72year-old Goethe, emerged from this intensity, a root, a common emotional ground.

During the first three visits we find Mendelssohn intent on pleasing Goethe and it is interesting to consider the development that had taken place in Mendelssohn prior to his final visit, which took place between 21 May to 3 June 1830 on the threshold of Mendelssohn's Italian journey. Buoyed by the success of the *St Matthew Passion*, his publications and English tour, Mendelssohn now greeted the poet as an established artist, asked for and was granted the familiar 'du' – a form of address which Goethe rarely granted after 1800. (Even Schiller and Goethe had always remained on 'Sie' terms, though their correspondence shares an intimacy different from that of the Goethe–Zelter letters.)

For Goethe, Mendelssohn's visit was a welcome interruption to the naturally increasing solitude of old age. The gratitude Goethe expressed, and the willingness of the 80-year-old poet to learn from the 22-year-old composer,[119] provides a counter-image to the portrayal of a conservative poet in musical literature. For Mendelssohn, Goethe was an important figure in the question of artistic identity. In his writing and in person Goethe offered Mendelssohn important lessons on how an artist ought to conduct himself. The high standards he set were the usual

---

[117] Mozart's C minor Piano Sonata K457 (1784) has also been sourced as a model by Todd. Felix was familiar with Mozart's two piano quartets (K478 and K493) whose imprint is on Felix's score.

[118] *GM*, p. 50.

[119] GZ 3 June 1830. See also *GM*, p. 36.

basis for the attainment of durable distinction in any life or art: openness, courage and complete commitment to one's art. Goethe's courage was evident not only in his embrace of solitude, both personal and intellectual, in his later years, in order to produce *Faust II*, but also in the writing of *Werther*, the novel that made his name at 22 – the same age as Mendelssohn on this final encounter. Such accidental resemblances between Goethe's formative years and Mendelssohn's own experiences added intimacy to this final encounter with the Olympian patriarch, whose wisdom, abundance and acuity were made available to the composer.[120]

For Mendelssohn, Goethe was a *rara avis*, an artist whose note was uniquely beyond the common scale.[121] Mendelssohn could grant this inimitable status to his art and, on his final visit, still recognize the process that produced it as the usual, uncertain, hopeful, needy, half self-surrendering, half self-priming process that he, like every artist, had also experienced. Perhaps the final thing to be learned from this extraordinary relationship is that in the realm of art, as in the realm of consciousness, there is no end to the possible learning that can take place. When Goethe embraced his friend, knowing it might be the last time they would meet, Mendelssohn took with him an image of an exemplary poet who showed him how the artistic vocation entails the disciplining of a habit of expression until it becomes fundamental to the whole conduct of a life.

## Zelter's Nobility of Spirit: A Forgotten Ideal

One of the incidental pleasures of the pages is the constant stimulation of the wily remarks and upfront judgements that Zelter made with such relish. In 1827, for example, he refers to Couperin's ornamentation as 'French froth',[122] a remark which is understandably levelled against him when cited without reference to the following letter where he explains to Goethe how Couperin's style of ornamentation became ingrained in J.S. Bach's compositional style.[123]

In a similar fashion, Zelter's rejection of Berlioz's 1828 setting of *Huit scènes de Faust* (Eight Scenes from [Goethe's] Faust) is cited out of context. First, Goethe's request is usually cited as an example of his inability to judge a musical work, yet the poet's openness to the composer is evident in these letters: 'A Frenchman has set eight passages of my *Faust* to music, and sends me the score which is very beautifully typeset; I should much like to forward it to you and hear your

---

[120] An important reference on the reciprocity of Goethe and Mendelssohn's relationship is found in Claus Canisius, 'Stranger in a Foreign Land: Goethe as a scholar in music', in *Goethe and Schubert: Across the Divide* (Dublin: Carysfort Press, 2003), p. 36.

[121] Albert Bielschowsky, *Goethe, sein Leben und sein Werke* (2 vols, Munich: Beck, 1922), vol. 2, p. 683.

[122] ZG 5 to 14 April 1827.

[123] GZ 21 to 22 April 1827; ZG 8 to 9 June 1827.

*favourable* opinion.'[124] Goethe's receptiveness to Berlioz's musical realization in this passage is indicative of his openness to French interpretations of his *Faust* in general. Through the translations of *Faust I* (1828) and parts of *Faust II* (1840), which inspired Delacroix (paintings and etchings) and Berlioz (*La Damnation de Faust*, 1846), Gerard de Nerval (1808–55) succeeded in presenting a 'French Faust' which Goethe preferred to his own: 'I don't like reading Faust in German any more; yet in this French translation everything makes a refreshing, novel, and spirited impression.'[125] Zelter's reply to Goethe's request and subsequent diatribe against Berlioz's *Huit scènes de Faust*[126] should also be placed in context, for his remarks tell us as much about Berlioz as about Zelter's prejudices. Berlioz's first pieces submitted for the Prix de Rome met with a similar reaction from the judges; Paganini rejected Berlioz's ideas for a violin concerto including a programme based on the sad fate of Mary Stuart, and the Paris Opéra, which paid extraordinarily high royalties to composers, consistently rejected his works. Berlioz was a caustic, provocative writer who disagreed with the musical standards of his time: in every sense, he fought an uphill battle, not just with Goethe and Zelter but also with his most of his contemporaries.

In Goethe's letters to Zelter, by comparison, one is aware of the strictness of his mind of his scrupulousness in respect to what he withholds. In Zelter's letters to Goethe he gave free reign to his prejudices, and such passages parade Zelter in full flight. But as attractive as this off-the-cuffness may be, the real attraction of Zelter lies in the nobility of his mind, the way he combined ardour with rigour, the ideal of service behind and beneath the attitudizing. 'Could I but achieve something great! My life is passing and nothing comes of it',[127] he writes to Goethe after he administers a rebuke to himself for failing to produce work of lasting substance.[128] At the same time he was well able to discover and acclaim musical ability in those around him. In a letter to Goethe on 11 June 1826 he compares his own setting of a poem by Voss to a setting by his student, Fanny Mendelssohn, and admits, 'She has really caught the spirit of it better than I have.'[129] It was this crystalline purity of motive and conduct that redeemed much of the egotism and common clowning.

**Song and the Art of Identity**

The happy entertainer in Zelter got wonderfully into his stride in Weimar and besides earning the respect of Goethe and Schiller, he also won the love of a great number of men and women who encountered him during these years. What

---

[124] GZ 28 April 1829.
[125] Eckermann, 3 January 1830, p. 396.
[126] ZG 21 June 1829.
[127] Ibid.
[128] ZG 3 February 1803.
[129] ZG 11 June 1826.

gratified Zelter most was the feeling of being privy to an atmosphere of artistic and intellectual endeavour, a cultural climate generated by an art so boldly and unpredictably written. Goethe was a *rara avis*, one whose note was uniquely beyond the common scale, and his friendship with Zelter elevated the composer's sense of personal and poetic destiny. In such settings as *Rastlose Liebe* and *Um Mitternacht*,[130] Zelter was true to the impact of Goethe's poetry and sensitive to the inner laws of his composer's being. At the same time Zelter perceived song as irreducibly an event of language, and he was invariably true to Goethe's muse, if not to himself. In *Wandrers Nachtlied*,[131] for example, the sense of evanescence, of the transitoriness of things, of the stillness behind things into which they eventually pass, resounds in the music. In the composition of this lyric there is a deep, emphatic appreciation of the ephemeral beauty manifested in nature, human life or a song. A different economy of means, a sense of a huge encircling stillness, a strong sense of another world within worldly surroundings, are evident in Schubert's setting of this poem. Both Schubert and Zelter felt a need to extend the alphabet of expressiveness in setting Goethe's poetry. Yet in contrast to Schubert's *Gretchen am Spinnrade*, which has come to represent the kind of untrammelled, radically unaligned work we associate with music of high artistic purpose, Zelter's Goethe settings unveil a natural inclination to make himself an echo chamber for the poem's sounds. At the same time he knew what the creative demands entailed and it was this essential knowledge that punished him when his compositional work began to lose its sense of inevitability, and he had to labour towards a power rather than ride upon it.

As a figure of his times, Zelter may have lived out a certain cliché: the self-educated musician who studied music against his father's wishes. And in biographies of his early years we are confronted with an artistic isolation that is painful and resistant, a figure painfully displaced within himself and yet familiar. In these letters to Goethe we witness the way in which he envisaged and conducted his life. The exchange of poems to be set and their musical reply verifies song as a domestic art, where Zelter has drifted into a certain vein of musical thought. The songs exchanged in these letters corroborate the creative purpose of early German song and it was Zelter's historic good fortune to have not only his own compositional talent but also the genius of his good friend Goethe to sponsor it. During these years, Goethe's poetry was both the ship and anchor of Zelter's talent – a buoyancy and a steadying. Through Goethe, Zelter extended the idiom of his art and left behind no ignominious legacy.

---

[130] Carl Friedrich Zelter, *Fünfzig Lieder für eine Singstimme mit Klavier* (Mainz, London, New York, Paris, Tokyo: Schott, 1932, 'Rastlose Liebe', pp. 5–8 and 'Um Mitternacht', pp. 34–35. Hereafter referred to as Zelter, *Fünfzig Lieder*. A exemplary performance of Zelter's 'Um Mitternacht' by Ann Murray (soprano) and Graham Johnson (piano) is can be found (along with other songs by Zelter) on *Songs by Schubert's friends and contemporaries* (London: Hyperion Edition, 2006), CD1, CDJ33051/3.

[131] Zelter, *Fünfzig Lieder*, 'Wandrers Nachtlied', pp. 1–2.

## The Lure of the Poet: Zelter's Relationship with Goethe

The original object of Goethe's correspondence with Zelter was correctly recognized by Kayser and Reichardt, who believed Goethe found in Zelter the musical correspondent he had been seeking. In Zelter Goethe found an intelligent and reflective musician whose natural outspokenness, sharp wit, and ironic sense of humour engaged the poet. Zelter provided Goethe with the sounding board and support he lacked after his return from Italy, in ample measure and in various forms – a sympathetic understanding and musical realization of his poetry, an engagement with musical life outside Weimar. Far from becoming dependent on Zelter's musical opinions, in the early years of the correspondence Goethe clearly recognized Zelter's contradictions and limitations: in the very first letter he wrote to Zelter, Goethe requested Zelter to set 'Die erste Walpurgisnacht', a task Zelter was unable to fulfil; similarly, plans to write a cantata for the Reformation Jubilee together[132] or provide music for a commemorative performance of Schiller's *Lied von der Glocke*[133] were impeded by Zelter's inability to realize a large-scale commission.

Despite such failings Goethe found his belief in man's essential goodness and continual progress embodied in Zelter, a recognition symbolized in the coat of arms he designed for Zelter: 'Zum Werk und Kunst treu'. As W.B. Yeats later wrote, 'The intellect of man is forced to choose/Perfection of the life, or of the work';[134] Zelter chose the latter and his letters to Goethe envelop us in a musical life that is honour-bound and assiduous. In 1804, when Zelter was in the full summer of his power, he established the Ordentliche Singschule:[135] the first state-supported programme of music education in Prussia. Four years later, in December 1808, he founded the Berlin Liedertafel, a choral society of 25 men, who composed and performed works for each other, and which became a model for the formation of other such societies throughout Germany. Zelter was also responsible for the foundation of the Musikalische Bildungsanstalt, which became the Institut für die Ausbildung von Organisten und Musiklehrern in 1822,[136] and he also established various institutes for teaching church and school music in Königsberg (1814), Breslau (1815), and Berlin (1822). As founder of the Royal Academy of Religious Music in Berlin (1822) and director of the Sing-Akademie (1823), Zelter was responsible for introducing significant works to the general public,[137] thereby

---

[132] GZ 14 November 1816.

[133] GZ 22 July 1805; ZG 30 July 1805; GZ 4 August 1805; ZG 25 August to 8 September 1805; GZ 12 October 1805; ZG 26 October 1805; GZ 18 November 1805; ZG 14 December 1805; GZ 5 June 1806.

[134] W.B. Yeats, 'The Choice' in *Collected Poems* (Dublin: Macmillan, 1933), p. 278.

[135] ZG 8 December 1824.

[136] This in turn became the Königliches Akademisches Institut für Kirchenmusik in 1875.

[137] See for example the performance of Bach's B Minor mass, ZG 19 February 1831.

earning the composer a reputation as an authority on early sacred music. Under his guidance, the Sing-Akademie became a model for the performance of early sacred choral works with instrumental accompaniment provided by the Orchester-Schule or Ripienschule, which he founded in 1809 to supply string players for his concerts in the Sing-Akademie.[138] In recognition of this musical distinction, Zelter received an honorary doctorate from the University of Berlin in 1808. At the suggestion of Wilhelm von Humboldt, the first chair of music was created at the Akademie der Künste in 1809 and Zelter was made responsible for the city's sacred and secular music education.[139] Zelter held the first academic music position in Berlin in 1815, when appointed director of music at the Friedrich-Wilhelm University, founded five years before. In 1830 this position was changed to that of a university lectureship; only the second of its kind in Germany. Zelter was appointed Professor of Music and two years later Marx became his successor.

Inexorably Zelter was driven to raise musical standards across Germany. It was this unceasing energy, his activism and passionate devotion to music, his horse-sense and perspicacity which drew Goethe to him. Goethe also admired Zelter's ability to encounter the harsh realities of life without jeopardizing traditional order. Following the suicide of Zelter's stepson, Carl Flöricke, when Zelter writes under the shadow of death, his letter to Goethe is a nightmare glimpse into the mind of a man who has survived traumatic events and is now exposed to a comfortless future.[140] We immediately recognize his predicament and the pitch of his grief and find ourselves the better for having them expressed with such dignity and unforgiving truth. So, too, Goethe's letter marking the sudden death of his only living child, 'In Memoriam (August von Goethe) – In Friendship and Sympathy',[141] may be read as a projection of his wisdom, refined, as it was, in the crucible of experience.

## Epilogue: Numbered Days

In an age such as ours, when 'the instability of the human subject' is constantly argued for if not presumed, there should be no problem with a correspondence which is woven from two such different psychic fabrics. In fact the Goethe–Zelter letters perfectly answer the modern conception of a work of creative imagination as one in which conflicting realities find accommodation within a new order; and this reconciliation comes most poignantly and most profoundly in the final years of the correspondence when the poet in old age gathers in his harvest and begins to plan the posthumous publication of their letters. The final five years

---

[138] This gave rise to the Spontini's Königliche Theater-Instrumental-Schule (1822) which trained musicians for the royal theatres.

[139] ZG 19 June 1825; ZG 19 May 1831.

[140] ZG 14 to 17 November 1812; GZ 3 December 1812.

[141] GZ 23 February 1831.

of the correspondence are imbued with a strong sense of death hovering close, unknowable but certain, and yet, because it is imagined within a consciousness which has learned to expect that the correspondence will find an ultimate home among the poet's published papers, this primal human emotion is transmuted into something less shadow-line, more metaphysically tempered. As Goethe prepares the letters for publication, he looks beyond the grave, resolved to immortalize a composer who lived a singularly individual life. Goethe's correspondence with Zelter commemorates the composer not as an Orphean musical voice but as an exemplary practitioner, one whose history was the musical history of his times. Yet these late letters are not just a narrative full of musicological interest; they are also literature of a high order, in which such letters of great intensity – such as 'In Memoriam (August von Goethe) – In Friendship and Sympathy'[142] – rise like emanations from some fissure in the bedrock of the human capacity to endure.

This 35-year correspondence with Zelter endorses the perception of Goethe as a toiling intelligence, a Dantesque spirit pushing toward ever higher levels of understanding and mastery. Yet it also bequeaths an enduring profile of Zelter as a noble musician working towards high national purposes, a profile which, will, I hope, persuade readers to suspend their disbelief in Zelter, and will be part of the redress that the composer deserves. But is not enough for musicologists to be what Osip Mandelstam once called 'purveyors of the paraphrasable meaning', not enough to have the will doing the work of the imagination. Some shift in the mindset or reception has to occur, some startle of insight or originality that may prompt an exegesis of Zelter's life and work and the reinvention of Goethe and Zelter's musical world. My aim in writing this translation is, therefore, to rebalance truth that has been regarded for two centuries as self-evident by garnering together a critical record that might be hung in the scale as a counterweight to the current musicological reception of their lives.

Lorraine Byrne Bodley

---

[142] Ibid.

# Section I
# Early Years' Correspondence 1796–1814

### 1. Goethe to Madame Unger

Weimar, 13 June 1796

Your letter, dear lady,[1] and the enclosed songs gave me very great pleasure. Herr Zelter's admirable compositions reached me while I was with people who first made me acquainted with his work. His melody to the Lied 'Ich denke Dein'[2] had an unbelievable charm for me, and I could not help writing that text for it, which stands in Schiller's *Musenalmanach*.

I am no judge of music, since I don't have a grasp of the means it uses to achieve its ends; I can only speak of the effect it produces upon me, when I give myself over to it fully and repeatedly; and so I can say of Herr Zelter's settings of my poems: that I could scarcely have believed music capable of such heartfelt tones.

Thank him very much for me, and tell him that I should very much like to get to know him personally with a view to mutual discussion. Although it is true that in the eighth volume of my novel there will not be any room for [new] settings; still, the legacy of Mignon and the old Harper is not yet exhausted, and all of it that can be allowed to see the light I should most gladly entrust to Herr Zelter.

Meantime, I may, perhaps, send some other poems soon, with the request that they be set to music for Schiller's *Musenalmanach*; I had hoped to enclose them in this letter, which, as a result, has been longer in coming than it ought to have been.

Accept my thanks, dear Madam, for the trouble you have taken, and believe that I appreciate the interest which kind and enlightened minds take in me and in my works, through which I can also bring a part of my existence near to persons far from and unknown to me.

Goethe

---

[1] The wife of Goethe's publisher in Berlin. Goethe had written his 'Nähe des Geliebten' as a musical parody to Zelter's setting of Frederike Brun's 'Ich denke Dein', and incorporated the new song into a production of *Claudine von Villa Bella* in Weimar in May 1796. Hearing of this through a mutual friend, J.F. Latrobe (1769–1845), Zelter was encouraged to send Goethe (through Unger) some of his compositions, including his *Wilhelm Meisters Lehrjahre* settings.

[2] Frederike Brun (1765–1835), 'Ich denke Dein'.

## 2. Zelter

Berlin, 11 August 1799

Noble Sir!

My good friend, Herr Unger, brought me ineffable joy through something you wrote in your letter to him. The favour which my [compositional] endeavours have received from you is a great joy to me, something I had hoped for but without any confidence, although I have no doubt about the quality of some of my work; the unsolicited approbation of a man whose works are held sacred in my home has given me reassurance such as I have never felt so purely and as strongly as now.

It would be a great boon to me if you would entrust the composition of more of your poems to me, for I don't know how to commend them more than through my own pure inner response; and I may say that with great dedication I have worked on your poems according to the measure of my talent.

Apart from the settings which were published in the Schiller Almanach, I have also composed: 'Der Zauberlehrling'; 'Die Braut von Corinth'; 'Die Erinnerung'; 'Das Blümlein Wunderschön'; 'Der Junggesell und der Mühlbach' and 'Bundeslied', which I would gladly send you if it were agreeable to you. I have thought about sending them for a long time and never dared. As soon as you give me the nod, they will be in your hands as quickly as possible.

Sincerely
Zelter

## 3. Goethe

Weimar, 26 August 1799

It is with deep gratitude that I reply to your friendly letter, by which you express in words that of which your compositions themselves have long convinced me: namely that you take a lively interest in my works, and show that you respond with genuine empathy. The beauty of an active participation is that it is itself in turn productive, for if my poems called forth your melodies, I can say that your melodies have stirred me to many a song, and doubtless if we lived nearer to one another, I should more frequently than at present feel myself inspired by a lyric mood. Every kind of communication with you will give me great pleasure.

I enclose a work[3] that has rather a strange appearance. It was suggested by the question: whether dramatic ballads might not be worked out in such a manner, as to

---

[3] Goethe's ballad 'Die erste Walpurgisnacht'.

furnish a composer with material for a large-scale choral work. Unfortunately this particular ballad is too insignificant to deserve being treated on so large a scale.

Warmest greetings to Herr Unger.

Goethe

## 4. Zelter

Berlin, 21 September 1799

It is against my wishes to have delayed this consignment, and even for these few settings I had to push the copyist. I am holding several settings back and console myself with the pleasant hope of being able to write to your Excellency more often.

The manner in which 'Der Zauberlehrling' is performed is essentially how I like to read the poem: namely, I begin not too quickly, here and there the tempo accelerates so that a powerful rendition of incantation remains possible and flows from the singer until the sorcerer appears, at which point I underscore the setting with a higher, commanding tone. The musical climaxes lie mainly in the power of the singers, who must remain serious and take great care not to labour the words. I took the Lied 'Thekla'[4] from the *Musenalmanach*. It is performed by a 'harp-strummer', who sometimes narrates and sometimes is moved to use gesture. If I had in those days already known the *Piccolomini*,[5] then it is very likely that it would have turned out differently, although the weight and depth of the lament should be effective even without the context. 'Die Erinnerung'[6] ought to have a secretive, uneasy, tender character and that should be conveyed by the music alone, without the singer having to demonstrate any special agitation. For that reason it is indicated *comodetto*.

The sonnet is a daring venture. I am ill-versed in the theory of poetry and thought that the sonnet, with its architectonic structure as Sulzer[7] sees it, is especially suitable to be set to music. However, although this setting is the best of several attempts, I cannot consider it successful. The melismatic phrases which occur here and there in the melody are most suited to the expression and at the same time misplace the outer proportions of the poem, which I strove to maintain. There are perhaps still metrical rules for the sonnet which I did not discover in theories known to me: the poet must have observed the enjambments, for example,

---

[4] Zelter's setting of Schiller's poem 'Des Mädchens Klage' from Schiller's *Wallenstein*.

[5] Part Two of Schiller's *Wallenstein* Trilogy; first performed on Anna Amalia's birthday on 30 January 1799. The Berlin premiere took place on 18 February 1799.

[6] ZG 11 August 1799.

[7] Johann Georg Sulzer, *Allgemeine Theorie der Schönen Kunste* (Leipzig, 1774), 'Sonnet', p. 1095.

in the first quatrain and Schlegel's sonnet 'Gesang und Kuß', which I have also composed, closes with a question.

I received your most precious letter of 26 August on 30 August. 'Die erste Walpurgisnacht' is a very suitable poem.[8] The verses are musical and singable. I wanted to set it to music which I could send to you here and have worked on a good portion of it, but I cannot quite capture the tone of the entire poem and so it is best to let it lie for a while. Herr Unger sends his best wishes and I have the honour of being your respectful

Zelter

## 5. Zelter

Berlin, 30 January 1800

I haven't forgotten to send your Excellency a few of my compositions again, and even if, apart from the serenade,[9] nothing among them is entirely new, neither are they known through publication. Nearly all of them observe the metrical patterns and verse forms and I would like to be in a position to acquire a thorough grounding in this area of the art. The short verses in the middle of long strophes are the most difficult to set to music, if one strives to preserve the [correct] tone and poetic disposition.

'Das Herbstlied'[10] calls for a lively tempo. 'Der Jungesell und der Mühlbach'[11] works well especially when it is sung antiphonally. 'Das Blümlein Wunderschön'[12] could also be sung as a duet. Of 'Die Braut von Corinth'[13] I don't quite know what to say. Friends of mine who have performed it really like it and I don't have anything to say against it. It could be that this poem can only be performed in this way. I sing it almost in a quasi speech-like manner, and if it is sung in a hollow voice, as if one is bound to tell something dreadfully mysterious, then the essence of the poem really comes forward. I strove to observe the short lines among the long sentences and because of this a rather adventurous musical metre has evolved.[14] The most difficult thing for the singer is to handle all the verses

---

[8] Goethe had enclosed this ballad in his first letter to Zelter: GZ 26 August 1799.

[9] Zelter's setting of an anonymous text ('Zu meiner Laute Liebesklang …') published in *Zwölf Lieder am Clavier zu singen* in 1801; the composition is not in Goethe's music collection.

[10] Zelter's setting of Ludwig Tieck's 'Herbstlied' ('Feldeinwärts flog ein Vögelein …') published in *Zwölf Lieder am Clavier zu singen* in 1801.

[11] ZG 11 August 1799. The setting is not in Goethe's music collection.

[12] Ibid.

[13] Ibid.

[14] Zelter originally scored the song in 6/2 but revised it as 3/2 for publication in 1802.

in such a way that the poem remains animated though the melody is repeated so often. When all is said and done it is not a poem for everyone: so not everybody can sing it. 'Bundeslied'[15] I have heard sung by 112 voices at the Liedertafel and [through it] have experienced how powerful a German poem can be. A serenade is not the best poetic form: so I was more interested in the actual form of a serenade which, when strummed outside a beloved girl's window, is the most important aspect of it.

I don't know whether I should fear that my scribblings will be too tedious for your Excellency. I have long enough repressed a desire, which I will still finally dare to utter. For a long time rumour has it that you have written the libretto for a serious opera.[16] Perhaps I am ill-informed; but how it would delight me alone if I could assist you to produce such a meritorious work! And what an agreeable task would the composition of such an opera be for me! I don't want to give the impression of being a braggart, but I know what I can accomplish and under such guidance I would not produce anything mediocre. Through your *Iphigenie* I have been almost convinced that we would find each other through such a collaboration, perhaps never to be parted again. Through my own affinity for dramatic music, which is being developed generally but without good fortune, it was inevitable that a number of dramatic attempts came to me spontaneously. Several of them confirm to me that I am capable of producing a large scale work.[17] Through this I haven't composed anything well-known, but I will send you samples of my work and would really value your opinion. I have edited more operas because the libretti only partly met my own inclinations. It is very likely that we will be granted a new, large theatre here[18] very soon which allows one to imagine that this great event will give rise to even greater things. I would not use this information lightly because I don't want to stand with empty hands among the children of Parnassus and bemoan the common taste of our time!

Herr Unger told me of late that your Excellency had some questions he wished to discuss with me.[19] As far as it goes my knowledge is at your service and what

---

[15] ZG 11 August 1799. A copy is contained in Goethe's music collection.

[16] Goethe's fragment, *Der Zauberflöte zweiter Teil*. Goethe listened to Schiller's words of caution about writing a sequel to Mozart's *Die Zauberflöte* and did not complete the libretto.

[17] Zelter's settings of Gellert's *Das Orakel* (operatic fragment); scenes from Metastasio's libretti by and scenes from the opera *Olympia*: 'Misero me! Ah! Che veggo?' and 'Oh Dio, se in questo istante'.

[18] In 1801 the Königliches Nationaltheater replaced the Französiches Komödienhaus (founded in 1786) on Gendarmenmarkt. A new 2,000-seat theatre was opened on 1 January 1802.

[19] In his letter to Johann Friedrich Unger on 4 November 1799, Goethe had expressed the desire to discuss some theoretical issues with Zelter.

I don't know, my fatherly friend, Fasch,[20] a very thorough and fine theorist, will supplement with pleasure. I recommend myself best through my songs, because I don't know a better way to serve you as when I follow your own judgement and remain with the most sincere esteem yours sincerely

Zelter

## 6. Goethe

Weimar, 29 May 1801

You have accomplished a very valuable piece of work in the book you have written about Fasch,[21] as well as given me great pleasure. The remembrance of a human life that has passed away is so condensed, that feeling reanimates the ashes and presents the transfigured Phoenix to our eyes. Every worthy fellow may live in hope that some day or other he will be represented in this way by his friend, his pupil, his fellow artist.

When you compare how lovingly the individual is here restored to us, what a poor picture is given by those necrologists, who, immediately after one's death, carefully balance the good and bad as perceived and applauded by the majority. They touch up his so-called virtues and vices with hypocritical righteousness, and thereby are worse than death in destroying a personality, which can be imagined only in the living union of those opposing qualities.

I was particularly delighted with your account of the creation of the Mass in 16 parts,[22] and of the Sing-Akademie to which it gave rise; how pleased I was that the good Fasch should be so fortunate as to have lived to see such an idea realized.

In an earlier letter – for which I regret I still owe you an answer – you ask whether there is anything resembling an opera among my papers? In the next edition

---

[20] Carl Friedrich Christian Fasch (1736–1800), harpsichordist (accompanist to Frederick the Great in 1756), composer, teacher, founder of the Sing-Akademie (1791), was an important figure in the revival of choral singing in Germany. He performed numerous choral works by J.S Bach with the Sing-Akademie, the first of which was the motet, *Komm, Jesu, komm*; this practice reached its pinnacle in Mendelssohn's revival of the *St Matthew Passion*.

[21] Zelter's biography, *Karl Friedrich Christian Fasch* (Berlin: Unger, 1801); Unger had sent a copy of the book to Goethe on 5 May 1801.

[22] In his biography Zelter reports how Fasch, inspired by a mass by Orazio Benevoli which Reichardt brought back from Italy in 1783, wrote a *Missa a 16 voci in quattro Cori* (a mass for four choirs (16 vocal parts)) in a few weeks, Zelter, *Karl Friedrich Christian Fasch*, p. 25.

of Wilman's *Taschenbuch*[23] you will find the first scenes of *Die Zauberflöte II*.[24] Some years ago I sketched a plan for a serious cantata, *Die Danaiden*, in which, in the manner of the ancient Greek tragedy, the chorus was to appear as the principal subject; but neither of the two pieces will, I expect, ever be finished. One would have to live with the composer, and work for some particular theatre; otherwise not much can come of such an undertaking.

From time to time be sure to send me some of your compositions. They give me great pleasure. Besides, I do not live in a musical atmosphere; throughout the year we reproduce first one, then another piece of music, but where nothing new is actually produced, an art cannot make itself vividly felt.

### 7. Zelter

Berlin, 7 to 13 April 1802

[...] Of your poems, I have only set to music the ones I have enclosed. In 'Frühzeitiger Frühling'[25] the three strophes automatically became one, since with all your songs the composer rarely acts on his own volition, if at all, because they always determine themselves. Whoever wants to sing it well, must know it by heart. I have a copy of 'Schäfers Klagelied'[26] from Frau Hufeland[27] and have already composed it in Leipzig.[28] It should not be performed too loudly but as lightly as possible. I have also composed a song for her friend de Mappes,[29] but

---

[23] *Taschenbuch auf das Jahr 1802. Der Liebe und Freundschaft gewidmet* (Bremen: G.F. Williams), pp. 15–36: 'Zer Zauberflöte zweiter Teil von Goethe. Entwurf zu einem dramatischen Märchen'.

[24] For discussion on Goethe's unfinished sequel to *Die Zauberflöte*, see Eckermann, 13 April 1823, p. 546.

[25] Zelter's setting of Goethe's poem 'Frühzeitiger Frühling' ('Tage der Wonne ...'); Zelter had received the poem from Goethe on his first visit to Weimar in February 1802. The setting is not in Goethe's music collection.

[26] Zelter's setting of Goethe's 'Schäfers Klagelied' ('Da droben auf jenem Berge'); the song is no longer in Goethe's music collection.

[27] Conradine Louise Wilhelmine Hufeland (1776–1823), wife of Privy Councillor Gottlieb Hufeland (1788–1803).

[28] Zelter composed it on his return journey from Weimar, on 28 February or 1 March 1802.

[29] Walter Map (Gualterus Mapes) (1140–1209), English poet. 'Das Schenklied' ('Mihi est propositum in taberna mori ...') was, at this time, attributed to him; later Jacob Grimm traced it back to the work of the medieval poet 'Archpoet': *Carmina Burana* 191 'Estuans intrinsecus ira vehementi'. Goethe was familiar with the text through Bürger's adaptation 'Zechlied', written in 1777 and published in his *Gedichte* of 1780. The song which Zelter has composed is an early setting of Goethe's 'Tischlied', which was written as a parody of

he is not too happy with it. Schulz's melody[30] is as good as it gets, but she didn't perform her German Lied with enough dignity and worse than Schulz would have wanted; I, too, was unhappy with it. I had more luck with Schiller's 'Die vier Weltalter';[31] at least I achieved what I can make of it. I have also set Schiller's romances to music once again: 'Der Kampf mit dem Drachen',[32] which I must be happy with because the 12-line verses are infinitely difficult to vary. If only the poem were not so long that the singer nearly collapses, then I would rate it in my works alongside 'Der Taucher'.[33]

As a result of all the sunshine and glory that I enjoyed in your home, I left the five strophes of your new romance[34] behind me, which pleased me infinitely and I would be immensely grateful if you could forward them on to me. Perhaps the composition will encourage you to complete the work if it hasn't happened already. I thank God hourly on bended knee that I have finally met you. The memory of those days is imprinted on my mind. Through the encounter a new spirit has awakened in me and if I brought or if I bring something forward which is worthy of the muses, I know it is a gift and recognize from where it comes.

13 April: [...] I enclose a copy of a little song for your noble honourable princess,[35] which, in my name, you will be so kind as to lay at her feet in my name. I would have sent it myself had I not thought that this little thing would appear better and more valuable if delivered by more worthy hands than mine.

Last Saturday Reichardt's setting of *Der Tod des Herkules*[36] was performed at the Nationaltheater. The libretto is treated à la Sophocles by the composer, like Gotter's *Medea*,[37] except that there are choruses interspersed which, by their grouping, give an uncommonly clear and advantageous coherence. The

---

Schulz's setting. Zelter's manuscript is dated 19 October 1823 (Ms. autograph 10); there is no copy in Goethe's music collection.

[30] Johann Abraham Peter Schulz (1747–1800), composer, Kapellmeister in Berlin, Rheinsberg and Copenhagen. His setting of the Map/Bürger text was published in his *Lieder im Volkston* (1st edn, Berlin, 1782; 2nd edn, Berlin, 1785).

[31] Zelter's setting of Schiller's 'Die vier Weltalter' ('Wohl perlet im Glase der purpurne Wein ...') from Cotta's *Taschenbuch für Damen auf das Jahr 1803*, pp. 205–08, was published in Zelter, *Sammlung kleiner Balladen und Lieder* (Hamburg: Böhme, 1803). Zelter's composition is no longer contained in Goethe's music collection.

[32] Zelter's setting of Schiller's ballad 'Der Kampf mit dem Drachen' ('Was rennt das Volk ...') from Schiller's *Musen-Almanach für das Jahr 1799*, pp. 151–64, was also published in the *Sammlung kleiner Balladen und Lieder* (1803).

[33] Zelter's setting of Schiller's 'Der Taucher' ('Wer wagt es, Rittersmann oder Knapp') was first published in 1803.

[34] Goethe's ballad 'Hochzeitlied' ('Wir singen und sagen ...').

[35] Princess Caroline Luise von Sachsen-Weimar-Eisenach (1786–1816).

[36] Melodrama by Johann Friedrich Reichardt (1752–1814) premiered on 10 April 1802, with a second performance on 12 April.

[37] Friedrich Wilhelm Gotter (1746–97), one-act drama set to music by Georg Benda, which was part of the repertoire of the Berlin Nationaltheater from 1787 to 1832.

music is stamped with Reichardt's genius, which is always announced through great courageous strides; it appears at its best in the quiet moments, which are exceptionally moving and very resolute. Iffland[38] plays the part of Hercules so well and so nobly and he is able to make the gradual transitions to the pinnacle of agony to which only the body succumbs, so that everywhere an advantageous mixture of suffering humanity and divine power develops. The finale is particularly beautiful: Hercules climbs the [funeral] pyre which is kindled by a bolt of lightning; his head is lit from above and his death is a visible crossing of the transfiguration into Olympus.

## 8. Zelter

Berlin, 9 May 1802

[...] Now I have something on my mind that you will easily guess from the enclosure. *Hercules* has had a very cold reception. The reasons for this [reception] lie partly in the subject, which is not easy for the general public to digest, and in the current prejudice against the composer, who years ago was praised to the heavens at the expense of other good composers. It would be all right to leave both sides to their opinions, if art were not to suffer thereby, which, with its moderate progress to perfection, has to survive the war against whims, arrogance and ignorance. I myself can no longer bear it that an industrious, skilful well-intentioned work which is staged with unspeakable efforts and much expense should be thrown away in such a disdainful, capricious manner, and be dismissed as worthless.

Therefore I have a request: that you read my description of *Hercules*.[39] I would be very proud if you could give even one word of recommendation; then I would feel I had the right to speak, where others, who ought to speak, remain silent.

Would you be so kind as to deliver the single page of manuscript to Schiller? If you have both of these *Tafellieder* transcribed,[40] you could try them out some morning at the theatre rehearsals; the soloist must do his best thereby.

---

[38] August Wilhlem Iffland (1759–1814), actor and (from 1795) director at the Mannheim Nationaltheater; Artistic Director and General Manager of the Königliches Theater from 1811 until his death in 1814.

[39] Zelter's essay on Reichardt's melodrama, *Der Tod des Herkules*; the manuscript has not been preserved with these letters.

[40] Zelter's settings of Schiller's poems: 'Punschlied. Im Norden zu singen' and 'Punschlied'.

## 9. Goethe

Weimar, 31 August 1802

During the time you heard nothing from me, dear Zelter, while I have not travelled very far, I have mostly been away from home. I had to oversee the building of a new theatre in Lauchstädt[41] and direct the inauguration, whereby, as is usual in such cases, one caters for the enjoyment of others at the expense of one's own pleasure. Then I stayed in Jena for a while, in literary seclusion in the library; this time neither noise nor silence inspired anything in which a composer could take pleasure. Let us hope that the friendly social life of the winter will put us in a lyrical frame of mind, which would most certainly be secured if you put your good intentions into practice and came to stay with us once again. Give me your kind reassurance in due course.

You will soon see in print the prelude[42] that I wrote for the inauguration of the Lauchstädt theatre. At the beginning I had no desire to publish it, because everything was inspired by the occasion, the moment, the individual members of the company, the power of the music,[43] and all that is connected with external production; now, may all that remains on paper be published and have whatever effect it can.

Let me know soon that I am in your thoughts.
Goethe

## 10. Zelter

Berlin, 16 September 1802

[...] I very much look forward to the appearance of your prelude and repeat my request that you send me the romance[44] from which you read five strophes to me. This winter I am unable to make plans for a short trip because almost everyone at home has been sick during the summer. God knows how much I like to be with you; I have never felt the sun shine so warmly as in Weimar. I am greatly indebted

---

[41] Goethe travelled to Lauchstädt on 21 June 1802, where Joseph Bellomo had founded a provisional summer theatre in the new theatre designed by the architect, Johann Heinrich Gentz (1766–1811). Goethe had opened the theatre with his prologue, *Was wir bringen*, and a performance of Mozart's *Titus* given by the ensemble of the Weimar Court Theatre. The ensemble remained in Lauchstädt until the middle of August.

[42] Goethe, *Was wir bringen. Vorspiel bei Eröffnung des neuen Schauspielhauses zu Lauchstädt*.

[43] Mozart's *Titus*, libretto by Caterino Mazzolà after Pietro Metastasio, *La clemenza di Tito*; German translation by August Vulpius.

[44] Goethe's 'Hochzeitslied'.

to you for your response to *Hercules*;[45] for me, it is the seal of your affection which I know how to treasure.

## 11. Goethe

Weimar, 6 December 1802

When, during these dark days, I thought of happy circumstances, I often looked back to the time of your delightful presence amongst us last year. I have but slender hope of seeing you again soon; yet it is my wish that a thread should continue to be spun between us.

Therefore give a friendly welcome to the count and the dwarfs,[46] who arrive with this letter; for the first time, I think, they show style and ingenuity. Cherish these merry imps in your true musical sense, and prepare for yourself and us some diversion for the winter evenings. But do not let the poem out of your hands; if possible, keep it secret.

My whole household thinks of you with affection and love
Goethe

## 12. Zelter

Berlin, 12 December 1802

A group of Sing-Akademie members organized a pleasant surprise in celebration of my birthday. A little play with many of my songs woven into its fabric was staged very nicely; all of my children were given parts. The finale was a little *Lustspiel*,[47] at which you yourself would have been quite amused to come across our carpenter, Steffani, dressed up in the most outrageous costume – a low-cut dress – as a lady-in-waiting to the Queen of Bathsheba. This had the whole house in hysterics. Among the many lovely presents of the day was your dear letter, which I recognized from the address and which I guessed was from you by the exceptional size of its contents. I will not leave your lovely wedding song out of my hands and as soon as it is composed, you shall have a copy. [...]

---

[45] ZG 9 May 1802.

[46] A copy of Goethe's 'Hochzeitslied' which Zelter had left behind on his visit to Weimar in February 1802.

[47] *Lieder und Gesänge aus dem Liederspiele: die Mühle, in einem Akt. Aufgeführt zur frohen Geburtstagsfeier am 11. Dezember 1802.* The play contains settings by Zelter which were performed by members of the Sing-Akademie. A copy of the first publication is held in the Preußischer Staatsbibliothek, Berlin (SBB PK: Mus.Ms 1164).

The pleasant news that you are going to share your treasures with the world has inspired me again, and since then I have set to work on your poems again. What you once wrote to me about the dramatic form of the romance in relation to 'Die erste Walpurgisnacht', confirmed to me a direction which I had already sought to develop in 'Der Zauberlehrling'. 'Walpurgisnacht' remains unfinished because it always imposed on me the old worn-out cantata form.[48] Now I have attempted [to set] 'Der Müllerin Reue' and I wonder what you would think of it.[49] As it must be sung by two people, it would be good if one of them were a tenor. Unfortunately the piece is difficult to produce and must be learnt well, so that neither breathing nor diction fails. The tenor must declaim his rumbling lines very boisterously and the [soprano] descant [should be sung] gently but coherently and full of feeling.

I have thought of setting Cupid's song as a little intermezzo in the Italian style:[50] if three young girls, lightly dressed with net cages on their backs, appear on stage friendly and blithe in a circle, cry out, 'Wer kauft Liebesgötter!' and then sing the poem to a light and playful melody, then it cannot fail to work. The fortepiano, which at the very least requires the lightest accompaniment (without any passionate expression), could be placed behind a screen or even in the same room.

And so accept what I so willingly give. I would like to send the peace of the blessed to you, for where there are no gods, there is no heaven. Remember me warmly to Schiller. I would like to surprise myself with the joy of going to my dear Weimar. I can't yet fix a date, especially with the carnival approaching, when the royal family is in Berlin. I must be mindful of my duty, to which I naturally apply myself when it concerns the Sing-Akademie. This institute enjoys a special hospitality in a king's household[51] and it would be very painful to me if a request came from a higher source in my absence and there was no one there who knew what to say on behalf of 200 members, no one who knew how to say the correct thing about an unfamiliar project and so would give a very confused impression by mixing up ends and means. For who will know, in this day and age, how to

---

[48] Berlin composers and theoreticians – among them Reichardt and Zelter – recommended a cantata-like form, when there were heterogeneous emotions in the text and when a change in emotions was dominant because it would be unreasonable to expect a poet to write an ode which maintains the same feeling through many verses.

[49] Zelter's setting of 'Der Müllerin Reue' first appeared in Schiller's *Musenalmanach* in 1799 and subsequently in *Goethes Schriften*, vol. 7, pp. 77–81. An original copy of the setting is neither in Goethe's music collection nor housed with Zelter's manuscripts in Berlin.

[50] 'Wer kauft Liebesgötter' from Goethe's sequel to *Die Zauberflöte*. Zelter's setting is in Goethe's music collection (GSA, 32/32).

[51] From the end of 1793 the choir was granted use of the round room in the building of the Königliche Akademie der Künste, and from this point on they called themselves the Sing-Akademie.

bring together bright young people and dignified men and organize them to sing a devout Kyrie together. [...]

Enclosure: Zelter's settings of Goethe's poems, 'Der Müllerin Reue' and 'Wer kauft Liebesgötter?'

### 13. Zelter

Berlin, 18 December 1802

I haven't forgotten to send you the setting of the 'Hochzeitlied'.[52] It was finished before I sent my last letter, but I wanted to wait until I was happy with it. You will find that the strophes in which there is a full stop after verse seven are the clearest and the three rhymes of verses five, six and seven appear to establish the intention of this metre which is new to me,[53] so I have developed the modulation of the entire setting not on the first but on the second strophe.

'Der neue Amadis'[54] can now go back to you with 'Hochzeitlied'. I have set it as an exercise because of its fifth unrhymed verse.

I have not let any of your unpublished poems out of my hands. I did not receive 'Schäfers Klagelied' from you and when Frau Privy Councillor Herz[55] requested a copy of my setting and already had a copy of the poem, I gladly acquiesced. In a new song collection by Reichardt, the manuscript of which I saw through Sanders, I caught sight of 'Frühzeitiger Frühling', which Reichardt probably received from you.[56]

They say the king is coming to Berlin on the 21st of this month and so the carnival can end towards the end of January. The queen's close delivery [date]

---

[52] Zelter's setting of Goethe's 'Hochzeitlied', published in Zelter's *Sämtliche Lieder, Balladen und Romanzen*, vol. 2. The enclosed composition is no longer part of Goethe's music collection.

[53] Zelter's setting of 'Hochzeitlied' for solo voice and piano is composed in 6/8 time; the choice of metre is rare among his settings.

[54] An autograph of Zelter's unpublished setting of Goethe's poem 'Der neue Amadis', dated 18 December 1802, is housed in Berlin (SBB PK: Mus. ms. Autogr. Zelter 22, no. 2). The enclosed copy is no longer contained in Goethe's music collection. As Zelter's previous letter suggests, the setting was notated on the same manuscript page as 'Hochzeitlied' (GSA 95/I, 9).

[55] Henriette Julie Herz, née de Lemos (1764–1847); the setting was presumably composed for her salon.

[56] Goethe's poem 'Frühzeitiger Frühling', set to music by Johann Friedrich Reichardt in 1802, was first published in *Le Troubadour italien, français et allemand* (Berlin: Heinrich Fröhlich, 1805/06). The publication of Reichardt's setting by the Berlin publishers, Johann Daniel Sanders, which Zelter mentions, cannot be sourced; *MA* 20.3, p. 136.

confirms my suspicions,[57] which means I could be in Weimar in early February, if this pleasant calculation is not by chance proven wrong. You have opened your house to me with such a warm welcome and I will accept in so far as I do not inconvenience you in any way. [...] Like a child I look forward to being with you and have nothing else on my mind.

Enclosure: Zelter's settings of Goethe's 'Hochzeitlied' and 'Der neue Amadis'.

### 14. Goethe

Weimar, 24 January 1803

I cannot contemplate the hope of your visit with such silence,[58] especially as there are some things for which I have to thank you.

The songs you sent gave me, and others, much joy and have already been carefully performed in little concerts, which I arranged in anticipation of your visit. Naturally their performance awaits your own finishing touches.

Would it be possible to bring with you some SATB settings which are not too difficult? That way your presence will have an effect on us in many ways.

I will close here for now, so that this page, which has already missed the post, will not be delayed any further. Your room, which you know, has been arranged beside a little bedroom, so you can come and go as you please. I myself am in a good position to be able to relax and enjoy your visit next month in peace [...] In the hope of looking forward to some interesting talks with you soon, I wish you good health and a good journey.

### 15. Goethe

Weimar, 31 January 1803

Only one line to tell you briefly that good Dr Chladni is here[59] and will remain in the area until about 9 or 10 February. Perhaps this may have some bearing on your

---

[57] Queen Luise Augusta Wilhelmine Amalie of Prussia (1808–77) bore a daughter, Princess Friederike Wilhelmine Alexandrine Maria Helene, on 23 February 1803.

[58] Goethe's diary on 24 January 1803 mentions Zelter's visit: 'To Herrn Zelter, regarding his arrival here', *WA* III/3, p. 69.

[59] Ernst Florens Friedrich Chladni (1756–1827), physicist and music theorist. Author of the theoretical work *Die Acoustik*, 1802. Goethe's diary on 31 January 1803 mentions his visit: 'To Herrn Zelter regarding Chladni', *WA* III/3, p. 70. See also the section, 'Chladnis Tonfiguren' in Goethe's essay *Entoptische Farben*, vol. 12, p. 501f.

journey. If you could meet him while he is still here, we would have some lively discussions about music.

Only this much to confirm once more my eager wish to see you under my roof.

## 16. Zelter

Berlin, 3 February 1803

I must relinquish any hope I had of spending some days in Weimar this winter; so I will take the opportunity of sending you what I would have brought myself. For years I have been dissatisfied with my setting of the enclosed 'Reiterlied'.[60] Therefore you receive it in score, in order to be able to make use of it perhaps for the theatre. If you want it, would you be so kind as to return the score to me when you have it copied for the various voices,[61] for I haven't kept back a copy. You will probably decide that the performance of this piece should be free, lively and light rather than heavy and dragging – this goes for the orchestra as well as for the singers – and I have nothing else to add than that it would be very nice if it were to appeal to Schiller as it stands,[62] because all of the settings of this song, with which I am familiar,[63] are unsuccessful.

Madame Mara has arrived here,[64] and, after so many years, I long to hear the divine singing of this artist. In all that time I have heard no other singer who can do everything with her glorious voice, never delivering anything less than perfect.

---

[60] Zelter's setting of Schiller's 'Reiterlied' from *Wallenstein*. Schiller had sent the poem to Zelter on 6 July 1797 and asked him to compose a setting for the play, *SNA* 29, p. 96.

[61] In Goethe's music collection there is a five-page copy of this song, with the choral voices indicated by the names of the actual singers: H. Spitzeder, Ehlers, Brandt, Benda, Eilenstein (GSA 32/34).

[62] On 28 February 1803 Schiller wrote to Zelter: 'Goethe has been telling about a number of lovely melodies you have sent him; he is having them rehearsed and promises us a real feast of them this week. I will hear 'Der Kampf mit den Drachen' as well as 'Reiterlied' this week', *SNA* 32, p. 17.

[63] Settings by Christian Jakob Zahn (1797), Christian Gottfried Körner (1797), Johann Rudolf Zumsteeg (1802), Bernhard Anselm Weber (1803): see Max Friedländer, *Das deutsche Lied im 18. Jahrhundert. Quellen und Studien*, 2 vols (Stuttgart and Berlin: Cotta, 1902), vol. 2, p. 397f.

[64] Gertrud Elizabeth Mara, née Schmeling (1749–1833). Goethe was mesmerized by this diva's performance in Leipzig in 1767 and later recalled it in the poem 'Sangreich war dein Ehrenweg' for her, GZ 19 February 1831. Mara arrived in Berlin on 1 February 1803. During this visit she gave two concerts with the Königliche Kapelle in the opera house on 13 February and 6 March, which were reviewed by Zelter in the *Spenersche Zeitung*, 8 March 1803. She was also soloist for Zelter's performance of Graun's Passion

Your dear kind letter of 24 January saddened me. I was unwilling to come empty-handed to Weimar and therefore I have not been idle. I hoped that several quite new settings of your poems would win your favour. 'Sehnsucht' ('Was zieht mir das Herz so?')[65] and 'Der Sänger'[66] are quite new and, in my opinion, are even better than Reichardt's settings. Since Part I of *Wilhelm Meisters Lehrjahre* was published, I have had 'Der Sänger' constantly on my mind, and finally here it is on paper. Reichardt's setting[67] is like a march, and starting rather imperiously, should at all events end as it began; I have restored the ballad form. After that I finished several of your songs and have added four new strophes to 'Das Blümlein Wunderschön'. 'Der Junggesell und der Mühlbach' has, at the suggestion of a critic in the *Apollon*,[68] been given more musical substance. Schiller's 'Hero und Leander', 'Worte des Glaubens',[69] 'Der Kampf mit dem Drachen', 'Die Sänger der Vorwelt'[70] have received the final touches; I have reset some new sonnets, including one by Herder,[71] as well as several old German songs from the seventeenth century

---

in the Nicholaikirche, Berlin on 11 March; see *AMZ* 5 (1802/3). Rochlitz's *Für Freunde der Tonkunst* (4 vols, Leipzig: Carl Cnobloch, 1824–32) contains an interesting memoir of her.

[65] Zelter's setting of Goethe's 'Sehnsucht', *MA* 6.1, p. 76. As the poem was first published in 1804, these verses belong to an unpublished edition given to Zelter on his visit to Goethe in February 1802. Zelter's setting is in Goethe's music collection. A Berlin autograph (SBB: PK: Mus. ms. autogr. Zelter 22, no. 1), dated 18 December 1802, is unpublished.

[66] Zelter's setting of the Harper's first song in *Wilhelm Meisters Lehrjahre*. Zelter's setting is not in Goethe's music collection; the Berlin autograph (SBB PK: Mus. ms. autogr. Zelter 22, no. 1), dated 18 December 1802, is still unpublished.

[67] Reichardt's 'Sehnsucht' was published in the *Romantischen Gesängen* (1805) and in Goethe, *Wilhelm Meisters Lehrjahre* (Berlin: Unger, 1795) where all the settings appeared as inserts in the book.

[68] 'For a fuller definition of the latter we would like to add that it is, what music in a genuine *Romanze* always is and has to be, namely genuinely romantic', *Apollon. Eine Zeitschrift*, (ed.) Julius Werden (pseudonym for Johann Gottlieb Winzer), Adolph Werden (pen name adopted by Friedrich Theodor Mann) and Wilhelm Schneider (Penig, 1803), p. 69f.

[69] Zelter's settings of Schiller's ballad 'Hero und Leander' (*SNA* 2/I, p. 298) and his poem 'Die Worte des Glaubens' (*SNA* 2/I, p. 329) are not in Goethe's music collection and remain unpublished.

[70] Zelter's setting of Schiller's poem 'Die Sänger der Vorwelt' (*SNA* 2/I, p. 298) is not contained in Goethe's music collection. It was published in Zelter's collection *Sechs Deutsche Lieder für die Baß-Stimme* (1826).

[71] Zelter's setting of Herder's sonnet 'Ach könnt ich, könnte vergessen Sie', which he discovered through Wilhelm Schneider's setting published in the *Apollon*, is no longer in Goethe's music collection. The Berlin autograph is dated 31 October 1802 (SBB PK: Mus. ms. autogr. Zelter 22, no. 3); the setting was first published in Zelter's *Neue Liedersammlung* in 1821.

by Abschatz,[72] Zinkgref,[73] Paul Gerhardt.[74] I recount my small glories to you like a child who has had Christmas presents from the Muses, and when all is said and done, does not know what to do with all his treasures. Could I but achieve something great! My life is passing and nothing comes of it. Could you possibly suggest something by Herder, whom I esteem most highly?[75] I read so little, and re-read my old favourites so often, that poetic gems often escape me. And now, 'Enough, ye Muses!' But pray be on your guard, that your house is not haunted! It is my spirit which has taken up his quarters with you, and is settling down and making its nest by degrees.

Of the settings I have sent you there is one, 'Die Erinnerung', of which I have given away all the copies I had. Could I possibly ask you to have a copy made and dispatched to me, as I would like to have it published? As far as I remember it is in B flat major or E major.[76]

## 17. Goethe

Weimar, 10 March 1803

I can understand very well that it requires some resolution to leave one's own circle, and to look up distant friends at this time of the year; yet I am troubled in more ways than one by your letter of refusal. Apart from what we should have gained for the general and higher aims of art by personal communication, it so happens that this winter I am preoccupied with the organization of the opera and orchestra[77] more with a view to the future than the present; and I thought your help would be absolutely indispensable in this matter.

The significance of the old proverb, 'Go straight to the right smithy', was clear enough to me long ago; but what use is this knowledge if the smithy is so far off that one cannot reach him with one's harness?

---

[72] Zelter's setting of 'Mut', written by Baron Hans von Aßmann (really Johann Erasmus) von Abschatz, is not in Goethe's music collection. The Berlin autograph, dated Berlin 13 January 1803, is unpublished (SBB PK: Mus. ms. autogr. Zelter 22, no. 4).

[73] Zelter's setting of Julius Wilhelm Zinkgref's 'Klage' is not in Goethe's music collection. The Berlin autograph (SBB PK: Mus. ms. autogr. Zelter 22, no. 6), was first published by Landshoff in 1932.

[74] Zelter's setting of the poem 'Sonnet' (Berlin autograph (SBB PK: Mus. ms. autogr. Zelter 22, no. 7) is not in Goethe's music collection. It was first published in Zelter's *Sämtliche Lieder, Balladen und Romanzen*. Here and in the published version Zelter names the poet as Gerhardt; on the manuscript copy he attributes it to Paul Fleming. The poem could not be traced to either author.

[75] See Goethe's letter to Amalie von Imhoff, *WA* IV/51, p. 171.

[76] The setting in B flat was first published in Zelter's *Neue Liedersammlung* in 1821.

[77] Goethe was Director of the Weimar Court Theatre from 1791 to 1817.

So as I cannot give up the hope of seeing you, I make a proposal that I trust you will welcome. If you could possibly find the time to make the trip to us, I would feel obliged in my present position, and in view of the benefit I expect for the plans to which I am committed, to cover your travelling expenses here and back, and to provide for you during your stay. Now, if you were to weigh the inconveniences of the journey, and the loss of your valuable time against the enjoyment you would have through a visit here, we would not remain too much in debt to you, and perhaps we could arrange to meet more often in the future; this might not be of any great advantage to you, but at least you would not suffer any monetary loss.

Think it over and tell me what you think of the proposal to which I hope you will give a favourable answer; and all the more so since you are in no way restricted as to the time of your visit, and we should be ready to welcome you any day between this and Whitsuntide. Your room is still unoccupied and ready to receive you.

All your friends think of you with enthusiasm, which was rekindled by your new compositions –'Reiterlied' and 'Der Zwerg' – which were performed again only yesterday.[78] Schiller thanks you most sincerely.

A new tenor has come here;[79] he has a very beautiful voice, but is in every sense a novice. What a thing it would be for him and for us if you could advise on his future development! I mention but this one link in the chain of obligations we should gladly owe you.

I need not tell you how seriously we are taking the improvement of our theatre, and particularly of the music, for the wedding of our crown prince,[80] and the celebrations which have to be given in the last quarter of the present year, and so on. Nor is there any need to repeat the proposals and requests I have already made.

I enclose the delightful composition you asked for.[81]

If you look through Herder's early publications of *Volkslieder*,[82] as well as his miscellaneous poems, you are certain to find much that will interest you. When my small concerts are given, I am very anxious that every one of my friends should be astonished at himself, when he hears his works reproduced in your music.

Can you give me your considered opinion of Madame Mara?

                       Farewell and let me have your favourable answer soon,
                                                    Goethe

---

[78] Zelter's settings of Schiller's 'Reiterlied' and Goethe's 'Hochzeitlied'; ZG 3 February 1803.

[79] Franz Brand, tenor and actor, made his first appearance on the Weimar stage on 26 February 1803; he remained in Weimar until 1807.

[80] Carl Friedrich von Sachsen-Weimar-Eisenach (1783–1853) married the Tzar's daughter, Maria Pawlowna (1786–1859) in St Petersburg on 3 August 1804.

[81] Zelter's setting of 'Die Erinnerung'. Goethe sent back the original manuscript; a copy remains in his music collection (GSA 32/14).

[82] Collections of folk songs translated into German by Herder, published in 1774, 1778 and 1779.

## 18. Zelter

Berlin, 1 April 1803

I will definitely come to Weimar, at the very latest in June, and I look forward to it like a child. For six weeks I have been watching my mother dying, suffering appallingly day and night, whereby my whole house has been in disarray.[83]

On 21 March my son[84] left here for Dresden. From there he will travel on to Weimar. I haven't given him a letter of introduction; he will announce himself in person and ask your blessing.[85]

The enclosed reviews about Madame Mara were written by me; more about that again.[86]

## 19. Goethe

Weimar, 1 July 1803

Accept with affection, dear friend, a little present, which Privy Councillor von Wolzogen[87] will bring you from me. You enjoyed von Knebel's Spanish snuff, and a further supply was found. Where? You shall find out when it is safely in your hands. Fill your box with it, and sometimes when you take a pinch, whether you are alone or in good company, think of my affection and esteem for you. That is always an enjoyable moment.

The sower, when he has sown his seed, goes away and lets it sprout;[88] what a pity you cannot see how much good is springing up from what you have sown among us.[89]

---

[83] Zelter's mother, Anna Dorothea Zelter, née Hintze (1731–1803), died on 30 April 1803.

[84] Zelter's stepson, Carl Flöricke (1784–1812).

[85] See Goethe's diary entry on 14 May 1803, *WA* III/3, p. 73.

[86] Zelter's reviews of two concerts given by Gertrud Elizabeth Mara in Berlin appeared in the *Spenersche Zeitung*, no. 21, 17 February 1803 and no. 29, 8 March 1803 (GSA 28/1014); *MA* 20.3, p. 143.

[87] Baron Wilhelm Ernst Friedrich Franz August von Wolzogen (1762–1809), architect, diplomat and minister in the service of the Duke of Sachsen-Weimar-Eisenach.

[88] Reference to the biblical parable of the sower (Matthew 13, 18–23; Mark 4, 26–29).

[89] Zelter stayed with Goethe from the end of May until 11 June 1803.

## 20. Zelter

Berlin, 1 to 9 July 1803

[…] In Dresden I met Madame Mara, who was overjoyed to see me.[90] She was just about to give a concert that I attended. There, as everywhere, she has admirers and enemies. The thing she liked best was the unexpectedly good reception which appears to be her main priority just now.

The first thing that caught my attention in Berlin was a short biography of the late Mozart, half dedicated to you,[91] to which is appended an anything but short, aesthetic description of his works, together with a poor portrait of him. Could you possibly find out for me who is the Neudietendorfer author of this educational work for young composers?[92] The Neudietendorfers may benefit by it […]

4 July: Yesterday, I saw a performance here of Schiller's *Die Braut von Messina* for the first time.[93] It was the third performance of the work. Madame Meyer[94] did everything that was possible for her as Donna Isabelle; Madame Fleck was somewhat better as Beatrice. Manuel H. Beschort sometimes showed noble attitude; Iffland played Bohemund suitably and Bethman gave the best performance as Cesar. The entire production was a highly polished and glorious spectacle and the entire cast, apart from the choruses, displayed knowledge of the theatre and attention to detail. Almost every grouping of the two brothers, the mother and the sister betrayed a special artistic touch and the costumes were beautiful, as were the sets, four of which were new. The final scene with the sarcophagus and its newly composed incidental music were both superb.

The play itself is distinguished here by its length rather than by its breadth. Long speeches in verse rhythm are not Madame Meyer's thing. She has neither breath nor tone to carry the modulation of Schiller's lines and consequently a

---

[90] Zelter travelled from Weimar to Dresden on 11 June 1803. Mara was away for several months on a concert tour throughout Germany which brought her to Frankfurt am Main, Gotha, Weimar, Leipzig and Dresden; there are no accounts of any concerts given by her in the Dresden newspapers. She arrived in Berlin in August where she gave a concert with Giovanni Carol Conciallini (1742/45–1812), Italian singer at the court opera, Berlin; see *AMZ* 5 (1802/03), no. 19, 2 February, column 322–4 and no. 50, 7 September, column 850.

[91] *Mozarts Geist. Seine kurze Biographie und ästhetische Darstellung seiner Werke. Ein Bildungsbuch für junge Tonkünstler* (Erfurt, 1803). The book was jointly dedicated to Goethe and August Eberhardt Müller, Cantor of the Thomas-Schule in Leipzig.

[92] This book, written by Ignaz Ferdinand Arnold from Neudietendorf/Erfurt, was published anonymously.

[93] Schiller's *Die Braut von Messina* was performed for the first time in Berlin in the Königliches Nationaltheater on 14 June 1803; further performances were given on 16 and 20 June, and 3 July 1803. Zelter had, in fact, attended the fourth performance.

[94] [Johanna] Henriette Meyer, née Schüler (1772–1849), actress.

substantial part of the first and final acts were drawn out and very unclear. From time to time she tried to pull herself together and aim at the sublime, but she had no idea how to achieve this. With great confidence in the author, audiences here take every opportunity, through loud and sustained applause, to encourage the artists in their quest and seem unable to hide their thirst for what is better and higher. There was a full house and it didn't hold back.

I would prefer not to say anything about the choruses because everything is unclear and rather vague. I bet Schiller was justified and that there is something behind it which we don't yet recognize. Perhaps I will write more about it to you again when the play is published and I have it before me in black and white.[95] Several choral passages were really effective, which many of my friends in Berlin had already told me. When I think that, year in year out, day in day out, our company must play around with so-called domestic pieces, with the study of frivolous, ordinary, everyday material and a lot of the most common local pedestrian events, I must admit I am amazed that they can act so expertly. Schiller himself would not be dissatisfied with the individual performances.

The positioning of the chorus was not to my liking. I thought the chorus should be tightly grouped on both sides of the stage and, as far as possible, in the background, thereby separated from the main groups by the greatest distance possible. In this way the chorus would have, as it were, the main part of the entire play and bring the whole play to life. Metre controls delivery of the text – at least that's the way it seems to have been rehearsed, and through his movements Iffland indicates the rhythm. The passages which are true to the metre are the most effective. It would be worth investigating whether the metre would not be better maintained and the entire play would benefit if a damped beat was marked on the drums. The chorus should be divided into two, placed on both sides. They would alternate like the strophes and antistrophes of the ancients, and could also consist of questions and answers.[96] In any case a composer should be brought in who would know what needs to be done. Also there should be some attempt to raise the chorus up on a platform to make it immobile; because the mobility they have here is neither to their advantage nor to that of the work. They could set the tone, create the general mood to contrast with the action. I don't know how to make my feeling clearer here; rehearsals are needed using real singers to make things easier and the whole of it needs to be invented anew.

I would like to be instructed about the role of the Greek chorus by you.[97] I never imagined it as anything else but a living backdrop and believed, therefore, that the chorus must be immobile. One could, of course, think of another interpretation of the chorus, if it is not too fine or speculative: in the earliest stages of theatre, there cannot have been an audience capable of understanding the poet. Therefore,

---

[95] Schiller's play was published in four episodes (Tübingen: Cotta, 1803).

[96] Antiphonal song for two singers or two choirs (or a divided choir) following the practice of ancient Greek music, later developed in settings of early Christian Psalms.

[97] Goethe's reply is given in an enclosure to GZ 28 July 1803; *MA* 20.1, p. 44.

the poet was compelled to create everything himself: the language, the play, the characters and also the public, and the latter could have been represented by the chorus. At the very least the chorus has to have been of ancient origin, predating the Greeks. They gladly took on the chorus to place it in front of their audience to teach them how to feel and to think as the poet wishes them to and not to demand what the poet is not prepared to give. [...]

The glorious snuff, redolent of the fragrance of all muses, is real refreshment to me; it will be no surprise now if I write something good.

## 21. Goethe

Weimar, 28 July 1803

So often have I followed you in thought that I have unfortunately neglected to do so in writing; today only a few words to accompany the enclosed sheet. I shall continue my reflections and only touch the main points as briefly as possible; you yourself will, of course, supply the details.

Of Mozart's biography I have heard nothing further as yet, but shall inquire about it and about the author too.[98]

Could you outline for me the duties of a Kapellmeister, at least in so far as it is necessary for one like me to know, so that I may to some extent be able to judge a man in this position, and in any case give him direction.[99]

Madame Mara sang last Tuesday in Lauchstädt; I have not yet heard how it went.[100]

Thank you sincerely from myself and my friends, for the songs I received through von Wolzogen.[101]

---

[98] The book appears to have arrived in Goethe's library only at a later stage; *Goethes Bibliothek. Katalog*, (ed.) Hans Ruppert (Weimar: Goethe Sammlung zur Kunst, Literatur und Naturwissenschaft, 1958, reprint Leipzig 1978), no. 176. Hereafter referred to as Ruppert.

[99] On 7 August 1803 Zelter sent Goethe a manuscript with his remarks on the nature of an orchestra, for which Goethe thanked him on 29 August. Six months later, on 28 March 1804, Goethe asked Zelter's permission to publish it in the *Jenaische Allgemeine Literatur-Zeitung*, hereafter referred to as *JALZ*. Zelter consented, though with some hesitation. At first nothing happened; only when Reichardt took up the manuscript to have it printed in the *Berliner Allgemeine Musikalische Zeitung*, which he edited, did Goethe realize that 'he could not withhold the essay from an intellectual literary journal'; in June and July the essay appeared in the *JALZ*.

[100] The performance took place on 26 July 1803.

[101] Presumably in Zelter, *Sammlung kleiner Balladen und Lieder* (1803).

There was no time to think of producing anything new. Soon I hope to send you the proof sheets of my poems, with the request that you will keep them secret until they are published.[102]

Enclosure: In Greek tragedy the Chorus is seen in four Epochs. In the first Epoch a few characters calling up the past into the present are introduced between the singing, in which divinities and heroes are exalted and genealogies, mighty deeds, portentous destinies, are brought before the fancy. Of this we have a proximate example of the *Seven against Thebes* by Aeschylus. This was the beginning of dramatic art – ancient style.

The second Epoch shows us the whole Chorus as the mystic leading character of the piece as in the *Eumenides* and *Supplices*; I am inclined to think these represent the lofty style. The Chorus is independent, the interest rests upon it; it is, one might say, the republican period of dramatic art; the rulers and the gods are mere supplementary personages.

In the third Epoch, the Chorus becomes supplementary; the interest is projected upon the families, their respective members and chiefs, with whose destinies the destiny of the surrounding people is slightly connected. The Chorus is subordinate, and the figures of Princes and Heroes step forth in their isolated majesty. I am inclined to think of this as the grand style. The tragedies of Sophocles stand on this level. Inasmuch as the multitude has only to watch the hero and Fate, and cannot influence Nature either in special circumstances or generally, it falls back upon reflection and undertakes the office of an appointed and welcome spectator.

In the fourth Epoch, the action continues increasingly to confine itself to private interests; the Chorus appears often as a wearisome tradition, as an inherited piece of the dramatic inventory. It becomes unnecessary, and therefore is equally useless, tiresome and disturbing in a living, poetical whole – as, for example, when it is called upon to keep secrets in which it has no interest, and so on. Several examples of this are to be found in the plays of Euripedes, of which I might name *Helena* and *Iphigenie in Tauris*.

In order to return again to the musical thread, you will see from the above that any attempts must be made in connection with the first two Epochs and this could be realized in very short oratorios.

---

[102] Goethe's 'Der Geselligkeit gewidmeten Liedern' which appeared in Goethe and Wieland (eds), *Taschenbuch auf das Jahr 1804*, pp. 87–152.

## 22. Zelter

Berlin, 15 July to 7 August 1803

Privy Councillor von Wolzogen has very obligingly, through an acquaintance, sent off six copies of my songs for you. One of them is for Schiller and one is intended for Ehlers.[103] [...]

When I received your kind letter of 28 July, I had just been reading at my leisure Schiller's preface to *Die Braut von Messina*, and had already begun to try a musical arrangement of the choruses. This much I have divined: that to come to grips properly with the new genre, I should need a quiet year. As soon as I have completed enough for it to be recognizable, I will write to you about my discovery. What you wrote to me about the choruses has been extremely useful, for I am more concerned with an accurate view of the ancient Greek chorus than with one of my own invention. The musician is so horribly subordinate to the poet, and besides that he needs the whole strength of his art. Your idea of attempting a small oratorio is excellent and, for more than one reason, I should like to see it carried out. It is a new way to [access] the heart and I constantly think about it.

That someone could dedicate a book to you without sending you a copy[104] is totally inconceivable to me. It is dedicated to you and to Müller (probably Cantor of the Thomasschule in Leipzig).[105] [...]

Your songs should be highly welcome to me especially as I cannot compose because there is too much work to do. I have had a painful wait for the publication of *Die natürliche Tochter*, but it is not yet available.[106]

What I have written down about the orchestra, I have enclosed for you here.[107] Something more complete could only be accomplished if one worked continually with an orchestra. I would like to know whether this small piece is of any interest to you and whether, from time to time, I might write to you on the subject; if so, I would need to get the pages back from you as I haven't made a copy. There is much to say on the subject and if you require information, I would gladly accommodate you. I believe I know the essentials as well as anyone does and would be able to speak about it just as well as others. A completely new discipline would have to be introduced if anything is to be achieved.

---

[103] Johann *Wilhelm* Ehlers (1774–1845), actor, singer, guitarist, composer; in Weimar from January 1801 to Easter 1805. Goethe valued him as an interpreter of his *Gesellige Lieder*, *Tag- und Jahres-Hefte*, 1801, *MA* 14, p. 65.

[104] Ignaz Ferdinand Arnold, *Mozarts Geist* (Erfuhrt: Henning, 1803).

[105] August Eberhard Müller (1767–1817), organist at the Nicholaikirche in Leipzig from 1794; Director of Music at the Thomaskirche from 1800; appointment as choirmaster and organist at the Thomaskirche in August 1804.

[106] Goethe's tragedy was first published by Cotta in the *Taschenbuch auf das Jahr 1804*.

[107] Zelter's manuscript has not been handed down.

## 23. Zelter

Berlin, 10 August 1803

[...] You ask me about the music to the second part of *Die Zauberflöte*. I take you to mean by that our new representation of Winter's music.[108] It is being staged with great pomp and will be a huge theatrical undertaking.[109] An immeasurable amount of new scenery, air and earth apparitions which follow one another almost from minute to minute – so that the cast can barely fit their arias in – dominates the piece and keeps the machine operators busy, so that they are seen here and there and heard before they are meant to be. The music suits the play about as much as *Die Zauberflöte II* fits with Part I. The score is very full and crammed with effects that startle and overwhelm one's ears and senses. There is a full house every time, though I see no signs of real satisfaction from that part of the audience for which the piece seems to have been written; I suppose it will come in time [...]

The amount of expensive props for this opera as well as the noisy and disturbing machinery are so mindlessly and unprofessionally put together and so badly painted that one would turn away one's face with annoyance if one were not attracted and drawn in at the same time. In a disturbingly dangerous way the figures of three beautiful young women are suspended over 20 feet in the air on thin ropes for more than half an hour and sing with such fear and trepidation, that one's heart would skip a beat. The end of these four hours of childish pranks, which are protracted through the insertion of three long musical scenes, consists of the fall of the empire of the Queen of the Night: a King of Paphos, named Tipheus, to whom the Queen of the Night wants to marry off her daughter, Pamina, is eventually killed by Tamino and thrown into the jaws of a fire-spitting mountain, from which the flames shoot high into the sky [and] join with a rain of fire from above. Amid horrific crashes and bangs which completely drown out the music, the Queen of the Night is flung down from her high perch.

One part of the libretto is not without humorous appeal: Papageno, who is again bereft of his new-found Papagena, searches for her, among other places, in a rural region where he encounters, by chance, his father, his mother and an innumerable multitude of younger and older siblings, aged from 2 to 20, who are all his father's children, which gives rise to much farce and comical situations. Apart from that the libretto is incredibly bad. [...]

---

[108] Peter von Winter's opera *Das Labyrinth, oder Der Kampf mit den Elementen* composed in 1797 (libretto by Emmanuel Schikaneder). Considered a sequel to Mozart's *Zauberflöte*, it was first performed on 18 July 1803 at the Königliches Nationaltheater, Berlin. Goethe's question on 4 August 1803 relates to Zelter's music for Goethe's published fragment *Der Zauberflöte Zweiter Teil* which appeared in Willman's *Taschenbuch* (1802), *MA* 6.1, p. 101.

[109] The performance was reviewed in the *Spenersche Zeitung*, 21 July 1803, *MA* 20.3, p. 152.

Regarding the composition of the chorus [from *Die natürliche Tochter*] I have now made a definite decision. Namely, all the chorus lines must be sung. It is bad luck for me that I have to do without you. When I flick through it, thousands of ideas occur to me and the [real] question is whether I should give a singer the bride's part at the end, not whether she should sing everything – but here and there she will have to sing. Let me know what you think of this. In addition, I am thinking that something has to happen with the libretto, which I can't explain clearly because I have to handle the music in a fragmentary way. Schiller would not be in favour of any alterations. But, to my mind, towards the end the libretto becomes very diffuse rather than compressed; and so I would suggest that, instead of what is in Act Four of the manuscript, you include a kind of epilogue where the chorus, noble and detached, appears as the main character, and finds itself at home in the highest regions that the musician can create. I would also like to know what you think of this.

Madame Mara is due to arrive today or tomorrow, 14 August.[110] They say that she experienced terrible aggravation at Lauchstädt, even though – thanks to Reichardt – her concert went off well. She had announced in Dresden that she wanted to entertain the Electoral Prince with her talent, but when she was told His Royal Highness was pleased to hear music during dinner, she was forced to confess that she could not sing at a banquet. This decision cost her a hundred ducats, and the Electoral Prince an aria.

## 24. Goethe

Weimar, 29 August 1803

First, let me thank you for your songs,[111] which are distributed according to your instructions and otherwise are well-housed; thanks also for the pages on musical direction.[112] As soon as our musical exercises are taken up again, I will put them into practice and hopefully come to the point where I can ask you for more guidance. [...]

What do you think of the plans to transplant the *Jenaische Allgemeine Literatur-Zeitung* to Halle? We others, who are behind the scenes, never cease to be amazed that a Royal Prussian Cabinet, just like any other public body, should allow itself to be fooled by names, shams, charlatanism and importunity. As if such an institution could be taken over and transported like the Laocoon or any other movable work of art! [...]

---

[110] The concert is reviewed in the *AMZ* 5 (1802/3), no. 51, 14 September 1803, *MA*, 20.3, p. 152.

[111] Zelter's *Sammlung kleiner Balladen und Lieder* (1803).

[112] Zelter's essay on the orchestra sent to Goethe on 7 August 1803.

For the moment things continue as usual in Jena, and as we still have Court Councillor Eichstädt,[113] the most active editor, everything will go on in its own course. [...]

If you care to join us, you are very welcome. How good it would be if you could use your role as reviewer to tell the public, in an orderly way, what at present so badly needs to be said about music.

I shall share in the undertaking, giving advice, and actively participating.

### 25. Zelter

Berlin, 7 September 1803

[...] I am inclined to recommend young Mendelssohn[114] as a thoroughly useful correspondent in Paris. He was fortunate enough, a few years ago, to have been speaking with you at Frankfurt am Main. He is a fine young man, well read, with good taste. He is now in Berlin, and hopes to pass through Weimar on his return journey to Paris. If you approve, I might give him a letter [of introduction] to you. Whatever else I can do in the interests of the *Jenaische Allgemeine Literatur-Zeitung* I will do gladly in the course of time.

### 26. Zelter

Berlin, 1 October 1803

It is true that our theatre is in danger of being split up. The singer, Ambrosche, is dead; Beschort should be dead; Madame Fleck is getting married and will leave the theatre; Madame Meyer is married already but is still leaving; Madamoiselle Eigensatz is moving to Vienna, and Eunicke and his wife have found work elsewhere. What truth there is in all of that, time will tell!

---

[113] Heinrich Karl Abraham Eichstädt (1772–1848), editor of the *Jenaische Allgemeine Literatur-Zeitung.*

[114] Abraham Ernst Mendelssohn (1776–1835), second son of the philosopher, Moses Mendelssohn, and father of Felix Mendelssohn and Fanny Hensel. Goethe had met him in August 1797 in Frankfurt; see Abraham Mendeslssohn's letter to Zelter, 1 September 1797, *Jahrbuch der Sammlung Kippenberg* 4, 1924, pp. 72–6. Hereafter referred to as *JbSK*.

## 27. Goethe

Weimar, 10 October 1803

My theatre school, founded on Unzelmann's advice, has now grown to 12 members.[115] The first fully staged performance will be given next Thursday but it will not be open to the general public. I hope much good will come from this venture.

Could you enquire after young Lauchery, the choreographer's son?[116] He is employed at the cadet's house in Berlin. In our circumstances we need a man who understands dance more than one who dances, one who has good teaching methods and a feeling for theatrical arrangements and divertissements. He is recommended here and I would like to get to know more about him through you. [...]

Would you not like to take on this year's edition of the musical journal, which is now finished, in line with what has gone before?[117] It seemed to me a good opportunity to say something in general about the nature of music and introduce aesthetic judgements.

## 28. Zelter

Berlin, 24 to 28 October 1803

[...] I will gladly take up the opportunity to write something for the music column in the *Jenaische Allgemeine Literatur-Zeitung*.[118] I am working on something, which it would be important for me to discuss with you in person.[119] When I have finished it, I will forward it to you to get your opinion; it involves some important issues in the art [of music] and for me personally.

---

[115] Goethe had started to give acting lessons the actor Friedrich Unzelmann's son, Carl Wolfgang Unzelmann (1786–1843), on 14 March 1803. In July 1803 two further students emerged in Bad Lauchstädt: Karl Franz d'Akácz and Pius Alexander Wolff (1782–1828), *Tag- und Jahres-Hefte* (1803), *MA* 14, p. 102. See also Goethe's *Regeln für Schauspieler*, *MA* 6.2, p. 703.

[116] Albert Lauchery (1779–1853), dancer and choreographer in the *école militaire* in Berlin; son of the court choreographer, Etienne Lauchery.

[117] Zelter agreed to write a review in the *Leipziger Allgemeine Musikalische Zeitung* (1802/03) on 28 October and several times remembered the promise, but the idea was never carried out.

[118] The promise to write a review in *JALZ* was never fulfilled.

[119] Zelter's second memorandum to Minister Carl August von Hardenberg.

Would Schiller be willing to compose some hymn-like verses which I could set to music to welcome my King when he visits the Sing-Akademie?[120] The King, who has expressed his wish and desire to subsidize us, has never visited the Sing-Akademie before. It is possible that he will visit soon and I would like to receive him worthily. It is up to the poet; four or five verses would be sufficient and a fairly strong choir of at least 150 voices could sing like one person producing the whole. I want to keep it a secret; you can imagine how things are here.

### 29. Goethe

Weimar, 27 February 1804

How long have I been silent to you, dear friend, and how often have I wished to be with you on Mondays and Tuesdays.[121] I have hardly heard any music this winter and through it I feel I am missing out on one of life's great pleasures. [...]

Our newspaper is going exceptionally well.[122] If you would like to take the opportunity to write something really fundamental about music, we would gladly publish it. Do it this winter before you get caught up with work in the spring and the summer. [...]

### 30. Zelter

Berlin, 5 March 1804

I should have written to you a long time ago, even before I received your second letter, and so your apologies for not being in touch are doubly embarrassing. [...]

Heartfelt thanks for the seal. I heartily hoped for this little thing which will soon be indispensable to me because my Sing-Akademie is now thriving more than ever. Our Queen was with us on 3 January and on 14 February the King paid a visit with his whole court, which gave me tremendous joy. I entertained the King with an eight-part *Te Deum* for double choir, which I composed for his birthday two years ago.[123] He was obviously very pleased and paid me many personal compliments, which I lapped up from him.

---

[120] Friedrich Wilhelm II of Prussia (1770–1840) visited the Sing-Akademie on 14 February 1804. It is not known whether Schiller received Zelter's request.

[121] The weekly rehearsals took place on Mondays and Tuesdays in the Sing-Akademie.

[122] *JALZ*.

[123] Zelter's *Te Deum* for two choirs and soloists in D major; the manuscript is now lost.

[...] The minister has actually written to me [...] In the enclosed I have recommended my beloved Sing-Akademie to the minister[124] and expressed my wish that he sanction it and place it under the curatorium of the fine arts. This same Sing-Akademie has 200 members and consequently is a constant heavy workload, because I have to work day and night for it. I have brought it on so much that it will be able to sustain itself in future times if the King can house it in the academy as happened before; and this was not exactly easy, because the mere upkeep costs 1,000 thaler per annum and I perform my service free of charge. [...]

## 31. Goethe

Weimar, 28 March 1804

Many a traveller testifies to your works and deeds, in so far as they are in the public forum and have a public impact; your refreshing letter gives me a glimpse into your inner life, worked by no steel spring but animated by a living spirit. I think you are lucky to be exerting a growing, formative influence on that environment which you have yourself created, and to have the hope that you have also achieved something that will last. [...]

What our little company is able to accomplish was shown in the production of Schiller's *Wilhelm Tell*, which was very fittingly performed. However, our opera is not as satisfactory. Yesterday I recognized your remarks about so many orchestral points, which I could make no use of because I had to abandon the chaos. May I perhaps publish the little essay in the cultural column of the *Jenaische Allgemeine Literatur-Zeitung* in the section at the end, where you will have discovered many insightful observations about art and language? May I put 'Weimar Arts Circle' at the end, whereby we designate the essay as ours or at least link it with our way of thinking? If possible could you also soon write a review for us?

I just found your letter in which you enclosed your remarks about the orchestra. Certainly if you saw it in print you would be encouraged to go further along this track and to discuss it further. I would love it if you agreed. It would benefit us all if a thing like that were brought to the attention of the general public.

Bye for now. I am wondering how it may be possible somehow to see you this year?

Goethe

---

[124] Zelter's second memorandum to Minister Hardenberg. Both memoranda are published in: Georg Schünemann, *Carl Friedrich Zelter der Begründer der Preußischen Musikpflege* (Berlin: Hesse, 1932), hereafter referred to as Schünemann; subsequently in extracts and with the pertinent correspondence in: Cornelia Schröder, *Carl Friedrich Zelter und die Akademie. Dokumente und Briefe zur Entstehung der Musik-Sektion in der Preußischen Akademie der Künste* (Berlin: Akademie der Künste. Monographien und Biographien 1959). Hereafter referred to as *Carl Friedrich Zelter und die Akademie*.

## 32. Zelter

Berlin, 1 May 1804

My essay to Minister von Hardenberg[125] would soon be in your hands if I could have taken the time to write a fair copy and so I send you a copy my wife made from the original draft, which I have handed in and for which I ask to have back in case I might need it. As yet there has been no response and perhaps there never will be. However, it is necessary to know that this essay was prefaced by a letter to the minister, in which two of the minister's questions were addressed: how an arts academy can have influence on manufacture and industry, and how the academy can be perfected in its own right. My proposal to the minister implied that the latter must be a priority if the first objective is to be realized and also that the artists must be masters of their art if they are to have any influence at all; that all the arts in an academy must be developed simultaneously and that in our academy one art (music) is completely wanting in that it is not scientifically grounded; that I could make many useful proposals if permitted and so on. The minister answered very graciously and asked me to outline my ideas and so that was how the following essay came to be written. [...]

The greatest joy that my little piece of writing could give me is this: if you should find it of value, the whole article or just in places, and would read it yourself to Anna Amalia, because only you could convey my feeling and intent.[126] [...]

The difficulties you experience with your opera are the same as here, where the situation also leaves much to be desired; however, despite that we still enjoy it. We have a right to discuss something which costs us money and we have to swallow it down whether it tastes good or not.

I did not write the comments about the orchestra with a view to publication. What you consider practical or beneficial could be included, if you don't find the corrections too tedious. I am happy for you to publish in the *Jenaische Allgemeine Literatur-Zeitung* whatever you find useful among my report and artistic views (in so far as they do not directly concern the Sing-Akademie about which I don't want to say anything publicly) and reports; I will also be looking for any interesting artistic reviews. The article in the *Jenaische Allgemeine Literatur-Zeitung* is a good idea: alternation between art and science is in any case advantageous, while it has to be said that the public is currently more concerned with art. [...]

My plan to create something of lasting value for music and in general occupies me day and night and is increasingly aimed at establishing principles. One cannot hope for much from a public that is still in the making. It has to be made and created and that can only ever be done by one person, and he has to be able to

---

[125] Zelter's first memorandum to Minister Hardenberg on 28 September 1803.

[126] Anna Amalia (1739–1807) thanked Goethe on 13 May 1804 for 'passing on Zelter's essay on music' (*Briefe an Goethe. Gesamtausgabe in Regestform*, (ed.) Karl-Heinz Hahn (Weimar: Regestausgabe, 1980ff), 4, no. 1526). Hereafter referred to as *RA*.

hold his own against the crowd. I would really like to discuss the matter with you further.

Enclosed: Copy of Zelter's second memorandum to Minister Hardenberg in Julie Zelter's hand.

### 33. Zelter

Berlin, 12 July 1804

Has Reichardt shown you his attempt at setting your *Iphigenie* to music?[127] If so, I would like to hear a word from you about it. It seems to me like an operation carried out on a healthy developed body and the body is like a patch applied where there is no hole. But your opinion is dearer to me than my own.

Everyone in Berlin is going on holidays and I remain here. If only I could spend once more just six hours with you sometime, it would keep me going the entire year.[128] […]

I have composed Schiller's 'Berglied' and enclosed it with this letter with the request that you pass it on to him.[129] If only I could sing it for him as well, because it would be hard for someone to get it right.

Enclosed: Zelter's setting of Schiller's 'Berglied'

### 34. Goethe

Weimar, 13 July 1804

Your essay, my honourable friend, has given me and a few of the initiated to whom I showed it much pleasure;[130] even more it has enlightened and strengthened us

---

[127] Zelter's enquiry was prompted by the publication of a single setting, 'Heraus in eure Schatten', from Reichardt's *Monolog aus Göthes Iphigenie also eine Probe musikalischer Behandlung jenes Meiserwerkes* (Leipzig, 1798).

[128] Goethe and Zelter did not meet until August 1805 in Bad Lauchstädt.

[129] Zelter had received the poem from Schiller during his visit to Berlin (1 to 17 May 1804). In Schiller's diary he notes meeting Zelter twice: on 3 and 15 May. Zelter's autograph manuscript is in Goethe's music collection, dated 21 May 1804. It was first published in Zelter's *Sämtliche Lieder, Balladen und Romanzen* (1812).

[130] Zelter's second memorandum to Minister Hardenberg which Goethe had shown to Schiller and Anna Amalia on 1 May 1804. Schiller responded to Zelter directly in a detailed letter on 16 July 1804 (*SNA* 32, pp. 153–55) which Goethe enclosed with his own. In Anna Amalia's letter to Goethe on 13 May 1804, in which she thanked him for sharing Zelter's

in our convictions of what is good and right. It has come from the depth of your character and talent and must make the most vivid impression on those who are in any way receptive. But what will the world think of it and make out of it? – the world which does not care to listen when complaints are formally made against it, and which, of course, cannot dream of finding a worthy enjoyment which it does not know, but rather snatches at some fleeting joy, which is created out of the world itself and therefore conforms with it.

It is a great pity in our times that every art, which after all is surely meant first and foremost for living, should, in so far as it is excellent and worthy of eternity, find itself in conflict with the time, and that the true artist frequently lives alone and in despair, in the conviction that he possesses and could impart to men what they are seeking.

We agree with you that first and foremost music must be improved through hymns, and that even for a government nothing could be more desirable in every sense than to foster an art and suitable higher feelings, and to purify the sources of a religion which is suitable for the cultivated and uncultivated alike. You have expressed yourself so admirably and concisely on this point that nothing can be added to it. But what we now wish you to take to heart, for practical purposes, is that you should, if possible, conceal your opposition to the time, and generally that you should dwell more upon the advantages that religion and morals would derive from such an institution, and less upon those that art has to expect from it. We should not use our arguments to move men to the good of which we are convinced, but we should consider what their [arguments] might be. [...]

If you have composed any poems of mine or my friends, I would ask you to send them to me at your leisure. There is no music around here at the moment, but I would make sure I heard anything which comes from you and would again feel renewed by for a long time. [...]

Enclosed: Copy of Zelter's second memorandum to Minister Hardenberg; Schiller's letter to Zelter, 16 July 1804; Schiller's poem 'Der Alpenjäger'.

---

musical essay, she agreed with the author's opinion and passed on her good wishes for the 'implementation of his humanistic ideas'. Later Goethe showed the essay to Friedrich August Wolf; see Goethe's diary, 10 September 1804, *WA* III/3, p. 107.

## 35. Zelter

Berlin, 29 July 1804

[…] As your letter has been lying around for another day, I will send you a song which I have just composed.[131] Reichardt has set the Italian poem to music so successfully, that I wouldn't consider composing it;[132] instead of which I found your parody[133] and set about composing it and I will be really happy if my melody ranks with Reichardt's setting as your parody does with the original.

Enclosure: Zelter's setting of Goethe's 'Nachtgesang'; Letter from Zelter to Schiller, 24 July 1804.

## 36. Goethe

Weimar, 30 July 1804

Thank you very much for the programmes you sent me through Mademoiselle Amelung. I look forward with pleasure to your Schiller setting,[134] which we will perform as well as possible […]

In a month's time I hope to have a reading of my *Götz von Berlichingen*.[135] I am entirely indebted to you that it is so far advanced. I could not understand why, over a year past, I had dealt with my work like Penelope, forever unravelling again what

---

[131] Zelter's setting of Goethe's 'Nachtgesang' is no longer part of Goethe's music collection. It is contained in the songbook which Zelter put together for his wife (SBB PK: Mus. ms. autogr. Zelter 22, no. 17), dated 29 July 1804, originally only with Goethe's text, but with the Italian text added in red pen. The song was first published by Landschoff in 1932.

[132] Zelter knew Reichardt's 'Notturno', a setting of the Italian folksong 'Tu sei quel dolce fuoco', presumably from the first edition: *6 Canzonette con accompagnamento de piano o arpa* (December 1803, no. 1).

[133] Presumably in Goethe/Wieland, *Taschenbuch auf das Jahr 1804* (Hagen, no. 486), which appeared in October 1803. Reichardt's setting of Goethe's text, a parody of the Italian folksong 'Tu sei quel dolce fuoco', first published in *Gesänge mit Begleitung der Chitarra*, (ed.) Wilhelm Ehlers (Tübingen, 1804), where it appeared under the title 'Notturno', though only the first stanza was published and without identifying the author (because the songs were intended as a supplement to the *Taschenbuch*); obviously Zelter did not know this publication.

[134] Zelter's setting of Schiller's 'Berglied'.

[135] From mid-February Goethe was reshaping this play; see Goethe's draft letter to Wilhelm von Humboldt, 30 July 1804, *WA* IV/17, pp. 171–5.

I had woven. Then in your essay I found the words,[136] 'What one does not love, one cannot do'.[137] My eyes were opened, and I saw clearly how up to that point I had treated the work as a piece of business, which, along with everything else, had to be got rid of; this explained how I approached it, and why it had no lasting value. From then on I devoted more attention, sympathy and concentration to this subject; so that the work is now – I will not say good – but at least finished.

Now I would like to ask you for a couple of small pieces of music, first, for George's song, 'Es fing ein Knab' ein Vögelein',[138] which I believe you have already set. Secondly, I want a quiet, devotional and elevating four-part hymn – with Latin words – that would take around eight minutes to perform; it may be a piece from a mass, or anything else of the kind.[139]

How I wish we lived nearer one another, or that we were both more mobile; the benefit of a continual exchange of ideas is incalculable. Anyhow, let us write to one another from time to time.

A thousand farewells.
Goethe

### 37. Zelter

Berlin, 4 August 1804

The song from *Götz* is not among my early compositions, but I have already composed it in the joy of this morning. I would like to know whether the song can be accompanied by orchestra or whether the boy should sing it alone without accompaniment? And another question: would the following passage be suitable for what you want: 'Domine Deus rex coelestis, pater omnipotens; Domine fili Jesu Christe, qui tollis peccata muni, Miserere nostri!'[140] I will try to keep within eight minutes. The Latin words are from the Catholic mass and if you are not happy with them, I could also choose words from a Latin Psalm.[141]

Now I will ask you for a reply by return of post so that you should receive at least one of the pieces in the next mail. [...]

---

[136] Zelter's second memorandum to Minister Hardenberg which he had sent to Goethe on 1 May 1804.

[137] This citation is not in the editions of Zelter's memoranda edited by either Schönemann or Schröder.

[138] Goethe, *Götz von Berlichingen*, Act 4, scene 16.

[139] In response to Goethe's request, Zelter set Psalm 111.

[140] *Domine Deus*, from the Gloria of the Ordinary of the Roman Catholic Mass, was set to music by Zelter in 1804; it was not used for the stage music to *Götz*.

[141] Goethe decided upon this option and in the next letter Zelter sent him his setting of the words 'Beatus vir' from Psalm 111.

It will be best if I enclose the little song here. If it needs to be altered or composed differently, I will follow your instructions; I will compose it as you would like it. One more observation: eight minutes' devotional music is quite a long time on the stage. Obviously it depends on the circumstances and so I will leave it to your judgement.

The King's birthday was celebrated yesterday.[142] We gathered together a group with Hufeland, Müller, Tralles, Woltmann, the Fichtes,[143] a few strangers and a few members, myself and family and toasted the occasion well. This Tuesday I will hold a birthday celebration in the Sing-Akademie and give a speech which is still not written down.[144]

Bye for now. I will expect your instructions by return of post.
Zelter

Enclosure: Zelter's setting of 'Georgs Lied' from Goethe's *Götz von Berlichingen*

## 38. Goethe

Weimar, 8 August 1804

I thank you most heartily for sending me the little song so promptly, and will now go more into detail about the chorus in *Götz*. It is really meant to be sung at the nuptials of Maria and Sickingen. The simple church procession moves across the stage to the sound of a hymn, an organ can be clearly heard in the distance, and as the chapel is close by, the chanting may continue to be heard while a scene is being played outside. Be so kind as to choose some words from a psalm. The character of it, as you will observe, is gentle and solemn, inclined to sadness on account of the circumstances; a prelude to the following scene, where those who are just married are, so to speak, chased away by Götz. All things considered, I think you are perfectly right in saying that eight minutes is too long; we will be content with four. It lies within my power to fill out the rest. [...]

I am very pleased with the melody to my serenade[145] and it is certainly better suited to my poem than my poem is to Reichardt's very praiseworthy melody.

---

[142] Friedrich Wilhelm III of Prussia (1770–1840); his birthday was 3 August.

[143] Christoph Wilhelm Hufeland (1762–1836) and his wife, Juliane Wilhelmine Friederike Hufeland née Amelung (1771–1845); Johannes von Müller (1752–1809); Johann Georg Tralles (1763–1822); Carl Ludwig Woltmann (1770–1817); Johann Gottlieb Fichte (1762–1814) and his wife Maria Johanna Fichte née Rahn (1755–1819).

[144] *Rede zur Feier des Geburtstages Seiner Majestät des Königs Friedrich Wilhelm III. Gehalten auf der Singakademie zu Berlin am 6ten August 1805 von Carl Friedrich Zelter* (Unger, 1805). A copy is preserved in Karoline Schulze's papers (SBB PK: Mus. ms. theor. 1540).

[145] Zelter's setting of Goethe's 'Nachtgesang'.

The little song for Georg is quite deliberately without accompaniment; we will see how the little fellow handles it!

I am very anxious to get this new version of *Götz* out of me. I should have finished it long ago had its length not delayed me; for in trying to make the play more theatrical, it became longer rather than shorter; what was diffuse has certainly been condensed, but what was transitory has become fixed; it will still take nearly four hours to play. If it is performed in Berlin, let me know your first impressions and what you make of it; for with the exception of the exposition in the first one and a half acts, which have been left almost entirely as they were, the piece has been altogether dismantled and recomposed [...]

Farewell and forgive my rambling letter.
Goethe

## 39. Zelter

Berlin, 12 to 18 August 1804

I am taking the liberty of sending you another copy of 'Georgs Lied'.[146] It is transposed down a semitone and is tighter and more polished, and so I think it should be sung in a more carefree manner. In the event that it is not sung by a young boy, the song would work if transposed into a lower key again, which would be suitable for the voice in question. If you don't agree with the freedom I have taken with 'So! So! Hm! Hm!',[147] it could be composed strictly following the words, although it would lose some of the feeling of ease.

In relation to the Latin church song,[148] I would like to have as exact information as possible regarding the situation and occasion. My work is, in fact, finished; but since I don't have the right viewpoint, I don't know myself what to make of my work and in short I am not too happy with it. I could recommend better pieces by other composers to you, who do what they do quite well but who would not be suitable for a new occasion [...] If you haven't fully planned the scene yourself, then perhaps the composition of this section could wait until everything is finished and then I promise to deliver the composition into your hands from one post-day to the next.

---

[146] Zelter's revised setting is not in Goethe's music collection. A copy, entitled 'Georg', dated 5 August 1804, is in Zelter's collection: *Lieder für eine Mutter und ihre elf Kinder* (SBB PK: Mus. ms. autogr. Zelter 22, no. 18).

[147] Goethe's refrain; in his setting Zelter abandoned this plan and inserted further repeats, in part omitting this interjection.

[148] Zelter's setting of the Latin text 'Domine Deus rex coelestis'; Goethe decided on the composer's second suggestion of a Latin psalm.

18 August: I am to blame for not having written the review, since I promised to;[149] but the fact that it hasn't happened is also not entirely my fault. Things continually crop up here which are not more important but are more pressing at the moment. I am much more preoccupied with myself than ever before. I have written to the King[150] and have received a very promising reply.[151]

If, my dear friend, you could arrange for my little piece on Fasch to be published in the *Jenaische Allgemeine Literatur-Zeitung*, it would be very advantageous for me because the paper is highly regarded.[152] There has been no notice about it in the *Hallische Allgemeine Literatur-Zeitung*,[153] at least not that I am aware of. Perhaps I could find out through the editors at Jena.

Enclosed: Zelter's revised setting of 'Georgs Lied'

## 40. Zelter

Berlin, 21 to 24 August 1804

My feeling has not deceived me. In the same moment as I read your letter of 8 August, I realized that my complete choral piece was worth nothing.[154] What I wrote to you about the sound of an organ appears to me to be no longer relevant, even confusing, because the sound of the organ can't come from the same place as the church procession, but should come from where it is going. The current arrangement is simpler[155] and will hopefully perform its function by not saying more than it should. The orchestra begins to play as the procession approaches. The chorus enter at bar 5; the choral procession must be arranged so that at least the singers are all visible by the time they sing their first note, even if the largest part of the procession is still off stage. Their entrance must be arranged so that four steps are taken to a bar: a step to every crotchet. The bigger the chorus is, the better; it must contain at least 12 singers: 3 sopranos, 3 altos, 3 tenors and 3 basses. They must articulate all the words very clearly and the orchestra must interject powerfully, not sluggishly and not aggressively. The music takes exactly four minutes to perform; should it happen in this performance that the moment is

---

[149] Nothing came of the promised review.

[150] Zelter's fourth memorandum, dated 1 August 1804 and sent directly to the Prussian King Friedrich Wilhelm III, is a very personal letter, in which Zelter describes his career and his work for the Sing-Akademie, with a view to obtaining a fixed salary; excerpts are printed in Schröder, *Carl Friedrich Zelter und die Akademie*, pp. 104–108.

[151] 11 August 1804; Schröder, p. 108.

[152] There is no mention of Zelter's Fasch biography in *JALZ* (1804) or *JALZ* (1805).

[153] *Allgemeine Literatur-Zeitung* (ed.) Christian Gottfried Schütz in Halle.

[154] Zelter's setting of the words 'Domine Deus rex coelestis'.

[155] Zelter's setting of Psalm 111.

too short or over-hasty, a reprise is marked in the score where ten bars could be repeated, but only if it is necessary. The choral entries must be very secure, not tailing each other, as is often the case here, but they should appear as one voice. Wind instruments are not woven into the piece because the singing would suffer; only at the very end do two bassoons enter one after the other. As the chorus withdraws at the end, the orchestra becomes quieter, just as at the beginning it became louder. The words are taken from Psalm 111 as it appears in the 1554 Vulgate.[156] I have, therefore, included the Gloria because it is used in all religious ceremonies of the Catholic Church. The audience – assuming they are probably situated on the stage – could speak a few appropriate words in between the Gloria and the Psalm; I have marked a fermata on the score at this point and expect it will work well. That's my sermon, which is longer than my music, though I hope the latter is better and the former would be unnecessary.

Let me know whether the revised version of *Götz* also begins with the inn scene as in the old one; when I can find enough time and peace, I would like to write a new overture to it. Perhaps it would earn me a free ticket to the Iffland production at our theatre. If you find you have a feeling, preparatory to Act One, which is not closely identifiable with the first scene, I would like you to tell me, because the overture should be attached to the hostel scene. Although it will take care not to paint the first scene, it should try to capture much more the spirit, life, moral weight and strength of the hero.

24 August: Tonight I have drawn up a plan for setting *Götz* to music.[157] The new piece will be set in acts or large masses of material, with artistic punctuation added not for its own sake but to enhance understanding. The overture is as good as finished and in order to finish it, I just need a response to the questions I asked you; I have also thought of a musical epilogue which would really add closure to the piece, in case old Götz were to be the last person on the stage, who in your play appears like a setting sun. To finish it I must have a copy of the complete manuscript, which you probably won't want to let out of your hands until you send it off. Meanwhile I would only need to have it for a few days and I could send it back to you by return of post. Admittedly I could wait until Iffland had a copy[158] but then Reichardt or Weber would fall on it[159] and I would end up with nothing once more. This epilogue is only 25 bars long and gains its meaning

---

[156] *Beatus vir qui timet Dominum: in mandatis eius volet nimis*: the opening words of Psalm 111. The composition, listed in Kruse's catalogue, is now lost.

[157] As with many of Zelter's plans for large-scale works, this remained unrealized. Zelter's only settings for this play are: 'Georgs Lied'; incidental music for the Wedding ceremony scene of Maria and Sicklingen (Psalm 111); a Gloria and the overture.

[158] Zelter is referring to Iffland's production of the play in Berlin.

[159] Reichardt had already published an overture and some songs from Goethe's *Götz von Berlichingen* in the *Musikalisches Kunstmagazin* 2 (1791): 124, as volume five of his *Music zu Göthes Werken* series, but never expanded his incidental music beyond this publication. Bernhard Anselm Weber never composed incidental music for this play.

(for the unskilled especially) only through repeated performance of the entire piece. For this epilogue is at the same time the prologue and precedes the overture, immediately suggesting what type of character one can expect in the course of the play. It would also be a pleasure to find the prophecy fulfilled at the end. What do you think of all this?

### 41. Goethe

Weimar, 10 September 1804

Just to let you know that your overture should work very well. The piece begins with the hostel scene. I am caught up in rehearsals. All would be well except that I am worried about the length. You will hear as soon as it is finished and then we can discuss the intermezzo. A thousand greetings and thanks for your heartening and encouraging letter.

Goethe

### 42. Goethe

Weimar, 24 September 1804

Once again through Levin[160] I am sending you a packet of snuff, which our dear Duchess Amalia gave me for you with best wishes. [...]

Levin will tell you that your choral hymn came across as very charming and beautiful, and gave prominence to the important moment.[161] I enclose an advertisement for our art exhibition this year. I shall write again in a few days. Let me hear from you soon.

Goethe

---

[160] Liepmann Levin, later Ernst Friedrich Ludwig Robert, and from 1814: Robert-Tornow (1778–1832), brother of Rahel Levin, later Varnhagen von Ense (1771–1833).

[161] Zelter's setting of Psalm 111 and *Gloria*, premiered in Goethe's revised version of *Götz von Berlichingen*, on 22 September 1804 in the Weimar Court Theatre.

## 43. Zelter

Berlin, 27 to 29 September 1804

*Egmont* was due to be performed on the 13th of this month but nothing came of it.[162] Madame Unzelmann told me that Schiller was not happy with Reichardt's composition of the song in *Egmont*,[163] so I took it on and my music is included here.[164] I had to repeat the first word, 'Freudvoll', which has a dipthong and cannot be treated melismatically. The two words which directly follow one after the other, 'Freudvoll und Leidvoll', are musically difficult to set; it depends on how you see it. The little introduction is nothing more than a single chord: then the voice enters vehemently, and at the word, 'Leidvoll', changes to melancholy. It becomes livelier towards the end and the words 'Glücklich allein ist die Seele die liebt' must be sung with increased animation. You will see how the song is received in the theatre, where it has the failing that it does not fit in with Reichardt's intermezzo, because for the following intermezzo Reichardt has written variations on this theme for the orchestra which are even more beautiful than his song.[165]

Your Court Chamber Councillor Kirms[166] has written to me to ask my opinion on the Silbermann grand piano which I saw at your ducal palace. I would advice him to hold onto this instrument. You would get very little for it and the instrument is good, even if it is out of fashion. In a palace where the good and the beautiful have so much room, there is bound to be a remote room somewhere where this old instrument, which is not lacking in taste, could find a modest home underneath portraits of some old heroes of the dynasty until there comes a time when a connoisseur takes it away and replaces it with a beaten-up fortepiano.

---

[162] There is no mention of a performance (or its cancellation) in the Berlin newspapers in 1804.

[163] Reichardt's setting of 'Clärchens Lied' ('Freudvoll und Leidvoll') from Goethe's *Egmont*, Act 3; first published in Reichardt's *Lieder der Liebe und der Einsamkeit, zur Harfe und zum Klavier zu singen* (Leipzig: Fleischer, 1798).

[164] Zelter's setting of 'Clärchens Lied' is no longer in Goethe's music collection. An autograph in Berlin (SBB PK: Mus. ms. autogr. Zelter 22, no. 19) is dated 5 September 1804. The song was published in Zelter's *Sämtliche Lieder, Balladen und Romanzen* (1810), vol. 1.

[165] The publication was planned in Reichardt's *Musik zu Göthes Werken*, vol. 5 (Berlin: Verlag der neuen berlinischen Musikhandlung, 1793). The *AMZ* reported Reichardt 'is also working on music for Goethe's *Egmont*, which will be performed this winter'; *AMZ* (1801), no. 11, 7 January, column 255. The performance took place on 25 February 1801 in the Berlin Nationaltheater; Reichardt's music was not reviewed in the *AMZ*.

[166] Franz Kirms (1750–1826), court official in Weimar, 1791–1824: member of the board of management for the Weimar Court Theatre, finally theatre manager and artistic director. Zelter's reply to Kirms is in the Weimar Archives (GSA 95/N 10); *MA* 20.3, p. 173.

I have indeed completed a sketch to your *Götz* overture, but I have been out and about so much and have had so many distractions that I won't have it for you before the performance of the play (which apparently is just around the corner).[167] If you could let me know when the premiere of *Götz* will be, perhaps I could find a time where I would be in the mood to complete the work I have begun. I am on tenterhooks and a word from you would be a great boon and comfort. There is no word from Schiller. There was news in the papers yesterday that recently he is seriously ill again.[168] I had so hoped that we would welcome him here without your losing him, and in the end perhaps we will all lose him.

Enclosed: Zelter's setting of 'Clärchens Lied'

## 44. Goethe

Weimar, 5 November 1804

Levi, a young man whom I got to know in Lauchstädt, departed immediately after the first performance of *Götz von Berlichingen*. I gave him a sealed box of the famous Spanish snuff and he promised to give you as detailed an account of the performance as is possible. As I haven't heard from you for a while, I fear that the journey has taken him longer than he planned and he has not yet arrived in Berlin. [...]

One more thing. Would you send me the score of your 'Wohl auf Kameraden';[169] I don't have a copy to hand and it is to be rehearsed for performance in the winter and is to replace the old popular song.

Warmest greetings from Schiller and myself.

Goethe

## 45. Zelter

Berlin, 7 October to 15 November 1804

Your *Götz von Berlichingen* is now a reality.[170] I was especially pleased that our choir gave a good performance because it is the first piece of theatrical music

---

[167] Zelter's overture was never completed.

[168] On 24 July 1804 Schiller suffered a severe colic attack, probably caused by bowel spasm.

[169] Through lack of time, Zelter could not, at first, accede to Goethe's request for the score of Schiller's 'Reuterlied'; in the end Goethe had the score copied from the parts.

[170] The premiere took place on 22 September 1804.

which I have composed.[171] I heard from Levi and from other quarters that *Götz* was given a good performance in Weimar. The grand length of it, by the way, should not be burdensome to us. It is the container for the whole and if it is too big for anyone, he can drink out of bottles. The rest of us are ready to drink in one draught what is prescribed for us! [...]

I will put the 'Reuterlied' score in the next post for you. [...]

## 46. Zelter

Berlin, 8 December 1804

The reasons you have still not received the 'Reuterlied', even with this letter, is because of unpleasant work which I myself, of course, have imposed on myself. I had let it be known among friends that I would be willing to give a type of workshop on the art of singing.[172] Soon there were many participants and for the last two weeks I have needed nine hours a week in which I had to prepare with great diligence to fulfil the expectations which, without my intending it, have been roused. Meantime I got into my stride more quickly than I would have imagined possible and I have no doubt of a successful outcome. Well, it would have given me much more enjoyment if I were now not forced, because of this venture, to read a pile of terrible books on singing. More later; the post is going now!

## 47. Goethe

Weimar, 13 December 1804

I have created the score of 'Reuterlied' from the parts: don't worry yourself about it any longer. [...]

---

[171] Zelter's setting of the psalm 'Beatus vir'.

[172] While his teacher, Fasch, was still alive, Zelter had begun to hold additional singing classes in 1792 with members of the choir founded by Fasch, and 'with those who wanted it, to do solfege and other useful exercises'; see 'Fragen die Sing-Akademie betreffend', namely Reichardt's questions about the origins of the Sing-Akademie, answered by Zelter (GSA 95/ii, 7, 5). See also Zelter's report regarding musical and singing institutions, 'Über den Zustand des allgemeinen Gesangswesen', 11 February 1811, *Akten des Kultusministeriums*, Berlin 158 I–III, in Alfred Morgenroth, *Carl Friedrich Zelter: Eine musikgeschichte Studie* (Berlin: Unpublished Doctoral Dissertation Friedrich-Wilhelms-Universität, 1922), vol. 1, p. 62. See also Zelter's letter to Goethe, ZG 8 May 1816. Zelter's student Emil Fischer pays homage to Zelter as singing and composition teacher in his *Rede beim Wohltätigkeitsfeste des Berlinischen Gymnasiums am 20 Dezember 1834* (Berlin, 1836), pp. 7–29.

16 December: I am really sorry that I am unable to take part in your lectures.[173] It is according to my nature to live in a small place; but the worst thing about it is that one has hardly anything to enjoy apart from what one dishes up oneself, whereas in a bigger place one can easily and often be entertained by others. [...]

## 48. Zelter

Berlin, 22 December 1804

Today I am trying to digest an incredible operatic mêlée, *Die Sternenkönigen*,[174] which I saw for the first time yesterday and which is so immeasurably bad that we are all at war with it while playing and seeing it.

My [singing] course progresses nicely. The best I can hope for it is that it will introduce me to things in art and science that I don't yet know and then I will have fulfilled more than one aim.

If you were to have a free hour then I would recommend a little task for you: to think up a plan for a little roguish Singspiel of one or two acts which is also quite frisky.[...]

## 49. Zelter

Berlin, 19 January 1805

Just before my arrival home, Ehlers was here[175] and brought greetings from you and from Schiller. He didn't want to delay so I don't know whether I will get to speak to him. He has arrangements made for today and tomorrow and didn't leave any indication as to how I might see him.

Recently I have composed a new song by Schiller, 'Die Gunst des Augenblicks',[176] in which an increasingly larger musical form is attempted; I will send it with Ehlers if I see him. [...]

---

[173] The public lectures and classes Zelter gave on the art of singing.

[174] Romantic fairytale with songs by Ferdinand Kauer (Libretto after Leopold Hubers *Das Sternenmädchen im Meidlinger Walde*) premiered in the Königliches Opernhaus on 17 December 1804. Zelter attended the performance on 21 December.

[175] In January 1805 Wilhelm Ehlers travelled to Berlin to give concerts with a letter of recommendation from Goethe.

[176] Zelter's setting of Schiller's 'Die Gunst des Augenblicks', cantata for four soloists, choir and orchestra.

## 50. Zelter

Berlin, 2 April 1805

A few words to accompany the enclosed documents which I ask you kindly to pass onto young Voß.[177]

I have now set the song to music three times.[178] I am sending you the final product, since it is probably needed. If I come up with something better, I will send it on. The singer will do her best with it and she must see to the insertion of the melody into the spoken dialogue with a natural, quiet expression. I will write to Voß as soon as I can free myself from all diversions and all the running around.[179]

## 51. Goethe

Weimar, 1 June 1805

Since I last wrote to you,[180] I have had very few good days. I thought I was losing myself, and now I lose a friend,[181] and in him one half of my existence.[182] In truth, I ought to begin a new way of life, but at my age there is no longer a way. Therefore each day I can only look straight ahead of me and address immediate concerns without worrying about the future.

As people try to turn every loss and misfortune into some diversion for themselves, I am being urged by our theatre company, and many others, to honour our departed friend's memory by a stage performance.[183] I shall say nothing further about this, except that I am not against it and all I should like to ask you just now is, whether you would be willing to assist me in this, and first of all – if you

---

[177] Johann *Heinrich* Voß (1779–1822), eldest son of Johann Heinrich Voß, teacher at the Weimar Gymnasium from 1804 to 1806.

[178] Schiller's 'Die Gunst des Augenblicks'; the setting, which was published in Königsberg and Berlin in 1809, is not part of Goethe's music collection.

[179] On 25 May 1805 Zelter wrote to Voß thanking him for his report about Goethe and enquiring whether he had received the manuscript of his setting from *Othello*.

[180] GZ 29 January 1805.

[181] Johann Christoph *Friedrich* Schiller (1759–1805) died in Weimar on 9 May 1805.

[182] Quotation from Horace's *Carmina* I, 3/8, where Virgil is described as 'animae dimidium meae' (the half of my soul).

[183] Goethe's original plan was to complete and stage Schiller's *Demetrius, Tag- und Jahres-Hefte* 1805. The memorial performance for Schiller was, in fact, staged in Bad Lauchstädt on 10 August opening with a scenic performance of Schiller's 'Das Lied von der Glocke', to which Goethe had written an *Epilog zu Schillers Glocke*.

would be so kind as to let us have your motet, *Der Mensch lebt und bestehet*,[184] for which I see a notice in the twenty-seventh edition of the *Berlinische Musikalische Zeitung*.[185] Would you also either compose something else in a solemn style, or search out and forward to me some compositions, whose character I will specify to you, in order that suitable words may be added? As soon as I hear your response to this, you shall have further details.

Your admirable series of short essays on the arrangements of the orchestra I have kept by me up to now,[186] not least because they contained a sort of satire upon the state of affairs here. Reichardt now wishes to have them for the [*Berlinische*] *Musikalische Zeitung*.[187] I am going back to them, looking at them, and I cannot possibly withhold them from the review section of our [*Jenaische Allgemeine*] *Literatur-Zeitung*. Some of our circumstances have changed somewhat and in the end we are allowed to criticize even what we ourselves have brought about.

Privy Councillor Wolf of Halle is here at present.[188] If only I could hope to see you too this year. Is there no possibility that you would come to Lauchstädt at the end of July, to assist preparing and carrying out the work mentioned above?[189] Think it over, and tell me whether it is possible; the means we can think about afterwards. [...]

---

[184] The opening words of Matthias Claudius's poem, composed as a motet for double choir (both SATB) by Zelter in 1803.

[185] Founded by J.F. Reichardt, Berlin's first notable journalist. The journal was short-lived (1805–06). In this journal Reichardt and others had reported a celebration in memory of the deceased Academy director, Johann Wilhelm Meil, on 12 February 1805, at which Zelter's Requiem, a Haydn motet and Zelter's eight-part motet *Der Mensch lebt und bestehet* were performed. The latter was analysed in detail by Reichardt.

[186] Zelter's *Bemerkungen über das Orchesterwesen* were enclosed in a letter to Goethe on 7 August 1803. They were, in fact, published – issued in separate articles – in June and July 1805: 'Planiform des Orchesters', *JALZ* 66 (1805), 17 June, column 567f; 'Direktion des Orchesters', *JALZ* 67 (1805), 19 June, column 575; 'Der erste Violinist', *JALZ* 68 (1805), 22 June, column 583f and *JALZ* 69 (1805), 24 June, column 591f; 'Stärke des Orchesters', *JALZ* 70 (1805), 26 June, column 599f and *JALZ* 71 (1805), 29 June, column 607f; 'Stimmung des Orchesters', *JALZ* 72 (1805), 1 July, column 615; 'Proben', *JALZ* 73 (1805), 3 July column 623f; 'Tempo', *JALZ* 74 (1805), 6 July, p. 631; 'Stellung der Instrumente', *JALZ* 75 (1805), 8 July, p. 639f.

[187] See Reichardt's letter to Goethe, 8 April 1805, *GJb* (1925), p. 226.

[188] Christian Wilhelm *Friedrich August* Wolf (1759–1824) arrived in Weimar on 30 May and remained there until 14 June.

[189] Goethe's request is reissued on 22 July; Zelter declined on 30 July due to an overload of work and also financial commitments.

## 52. Zelter

Berlin, 8 to 11 June 1805

I have not written to you, dear friend, for so long that it is a source of anxiety to me. Although I have written many a letter in that time, it would have been perhaps impossible for me to write you a proper letter without some special reason. Your dear letter of 1 June woke me up. I have just received it and am answering it straight away, even though it can only be posted from here next Wednesday the 12th.

My motet is enclosed,[190] but I doubt that it will suit your present purpose[191] because it is in eight parts and needs a choir of at least 32 good choral singers if it is to be effective. As a result I did it mainly to try my hand at a type of music which is rarely used or looked for today. It would also work well if the vocal parts were doubled by an orchestra (however, without wind instruments). By the way, I also enclose the opening movement of my Requiem,[192] which perhaps might also be useful in so far as it only requires a choir of 16 to 20 singers and four soloists; the choir could also be supported by the orchestra. But why do we want to make do with borrowings? I should think it would not be difficult for you to make something special or arrange for it, and I could send you the music as soon as it is possible.[193] The pieces mentioned above are really intended for the church and I am afraid they won't be suitable outside this context. [...]

I read *Rameaus Neffe*[194] for the first time yesterday and really enjoyed it and it really hurt to realize that you know more about the art of music than I do. I have never read anything that had my eyes so out on springs as this book. One can be astonished at oneself in understanding this book and I think to myself: you could not resist translating it, if translating it you did. Your remarks about the people in the book are so admirable that I would have to admire you, even if you had written nothing else.

The unexpected death of our beloved Schiller has caused a general sensation here in Berlin [...] for just now, when Schiller is played, the house is always full – a rare thing for this time of year.

Then let us too do something in this matter, something which shall be a lasting connection with a lasting subject. (Natural for us.) If you are not under too much

---

[190] Zelter's setting of Matthias Claudius's *Der Mensch lebt und bestehet*, motet for mixed double-choir; the score is not in Goethe's music collection.

[191] A memorial performance for Schiller.

[192] Presumably Zelter's Requiem composed in memory of Fasch and first performed on 3 August 1802; the manuscript is now lost.

[193] Zelter's promise was not realized.

[194] *Rameaus Neffe. Ein Dialog von Diderot aus dem Manuskript übersetzt und mit Anmerkungen begleitet von Goethe* (1805).

pressure, it might be a soothing, healing employment for you, and I will pull myself together and do what I can.

I would love to pay a visit to Lauchstädt. Just finding you there would be reason enough; however, I will not be able to manage it. My wife has been so sick this winter, that she has to drink pyrophosphate at the spa itself; as a result I am alone with all my children and work and have no help.

The Requiem that I enclose is the one we performed in Schiller's memory at the Sing-Akademie on 21 May, at which our good friend Jacobi attended.

Farewell and give me the happiness of hearing reassuring news of you.

Zelter

## 53. Goethe

Weimar, 19 June 1805

Many thanks for your prompt dispatch of the music I requested.[195] As soon as possible I will try to find an opportunity to hear it. Furthermore, I share your conviction, that we should have no patchwork on this occasion but should create something out of the whole piece. Unfortunately, I have never been so lucky as to have a first-rate musician by me to collaborate with, so in cases like this I have always been obliged to keep to cobbling and patching, and on this occasion I had expected it to be the same again.

You shall now at least hear about my plan[196] as soon as possible and do let me know what you think of it. But our intention, as well as our work, must be kept a secret until we are ready and can proceed to performance with an easy mind.

While working on *Rameaus Neffe*, and things related, I often thought of you, and wished for only a few hours conversation with you. I know music more by reflection than by enjoyment and therefore only in the general sense. I am glad you found this little volume entertaining; the dialogue is also a genuine masterpiece. [...]

Privy Councillor Wolf of Halle was with me for a fortnight.[197] The presence of this highly capable man has supported me in every sense. I am expecting Jacobi to arrive any day.[198] Why can I still not hope to see you this year?

Farewell, and write to me again soon so that such long pauses may not arise.

---

[195] Zelter's motet *Der Mensch lebt und bestehet* and the opening movement of his Requiem.

[196] Goethe's notes for an oratorio libretto for a memorial celebration for Schiller on 10 November 1805, *Schillers Totenfeier*, WA I/16, pp. 561–9. Although in principle he agrees with Zelter about the creation of a new work, Goethe eventually considered the project unrealistic from a practical perspective.

[197] Friedrich August Wolf was in Weimar from 30 May to 14 June 1805.

[198] Friedrich Heinrich Jacobi (1743–1819) was with Goethe from 23 June to 1 July 1805.

### 54. Zelter

Berlin, 2 July 1805

I am perfectly prepared for your plan and await its arrival. As soon as I know your thoughts, you will have my response by return of post. I will put all other work aside in order to perform what I can with diligence and at leisure. I am rushing to get this letter into today's post.

### 55. Goethe

Lauchstädt, 22 July 1805

At the moment I have in mind to do a dramatic production of Schiller's *Glocke*; what might come of it if I had your help! Do come!

### 56. Zelter

Berlin, 30 July 1805

My desire to be with you and your recent invitation to join you at Lauchstädt, brings me almost to the point of despair. I am up to my neck in so much work and drudgery that I cannot leave the place and must stay at home. Apart from that, a week from today the King's birthday will be celebrated at the Sing-Akademie,[199] for which I have made all kinds of preparations and am not quite finished yet. [...]

### 57. Goethe

Lauchstädt, 4 August 1805

Up to today I have been flattering myself, though with only a faint hope, that I would see you here. It is one of the saddest conditions under which we suffer, that not only death, but even life separates us from those we most esteem and love, and whose assistance could be most beneficial to us.[200]

---

[199] The birthday of King Friedrich Wilhelm III on 3 August was officially marked by the Sing-Akademie on 6 August.

[200] After the celebration of the king's birthday, Zelter made a rash decision to travel down to Goethe and he arrived in Bad Lauchstädt on 9 August 1805, a day before Goethe's memorial celebration for Schiller. Carl August wrote to Goethe on the same day: 'As I am

So that this letter may be dispatched at once, I will move immediately from such sorrowful reflections to a request. I am going to give a dramatic representation of Schiller's *Glocke*,[201] and beg you to help me with it. Read the poem through, and send me an appropriate overture for it, by any master.[202] Then, in the middle of the fifth verse, declaimed by the master, after the line, 'Say a holy word', I should like a short chorale, for which the words, 'In all we strive to do Thy grace, O Lord, be near' might form the text. Then the following four lines, as far as 'With waves of fiery brown' would be spoken again. The chorus would then be repeated, or, if you like, musically developed.

In the final chorus, I should like to hear the words 'Vivos voco. Mortuos plango. Fulgura frango'[203] in a fugue, which, as far as possible, should imitate the pealing of bells, and, as suits the occasion, lose itself in 'Mortuos plango'.

If a good idea should occur to you, do me the favour of elaborating it, and send me the scores direct to Weimar where I shall soon return.

If it were possible for this gift to reach me by 19 or 20 August, its arrival would be very timely; for I should like to open the season in Weimar with this performance.

I hope then to send you the other poem, or at all events a sketch of it,[204] which could be given on 10 November, in honour of our friend's birthday.

More in the next few days,<br>Goethe

---

writing this, Zelter walks in [arriving] from Berlin. My joy at seeing this superb man and to have him for several days is immense.' Zelter's visit was very short, as the next letter he wrote was from Berlin on 13 August.

[201] The memorial performance took place in Bad Lauchstädt on 10 August. The evening included performances of *Maria Stuart* by the Weimar Court Theatre, Schiller's 'Das Lied von der Glocke' and Goethe's *Epilog zu Schillers Glocke*. Zelter's music was not ready in time. When the memorial performance was repeated on 19 August, Zelter's choral finale was performed for the first time. The first Weimar performance of Schiller's *Glocke* with Goethe's *Epilog* took place on 10 May 1806. Goethe's *Epilog* was later composed by Bernhard Heinrich Romberg (1767–1841) and Max Bruch (1838–1920).

[202] Zelter could not deliver an original composition or another suitable piece on time. On 25 August he informs Goethe of his completion of the overture for Schiller's *Glocke*. After many attempts to finish the music, he seems to have finally given up the project around the beginning of 1806.

[203] 'I call on the living. I mourn the dead. (lit.) I break the flashes of lightning': Schiller's motto in 'Das Lied von der Glocke', from an engraving on a bell in Schaffhausen (1468).

[204] The planned libretto with music by Zelter for Schiller's memorial celebration. Goethe's sketch is not published. In Goethe's view, 'this was mainly due to his musical friend', as he wrote to Friedrich August Wolf on 5 January 1805. For his part Zelter justified himself by saying, 'I had already started the work. I don't know what Goethe had completed – he was seriously ill' (Zelter to David Friedlaender, 27 October 1808, on the occasion of sending a schematic plan – written in Goethe's own hand – for *Schillers Totenfeier*).

## 58. Goethe

Lauchstädt, 1 September 1805

I have arrived back in Lauchstädt, and am dictating this in the rooms where your presence made me so happy.

I have been to Magdeburg with Privy Councillor Wolf and from there went on to Helmstadt, where I found many interesting people and things. Afterwards we went via Halberstadt, past the Harz and returned to Halle via Aschersleben.[205]

Here I am quite alone again, after sending my son August, who has accompanied me so far, back to Weimar,[206] and I am looking back on all the good that has happened to me during the last eight weeks and trying by degrees to remember what we agreed upon.

An ancient work that fell into my hands,[207] almost accidentally, will be useful for this purpose; you will receive with this letter my translation of a translation.[208] As soon as I can revise it according to the original, the wording will, of course, sound quite different, but I dare say you will find no more food for thought in it then than you do now, since the expressions are still a bit halting.

Do write, and send your letter soon to Weimar. Before I leave these parts you shall hear more from me. In particular, I am now dictating something about the underlined passage of the old mystic.[209] A thousand farewells and thanks for your visit, which made me glad to be alive again and increased my happiness.

---

[205] This journey took place between 14 and 27 August and is recounted in unusual detail in his *Tag- und Jahreshefte* (1805).

[206] Goethe's secretary, Friedrich Wilhelm Riemer (1774–1845), Goethe's wife (from 19 October 1806), Christiane Goethe, née Vulpius (1765–1816), and Goethe's 16-year old son, August (1789–1830), had accompanied Goethe to Lauchstädt. Christiane and Riemer went back on 12 August; August travelled to Halle and Helmstedt, returning home on 29 August.

[207] An unknown Latin edition of Plotinus's works, most likely *Plotini, Platonicorum coryphaei, opera quae extant omnia* trans. Marcellus Ficinus (Basel, 1515), which Goethe had borrowed from the Weimar Library on his return from Lauchstädt on 18 September 1805.

[208] Goethe's translation of Plotinus, *Ennead*, V, Book 8, chapter 1, (ed.) Marcellus Ficinus, (Basel, 1515).

[209] What Goethe dictated was his critical response to the content of this passage: three aphorisms which he later integrated in the collection of aphorisms, 'Aus Makariens Archiv' in Goethe's *Wanderjahre*.

## 59. Zelter

Berlin, 25 August to 8 September 1805

In your letter dated 4th of this month, which arrived here while I was still in Lauchstädt, you wished to have the music to [Schiller's] *Glocke* by 19th or 20th of this month. Today is already 25 [August] and I have just finished the overture. But I did arrive back here on the 13th and needed a week to settle myself back into my regime as well as to tie up the many loose ends in my affairs, which had got quite out of hand.

I am continuing to work on it every day and so the thing will be ready in time; when exactly I really can't say. Work is very slow when one is not able to stay with it and is disturbed by many external matters.

## 60. Goethe

Jena, 12 October 1805

Above all, I need from you an indication as to how far the music for [Schiller's] *Glocke* has progressed. I don't want to produce it in the old way because you always establish a work through its first performance and afterwards the public, even the more educated [public], is no longer receptive. Meanwhile time has moved on and the prologue will probably be published before I have it performed. At the same time that doesn't matter very much as long as we are not too late. So please tell me soon what the prospects are. [...]

## 61. Zelter

Berlin, 26 October 1805

[...] Meanwhile I have finished the music to Schiller's *Glocke* as far as the finale, but I will need some quiet days before I can be back on track, something which is difficult in my present circumstances. Today is already 26 October and the question is whether late November will be time enough? Whatever happens I will start on it again next week and try to get into it. I will keep you informed of my progress.

## 62. Goethe

Weimar, 18 November 1805

On 9 November, the same day we wished to commemorate Schiller in our theatre, the Royal Russian Emperor was happy with our performance of *Wallensteins Lager*. As soon as you kindly send us your work we will make up for lost time.

How are your music classes going? I, too, have set aside one morning in every week, where I lecture to a small circle on my experiences and convictions, relative to natural history.[210] This opportunity will enable me to realize for the first time what I possess and what I do not possess.

Madame Jagemann has also finally arrived back. The programmes had arrived earlier and they, too, as a sign that you are thinking of me, brought me happiness. Let me hear from you again soon. Before long, the results of my own quiet activities will give you some pleasure.

## 63. Zelter

Berlin, 14 December 1805

With this letter you will receive a packet of fresh morsels, given to me on the occasion of my birthday, so lovingly celebrated last Wednesday by all the members and friends of the Sing-Akademie, amounting to 250 in total.[211] [...]

My building projects are continuing into the winter and for almost three months I have felt so unwell that a persistent feverish tension has rendered me incapable of attending to matters of the spirit; as a result the music for *Glocke* is not yet finished.[212] Not that I can say that I feel any better. Instead, everything is

---

[210] The so-called *Mittwochgesellschaft*, consisting of Duchess Luise Augusta (1757–1830) and her daughter, Caroline (1786–1816), Maria Pawlowna (1786–1859), Charlotte von Stein (1742–1827), [Luise Antoinette] Charlotte von Schiller (1766–1826), Frau Friederike Sophie von Schardt (1755–1819), [Magdalena] Henriette von Knebel (1755–1813), Luise von Göchhausen (1752–1807), sometimes also in the presence of the Duke, Carl August (1757–1828), Karl Ludwig von Knebel (1744–1834) and Christoph Martin Wieland (1733–1813). The lectures on his research and experiments in natural science took place on Wednesdays from 10 a.m. to 1 p.m.; see Goethe's *Physikalische Vorträge schematisiert*, *MA* 6.2, p. 1271.

[211] Zelter's 57th birthday on 11 December 1805 was celebrated in the grand hall of the Englishes Haus, the celebratory speech was published by Dieterici: *Rede bei der Geburtstags-Feier des Herrn Zelter, im Kreise der Sing-Akademie gehalten von August Hartung* (GSA 143/22).

[212] Up to 1810 Zelter's work for the Sing-Akademie was unpaid. In order to earn a living for himself and his family, he continued his building business. As a result of the war in 1806, building work in Berlin had almost come to a standstill and in December 1808

immeasurably sour for me, because a wretched sluggishness in my bones makes me tired every time I move.

But that doesn't mean that my part in this work has lapsed, and as soon as I am up on my feet again it will be finished with all haste.

### 64. Goethe

Weimar, 5 January 1806

It belongs to the perverse ways of the world, that you, whose birthday I ought to be celebrating, should celebrate your birthday with me by sending me precious foods to savour. You have our thanks daily as we eat them. If only we were not separated by such a great distance, that we could hope to see you among us sometimes.

The good effects of your Lauchstädt visit[213] have lasted well and within the first six months of the year you will get to see things which I can recommend to you in advance. Since I hadn't heard from you for a long time, and the work you promised hadn't arrived,[214] I regretfully assumed that you must be unwell this winter, for I know that you do much out of love for me even when it inconveniences you. Don't leave the good work aside; surprise me with it later on.

You have a copy of *Wunderhorn* at home.[215] Does it stir up any strong feelings? Share with me the melodies which it must certainly have inspired. That's enough for today; it is just to show that I am thinking of you and to break the silence.

### 65. Goethe

Weimar, 5 March 1806

I haven't heard from you for so long, my dear, excellent friend, and I understand that things are for you much the same as they are for us. Everybody has so much to do in his own circle that there is hardly any time to look around outside.

---

Zelter realized that for 26 months he had earned virtually nothing professionally and had as good as resigned from the building trade; the appointment to Professor of Music at the Akademie der Künste in July 1809 finally put him in a position to give up his practice as a builder; however, it was only in 1815 that Zelter officially resigned from the builder's guild.

[213] Zelter had surprised Goethe with a visit to Lauchstädt from 9 to 11/12 August 1806.

[214] Zelter's music to Schiller's *Das Lied von der Glocke*.

[215] *Des Knaben Wunderhorn. Alte deutsche Lieder gesammelt von Achim von Arnim und Clemens Brentano* (2 vols, Heidelberg, 1806), vol. 1. Volume one was dedicated to Goethe; volume two was published in 1808.

Meanwhile I have been busy in various ways[216] and before too long I hope what I have in progress will bring you some joy. You, too, are, no doubt, busy tending to the pleasure and edification of many people, which unfortunately I am not able to partake in so easily.

The idea of visiting you and Berlin has often attracted me; but so many things detain me here and of course I cannot see when it will all come to a merciful end. As I feel a pressing need not merely to see you but also to get a clear picture of your surroundings and to give you a clearer picture of mine, the thought occurred to me that I might send my son to you.[217] He could bring you my greetings and in the full bloom of youth, at which time worldly matters make a strong impression, could take in the image of such a great city and also bring it back fresh for my pleasure.

Although he is already a steady and self-contained boy, I still wouldn't like to send him alone and think of him in an urban whirlpool. I was wondering whether you might find accommodation for him near you and look after his needs in the beginning. I will send you a letter of credit so that all the money he needs won't be in his pocket. I won't say any more, because everything else depends on the circumstances. The main question is: whether such a visit would be too inconvenient for you. I would give him letters of introduction to my other friends in Berlin and the rest would work itself out. But above all, I would like to know that he is set up in a safe place. The visit would not last more than a fortnight or three weeks. He could arrive in Holy Week. A thousand greetings and please let me have an answer soon.

Goethe

## 66. Zelter

Berlin, 12 January to 11 March 1806

It is bad when in the dispersive confusion of the world, the excitement from outside interferes with artistic production. Under such circumstances there are times when one forgets his capital when no creditor appears to remind him of it. So it has happened to me, more or less. I am everywhere in debt and since the summer I have hardly – or not even – thought of composing.

In recent days I have got rid of a very uncomfortable sore throat which my illness of over three months appears to have developed into. I feel freer now and my old cheerfulness seems about to be restored. Your letter, which I have just received, will hopefully reinforce what my own sturdy constitution has begun, and so work will start again on our *Glocke*, so that it can soon be performed.

---

[216] Goethe's *Farbenlehre* and *Faust I*.

[217] The visit was always postponed and plans for August von Goethe's visit were finally relinquished in June 1806.

Our court enjoys the illustrious presence of your heir to the throne and the grand duchess.[218] Today, for the first time, I spoke to von Wolzogen[219] in Professor Fichte's Sunday colloquium.[220] He told me that the heir to the throne had asked for me, but since he is staying in the King's palace, I didn't want to visit him unannounced. There is no end to the comings and goings there. Next Tuesday or the Tuesday after, I am thinking of entertaining him at the Sing-Akademie and then I will definitely get a chance to speak to him.

My Sing-Akademie is flourishing and awaits your arrival. Come soon and come before my summer is over.

...and so here I take up this letter on 11 March, two months later, which even today perhaps would not happen if I didn't have to answer your dear letter of 5 March. Everything is taken care of for your son's arrival. If he doesn't come earlier than Holy Week I will take him into my home, and, whatever things are like here, he will be with me where I can look after him well. If he were to come earlier everything is still taken care of and you can be fully confident sending him off. My wife is about to give birth and is due any moment. All the signs are good. I would love your son to be here at the latest by Holy Thursday so that he could hear Graun's Passion Music,[221] which he won't hear anywhere else and will never again hear performed with such perfection. Everything else will be looked after when he arrives and you can count on it that you won't be under obligations to anyone in Berlin as a result of your son's visit. In any case, as soon as he arrives he must come to my address, no.1 Münzstraße, so as not to be wandering around unnecessarily.

---

[218] The heir to the throne, Carl Friedrich von Sachsen-Weimar-Eisenach (1783–1853), and his wife, Maria Pawlowna, née grand Duchess of Russia.

[219] Baron Wilhelm Ernst Friedrich Franz August von Wolzogen (1762–1809), architect, diplomat, resident in Weimar from 1801.

[220] Fichte had advertised his Sunday lecture series in the Berlin newspapers on 7 January 1806. The first lecture took place on 7 January, 12–1 p.m. in the round hall of the Akademie buildings; a second lecture took place on 26 January 1806; no further dates are known.

[221] Carl Heinrich Graun (1703/4–59), Kapellmeister to the court of Friedrich II, best-known for his Passion Music. Princess Anna Amalia commissioned the libretto from Carl Wilhelm Ramler and suggested to Graun that he compose it. The first performance, which was given by J.P. Sack's *Musikübende Gesellschaft* in the Berlin Cathedral on 26 March 1755, marked the beginning of performances in the main churches of Berlin on Good Friday which lasted until the end of the nineteenth century. The first performance of the work by the Sing-Akademie, which took place on 12 April 1796, was also the first official performance of a large-scale work with orchestral accompaniment presented by the singing society, founded in 1791. From 1801 performances took place in the hall of the Königliches Opernhaus and later in its own building on Unter den Linden. Long after Zelter's death the work was part of the standard repertoire of the Sing-Akademie. The performance mentioned in this letter took place on 4 April 1806: *AMZ* 8 (1805/06), no. 30, 23 April, column 478; *MA* 20.3, p. 193.

I had made a wonderful plan. The music for *Glocke* is finished to the point where it can, as it were, be tried out by and made suitable for a particular orchestra. With that in mind I wanted to come to Weimar and perfect it there; this has all been thwarted by this mild, crazy winter, for I have had to work almost every hour so that my family would not go hungry. Finally, I confess that for the sake of your Prince and Grand Duchess I didn't want to leave here, for I hoped they would want to hear some proper music done very professionally. [...] Yesterday evening I finished a very good piece of church music, which, in memory of a worthy preacher who passed away five weeks ago, will be performed next Sunday.[222] [...]

Now I will make a suggestion: when you son is here, collect him from Berlin. Naturally I can't offer you my house, but think about it. I don't think it is such a bad idea.

## 67. Zelter

Berlin, 18 March 1806

Instead of being able to report something joyful, something pleasant to you, I lift myself out of the depths of sorrow to tell you that yesterday, without any warning and contrary to all expectations, I lost my lovely, beloved wife just before childbirth.[223] The child was brought into the world after her death and was also dead.

I don't know yet what I am going to do or how I will bear it. I am alone again now.

If I say that in the ten years of our marriage we were always of one mind and felt the same about everything, whether it was within us or external to us; that there was no fibre of her that did not love me, I am able to say that she really deserved to be known by you, for that was one of her wishes.

She will be buried tomorrow morning. I am alone and have plenty of room. Send me your son as soon as you can; he should be nowhere else but with me. My address is: 1 Neue Münzstraße.

---

[222] Zelter's cantanta, *Der Fromme geht dahin*, composed in memory of Theodor Karl George Woltersdorf (1727–1806).

[223] Zelter's second wife, Juliane Karoline Auguste (1767–1806), died on 16 March 1806. Their son, Felix, was stillborn.

## 68. Zelter

Berlin, 19 to 20 March 1806

[…] I am using my new solitary state and the need to keep busy to write to you and gather my thoughts bit by bit, which have been scattered as a result of my tragic circumstances. I am healthy and will regain my strength, once the next difficult days are over in which every new sight reminds me of my deepest sorrow, which I treasure as if it were healing me.

In Lauchstädt it was said to me, your *Farbenlehre* would appear in the Easter exhibition.[224] You don't seem opposed to the idea of sending the director of our Kunstakademie, the court painter Frisch,[225] a signed copy through me. Without this fine fellow the Sing-Akademie would perhaps have gone under this year, and I would like to do something to delight him. He is very old. As I am certain that he holds you in very high regard, I am sure I can be very nice to him in this way, which is the reason why I am taking the liberty of reminding you.

## 69. Goethe

Weimar, 26 March 1806

I had hardly sent off my letter announcing the postponement of August's journey, when yours arrived with this unexpected and traumatic news which has really dismayed me. At the very time when Berlin is on my mind more than ever, when we were planning a visit in the new Münzstrasse[226] and I am hoping to get a clearer picture of yourself and your surroundings from my boy just as he brought me back the picture of my mother last year,[227] you are experiencing a violent wrench which I feel with you in every sense. I must now think of you as lonely in a large household with many demanding tasks to attend to, or else my thoughts turn to myself and I imagine this happening to me. Unfortunately the obstacle which delays my deputy cannot be cast aside,[228] otherwise I should send him at once, for the presence of a new, friendly and loving person, would perhaps be a comfort to

---

[224] Although Goethe's *Farbenlehre* (Part One) appeared in 1805, the complete work did not appear until 1810.

[225] Johann Christoph Frisch (1738–1815), Court Painter under Friedrich II, Director of the Akademie der Künste, Berlin.

[226] Zelter's home in Berlin until September 1817.

[227] August von Goethe visited Goethe's mother in Frankfurt from 7 April to 2 May 1805; see the letters from Katharina Elisabeth Goethe to her son on 8, 11 and 21 April, 2 and 11 May 1805 and Goethe's letter to his mother on 6 May 1805, *WA* IV/17, pp. 282–3.

[228] August von Goethe was, in fact, unable to travel outside Weimar under his father's name, because he was considered illegitimate.

you, and the good to which it would give rise, would probably counterbalance any inconvenience it might occasion. It would also be a comfort to me to know that a representative of my sympathy and of my heartfelt concern was with you; but even this is not to be, and all this happens at a time when I, too, have many burdens to bear. No more! Let me hear from you soon.

Goethe

### 70. Zelter

Berlin, 20 to 29 March 1806

I have resumed work but cannot get back on track; above all, it won't come; no matter what.

I am like a split tree. The lovely half, that of summer, is separated from me and this half is beset by everything that causes pain.

My friends want to get me out of the house, to bring me out of myself, but I won't do it. Only I can make myself whole again and I will overcome [my loss]. I feel my strength and hope to retain some of it, but I want the full experience of my present condition.

Five days ago I had no premonition of my misfortune and I can honestly say it made me happy to be having another child and to make up the dozen again.[229] My youngest son was born on Good Friday and as a result she called him Raphael.[230] She believed she was carrying another boy, which was to be called Felix, and now it has come to this.

On Saturday, the day before she died, she went into the church to hear the rehearsal of my music.[231] I was not meant to know, and how overjoyed I was to see her there. She said so many pleasant and intelligent things about it afterwards, that it was only then that I knew what I had achieved. She said she had felt the weight of her body for the first time, which was the reason she couldn't sing along.

O my friend, why have you not heard this sweet, powerful voice [...] which she has now taken with her to the grave. Her pure heart poured forth from her mouth like a fresh, enlivening zephyr; it was touching, bringing ease. When she sang in the choir of the Sing-Akademie, I could recognize her voice in a choir of 150 without her having to project. The sound was light and flowed easily when she opened her mouth. Two years ago even when her voice was affected by nerves, she sang with Madame Mara in a local church.[232] Friends of Mara's contested and

---

[229] Zelter's family consisted of three stepchildren: Henriette, Caroline and Carl Flöricke; six children from his first marriage: Adelheid, Georg, Julie, Doris, Rosamunde und Auguste; two children from the second marriage: Adolph Raphael and Clara.

[230] Adolph Raphael was born in Berlin on 22 March 1799.

[231] Zelter's cantata *Der Fromme geht dahin*.

[232] *AMZ* 5 (1802/03), no. 27, 30 March 1803, column 453f; *MA* 20.3, p. 195.

believed the heavenly voice belonged to their favourite. One of our connoisseurs had said: now you see ...

You know, my noble friend, my opinion of Mara, whom in terms of ability, basic virtuosity, and taste, no other German singer has matched, but her voice had two dangerous breaks, which sometimes like an evil fate, even when she is well-prepared to sing, come between what she intends and what she produces and cause embarrassment even to her great talent. My wife's voice, in a range of two and a half octaves, was like a series of equally polished [notes] which flowed into one another and at the same time were distinct, resulting in a cantilena, which didn't surprise you but always enraptured you the more you heard her sing. [...]

It is Saturday and I will say farewell; the letter must go in the post.

### 71. Goethe

Weimar, 19 April 1806

[...] Many thanks for your letter. Write to me from time to time. I will let you hear from me from time to time, even though I can, at present, be quite withdrawn. I have not been in great form lately. I must seek out time to make progress with editing works of mine that are to be published.[233] [...]

### 72. Zelter

Berlin, 21 to 26 April 1806

As I haven't heard from you at all, I cannot stop thinking about you without anxiety. I imagine you afflicted by your old complaint, alone, brooding, turned in on yourself. I am now as frightened as a child; the slightest unsuspected thing frightens me. On the 13th of this month, my wife's mother arrived in time for lunch. We had a friendly happy meal together; the following morning she was dead.[234] She was 82 years old, and with that, lively, sociable, active, and I can also say beautiful – and so she was taken from us. Two months ago my sister died[235] – I don't know what I am to do. I ask you earnestly to let me hear from you. Also your son is not coming. I had forgotten that if your son came in the company of

---

[233] In March and April 1806 Goethe worked with Riemer on the revision of *Faust I*, which was originally planned by Cotta as volume 4 of Goethe's collected works, though it, in fact, appeared as volume 8.

[234] Dorothea Luise Pappritz, née Hildebrandt (1725–1806) died on 14 April 1806 in Berlin.

[235] Marie Charlotte Syring, née Zelter (1754–1806), Zelter's second sister, died in Calbe on 16 January 1806.

a guide or an attendant, that I would be perfectly equipped to put up both, since a bright, healthy, warm room, two beds and whatever else my house provides, is ready to receive dear guests.

23 April, evening: I have just received your dear letter of the 19th of this month, which has calmed and comforted me now that I know you were occupied with such pleasant work. [...]

We have a new magic opera. Levi, who calls himself Robert on the book, created the text and our Kapellmeister Himmel a really nice score.[236] The public are still not too sure how to receive the work, in so far as they are embarrassed to consider such magical works as good [...] If only this opera were not so long for what it is (it plays for four hours) and the music were not always impossible to play, I would consider it the best of its kind, although I have only seen it once. The whole production has a truly modern tendency in that it represents the theatrical character of our time in a nutshell. The beautiful, the good, the high, the low, the fluctuating, the charming, the complex, the intoxicating, the grotesque, the glorious, the rollicking, the dark, the adventurous, the unbridled – in short, the individual externalities of contemporary art that must always resort to old marvels to relight its torch which will not burn because it has no new oil – speaks very clearly to him who will listen. The author is a Jew, so you can imagine what he must put up with because in addition to this he is one of the poetic poets. The Berlin state and learned newspaper critics will not forgive him for this, even if they wanted to show mercy to a Jew.

## 73. Zelter

Berlin, 1 to 21 June 1806

[...] My loneliness has its good moments in that I get a rest from life, so to speak. I gathered everything around me that belongs to my wife and so I keep myself busy in my own way and to me it is as if she was still alive. Sometimes it hits me really hard when I must recall the past and yet I must move on, bear the loss and be silent. I am healthy. In two months I expect to marry my daughter to my sister's son;[237]

---

[236] *Die Sylphen* by Friedrich Heinrich Himmel (1765–1814), pianist and composer for the Berlin Court. The libretto, after Gozzi's *Zobeis*, was written by the Berlin writer Ernst Friedrich *Ludwig* Robert (formerly Liepmann Levin and from 1814 known as Robert-Tornow). The premiere was on 14 April 1806 at the Königliches Nationaltheater, Berlin. Zelter had attended either the premiere or the performance on 20 April. The opera was performed five times in Berlin (between 14 April and 30 May 1806).

[237] Zelter's eldest step-daughter, Henriette Flöricke (1780–1849), married Johann Ferdinand Syring, a son of Zelter's sister Luise, on 14 September 1806.

then I will have more room. My eldest son[238] works as a foreman, the second[239] is learning to be a bricklayer, the third,[240] who goes to school, is not without talent, wild, learns with difficulty, is physically strong and teases his sisters. The girls, of whom there will be six when the bride has gone, all go to school and are all healthy. I dare not think what it will be like when our bride is gone. I have a very hard life ahead of me, but let it come and I will not be afraid of anything transitory. […]

Saturday evening, 21 June: On 12 June the Academy of Arts and Mechanical Sciences appointed me as an honorary member and assessor[241] and has given me an official certificate. You can imagine how dear this is to me because of the Sing-Akademie and I ask you to draw attention to it in the [*Jenaische Allgemeine*] *Literatur-Zeitung*.

I'll close so this letter doesn't miss the post again

Z

## 74. Zelter

Berlin, 23 June 1806

[…] The most recent news I can give you is that everything is as it was in the past, that I'm healthy and I that I think about you every hour, every day.

Tomorrow evening after the Sing-Akademie I think I will go to Potsdam for a few days to have a look at the musical treasures of the deceased king.[242] I have something in mind which I will let you know about if it transpires. […]

---

[238] Zelter's stepson, Carl Flöricke (1784–1812).

[239] Georg Friedrich Zelter (1789–1827).

[240] Adolph Raphael Zelter (1799–1816).

[241] *Vossische Zeitung*, 19 June 1806.

[242] Nothing is known about the fruits of Zelter's research on the musical scores bequeathed by the Prussian King Friedrich Wilhelm II. Zelter pursued intensive catalogue work over a number of years; from 1800 to 1803 he completed a catalogue of the music in the possession of Princess Anna Amalia of Prussia. The sheet music in the libraries of Friedrich II and his successors was later categorized by Georg Thouret, *Katalog der Musiksammlung auf der Königlichen Hausbibliothek im Schlosse in Berlin* (Leipzig, 1895).

## 75. Zelter

Berlin, 17 December 1806

My Sing-Akademie has been suspended since 14 August.[243] I have left the thread lying so that when it is possible I can take it up again where I left it, but there is no prospect of this to date. [...]

Let me know whether your art treasures were spared. In the local academy where I had left my lovely scores, I found the cabinet broken into, but I haven't missed anything yet. The main works and monographs are there and because the collection is very large, I would need a few weeks to go through it and I have neither sufficient time nor sufficient light because the days are so short and dark. [...]

Apparently, Schmidt wants to enlist actors and singers for the Viennese Theatre, though he has not said anything to me about it yet, nor have I asked him about it.[244]

Bye for now. If only I had the chance to speak to you again.
Zelter

---

[243] On 20 October 1806 Zelter had issued the following circular to the members of the Sing-Akademie: 'In recent times the general concern of patriotic people is affected by external circumstances, which are important enough to hinder our artistic endeavours. For that reason we are cancelling our usual rehearsals in order to continue them in more favourable circumstances. I, myself, will attend for my usual hours and will personally look after the welfare of the institute, since it is so close to my heart.' In Martin Blumner, *Geschichte der Sing-Akademie zu Berlin* (Berlin: Horn & Raasch, 1891), p. 37. Hereafter referred to as Blumner. The society reassembled for the first time on 10 February the following year in the usual venue.

[244] As a result of Schmidt's conversation in Weimar, in January 1807 offers were made from Viennese theatres to the Weimar actors and singers Henriette Beck, Friedrich Haide, Karl Unzelmann, Heinrich Stromeyer and Friederike Vohs. It led to an engagement for Henriette Beck and Friedrich Haide; the former did not take up the post and the latter resigned after a few months.

## 76. Goethe

Weimar, 26 December 1806

A thousand thanks dear friend, for having finally broken this painful silence.[245] I have been thinking of you every day since 14 October,[246] and even as I write to you, a sealed letter, addressed to you, is lying on my desk, which I didn't have the courage to send off. For what can we say to one another? On 12 December I celebrated your birthday in silence[247] and so too in the future we shall only be able to celebrate what is dear to us in silence.

Anyhow I have got through these bad days without much damage. It was not necessary for me to take part in public affairs, as they were sufficiently well-attended to by excellent men;[248] and so I was able to stay in my cell and brood over my inmost thoughts.

During the worst hours, when one could not but be anxious about everything, my greatest fear was losing my papers, and since then I have been sending everything I can to the printers. My *Farbenlehre* is making big strides. [....]

Some proof sheets of my works, published by Cotta, have arrived. Some of the poems of the first volume will, I hope, call forth melodies from you, which will make us feel we are the same as ever. It is wonderful that you found your musical treasures unharmed. I am sorry that you are so bogged down by administration and so many other things Schmidt tells me of. However, in the current situation, it is not in our power to say how we would like to be active. Your good spirit will never leave you; likewise may your good courage never fail you. Let me hear something from you occasionally; I will write too.

---

[245] The exchange of letters between Goethe and Zelter was interrupted from the end of August to mid-December on account of military events surrounding Napoleon's invasion of Sachsen-Weimar and Prussia. Zelter broke this silence in the previous letter, recounting affairs in Berlin.

[246] The date of the battle of Jena and Auerstedt. On 15 October Napoleon entered Weimar, on 16 October he ordered that the plundering should cease and on 17 October he departed. On 26 December, the day he wrote to Zelter, Goethe reopened the theatre.

[247] Zelter's birthday is 11 December; Goethe's diary for 1806 observes his friend's birthday, *WA* III/3, p. 182.

[248] Privy Councillor Christian Gottlob Voigt (1743–1819) and Privy Councillor Baron Wilhelm Ernst Friedrich Franz August von Wolzogen (1762–1809), who, as members of the Privy Council (without the collaboration of Goethe, who was excused on account of illness), had an audience with Napoleon in the Weimar Palace on 16 October in which they asked the emperor that the plundering be stopped for the sake of protecting the State of Sachsen-Weimar.

## 77. Goethe

Weimar, 27 March 1807

I have a good opportunity to send you here the first delivery of my [collected] works.[249] I had hoped that they would reach you in peaceful times, but since even in the worst times there are hours of boredom which one can relieve by reading, then perhaps this volume will arrive at a good time.

Let me hear from you soon. I don't know what to write about myself, other than I use the quiet times, which are granted to us at present, as best I can, in order to protect from oblivion and transitoriness what I have thought and what I have achieved.

If you could be inspired by some of my songs to compose them, it would be a very welcome sign of your existence and your empathy

Enough for now, with heartfelt greetings from my family

G

## 78. Zelter

Berlin, 4 to 18 April 1807

When I read the first edition of the [*Jenaische Allgemeine*] *Literatur-Zeitung* in January,[250] my old determination rose up powerfully in me and I decided to compose music for which the lovely long nights would have to yield up the time. I composed the enclosed poem[251] for want of a better one, and I have done with it what I can.

On Easter Sunday I performed the work in public.[252] It was received favourably even by our guests and I earned nearly 800 thaler for the work, with which I will pay my debts and establish new credit.

---

[249] The first four volumes of Goethe's collected works published by Cotta containing poetry (vol. 1), *Wilhelm Meisters Lehrjahre* (vols 2 and 3) and theatrical works (vol. 4).

[250] Zelter is referring to the article by Johann Heinrich Meyer and Goethe, 'Unterhaltungen über Gegenstände der bildenden Kunst als Folge der Nachrichten von den Weimarischen Kunstaustellungen', *JALZ* 4 (1807): pp. i–xii.

[251] Presumably the libretto to *Die Auferstehung und Himmelfahrt Jesu, eine geistliche Kantate von Carl Wilhelm Ramler, komponiert von Carl Friedrich Zelter* (Berlin: Unger, 1807). The work is neither in Goethe's music collection nor in his library; a copy is held in the Goethe Museum in Dusseldorf (KK 1774).

[252] The oratorio was performed for the first time on 29 March 1807; *AMZ* 9 (1807), no. 29, 15 April, column 464; *MA* 20.3, pp. 208–09.

What would I have given for you to have been able to hear the music! I tried to realize our idea of a chorus in my own way, and despite the poem, have not been unsuccessful [...] Perhaps it has even enhanced it in the most meaningful parts.

The choir performed the whole resurrection episode as well as the ascension into heaven, and the whole thing came across forcefully and with clarity. By the way, this chorus is a permanent presence throughout the work and is interposed at crucial points to make its presence felt – and without it nothing can happen.

The desire to write a choral work has awoken in me but I cannot find a [suitable] subject. If only I could find someone here who would write me the verses. Think of a [suitable] subject and tell me. Among my local acquaintances, there is a man who can write quite nice verses and who could be useful to me and I could send you what he produces before I set it to music. It doesn't have to be spiritual in nature, as long as it is heroic. Since it will be a while before any proper building can be done, for the time being I will have to write music to earn a living.

I have repeatedly received proposals from Vienna, which I have, admittedly, not even declined, but I cannot leave here yet, nor do I want to – even if the conditions offered were favourable. I have been sent a melodrama from there containing choral sections (Hypermestra, the noble Danaide) but it is so modern, so shallow and so empty that I will take care not to waste my efforts on such a libretto.[253]

I am waiting impatiently for the first volumes of the new edition of your works. Make sure I get a copy straight away. Since the invasion[254] I haven't read anything other than *Die Propyläen*,[255] which have helped me in the composition of my music; if perhaps a genuinely musical book might have seduced me into wanting to write something better than I am capable of.

## 79. Zelter

Berlin, 23 to 25 April 1807

While I was thinking this morning that you could well have received my last letter by now, Privy Councillor von Müller sent me your delightful package with the lovely books and your letter of 27 March. The enclosed setting[256] composed itself

---

[253] The text sent to Zelter could not be established. A work of the same title by Heinrich Schmidt was later published in the *Wiener Hof-Theater Taschenbuch auf das Jahr 1814* (Vienna, 1813), pp. 109–31; neither a setting nor a performance could be traced. See Wolfgang Schimpf, *Lyrisches Theater. Das Melodrama des 18. Jahrhunderts* (Göttingen: Palasetra, 1988), vol. 2, p. 239.

[254] The occupation of Berlin by Napoleon's troups from 27 October 1806.

[255] Goethe's art history journal, *Die Propyläen* (1798–1800).

[256] Zelter's setting of Goethe's poem 'Vanitas! Vanitatum vanitas' from Goethe's collected works published by Cotta, vol. 1, p. 98. The copy in Goethe's music collection is

on the spot as I was reading the poem. When I was reading sorrow fell like a dead weight from my heart, and if the melody is suitable then it is hardly surprising and no thanks to me.

After I sent my last letter off in the post I heard the news about the Grand Duchess Amalia's death.[257] I will never come across another like her. Who will our dear songs appeal to from now on when everything worth loving is no more? I knew well that she was old and was full of dread for a time that could not be averted, but still I must mourn at a distance.

25 April: Since yesterday I have set to music another five of your poems[258] and am working on another: 'Stirbt der Fuchs, so gilt der Balg'.[259] I have, as you might say, through-composed this but am not exactly unhappy with it. The title suggests to me a party game with which I am not familiar. Let me know the nature of this game. Something is missing from my setting and I guess it is the knowledge of this game. I need to know soon while the idea of the composition is still fresh and new.

Of the poems in volume one, I have now set 36 and several more will follow later. There are some I will not set since Reichardt has done them unsurpassably, for example: 'Das Veilchen'; 'Heidenröslein'; 'Der untreue Knabe'.[260] [...]

I am impatiently waiting the approaching spring, and God only knows what it will bring. But we live in hope: *pacem te poscimus omnes*.[261]

## 80. Goethe

Weimar, 4 to 7 May 1807

Warmest thanks for setting my song.[262] Just now it is most refreshing to be able to take refuge, if only for a short time, in a light and easy mood. [...]

---

dated 23 April 1807 (GSA 32/16). The song was published in vol. 2 of Zelter's *Sämtliche Lieder, Balladen und Romanzen*.

[257] Anna Amalia von Sachsen-Weimar-Eisenach (1739–1807) died on 10 April 1807.

[258] In addition to 'Stirbt der Fuchs, so gilt der Balg', the settings include: 'An die Entfernte'; 'Der Musensohn'; 'Die Spröde' and 'Die Bekehrte'. The texts are from vol. 1 of Goethe's collected works by Cotta. The manuscripts are all dated 24 and 25 April 1807. Autograph copies are contained in Zelter's unpublished papers (SBB PK: Mus. ms. Autograph. Zelter 22).

[259] Zelter's manuscript is dated Berlin, 24 April 1807.

[260] J.F. Reichardt, *Goethes Lieder, Oden, Balladen und Romanzen mit Musik*, I–IV, (4 vols, Leipzig: Walter Salmen, 1809–11), nos 104, 10 and 110 respectively.

[261] 'We all ask peace of you.'

[262] Zelter's setting of Goethe's poem 'Vanitas! Vanitatum vanitas'.

Our Grand Duchess [Anna Amalia] is a great loss,[263] at a time when so much is turned upside down and chaotic. We must reflect no further on this subject, nor on anything else at the present time. We must live on from one day to another, and do and accomplish what is still possible. [...]

7 May: Your letters, which arrived one after the other, really delighted me and I will continue to reply to some points. How I would have loved to have been able to hear your oratorio:[264] but I am, unfortunately, so cut off from music and although we sometimes have really good voices, the little bits of operetta here and there are not enough. And so it seems as if all sound, all song in me has disappeared, and with it all my musical imagination. Perhaps good fortune and a reasonable project will bring us together again and we will be in a position to collaborate on something.

That you liked my *Elpenor*[265] gives me the greatest pleasure and the object of those pages has now been achieved. [...] I am looking forward to the enjoyment you will get from the continuation of my *Faust*;[266] it contains things that will also interest you from a musical point of view. [...]

Farewell, and write again before Whitsuntide, and then send me news of yourself to Carlsbad.

Goethe

## 81. Goethe

Carlsbad, 27 July 1807

It is a long time, my very dear friend, since you heard from me. [...] Write and tell me how you are getting on. I have thought of you a thousand times, and of what you have accomplished as a private person, without the support of the wealthy and powerful, and without any special encouragement. Perhaps what we have most to regret from political change is mainly this: that under its old constitution Germany, and especially the Northern part, allowed the individual to cultivate himself as far as possible, and it allowed everyone to do what was right in his own way, without, however, there ever being any special interest shown in him by the community at large.

To these general and certainly inadequate reflections, which I should like to discuss further with you in person some day, I wish to add a special request, which I beg you will kindly comply with soon. Although we have both voices and

---

[263] See Goethe's obituary, *Zum feierlichen Andenken der Durchlauchigsten Fürstin und Frau Anna Amalia*, MA 9, p. 929.

[264] Zelter's cantata *Die Auferstehung und Himmelfahrt Jesu*.

[265] Goethe's tragedy *Elpenor*.

[266] *Faust: Ein Fragment* was published in 1790; *Faust I* was first published by Cotta in Goethe's collected works (1808).

orchestra in Weimar, in addition to which I am the person in charge,[267] I could never secure musical enjoyment with any definite regularity, because the terrible relation between life and the theatre invariably destroys the higher purpose for which alone they exist or ought to exist. Schleswig has sent us two new people again: a very good tenor[268] and a kind of *répétiteur*.[269] I have not yet made their acquaintance, but they seem to be good, intelligent people.

I do not care to concern myself with opera as it exists here at the moment, particularly as I do not have a complete knowledge of such musical matters. I should therefore prefer leaving the secular age to itself and withdrawing into the spiritual.[270] I should like now once a week to have sacred part songs performed at my house, in the same way as at your Sing-Akademie, though it would be a pale reflection of it.[271] Help me to achieve this, and send me some part songs for four voices,[272] not too difficult, and with the parts already written out. I will gratefully reimburse you for any expense involved. Let me know whether such scores are available in print or engraved. Canons, too, and whatever you may think useful for the purpose. You will always be in our midst in spirit, and heartily welcome whenever you care to appear in person. Write me a few lines here, for I shall remain here another month, and send me a parcel to Weimar, that I may begin at once when I get home. Farewell, and rest assured of my lasting friendship.

Goethe

---

[267] Goethe occupied the position of Senior Director of the newly-founded Weimar Court Theatre, where plays as well as operas and Singspiele were staged.

[268] Otto Morhardt (d.1813/14), singer in Weimar from 1807–09.

[269] The opera singer Rudolf Karl Heß (b.1769), singer and actor; in Weimar 1807–8/9. See Goethe's *Tagebuch*, 14, 20, 21 and 27 September 1807, WA III/3, pp. 275, 277 and 279.

[270] Goethe pointedly compares the opera-loving century and its secular music to the practice of religious music.

[271] On his return from Carlsbad, Goethe immediately implemented this plan; see Goethe's diary on 27 September and 1 October 1807, WA III/3, pp. 279 and 281. For the time being Rudolf Karl Heß arranged rehearsals, took on the role of music director and performances took place on Sunday at lunchtime; see Goethe's diary: 4, 11 and 18 November 1807 WA III/3, pp. 292, 294 and 297. The first Sunday concert (for an invited audience) took place on 20 December 1807 in Goethe's home; see *Tag- und Jahres-Hefte* 1807, where Goethe mistakenly dates the concert 30 December 1807, MA 14, p. 196.

[272] Zelter, who had nothing suitable to hand at that time, at first recommended songs by Josef Haydn which were available in publication and which Goethe immediately ordered. Zelter in fact sent Goethe the promised setting for a small choir in the following letter.

## 82. Zelter

Berlin, 6 to 8 August 1807

[…] I set up a ripieno school[273] in March, which gave me a lot of work without too much to show for it. Finally I am continuing the Sing-Akademie two days a week. I am doing it so quietly that the members I don't want there won't notice, and this is what I am working on from week to week. […]

And to turn to what you requested again: I don't have many spiritual works which you could perform at your home with less than four or six people because the majority of what I possess are for a large, well-established choir, and they are also old works, which contemporary singers are not very favourable towards, because they never learn to sing them well without wanting to, without perseverance and thorough direction. But I will send you what is appropriate. For the time being I would recommend a collection of four-part choral works by Haydn, which are, in their own way, very good and which were published by Härtel in Leipzig[274] about two years ago and which you could probably buy in Weimar. Then I will also send you some short songs from here, the majority of which, however, have bad German texts. As I don't possess copies of them myself, I will have to search them out and send them to you from time to time. But if you would like to spend the autumn in Berlin, then you would hear something which is not too bad. After that I will leave for Italy; that means the Sing-Akademie is as good as lost for it can't survive. I can see that and it makes me sad. It is now 250 strong and I cannot see who will keep this ship afloat. It is one thing to maintain a paid orchestra and another to keep a group of so many amateurs together. Do come! You should find a good excuse. Privy Councillor Wolf is here.[275] He swallows down a piece of

---

[273] To counter the difficulties of performing old music with instrumental accompaniment, Zelter had formed the Sing-Akademie's own *Collegium Musicum*, which had commenced with his seminars on 10 April 1807 and met every Friday (additional rehearsals on Thursday at midday for older music works connected with the Sing-Akademie). In his diary, kept from the beginning of the rehearsals, Zelter names the players: 10 first and 10 second violins; 8 violas; 8 cellos; 4 double bass; 3 flutes; 2 oboes; 2 horns; 3 bassoons; 3 trumpets and timpani. Instrumental works by Handel, Johann Sebastian Bach, Hasse, Albinoni, Geminiani, Quantz and others were studied. The accompaniment of arias performed by members of the Sing-Akademie was part of the programme. In accordance with its original remit, the ripieno school played for the Sing-Akademie performances, for example, the performance of Handel's *Alexanderfest*. See Georg Schünemann, *Die Singakademie zu Berlin 1791–1941* (Regensburg: G. Bosse, 1941), pp. 27–9; Schünemann published the diary with Zelter's entries, the manuscript of which is still missing today.

[274] Joseph Haydn, *Drei- und vierstimmigen Gesänge mit Begleitung des Pianoforte* (Leipzig: Breitkopf und Härtel, 1803).

[275] Following the battle of Jena, Wolf moved from his position as Professor of Eloquence in Halle to Berlin in 1807, where he was soon named a member of the Academy of Science and was invited to play a role in establishing the future university.

work that history has worked at for a thousand years as if it were a cup of tea. That can't be healthy. For the rest, he feels at home in Berlin and whether we keep him [here], time will tell.

## 83. Zelter

Berlin, 23 to 24 August 1807

Enclosed is a package of choral works of all kinds.[276] They are all short and therefore it won't be too difficult to use them in a small and narrow circle. Admittedly one should have for a small sociable group pieces which are other than spiritual – really cheerful and also easier ones than this package contains. Meanwhile a start must be made somewhere; all is well where music is.

Here in Berlin there are perhaps more than 50 such family circles, who enjoy singing together and which are called 'singing teas'. I myself am not able to take part in any of them, because they are the most lethal enemies of the Sing-Akademie. As a result I am not familiar with their repertoire. I have, however, already been given a commission for a second consignment. Admittedly the Sing-Akademie came into existence through one such circle; but extreme care must be taken not to see it dissolved into a Singtee once again, where for everyone there is total freedom and no law. As a result the Sing-Akademie is only concerned with large-scale works for many voices and if, my friend, you should need anything of this nature, I can serve you with a rich and excellent repertoire.

If only you could be here this October, you would hear something of real value. The Sing-Akademie has had a white marble bust of my wife sculpted.[277] It will be ceremonially unveiled in the Sing-Akademie and on this occasion I will perform a work[278] which Handel has written for the feast of Saint Cecilia.[279] What happens

---

[276] In Goethe's music collection there are two bundles of papers with four sets of choral parts, whose inscriptions (SATB) are in Zelter's hand (everything else is by a copyist). One of these (GSA 32/19) contains 12 settings of religious texts by Fasch, Gluck, Haydn and Reichardt, among others; no. 13 is a copy (by a different copyist) of Pertis's *Adoramus te Christe*. The second package (GSA 32/183), written by the same copyist as the first dispatch, contains 15 songs by Haydn, Himmel, Mozart, Reichardt, Righini and Zumsteeg among others. Of the two collections mentioned here, the second was presumably the dispatch sent in January 1808.

[277] The bust of Julie Zelter, who had died on 12 March 1806, was commission by the Sing-Akademie from Gottfried Schadow. He modelled it on her death mask by Beyer and the work was completed by the beginning of March 1807. A marble copy, undertaken by Schadow's son Rudolph, was unveiled in the Sing-Akademie on 13 October 1807; *AMZ* 10 (1807/08), no. 6. 4 November 1807; *MA* 20.3, p. 219.

[278] George Friedrich Handel, *Alexanderfest*; text by John Dryden, German trans. Carl Wilhelm Ramler.

[279] 22 November.

otherwise in this world, I will leave to others; for my part I will carry on from where I left off. No one can stop me, even if no one thanks me; in the end you will do the same and if everyone does what he must do, according to where the spirit drives him, then I imagine things will only become better rather than worse. [...]

24 August: I must tell you, whenever you sing though these pieces, you must go back to the beginning each time; otherwise the singers, according to new practice, will sing the piece through to the end, have their opinions about it, swallow one piece after the other, and then they are finished and look around for something else, for they are generally convinced that art is only there to justify their opinion, whereas the good and the best cannot be discerned until one knows the work by heart and is possessed by it. As it doesn't require much to get four voices together, people soon become familiar with this and bored with it the more appealing and the simpler it is; in such a circle there has to be something else to change the singers around and to give them a breather. Finally, the room cannot be too small where music in several parts is being sung. One can begin by singing in a room, but then where possible change to a bigger space so that the voices can reverberate. Automatically they limit themselves, or expand, according to the space.

In a future dispatch you shall receive a *Stabat Mater*, which consists entirely of canons: 22 in total.[280]

## 84. Goethe

Carlsbad, 30 August 1807

Let me thank you from the heart, my dearest friend, that you let me look so deeply into yourself and how you really are. There is really something Promethean in your nature,[281] which I can only be amazed at and admire. While you were calmly and patiently bearing that which can hardly be endured, and making future plans for a happy and creative activity, I have been acting like one who has already crossed Cocytus, and has at least tasted the waters of Lethe.[282] Otherwise, in as far as I still consider myself an inhabitant of this world, I, too, have done what I can do, in my own way, taking in many experiences, doing some reading, learning, making notes, working things out and taking things as they come.

---

[280] A motet, *Stabat Mater Dolorosa*, by Zelter is unknown.

[281] A reflection of Goethe's preoccupation with the Pandora myth, already mentioned in his diary in July 1807 and which lead to the Festspiel *Pandoras Wiederkunft* later that year.

[282] Cocytus and Lethe, rivers of the underworld in Greek mythology.

## 85. Goethe

Weimar, 15 September 1807

You really are a good friend! When I returned home, I found the songs, and we have already started our little singing school.[283] We shall by degrees attract our stage singers and chorus, besides people from the town; then we shall see how far we have got. We have a good [rehearsal] venue in our theatre.

Your renewed invitation makes my heart heavy. It is unpardonable that I should still be unacquainted with your institution, but for several years past I have felt a certain attachment to the place I live in. This has mainly arisen from the way so much has been aroused in me but not developed. So throughout the year I am busy merely trying to get things cleared up here and there, quite apart from the circumstances of my health and the time we live in. The latter, however, would be less likely to prevent my coming were it not for the former. But if the truth were known, I feel a dread of new influences and excitements, and therefore, of my own free will, deny myself many a pleasure.

The reception our theatre received in Leipzig[284] inspires me with energy and inclination to devote myself eagerly to the business this winter once more. We have, in this instance, been rewarded for our perseverance, and shall go on in the old way with confidence and hope; and thus, even the worst slander and opposition, such as we once had to experience from Berlin, will have no effect. Your perseverance, too, my worthy friend, is ever before my eyes. I am only afraid, that if you do go to Italy, the glorious bond of so many years will be dissolved. It is pleasant and natural that some of the grains of seed scattered abroad by you should have fallen upon the tea tables.[285] Please get me some such songs; they might be the very thing we need!

I shall not tell you anything about my other activities, but hope soon to be able to send you some of the fruits of my quiet industry.[286] Farewell, and let me also have a song now and then. I could enjoy such little things more readily now if you

---

[283] Goethe's diary: 14 and 16 September 1807, *WA* III/3, pp. 275–769.

[284] The Weimar Court Theatre had a guest performance for the first time in Leipzig from 14 May to 5 July and 4 to 31 August 1807. Goethe was informed of its great success by Friedrich Rochlitz, who wrote to the poet about it on 30 May and 4 July 1807.

[285] A reference to the small vocal societies in Berlin, called *Singe-Tees* (the musical equivalent of a glee club.) There were approximately 50 of them and Zelter viewed some of them with suspicion, as being 'the most dangerous enemies of the Sing-Akademie', though it owed its origin to one of them.

[286] Around mid September Goethe was working on the *Vorspiel zu Eröffnung des Weimarischen Theaters* which was published on 22 and 22 October 1807 in the *Morgenblatt für gebildete Stände*, *MA* 9, p. 235.

would set them to an easy accompaniment for guitar,[287] as I have several guitarists at hand.

### 86. Zelter

Berlin, 20 to 22 September 1807

A longer, not unpleasant visit detained me from sending this letter yesterday evening. My foot is still not completely healed, but I was still able to go into the Academy and hold the rehearsals, from where I have now returned. If only you could have heard Handel's choruses in *Alexanderfest*! I am certain that the glory, the power, the life and the peace would have shown you another aspect of the music, as very few people see it – and then only very seldom. The text, which is by Dryden and originally in English, recounts how Timotheus moves Alexander[288] through his art and has won a victory over this violent war-like character. If only I, too, could also relate what always makes me rather sheepish and speechless: the naivety, the clarity, joy and the life! I cannot possibly conceive how one can exist without these qualities and yet one lives – but that's the way it is. […]

Our theatre begins to hoist itself up after a very sad summer, where one almost feared we would see it closed. The house is full at every performance; above all the ballet and opera are popular, which overall and in their own way are also better than the rest, especially as we now do without our best female leads, because Madame Bethmann is away and Madame Fleck heavily pregnant.

I can no longer remember whether I have sent you the composition of the 'Generalbeichte',[289] so I am sending it to you now. You might be in need of it for your choir. I have handled the poem in a very dramatic way, and you will find that it has achieved our usual standard. Because it is so easily written out, I will just send you the score, so as not to send such a large letter again. I have marked it up very exactly, and you yourself can see to it that it is sung with the correct dignity and will not be raced through.

I look forward eagerly to the next volumes of your works,[290] and I hope that they will appear at the next fair.

---

[287] One of the guitarists was Wilhelm Ehlers; in Weimar from 1801-05.

[288] Alexander III, the Great (356–323 BC).

[289] Zelter's setting of Goethe's 'Generalbeichte', for solo voice, choir and accompaniment is in Goethe's music collection (GSA 32/6). The setting was not sent in an earlier letter.

[290] Cotta's new edition of Goethe's works, vols 4 to 12.

## 87. Goethe

Weimar, 28 September 1807

[...] We have diligently studied the four-part choral works which you have sent. Every Sunday morning people gather here. I have had the Haydn pieces you recommended sent from Leipzig. Send me more from time to time and you will do me a special favour, and let me know what I owe you, so I don't add to the debt for accommodation. Next time, news about other matters.

## 88. Zelter

Berlin, 6 October 1807

Some more music for your new choir, if I have not sent it already! More will follow as soon as my messenger has returned from Leipzig.

## 89. Goethe

Jena, 16 December 1807

First of all, dear friend, I could not ask enough of you; first it was one thing, then another; I plagued you with my commissions,[291] though you have enough to do without them, and now that everything has come – songs, price list, turnips – I am like those whose prayers have been answered, and with no more thanks turn from the giver to the gifts.

I will not excuse this, for there is always time to send a few lines to a friend, but since my return home from the baths I have felt strangely oppressed by the present, as if I had to pay another penalty for those four months which I spent upon the unclouded mountain heights like a retired gymnosophist. It is true nothing disagreeable has happened to me, but yet so much that I like and disliked forced itself upon me that neither my physical nor my moral powers were quite sufficient to the task.

My small choir, which, of course, consists of hardly more than four voices, is shaping up quite nicely and already shows its influence upon the theatre. Shortly before I left home,[292] it was greatly improved by the acquisition of a young female

---

[291] Goethe refers to his repeated requests for music for his newly-founded choir, as well as his requests for the Berlin theatre programmes, and for a price list for Berlin porcelain.

[292] Goethe was in Jena from 11 November to 18 December 1807.

voice,[293] which might almost pass for a countertenor. Might I ask you, at your convenience, to let me have Schiller's 'Punschlied'?[294] Unfortunately I have but one voice part left; the others have been removed. […]

So much, my dearest friend, for the moment. I am packing up to return to Weimar. I have been very happy here, and you would never guess it: I have been drawn into sonneteering.[295] I shall send you a dozen some day soon,[296] on the one condition that no one sees them, and that they are not copied. But should you care to set one of them to music, I should be very much pleased; I am only too glad to see my productions floating in your element. Write to me again, if only a line or two. A word from a friend is doubly enjoyable in these gloomy, short days.

Privy Councillor Wolf has given us an excellent book on the study of antiquity, which is very rich and reminds us of everything we know, and gently points out to us what we should know and how we should deal with it all.

### 90. Zelter

Berlin, 9 January 1808

A second parcel of songs has been ready for a good while and awaits dispatch. Of Schiller settings, I enclose two 'Punschlieder' which I composed. You will find your way into it and be able to write the following strophes. […]

I received your kind letter from 16 December last year on 23 December. I am overjoyed about the sonnets and please send me them soon. The conditions shall be fulfilled. No one is to see them or write them out, and what will lend itself to composition by me you will have immediately.

---

[293] Regina *Henriette* Häßler (1790-1849), daughter of the pianist, composer and music dealer Johann Wilhelm Häßler in Erfurt; in Weimar from 1807; wife of Carl Eberwein from 1812.

[294] As Zelter was not clear which of Schiller's *Punschlieder* Goethe meant – 'Punschlied. Im Norden zu singen' ('Auf der Berge freien Höhen') or 'Punschlied' ('Vier Elemente, innig gesellt') which he had already sent the poet on 9 May 1802 – he enclosed both compositions in the following letter.

[295] Around the end of his time in Jena, Goethe attended August Wilhelm Schlegel's lecture on the sonnet and had become preoccupied with the form; the origin of his sonnet cycle is traceable to the beginning of his time in Jena.

[296] Goethe eventually kept his promise (after Zelter reminded him several times); on 22 June 1808 Goethe sent Zelter six poems out of a total of 17 from the cycle, composed in the winter of 1807/08.

## 91. Goethe

Weimar, 22 January 1808

[...] The music has already been handed over to our little [singing] school; your first consignment is still the best thing we have had for some time past. The greater part of it was performed yesterday before our princesses,[297] who really enjoyed it.

You once spoke about a *Stabat Mater*; pardon me for reminding you of it. My little institution is getting on well; but the young people, as you well know, are very fond of stepping out of line, and each one imagines himself to be better off when he is singing some pitiful or mournful lament of unrequited love as a solo. I allow such things towards the end of each session and yet, at the same time, execrate men like Matthisson, Salis, Tiedge[298] and the clerical body who show us heavy Germans – even in songs – a path beyond the world, which we leave quickly enough as it is. Add to this that musicians themselves are often hypochondriacal, and that even joyous music may descend into melancholy. I praise what you produce, dear friend. Again yesterday, during the 'Niemals erscheinen die Götter allein'[299] and in the 'Liebe Freunde, es gab beßre Zeiten',[300] it almost seemed as if everyone was shaking from his head the dust and ashes of the century.

I owe so much to you; perhaps I shall be able to repay you some day.

## 92. Zelter

Berlin, 27 January to 20 February 1808

[...] But where are the sonnets that my heart longs for? Don't let me languish after them any longer and send me no fewer than the promised dozen; otherwise I compose elegies and hymns by Tiedge, and send you them to you as a plague on the land.

---

[297] Louise Augusta (1757–1830), wife of Duke Carl August, and Maria Pawlowna (1786–1859), Grand Duchess of Russia and sister of Alexander I; wife of Carl Friedrich of Sachsen-Weimar-Eisenach.

[298] Friedrich von Matthisson (1761–1831), Baron Johann Gaudenz von Salis-Seewis (1762–1834) and Christoph August Tiedge (1752–1842): representative of a generation of lyric poets between Sentimentality and Romanticism. Their poetry was very popular, especially in almanacs, and was often set by Reichardt, Zelter and Zumsteeg.

[299] Zelter's setting of Schiller's 'Dithyrambe', which appeared under an earlier title 'Der Besuch', in Schiller's *Musenalmanch für das Jahr 1797*.

[300] Zelter's setting of Schiller's 'An die Freude'; there are numerous handwritten copies of Zelter's song in Goethe's music collection.

In actual fact I have composed a hymn to the sun by Tiedge,[301] because he is here at the moment with his patroness, Frau von der Recke, whose favour I also have to boast. I have also composed a spiritual poem by Frau von der Recke[302] and let her hear it in the Sing-Akademie.

It is said here that Reichardt is performing his operas in Weimar all through the winter.[303] Here there are nothing but translations from the French, which also have their good points, all the more so because, in general, they are always still the pick of the crop. In addition we mostly enjoy ballet, where one can take pleasure in beholding physical prowess.

### 93. Goethe

Weimar, End of March, beginning of April 1808

[…] When I look at my latest short poems,[304] I unfortunately find nothing singable among them, and so I don't want to send them to you. On the other hand, you will soon receive some work from a young composer,[305] who has been a collaborator in my choir this winter. Will you be so kind as to write me a report about it? They are four-part songs and if they impress you, I will send the young man himself perhaps this coming September, whereby he could enjoy your direct influence.

Since, instead of communicating something to you or offering you something pleasant in my letters, I am always wanting and expecting something new from you, so I look around to see if I can find something to give you pleasure, and that's when the delay with my new volumes is irksome. I suspect Cotta will publish the eight remaining volumes together. As soon as they are in my hand, your copy will be in the post. There are some things in it that will certainly give you pleasure.

---

[301] Zelter's setting of Christoph August Tiedge's 'Hymnus an die Sonne', for two choirs, bass solo and piano accompaniment, was performed on 16 February 1808 by the Sing-Akademie.

[302] The poem has not been identified; it is not the poem ascribed to von Kubik/Meier Elisa von der Recke which was reviewed in the *Berlinische Musikalische Zeitung*, 15 June 1793, in connection with Zelter's published setting of the verse 'Allgütiger! Ich bringe dir ein Herz'.

[303] Rolf Pröper, *Die Bühnenwerke Johann Friedrich Reichardts: 1752–1814* (Bonn: H. Bouvier, 1965) does not refer to any performances of Reichardt's operas in Weimar. Zelter is most likely referring to Reichardt's Singspiel *Jery und Bätely*, which was in the Weimar repertoire from 9 June 1804 and appears once in the theatre programmes of 1807/08, on 21 December 1807.

[304] The cycle of 17 sonnets written between December 1807 and early 1808.

[305] Franz *Carl* Adalbert Eberwein (1786–1868).

Reichardt, as you know, has employment in Cassel.[306] Nothing has become of the performance of his operas here, about which there was a great deal spoken. I hear Himmel died in Rome.[307] It is truly a pity for such a fine talent! [...]

## 94. Goethe

Weimar, 20 April 1808

Here are the songs,[308] dearest friend. Cast an eye over them! Perhaps you will make some remarks in red ink, and say generally what you think of the young man's talent, and in particular let me know how far he seems to have progressed in this difficult art. I shall perhaps send him to you for Michaelmas, as next winter he would like to become the conductor of my little musical choir. As I was not fated to revel at ease at the rich table of a great city, I must cultivate and plant on a small scale, and produce and accomplish what is possible at the time, under the given circumstances.

Please tell me, when you have time, something about early Church music in Constantinople, which, with the Greek Church, seems to have spread in the East, and to have influenced the Slavonic people.

Where do you think the universal tendency towards minor tones originates, which can be traced even in the Polonaise?

This Easter, eight Choristers passed through here on their way from St Petersburg to Paris and the Chapel of the Russian Ambassador. They sang in the Greek Church[309] here on both feast days, when – as her Royal Highness[310] told me – they performed nothing but genuine, ancient church compositions. The nearest thing that I have heard to it is the *canto firmo* of the Italians and the way

---

[306] Reichardt was employed as court composer by King Jérôme in 1808; he soon left Kassel for Vienna and from there travelled back to Giebichenstein.

[307] Friedrich Heinrich Himmel died on 8 June 1814; the rumour stemmed from a death notice in the *AMZ* 10 (1808), no. 27, 30 March announcing the death of a Leipzig Kapellmeister Himmel, who was employed in Rome, *MA* 20.3, p. 227.

[308] Settings by Carl Eberwein, mentioned in the previous letter. Zelter returned them in his letter of 6 April to 7 May, in which he writes a critical report on them.

[309] The Russian orthodox church of the Grand Duchess, Maria Pawlowna, was on the ground floor of Ackerwand 25, the property in which Charlotte von Stein lived. After Maria Pawlowna's move to Weimar, a magnificent private chapel was founded in November 1804 by the family and by the Russian community in Weimar. This small Russian group, which consisted of four choristers and a conductor, was directed by the father confessor of the Grand Duchess, Proto-Presbyter Nikita Jasnwskij, for whom lodging was also prepared in the same house.

[310] Maria Pawlowna von Sachsen-Weimar-Eisenach.

in which the Passion is performed in the Papal Chapel, namely to the actual text of the Evangelists.

I still haven't any [volumes] of my published works to send. I attach the first section of *Faust*; no more of it has been sent to me. I ask you not to let anyone see it and to send it back to me with the music, because otherwise something will be missing from a copy.

### 95. Zelter

Berlin, 6 April to 7 May 1808

[…] Telemann (a composer from Hamburg of the last century) said, 'A good composer must be able to sing a public notice.'[311] That I should disgrace my Emperor[312] by not being able to sing a sonnet? God forbid! And so bring on the sonnets; I will toss them like a salad.

It is not at all a pity about Himmel's talent. Not that many would be his equal, but he is alive and if God lets him live as long as me, he can watch [how things develop.] I am told he has left Rome for Munich; perhaps you will meet him in Carlsbad.[313]

I am waiting to see the work of your young composer[314] and he himself will be welcome if he visits us.

At the moment I am busy with [the] preparations for two concerts,[315] through which I intend to coax a few thaler out of my dear fellow citizens. If only the path to Carlsbad was via Berlin. […]

1 May: Of Eberwein's songs, which I return with the first section of *Faust*, 'Am Neujahrstage'[316] pleases me most. One recognizes a definite sentiment in it and, more to the point, this sentiment is homogeneous throughout. The piece begins, it develops, it reaches a pinnacle through the climax at bars 36 and 37, and

---

[311] This saying can be sourced back to Johann Friedrich Reichardt's essay 'An junge Künstler', which appeared in the *Musikalisches Kunstmagazin* (Berlin 1782), p. 4. Goethe adopts this expression in a letter to Zelter on 15 January 1814 without realizing that he had received this anecdote from Zelter.

[312] Napoleon I. By 'my' emperor Zelter is referring to his membership of the administrative committee set up by Napoleon.

[313] Goethe met the Berlin court Kapellmeister in July 1808 in Franzensbad; see Goethe's diary, 12 and 16 July 1808, *WA* III/3, pp. 359 and 361.

[314] Carl Eberwein.

[315] On Good Friday 1808 the Sing-Akademie performed Graun's Passion *Der Tod Jesu* and on Easter Sunday they performed Zelter's cantata *Die Auferstehung und Himmelfahrt Jesu*.

[316] A five-part song of praise to Goethe with words by Friedrich Wilhelm Riemer, composed by Carl Eberwein and dedicated to the poet.

ends quietly. The five-part passage in it follows logically and is at least studiously developed.

The composition is pure but meagre. I say meagre because here one is dealing with a developing composer, although I must state again that the middle voices move naturally enough. All that is missing is freedom and assurance which only a good schooling can give – and at present this is nowhere to be had.

The main criticism would be directed against the modulations or the cadences. But this is such a broad subject that it cannot be dealt with by letter. Let me attempt some comments:

The beginning of the poem consists of an invocation, which I feel is incorrectly handled here [...] the first bar is rather unmelodic, disjointed, so that the opening appears incomprehensible. In order to make myself clearer, I have sketched it in, in my own way, in red notation. The second line of the poem I have altered, not to improve upon the poem, but to show the composer how he should punctuate musically. As mentioned, it is difficult or impossible to write about this. Eberwein must think it over until he has grasped it; therefore, I have mapped out the first four bars.

I have marked some unacceptable harmonic progressions with red crosses. They appear hidden from the eye, but a practiced ear finds them offensive, although one is constrained to hear them often enough today. They are more disagreeable to me than obvious mistakes because there is something wretched about them, against which I warn my students daily. The faults of a master are always the outcome of mastery, and therefore do no harm, whereas disjoined work is only a cover-up for incompetence. [...]

One must also avoid repeating words unnecessarily – especially in works for a number of voices – because the cantilena suffers through it.

The other pieces appear to me less suitable to part settings; on the other hand one could still have an infinite number of parts; I also sing along even where I would have to supply the sixth voice by myself alone.

One must accustom oneself early to consider art not as an essential luxury, but the result of cause and effect; otherwise a false taste develops, on which what is false continues to build until the whole construction collapses.

The song 'Ich denke dein'[317] has something rather church-like about it and thereby is rather like a lament. I would imagine it could be hopeful instead. I don't see any justification for the minor key; besides I generally don't like to permit a sad tone unless it is based on the deepest sorrow. Above all, one can let art partake of nature's overwhelming and shattering emotions, for its purpose is to edify, not to overwhelm and destroy. In such circumstances art appears to me misplaced, like the best wine to someone who is drunk. Admittedly, this depends much on the individual character of the artist; but that is what art is for; otherwise the artist wouldn't need it and also could not be an artist. By the same token an

---

[317] Eberwein's setting of Goethe's 'Nähe des Geliebten'.

actor cannot be allowed to play a comic role sadly or to play a moderate character as an exaggerated one; the composer is no less constrained in his own way.

2 May: You ask where the universal tendency towards minor tones originates, which is traceable even in the Polonaise?

I have had the same experience, but musicologists give no satisfactory answers on the subject. The minor key is distinguished from the major tonality through the minor third, which takes the place of the major third. Our present diatonic (natural) scale originates in the way a string is divided. If it is divided in half one gets an octave; if one divides it into three, a perfect fifth results; if one divides it into five, one finds the major third. The string may, however, be divided into as many parts as one likes, yet this will never produce a minor third, although by so doing one can always get nearer to it. Accordingly this minor third is no immediate given of nature but a work of more recent art, and it must be regarded as a diminished major third, just as – even by the strictest composers – it has been treated as a consonant interval. Namely, it may, like the major third, be introduced everywhere, freely and without preparation, which, in a pure style, is not permissible for a dissonance.

I think I first met with the almost universal bias towards minor keys in the songs of northern nations, especially among island dwellers and along the coasts. The history of the art of music says next to nothing about the songs of the far north; travellers, who may have had some musical knowledge, have written them down so unsatisfactorily that we can conclude more about the limitations of their knowledge than about the true spirit of the songs, for only good musicians can record such things correctly. The hunting and fishing songs of Russia, Livonia, Norway and Scotland are the first that lead us to draw some conclusion about character; even more so the dances, which are capable of more outward expression than the songs, which demand inner feeling. This is why the Scottish, Russian, and Polish dances are so beautiful, and so truly national, that they are imitated, though awkwardly enough, among all cultivated nations. But even these dances, as far as I thought them to be genuine, were always set to minor keys, the best of them anyhow. It is well known that the Russians and Poles love dancing, and that they dance beautifully, with grace, agility and expression, showing much more dignity and life than one would ever suppose from their ordinary habits. The Russian songs and dances that I have heard were, without exception, in minor keys, though at the same time very lively, consisting of many quick notes and short metres. Had these dances been in major keys, I should have thought them extravagant and wild in their elation, whereas in the minor key they become serious, tender, more yearning, as if they are in search of the cheerfulness which is hindered by the damp, cold air and spicy food.

The genuine Polonaise inclines already to the south; an easier passion seems to awake in it. The uneven or triple time, which is already more an artificial than a natural metre, gives it a special character and the many melodic stresses that dominate the polonaise and always cut across the middle of the measure seem to even out this uneven metre, which betrays a tendency towards the more northern style, or derives from it. This will also be the case with the minor keys which can be found here, but not so commonly.

Now, if we leap from the north to Italy, minor keys are found – especially in the best musical epochs – only in temples and churches, where they were indispensable on account of the so-called Greek or Ecclesiastical modes. In songs, dances and theatrical pieces, a light, flexible melody is most common, even in the expression of the fiercest passion (with few exceptions), and in more recent times the Italians have gone so far that even an air such as 'Tu mi da me dividi' is set to the brightest melodies, to prevent the slightest suggestion of anything melancholic. These airs are then the most popular of all. On the whole, *opera buffa* enjoys far greater perfection than *opera seria*, for which no greater texts exist than those of Metastasio,[318] Apostolo Zeno[319] and others of the same ilk. Yet in *opera buffa* minor keys are used to heighten the comic and resist the serious.

To judge by this, one might look for a minor key tendency in relation to climate. Now, the North Germans stand in the centre, eagerly reaching out to every point of the compass in order to enrich their flat territory. Since they learn to do everything, ultimately they are just looking for spices to free up the blood, and then they call that passion. It is another matter with shepherd folk and mountaineers. These seem to take their scales from their horns, for they know no other instrument, so their songs and dances are either major or minor, according to what the horn can produce. A good example of this is the Scottish hornpipe, as is found in the following melody:

This dance is in a major key, but I have met with Swiss songs, also in minor keys, which presently escape my memory.

As for music in Constantinople, I know as much as my historians, namely nothing at all. An Oriental Emperor, Constantine IX, surnamed Porphyrogenitus, who made emperor when he was seven years old and was poisoned in the year 959, is said to have been a great musician. Then Nicolai tells me, a Greek Emperor,

---

[318] Metastasio's libretti are quintessential examples of eighteenth-century Italian drama. The stylization process beginning with Zeno is continued; the music had to be subordinate to the text. Mythological and allegorical figures were replaced by historical heroic figures. Independently of their geographical origins, they act according to the eighteenth-century courtly ceremonial, in crassly distinguished, contrasting emotional qualities, determined by conflicts that arise from the demands of duty and love.

[319] Zeno had endeavoured to bring the libretto back to the classical norms for drama, especially the literary norms of French tragedy.

Constantinus,[320] wrote a work in the tenth century on the court ceremonies at Constantinople, which was printed at Leipzig in 1751 in two folio volumes of Greek and Latin and, according to him, must certainly be in the Weimar Library. Perhaps this book might contain something about music in Constantinople. You may possibly get further information in the Abbot Gerbert's Latin work, *De cantu et musica sacra*,[321] which, unfortunately I do not possess. The same author also published a work called *Scriptores ecclesiastici de Musica sacra potissimum. Ex variis Italiae, Galliae, et Germaniae, codicibus manuscriptis collecti*.[322] [...]

### 96. Goethe

Carlsbad, 22 June 1808

Your dear letter of 6 April did not reach me until I arrived here. I immediately sent back Eberwein's songs, and afterwards a copy of your favourable criticism. What a good thing it would be for that young man to study under you for a good while! Just now, however, he is experiencing the fate of all beginners: they go astray like sheep, and each takes his own line.

My warmest thanks for what you have said, to my comfort and instruction, in reply to my questions. It is only with regard to your theoretical statements, which, as I well know, square with the convictions of the physical and musical world, that, as is usual with me, I have something (in my own way) to remind you of. How dearly I should like to converse with you on this subject, which is so closely connected with others I am pondering; then some of the chief knots would surely be unravelled for me. I enclose a sheet of paper on which your statement is repeated, followed by my doubts, objections and questions, in so far as I was able to summarize my thoughts upon so complicated a subject. As I have numbered the points of argument and kept a copy of them, you might be so kind as to answer them one by one. That way I should be able to keep your explanations together with my draft. [...]

If you find Voß's sonnet objectionable, we are completely agreed upon that point as well. In Germany we have had several instances of very gifted men who end up losing themselves in pedantry, and it is the same in his case. Through sheer prosody his poetry has entirely vanished. And what is the point of pursuing with hatred and rage an individual rhythmic form – the sonnet, for example – when after all it is only a vessel into which anyone can put whatever substance he likes?

---

[320] They are both the same person: the Kaiser von Byranz, Konstantin VII. Porphyrogennetos, who was also known as a writer of hymn texts; his treatise *Libri duo de ceremoniis aulae Byzantinae* appeared in a two-volume edition in the eighteenth century.

[321] Martin Gerbert, *De Cantu* [About Song] (2 vols, St Blasien, 1774).

[322] Ecclesiastical writers on sacred music, collected from various handwritten codices from Italy, France and Germany (3 vols, St Blasien, 1774).

How ridiculous it is to be forever returning to that sonnet of mine,[323] in which I spoke rather unfavourably of sonnets, to take sides on an aesthetic subject, and to see me as taking sides, without considering that one may quite well jest and joke about a thing, without at the same time despising or denouncing it on that account.

I hope, therefore, that the accompanying sonnets will meet with a warmer reception from you; only I urgently beseech you not to let them out of your hands.[324]

I have nothing further to write to you from here, except that I am in good health and as industrious as I can be. […]

*First Enclosure*

1. 'The minor key is distinguished from the major, by the minor third.' Is it not also distinguished by diminishing or narrowing the other intervals?
2. 'Which takes the place of the major third'. This expression can only work if we start from the major key. A theorist of northern nationality, when speaking of the minor tones, could just as well say that the major third takes the place of the minor third.
3. 'Our present diatonic (natural) scale'. That the diatonic scale should be the only natural one – my opposition is really directed against this opinion.
4. 'Originates in the way the string is divided. If it were divided in half and so on.' That the division of the string into different parts should produce sounds harmonious to the ear is a nice experiment which might even be made the foundation of a certain scale; but if it cannot be accomplished in this way, might it not be possible in some other manner?
5. 'The string may, however, be divided into as many parts as you like and yet this will never produce a minor third, although by so doing, you can always get nearer to it.' You ask too much of an experiment when you require it to do everything. Electricity was at first only produced by friction, whereas its greatest manifestations are now produced by mere touch. Our aim should be an experiment by which one could also represent the minor tones as original.
6. 'Accordingly, this minor third is no immediate given of nature, but a work of more recent art.' I deny the conclusion as I do not admit the premises.
7. 'And it must be regarded as a diminished major third'. This is a subterfuge to which theorists usually resort when they have established something that

---

[323] 'Das Sonnet', written in 1800 in response to Voß's programmatic sonnet. It first appeared in the *Morgenblatt für gebildete Stände* in 1807. Later Goethe revised his opinion, composing a cycle of sonnets, one of which, 'Die Liebende schreibt', was set to music by Schubert and Mendelssohn.

[324] Six sonnets by Goethe from a group of 17 sonnets which he later completed in Jena in 1817; the six enclosed sonnets are 'Mächtiges Überraschen'; 'Freundliches Begegnen'; 'Wachsende Neigung'; 'Gewöhnung'; 'Entsagung'; 'Jähe Trennung'.

restricts nature: for they are then obliged to retract and annihilate what they formerly maintained in a very paradoxical fashion. If a major third is an interval that nature gives us, how can we diminish it without destroying it? How much and how little can it be diminished and not be a major third and still be a third? And, ultimately, at what point would it cease to be still a third? My imaginary northern theorist might with equal justification affirm that the major third is an augmented minor third.

8. 'And so – even by the strictest composers – it has been treated as a consonant interval.' We have a clear instance here of what happens so often both in art and technique: that the practical sense knows very well how to dispense with theoretical limitations without making too much fuss about it.

9. 'That is: it may, like the major third, be introduced everywhere, freely and without preparation – which, in a pure style, is not granted any dissonance.' 'If it is treated as a consonant interval, it is consonant, for such things cannot be established primarily by convention. If it occurs freely and without preparation, then it is not dissonant: it is by nature harmonious as is everything which springs from it.'

Here a very remarkable consideration comes into play in respect of all physical inquiry – one which has been already touched upon before. When he is in full command of his senses, man is the greatest and most perfect physical apparatus that there can be. And it is, in fact, the greatest failing of modern physics that the experiments are, as it were, separated from human beings and only acknowledge as nature what artificial instruments demonstrate – and thereby want to limit and prove what nature is capable of. It is exactly the same with calculations. Much that is true cannot be calculated, just as there is much that cannot be clinched by experiment. On the other hand, man stands so high, that what otherwise defies representation finds its representation in him. What then is a string and all its mechanical divisions compared with the ear of the musician? It may even be asked, what are the elementary manifestations of nature herself compared to man, who must first control and modify them in order to be able to assimilate them to some extent? However, I do not intend to lose myself in these considerations just now. I would prefer to discuss them in detail first and to ask you for more information on a few other points.

*A simile as postscript*

All the arts, seeing that they could only work themselves upwards by exercise and thought, practice and theory, seem to me like towns where the ground and soil on which they are built can no longer be detected. Rocks have been blasted away, and these same stones carved into shape and made into houses. Caves were found very convenient and converted into cellars. Where the earth gave way, it was entrenched and walled up; perhaps right beside the original rock a bottomless piece of swamp was encountered where stakes and piles had to be driven in. When at last all is completed and made habitable, what part of it can be called nature, and what art? Where is the foundation and where are the accessories? Where is the substance, where is the form? How difficult it is, then, to give reasons, if we would assert that in the earliest times, if one had had an overview of the whole, everything could have been done more in accordance with nature and art, and with more purpose. If you consider the piano or the organ, you might imagine you had the simile of my town before you. I wish to God that I could live beside you some day and attain true enjoyment of life; I should then be heartily glad to forget all questions about nature and art, theory and practice.

## 97. Zelter

Berlin, 8 May to 14 July 1808

My ripieno school, about which I wrote to you last year, has had to be shelved for a long time, because the Academy of Fine Arts is planning an exhibition, which is to open already this month. Needless to say this interruption is not agreeable to me. I have spent a whole year teaching the basics of musical practice and have achieved hardly anything. [...]

15 May: Meanwhile I continued work I had begun earlier, especially the attempt to handle special artistic verse metres musically and to lay them in the mouths of the choir. I thought I would make good use of the time Privy Councillor Wolf is here. [...]

I found the repercussions of your observations on music theory electric because so many of these objections have also been stirring in me for a long time. I can only state what we already know. I lack the mathematical patience to investigate further, and when I am striving for clarity, it suits my own purposes, since in my compositions there is a certain striving towards the classical.

Our theory [of music] has become a system that one should learn and be able to teach. That thereby violence is done to nature cannot be doubted. True, it is a rich web of modification which one can hardly contemplate without admiration, so that the musicians are led to believe that what is not achievable through this system cannot be achieved at all. This much is certain: if one moves individual pillars of this theory away from their foundation, then one runs the danger of damaging the building. Now to your questions:

1. The minor key is distinguished from the major 'only by the minor third'. The fifth and octave remain unchanged in both tonalities, hence both of these form perfect consonances, whereas the third, because of its variability, is called an imperfect consonance, because it can be great or small (major or minor).
2. The experiment of the division of a string, from which the intervals of our scales originate, includes yet another a physical phenomenon: the appearance of overtones. If one sets a deep string vibrating, one doesn't just hear the sound

of the string but at the same time several tones automatically resounding above it. If one looks for these overtones, the numbers 2, 3, 4, 5, 6, 7 and so on are found, which the human ear can still distinguish. The same experiment can be performed on the Aeolian harp since, especially with stronger and prolonged air movement, the higher numbers 8, 9, 10, 12, 13 and so on also become audible and resound discordantly. The wonderful effect of the Aeolian harp is that these sounds appear essential and arbitrary at the same time. All of these resounding sounds share a common tonic (to which the harp is tuned) and in this tonic the third never appears other than great (major), so never small (minor). Therefore, I have called the minor third a work of art, a diminished major third, because of the way it is handled by musicians as consonant (like the major).
3. That our diatonic scales are the only natural ones, I have at least not wanted to maintain, because it cannot be proven. True we possess right now two different temperaments for scales of which one is called equal temperament and the other is called unequal temperament. Neither is completely natural and we don't know whether the Greeks had a natural scale, because we know so little about the past.
4. Should it not be possible by other means? – By all means! The minor third is there, but not as a product of the tonic, so it cannot automatically resound. The minor third develops much more from the relationship: $6/6:5/6 = I: 5/6=6:5$; otherwise one could not tune it at all. The perfect fourth also exists in this way: $4/5:3/4$ or $I: 3/4 =4:3$; and so it also does not resound automatically and yet it is truly consonant.
5. and 6. If an experiment provides everything to achieve a complete picture, one can ask what more is required? The minor third is not among the natural overtone series. It is a composite relationship and I doubt any external cause could make this interval appear naturally of itself. If it were possible, however, all remaining intervals would alter themselves at the same time and we would then indeed have a completely new and completely different system for minor tonalities, which most likely would not tolerate being within the major tonality, whereas our present system combines both in an unlimited wealth of modifications.

Electricity [sic] could well be applied to the Aeolian harp. Furthermore friction could be applied but only to resounding bodies and the result would, I imagine, only be significant for the major third, for the ear can accept all dissonances a step apart: the tonic beside the second, the second beside the third, the third beside the fourth, the fourth beside the fifth and so on. But the minor third is intolerable beside the major third because it cannot be resolved, which is the reason why I had considered the minor third as an indirect given of nature.

The following three points arise from the previous one. All intervals that lie between the usual ones are possible; but if we are to use them and teach them with proper respect for order and art, then we must have a new system. However, what our accepted – though imperfect – theory dictates is exactly what you yourself add. For the above phenomena are not only not separate from man in his physical and spiritual make-up, but rather they marry him to those elements of nature which are outside him. His nerves, the most secret powers of his mind resound with kindred tones and attract him, they lead him forward; they would really torture, depress and destroy if they were not what they are and have remained that way for so long.

The horn and the trumpet are among the instruments that do not freely produce all the natural overtones of our scale. The major third is freely sounded on horn as on the trumpet. But the minor third can only be acquired through stops with the hand, and so since it does not freely appear, it is also never completely pure: the ear misses something. Finally, I recall a bell that is situated here in the city. This bell, which must have disparate parts, lets a third be heard that is smaller than the major and therefore is closer to the minor than the major, yet every time the bell is struck, this third purifies itself while swinging in the air and gradually approaches the major third until it is pure. I have often observed this experiment myself for a quarter of an hour at a time. Now, since this resounding tone is nearer to the minor third than to the major, then why does the lingering sound not merge into the minor third?

13 July: The last eight volumes of your works arrived on the 5th of this month. […] The sight of the unfortunate Gretchen made me disconsolate. It is so subtly implied and yet has a tremendous effect. Will you clarify for me so much that is new in *Faust*, which I have read so often, for example the intermezzo? But first I will read the whole poem once again.

I have read your *Pandora*[325] and am agitated because since then I cannot sleep until I know the entire play. In order to calm myself, I have already composed these scenes and committed them to paper.[326] I hope to present the two brothers alongside one another so they should be recognizable, but I don't know the children yet and to guess at the mother is so dangerous; for once the wrong character is given melodic forms, nothing can be done to set it right.

---

[325] Goethe's Festspiel *Pandoras Wiederkunft* was in the first edition of the journal *Prometheus* (1808). Goethe had referred Zelter to the publication on 22 June.

[326] Zelter's setting of *Pandora* was left lying for the time being because of the problems referred to but also because Zelter did not have the continuation of the text. Work on this setting was resumed when Zelter received the complete text during their time together in Bohemia in July and August 1810, but, once again, Zelter's compositional work came to a halt under the pressure of everyday life. The work was taken up again in May 1811, at which point Zelter discarded everything he had composed to date. Even Goethe's encouragement to continue composing the work could not prevent it from being unfinished in the end.

## 98. Zelter

Berlin, 9 to 11 September 1808

The young Eberwein arrived on the 19th of last month, and the next day we began our scholarly discussions, which in the last few days have taken an easier path, after having gone rather astray into a general wilderness. As he has only a short holiday, it will be difficult to fit in some of the preconditions of art which should get into the blood from one's youth; and so he wants me to ask you, my friend, for a longer period of leave. I do this gladly, all the more as I hope that, on his return, he will compensate for the extra time. So I ask that you leave him at least next winter in Berlin, which will bring some musical benefit.[327] Even his participation in the Sing-Akademie can only be of use to him as an artist if he attends a *series* of lectures, whose product he sees develop and grow, but especially if he hears solid and masterly compositions in the plain German style, which will either make him aware of his shortcomings or spur him on to compete. It has taken hold of him, that I can see, but he is not finding it because he is looking from the outside. He has already made many friends. Yesterday, for the first time, he performed publicly on the violin, not without applause.[328] His tone is good and pure, but he has, God knows from whose example, acquired the habit of a tearful, retarding cantilena, the drawbacks of which I will suitably explain to him. To his question of how much he has to pay me for the lessons I have explained that I am thinking of arranging this matter with you: to you I will say to begin with that the more he learns, the less he has to pay, and his longer stay with me in Berlin will not cost more if he is not well off.

11 September: Since this letter was left behind yesterday and can only be sent next Wednesday, I must ask you for an answer by return of post with regard to young Eberwein. I have said to him I had a letter from you in which you requested we set up a diary recording his progress.

It is necessary that the young man stays on course; to this purpose I myself am giving him the opportunity and for that reason he has been accepted [in the Sing-Akademie]. However, as his time is also limited, I have also made it clear to him not to lose himself; apart from that he can enjoy applause and friendship in great company every day, about which nothing should get back to Weimar.

---

[327] Goethe had to deny Zelter's request but he did grant Eberwein eight months leave the following year from mid February to October.

[328] Eberwein performed 'with real skill and precision', *Vossische Zeitung*, 10 September 1808, at a summer concert entitled 'Musikalische Divertissement' arranged by the court chamber musician Georg Abraham Schneider. The performance took place in the Georgian [Georgeschen] Gardens, Friedrichstrasse 141.

## 99. Goethe

Weimar, 19 September 1808

You make me your debtor yet again, dearest friend, through the good reception you have given Eberwein. When I granted him the short holiday in Berlin,[329] I could only do it with the intention of making him aware that art has a height and a depth of which he seemed to have only a remote understanding, and a law of which, if one comes from the outside and like the young people only scratches the surface, one can have only the faintest notion. Unfortunately I cannot extend his holiday this time and I will be satisfied if he, in the language of Pietism, comes back as a sinner, if he feels that much is to be discarded which he had considered good, if he notices that what the world considers roads to success are often wrong paths, if an insatiable desire is activated in him to see you again and to be educated by you. If I find him so disposed, I will provide for him in the future what he must for the time being do without.

I am back safely from Carlsbad and accomplished a great deal there, which sooner or later I will confide to you. [...] As soon as I am easier in my mind you will hear more from me. When Eberwein's leave is over, send him on his way.

Goethe

## 100. Zelter

Berlin, 30 September to 15 October 1808

So I am sending Eberwein back to you a little better than when he arrived. He has only seen the entrance; whether he will find even the inner courts, time will tell. I have diligently given him work which appears dry to beginners in order to isolate him first and to cut him off from the age, for if he doesn't learn to do anything better than what the crowd has always wanted to hear, then it doesn't matter much how he wastes his time. I have given him the task of sending me something of this kind at least every month; then I will answer him promptly. I rely on your encouragement, since he has to keep up the work [...]

Your letter of the 19th of this month arrived here on the 27th. I considered it appropriate to let young Eberwein read it himself, partly so as not to be the bearer of sad news and partly to show him how you yourself think about art. [...]

15 October: This letter, which awaits the departure of Eberwein, is still lying here in front of me as he is also still here because a letter and money from Weimar

---

[329] From 19 August to 16 October 1808, during which time Eberwein studied compositional techniques and performance with Zelter.

are outstanding. As he is becoming more and more anxious, I have advanced him six Friedrichs d'or,[330] which will enable him to depart from here tomorrow.

## 101. Goethe

Weimar, 30 October 1808

Accept my best thanks, dear friend, for all that you are able to do and for all that you mean to do for young Eberwein. The world of art has certainly gone too much towards the bad for a young man to see easily what is crucial. They always look for it anywhere but where the real source is; and even if they once catch a glimpse of the source, they are unable to find their way to it.

For this reason, some half-dozen of our younger poets put me into a state of despair; in spite of their extraordinary natural gifts, they hardly manage to write anything that I can admire. Werner, Oehlenschläger, Arnim, Brentano[331] and others work and toil away; but everything they produce is completely lacking in form and character. No one will understand that the highest and sole operation of nature and of art is form and in form, specification, so that each thing may be and remain something special, something significant. It is not art to allow one's talent to act capriciously, according to one's individual whim; something should always arise out of it, as from the scattered seed of Vulcan, there arose a marvellous serpent-boy. [...]

Have the kindness, dear friend, whenever you have a quarter of an hour to spare, to give me a brief sketch of the errors of young musicians; I should like to compare them with the blunders made by painters, for one must, once and for all, calm oneself about these matters, denounce the whole system, not think about the education of others and devote the short time that remains to one's own works.

But while expressing myself in so ungracious a manner upon these points, I must nevertheless, as good-natured grumblers are wont to do, at once recall my words and beg of you to continue devoting your attention to Eberwein, at all events until Easter when I shall send him back to you again. He feels great confidence in you, and great respect for your institute; but even this, unfortunately, does not mean very much for young men because secretly they still think that something outstanding can be equally well produced in their own silly way. A good many men have an idea of the goal, only they would like to reach it by sauntering along the labyrinthine ways.

---

[330] The contemporary currency, namely gold coins; one Friedrichs d'or was worth five German Reichstaler.

[331] Zacharias Werner (1768–1823); Adam Gottlieb Oehlenschläger (1779–1850); Achim von Arnim (1781–1831) and Clemens Brentano (1778–1842).

## 102. Goethe

Weimar, 7 November 1808

Yesterday we feasted on some of your gifts, on your compositions, as on your turnips. I was also so grateful to you in that Eberwein appears to have brought back with him something of your gravity. He seems to me like Moses when he came down from the mountain with his face shining.[332] If that is only an outer manifestation, we can suspect that something is also likely to have happened inside. I thank you for your kind help towards his progress because his return here is advantageous for him and for us. Our little choral singing would be completely gone to ruin during the winter. Now he can take stock and make his pilgrimage to you around Palm Sunday.

Reichardt from Cassel was here yesterday:[333] he is visiting the theatres of southern Germany to get personnel for Cassel Theatre, which of course must be very strangely organized. He wants people who can perform two functions [as actor and singer].

## 103. Zelter

Berlin, 12 November 1808

[...] Eberwein departed from here on 16 October and I also received a letter from him on the 7th of this month. He must remain very focused if he is to have any success. The technical aspects of an art really must be properly learnt in the early years. If it is true that the spirit only stirs from within, concern for the outer presentation must be eliminated. He who knows the trade will admit that it is a help to the writer because it nourishes his joy and liberates the inner drive.

What you say in your letter in relation to specification in the shaping and in form and character is perhaps more true of music (at least in music it is more difficult to achieve) than of the plastic arts. For each of the poetic spirits named by you, I could name a musical counterpart, and so confirm your judgement that one sees with admiration and terror, will-of-the-wisps, and signs of blood on the horizon of Mount Parnassus. Men so brilliantly gifted as Cherubini, Beethoven, and several others steal the club of Hercules to smash flies with; at first one marvels and then directly afterwards one shrugs one's shoulders at the amount of talent

---

[332] Moses descending from Mount Sinai; Exodus 34, v. 29.

[333] Reichardt had found a position as Directeur général des théâtres et de son orchestre and music teacher to the queen in Westfalen at the beginning of 1808, but the position was not artistically satisfying. By the end of October 1808 he was sent to Vienna with the task of engaging singers for Italian *opera buffa*. En route he passed through Weimar on 6 November; his visit is not recorded in Goethe's diary.

wasted in making minutiae important and exalted ways common. I really could despair when it occurs to me that new music must perish if art is to come out of [new] music.

No art can exercise a positive influence, which wanders about in endless space, shameless and shapeless like the more modern music, exposing its highest and most secret charms, out of context, to the public gaze of the common and vulgar, like an anatomical cabinet or a collection of anecdotes about illicit affairs which oversatiate common curiosity. Let people object as they will to the composers of earlier centuries (for who is not obliged to learn more than he knows?); they never threw art away nor surrendered the inner sanctuary. Whoever appreciates this side of them also learns to respect them. This much is certain: had we built on their foundation, we would have an art and we would be very different people from the way we must view ourselves now.

### 104. Goethe

Weimar, 15 December 1808

You receive here, dear friend, the requested manuscript. It contains a couple of my songs which I looked for and found at your prompting.[334] By the way, I myself possess a very fine collection of original manuscripts and sometimes double copies, especially in the case of German writers. [...]

With the next post you will receive a vellum copy of my works,[335] which has finally arrived here. [...]

### 105. Zelter

Berlin, 26 December 1808

[...] In honour of the King's return, I have established a Liedertafel: a society of 25 men, the twenty-fifth of whom is the appointed master, gathers once a month for a supper of two courses and entertains itself with jovial German songs.[336] The

---

[334] 'Trost in Tränen' and 'Vanitas! Vanitatum vanitas!'

[335] *Goethes Werke* (Cotta, 1808), vols 1–12.

[336] Zelter reports here a few days after a gathering of the founder members in Voitus's house on 21 December 1808, but before the official formation, on 24 January 1809, of a new Liedertafel, an assembly of 25 men from the Sing-Akademie who came together once a month to sing and eat a light meal: 'the idea a forming a male-voice choir combined with the idea of a place for honouring the monarch, which is characteristic of the Liedertafel, would have been partly inspired by the king' (Peter Nitsche, 'Die Liedertafel im System der Zelterschen Gründungen' in Carl Dahlhaus (ed.) *Studien zur Musikgeschichte Berlins im*

members must either be poets, singers or composers. The writer or composer of a new song reads or sings, or has it sung at table. If it is well received, a box is passed round the table, into which everyone (if he likes the song) puts a groschen or two, as he wishes. The money is counted on the table; if it is enough to purchase a silver medal to the value of a good thaler, the conductor awards the winner the medal; in the name of the Liedertafel they drink the health of the poet or composer and discuss the beauty of the song. If a member can show 12 silver medals, he has a supper at the expense of the group, he is crowned with a garland, can ask for any wine of his choice, and is presented with a gold medal worth 25 thalers. All other arrangements are mentioned in the plan, which right now is being circulated. Anyone blurting out words that are dishonourable or offensive to any member or to the society pays a fine. Satirical verses about individuals are not performed; everyone has complete freedom to be himself provided that he is liberal. The maximum number of rules is 12; there can be less, not more. Now draw me a sketch for an attractive scroll, rather a big one, containing the word 'welcome' – and one for a small medal and one for a gold medal; I ask you urgently because we must strike when the iron is hot. All the members are enthusiastic and can hardly wait for the King's arrival.

[…] Your poems have brought great joy!

Zelter

## 106. Goethe

Weimar, 16 February 1809

Dear friend, you will receive only this short note of greeting through Eberwein, who is leaving now.[337] Having put it off long enough, he has reminded me about a letter to you exactly at a time when I don't have my thoughts together. Give him a warm reception and help him to develop further through advice, teaching and example. If what we wish for is not produced in our students, we still won't be rid of them, so we have no other recourse but, with resignation, to reproduce ourselves in this imperfect way. I am working on something that will also give you

---

*frühen 19. Jahrhundert* (Regensburg: Bosse, 1980), pp. 11–26, here p. 15). According to their statutes, the first meeting was scheduled to take place the day after the king's return, which was long anticipated; the meeting was, however, postponed, and the first proper assembly took place on 2 May 1809 – more than seven months after the king's arrival on 23 December 1808. See also Hermann Kuhlo, *Geschichte der Zelterschen Liedertafel von 1809 bis 1909* (Berlin: Horn & Raasch, 1909).

[337] Eberwein's second study trip to Berlin, to take composition classes with Zelter from February to October 1809.

joy some day.[338] Therefore, forgive my silence and in your own time let me hear something from you once again.

### 107. Zelter

Berlin, 9 May 1809

My dear friend, you have sent me quite a fine young man in Eberwein, for whose acquaintance I remain newly obliged to you and you shall receive him back more competent than when he arrived. I must praise not only his diligence and his perseverance, but also for six weeks his eye is beginning to search for the kernel of art, and his desire is being transformed into a sense that what is right and beautiful has to be found for each individual thing. We have taken a serious path which initially does not exactly go smoothly, yet we have made considerable progress in a short time and we hope to settle comfortably into our routine. Already we understand that the rule does not stand alone and itself has a rule we can intimately approach by finding its foundation in the depths of our heart. In this way a feeling for art develops, which recognizes that the cycles of everyday life cannot be directly translated in art. The wonder at artistic craft merges into deep admiration and love of truth and so we hope to arrive on a path where perception is clearer and the goal more certain.

I must confess now that I myself am beginning to feel more and more affinity with the young Eberwein, and since he is working so well, I would like to be able to extend his visit. Now the question is whether he could stay here for another four, five, six months? If he remains as diligent, I can vouch that the time will be put to good use; if he doesn't, I would rather write and tell you. It is really terrible to be pressed by time in such circumstances, because it is also true that all days cannot be called good days.

### 108. Goethe

Jena, 1 June 1809

I consider Eberwein fortunate; I even envy him that he lives near you and can be enlightened by you on life and art. As our opera company is not going to Lauchstädt this summer, he is not needed and may stay away, but only until his presence is required here again. I enclose a short poem, which you might like to accompany with the necessary musical declamation;[339] or perhaps you will give it

---

[338] Goethe's *Farbenlehre*.
[339] 'Johanna Sebus', published by Frommann in Jena in 1809; Zelter's setting of Goethe's ballad as a cantata for soprano, baritone and bass solo with SATB choir was

to Eberwein to try his hand at it. I was induced to write it by good people of that district, who, in an all-devouring age, wished to preserve the memory of a pure act of humanity. [...]

Since Eberwein left and I have been occupied with all kinds of theatrical matters, I am rather cut off from music. I hope in future to have all the more enjoyment of it through him – echoes from your heaven, which alas! I am destined never to enter, a thought that sometimes annoys me. In times of war we see for the first time how clumsily and awkwardly we behaved in times of peace. When you have set it to music, let the little ballad be as widely known as you like, and do not leave me too long without a word of encouragement.[...]

## 109. Zelter

Berlin, 12 June to 14 July 1809

Eberwein is just as delighted with his extended leave as am I. He is making progress and this time you might find it harder to get him back. He is more familiar with things which used to amaze him and he now sees in art, which seemed to confine him, an open sea in which one can fish to one's heart's content. His violin playing has also improved and ascends gradually from the dreary moaning and whining to a brighter expression of life. He attends all my singing lessons daily at the academy[340] and will educate good students for you if he stays with it and does not move away from the fundamentals. So as not to distract him with sensibility, I have set the ballad to music myself. [...]

10 July: You will have seen from the papers that I have been made Professor of Music at the Akademie der Künste.[341] I had as good as resigned from industry[342] and I am now in my element and want to see what success is possible at our time of

---

enclosed in a letter to the poet on 17 February 1810 and published by Ambrosius Kühnel in Leipzig in 1810.

[340] The vocal group established by Zelter, about which he wrote in his sixth memorandum: 'For five years I have a held a proper Singschule like those of Italian conservatories, in order to be able to teach the individual members of the Sing-Akademie' (Schröder, p. 120).

[341] The *Spenersche Zeitung* (also read by Goethe) had reported on 8 July 1809: 'Persuaded by the unmistakable influence which public music has on the nation's [cultural] education, his Majesty the King has, following an application from the Head of the Department of Culture, set up a Professorship of Music at the Akademie der Künste, and this Professorship has been granted to the well-established composer, Herr Zelter [whom] his Majesty has also deigned to appoint an official member of the Academy.' The appointment was made on the recommendation of Goethe and Wilhelm von Humboldt.

[342] Zelter's practice as an [architect and] master builder.

life and in our [present] times. Hopefully our misfortune will bring us the benefit of banishing the costly foreign parasites and their tastes.

14 July: I am just about to travel to Königsberg[343] and you will not yet receive the ballad[344] but only this letter. The composition is in fact finished, but I want to send it to you only after my return, because I intend to make all kinds of improvements in it. I haven't forgotten what you wrote to me once about dramatic ballads;[345] in some ways this idea has formed the basis here, and since I employed it, the realization has thereby become more mature. Good work also requires good hands and only since I have it in front of me do I see exactly what is to be done. There is nothing for it but to busy myself with architecture;[346] if only I were 30 years younger!

## 110. Goethe

Jena, 26 August 1809

Accept my warmest thanks for the good care you are taking of Eberwein. I will be very happy if he brings us back something really fruitful in his subject. [...] I am very grateful that you have taken on poor Najada;[347] I am really eager to hear your composition.

---

[343] Zelter combined many tasks on this journey to Königsberg, to where the Prussian king had escaped before Napoleon's arrival in Berlin. The need for his journey arose through the conflict with the Royal Kapellmeister, who wanted to refuse Zelter the use of the opera house for his Good Friday and Easter Sunday performances; a decision by the cabinet to allow Zelter the use of the room was the first outcome of the journey. The next issue was the long-overdue payment of Zelter's salary, which was due to him after his appointment as Professor of Music; this, too, was agreed with Minister Altenstein to Zelter's satisfaction. The most difficult task concerned his own business, namely the collection of long-outstanding rental debts from General Scharnhorst and the royal physician, Hufeland. Zelter's experiences on this journey, from which he returned on 24 September, are documented in detail in his daily letters to his sister Luise Syring. See Joseph Müller-Blattau, 'Karl Friedrich Zelters Königsberger Briefe 1809' in *Altpreußische Forschungen* 12 (1935): 256–76. Hereafter referred to as 'Zelters Königsberger Briefe'.

[344] Zelter's setting of 'Johanna Sebus'.

[345] GZ 26 August 1799.

[346] Here Zelter means musical structure and compositional theory.

[347] Goethe uses the name of the Greek water nymph to refer to his ballad 'Johanna Sebus', which commemorates a young girl who loses her own life in a storm tide through saving the lives of others.

## 111. Goethe

Jena, 16 September 1809

If Professor Zelter has returned to Berlin, I cordially beseech him to send news of himself and our Eberwein.[348] If he has not returned, then I will ask his family. [...] It would be very nice if Eberwein would let me know how he is and what are his current wishes and prospects.[349]

## 112. Zelter

Berlin, 11 to 23 October 1809

And so gladly yet reluctantly I am sending Eberwein back to you: gladly because I hope that what he now has and knows will have an effect, develop and do him justice, which best happens away from the school and in freedom; reluctantly, however, because I would still prefer to keep him here. He takes with him all kinds of knowledge about the nature of his art, of which he has not yet fully taken possession, because as yet he hasn't felt the need for it. It will awaken after a time and come to fruition in him and perhaps appear to him in the form of completely new ideas. If he is actively engaged as soon as possible, he will generally be able to cope, especially if he has to, and what he finds lacking I will then supply. I therefore advise that he be employed in an official post. If the directors were to give him the task of creating the intermezzos of a comedy in three acts together with a proper overture (yet in a set time frame which is not too long), he would be suitably encouraged; and if he has some success, one could reward him with a small gratuity. It takes a great fountain of genius for an artist to occupy himself completely and to find his own way. Eberwein's talent is not so rich, but he appears to me to be the man who does what one needs and there have to be such people, especially with a standing orchestra. [...]

In Königsberg von Humboldt told me you put in a good word for me with someone influential.[350] I have been made Professor of Music; however, because of the disruption of the whole system I still don't know how to measure my situation. Plans for the university are in hand except for their execution, which, as it appears, is dependent on the King's return. I shall be salaried – that goes without saying; how and whether I am to earn my bread on the side and do most of it without being

---

[348] Zelter returned from Königsberg at midnight on 24 September 1809.
[349] There is no record of the letter Goethe requests from Eberwein.
[350] Zelter had met Wilhelm von Humboldt many times in Königsberg, mostly over lunch at Minister Dohna's.

paid, time will tell.[351] I know the way it is and I am in no way capable of being importunate. There is enough to do, but, knowing the situation and the people as I do, I doubt whether the right things will happen. Meanwhile I go on in my old way, come what may. Quite apart from what we didn't know or didn't have, we have lost too much for me to be able to entertain great hopes; for as you say in your letter, they are only despairing that they are no longer to lead the old sinful life; and everyone only thinks that the right thing is what is right for him.

23 October: I have had to make a necessary journey which is why this letter was left lying here and Eberwein departed without saying goodbye. [...]

A musician from the Königliche Kapelle called Schneider,[352] who can no longer get work here, is setting out on a musical tour with his wife and will pass through Weimar. He asked me for a letter to you, that he might see you. I didn't give it to him, because I knew that you are not in Weimar. He is a skilled horn player and he has composed an enormous amount of good music, including a short German opera. He was very accommodating to Eberwein, as he is generally a true phoenix among his peers. As he has no letter of introduction, he will announce himself in person to you. If you would like to see him and at all events give your consent that the Weimar orchestra facilitate him in case he wanted to give a concert, or help him to have his little opera be heard in your theatre, you would certainly give him great pleasure. His pretty little wife[353] is one of my students and has a nice voice, but she is really timid and lacks experience.

## 113. Goethe

Weimar, 21 December 1809

[...] On Thursdays and Sundays Eberwein plays for us much of the music he has brought back with him, and whatever he can communicate to us by virtue of your

---

[351] On 23 August 1809 Zelter discussed his salary with Minister von Altenstein: 'Yesterday Minister von Altenstein spoke favourably and in very friendly terms about my academic existence. I can be happy about this, since I can see that they cannot do what they would like to do' ('Zelters Königsberger Briefe', p. 273). In a further letter to his sister it emerges that he is promised 600 thalers in addition to the 400 thalers he had received from the Sing-Akademie since Easter 1809.

[352] Georg Abraham Schneider (1770–1839), cellist, conductor and composer, horn player in the Königliche Kapelle in Berlin, and his wife were Goethe's guests on 17 November and gave a concert in Weimar on 21 November; see Goethe's diary entry on 17 November 'Die Berliner Musici' and 21 November, WA III/3 pp. 400–401.

[353] Caroline Schneider née Portmann (1774/75–1850), singer.

input and blessing.[354] Schiller's poems have been most admirably composed.[355] The music supplements them, for really no song is perfect until it has been set to music. Here, however, is something quite peculiar. Thinking or enthusiasm is now for the first time dissolved, or, I should rather say, melted into the free and lovely element of sensuousness. One thinks and feels, and is carried away by it.

You can also imagine that the light-hearted songs[356] do not fail to produce their effect, as I am much more fond of such things, and in fact everybody is glad to be happy or to be put in good humour.

Eberwein is doing really well. Through your help he has come further in everything than those he has to conduct in the small school, and he is making good progress, in so far as I can judge in a subject which I don't understand. The supply of music in our small musical archive is for our purposes already quite considerable, and as slight as everything is, compared to what you have done and do, it is still something. How we treasure a copperplate engraving of a painting we cannot see. [...]

Write and tell me something about yourself when you have the opportunity, and send me something to enjoy. It is true, we have plenty of the old and unexplored; however, the newest and most immediate has the greatest attraction.

### 114. Goethe

Weimar, 4 January 1810

Don't forget 'Johanna Sebus' and don't let it be submerged again,[357] now that you have passed her a helping hand.

### 115. Zelter

Berlin, 30 December to 26 January 1810

I am in complete agreement with you with regard to the tone and spirit of social songs. I, too, prefer cheerful, light songs and Privy Councillor Wolf claimed

---

[354] Rehearsals were on Thursdays with concerts at Sunday lunchtimes in Goethe's home; on Eberwein's return from Berlin he took over the role of Director of Music of Goethe's Hauskapelle.

[355] Most likely, Zelter's setting of Schiller's 'Die Gunst des Augenblicks' and the two *Punschlieder* (first sent to Goethe on 2 April 1805 and again on 9 January 1808).

[356] 'Urians Reise um die Welt' and 'Die Gunst des Augenblicks' mentioned in the following letter.

[357] Zelter had mentioned his completion of this setting on 12 June 1809, but failed to send it; it is enclosed in his letter to Goethe on 21 February 1810.

recently that he had only fully recovered from his terrible illness[358] through the cheerful songs of the Liedertafel. I, too, would be inclined to complain to you about the German poets, who are too serious in their poems, and I imagine you could talk to these good people cheerfully and tell them not to express themselves too pensively and gloomily. One should get one's fill of moaning and groaning in everyday life.

I am delighted that Eberwein is getting on well because he must be very industrious, especially if his stay in Berlin is to be useful to him. A talent must become fully developed and that can only happen through constant activity.

*Macbeth* is being performed here in Schiller's translation as well as the cast will allow.[359] [...] Then finally, after a long wait, we are going to have *Iphigenie* with Gluck's music at the theatre.[360] The general public show no great enthusiasm because we are not so lucky as to be able to cast the two female roles suitably.

24 January: [Wilhelm] von Humboldt has sent me by post your letter dated 4th of this month as a sign that he will be absent longer than he wanted. I was really delighted to see my songs praised by you. 'Herr Urian' is well received here and is sung at almost every gathering. The song included here belongs to the melodramatic[361] and will not scare off singers if it is performed perfectly. Eberwein will see to it that it is performed in the correct way [...].

Eight years ago I left a composition, 'Der Müllerin Reue', with you in Weimar without retaining a copy. I remember this composition only in so far as it appeared to be successful and you liked it. Could you look for this piece and send me a copy? I want to look for and have [in my keeping] what I would wish to retain. When you are in full health and feel inspired, you think only of [creative] work and form. What you liked I will preserve in love, even if it is the smallest thing:

---

[358] Wolf had been seriously ill with malaria.

[359] Following Burger's translation of *Macbeth* in 1806, Schiller's adaptation of the translation was first staged in Berlin on 11 December 1809, with an overture and incidental music by the music director Friedrich Ludwig Seidl (1765–1831). Further performances were given on 18 and 31 December 1809.

[360] Christoph Willibald Gluck's *Iphigenie in Aulis* was first performed in the Königliches Opernhaus in Berlin with ballet music composed by Bernhard Anselm Weber (1764–1821). The festive occasion (not mentioned by Zelter) marked the return of the royal couple from East Prussia, where they had stayed during Napoleon's invasion of Berlin. The reviewer in the *Vossiche Zeitung* (28 December 1809) only devoted a few lines to the performance, noting the full house. A longer report appeared in the *AMZ* 12 (1810), no. 16, 17 January, column 253.

[361] Zelter's setting of Goethe's poem 'Weltseele', which bears the performance direction 'melodramatic (pathetisch) and spiritual (spirituos)'.

Love and art make the every small thing great
He whom the poet lauds is given a forum; the individual
Allies himself to the choir of heroes.[362]

In 'Johanna Sebus' I have tried to do what you once wrote to me about the dramatic form of romances.[363] The composition is sketched and finished but not in an accomplished manner, and since my journey to Königsberg I have not been able to find a quiet hour to devote to it. If one goes out from oneself every time, out from the same point, then life and art will always lead onto new radii, new forms, and it is hard, so to speak, to enter in again from the beginning. [...]

## 116. Zelter

Berlin, 17 to 21 February 1810

Here, my divine friend, is my – our – 'Johanna [Sebus]'[364] to whom, at all costs, I wanted to do no harm [...]

Apart from the fortepiano I am asking Eberwein not to rehearse the other instruments[365] until the choir (which should not be more than nine members) perform really well. The singers must vocalize uniformly: that means if two or more people sing the vowel 'o' together and one sings 'a' and the others sing 'o', the expression is unclear; therefore, they must accentuate all the same vowels together.

The dam bursts [...] melts [...] disappears [...] disappeared [...][366] If this is performed properly, the composition will be effective. It is written that way.

I ask you then not to let the music out of your hands as I have already sent it for publication in Leipzig.[367] It should come out at Easter. It can, of course, be transcribed in your home.

---

[362] Quotation from Goethe's elegy 'Euphrosyne'.

[363] GZ 26 August 1799.

[364] The autograph, dated 30 January 1810, is in Goethe's music collection (GSA 32/74).

[365] In contrast to Zelter's published version, this manuscript is scored with additional instruments in the coda ('Bedeckt ist alles mit Wasserschwall ...'): flute, violin, viola, cello, drums and timpani. An arrangement for orchestra, scored by Zelter's friend Johann Christoph Schultz and published by Johann-Wolfgang Schottländer, makes the false assumption that it is the first orchestral setting of the cantata; see Zelter, 'Johanna Sebus', *JbSK* 9 (1931), pp. 291–94. The manuscript sent to Goethe in this version is, in fact, the first orchestration of the cantata.

[366] Here Zelter indicates the slight variations made with each refrain.

[367] Contrary to his original desire to have the cantata published by Cotta, Zelter sent the manuscript to the publishers Ambrosius Kühnel in Leipzig on 17 February 1810. The

I cannot express in words the joy you gave me on the 14th of this month with the poem[368] received for my Liedertafel. I have set it to music already. It shall be performed next time, on 10 March on the birthday of our Queen and than you will receive it directly. [...]

We usually print the words of songs which we sing during festivities at the Liedertafel. As I look upon your song as our property, I shall have it printed with the rest, unless you expressly forbid it; so, if you do not wish it to be printed, let me know in the course of the month.[369]

I don't know whether Eberwein brought you 'Trommellied' by Voß[370] and whether you already know it? It is completely cheerful, but there is a fatal transcription mistake in the score: the last note of the melody should be in all voices, not a minim with a fermata, but a short staccato crotchet and the final drum beat must fall on this crotchet. I will ask Eberwein to correct this detail in his manuscript and the singers must practice to catch this final beat exactly.

21 February: While we are on the subject I am sending you the music to your poem[371] with this [letter] before I have heard it. Should I find something to improve in it, it can be inserted later. Would you like to give it a title?[372] It must have a name. The post is leaving. God be with you!

---

work appeared in 1810 with a commemorative title, 'Johanna Sebus' by Goethe. In memory of the 17-year-old beautiful girl from Brienen, who, on 13 January 1809, perished in drift ice on the Rhine, while saving others. For voice and piano, set to music by Zelter.' The first edition was published by A. Kühnel in Leipzig in March 1810, the second was published by Kühnel's successor, C. F. Peters.

[368] 'Frisch! der Wein soll reichlich fließen'.

[369] Zelter's through-composed choral setting, 'Rechenschaft', was published by C. Salfeld in Berlin in 1810.

[370] 'Tafellied für die Freimauerer'. Zelter's setting is entitled 'Tafellied' (GSA 32/44). The title 'Trommellied' comes from the refrain, 'Trommelt auf den Tisch!', where Zelter gives the direction, 'everyone drums on the table here and ends with a strong accent on the last short note'.

[371] Zelter's through-composed setting of Goethe's poem 'Frisch! der Wein soll reichlich fließen' for mixed choir and soloists; the autograph is in Goethe's music collection (GSA 32/13).

[372] The poem, of which there is no manuscript copy in Goethe's hand, is written without a title in Zelter's handwritten copy. In the following letter, Goethe suggests the title 'Pflicht und Frohsinn'; Zelter referred to it as 'Ächzlied' on 4 April; eventually it was published with the title 'Rechenschaft' and Goethe adopted this in Cotta's second edition of his works.

## 117. Zelter

Berlin, 25 February 1810

In the manuscript of 'Johanna Sebus', which should be in your hands by now, I have just discovered all kinds of mistakes which I entrust to Eberwein for correction:[373]

In all four *piano* repeats of the first choir 'Der Damm ...' in the tenor part, eighth bar, the fifth note should not be G but a minor third lower: E.

In the third choral repetition, 'Der Damm verschwindet! Die Welle braust!', in the soprano line, second bar, third note, the word 'braust' should not be B but a fifth higher: F sharp.

In the timpani part some notes are missing, therefore I enclose the page.

When you have heard the music sung through a few times, I would like to know from you: whether your idea is fulfilled and whether anything has got lost and doesn't come through. [...]

There is no lack of successful passages. You should make your judgement about the whole piece. Perhaps the plastic arts are a more advantageous field, as they place all the elements before the eye and can give it a complementary effect. I hear Bury has painted the scene but I haven't seen it. Let it be what it will; we have done our best.

'But enough, you Muses! In vain I strove to portray what does not sing in the song; what you haven't granted to the song; so you gave me the writer friend, the friendly poet. Just as everything comes from you, I have everything from him.'[374]

## 118. Goethe

Weimar, 6 March 1810

Your music to 'Johanna Sebus' I have as yet only heard imperfectly, but enough for me to assure you that I think it is excellent. I would have to write at some length, if I were to try and tell you everything that went through my mind on this occasion. I will only say one thing: that you have made very important use of something for

---

[373] In the manuscript bequeathed to us (GSA 32/74) Zelter's corrections are all carefully inserted (in pencil, with the original entries recognizable in ink), and the timpani part has been completed.

[374] Zelter's poetic thanks to Goethe in the form of a parody of the last four lines of Goethe's elegy from *Alexis und Dora*: 'But enough, O Muses! In vain you attempt to portray how misery and happiness succeed one another in a lover's heart. When love has inflicted its wounds, you cannot heal them; but they can be soothed, dear Muses, only by you.'

which I have no name, but which is called imitation, word painting, among other things – something which with other composers leads to error and goes astray.

It is a kind of symbolism for the ear, where the subject, in so far as it is in motion or not in motion, is neither imitated nor painted, but produced in the imagination, in a way that is quite peculiar and impossible to grasp, so that the thing described and the describer appear to stand in scarcely any relation to one another.

It is a matter of course that in music thunder can roll and waves roar quite naturally. But it is surprising how you have expressed the negation, 'Kein Damm, kein Feld' by a disjointed, interrupted passage[375] and also the anticipation of pleasure before the passage 'Doch Suschens Bild'.[376] Let me stop here, as I should have to discuss the whole [setting] as well as the details. I hope to hear it again several times soon and to enjoy it completely – which is better than reflection and criticism. Your corrections arrived safely and have been inserted.[377]

As for the song,[378] it could be called 'Pflicht und Frohsinn'. Continue as you are doing, and as often as it is sung, let some genial fellow add a new verse or sing it instead of some other one. I have not yet heard the melody; lately things have been too unsettled around here.

Now goodbye, and let me have Voß's 'Trommelied', for Eberwein did not bring it with him. Our little society arranged a musical performance the other day in the theatre,[379] when your 'In Flammen nähet Gott'[380] and 'Die Gunst des Augenblicks', among other things, were most effective.

---

[375] Before the choir sing the words 'Kein Damm! Kein Feld!', the choir and soloists have five bars rest as the piano accompaniment leads into the final passage.

[376] The music for the verse, 'Doch Suschens Bild schwebt überall', is a variation of what has gone before, which is next heard in the solo setting of the verse 'Bedeckt ist alles mit Wasserschwall' before being taken up by the piano and finally voiced by solo voice accompanied by piano.

[377] See Goethe's letter to Eberwein, 3 March 1810, *WA* IV/51, p. 282.

[378] Zelter's setting of Goethe's poem 'Frisch! der Wein soll reichlich fließen'.

[379] On 22 February 1810 Goethe's domestic chamber choir mounted a concert under Eberwein's direction in the Weimar theatre. Goethe's diary records 'an evening of musical entertainment' in the theatre. In addition to the two songs mentioned in the letter, the programme included further compositions by Zelter ('Das Vaterland'; 'Generalbeichte' and 'Herr Urian'); Mozart ('Liebes Mädchen wir sind hier'; 'Ich armes welsches Teufel' and 'Bandel-Terzett') and Carl Eberwein ('Lasset eure Lieder hören'; 'Willkommen Dir, des neuen Jahres Sonne!' and 'Holder Genius des Landes') as well as music by Jommelli, Kaiser, Salieri, Cauer, Ferrari and Wenzel Müller.

[380] Zelter's setting of Christoph August Tiedge's 'Hymnus an die Sonne'.

## 119. Zelter

Berlin, 14 to 20 March 1810

Our little song[381] made quite a sensation in that some are secretly delighted with it and at the same time also get annoyed by it. Actually we are not so bad: we only act that way now and again. It was sung at the birthday of Queen [Luise][382] at the Liedertafel and already I hear it sung again here and there and cannot prevent it. Most of all it pleased Prince Radziwill,[383] who was among my guests on the day. This man takes great pains in setting your verses to music and for a foreigner he has hit the right tone happily enough.

Your letter dated the 6th of this month has just arrived, which I read with great edification. It is really satisfying to be in agreement with the poet about the fundamental meaning of the poem. If the poet understands the composer, then the latter has also understood the poet and everything else is the ordinary material that everyone is capable of who understands his trade.

Your thoughts about the composition of 'Johanna Sebus' are very informative for me in so far as they highlight the points in the piece which the composition has to separate before achieving a totality. If I have not failed here, then I will not worry about the rest, which has its own direction.

Since the beginning and the end of the poem are of different sentiments, but such that the latter follows from the first, filling in the not too considerable space between both ends always remains a challenge, if the stages of change and intensification are not to appear disconnected or feeble, to which end the chorus is industriously employed as you will probably notice at the passage: 'verloren sein – sind alle fern'.

If you would only be inclined to entrust a larger work to me where one would be able to really let go. It would be a real shame if we would some day have to

---

[381]  Zelter's setting of Goethe's poem 'Frisch! der Wein soll reichlich fließen'.

[382]  10 March 1810.

[383]  Prince Antoni Heinrich Radziwill (1775–1833), Polish cellist and composer, important patron of music. Radziwill was one of seven people who responded to Beethoven's request to act as patron to the publication of his Mass in D; Beethoven dedicated his *Namensfeier* overture to him, op. 115, and he was also an important patron to Chopin. As a composer he is best known for his music to Goethe's *Faust*. Scenes from Radizwill's *Faust* – which is the first setting of Goethe's *Faust* – were performed at a private performance in Berlin in 1816; they were performed again at Monbijou, near Berlin, on 10 June 1819 and the entire performance was repeated on 24 May 1820. Radziwill worked on the score until his death in 1833. The complete work was performed by the Sing-Akademie on 25 October 1835 and the score was published the same year. It was performed by the Sing-Akademie 25 times between 1835 and 1888. It was also used as incidental music for the first official performance of *Faust* in Berlin in 1888.

part without producing such a work for the world, which we had set about together with proper collaboration.

You will show little interest in an opera or suchlike, given the frenzy of musical production. [...] In any event a German subject would be the most appropriate: a Hercules would not be scoffed at and ultimately I would put up with Orpheus, who could still be presented as he has not been seen before.

'Trommellied' is enclosed.[384] I have not written out the words so that the letter will not be too large. The poem is in the new edition of Voß's collected works published in 1802, second volume, page 132.[385]

19 March: [Wilhelm] von Humboldt[386] sent me your verses of 30 January, in which I take the greatest pleasure. I cannot comprehend how you clothe such marvellous ideas in such a calm style of writing. When I have your verses in front of me, it always seems to me as if they themselves are nestled in melodic forms and need to be sung. [...]

20 March: As you have to forgive so much, perhaps you will forgive your verses when you find them planted on my territory. For I can only enjoy the beautiful if I myself assimilate it. What function has beauty in the world, if not to make it more lovely?

## 120. Zelter

Berlin, 4 to 5 April 1810

For some weeks past I have not been myself; perhaps it was the withering March wind, or some other outside influence, that made me, not exactly ill, but rather depressed and out of sorts. I eat without relish and life, which I value, holds no joy.

So yesterday afternoon I took no wine; I did not want it and went to sleep after dinner on the couch. Meanwhile my understanding postman laid your blue envelope on my chest and I joyfully recognized it on awaking. Before I opened it, I called for a glass of wine to complete my good cheer. As my daughter was pouring it out, I broke open the letter and shouted: 'Ergo bibamus'.[387] She was so startled that she let the bottle fall; I caught it, once more I was blithe and cheerful, and the wine, probably from gratitude for its salvation, did its job.

---

[384] Zelter's four-part setting of Johann Heinrich Voß's 'Tafellieds für Freimauer'. The autograph is contained in Goethe's music collection (GSA 32/44).

[385] Johann Heinrich Voß, *Sämtliche Gedichte* (6 vols, Königsberg: Friedrich Nicolovius, 1802). The poem is in vol. 4, *Oden und Lieder*, pp. 132–7. The first five volumes of this edition are in Zelter's library.

[386] Goethe, *Die romantische Poesie*, MA 9, p. 245.

[387] Title and refrain from Goethe's poem, 'Hier sind wir versammlet zu löblichem Tun ...' (*MA* 9, p. 35) which he sent to Zelter on 27 March 1810.

So that the first impression might not ebb away, I sent for pen and ink and set your poem to music there and then. Looking at the clock, I found it was time to go to the Sing-Akademie and after that there was a meeting of the Liedertafel. Forty members were present. I read the poem aloud; at the end of each strophe, they all shouted of their own accord in unison, as though in a double chorus, 'Bibamus!', laying such a significant stress on the long vowel, that the floors resonated, and the vault of the great hall seemed to lift off. This gave me the melody at once, and here you have it, exactly as it composed itself.[388] If it is all right the way it is, I claim no part in it; it is all yours, and yours alone.

Your interest in the Liedertafel will inevitably bear fruit. The powerful German songs increasingly have the desired effect. Instead of a weary, tired life, a lively reinforced sense emerges, which no one before dared to show. One can stand up straight: the path becomes more certain through sheer joy. [...] There is nothing but good prospects here.

The delight that you thought of us so soon again enlivened everyone. Your health was toasted like no one else's. The groaning song was called for and they sang it as animatedly as the last time. They understood it much more today. Between every verse they tippled and shouted, 'Long live duty!' and the last stanza was repeated with hearty determination.

Amid the hustle and bustle that holds us back and makes us weary of work, I have thought up a secret aspiration, which I now nurture every day. For a considerable time I have already been plagued by gout in my wrist, which has got so out of hand that I can hardly grip anything without pain. Apart from the piano I cannot play a single instrument any longer and must live in fear of losing that one. I have always heard the baths at Teplitz praised and I would like to visit them. [...]

5 April: Yesterday my work was interrupted by Reichardt, who had just arrived. We would have four Kapellmeister together here again.[389] If the senior Kapellmeister in the south[390] wanted to accept their rotation, he would be helpful to us. I'd be surprised if he is not looking for something we don't have. I am more sorry for him than for many others. I have become accustomed to his peculiarities. I would not want him to be other than he is. But not everyone thinks the same and he will have to see where he stands. [...]

---

[388] Although enclosed with this letter, Zelter's setting is not in Goethe's music collection.

[389] Johann Friedrich Reichardt (1752–1814), Vincenzo Righini (1756–1812), Bernhard Anselm Weber (1764–1821), Friedrich Heinrich Himmel (1765–1814).

[390] Zelter is alluding to Reichardt, who, from 1810, no longer held a position as Kapellmeister in Berlin. Two years previously (November 1808 to April 1809) he had travelled to Vienna and had tried in vain to find a new position as Kapellmeister in one of the opera houses. The reference to the south refers to this Viennese visit.

I am busy with my Easter concerts at present,[391] which I don't have the heart for this time. If I knew you were among my audience, then the rest could go wherever they liked.

### 121. Goethe

Jena, 17 April 1810

The warmest thanks for your practical reply. Unfortunately I am separated from my little choir and so I can only celebrate 'Ergo Bibamus' with the eyes and with the throat. Tell me first of all what songs are repeated most often at your Liedertafel, so that I can get a feeling for your guests and discover what type of poetry pleases their ear. When one knows that, one can give all kinds of fun to one's friends.

Follow up your idea of going to Teplitz. I am convinced that this spa would be very beneficial for me, after Carlsbad. [...]

### 122. Zelter

Berlin, 24 to 30 April 1810

As our Liedertafel is officially concerned with song, everything performed by the members of the table must be sung.

Every time the newest pieces form the beginning as a rule and the poet and composer are able to demand that anything that doesn't succeed immediately or isn't understood is repeated as often as they find necessary. Until now I have been very concerned that something new came to the table every time; we have certainly had much that is new.

Song has the capacity to bind entertainment together and to maintain focus on a subject. From it the memory of a passage from a lovely popular poem often arises which is then called for and immediately sung. [...] The songs which automatically come up in this way most often are: 'Bundeslied'; 'Generalbeichte'; 'Herr Urian'; 'Freude schöner Götterfunken'; Voß's 'Trommellied'; 'Ein Musikant wollt' fröhlich sein' from the second part of *Des Knaben Wunderhorns*;[392] an old Latin song in the style of Suetonius:

---

[391] On Good Friday, 20 April, Zelter conducted Graun's *Der Tod Jesu* and on Easter Sunday he conducted a performance of his oratorio *Die Auferstehung und Himmelfahrt Jesu*.

[392] Zelter's settings of 'Bundeslied' ('In allen guten Stunden'); 'Generalbeichte' ('Lasset heut im edeln Kreis'); 'Herr Urian' ('Wenn jemand eine Reise tut', Matthias Claudius); 'An die Freude' ('Freude schöner Götterfunken', Schiller); 'Trommellied' (Voß) and 'Fuge' ('Ein Musikant wollt' fröhlich sein ...').

Gallias Caesar subegit
Nicomedes Caesarem.
Ecce Caesar nunc triumphat
Qui subegit Gallias.
Nicomedes non triumphat
Qui subegit Caesarem.[393]

And lots more! The last work is sung splendidly by two choirs and Privy Councillor Wolf, who wrote the poem, appeared happy with the metrical treatment. It was repeated many times – six to eight times – because everyone really felt like doing it as the metre catches on wonderfully.

If I am looking forward to something, it is this: finally to embrace you again after five years.[394] Everything must be done to bring this about. My Easter concerts are over[395] and I am happier with my income than with what has been achieved. I could say I was rich if I didn't have to pay debts. […]

## 123. Zelter

Teplitz, 30 June 1810

[…] Kaufmann is the inventor of an instrument which he calls a harmonichord.[396] This instrument has many similarities with the common-place harmonica and at the same time [has] something of the organ. It seems to me, however, much more perfect than the harmonica because it plays lighter and more purely. At the right distance – especially in the evening in the open air – it must be an unbelievably beautiful effect and so I have not wanted to delay directing this fine young man to you. One cannot hear anything purer than the beautiful tones of this instrument

---

[393] Zelter's setting of 'Cantus martialis Romanus' from Gaius Suetonius Tranquillus's biography on Caesar (chapter 49): 'Caesar subjugated the Gauls/ Nicomedes subjugated Caesar./ Behold, Caesar now triumphs/ who subjugated the Gauls./ Nicomedes does not triumph/ who subjugated Caesar.'

[394] The last time Goethe and Zelter met was in Lauchstädt in August 1805.

[395] Zelter was unhappy with both performances, as were the critics. Unfavourable reviews – especially of Zelter's oratorio – were published in the *Spenersche Zeitung* and the *Vossische Zeitung* on 24 and 26 April. Friedrich Rellstab's review in the *Vossische Zeitung* was publicly answered on 1 May 1810, signed by 37 members of the Sing-Akademie and published in: *AMZ* 12 (1810), no. 33, 16 May 1810, column 527; *MA* 20.3, p. 262.

[396] In 1808 Johann Gottfried and Johann Friedrich Kaufmann (father and son) invented the harmonichord, a kind of upright (giraffe) piano, in which the strings are set in vibration not by the blow of the hammer but by indirectly transmitted friction. Carl Maria von Weber explored the possibilities of the harmonichord, which in tone resembled the glass harmonica, in his Adagio and Rondo for harmonichord and orchestra.

and the harmonica, which is unpleasant to play and hardly ever so well tempered, will very likely be supplanted through it.

### 124. Goethe

Carlsbad, 4 July 1810

[…] I intend to visit the master of the harmonichord at his invitation, and introduce him to other music lovers.[…]

### 125. Zelter

Teplitz, 8 July 1810

With regard to a social life, it is very impoverished here, especially since Privy Councillor Wolf departed. Still, yesterday I made the acquaintance of the poet Carpani, who, from now on, will compensate me through his operas and spiritual poems.[397]

Will you be so kind as to send the enclosed letter to Körner,[398] as it contains something musical? […] I am now thinking seriously of the trip to Vienna because I don't see how I can arrange it if it doesn't happen now.[399]

### 126. Zelter

Prague, 28 to 30 July 1810

I arrived here on Sunday 22nd, just in time to go to the theatre. To my delight I suddenly saw before me my former student, little Minna Unzelmann,[400] who

---

[397] Before Zelter met the Italian writer Giuseppe Carpani in Teplitz, he had contributed to a collection of arias edited by the writer: *In questa tomba oscura. Arietta con accompagnamento di Piano-Forte composta in diverse maniere da molti Autori* (Vienna, 1808). Later, in July 1819, Zelter met Carpani again in Vienna; in his account of his travels he mentions *Le Haydine*, the well-known Haydn biography in epistolary form.

[398] The letter has not been handed down.

[399] Zelter did not travel to Vienna: from 14 to 21 July he was in Carlsbad; from there he travelled to Prague, returning to Teplitz where he remained until 23 August.

[400] Wilhelmine Unzelmann (1802–71), actress in Berlin and Prague; daughter of the actress Friederike Bethmann. Of the performance Zelter wrote to his sister, Luise Syring: 'She recognized me immediately in the stalls and from then on she performed so that her body was always turned to me' (GSA 95/I, 8. 16, no. 27).

happily played the pleasant role of the cobbler's wife (in the opera *Die verwandelten Weiber*)[401] to applause. She has really come on in a short time. She sang purely and performed with ease. After the finale she was called for and applauded. On Monday Kotzebue's Intermezzo was performed; I was not exactly impressed by it; and on Tuesday *Die Schweizerfamilie*[402] [was performed], which I found delightful. The music for this opera is exceptionally charming and entertaining and I would say, for the most part, with the most excellent forces. Mademoiselle Müller,[403] daughter of the famous composer Wenzel Müller,[404] makes a great Frau von Heygendorff.[405] Attractive figure, light movements, ease in speaking, control of the voice are natural to her. Just as she doesn't do anything that is too much with these rare resources, neither does she do anything wrong. Yesterday she played Sargin.[406] I cannot stand this work or the laboriously rich music. I listened through it yesterday purely because of this girl. One cannot see anything more noble, more agreeable than this young girl in traditional male costume. Feet and hands, thighs and upper body are in perfect proportion and move with unbelievable daintiness. Only the youth and sweetness of the voice betrayed the woman. I will make an effort to speak to her and especially to congratulate her. At the same time I was sad that her voice will not hold out. [...]

Yesterday lunchtime I was invited to a Lenten supper by the prelate of the Strahofer convent,[407] by the name of Milo Griem.[408] That's the way one likes to fast! For a private library, the collection of books appears very significant and contains interesting manuscripts of Bohemian history. The church is splendidly laid out and has the best organ gallery I have ever seen. In the librarian, Father Gottfried [Dlabacz], and an approximately 60-year-old Father Octavian [Joseph Prutky], I found a couple of people I can identify with.

---

[401] *Der lustige Schuster oder die verwandelten Weiber*, comic opera by Ferdinando Paer (libretto from the Italian, *Poche, ma buone, ossia le Donne cambiate* of Giuseppe Maria Foppa).

[402] Joseph Weigl, *Die Schweizerfamilie*, Singspiel (libretto from the French, *La Famille Suisse* by Ignaz Franz Castelli).

[403] Therese Grünbaum, née Müller (1791–1876), singer, engaged in Prague from 1807 to 1816.

[404] Wenzel Müller (1767–1835), composer and Kapellmeister in Vienna and for a brief period in Prague (1807–1813).

[405] Henriette *Caroline* Friederike von Heygendorff née Jagemann (1777–1848), singer and actress in Weimar (1797–1828), Carl August's lover, ennobled with the name 'von Heygendorff' from 1809.

[406] The title role in Ferdinando Paer's opera, *Sargines, oder Der Zögling der Liebe* (libretto from the Italian, *Sargino ossia l'Allievo dell'amore* by Giuseppe Maria Foppa).

[407] Premonstratensian monastery in Strahov, Prague.

[408] Johann Nepomuk Grün (1751–1816).

Monday, 30 July: I have already had some fun with our canon.[409] I wrote it in the family album of a [female] singer, who didn't know what I meant by it. Apropos it occurred to me that I wrote it out in four parts on your manuscript paper, at least that's how I remember it. However, it is in fact for six voices and a voice can enter on the second crotchet of every bar. The canon can also be sung solo or in two, three, four, five and six parts. [...]

### 127. Zelter

Berlin, 3 November 1810

Along with the new composition which I enclose, you will receive 'Schneidercourage',[410] once again, because I think I made some alterations; you can destroy the old copy.

### 128. Goethe

Weimar, 18 November 1810

[...] And to add on immediately now, how much joy you have given us through the last consignment of compositions[411] as well as through 'Diogenes',[412] which has become a favourite of our small audience.[413] I hope your Liedertafel will have had no less pleasure in the same [pieces].

The weekly musical meeting, as small as the institution may be, provides me the invaluable pleasure, which I otherwise would have to forgo, of hearing your

---

[409] Zelter's canonic setting of Goethe's verse 'O, wie lallt das Kind so faul', first published in *WA* (1893) under the title 'Singschule'; *MA* 9, p. 49. Zelter's manuscript, entitled *Canone perpetuo a 4 Voci* (GSA 32/23), is corrected in Goethe's hand to: *Canone perpetuo a 6 Voci*.

[410] Zelter's setting of Goethe's poem 'Schneidercourage' ('Es ist ein Schluß gefallen'), which Zelter had perhaps received from Goethe in Teplitz or Carlsbad.

[411] Zelter's settings of Goethe's poems 'Es ist ein Schuß gefallen' and 'Zwischen Weizen und Korn'.

[412] Zelter's three-part canonic setting of Goethe's poem 'So wälz' ich Unterlaß' (published in 1815 under the title 'Genialisch Treiben' in Goethe's collected works). The composition is not in Goethe's music collection; the enclosed manuscript is possibly the Düsseldorf autograph which is dated 'Teplitz, 22 August 1810', but incorrectly dated '1820' in the catalogue (GMD: *Katalog der Musikalien*, Nr. 1544a).

[413] Riemer later wrote of Zelter's 'superb as well as humorous canon' which was 'premiered by Goethe's *Hauskapelle* on the 4 November 1810 and from then on performed repeatedly as one of their favourite pieces', *Mittelungen über Goethe*, vol. 2 (Berlin, 1841), p. 542f.

superb works repeatedly and becoming acquainted with them. 'Johanna Sebus' and 'Die Gunst des Augenblicks' will be performed today and I am already looking forward to it. Let me know soon how *Pandora* is going[414] or whatever else you have taken up to work on. The writer of this letter[415] has dug out some songs and jokes again,[416] which will reach you in good time and are likely to give pleasure both to you and to others. 'Der Schneider'[417] is really excellent and always gives great satisfaction.

At the end of this week we are to hear Paer's *Achilles* in Italian;[418] Brizzi has arrived,[419] and will sing the part of the hero for us. Our other singers are either polishing their Italian, or beginning to learn the language; whatever happens, we shall have a nice performance [...]

In conclusion, let me tell you about a curious plan we have, that is, a performance of *Faust* just as it is – insofar as it can be done.[420] Perhaps you could help us with some music, more especially for the Easter song[421] and the slumber song, 'Schwindet ihr dunklen Wölbungen droben'.

---

[414] Goethe is enquiring about Zelter's setting of *Pandora*, which the composer had taken up in Teplitz once more; on his return to Berlin the work was put aside again due to a heavy workload for the Sing-Akademie.

[415] Goethe's amanuensis, Friedrich Wilhelm Riemer, who later prepared these letters for publication.

[416] Perhaps Goethe's poem 'Problem' (*MA* 9, p. 50) which Zelter set on 22 November 1810.

[417] Zelter's setting of Goethe's poem 'Es ist ein Schuß gefallen'.

[418] Ferdinando Paer (1771–1839), Italian composer, and one of the leading representatives of the Italian operatic school at the close of the last century. He settled in France and became Maitre-de-chapelle to Napoleon, whom he accompanied to Warsaw and Posen in 1806. His most famous operas include the sequel to Mozart's *Marriage of Figaro* (1797) and *Leonora*, which has the same plot as Beethoven's *Fidelio* (pre-dating it by a year). Paer's opera, *Achilles* (libretto by Giovanni De Gamerra), was performed on 28 November 1810 in Weimar, with further performances on 1, 15 and 19 December.

[419] Antonio Giovanni Maria Brizzi (1770–1854), Italian court and chamber singer in Munich. Carl August had got to know him in Eisenberg through Prince Lobkowitz and asked Goethe to engage him as a guest performer in November. Difficulties in rehearsals of the Italian opera *Achilles*, proposed by Brizzi, caused Goethe to reject, or to be precise, 'postpone' Brizzi's appearance until the following year; since Brizzi did not consent and demanded full salary, he was engaged nonetheless. Brizzi arrived on 16 November. In November and December 1810 he appeared many times in Paer's *Achilles*. See Goethe's correspondence with Carl August between September and December 1810 and also Goethe's letter to Brizzi on 4 and 22 October 1810, *WA* IV/30, pp. 155–7.

[420] Goethe noted down ideas for a performance of *Faust* in his diary on 13 November. The idea was put aside at first and then abandoned. The first performance of *Faust I* in Weimar took place on 29 August 1829.

[421] 'Christ ist erstanden', *Faust I*, v. 737ff.

## 129. Zelter

Berlin, 16 to 20 February 1811

At last I have had enough time to myself to be able to consider my debt to you. I have to observe, report and make arrangements and can neither find the beginning nor the purpose in the accursed music world, in which everyone is so self-satisfied that my flesh creeps. Everything would go well if we could do everything in peace and move forward step by step; but everything has to be reported and we have to fill up reams of paper. This is at the cost of joy and courage. [...]

As to *Pandora*, as good as nothing has happened the whole time, although I have, at the same time, finished a fine number of little songs, which come [to me] short but complete and instantaneous outpourings. I will send you what is finished of *Pandora*, when I get to it. [...]

But the real reason why I have not written for so long is that I wanted to send you straight away what you wanted for *Faust*[422] and had just started to do so when I received your letter; then irksome things occurred and the thing had to remain lying and is still there. So you will have to get music from elsewhere; I cannot do it now because it needs an uninterrupted stretch of time; also I would have to speak with you about it in person, because the thing is no trifle in so far as it has to fit into the whole: one must do that; all the rest comes from the gods. Your undertaking is as beautiful as it is audacious. Prince Radziwill will arrive with you around the time of the performance.[423]

## 130. Goethe

Weimar, 28 February 1811

[...] I cannot quarrel with you for declining to compose the music to *Faust*.[424] My proposal was rather whimsical like the project itself. [...] Now farewell, dear sun, and continue to give forth warmth and light.

Goethe

Enclosed: 'Sicilianlied', 'Finnisches Lied', 'Schweizerlied'

---

[422] The incidental music for *Faust*, including settings of 'Ostergesang' ('Christ ist erstanden') and 'Einschläferungslied'.

[423] As with the planned performance, Radziwill's meeting with Goethe was postponed; his first visit to the poet was not until 25 November 1813.

[424] Zelter had relinquished Goethe's request for incidental music for *Faust I* on 16 February 1811; plans for the performance seem to have been pushed back by other scheduled performances, namely Brizzi's appearance in *Achilles* and *Der standhafte Prinz*.

## 131. Zelter

Beginning of March 1811

[...] Everyone here is talking about your performance of *Der standhafte Prinz, Don Fernando von Portugal*;[425] it must have been excellent. I have a similar work in front of me: I will perform an old, very fine piece of music, which the members have brought to my attention. But they want their old licentious way, which I will not endure and that causes quarrels and is very painful. [...]

At last I have also seen and heard the recently acclaimed Parisian Opera, *Die Vestalin*.[426] It is a real joke and the gentlemen of the Paris Conservatoire – who would not make up their minds as to which of two excellent people they should award the prize because they really have no critical standard and trilling and chirping is all they are interested in – were forced to see the Emperor put his finger into the pie and award the prize to a young artist, who, if he is past 25, will never do anything much. The libretto is flexible enough for an opera and there is room for music. Spontini[427] has used it like a boy, whose hands have just been set free from swaddling bands for the first time, and he lays about him with both fists so violently that the pieces fly about one's ears.

Bettina wanted to be married last Sunday week.[428] However, both parties had forgotten a few trifles, such as the calling of the banns, the hiring of lodgings, the procuring of a bed and similar preparations. I imagine, therefore, that things must remain as they are until after Lent.

---

[425] Goethe's production of Calderón's tragedy *Der standhafte Prinz, Don Fernando von Portugal* (in August Wilhelm Schlegel's translation) was first performed on 30 January 1811, with a second performance on 6 February.

[426] *La Vestale* (1807) and *Ferdinand Cortez* (1809), two of Spontini's best-known operas, were written for Paris and were the first stage works to reflect the taste of the Napoleonic era for operas with sumptuous production and plots with historical and political significance. The Berlin premiere of *Die Vestalin* (libretto by Etienne de Jouy, translated by Carl Herklots) took place on 18 January 1811 in the royal opera house. See *AMZ* 113 (1811), no. 7, 13 February, column 132 and no. 11, 13 March, column 195. Zelter went to the fourth performance on 27 February.

[427] The Italian theatrical composer Gaspare Luigi Pacifico Spontini (1774–1851).

[428] Elizabeth *Bettine* Brentano (1785–1859) married Achim von Arnim (1781–1831) on 11 March 1811.

## 132. Goethe

Weimar, 18 March 1811

[...] May you succeed in every way, in all you do, and in all you write. I imagine how you manage in your Sing-Akademie. Just educate a certain number of pupils and you will be cultivating almost as many adversaries. Every genuine artist must be regarded as one who is protecting something acknowledged as sacred, which he intends to propagate with thoughtfulness and with care. But every age, in its own way, tends towards what is secular, striving to make what is sacred common, what is difficult easy, what is serious amusing: and nothing could be said against this, were it not for the fact that sincerity and humour are thereby utterly destroyed. So much for today! Let me hear from you frequently. 'Johanna Sebus' is often enough asked for at our musical gatherings on a Sunday,[429] and is delightfully performed; I might almost hope that you yourself would be satisfied. We have not yet had it performed with instruments. Eberwein is doing admirably; I wish he could have the good fortune to enjoy another six months of your company and teaching. Our Kapellmeister Müller[430] has a good grip on his orchestra and chorus, as well as the soloists; and with regard to musical enjoyment we certainly have been well off this winter. And for now, from my heart, farewell! I am busy in various ways, and am quietly easing myself away from things, so that I may soon be able to set out again on my summer tour.[431]

## 133. Zelter

Berlin, 21 March 1811

Thanks for the beautiful poems. The Swiss one has been written in a good Swiss; I will just let it ferment, then you will have it.

---

[429] The performances given by Goethe's chamber choir before an invited audience.

[430] August Eberhard Müller (1767–1817) took over the position of Director of the Weimar Court Ensemble, a position which combined teaching duties in the Gymnasium in Weimar (including giving teacher seminars) with the position of Director of Music at the Herderkirche.

[431] Goethe's trip to Carlsbad from 12 May to 1 July 1811.

## 134. Zelter

Berlin, 8 April 1811

This winter our theatre has been very lively. Many new pieces and a number of foreign actors have enlivened it. Reichardt had a new opera performed, *Der Taucher*,[432] which will not appear again. The libretto is too mediocre[433] and the composer, who thinks less of the witchcraft than of the pace, would have done well to have taken more time and fill it in somewhat better, instead of which he runs from one thing to another and collects or spreads political anecdotes.

Madame Schütz (formerly Madame Hendel, before that Madame Meyer and before that Madame Eunike, née Schüler)[434] is here now and her performance is all storm and bluster. I have seen Benda's *Medea*[435] and Kotzebue's *Oktavia*.[436] For a woman who is already sleeping with her fourth husband, something so natural would not be too much. She makes enough effort and screeches and runs and wrenches; I don't like it when context and melody are missing. Essentially it is like a disjointed work soldered together from a hundred fragments which clash horribly.

## 135. Zelter

Berlin, 17 to 25 May 1811

23 May: On 19 May *Ariadne auf Naxos*[437] was performed very proficiently by Madame Wolff. The dialogue in this so-called Duodrama is just too deplorable and our Theseus[438] was like a commercial attendant in disguise. It says much for

---

[432] Johann Friedrich Reichardt's two-act opera, which was unfavourably received, lasted only two performances in Berlin, on 18 and 24 March 1811; see: *AMZ* 13 (1811), no. 16, 17 April, column 275f.

[433] The libretto by Samuel Gottlieb Bürde was inspired by Schiller's ballad.

[434] Henriette Schütz née Schüler (1772–1849), worked as an actress in Berlin from 1796 to 1806. Between 26 March and 27 April 1811 she appeared in no less than ten guest roles as well as in two pantomimes. In contrast to Zelter's harsh criticism, she was very favourably received by the press: *Vossische Zeitung*, 6 November 1811, *MA* 20.3, p. 280.

[435] Georg Benda's melodramatic setting of Friedrich Wilhelm Gotter's tragedy *Medea*, performed at the Königliches National Theater on 28 March 1811 with Henriette Schütz in the title role.

[436] Kotzebue's *Oktavia* was performed on 30 March with Henriette Schütz as Octavia and Iffland as Antonio.

[437] Georg Benda's melodrama *Ariadne auf Naxos*; libretto by Johann Christian Brandes.

[438] The role was played by Franz Mattausch (1767–1833).

Madame Wolff that she could hold herself in her position without bursting into loud laughter over her beloved Theseus. Straight after this Madame Wolff played alongside her husband in the confessions, which ran smoothly and went well and made a suitable impression.

[...] I have resumed work on *Pandora*[439] and a good section from pages 50 to 57 inclusive is almost finished. And what's best is that it appears it will be all of a piece. You will remember that I had already written the opening to this section in Teplitz: 'Mühend versenkt'.[440] On the other hand, I can use nothing at all that I composed two years ago and I would prefer to set it again and relate it to the whole than to patch it up. I must leave pages 58 to 64 (where Eos appears)[441] until the whole is ready in order to set off the light side of the work against the dark. What's really important to know is how Eos' apparition will take place in the theatre, for it should not work like copper: impetuously, in spurts.

### 136. Goethe

Carlsbad, 26 June 1811

May you also in some way be rewarded for what you are doing for *Pandora*. Could I have foreseen your interest in this work, I should have treated the subject differently, and tried to free it from the difficulties for both music and performance which it now has. But now that's the way it is. Continue with it, as it pleases you, and I will see if I can undertake the completion of Part Two.[442] I have planned and sketched out everything, but the figures themselves have become rather distant from me, and I am somewhat astonished at their titanic shapes, when – as yesterday, by chance – I happen to declaim something from it.

May good fortune accompany you on your journey to Silesia, and may your active perseverance be rewarded by proper results – for truly, when one reflects how little the world has responded to your fair and noble achievements, one might well say that the response has not been appropriate. [...]

[...] Himmel has been here for some days[443] and, though suffering, is still the same as ever: cheerful and communicative, and by his playing improving even the roughest instruments. All along I have heard and seen too little of him, and we do not meet very often, owing to his convivial way of life; yet it has occurred

---

[439] Zelter had begun work on this composition during the days spent with Goethe in Teplitz: 7 to 23 August 1810.

[440] 'Mühend versenkt ängstlich der Sinn/ Sich in die Nacht', *Pandora*, v. 949f.

[441] *Pandora*, v. 749f.

[442] In time Goethe believed he had planned *Pandora*, Part One, on too large a scale for continuation and, as a result, Part Two was never written.

[443] In his diary, Goethe records a visit from the Kapellmeister Friedrich Heinrich Himmel on 23 and 24 June 1811, *WA* III/4, p. 214.

to me recently whether I might not be able to publish the maxims, convictions or passions, or whatever you wish to call them, around which he centres his musical settings of lyric poems or by which he is guided. This does not seem to me impossible, and I think I am well on the way; still I have too many deficiencies to be able quit my task so easily. If, at your leisure, you can help me occasionally, you would be doing me a kindness.

### 137. Zelter

Breslau, 12 August 1811

[...] It is generally believed that Himmel has been dead for three weeks.[444] He must have died just after your letter of 26 June, yet the papers would have reported it. His death would have hit me very badly because I have never experienced a better, more comfortable handling of the fortepiano. Nature and opportunity proved themselves very loving in this happy youth and it would be no wonder if the world were to lose the best musician in him.

To go through life supported by the remains of a king, schools and universities, in artistic lands, the castles and chapels of princes is a lot which can support an artist's cheerfulness and humour. In the process he attempted much and could have even been luckier therein, if he had not started where art breaks off. I considered his lyrical talent crucial. If only his boldness and brazenness were quiet and certain, his works would lack nothing. In recent times he would have learned much, if only he had not despised schooling, without which mastery cannot occur. Therefore, like Reichardt he venerates what he could have improved. Ultimately what every artist needs must be learnt first and you yourself have said it clearly enough in 'Künstlers Apotheose': namely that art remains art and natural talent and instinct are not enough without it.

### 138. Zelter

Berlin, 25 October 1811

[...] Since the end of last month I have been in Berlin again, after I had almost spent three months in the Silesian mountains in order to dig up old musical treasures from the dust.[445] The business was not altogether thankless [...] I had only one volume of your works with me on my journey and from this I set

---

[444] This was the second rumour to circulate claiming that the piano virtuoso was dead; he died three years later, on 8 June 1811.

[445] Zelter's journey was recorded in the *AMZ* 13 (1811), no. 34, 21 August, column 580f.

'Die Geheimnisse'.[446] I should be surprised if you will recognize your octaves again; if only I could sing them to you. Some friends didn't find the composition too bad.

[…] I always invite a couple of guests to the Liedertafel; 'Ergo bibamus' is sung so that the hall resounds. This little piece is not bad, so that even Reichardt had to praise it, though he is envious of my songs and he will not gladly acknowledge them. He gets annoyed that you waste your time with all kinds of vermin: I know who he means by that and laugh about it. He pinches your poems from me, shits them onto a piece of manuscript and sends them warm to the press in order to be the first. Or else they are composed afterwards: since he treated 'Der junge Jäger'[447] and many others in a very careless manner. He likes to make every good-natured fool his obedient servant, as I was for a long time, and then he thinks one is ungrateful.

### 139. Goethe

Weimar, 11 November 1811

[…] Brizzi is here again and tonight we listen to 'Ginevra, Queen of Scotland'.[448] I wish that you were here with us, partly to enjoy this festival with us, partly to give me explanation of the composition, whereby my enjoyment would be at the same time judicious and intelligent. […]

If there were to have been some talk about the composition of one of my works, I would not have easily guessed 'Die Geheimnisse'. This news of yours makes me very curious.

---

[446] Zelter's setting of Goethe's epic fragment 'Die Geheimnisse'; the Berlin manuscript (SBB PK: Mus. Ms. Autogr. Zelter 21/3) is dated Breslau, 19 August 1811. There is a second copy in Goethe's music collection (GSA 32/30) scored by a music copyist on a double page which contains two compositions: *Prolog zu den Geheimnissen* and *Die Geheimnisse*. When Zelter sent this manuscript to Weimar is unknown.

[447] Reichardt's setting of Goethe's poem 'Es ist ein Schuß gefallen' (first published in Zelter's setting in the 1810 edition of his *Sämtliche Lieder, Balladen und Romanzen*). Reichardt's setting was published in his *Oden und Lieder von Goethe* vol. 4 (1811). It later appeared under the title 'Schneider-Courage' in vol. 1 of Goethe's collected works (1815).

[448] In his second appearance as guest artist, the Munich singer Antonio Brizzi played the part of Polineso in Simon Mayr's *Ginevra* on 11, 16 and 27 November, followed by a single performance in the title role of Ferdinando Paer's opera *Achilles* on 30 November.

## 140. Goethe

Weimar, 8 April 1812

[…] As the work of my little musical institute[449] has been interrupted this winter, I have been able to enjoy the usual exchange of ideas with you less than usual. […]

At Easter our friend Riemer was appointed Professor at the Gymnasium here;[450] and although I am sorry to lose him, I am happy in the knowledge that he is active, and, what's more, in a way which is suited to his powers and talents. His abilities surpass what is demanded of him here, so he cannot but feel at home in his appointment.

## 141. Zelter

Berlin, 9 to 10 April 1812

[…] Dr Sibbern from Copenhagen[451] is asking me to deliver something to Weimar for him and so I am taking this opportunity to send our songbook,[452] which, as a favour to me, the gentlemen have had published during my absence in Silesia. I am almost ashamed to send it to you because it is teeming with misprints, which upset me every time I look at it. One would almost have to be everything and do everything oneself; no one is any good. That's how it is with the new edition of my collected songs.[453] In two years three volumes have been brought out and it should have been eight issues. I had ordered copies for you on holland paper and I have still not received them; on top of that, the publisher has gone to Leipzig[454] without paying me and so the whole saga continues.

---

[449] Goethe's house choir.

[450] Friedrich Wilhelm Riemer, linguist and tutor to Goethe's son until 1805; Gymnasium Professor 1812–20; in later years Goethe's secretary and collaborator, first editor of the Goethe–Zelter letters.

[451] Frederik Christian Sibbern (1785–1872), Danish philosopher and poet.

[452] *Gesänge der Liedertafel* vol. 1 (Berlin, 1811), a textbook for the organization of Liedertafeln (without compositions, only information on the composers in the subtitle of each poem); a copy is in Goethe's library (Ruppert, Nr. 917).

[453] Zelter's *Sämtliche Lieder, Balladen und Romanzen für das Piano-Forte* 3 vols (Berlin: Kunst und Industrie Comptoir: 1810, 1811, 1812), in Goethe's music collection (*GSA* 32/42).

[454] August Friedrich Kuhn was proprietor of the music publishers, Kunst und Industrie Comptoir, established 1807. A branch was opened in Leipzig in 1811, but shortly after the company's relocation to Leipzig in 1815 it went bankrupt.

## 142. Zelter

Berlin, 14 to 19 April 1812

I have given Dr Sibbern a copy of the first three volumes of my songs to take with him for you. I ordered an express copy for you on holland paper, but my publisher[455] is not a man of his word. You can't work with him. I'd like to be rid of him and have a better publisher. [...]

Madame Simonin-Pollet has arrived and has brought me your card.[456] She will give a concert on the 29th of this month and will probably have a good audience. I will show her around the Sing-Akademie next Tuesday.

## 143. Goethe

Weimar, 17 April 1812

[...] I have made up my mind to send you a something small I wrote last year,[457] so that we may have a new subject for regular discussion. I wrote this cantata, or scene if you prefer to call it that, for Prince Friedrich von Gotha,[458] who wanted something of the kind to show off his fine, well-trained tenor voice.

Kapellmeister Winter of Munich has set it to music very successfully[459] – with ability, taste and fluency, so that the Prince's talent is displayed in its best light. He is now, however, keeping the score for himself, for which I do not blame him.

---

[455] See footnote 189.

[456] The harpist Marie Nicole Simonin-Pollet, to whom Goethe had given a letter of recommendation on 27 February 1812. On 30 April 1812 she gave a concert in the Königliches Theater with the Königliche Kapelle, in which she performed: Nattermann's harp concerto *Les Papillons*, a rondo by Steibelt, variations on the popular duet from the play *Der Weihe der Kraft*, a fantasy and (together with her six-year old son) a Gavotte by Vetris.

[457] Goethe's cantata, *Rinaldo*, MA 9, p. 53.

[458] See Goethe's letter to Prince Friedrich von Sachsen-Gotha on 6 March 1811, *WA* IV/22, p. 419.

[459] It was performed in Goethe's home, with Prince Friedrich as soloist, on 15 November 1811 (see Goethe's diary, *WA* III/3, p. 242.). Years later, on 29 April 1829, Goethe asked Zelter to return Peter von Winter's score of *Rinaldo* which he had perhaps given to him on his last visit to Weimar in October 1827. Zelter had Philipp Christian Weyland deliver the score to Goethe and on 11 June received a requested copy of the score from Goethe. The original score by Winter is in Goethe's music collection (GSA 32/72). A detailed account of Winter's setting of Goethe's *Rinaldo* is in Achim Aurnhammer (ed.), *Torquato Tasso in Deutschland. Seine Wirkung in Literatur, Kunst und Musik seit der Mitte des 18. Jahrhunderts* (Berlin, New York, 1995), pp. 679–708.

But why should I not show the poem to you and with it bring some new life into our communications?

## 144. Zelter

Berlin, 25 April 1812

Yes, yes, my friend, you are certainly correct. Straight after your letter of 8 April my conscience was awakened and I swiftly took my letter and set three of your poems to music, which up to now I had never wanted to risk: 'Rastlose Liebe';[460] 'Neue Liebe, Neues Leben';[461] 'Mailied'.[462]

Unfortunately I am coming to these lovely things so late, as always, when others have already composed them incompetently and if these [settings] don't please you, I won't have done any better. What should come of restless love, new love, new life, at my time of life? And true: I'd like to see someone who loves you as I.

Your *Rinaldo* will not be an easy task,[463] if the full meaning hidden in it is to be brought out – [in particular] its enchanting delicacy, grace and charming rhythmic flow. One would have to take a lesson from the Italian school if one were not too old, but when the time is right let us try our hand at it.

The poem is suitable for the composer who knows what is to be done and protects himself from the danger of doing too much. Everything is light and freely intimated. The words are not pre-emptive and the musician has much input into the subject,

Far too often some supply the musician with words which, though they are intended to help, add superfluous, emphatic words which are sometimes negative and induce the poor devil, with the same expenditure of artistic means, to do the opposite of what is required. [...]

Finally the musician doesn't have it easy in collaboration with the poet or when he is subservient to him. He should be a man of genius, a poet himself, and be extremely dependent thereby. If the poet can carry on, as long as it is goes well,

---

[460] Zelter's through-composed setting of Goethe's 'Rastlose Liebe' for voice and piano. An autograph has not been handed down. It was published in volume four of Zelter's *Sämtliche Lieder, Balladen und Romanzen* (1813).

[461] Zelter's setting of Goethe's 'Neue Liebe, Neues Leben' for voice and piano. An autograph has not been handed down. It was published in Zelter's *Sämtliche Lieder, Balladen und Romanzen* (1813).

[462] Zelter's setting of Goethe's 'Mailied' ('Wie herrlich leutet'), first published under the title 'Maifest' and later renamed 'Mailied'. It should not be confused with Zelter's setting of Goethe's 'Mailied' ('Zwischen Weizen und Korn'), published in 1811.

[463] As with many settings of Goethe's large-scale poetic works, nothing came of Zelter's setting of Goethe's cantanta, *Rinaldo*.

the number of words is prescribed for the composer whether he can use them or not. In short, if the most difficult aspects go easily for him, then he has the greatest pains with minutiae. Often the trained musician himself is often unaware what artistry goes into them.

8 May 1812: A while ago, I found in Voltaire's works (the Gotha edition of 1785, volume nine)[464] a musical opera, *Samson*, which Rameau actually set to music,[465] though it has not yet been performed. I quite liked Voltaire's treatment, and the subject, assuming some necessary alterations, would be thoroughly suitable for an opera.

An opera, in my judgement, should not have more than three acts; two long and one short, or better still, one long act between two short ones. Here is my plan:

Act One:   The Chorus of Israelites lament their defeat but, encouraged by Samson, conquer the Philistines.

Act Two:   Triumphal entry of the Israelites. Reconciliation of Samson with Delilah. Recognition of the son. Treachery practised on Samson.

Act Three: Imprisonment and death of Samson, the known story; very brilliant.

Now what do you think of this? Would there not be enough scope there for plot and dramatic action? I thought you might set to work on it and at least amend this plan; at all events I will have verses made for me here.[466]

## 145. Goethe

Carlsbad, 19 May 1812

[...] Your kind words about *Rinaldo* are not only very pleasant to me but will, I hope, prove fruitful, for they have made me aware of that which by nature and inclination I have done, and should like to do, particularly for music on the stage. When you say, 'Everything is freely and lightly alluded to; the words are not encroaching, and the musician has to deal with the subject itself', this awards me the greatest praise I could wish for; for in my opinion, a poet ought to draw his sketch, upon a very widely woven canvas, so that the musician may have enough space to work out his embroidery with greater freedom and with coarse or fine threads as he thinks fit. The libretto for an opera should be a vessel, not a finished picture. This is certainly our opinion, but most of our good Germans have no comprehension of the matter, yet hundreds try their hand at it. On the contrary, how great our admiration of many of the Italian works must be, where poets,

---

[464] *Œuvres complètes de Voltaire* (Gotha 1784–90) in Zelter's library (no. 756–825).
[465] Rameau's lyric tragedy *Samson* (1733).
[466] Zelter's plan was never realized.

composers, singers and stage directors can all agree about a certain adequate technique. One new German opera after another fails for want of a good text, and the good Viennese,[467] who do not in the least know where the shoe pinches, offer a hundred ducats for the best opera which anyone in Germany could produce; however, they would be better off doubling the amount at the right smithy, and would then come out the winners.

The matter is, in fact, more difficult than people suppose; one would have to enjoy working in the theatre among all those who are contributing to the performance, and then, year after year, one should produce something new. One thing would lead to another and perfection might spring even from a failure.

Just now I should have no faith in *Samson*; it is one of the most monstrous of the old myths. A perfectly bestial passion of a supernaturally strong, divinely gifted hero for the most accursed wretch that the world has ever seen – the mad desire that always leads him back to her, though each time, owing to repeated acts of treachery, he is conscious of the danger of this lustfulness, which itself springs from danger – the mighty conception one must form of the supreme brilliance of this gigantic woman, who is capable of shackling such a bull! Considering all this, dear friend, it will at once become clear to you that we would have to destroy it, if only to choose names in accordance with the conventions of our time and stage. It would be much more advisable to choose a subject with less specific substance, if not indeed one of more immediate appeal to contemporary audiences. Look at *Die Schweizerfamilie* [468] and things of that ilk.

I must mention one other consideration. Subjects from the Old Testament produce a very strange effect here; I had occasion to reflect on this when Robert's *Jephtha*[469] and Alfieri's *Saul*[470] were given. They do not excite any disfavour, but still it is not popular; not disinclination, but lack of inclination. Those myths, truly grand as they are, present a respectable appearance in the solemn distance, and our youthful devotion remains attached to them. But when these heroes step forward into the present, it occurs to us that they are Jews, and we feel a contrast between the ancestors and the descendants that confuses and jolts us. This is the way I quickly explain it to myself after closely watching the effect of both pieces. This

---

[467] Joseph Fürst von Lobkowitz, of whom Goethe was a guest at the Eisenach Residence from 8 to 12 September 1810, and the singer Brizzi, whom Goethe had engaged as guest artist, had set up a competition 'to contribute to the furthering of dramatic art' (see Lobkowitz's letter to Goethe, 2 September 1812). Goethe had agreed to chair the panel of judges but afterwards showed very little enthusiasm; the project itself did not have much success.

[468] Joseph Weigl's Singspiel was performed in Weimar on 21 September and 26 October 1811.

[469] Ludwig Robert's tragedy *Die Tochter Jephthas*, performed in Weimar on 21 September and 26 October 1811.

[470] Vittorio Alfieri's tragedy *Saul*, performed (in Knebel's translation) in Weimar on 6 April 1811 and 8 April 1812.

last consideration would be set aside, were the myths transferred to other nations. But other difficulties would then arise; I shall think further about this.

In conclusion, I must ask of you not to withhold those compositions, and at the same time, for our old love's sake, to give our correspondence new life.

And I beg you, no such long pause again![471]

Goethe

## 146. Goethe

Carlsbad, 2 September 1812

In recent weeks, dear friend, I have longed for you very often and warmly. Through the performance on your songs and many other riches which he remembered, through the account of the delightful Sing-Akademie and the refreshing Liedertafel, and all the other things which are written about you and experienced, our good and highly esteemed Langermann[472] let me feel very acutely what I really lose as a result of living far away from you and as a result of the gulf between us, which the longer it lasts, the more it seems to widen. If I did not particularly avoid despair, these observations would make me very unhappy. Thank you for your lovely letter.[473] Next time write to me in Weimar, where I hope to come close to music again through your songs and other earlier gifts, from which, to my great dissatisfaction, the hustle and bustle of the world has driven me away. Admittedly, on my return I will find the old theatre and a new organ. However, I fear neither Belial nor Christ will have anything to blame me for with regard to either.[474]

If you could and would like to send me your composition of the memorial verse 'Invocavit', you would really make me happy. Langermann gave me a little taste of it. It was meant to celebrate your memory. [...]

I met Beethoven in Teplitz.[475] His talent astounded me; but unfortunately his natural temperament is completely uncontrolled, and although, indeed, not at all wrong in thinking the world detestable, still, in so doing, he does not make it more pleasant, either for himself or for others. However, he is to be greatly excused

---

[471] Between 7 December 1811 and 8 April 1812 the correspondence ceased; Zelter only received Goethe's greeting from 27 February in mid. April.

[472] Johann Gottfried Langermann (1768–1832), doctor, appointed State Councillor in Berlin in 1812 and subsequently a member of Zelter's Liedertafel. Goethe became acquainted with him in 1810; his diary for these weeks in Carlsbad record daily conversations with Langermann.

[473] Zelter's letter of 9–10 April delivered by Sibbern or possibly Zelter's letter from 14 to 19 April.

[474] Reference to 2 Corinthians, 6, v. 15.

[475] Goethe met Beethoven on 19, 20, 21 and 23 July 1812. His diary entry on 21 July reads: 'An evening with Beethoven. He played superbly', *WA* III/4, p. 305.

and much pitied for he is losing his hearing, which perhaps affects the musical less than the social part of his being. As it is, he is reserved by nature and is now becoming doubly so through this loss.

## 147. Zelter

Berlin, 30 May to 13 September 1812

The objections you raise against my opera plans are enlightening. As historical personae Samson and Delilah are offensive, even repulsive. One would have to alter much, which would be more difficult than it seems. Also, what you remember in general about Old Testament subjects we experience here with Joseph[476] and with Solomon.[477] One is only accustomed to seeing Jewish heroes ill-treated. If the words 'No matter. The Jew will be burnt!'[478] were spoken, the effect would be obvious. However, I would not be inclined to write an opera without a tragic subject. In any case the libretto would have to be written with an eye to the future. [...]

'Invocavit' is enclosed.[479] Unfortunately it is so tailored to our Liedertafel that I almost fear elsewhere it will have far too weak an effect. [...] I gladly send you the setting of 'Die heiligen drei Könige'[480] with it, which is of a somewhat lighter style and is enjoyed at nearly every table. However, you must excuse my brazenness, for I have botched up your words,[481] and tell me what corrections you want.

13 September: We have just had Siboni from Vienna here, who endeavoured to sing Paer's *Achilles* in German.[482] Last winter Tombolini sang an Italian aria

---

[476] Etienne Nicolas Méhul's musical drama *Joseph in Ägypten*, (libretto from the French, *Joseph* by Alexandre Duval, presumably in the version by Franz Joseph Hassauruk).

[477] Adrian Quaisin's musical drama *Salomons Urteil* (libretto from the French, *Le Jugement de Salomon* by Louis-Charles Caigniez, in a version by Matthäus Stegmayer).

[478] Quote from Lessing's *Nathan der Weise*, Act 4, scene 2.

[479] Zelter's setting of Goethe's 'Versus memorials'; a copy is in Goethe's music collection (GSA 32/11).

[480] Zelter's setting of Goethe's 'Ephiphaniasfest' ('Die heil'gen drei König'), first published under the title 'Ephiphanias' in Zelter's *Gesänge der Liedertafel* (1811); Zelter composed a second setting in 1812 with the title 'Die heiligen drei Könige'; a copy of the score is in Goethe's music collection (GSA 32/10).

[481] Zelter altered the second stanza of 'Versus memorials'; in lieu of the line of text 'O wär ich Braut', in *Gesänge der Liedertafel* Zelter wrote 'mir juckt die Haut' in his setting.

[482] Giuseppe Siboni (1785–1839), first tenor in the royal court theatre in Vienna, performed the title role in Paer's *Achilles* on 1 September 1812 in the Berlin opera house; see *Vossische Zeitung*, 5 September 1812.

in German translation.[483] You see how we advance in art and in nature. What we might have been able to learn from this would be how the Germans fare when they sing Italian.

Milder-Hauptmann is with us at present.[484] I have heard her in Gluck's *Iphigenie*,[485] the *Schweizerfamilie*[486] and the *Zauberflöte*, in which she sings the part of Tamino [sic].[487] The voice, figure and style of this young artist are so free, powerful and graceful, especially in the part of Emelina,[488] that we have seen nothing like it here for a long time. They criticize her vocalization as inartistic[489] and that kind of thing, but I find much to praise – warmth, truth, secure and appropriate singing and a kind of Swiss solidity most naively expressed – in any case I have never seen passions represented with such control and so effectively.

I am looking forward to your second volume and only wish to enjoy it soon. Have you also received our little book of songs? I hope it was delivered safely. I thought it might stimulate you to do something for our table once again. Come yourself and hear how your songs sound. I always imagine you don't yet know your songs well.

### 148. Zelter

Berlin, 14 September 1812

We have lost our very clever Italian conductor, Righini,[490] who died in his home town of Bologna on 19 August. He was to us much what Salieri was to Vienna;

---

[483] The programme for Raffaele Tombolini's concert in the Königliches Nationaltheater on 2 February 1812 gave a general indication of music performed, namely 'a Recitative and Aria with Chorus, translated into German'.

[484] *Pauline* Anna Milder-Hauptmann (1785–1838), soprano at the court theatre, Vienna, for whom the part of Fidelio was written. She played the leading roles in Gluck's classical operas and was largely responsible for the Gluck revival in Vienna and Berlin. Her greatest triumph was in this production of Gluck's *Iphigénie in Tauris*. Goethe wrote a short poem in her honour after hearing her in *Iphigénie in Tauris* and presented her with a copy of his drama on the same subject.

[485] Christoph Willibald Gluck, *Iphigénie in Tauris*. For reviews of Milder-Hauptmann's performance, see *AMZ* 14 (1812), no. 41, 7 October, column 670; *MA* 20.3, p. 295.

[486] Zelter went to the performance on either 6 or 9 September 1812; further performances were given on 15 and 22 September.

[487] Mozart's opera was performed with Anna Milder-Hauptmann in the role of Tamino [sic] in the Berlin opera house on 11, 13 and 18 September.

[488] Soprano role in the Singspiel *Die Schweizerfamilie*.

[489] Zelter is referring to the review in the *Vossische Zeitung* on 10 September 1812.

[490] Vincenzo Righini was court Kapellmeister in Berlin from 1793 and Director of Italian Opera until 1806; he was active as a Kapellmeister and composer until his death.

fresher than Salieri perhaps, but pretty equal in breadth and depth. For the moment I don't know any Italian composer whom we would want to see in Righini's position; but who knows what we will have to settle for? I have learnt much from him, although indirectly, especially through the present opposition with other conductors. The difference [of opinion] between excellent people often gives the best result.

What you say of Beethoven is quite natural; I, too, admire him with awe. His own works seem to cause him a secret shudder – a feeling which, in this day and age, is set aside much too lightly. His works seem to me like children whose father might be a woman or whose mother a man. The last work of his that I became acquainted with (*Christus am Ölberge*)[491] seems to me an unchaste thing, the foundation and aim of which is an eternal death. The music critics, who seem to be more at home in anything other than in what is natural and individual, have, in the oddest fashion, poured themselves out in praise and blame of this composer. I know musical people who formerly, on hearing his works, were alarmed, even indignant, and are now seized with a passion for them, like the devotees of Grecian love. How thoroughly one can enjoy them is conceivable, and what may come of it you have shown clearly enough in *Die Wahlverwandtschaften*. [...]

## 149. Zelter

Berlin, 14 to 17 November 1812

My eldest son,[492] who must have been well known to you since you were so good to him in Weimar,[493] shot himself tonight. Why? I still don't really know because his debts can be covered and his accounts are in order. He had just begun to be helpful to me, just as, in comparison with his relatives, he could be called competent. And now he leaves me when I wanted to draw him really close.

Sunday, 15 November: He wrote two letters on the day before his death:[494] one to his brother,[495] in whose presence he took his life. In it he recommended to the care of his brother his natural daughter,[496] a child of two-and-a-half years, and a beloved widow to whom he was engaged and who had already lost two husbands. The second letter is addressed to this widow. He gave his ring back in it, regretted

---

[491] Beethoven's oratorio *Christus am Ölberge* (1803); Zelter is referring to the Berlin performance on 2 September 1812, under the direction of Bernhard Anselm Weber, *AMZ* 14 (1812), no. 23, 3 June, column 378.

[492] Zelter's stepson, Carl Flöricke (1784–1812), son of Zelter's first wife, Eleonora, widow of August Wilhelm Flöricke.

[493] Carl Flöricke had been Goethe's guest in Weimar on 14 May 1803.

[494] The letters have not been handed down.

[495] Zelter's eldest son, Georg (1789–1827), from his first marriage.

[496] Louise Flöricke (1811–84); her mother's name is unknown.

that he had paid no heed to her loving admonition and bade farewell. *Don Carlos* lay open on his writing desk. On the pages was written: 'So is there no salvation? Even through transgression? – No!'[497]

At times I have had the unpleasant feeling: whether through my strictness I did him wrong. His many passionate, sensual relationships were acceptable. Although he lived completely with me and off me, he was completely free, had his good income and his own financial arrangements. In the letter to his brother he wrote that he had often tried to write to me, but in vain.

In pressing times, when he became of age, I paid him his father's inheritance which was in my care (because he is my stepson). His account was empty.

Sitting on his bed, beside his sleeping brother, he killed himself. He still sits there now in this position because I don't dare disturb the corpse before the post-mortem, but so lovely and noble as an experienced actor would like to appear to contented connoisseurs. The widow remarked to me that she had once wanted to release him, since just then she had the opportunity to get married properly. At that he pressed his pistol to his breast and said: then this is to be his beloved.

He shot himself in the mouth but lost little blood where the bullet went through. The mouth is intact and only marked by the gun smoke. His face is friendly. The other pistol is also loaded and the pan equipped with gunpowder. The letters were written a day before, but illegibly and covered by great big drops of tears. He has also made a form of will for his bequest. His acquaintances had not heard from him for weeks. I had not seen him for a week. My accounts which he kept for me were in the best order.

Now I must start to organize myself all over again. He had become indispensable to me. For his sake I had maintained all business projects from which he shared the profits. The day before yesterday he had received his tasks to qualify as a master, which he would have passed with honours before many others. So he leaves me in releasing himself. I would not have believed that I would be capable of the bitterest envy with which I looked at his lovely corpse after he passed away and would have thought of the other gun which lay in the desk in reserve. It is hard, cruel. If he had known how I love him, he could rest in peace.

Say something to ease this. I must pull myself together, but I am no longer what I was years ago. I have strength but for other things. Here I will be steady. In the last nine months I have lost my only dearly loved sister;[498] her son (who was also my son-in-law) and now this beloved offender. [...]

Monday Evening: Finally today, on the third day after the death, the official post-mortem took place. The pistol was not loaded with one bullet but with eight small ones [...] With them he was certain of hitting the brain through the mouth. A third pistol, mine, which he had taken with him, is also still loaded. Inwardly and

---

[497] Schiller's tragedy *Don Carlos*, Act 4, scene 21.
[498] Luise Syring died on 17 April 1812. Her son, Ferdinand Syring (married to Zelter's eldest step-daughter, Henriette), died on 23 January 1812.

outwardly the body was sound and healthy except for the bowels, which had signs of hypochondria. The stomach was empty. Tomorrow he will be buried.

Tuesday morning: Now he is being brought to rest. I am tormented and can only think I could have prevented it.

18 November. [...] Scold me that I write so often, when things are going so badly. I don't like to be on my own and I only feel at home with you.

21 November: Could you provide some historical information on 'Die erste Walpurgisnacht'? I began to set the poem to music some time ago and I am clear about the form of the poem, but I would like to learn something quite detailed about it. [...]

## 150. Goethe

Weimar, 3 December 1812

Your letter, my beloved friend, announcing the great misfortune which has befallen your house,[499] has greatly afflicted me and left me bowed down, for it came to me when I was in the middle of very serious meditations on life, and it was only through you yourself that I was enabled to rise again. In the face of death you have proven yourself genuine, refined gold. How glorious a character appears when it is penetrated with mind and soul, and how beautiful must that talent be that rests on such a basis.

As to the deed or misdeed itself, I can say nothing. When weariness of life seizes a man, he is only to be pitied, not blamed. Anyone who reads *Werther*[500] will not doubt that all the symptoms of this strange disease, as natural as it is unnatural, at one time raged furiously through my innermost self. I know full well what determination and effort it cost me in those days to escape from the waves of death just as, with difficulty, I saved myself to recover painfully from many a later shipwreck. And so it is with all sailors' and fishermen's stories. After the storm at night, the shore is reached again, the drenched man dries himself, and the following morning, when the glorious sun once more breaks forth over the glittering waves, the sea has once more an appetite for figs.[501]

When one sees how the world in general, and young people in particular, are not only given over to their desires and passions, but how, at the same time, what is nobler and better in them is dislodged and distorted by the serious follies of the time, so that everything which should lead to its happiness becomes its curse,

---

[499] The suicide of Zelter's son described in ZG 14 to 17 November 1812. Here, for the first time in this letter, Goethe uses the familiar *Du*, instead of the formal *Sie*.

[500] Goethe's epistolary novel *Die Leiden des jungen Werthers*.

[501] Reference to the Greek anecdote, whereby a merchant from Sicily dealing in figs suffers shipwreck. Looking from a rock over the peaceful sea, he says 'I know what it wants – it wants figs' (see Goethe's diary 21 May 1797, *WA* III/2, p. 22).

not taking into account the inexpressible external pressure, one is not astonished at the misdeeds by which man rages against himself and others. I would be capable of writing a new *Werther* that would make people's hair stand more on end than the first one did. Let me add one further remark. Most young persons, conscious of some merit in themselves, make more demands upon themselves than is fair. To this, however, they are urged and driven by their monstrous surroundings. I know half a dozen such persons who are certainly being ruined, and whom it would be impossible to help, even if one could enlighten them as to their real advantages. No one easily arrives at the conclusion that reason and a strong will are given to us that we may not only hold back from evil, but also from an excess of good.

Now let us pass on to other things in your letters, which have done me good [...] If some day or other you could send me *Rinaldo* unexpectedly, it would be a grand thing. I have no connection with music, except through you; for that reason let me thank you sincerely for the 'Invocavit' and 'Die drei Könige', though I have, as yet, only enjoyed reading through them.

Living here we spend quite disproportionately on music and yet we are really quite deprived of music. The opera, with its old repertoire and the novelties that are tailored to the needs of a small theatre and produced slowly enough, cannot be compensation to anyone. Meanwhile, I rejoice that both court and town are led to believe that there is some kind of enjoyment to be gained. The inhabitant of a great city must be deemed fortunate in this respect; for after all, it attracts many remarkable foreign artists. I would like to have heard Madame Milder. [...]

And now I still have to reply to your query about 'Die erste Walpurgisnacht'. The matter rests like this. Among historians there are some men, and more to the point, men whom we cannot but respect, who look for a real foundation for every fable, every tradition, however fantastic and absurd it may be, and always expect to find a kernel of fact within the fairy-tale husk.

A great deal of good has come of treating the matter this way, for the subject demands great knowledge; it is even necessary to have mind, wit and imagination to convert poetry into prose in this way. In this manner one of our German antiquarians has endeavoured to rescue and to give historical foundation to the story of the witches and devils on the Brocken, a legend which has been topical in Germany from time immemorial. His explanation is that the heathen priests and patriarchs of Germany, when they were driven from their sacred groves, and when Christianity was forced upon the people, used to retire at the beginning of spring with their faithful followers to the wild, inaccessible heights of the Harz mountains in order, according to the ancient custom, to offer prayer and fire there to the immaterial god of heaven and earth. And furthermore, in order to be safe from the armed spies and converters, he thinks, they found it necessary to disguise a number of their own people so as to keep their superstitious enemies at a distance, and that in this way, protected by the antics of devils, they carried out the purest of services.

I found this explanation somewhere,[502] a few years ago, but cannot remember the name of the author. The idea pleased me and I have turned this fabulous story back again into a poetical fable.

## 151. Goethe

Weimar, 12 December 1812

With the outgoing post you will receive a wonderful work[503] which will certainly give you some entertainment. It is by a remarkable though admittedly a somewhat strange man and contains a new system of music notation. Instead of the lines, intervals, little note heads and tails to date, he sets out numerical signs and maintains that this system is much more accessible. I cannot assess it because firstly I am used to the traditional notation from my youth and secondly no one could be more shy of numbers than myself. I have avoided and flown from all numerical symbolism – from those of Pythagoras to the recent mathematical mystics – as something formless and depressing. [...] Let me know what you think of this little book as you will easily assess what is favourable and unfavourable about it. [...]

I want to thank you now for the theatre programmes which you sent. They are bound now and I can follow the theatrical and musical delights of Berlin for the entire year.

## 152. Zelter

Berlin, 10 to 13 December 1812

[...] So my deep sorrow, which has turned me away from everybody, has doubled your support for me by openly showing you a dear brother to me; so I have gained though I suffered loss and scarcely thought I would get over it; so life stirs in me again – violent and human – and I will confess: I have felt happy again. [...]

Many thanks for your instruction regarding 'Die erste Walpurgisnacht'. I have taken the thing really according to your description, namely poetically, and the historical looks after itself. From much experience I have noticed that factual

---

[502] Decker offered this explanation in an essay in the *Hannöverschen Gelehrten Anzeigen* (1752).

[503] Johann Friedrich Werneburg, *Allgemeine neue, viel einfachere MusikSchule für jeden Dilettanten und Musiker. Mit einer Vorrede von. J. J. Rousseau* (Gotha, 1812). The book was not sent by post but delivered by Emil Osann to Zelter on 22 February 1813. Goethe's diary entry on 27 January 1813 reads: 'Werneburg's new system of notation brought to Prof. Zelter in Berlin by Dr Osann', *WA* III/5, p. 10. See Zelter's letter of thanks, 26 February 1813.

notes at times cause reverberations through which a type of clarity and truth enter into a melody. This excites understanding to such an extent that part of the work presents itself to me automatically, especially as I am so badly in need of external stimulation.

13 December: As I leaf through Part I of your memoirs, I wonder whether some of your sacred music texts written at that time still exist? I cannot conceal my curiosity to see some of them, because the period in which you occupy yourself with biblical subjects is very close to me, because I, too, was caught up with such things for a good part of my youth, although I neither knew what I was looking for nor found what I needed. It mainly interested me because it was ancient and dark. [...]

We will soon have to send home our French–Italian German Nationaltheater, which became our royal theatre [company] for quite a number of years [...] Opera must carry everything and for this [reason] plays are so badly supported that the few people who still go leave again because of the cold.

## 153. Goethe

Weimar, 15 January 1813

[...] Musicians have frequently been upbraided for liking bad librettos, and it has been said in jest that one of them offered to set a poster to music;[504] if the song were not independent of the words, how could the Good Friday music in the Sistine Chapel possibly have ended with the word 'vitulos'?[505] And there may be other instances. Many a programme, properly arranged, would make a better opera than the libretto itself.

---

[504] Goethe in fact knew this saying, 'A real composer should be able to set a public notice to music', attributed to Georg Philipp Telemann, from Zelter's letter of 6–7 May 1808.

[505] The last verse of Psalm 51 reads: 'Tunc acceptis sacrificium justitiae, oblationes et holocausta, tunc imponunt super altare tuum vitulos' (Now you accept the sacrifice of justice, offerings of holocaust, then they lay heffers on your altar). Goethe had heard the Good Friday liturgy in the Sistine chapel at the end of his visit to Rome; see Goethe's letter to Christian Friedrich Schnauß of 24 March 1788, *WA* IV/30, p. 41.

## 154. Zelter

Berlin, 24 December to 24 January 1813

[…] Recently I bought an original picture by Denner, a portrait of the composer Hasse,[506] whom I highly esteem. He died in Italy in the year 1783 aged 78, after a very fruitful artistic life. The picture was painted in 1740; it is two-and-a-half feet high and two feet broad, painted in oil and well preserved; it represents the artist as a handsome man, in the fullness of his strength and the zenith of his fame in Germany, but especially in Italy, where he was famous under the name of *Il Sassone*.[507] Eyes, mouth, chin and nose are beautifully chiselled and rounded, and the bearing of the man, with his expression and colour, confirms his character as an artist, who could feel quite happy only in Italy; for in Italy he learnt, loved, pleased, married and died, and he also adopted the religion of that country. His wife was the famous singer, Faustina.[508] […]

I knew Dr Werneburg[509] when he was in Berlin before the war. At that time he submitted his work (if I am not mistaken in manuscript) to the local academy,[510] through which it was brought to my attention and for which my opinion was sought (by Nicolai, I think).[511] The thing has its own value and it has never been denied that theory of musical notation is very extensive. But we possess it, we need it, we are used to it; our instruments sound as we have wished and even most accurate notation demands performers who achieve the best results of themselves. […]

The work by Werneberg has still not arrived with the post, and although I know it from the manuscript, nevertheless it would be important enough for me to see it published after many years. […]

---

[506] Johann Adolph Hasse (1699–1793), pupil of A Scarlatti in Italy, and the most popular composer of Italian opera in Neapolitan style of his time. Such a painting exists today in the Staatsoper (Semperoper) Dresden and was presumably passed down from the electoral estate. Zelter obviously possessed a replica.

[507] Hasse had acquired the epithet 'the Saxon' because he had mainly lived in Dresden from 1733 to 1763. It even appears in the title of Franz Sales Kandler's biography of the composer, *Cenni storico-critici intorno alla vita ed alle opere del celebre compositore di musica Gio. A. Hasse detto il Sassone* (Venice, 1820).

[508] Faustina Hasse née Bordoni (1700–81), Italian singer, married to Hasse from 1730; her success in Dresden and Italy and an invitation to perform for the French court in Paris made her internationally famous.

[509] Johann Friedrich Christian Werneburg (1777–1851), mathematician and physicist.

[510] Akademie der Künste und mechanischen Wissenschaften.

[511] The writer and publisher Christoph *Friedrich* Nicolai (1733–1811).

## 155. Zelter

Berlin, 12 February to 11 March 1813

26 February: I have also now read Werneburg's music tutor. Dr Ossan sent it to me on the 22nd of this month.[512] The enthusiasm and painful seriousness with which he goes to work would amuse musicians if they were to read the book. It is like our deceased preacher, Bierdemann,[513] who always scolded the absentees from the pulpit, so that the innocent had to listen to it.

If his new music theory were used and he wanted to introduce our current students to it, they would think he was mad. The world is as it is and it will be hard to influence it in his way. Now I don't know whether it is possible to advise him. Because if he had the desire to take an extract or form a catechism from the work – which is too wordy – and give it to this person or that person in order to apply it in schools, I think the thing could be lighter and I also would offer a hand.

27 February: The day before yesterday I heard a first-rate performance of Beethoven's overture to *Egmont*.[514] Every important theatrical work on the German stage should, by rights, have its own music. The benefit which would then accrue to poet, composer and public is immeasurable. The poet has the composer on his own territory, can guide him, teach him to understand, and learn to understand him; the composer works with an understanding of the whole and can know with certainty what he must avoid, without being limited, and it would be delightful for each to recognize himself through the other.

This time the overture was heard without the play,[515] just as the deceased Gleim always presented the hat of Friedrich the Great.[516] The overture in F minor

---

[512] See Goethe's diary note of 23 January 1813: 'Werneburg's new system of notation brought to Prof. Zelter in Berlin, by Dr Emil Osann', *WA* III/5, p. 10; presumably it was Dr Emil Osann (1787–1842) in Berlin, who had delivered the book.

[513] Heinrich Johann David Bierdemann (1725–86), preacher at the Sophienkirche in Berlin.

[514] On 25 February 1813 Beethoven's *Egmont* overture was the first item performed in a subscription concert in theatre hall; a review is published in the *AMZ* 15 (1813), no. 19, 12 May, column 318.

[515] In his review in the *Vossische Zeitung* 36 on 2 March 1813, Friedrich Rellstab raised some interesting ideas on the meaning and function of overtures in general and came to the conclusion that Beethoven's *Egmont* overture held more meaning in a concert performance than performed as an overture to the play.

[516] After his audience with the Prussian King Frederick II, Gleim expressed to Duke Friedrich August his wish to have the old hat which the monarch wore during his audience with him. After King Frederick's death the Duke sent the hat of the deceased Prussian King to Gleim with the words, 'My dear, here is the hat which the deceased king was wearing the morning before his death.' Zelter's reference is comparing the overture without the play to the hat without the king.

announces a tragedy in a series of dark chords, turns into a republican character with war-like overtones, becomes calm and wistfully nostalgic, dreamy, turbulent and finally victorious. One more merit in the music is the length: it is exactly as long as I would have wanted it and the first scene connects really well to the end of the overture. Now, I would like to persuade him to set the entr'acte to music, which must all come from the overture.[517] [...]

Reichardt's intermezzo, between Acts 3 and 4 of the tragedy, is first-rate – in spite of the slack performance. He has composed variations on the melody of the song 'Freudvoll und Leidvoll', which the orchestra play between Acts 3 and 4, at whose first hearing I was spellbound. [...]

## 156. Goethe

Teplitz, 3 May 1813

In Dresden Dr Sibbern told me he had seen you, that you had wished to give him something for me, but that you refrained from so doing as he would probably not go to Weimar. He certainly will not get there, but I should have been delighted to hear something of yours in Dresden. I enclose a short poem, a parody of one of the worst German songs, 'Ich habe geliebt, nun lieb' ich nicht mehr'.[518] If writing poetry were not an inward and necessary operation, independent of any external circumstances, these verses, of course, could not have arisen now; but as I imagine that one day or other you will be eating and singing again, I dedicate this unseasonable joke to you.

---

[517] Zelter obviously did not know at the time that Beethoven had composed incidental music for *Egmont* for the court theatre in Vienna, which was first performed on 15 June 1810. In addition to the overture, the music contains nine parts, among them the intermezzi, Acts One to Four. The orchestral parts for the overture were published in December 1810; the parts for the intermezzi appeared in January 1812. For Zelter's relationship with Beethoven, see Theodor Frimmel (ed.), *Beethoven Handbuch* (2 vols, Leipzig: Breitkopf & Härtel, 1926) vol. 1, pp. 470–73.

[518] A copy (in Carl John's hand) of the poem 'Ich habe geliebet, nun lieb' ich erst recht ...', later with the title 'Gewohnt, getan' (*MA* 9, p. 80); it is a parody of Christian Gottfried Solbrig's poem 'Ich habe gelacht', which Goethe had heard in Herr Solbrig's 'Deklamatorium' on 18 April 1813 in Leipzig.

## 157. Goethe

Weimar, 29 October 1813

[...] Tell me something pleasant about yourself. In the midst of so much trouble,[519] it is a great consolation not to be completely cut off from those we love. Blessings be yours – inwardly, if not outwardly!

## 158. Goethe

Weimar, 26 December 1813

At last, my old reliable friend, I see your dear handwriting again! [...]

First of all, if you will very much oblige me by setting the words 'In te, Domine speravi; et non confundar in aeternum'[520] as a vocal quartet with your usual great charm, your name shall be highly praised. When you have refreshed me through this, I will send you some quodlibets for your Liedertafel. [...]

Towards Christmas, I shall probably send you volume three of the thousand and one nights of my foolish life,[521] which looks almost more indiscreet in the telling than it actually was.

You will be amused when you see that I have been plagiarizing you. Were your profession not so utterly different from mine, it would happen more often.

This note was written some time ago [...] Lieutenant Mendelssohn[522] wants to take a few words to you from me. Here, therefore, is what I have written, with my best wishes and hopes. [...]

Let me hear from you soon. I have some lively songs to hand.[523] We have also been singing your 'Drei Könige' lately. This is the way we have to drive away the bitterness of death.[524]

---

[519] Following the Battle of Nations at Leipzig from 16–19 October 1813, in which the allied Prussian, Russian and Austrian armies had defeated Napoleon and forced his retreat, Weimar was again shaken by the wars surrounding the French and Cossack invasion on 20 and 21 October.

[520] The final verse of the Te Deum, the Ambrosian Hymn of Praise, based on Psalm 71, 1.

[521] *Dichtung und Wahrheit*, Part 3, Books 11–15.

[522] Nathan Mendelssohn (1782–1852), youngest son of Moses Mendelssohn.

[523] 'Die wackelnde Glöcke'; 'Die Lustigen von Weimar'; 'Viele Gäste wünsch' ich heut'...'; 'Meine Wahl'.

[524] Words of King Agog of the Amalekites; 1. Sam. 15, 32.

### 159. Goethe

Weimar, 14 February 1814

So that no post day will be lost, I am immediately sending you something singable[525] and something toneless;[526] let one please your artistic sense and the other your understanding. To say how infinitely your consignment has delighted and refreshed me, I would have to tell you stories; today, however, only heartfelt thanks.

### 160. Zelter

Berlin 21 to 22 February 1814

21 February: Your golden poems arrived early today. I spread them out like a Christmas gift in front of me at the round table by the oven. I am sending back a setting of one of them immediately.[527] [...] I don't know whether I told you that from time to time I have worked on something from your *Zauberflöte Zweiter Teil*. In the last few days I have also almost finished the overture.[528] It occurs to me now that in the gaps in the libretto some bright and cheerful text could be inserted and one could finally celebrate the peace when it comes about. But you would have to insert all that yourself. Other poets would not want to get it wrong and we can be grateful for that. How it would be if you were to take up the work once again and complete it. Let me know your thoughts on this suggestion.

---

[525] Songs for the Liedertafel mentioned in GZ 26 December 1813. The exact contents of this dispatch cannot be determined. Possible songs include the following: 'Offne Tafel'; 'Die Lustigen von Weimar'; 'Meine Wahl'; 'Eigentum'; 'Kriegsglück'; 'Wandrers Nachtlied' ('Über allen Gipfeln ist Ruh'); 'Gefunden'.

[526] Goethe's riddle 'Logogryph' ('Das erste gibt mir Lust genug'), *MA* 9, p. 100.

[527] Zelter's setting of 'Wandrers Nachtlied' ('Über allen Gipfeln ist Ruh'). The composition is no longer in Goethe's music collection. It was listed as no. 2 in Krauter's catalogue, *Zelters Compositionen*, but was later taken out by Walther von Goethe, as noted in the above catalogue and also in Goethe's music collection, GSA. The Berlin autograph (SBB PK: Mus. Ms. Autogr. Zelter 39) is dated 'Berlin, 21 February 1814'; the setting was first published in Zelter's *Neue Liedersammlung* (1821).

[528] Zelter's composition is unfinished.

## 161. Zelter

Berlin, 23 to 25 February 1814

Are you not becoming worried, old friend, once again to receive a note from me and a composition[529] with it? For I cannot refrain from giving you one of the happy moments back which your lovely poems give.

25 February: I have just set the chorale again for three voices.[530] If the poem had another strophe, one would have had time to establish the [right] feeling, where it is not possible to repeat any words. On the other hand it can be done if the melody is sung twice. Three male voices rehearsed to sing perfectly with one another will, in the clear stillness of the evening, have the best effect.

## 162. Goethe

Weimar, 23 February 1814

First of all, I must tell you that our little singing society has been feasting upon you and living off you alone, and after an unhappy break, has risen through you again.[531] We offered the transfiguration of 'Johanna Sebus'[532] as a sacrament of our rescue from the endlessly broad floods.[533]

I could also tell you a long story about the 'In te, Domine, speravi',[534] how I composed those words[535] in my Bohemian solitude,[536] among peculiar pressures

---

[529] Zelter's four-part setting of Goethe's poem 'Eigentum' ('Ich weiß, daß mir nichts angehört'). Zelter's manuscript, entitled *Hauschoral*, is dated 'Berlin, 23 February 1814'. An autograph copy in Berlin bears the same date (SBB PK: Mus. Ms. Autogr. Zelter 20).

[530] On the reverse side of Zelter's four-part composition, *Hauschoral*, is a three-part setting (TTB) of the same poem.

[531] Rehearsals had resumed at the end of November after an interruption caused by the war; see Goethe's diary, 21 and 28 November, 5 and 19 December 1813, *WA* III/5, pp. 84–6 and 88.

[532] Zelter's setting of Goethe's ballad 'Johanna Sebus'.

[533] As a metaphor for the French occupation and military manoeuvres during the Wars of Liberation.

[534] Goethe had requested a four-part setting of the first verse of Psalm 71; he received the composition at the beginning of February 1814.

[535] Clearly Goethe's composition attempt was merely a question of a rhythmic sketch. There seems to be no extant written record. Riemer reports in his diary on 11 February: 'In the evening visited Goethe, who showed me letters from Sartorius und Zelter. Discussed his composition. His setting of 'Domine in te speravi'. Goethe's composition of it for himself in Teplitz' *JbSK* 3, p. 59.

[536] Goethe's visit to Teplitz in the spring and summer of 1813.

from within and without; they had rhythm but no sound, were meant for four persons – not to say four voices – and I had no dearer wish than to hear these beautiful words musically realized by you. I was tempted into drawing four lines, one below the other, in order to illustrate the way I understood it. Now that I hear your composition, all is clear to me and it is a pleasant experience. The dilettante is only touched by that which is easily comprehensible and by that which has an immediate effect; this is also characteristic of his own productions, wherever he ventures into any one of the arts. My composition, which is fairly rounded and definite, resembles one of Jomelli's,[537] and it is wonderful and rather funny to catch oneself accidentally upon such paths, and to become aware of one's own somnambulism. In order to become clear about this in another form of art to which I have devoted myself more seriously, I am examining some old landscape sketches and perceive that it is much the same here.

Surely there must be some magic sounds in 'Die wandelnde Glocke'[538] for I really did write it in Teplitz, to where it seemed to call you. [...] Can you inform me about my little song concert so that it is a great success?

## 163. Zelter

Berlin, 9 March 1814

[...] Your observations about the composition of the words 'In te Domine [speravi]' excited many ideas in me: the melody came to me the moment I read the words in your letter and the fugal character of the words 'non confundar in aeternum' also work[539] – more because one is so accustomed to them in music from early times than that it simply is so and cannot be any other way. Whoever could do it, it is always daring to think up and use new forms in place of the accepted ones; and the listener, be he dilettante or artist, will want something of his own in it. Therefore, I think, like your own attempts, I always had to resemble a fine work of this type in order for it to be good itself and for it to address the feeling.

'Die wandelnde Glocke'[540] should, I think, be sung by a good contralto, such as I have often heard among elderly Bohemian women. In Bohemia the mountains are shaped like bells and when you drive past them at a certain distance, they seem, to a fantastic eye, to wander after you. Well, once a child, always a child.

---

[537] Goethe knew Niccolò Jommelli's composition of the psalm since 1808 from the motet *Confirma hoc dues* performed by Goethe's house choir; see Goethe's diary 6 March 1808.

[538] Goethe had enclosed this poem in a letter to Zelter on 29 December 1813.

[539] In Zelter's composition of the Psalm 'In te Domine speravi' the opening words are composed homophonically, with the words 'non confundar in aeternum' composed in fugal style, with the vocal entries rising from bass to tenor to alto to soprano.

[540] Zelter's setting sent to Goethe on 5 February 1814.

I enclose now a composition[541] which you will like even if it should appear somewhat confused. However, if you could sing the song of Sebus so beautifully, you may take this reflection to heart. [...]

In the future you will receive several things: 'Das Gastmahl';[542] 'Die Lustigen von Weimar'[543] and 'Wer sich nicht selbst zum besten haben kann'[544] are already composed; they should just be left to settle awhile.

Your suggestion that we see each other this summer is splendid. I had already thought of Teplitz because of my health, as I had hoped to relax my sinews. You will let me know a suitable time. I really long to chat with you about a hundred thousand things.

Regarding the canon, it is worth pointing out that the art is formed out of the dominant order of our Liedertafel, in that the rectangular table divides itself into two halves which sing at times as choir and counter-choir. From this, the most delightful animosities result, which would have given, especially you, the opportunity for really sound fun. As a rule, a canon is sung through three times.

While re-reading your letter, I am just reminded again of what I really wanted to say before, namely that I should like to see your composition for four voices,[545] or your plan, be it what it may. We are such slaves to the current forms, the subject or image of which our fathers had before them, that we cannot go beyond them without being unnoticed. If the occasion or the image which dictated and defined the form were before our eyes again, no one would have to strain every nerve to seem original. If we only lived nearer each other, no doubt many difficulties on this point would be cleared up, as certain things cannot be illustrated by words and are only made clear through the medium of art. I remember well that the music of the Leipzig Bach,[546] and his son the Hamburg Bach,[547] who were both quite new and

---

[541] Zelter's four-part setting of Goethe's 'Beherzigung', handed down in Zelter's collection for the Liedertafel (SBB PK: Mus. ms. autogr. Zelter II, 2, IV) as well as an autograph copy in an album by Edward Grell (Staatliches Institut für Musikforschung PK Berlin: RE 4 C.F. Zelter I). No copy exists in Goethe's music collection.

[542] Goethe's poem 'Das Gastmahl', later published under the title 'Offne Tafel'. The page with Goethe and Zelter's handwriting (SBB PK: Mus. ms. autogr. Zelter 15) was published in facsimile copy shortly after Zelter's death. The composition is not in Goethe's music collection.

[543] Zelter's setting of Goethe's verses 'Donnerstag nach Belvedere ...' for two soloists and choir; an autograph copy exists in Hamburg (SUB: CS 15, Zelter). A copy exists in Goethe's music collection (GSA 32/33).

[544] The opening line of verse three in Zelter's four-part setting of Goethe's poem, 'Ich liebe mir den heiteren Mann ...' which was enclosed in the dispatch of 14 February; it was published with the title 'Meine Wahl' by Cotta; the composition is in Zelter's 1813 collection for the Liedertafel (SBB PK: Mus. ms. autogr. Zelter II, 2 V).

[545] Goethe's plan for a setting of 'In te Domine speravi', which he mentioned on 23 February.

[546] Johann Sebastian Bach (1685–1750).

[547] Carl Philipp Emanuel Bach (1714–88).

original in their time, seemed to me almost unintelligible, though I was attracted by a dim recognition of their value. Then came Haydn, whose style was blamed because it, so to speak, travestied the extreme seriousness of his predecessors, so that good opinion reverted back again to them. At last Mozart appeared, who enabled us to understand each of the three men whom he had for his masters.

I enclose now the music to an ode by Horace,[548] over which I would be almost at odds with Wolf. The piece was written on the death of Dr Friedrich Ferdinand Flemming,[549] who was a loveable member of the Sing-Akademie and Liedertafel. All of Berlin grieves the loss of an eye doctor.

Our singers carry this piece softly to the end and the appoggiaturas indicated above notes are tiny stresses which moderate the strong beats, just as in a painting the colour contrasts with the contour. It must be sustained and flowing. That is not exactly easy in this piece; we have had to keep rehearsing it. In it lies, in my opinion, what some theorists consider a lack of a regular metre which could be called free time, because absence of measure is quite unphilosophical.

Now I want to admit that I have dabbled in your profession: I have attempted a transcription of the Latin[550] to give those of the academy who have even less Latin than I – but still have to sing it – a guide to its pronunciation. It would be nice if our friend Riemer could, without too much trouble, give a helping hand. I would not have been able to compose the Latin without thinking of it in German. Perhaps Riemer would like to give me a better word for 'Chorule', which I have put in the third stanza instead of Virgil.

I enclose the piece by Perti[551] as a remnant of a fine style from the late eighteenth century. Unfortunately I don't have more from this fine composer.

16 March: Professor Kiesewetter[552] wanted to take a letter with him and I wanted to give him last year's theatre programmes. He is still here now and today I set to music the last two poems you sent to give our Singtees[553] the opportunity to grumble about me with a full heart. This little joke would also like to go to you and when you have heard it, let me know whether the form is correct, especially as I have stitched both poems together.

---

[548] Zelter' setting of the verse 'Quis desiderio …' from Horace's *Carmina* (I, 24) for four solo voices and choir; the music is lost. The Ode is a lament for Virgil's friend, Quintilius Varus.

[549] Friedrich Ferdinand Flemming (1778–1813), amateur composer, died 27 May 1813.

[550] Enclosed with this letter; Goethe filed it in his archive under the title *Fremdliteratur*.

[551] Presumably the four-part setting of Giacomo Antonio Perti's *Adoramus te Christe*. The original could not be identified in Goethe's music collection. The setting is, however, handed down as an appendix to the choral setting, *Canzonette*, which was presumably sent by Zelter (GSA 32/179).

[552] Johann Gottfried Karl Christian Kiesewetter (1766–1819).

[553] Zelter's settings of Goethe's poems 'Die Jahre sind allerliebste Leute' and 'Das Alter is ein höflich Mann'; neither are in Goethe's music collection.

23 March: When I came home yesterday evening around 11[p.m.] I found your little letter and in the lovely stillness of the evening I immediately set to work on 'Der Totentanz'. The character had me terribly frightened, because just as I was about to write out the last notes, my loudmouth living room clock struck 12 – one after the other – so I went to bed and had to write the last notes out this morning. I enclose the little song. The singer must perfect the words as well as the music, read without emphasis and let one follow the other smoothly. Otherwise it is nothing. Admittedly, no one gladly gets involved in such conditions; I would think, however, one can pretend to be able to read well.

## 164. Goethe

Weimar, 15 March 1814

[…] I will turn my thoughts to *Die Zauberflöte*;[554] perhaps the spring air will breathe life into it again.

## 165. Zelter

Berlin, 21 April 1814

Through Professor Kiesewetter, who is going from here in the morning via Weimar to the army, you will receive some remaining things, including Fasch's Quintet for five singers which I had long laid aside for your collection of signature manuscripts.[555] As Fasch himself has not signed his name on the work, I have enclosed a report about the origin and intention of the piece[556] and I am already pleased that you will on occasion take delight in it. […]

---

[554] On 21 February Zelter had encouraged Goethe to resume work on *Der Zauberflöte Zweiter Teil*. The idea, which had formed in conversations with Iffland who wanted to perform it in Berlin, was discussed in correspondence with Schiller in May 1798 and gained new life upon publication of the fragment in Wilmann's *Taschenbuch auf das Jahr 1802*. Despite this and also Zelter's interest, Goethe heeded Schiller's caution and it remained unfinished.

[555] Carl Friedrich Fasch, *Versetto a 5 Voci Soli*, a late manuscript of *Meine Seele hanget Dir an* (in Fasch's hand and dated 4 November 96). The composition is no longer in Goethe's collection of autographs; see Hans-Joachim Schreckenbach, *Goethes Autographensammlung. Katalog* (Weimar: Arion, 1961); it is now held in the poet's music collection (GSA 32/46).

[556] The following notes, written in Zelter's hand, are enclosed with the composition: 'The five-part choral work, in the composer's hand and written by Fasch, is an attempt to apply the seventh degree of the scale, discovered by the mathematician Euler, which is not completely contained in the [tempered] scale. It is also remarkable that it was written

The day before yesterday I entertained their Majesties of Saxony[557] at the Sing-Akademie in our own way. The King and Queen openly showed satisfaction as experts and as I cannot be happier than when I do something good for fine people, you can imagine my own satisfaction. On this day the choir consisted of 152 singers not counting myself and the pieces went off well. What I liked so much about the King was that he didn't speak about the large number [of singers] but about the purity, the unity and the general impression.

### 166. Goethe

Weimar, 22 April 1814

Today just a word or two, dear friend, to tell you that, to my great delight, your last consignment reached me safely; the parts are copied out and are so far prepared that my household choir, with its adequate resources, will soon be able to give me a treat. Undoubtedly a special art is required to keep alive this mixed group from which now this, now that member drops off. The 'Ruhelied' is admirable;[558] our tenor[559] sings it very well, and in these times of unrest, it is all the happiness we get.

Enclosed: 'Gleich ist Gleich'

### 167. Goethe

Weimar, 4 May 1814

The most laughable scenes in *Wilhelm Meister* are serious in comparison with the tricks I have to resort to in arranging that your music should no longer only be visible but audible as well.[560] […]

---

when the composer came down with serious illness and was notated in the early days of his recovery. The words are written out in the music and after the setting.'

[557] Friedrich August I (1750–1827), King of Saxony and his wife, Marie *Amalie Auguste* (1752–1828).

[558] 'Wanderers Nachtlied' ('Über allen Gipfeln ist Ruh').

[559] Carl Melchior Jakob Moltke (1783–1831); in Weimar from 1809; see Goethe's diary 22 April 1809: 'An evening in the theatre: *Zauberflöte*; debut of the new tenor, Moltke', *WA* III/4, p. 23; his performances with Goethe's house choir are often mentioned in Goethe's diary.

[560] Zelter's settings written for performance by Goethe's house choir.

When an opportunity offers, I shall send you a full score by Christoph Kaiser,[561] some of whose music you know – in particular the Christmas cantata.[562] He was with me in Italy, and is still leading a secluded life in Zurich; I should like to hear in detail what you think of his style. I shall send you the Overture, and Act One of *Scherz, List und Rache*, the whole of which he has set to music. He is on my mind just now, as I am working at my *Italienische Reise*, and should like to be as clear about his art as I am about his studies and his character.

Briefly and hastily, let me thank you for the great pleasure which your parcel gave me. I succeeded this time in getting the ever-changing choir that meets at my house very well organized.

### 168. Zelter

Berlin, 15 May 1814

Your last letter of 4 May, from Weimar, arrived safely. Please let me have Christoph Kaiser's score as soon as possible, as I am already busy preparing for my journey to the spa, though for the rest of this month, at least, I am staying where I am. As yet I do not know a note of Kaiser's music, and if you happen to have his Christmas cantata at hand, please send that also. Reichardt wrote to me the day before yesterday, that he expects a complete recovery from his painful condition.[563] Abbé Vogler died suddenly in Darmstadt on 6 May.[564] Art would lose an excellent man by his death, had he not wasted the best time of his life in ploughing foreign acres, dissecting organs[565] and polishing up old trash. [...]

---

[561] Presumably the second edition of the autograph score of the overture and Act 1 of Philipp Christoph Kayser's music to Goethe's Singspiel *Scherz, List und Rache*.

[562] Kayser's *Weihnachstkantate* for two solo voices and strings (Zurich, 1810); the work was rehearsed by Goethe's house choir (see Goethe's diary, 1 and 4 November 1810, *WA* III/4, p. 146).

[563] Reichardt's letter has not been handed down; it was one of the last letters written before his death.

[564] Georg Josef Vogler (1749–1814), composer, organist, teacher to Weber and Meyerbeer.

[565] Zelter's reproach is aimed at Vogler's *Simplifikationssystem*. In Zelter's opinion, Vogler did not build organs in line with contemporary music practice. (*Die Musik in Geschichte und Gegenwart. Allgemeine Enzyklopaedie der Musik. Unter Mitarbeit zahlreicher Musikforscher* (...) ed. by Friedrich Blume vols 1–17 (Kassel, Basel: Bärenreiter Verlag, 1949–86; reprint Munich: Deutscher Taschenbuch Verlag, 1989). 13, column 1901). Hereafter referred to as *MGG*.

## 169. Zelter

Bonn, 6 to 11 September 1814

Cologne, 9 September: Yesterday I spent the whole day in the cathedral [...] The space in the church between the columns is very majestic and large. I have never seen anything so finely shaped; the sound is soft like the light and as clear as an unclouded starry sky. The effect of music without castrati would always be moderate in such spaces if the forces are not too large. Reichardt doesn't know what he is talking about when he speaks out against castrati.[566] There may be one castrato among a thousand men and the rock on which this church is built will not be the smaller for it. [...]

Early on Saturday: Music here is as quiet as the trade. Since I have been here I have hardly heard a note, not even on a barrel organ. [...]

## 170. Zelter

Berlin, 8 to 12 November 1814

[...] On my nocturnal journey there was no time to piece together all kinds of reminiscences on *Epimenides*.[567] The little song, 'Vorwärts! Hinan!'[568] crystallized and took melodic shape in my mind, as I have had your manuscript often enough before my eyes. I wanted to surprise you with this song: your choristers in Weimar should serenade you with it. On 11 October last Prince Blücher paid our Sing-Akademie a visit, and I thought I could not do better than greet him with the little song 'Vorwarts! Hinan!'[569] They sang it with such truth and delicacy of feeling that he was delighted. The 181 voices sounded so fresh and spirited that the old fellow could not help crying. Our friend Weber[570] was upset about it and I will have my

---

[566] For Reichardt's criticism of castrati see the following essays: Johann Friedrich Reichardt and Friedrich Ludwig Aemilius Kunzen, *Studien für Tonkünstler und Musikfreunde* (Berlin: Berlinische Musikhandlung, 1793), p. 21; Reichardt, *Vertraue Briefe aus Paris* (Hamburg: B.G. Hoffmann, 1804), vol. 1, p. 191. See also Reichardt's Schauspiel *Der Rheingraf oder das kleine deutsche Hofleben* (1806), p. 64.

[567] Goethe's Festspiel *Des Epimenides Erwachen*.

[568] The refrain from Zelter's choral setting of the song 'Brüder, auf die Welt zu befreien' from *Des Epimenides Erwachen* (Act 2, scene 7); the manuscript copy, entitled 'Vorwärts', is in Goethe's music collection (GSA 31/1).

[569] A manuscript of Zelter's setting bears the title 'Vorwärts. Blüchers Ehre' (SBB PK: Mus. ms. autogr. Zelter 10, no. 21).

[570] Bernhard Anselm Weber, composer and Kapellmeister of the Nationaltheater from 1792 until his death in 1821, during which time he keenly promoted operas by Mozart and Gluck.

work cut out to placate him. Perhaps he will complain to you himself because he has lent me his manuscript[571] in order to show it to Schulz[572] and believes I transcribed the verses from his score [...].

12 November: Please do not forget 'Gastmahl der Weisen'[573] and what you encounter on your travels, as next year I would also like to go through this district.

---

[571] Bernhard Anselm Weber's manuscript of the incidental music to Goethe's *Des Epimenides Erwachen*.

[572] Presumably Christoph Ludwig Friedrich Schultz (1781–1834), Chairman and financial manager of the Sing-Akademie.

[573] Zelter's setting of Goethe's poem 'Die Weisen und die Leute'.

## Section II
# Middle Years' Correspondence 1815–1825

**171. Goethe**

Weimar, 23 January 1815

[…] Eberwein's *Proserpina*, which you know, will be performed on 3 February.[1] We've put some real heat into this little work, so that it can rise up like a balloon and can still explode like a firework.[2][…]

**172. Zelter**

Berlin, 31 March to 1 April 1815

Finally yesterday *Epimenides* was successfully launched.[3] The effect was significant and it hit [the right tone], despite our spoilt audience, the delay in the work[4] and many minor details, which the poet himself would have wanted addressed. Yes, it appeared like a prophetic vision and, at the same time, like a test case. One

---

[1] Carl Eberwein's setting of Goethe's melodrama *Proserpina* composed in the Spring of 1814 (GSA 32/61). On the origins of the music and the rehearsals in Goethe's house; see 'Eberweins Erinnerungen' in Wolfgang Herwig (ed.) *Goethes Gespräche. Eine Sammlung zeitgenössischer Berichte aus seinem Umgang. Auf Grund der Ausgabe und des Nachlasses von F. Freiherrn von Biedermann* (4 vols, Zurich and Stuttgart: Artemis Verlag, 1965–87), vol. 2, pp. 901–903, and p. 991. Hereafter referred to as *Gespräche*. The performance took place in the Weimar Court Theatre on 4 February 1815, repeated on 6 February and 6 March 1815.

[2] See Goethe's recollections in the *Tag- und Jahres-Heften* (1814): 'The monodrama, *Proserpina*, in Eberwein's setting, was rehearsed with Madame Wolff, and a short, but highly significant performance was prepared which involved recitation, declamation, mime, and noble, dignified movement, and a large tableau portraying Pluto's Kingdom crowned the performance and left a strong impression [on the audience].'

[3] Goethe's one-act festival piece *Des Epimenides Erwachen*, set to music by B.A. Weber. Performances took place on 30 and 31 March in the Königliches Oper, Berlin, conducted by the composer; see *AMZ* (1815) no. 15, 12 April 1815, columns 257–9.

[4] A performance had been planned to celebrate the king's return from France on 20–14 July 1814 but was postponed because the score was not finished; Herklots's Festspiel *Asträas Wiederkehr* was performed instead of *Des Epimenides Erwachen* at the king's reception on 7 August 1814.

had believed (as the unbeliever is the most faithful) that the work would have no appeal to modern audiences anywhere. From the outset a good reception was not to be expected. I myself was embarrassed and had crept into the orchestra pit in order to be in the empty space between the stage and the audience. The opening was delayed, the full house became restless and I was worried.

The overture began: either Weber didn't have the time or he had considered that the muse itself voices the overture. In short he composed a modest, suitable, although somewhat lugubrious introduction to the work, which sounded very well. Even the first stanza, spoken rather broadly but well, caused quiet emotion, and with the departure of the muse[5] I noticed a better mood within myself and in the house which was perfected by the cheerful song of the spirits.[6]

The Daemon of Oppression[7] was spoken with emotion, clearly and steadily. His corruption of Love[8] and Belief,[9] as well as the wretched condition of lost freedom and innocence and the eventual emancipation through Hope,[10] make a deeply impressive scene. Both virtues cowered like trodden-on chickens and, as I said, the scene moved me tremendously and everyone felt it, thank God, even if they didn't recognize it. [...]

Saturday, 1 April: The second performance of *Epimenides* took place yesterday evening. If yesterday the piece received the usual applause for a good work, today the court, which was missing yesterday, was present. A significant section of the general public saw it for the second time today and the reception was warmer from the outset, more prepared, and yesterday's performance was to be considered a general rehearsal. Weber is delighted beyond words. He had to make every effort because Count Brühl pressed him[11] and one expected music that was arduous, cold and cobbled together. If he missed out sometimes and sometimes tried too hard, most of it succeeded admirably. The scene with the appearance of fire on the stage is perfect. He has composed much in the so-called melodramatic style and [it is] really first-rate; he is particularly skilled in this genre. With Cunning he has made much thankless effort and as a result this character is too lyrical. The licking and crawling which he wanted to express turns into sentimentality because he spends too long on it and stops the flow of the piece. Incidentally this character, Cunning,

---

[5] Played by Wilhelmine Maaß (1786–1834), actress and singer; in Weimar, 1802; resident actress at the Königliches Theater, Berlin, 1805–16.

[6] 'Wandelt der Mond und bewegt sich der Stern', v. 87–90.

[7] Played by Joseph Fischer (1780–1862), singer at the Königliches Theater, Berlin, 1814–18.

[8] Sung by Johanna Christiana Friederike Eunicke (1798–1856), singer and actress at the Königliches Theater, Berlin, 1796–1823.

[9] Love, Belief and Hope: allegorical figures in Goethe's *Epimenides*.

[10] Performed by Sophie Louise Schröck née Müller, (1776/77–1846), actress in Berlin.

[11] Count Karl Friedrich Moritz Paul von Brühl (1772–1837), Prussian Chamberlain, General Director of the Königliches Theater, Berlin (1815–28).

is a problem for every composer. The choruses, equipped here in the way they can be only in large theatres, made a very imposing impression, especially a visual one, through the entrance of the various ethnic tribes. Weber gave our leading lady a big magnificent aria with supporting choir, which ultimately is a work in itself. The piece lasts two and a half hours – but on both days it was held up as an endless amount of powerful phrases and sentences were clapped and called back, which was why the actors must pause so long. Sometimes it appeared as if the crowd formed themselves into two choirs in order to applaud this and that, here or there; then they all reunited briefly again and, in short, I really enjoyed it. On the first day the actors left out anything that referred to the King because the King had refused to tolerate – had even forbidden – all such connections: however, yesterday these had to be spoken and the cheering was furious. What's more is, where the group is formed for the finale, the triumphal chariot of the Brandenburg Gate is raised and displayed above the facade of the temple. Of all the speaking characters Epimenides made his mark through coherence, clarity, composure and dignity. Love was beautifully sung [though] spoken less well. Cunning, a slim, beautiful, smooth, tallish, humble courtesan, was exceptionally well and clearly sung. The chap has a tongue like a strip of tagliatelle. The performance was much more together than yesterday. The cast played more freely, fuller, with more eagerness. The appearance of Hope is really powerful. This scene really gripped me again, although it wasn't perfectly performed. It is the secret body to which all parts are fixed – it is calm but monstrous.

To me *Epimenides* was a good plaster on the wounds which struck me like cleavers before the despicable *24 February*.[12] The man[13] looks at fate like a cargo carriage onto which one can pack what one will, or as a charnel house for old bones. God preserve mankind from such poets! The clergy have laid a really good catch for themselves: he brings them all to the gallows.[14]

Now I have to I won't say 'apologize' that I have not replied to two of your letters.[15] The truth is I was out of sorts all the time and in pain, and have waited for the good weather which has now appeared. Could I go to a spa this summer?[16] God knows how badly I need it. I organized a really good Easter concert[17] and

---

[12] *Der vier und zwanzigste Februar*, tragedy by Zacharias Werner; the premiere took place on 23 March 1815; Zelter attended the performance on 29 March 1815.

[13] Friedrich Ludwig *Zacharias* Werner (1768–1823).

[14] Following his conversion to the Catholic Church in 1810, Werner was ordained in 1814.

[15] Goethe's letters on 21 November and 27 December 1814; whether Goethe's third letter of 23 January had reached Zelter at this stage is uncertain.

[16] Zelter was unable to accept Goethe's proposal of a visit to Wiesbaden; he spent a fortnight in Dresden in August 1815 and afterwards spent five weeks in Teplitz.

[17] On 24 August 1815 the annual performance of Graun's *Der Tod Jesu* was given by the Sing-Akademie under Zelter's direction; a report in the *Vossische Zeitung* on 20 March mentions 'the packed hall'.

made over 800 thaler pure profit from it. Also the department[18] has proven itself well disposed towards me. The extension of the State Chancellor's absence[19] is awkward for me because he must confirm my expected additional allowance.[20] It's no joke because it already involves 700 thaler. […]

Send me some songs. I have dressed your 'Hans Adam'[21] [in a way] in which he is fit to be seen.

### 173. Zelter

Berlin, 11 April 1815

The young Mendelssohn,[22] a student doctor, asked me for a letter of introduction to you so he could meet you in person. He has already taken part in the last war, and despite his indifferent health, he has decided to return to the army.

We are expecting our King here in Berlin and *Epimenides* will rest until then,[23] with whose interpretation I am occupied in all kinds of ways. […]

I avail myself of the opportunity to send you some original manuscripts of remarkable people. And even if you should already have something of theirs in your collection, from a historical point of view the compositions are important in

---

[18] The section for culture and public education in the Ministry of the Interior.

[19] Prince Carl August of Hardenburg was at the Congress of Vienna, which concluded on 9 June 1815.

[20] An annual payment of 600 thaler for Zelter's position as Professor of Music at the Berlin Akademie der Schönen Künste had already been agreed, but the first payment was made the following year. Already in his letter of 26 June 1811 Schuckmann, as director of the relevant Department for Culture and Education, had put in a request to State Chancellor Hardenberg for an increase in salary; see Cornelia Schröder (ed.), *Carl Friedrich Zelter und die Akademie. Dokumente und Briefe zur Entstehung der Musik-Sektion in der Preußischen Akademie der Künste*. (Berlin: Akademie der Künste Monographien und Biographien 3, 1959), p. 128f. Only in December 1816 could Zelter report to Weimar that he had received 'an additional annual allowance of 400 thaler'.

[21] The poem ('Hans Adam war ein Erdenkloß') from Goethe's *West-östlicher Divan* written in Berka an der Ilm; originally entitled 'Buchstabe Dal. 18te Gasele'. It was later published in the *Divan* as 'Erschaffen und Beleben'. Zelter's setting, which bears the title 'Der erste Mensch' (1815), was first published in his *Liedertafel* anthology of 1818.

[22] Georg *Benjamin* Mendelssohn (1794–1874), son of Joseph Mendelssohn and his wife, Henriette (Hinni) Mendelssohn, née Meyer.

[23] *Des Epimenides Erwachen* was given its third Berlin performance in celebration of King Friedrich Wilhelm III's return from Vienna.

themselves; particularly those of Sebastian Bach,[24] and Kirnberger.[25] In the life of Fasch[26] you will find an explanation of the piece headed *La Coorl*.[27] [...]

## 174. Goethe

Weimar, 17 April 1815

[...] I had already received some intelligent and detailed reports of the performance of *Epimenides*:[28] but now you come with your bold pen, and by dotting the i's and crossing the t's, for the first time make the writing perfectly legible.

Everything depends on a play of this kind being given a dozen times in succession. If you realize the elements that go to make up such a representation, you will almost despair of a happy result:

The work of the poet, whose basic position will always occupy the external senses and at the same time will stimulate the inner [senses] and demand from the audience that at every moment it look, notice and interpret.

The composer, who should accompany, carry, enhance and support and more or less fulfils this duty of his.

The orchestra, who should perform the intentions of the conductor perfectly.

Actors and singers, who, using the thread put into their hands, have to weave their way through so many perils. Everyone should do his duty and keep an eye on the rest.

Costumes, which are not just passable and are comfortable.

Many miscellaneous props, on which so much depends.

Scenery, whose invention must complement the whole and which must be changed without delays.

And then there is the audience who are assembled from so many classes and cultures, who, even with good will, come cold and unprepared. One can't take it amiss if in the present case they come together unconvinced and in the worst possible frame of mind.

[...] When the play is frequently repeated, it is quite a different matter [...] with more light-hearted nations; when any piece has once taken hold of them, it can be repeated endlessly because the actors, the play and the general public come

---

[24] No longer identifiable either in Goethe's music collection or his collection of manuscripts; Zelter describes the work in ZG 16 to 22 April 1815.

[25] Josef Philipp Kirnberger (1721–83) pupil of Johann Sebastian Bach, composer and violinist in Berlin; teacher to Fasch, Zelter and Anna Amalia von Preußen; music theoretician; author of *Die Kunst des reinen Satzes*.

[26] Zelter's Fasch biography.

[27] C.P.E. Bach, *Sonata in A minor*, third movement (GSA 33/33).

[28] Goethe had received letters about the performance of *Des Epimenides Erwachen* from B.A. Weber (1 April), Konrad Levezow (3 April) and Count Brühl (12 April).

to understand each other better and better; and then, too, one neighbour in the town stirs up another to go to the theatre until finally the common conversation of the day makes it necessary for everyone to see such a novelty. I saw an example of this in Rome, when an opera, *Don Juan* (not Mozart's),[29] was given every evening for a month, an event which so stirred the city that the humblest shopkeepers with the family all dressed up booked seats in the pit and boxes, and no one could exist without having seen Don Juan roasting in Hades and the governor rising towards heaven as a blessed spirit [...] That you should have held so firmly to the pivot upon which my play turns (but, as I hope, without grinding and creaking) and that you felt it so deeply pleased me greatly, although it is quite in accordance with your nature. Without these fearful chains the whole thing would be a failure. The fact that this example is proven in women makes the thing more pardonable and draws it into the domain of emotion; however, we will say nothing further about the matter, and leave its fortune to the gods. [...]

I do not doubt that you have succeeded in clothing Hans Adam's body in an excellent jacket; and I look forward to seeing him parade about in it. I will search out a later poem for you. I find orientalizing very dangerous work because before one is aware of it, the most solid poem slips out of one's hands [and] vanishes into air like a balloon filled with rational and spiritual gas. [...]

Just as I was wondering with what to fill up my remaining space, Mendelssohn[30] came in, bringing with him your kind greeting and gift,[31] both of them most welcome; I received him cheerfully, but distractedly, for when he first called I was more than a hundred miles away from the house. The music manuscripts are fantastic! I had no specimen of any of the three masters[32] in my collection. My very best thanks! As we have brought the Berliners to reflect and to make puns, let us stick to it for a time. Remember me very kindly to State Councillor Schultz. I have studied his treatises[33] again lately; both they and he have become so much dearer to me. Now adieu! May this letter be the happy beginning of new communication between us.

---

[29] Goethe had presumably seen Vincenzo Fabrizi's Opera *Il convitato di pietra* in the Teatro Valle, Rome, in 1787; Giuseppe Gazzaniga's opera *Don Giovanni Tenorio o sia Il convitato di pietra* was performed much later in Rome.

[30] Benjamin Mendelssohn.

[31] Zelter's letter from 11 April and the autograph manuscripts.

[32] J.S. Bach; C.P.E. Bach and Johann Philipp Kirnberger.

[33] Christoph Ludwig Friedrich Schultz, 'Über physiologe Gesichts- und Farben-Erscheinungen'. Schultz sent this essay to Goethe on 27 November 1814, and Goethe had it published in *Schweiggers Journal* in 1816.

## 175. Zelter

Berlin, 16 to 22 April 1815

How was the performance of your *Proserpina* staged and did it have a repeat performance?[34] Because such a piece, if it has also been rehearsed in the best possible way, will have something for the eye and the ear, as long as eye and ear are practised. One must help the best pieces to be well performed. [...]

I will hear 'Hans Adam' for the first time next Tuesday. It was ready quick enough though I went over it for a long time and now we want to hear whether it has not become only too much of a mosaic. As we must give a song a title, I have written 'Der erste Mensch' at the top. If you prefer another title, let me know. We will also sing the song 'Aus wie vielen Elementen soll',[35] which should stand out as more intellectual in so far as it was an exercise in bringing the different elements together under one melody. I have given the Lied the title 'Liederstoff'. I would have called it 'Die vier Elemente'[36] if Schiller had not written one with this title.

Next Tuesday we will perform Mozart's Requiem in the Sing-Akademie in memory of our deceased director, Frisch.[37] Why could I not be so fortunate as to expect you and Mozart among my audience? All that carping and toiling at minutiae (which are self-explanatory because they are lost in the whole) makes your body tired, if you are not listened to from time to time. Fortunately this is one of those pieces of music which, without opportunity, one takes into oneself like a beautiful artistic fragment, and when the opportunity is there, one can very innocently forget about it. There is just enough peace in the piece as is necessary to dismiss the memory of a pleasant, noble departed [person] in the shortest possible time. On the other hand, it is the same with the performance of *Der Tod Jesu*:[38] through performing it for many years the piece is firmly fixed in our choral repertoire and so I have little or nothing to do. What's more, the holy day arrives to which the people are accustomed and for which the theatre is closed. If the performance does happen to be praised, that just means that no one is disturbed and then I can be quietly satisfied [...]

---

[34] Goethe's monodrama *Proserpina*, with music by Carl Eberwein, performed on 4 February 1815 in the Weimar Court Theatre; a repeat performance was staged on 6 February.

[35] Goethe's *Divan* poem, 'Aus wie vielen Elementen', written on 22 July 1814; published under the title 'Elemente' (1819); Zelter's setting entitled 'Liederstoff' dates from 1814 and was published in the *Liedertafel* (1819).

[36] Schiller, *Vier Elemente*, SNA 2/I, p. 215.

[37] Johann Christoph Frisch (1738–1815), painter, since 1805 Director of the Akademie der Künste, died in Berlin on 28 February 1815.

[38] Passion Oratorio by Carl Heinrich Graun.

I am extremely delighted that you received young Benjamin Mendelssohn, as his disposition needs every encouragement if he is not to go under when he is not with others of his kind. His mother, an old friend and the loveliest female creature I have ever encountered, asked me for an address for you and as I had just laid out the fine autograph manuscripts for you, I was glad to save a few groschen on postage. The piece by Sebastian [Bach][39] is actually the Sunday recreation of its writer and considered by me like a drawing carried out by a great artist. If you should hear it said so often how I enjoy your *Epimenides*, you should praise me. It must be played vigorously and not be thrown away, because it is exactly as long as it should be and is completely united.

Now your obedient servant asks for something poetic. I have started many sketches of pieces I have to hand and sketched what, given a calm atmosphere, must work itself out. If the new [poems] arrive, the old will be made whole and the work is halved. I have still not finished 'Das Gastmahl der Weisen':[40] Riemer[41] is so good as to have it written out by his excellent lady,[42] for whom I will again send some of my eau de cologne.

### 176. Zelter

Berlin, 26 April to 13 May 1815

Yesterday our Requiem went like clockwork.[43] The Crown Prince, our entire court at present and the Ministry of Culture, and all the members of both the Academy of Fine Arts and the Academy of Science were present. Before the music for such a celebration can be thought about, there has to be a church, altar, catafalque, mourners and the office of the mass itself. There was no talk of all of these things because we enjoyed our music like good bread without meat. Our academy hall[44] which, by a long way, is not big or high enough to hold 500 people comfortably, was doubled in the absence of these things. That means with the mixture of daylight and light from 300 wax candles the resulting semi-light was very effective. The position of the catafalque was taken by the bust of the composer and that of the mourners was taken by friendship and gratitude. The mass was held; that means Schadow spoke of the merits of the artists and then I added the enclosed words.[45] As a result

---

[39] The piece cannot be identified as it is in neither Goethe's music collection nor in his collection of autograph manuscripts.
[40] Goethe's poem 'Die Weisen und die Leute'.
[41] Friedrich Wilhelm Riemer, Goethe's secretary and amanuensis.
[42] Caroline Riemer née Ulrich (1790–1855).
[43] The performance in honour of J.C. Frisch; see *Vossische Zeitung* 29 April 1815.
[44] The round room of the Akademie der Künste, in which the Sing-Akademie rehearsed until 1827.
[45] Zelter's speech is enclosed with this letter, *MA* 20.3, p. 351.

the mass was divided into three sections, which made a pleasant change. I was certain enough of the progress of my music and of my cheerful assistants to direct my attention to the audience. My enjoyment consisted in this: to take deep delight in the devotion and salutary atmosphere which lasted long after the music. Our Crown Prince, a cheerful, open, friendly youth, delighted me by his applause in so far as he had said to me earlier that he didn't think much of Mozart's Requiem. He came up to me full of joy and said: one should often hear good music, but one also has to hear it [performed] well, otherwise one learns not to listen. I ventured to give my applause to these good words, in that I replied: the good lies neither too deep nor concealed and a worthy investigation always reveals it. He praised the brevity of my speech and that I had mentioned Frederick the Great. – 'Had he not lived like us?' – 'Better!', I added and he bounded off happily.

### 177. Goethe

Weimar, 17 May 1815

I shall send you a few words at once, in return for your dear letter, so that you may be kept in the humour to write again and again. First of all, please let me have some news of the theatre from time to time; for as I am on good terms with Count Brühl, whom I knew as a boy, and as the success of *Epimenides* was due to his exertions, I should like to do him a favour, and in a general way, to remain on good terms with the Berlin Theatre. If there were only some incitement, it is very likely that I should write plays once more, and then Berlin is, after all, the only place in Germany where one has the courage to undertake anything. Owing to the numerous journals and daily papers, all the German theatres lie bare before our eyes, and when you think of it, which one can you turn to with any confidence? Only speak out like a good blunt German, as you were always inclined to, that I may not stumble about in the dark and squander my good intentions on false undertakings.

I have made my *Proserpina*[46] the carrier for everything which modern criticism finds and favours in works of art: (i) the heroic and decorative landscape; (ii) heightened recitation and declamation; (iii) Hamiltonian–Hendelian gestures;[47]

---

[46] A lyric monodrama, initially intended as a collaboration with Gluck in memory of his niece, and later initially introduced into *Der Triumph der Empfindsamkeit*. Goethe collaborated very closely with Carl Eberwein on the musical setting of this melodrama. See Nicholas Boyle's preface to Lorraine Byrne Bodley, *Proserpina: Goethes Melodrama with Music by Carl Eberwein* (Dublin: Carysfort Press, 2007), pp. xvii–xx. See also my own introduction to this score, pp. xxi–xl.

[47] Gestures and expressions imitating Lady Hamilton (née Emily Lyons, known as Emily Hart), whose performance Goethe had witnessed in March 1787 in Caserta (*Italienische Reise*, *MA* 15, p. 258) and the actress Henriette Hendel-Schütz, who had made

(iv) change of costume;[48] (v) change of scenery; and (vi) even a tableau for a finale that represents the realm of Pluto – all this, accompanied by the music you know, which serves as welcome spice for this immoderate feast of the eyes. It was received with great applause, and when foreigners come to us, it will be a tiny useful example of what we can do.

For some time past I have had just enough inclination to contribute articles to the *Morgenblatt*;[49] and that I may save you from wasting time looking for them, I will mark the numbers should like you to look them up. [...] nos. 75 and 76: Account of *Epimenides Erwachen*[50] [...] I shall also give an account of *Proserpina* and explain in more detail what I briefly touched upon above,[51] so that a similar, though more elevated representation of this little play may be given in several different theatres.

I have been glancing through my *West-östlicher Divan* in order to send you a new poem, but I now see clearly for the first time how this kind of poetry drives one to reflection; for I did not find anything singable in it, especially for the Liedertafel, for which, after all, it is our main business to provide. For what cannot be sung in company is in reality no song, just as a monologue is no drama.

[...] Meanwhile I am reading Winckelmann in the new edition by Meyer and Schulze,[52] who have immensely enhanced the value of his works, inasmuch as we see here what the author has actually accomplished and also what exactly is found to need correction and supplementation after so many years. [...] His own *History of Ancient Art*,[53] from the earliest down to the most recent times, has already been sketched from beginning to end, and some sections have been worked out in a masterly style. The merits of such men as Rubens [and] Rembrandt have never yet been expressed by anyone with so much truth and energy. One imagines oneself

---

her name through pantomime and Hamiltonian attitudes; see *Tag-und Jahres-Heften* (1810), MA 14, p. 218.

[48] In an essay on the performance of *Proserpina*, on which this sketch is based, Goethe wrote: 'Proserpina appears as Queen of the Underworld; she is characterized by glorious cloaks folded one over another and a veil and a diadem.'

[49] In 1815 and 1816 Goethe wrote 19 articles for the *Morgenblatt für gebildete Stände*, presumably out of a certain commitment to the publisher of the new edition of his works: the *Morgenblatt* was also published by Cotta.

[50] *Des Epimenides Erwachen. Ein Festspiel*, Berlin, 30 May 1815, *Morgenblatt*, nos 75 and 76, 29 and 30 May 1815.

[51] 'Proserpina, Melodram von Goethe, Musik von Eberwein', *Morgenblatt*, no. 136, 8 June 1815.

[52] Johann Heinrich Meyer and Johann Schulze (eds), *Winkelmanns Werke* 9 vols (Dresden, 1808–20).

[53] Johann Heinrich Meyer's *Geschichte der Kunst* was not, in fact, published in his own lifetime; it first appeared edited by Helmut Holtzhauer und Reiner Schlichting in *Schriften der Goethe-Gesellschaft* 60 (1974). Hereafter referred to as *SchGG*. Meyer's most important work was *Geschichte der bildenden Künste bei den Griechen von ihrem Ursprunge bis zum höchsten Flor*, 3 vols (Dresden, 1824).

in a gallery of their works: the effects of light and shade and colouring in these admirable artists speak to us from the black letters.

Now do make up your mind to write a History of Music in the same vein! You would hardly be able to resist doing so, were I to read out Meyer's work to you for only a quarter of an hour. From your letters and conversation I have already become acquainted with many of your first-rate masters. With the same idea and with the same energy, you would have to begin with an important period and work forwards and backwards, for the true can be raised and preserved only by its history, and the false can be lowered and destroyed only by its history [...]

Before I close this, I am again looking through my *Divan* and find a second reason why I cannot send you a single poem from it; this, however, speaks in favour of the collection. For every individual member is so inspired with the spirit of the whole, is so thoroughly oriental, referring to eastern customs, usages, and religion, and it requires explanation by one of the preceding poems, before it can produce any effect upon the imagination or upon feelings. I myself did not know in what a strange way I had made the anthology hang together. I have almost completed the first hundred poems; when I have finished the second, the collection will look more serious [...]

## 178. Zelter

Berlin, 22 May to 4 June 1815

[...] What you write about a history of music has lived in me for many years and what I have revealed to Johann Müller about it was also not rejected by him. Actually the purpose of describing my humble life was that I should be given the opportunity to present what I know from practical experience and history; as for writing a history of music which I have never seen, it would hardly be fitting for me as I have read little.

1 June: *Epimenides* has just been performed for the third time yesterday to celebrate the arrival of our King.

Each time the music, which is frequently rich in felicitous sections, is realized better. The overture is appropriately very serious and the song of the spirits moves along simply and cheerfully just as the first three scenes flow naturally from one to the other. Epimenides spoke with composure, clarity and grace.[54]

The fire episode in scene five, which was already effective, has improved further, although the Good Spirit of War almost does too much: a fine, brilliant actor[55] who plays Wallenstein and Götz to much applause took on slightly too

---

[54] The title role was played by Friedrich Jonas Beschort (1767–1846), actor and singer at the Königliches Theater, Berlin, 1796–1838.

[55] Franz Mattausch (1767–1833), actor employed by the Berlin Court Theatres.

much. The music for this scene is really first rate and links very well with the warriors' song.

If only the three Daemons, which admittedly do not appear together, were grouped together through the music, then I would say it was perfect. Cunning has lovely music: the actor is a natural,[56] of beautiful form and voice, smooth speech and holds his line well; only it is too long. Fischer[57] has a really oriental character and plays the part of an arrogant, contrary, despondent, spoilt, secure, courageous tyrant really well.

Something which has got tighter is [the performance of] the three virtues. There is still much to be desired and the freedom which should arise out of the redemption doesn't have any really brilliant music; otherwise the scene would be really effective.

From the nineteenth scene onwards, where the resolution of previous mysteries is meant to happen, it dawdles and seems as if it will never end.

I would prefer if Epimenides's song[58] were spoken, because he doesn't sing again through the entire piece. How would it be if it were sung offstage by some alto voices and only heard by Epimenides? It seems to me that it would be a good counterpart to the corresponding visual image and Epimenides could quickly join in and continue speaking.

To me the comet scene is also not right yet. It doesn't give any impression of the universe and doesn't correspond with the earth. I thought the scene should have a similar effect to the fire scenery. The naked light shaft on the horizon is not sufficient and would hardly be noticed if Epimenides hadn't announced its presence.

The twenty-first scene could be improved, although the different groups on foot and on horseback make an imposing impression. As the on-stage music is very strong, alternating with the music on stage and from time to time freshening the effect which is otherwise deafening, thereby becoming irksome..

The brilliant aria is really a concert aria[59] and as such belongs here really well. But it is cut off and stands apart and at the very least would have to be sung by a perfect, beautiful voice.

Miss Unity[60] doesn't know what she says and forces and pronounces in her old way, and as a result the piece suffers exactly where it should triumph. [...]

---

[56] Heinrich Blume (1788–1856), singer and actor in Berlin.

[57] Joseph Fischer (1780–1862), singer at the court theatres in Berlin from 1814 to 1818; later mainly employed in Italy.

[58] 'Hast du ein gegründet Haus', scene 20 (1816), later Act 2, scene 6, v. 759f.

[59] The Aria of Perseverance ('Wetteifernd komm' ich an') omitted from the 1816 edition.

[60] Wilhelmine Maaß.

4 July: Madame Milder from Vienna is here and will appear in 12 [different] roles.[61] She will perform for the first time on Thursday.[62] I am looking forward to her superb golden voice, which obviously belongs to those rarities that you will always be happy with. Admittedly we have a similar soprano, perhaps even as beautiful, in our Tombolini,[63] but the chap is Italian and has become so shallow, unfocused and cold that he is no longer to be enjoyed. Hasse may well have been justified in saying: a German artist would have to live from one year to the next in Italy if he wants to die blessed.[64]

### 179. Goethe

Wiesbaden, 16 June 1815

I am indebted to you for the repeated reviews of *Epimenides*. This is how I would like to express the result that emerges from it: on the whole it is lacking in imagination and feeling; exaggeration must occur, then absence. This would also happen with frequent repetitions now and then; because what the people cannot invent, they will surely discover. There's a great deal to be gained if you can see that Epimenides's song is sung behind the scenes if it is not recited by Epimenides. They will produce the piece again occasionally[65] and perhaps in the future it could be given an independent form.

### 180. Zelter

Berlin, 10 to 17 June 1815

Imagine a calm, really feminine form, fully formed, about 30 years old; with beautiful arms, white, gentle, German, reliable, unspoilt; whose lips are open so wide that a lightly expressive, rich, full voice can comfortably flow through: then you will see Madame Milder, who performed in Gluck's *Armida* yesterday.

---

[61] Anna Milder appeared in the title roles of Gluck's *Armide* and *Iphigénie en Tauride*; as Emmeline in Weigl's *Die Schweizerfamilie*; Antigone in Sacchini's *Oedip zu Colonos*; Susanne in Mozart's *Die Hochzeit des Figaro*; for reviews of her performances see *AMZ* 17 (1815), no. 29, 19 July and no. 46, 15 November, columns 772 and 490; *MA* 20.3, pp. 356–7.

[62] Anna Milder's first appearance was in Gluck's *Armide*, on 9 June 1815.

[63] The Italian castrato Raffaele Tombolini (1766–1839).

[64] The anecdote can be traced to either Hasse's writing or Kandler's biography of the composer.

[65] In addition to the Berlin performances, performances took place in Leipzig on 19 October 1815 and 5 April 1816.

If in your mind you add to such a figure an inner life of pure naivety that, in its innocence, reminds you of Pallas von Velletri (if I have the correct name),[66] then you will have Armida.

That such a creature, who is inhibited by no rules or acquired knowledge of the art, flows along like a fine stream, who doesn't come and go and stand as if an audience were present, but is rather like a blacksmith [who stands] before a forge in order to pull out hot what was placed in cold; that such a creature causes confusion and conflict for the connoisseurs of our art will become very evident perhaps because one says: a pretty woman – but colossal; a beautiful voice – but not what one calls singing; gentle and feminine – but cold and so on – and yet such sensational applause, as if they were really enthralled, moved and touched.

So one sees with joy how the appearance of sheer talent turns to water the ideas of an entire generation, who had become so accustomed to suspending the natural until there are enough words, notes about it and even attempts at travesty of it.

I did not have to change my old impression about the music and the libretto and understood even more that a true work is clearly recognized by a true performance.

This honest Pallas drops what does not impose itself and rises to the heavens with that which suits her. Gluck has clearly paid too much attention to minutiae and he would have been none too pleased if a woman had treated him like that. What he has done well is certainly good and he is to be excused on the grounds that he did not write the libretto.

The German translation[67] is so sluggish that it remains stuck in the singer's mouth. Milder knows how to free herself even from this.

Every week we have two, sometimes three, guest roles, which is not a bad thing because our [opera] house, which is too small in the winter, is often too big in the summer, and the general public are more interested in attending [the theatre] in the summer and getting to know the artists it wants, through which the directors have a better box office and other advantages. Incidentally if things go on like this for a year, we would take off by getting rid of debts and, given the technical set up which is there really for both theatres, great and noble objectives could be aimed at. Perhaps it will be possible to think that in time opera, operetta, comedy and tragedy will be kept separate from one another, for which purpose another house would have to be built, and then it would be possible to train the general public.

If the Queen were still alive,[68] we could certainly think about it, especially in a time of peace, because a court theatre is important where there is a court and when an audience do not show enough enthusiasm for their best poets. Such enthusiasm is completely absent. The oldest and best works are always new to the general public, in addition to which unity is missing on the stage and also in the

---

[66] Statue of Athena (*c.* 430 BC) from ancient Velletri, south of the Albanian mountains; it is housed in the Louvre, Paris.

[67] Translation by Julius Voß.

[68] Luise von Preußen, wife of King Friedrich Wilhelm III (1776–1810).

relationship between performance and audience. The general public is certainly better than the judges, who always only rebuke the mistakes and have nothing to say about the genuine, the fine, the lofty and the excellent. It is pathetic how these people must grapple with things they do not understand and by actual disposition can do nothing for an artist with natural flair except correct him, when he himself is already annoyed over what he hasn't managed to bring off. On the other hand, they make concessions to mediocrity and youth which they intend to encourage and out of which nothing will come. Likewise, they confuse both public and actors with their judgement of the plays, for what is the artist to do if there is no resonance of what he intended to do?

But why do I tell you about such things which you yourself know a thousand times better?

Yesterday (on 15 June) *Oedip zu Colonus*[69] was very successfully performed. One seldom sees such a slick production. The opera has never appealed to me and I listen to it repeatedly only because I have the judgement of France and Germany against me.[70] Yesterday I liked it and one sees what is possible for an excellent voice. The subject is obviously too large and mysterious for an Italian composer and the music contains little of the tragic. Everything is bright, cheerful, lively, without depths and will not grip [the audience]. And yet Gluck influenced this Italian because there are, however, faint Gluckean echoes in Sacchini. The effect of these is all the more pleasant in so far as they occur spontaneously and spice up the Italian cantilena, through which it is in fact enhanced. Although I am not like those who would wish for the mixture of talent and want to make one man out of Gluck, Mozart and Haydn, I don't want to have what God can't do and have enough in what is there.

### 181. Zelter

Berlin, 26 to 30 June 1815

[...] Imagination and feeling cannot be pushed or pressed into a work and, given the little attention to detail which artists and scholars of art pay to it, it cannot be otherwise, as long as musicians quibble with words and concepts over harmony and melody, and philosophers quibble over allegories and superstition. [...]

---

[69] The comic opera *Oedipe à Colone* by the Italian composer Antonio Sacchini (libretto by Nicholas François Guillard) was staged in Herklots's German translation on 16 October 1797 in the Königliches Opernhaus, Berlin; for a review of the performance; see *AMZ* 17 (1815), no. 29, 19 July, column 491f. Anna Milder sang Antigone.

[70] Sacchini's opera, which was premiered on 1 February 1787 in the Paris Opera House and hailed as the composer's masterpiece, remained in the repertoire until 1830, enjoying 583 performances, as well as countless sequels on European stages.

With regard to our friend Weber, I will try to come to an agreement with him about the inscription in question[71] (since I suspect that he continues to work at perfecting his work) and will give you information from time to time. I am pleased that you have taken up the idea which came to me, though so much depends on the performance. The ritornello to these words would have to commence as Epimenides still concerns himself with the contemplation of the family portrait [...]. Three good alto voices (supported intermittently by instrumental backing) would perform the eight verses briefly and audibly and, above all, like an old wise saying. The action remains flowing, which is particularly important.

Madame Milder continues to be applauded. I have never seen the theatre so full during the summer. She earned new friends even as Susanne in *Figaro*, and as Emeline in *Die Schweizerfamilie* she is thought to be unsurpassable. What pleases me most is that the crowd recognizes the talent as talent and exalts it.

## 182. Goethe

Weimar, 29 October 1815

I have not returned empty-handed from my crusade, and before long you will receive my printed observations upon art and antiquity in the districts around the Rhine and Maine,[72] with incidental remarks on science. [...]

I heard no public musical performances on my journey that gave me any pleasure. I met with some sympathetic voices that sounded very agreeable when accompanied by piano and guitar. I heard 'Der Gott und die Bajadere' given with all imaginable beauty and feeling.[73] However, is the first edition of your engraved songs no longer available?[74] I could not get it in Frankfurt, though the later ones were there. They know nothing about you on the Main, and the Rhine is not acquainted with you, so we have been preaching your gospel in these districts. In

---

[71] Zelter's suggested change to the Berlin production, of which Goethe approved.

[72] Goethe, *Über Kunst und Altertum in den Rhein und Mayn Gegenden* (Stuttgart: Cotta, 1816).

[73] Zelter's setting of Goethe's ballad, published in Schiller's *Musen-Almanach für das Jahr 1798*, was performed on 16 and 17 September by Marianne von Willemar (1784–1860). Her rendition of the aria 'Gib mir die Hand' from Mozart's *Don Giovanni* enchanted Goethe and he described her as a little Don Juan. A muse for Goethe's *West-östlicher Divan*, Willemar wrote the two Suleika settings made famous by Schubert, 'Was bedeutet die Bewegung' and 'Ach, um deine feuchten Schwingen'; the former was also composed by Felix Mendelssohn; Fanny Hensel composed settings of both poems.

[74] Zelter, *Sämtliche Lieder, Balladen und Romanzen* (Berlin, 1810–13); the publishers, August Friedrich Kuhn, had gone bankrupt and was taken over by the publishers Adolph Martin Schlesinger, who brought out a complete edition of Zelter's songs.

Heidelberg, on the other hand, you are fresh in people's memory.[75] You will, no doubt, allow me to send some of your canons and part songs there;[76] I should also like to forward the score of 'Johanna Sebus'.[77] They have a society of amateurs under [the direction of] a clever and able conductor.[78] A well-disposed young man has started a singing academy in Frankfurt,[79] which I hope to be able to assist and I wish you would test how good they are. These musicians suffer from the same misfortune as poets, for each one only brings forward his own work: that which is like him and within his reach. Fräulein Hügel[80] plays Handel's and Bach's Sonatas most admirably, and unfortunately, neither in that province of art, nor in any other, is there any central point after which everybody is sighing, since people are only accustomed to revolve around themselves. [...] And now a kind farewell, and do send me a little song or canon!

### 183. Zelter

Berlin, 8 to 11 November 1815

[...] In Giebichenstein I visited Reichardt's grave and his garden[81] and recalled the image of him when he was fresh and active. To turn to the living [...] from time to time I receive letters from around the place, [asking me] to send them some of my people to found and equip singing academies for them, with conditions which would not be too bad for myself. If I knew everything which is desired by these

---

[75] Goethe is referring to the Heidelberg lawyer and university professor Anton Friedrich Justus Thibaut (1772–1840), who as amateur musician and leader of a singing circle was known to Zelter, who later composed *Tenebrae factae sunt* for Thibaut's choir book (1816).

[76] On 16 December 1815 Goethe sent the following compositions by Zelter to Thibaut: (i) 'Wer kauft Liebesgötter' (Goethe), score and parts; (ii) 'Nimmer, das glaubt mir' (Schiller), score and parts; (iii) 'Lieben Freunde' (Schiller), score and parts; (iv) 'Berglied' (Schiller) score; (v) Two 'Punschlieder' (Schiller), (GSA/32/1509b).

[77] Zelter's setting of Goethe's ballad 'Johanna Sebus' (Leipzig: Kühnel, 1810).

[78] The choral evening which Thibaut had held in his home since 1806.

[79] Johann Georg *Heinrich* Düring (1778–1858), organist, flautist, composer and music teacher in Frankfurt am Main, founder of the Frankfurt choral society in 1809; see Goethe's *Kunst und Altertum am Rhein und Mayn*, MA 11.2, p. 40.

[80] Anna von Hügel (b.1789), daughter of Baron Johann Aloys Joseph von Hügel, an Austrian diplomat at the Nassau Court. Of her piano playing Goethe wrote to his wife, Christiane: 'At Baron Hügel's whose daughter played sonatas by Handel, which reminded me of the Bach sonatas [performed by Badeinspektor Schutz]'.

[81] Giebichenstein in Halle was Reichardt's place of residence from 1791; in 1804 he bought a manor house there on extensive grounds which he developed into a famous national park.

pretenders, then I could feel I was somebody. You are expected to be able to do all that they want, but nobody requests what you can do – either there or here.

    I will send you Part One of my songs […] when it can be obtained because I no longer have any more copies myself and my publisher is bankrupt. You need not be too secretive about my settings; they are intended to be brought to light and there is an engraving of 'Johanna Sebus' in Leipzig, so you can give your copy away.

    I will send several Tafellieder at the next opportunity.[82] It is impossible to find good copyists, otherwise they would be in your hands already.

### 184. Zelter

Berlin, 28 November 1815

Dr Chladni has also arrived[83] and I hope that we will keep this clever, good man. […] In the meantime I have read *Rameaus Neffe*[84] with admiration.

### 185. Zelter

Berlin, 18 February 1816

Our royal princes have made the heroic decision to stage and portray among themselves a full version of your *Faust*.[85] The preparations are projected so grandly that I almost fear it will come to nothing, as we have no venue where we would want to stage it.

    I have also been given the role of director, which I intend to play with as much dignity and clarity as is possible.[86]

---

[82] Zelter did not fulfil this intention.

[83] Ernst Chladni arrived to give lectures at the University in Berlin.

[84] Goethe's translation of Diderot's dialogues, *MA* 7, p. 567.

[85] Rehearsals for the performance of Radziwill's setting of Goethe's *Faust I* commenced on 30 March 1816, with further rehearsals on 6 and 13 April 1816. Radziwill's absence – arising through his appointment as Prussian governor in Posen in 1815 – put a halt to these rehearsals. Four years later two scenes were performed in Berlin on 24 May 1819, with a second performance in Schloss Monbijou on 7 June 1820.

[86] Zelter had taken on the role of director in 'Vorspiel auf dem Theater' and is referring to Goethe's position as Director of the Weimar theatre.

Everyone is delighted with the additional passages you sent in manuscript to Prince Radziwill.[87] I hear the Crown Prince[88] is completely absorbed in *Faust*, [the title role of] which, according to what I know of him, he will like very well. [The role of] Mephistopheles will be played by Carl von Mecklenburg.[89] [...]

In the meantime they have newly cast *Die Zauberflöte*[90] and provided it with 12 new sets, four of which are already on view. [...]

Dr Chladni is here and has concluded his second seminar on acoustics. [...]

Write to me about *Epimenides*: I am really keen. I can imagine what Müller[91] will say about it.

### 186. Goethe

Weimar, 11 March 1816

The presence of Messrs Schadow and Weber has brought me into closer rapport with Berlin;[92] for through personal conversation and friendly chat, even distant conditions can be brought nearer to us. A thousand times have I thought of you, and how you sail, swim, plunge in and plough through such a sea! [...]

My *Divan* has grown in bulk and in strength.[93] The style of poetry, which, without further reflection, I have adopted and made use of, has this peculiarity: that, like the sonnet, it almost resists being sung; it is also notable enough, that the Orientals distinguish themselves by writing not by singing. However, it is a kind of poetry that suits my time of life, way of thinking, experience, and view of things, while it allows one to be as foolish in love matters as one can only be in one's youth.

---

[87] Radziwill had visited Goethe on 1 April 1814 and performed excerpts from his *Faust* composition for the poet. Impressed by his 'strong talent' (Goethe to Knebel, 2 April 1814, *WA* IV/24, p. 213) Goethe gladly accommodated Radziwill's wish for additional verses, suitable for musical treatment. On 4 April Goethe was preoccupied with 'Paralipomena to *Faust*' (see Goethe's diary, *WA* III/5, p. 102) and on the 11 April 1814 he sent an additional scene and a newly revised scene to Radziwill ('Zwei Teufelchen und Amor', and a revised version of the 'Gartenhäuschen' scene; Anne Bohnenkamp, '...das Hauptgeschäft nicht außer Augen lassend'. Die Paralipomena zu Goethes 'Faust' (Frankfurt am Main and Leipzig: Insel Verlag, 1994), pp. 250–53 and pp. 257–9), hereafter referred to as Bohnenkamp.

[88] Friedrich Wilhelm von Preußen (1797–1888), later King Friedrich Wilhelm IV.

[89] Prince Carl Friedrich August von Mecklenburg-Strelitz (1785–1837), stepbrother to Queen Luise of Prussia.

[90] See *AMZ* 18 (1816), no. 7, 14 February, column 105; *MA* 20.3, p. 366.

[91] Presumably the Weimar Court Kapellmeister August Eberhard Müller.

[92] The recent visit of Gottfried Schadow and B.A. Weber to Goethe in Weimar.

[93] From the beginning of the year Goethe had added 25 poems to the *Divan*.

To close: a song that can be sung: 'Dir zu eroffnen/ Mein Herz verlangt mich'.

### 187. Zelter

Berlin, 9 March 1816

Once again I have received bad news. My youngest son[94] died of fever on 17 February in St Michel on the Aisne, after he had fought in the bloodiest battles without being wounded. He was captured in the last affair at Versailles. Two Prussian cavalry regiments fought against seven French cavalry regiments and four infantry regiments. He lost his horse and remained healthy. [He was only] sixteen. The beautiful boy. How will I get over it?

In the week since I received the news from his cavalry captain, I have thrown myself into my work and am copying out scores. In the evening I go to the theatre as writing in [poor] light makes my eyes tired. [...]

Chladni leaves here frustrated. I regret that we cannot keep this man here. [...]

### 188. Goethe

Weimar, 26 March 1816

Indeed you have had another hard task put upon you; unfortunately it is always the same old story, that to live long means to outlive many, and in the end, what is the meaning of it all? A few days ago, the first edition of my *Werther*[95] accidentally came into my hands and its song, long since forgotten, began to resound in me once again. And then one cannot understand how a man could bear to live another 40 years in a world, which in his early youth already appeared so absurd to him. One part of the riddle explains itself in the way everyone has something peculiar to himself which he proposes to develop by giving it free reign. Now nature makes fools of us day by day and so we grow old without knowing why or for what reason. When I consider the matter carefully [I realize] it is only the talent in me that helps me through all the unsuitable conditions in which I find myself entangled by false tendencies, accident and the adoption of foreign elements.

---

[94] Adolph Raphael Zelter (1799–1816), Zelter's second son from his (second) marriage to Julianne Zelter.

[95] *Die Leiden des jungen Werthers* (Leipzig: Weygand, 1774).

## 189. Zelter

Berlin, 18 to 19 March 1816

Your little song[96] made a big impression on me as I understand it and apply it to myself. It immediately inspired a musical form, for without this medium I would not have come to terms with it. As soon as it is written out and tidied up, you shall have it and then you can tell me gently whether my experiment matches your text or not! [...]

Chladni, who is leaving tomorrow, will take this letter with him. As a result I have finished the song[97] and send a little sample from the *Divan*.[98] One of your singers will easily be able to perform it for you, if he doesn't cause trouble for himself. I have not yet heard *Hafis* myself and still don't know how it will be in performance because it was set to music very recently. Pieces that are outside the spirit of our time I must carry around with me for a long time before I find a modern form in which they can be composed. And afterwards who should say whether one has succeeded because the others also cannot grasp it and prefer to pass over it? As a result a word from you about it should be very helpful because you live in it.

## 190. Zelter

Berlin, 31 March 1816

After several rehearsals with orchestra and chorus, there was also a reading rehearsal with music, yesterday evening. Prince Carl of Mecklenburg read the part of Mephistopheles, and the actor Lemm stood in for Faust;[99] the rehearsal was at Prince Radziwill's [palace] among his family circle. The Princess and her children were present,[100] the Crown Prince with his brothers and sisters, Prince

---

[96] 'Dir zu eröffnen' from Goethe's *Divan*.

[97] Zelter's setting of 'Dir zu eröffnen' for bass and piano accompaniment is in Goethe's music collection (GSA 32/24). A copy in Berlin is dated 18 March 1816 (SBB PK: Mus. ms. autogr. Zelter 26). Goethe mentions the setting in a letter to Jacob von Willemar on 5 April 1816, *WA* IV/26, pp. 324–5. The song was first published under the title 'Aus der Ferne' in *Sechs Deutsche Lieder für die Bass-Stimme mit Begleitung des Pianoforte* (1826).

[98] Zelter's setting of Goethe's poem 'So lang man nüchtern ist' for male-voice choir, written on the reverse side of the manuscript of 'Dir zu eröffnen'.

[99] In later performances the role was played by Pius Alexander Wolff.

[100] Princess Friederike Dorothea *Luise* Radziwill (1770–1836) with her daughter Elisa (1803–34) and her son Friedrich Wilhelm Ferdinand (1811–31).

George of Mecklenburg,[101] Frau von der Recke with her friend Tiedge, Frau von Humboldt,[102] and several artists who are to take part in the production.

For a start only those scenes were read in which Faust appears alone with Mephistopheles. Prince Carl reads this character in a way that leaves little to be desired – voice, tone, rhythm, figure and appearance – all is congruous, apart from the cloven foot. What is lacking in modulation and tempo will, I hope, be sorted out. His delivery, too, won universal applause, and the music jogged by his side like a donkey beside a horse.

The effect of the poem upon an almost entirely youthful audience, to whom everything was new and strange, is quite remarkable. They are amazed that it is all in print. They go and look at the book to see if that's what it really says. They all feel it is true; it is as if they were inquiring whether the truth is true.

Some of it the composer has brought off astonishingly well; where he goes astray is that he, like all artists at the beginning of their career, emphasizes what should be secondary.

'Christ ist erstanden':[103] performed well and with impetus, although not religious enough. Organ, choir and bells can still be produced, however. As [Radziwill] has no concept of the inner form of art, he searches in the distance for what lies at his feet. They offered him a bell which he also wants to use. However, he is not lacking in taste. I will let him try this and I am certain he will leave it out.

'Spaziergänger vor dem Tore':[104] In general, good, but it occasionally gets stuck in minor details. The beggar sings like a beggar and the orchestra play lavishly. With the soldiers he really let go: it never occurred to him that these soldiers are walking, not marching, soldiers but nothing is boring and good taste always has the upper hand.

The shepherd dressed himself up to dance: very popular and pastoral but not ephemeral enough.

'Drinnen gefangen ist Einer':[105] perfect! But the entire incantation needed music, although it was effective with just a mere reading. The swelling up of the monster, the mist, the sulphur, leading to the emergence of the fully grown form lends itself very well to music – and that with very ordinary means. Mephisto's explanation of who he really was had a great impact. Everyone was dumbfounded. It was grasped without, perhaps, being understood.

'Schwindet, ihr dunkeln': truly artistic. I would not know how it could be improved. The rat incantation, however, has to be described as excellent. It was rehearsed six times and was first rounded off in rehearsals. I found it appropriate that Faust, through the departure of Mephisto, did not simply wake but was awoken

---

[101] Grand Duke Georg Friedrich Carl Joseph von Mecklenburg-Strelitz (1779–1860).
[102] Caroline Friederike von Humboldt née Dacheroeden (1766–1829).
[103] 'Chor der Engel', *Faust I, Nacht*, v. 757ff.
[104] The scene 'Vor dem Tor'.
[105] The spirit's words ('There is something captive in there') in *Studienzimmer*, v. 1447ff.

as if by an electric shock. The bassoons, through a deep, short sound, made the thing natural to the amusement of all, and only the smell was missing.

'Weh! Weh! Du hast sie zerstört':[106] initially somewhat too heavy. The land of milk and honey presented from the words 'New life begins'[107] was really well and very originally realized.

The play is to be performed in three parts. The second section, which we are to rehearse soon, begins with 'Auerbachs Keller'; I shall keep you informed!

### 191. Zelter

Berlin, 4 April 1816

[…] In Paris our King bought the so-called 'Justina' picture collection,[108] which is really valuable. According to these happy circumstances we hope that the Kunstakademie, in which horses and stable lads had the upper hand up to now, will be converted into a museum, and also that a decent room will be granted to the Sing-Akademie, which is now in its twenty-sixth year.

Evening: I have come directly from *Clavigo*.[109] A foreign actor, Julius von Breßlau,[110] dedicated himself to Beaumarchais, but not convincingly. A rescuer-avenger must have a resounding voice. The work was neither really different nor really together and is a straightforward piece which should be tossed off easily. I fear it was not well directed in rehearsals. Not one person occurred to me who should direct it. The Wolffs[111] were expected, but they are not yet here. Madame Catalani[112] should also come and Milder should sing, yet we still never can be sure of having her because she has those against her who would wish for Italian opera. Admittedly German opera is very touch-and-go. The majority are translations and the majority of operas by Mozart are Italian. It can come to nothing here. There are too many cooks and not all who carry long knives are cooks. *Epimenides* is on tomorrow.

---

[106] The spirit's chorus, v. 1606ff.

[107] Ibid., v. 1622.

[108] In November 1815 the Prussian king purchased 157 works of old masters from the Galerie Giustiniani, founded by Vincenzo and Benedetto Giustiniani.

[109] Performance of Goethe's tragedy *Clavigo* on 4 April 1816, Berlin.

[110] Friedrich Julius (1776–1860).

[111] Pius Alexander and Amalie Wolff.

[112] Angelica Catalani (1780–1849), Italian singer, enjoyed an international reputation in Italy, Lisbon, Paris and London. She began a European tour in 1816 and gave her first concert in Berlin on 24 June 1816.

The bearer of this letter is the banker Abraham Mendelssohn.[113] He is the second son of the philosopher, and from the first years of his youth, after his father's death,[114] he has been attached to my house and its inmates. He is one of the right sort, and as such you will receive him. He has lovely children, and his eldest little daughter[115] could let you hear a thing or two of Sebastian Bach. This child was somewhat precocious, which she still is, and all of them are early developers. [His wife, Lea] is a most excellent mother and housewife; though unfortunately she is not very strong. The husband is very well disposed towards me, and I can borrow freely from him, for in times of general need he has grown rich without damage to his soul.[116]

## 192. Zelter

Berlin, 6 to 7 April 1816

*Epimenides* went well last night and the large theatre was full. There was much I wished you could have seen. Epimenides, Cunning, Oppression and Hope could not have been cast better, although the whole [work] will never be clear to us, since they always stumble around and almost naively miss the entrances. The opinions of the well-intentioned about it are so completely masked in silence that I prefer to remove myself when I can. Now they have to deal with the estates, and that always means: who will get this or that job and what will be paid for it. I have become almost anxious about it, which, observed from a neutral position, can be awkward and uncomfortable, for they are taken up with external concerns which they understand even less than the internal.

Right now a Parisian dancer with her husband[117] are gods and the talk of Berlin. That they can dance goes without saying, although you can hardly imagine more unattractive long-legged persons. They are of the best school and one is just astonished at the chasteness of their movements, whereas our people almost demonstrate more of their body than anything outside it. That is their whole art.

---

[113] Abraham Mendelssohn (1776–1835), banker in Berlin; father of Felix, Fanny, Rebecca and Paul Mendelssohn Bartholdy.
[114] Moses Mendelssohn (1728/29–86) died on 4 January 1786.
[115] Fanny Mendelssohn (1805–47).
[116] Reference to Matthew 16, 26.
[117] Constance Hippolyte Anatole and her husband Auguste Anatole; see *AMZ* 18 (1816), no. 16, 17 April, column 267; *MA* 20.3, p. 375.

I saw the ballet *Telemachus*[118] for the second time yesterday. The subject is more suitable to a ballet than a libretto,[119] which is lacking in meteorical style. Mademoiselle Düring, who should visit you,[120] plays Calypso and presents herself really well as a young pretty girl to the 36-year-old ramrod Telemachus. But she is able to match him with a series of unpleasant faces that would have made the departure easier for the true Telemachus!

Epimenides's song, 'Hast du ein gegründet Haus', was left out yesterday[121] and I must confess I was sorry about it. I didn't like to mention it to Weber as I know well that he is happy to be almost finished. He is like a coconut: one can only deal with him knife in hand. You will have seen him at close quarters.

Yesterday we had a first reading of *Faust*, and just as we were about to begin, all the young royalties announced themselves. As I had to read the beginning, it turned out that we didn't let ourselves be disturbed and the honourable guests took their places without much bowing and scraping. The thing went off as well as a first rehearsal can in such a mixed circle and I will really have to assert myself more and more [in order] to bring movement into the whole thing if no one else wants to do it. The 'jovial person' – one of the counts – didn't seem to know the poem at all. After the rehearsal he apologized to me for his bad reading, upon which he expected a compliment. I replied that reading would not have been a bad thing and that I feared his problem was the spelling. He made sheep's eyes at that.

Count Brühl played the poet quite decently. Lemm, the actor, improved and gradually settled into his part. However, Prince Carl deteriorated and fell into a preaching tone. We had finished Act One when the King arrived unexpectedly; most likely he could not endure home any longer, as his children had all gone off.

The whole of Act One was repeated, and the King, who at first, as is usual, kept quiet and in the background, after two hours of silence became sociable, chatty and really amiable.

---

[118] Anatole's adaptation, *Telemach auf Calypsos Insel*, from the French *Télémaque dans l'île de Calypso* by Pierre Gabriel Gardel, music by Ernest-Louis Müller; first performed (with Benda's *Pygmalion*) in the opera house, Berlin, on 28 March 1816, with a further performance on 5 April following the performance of *Epimenides*.

[119] Antonio Simone Sografi's libretto to Simon Mayr's opera of the same name: *Telemaco all'Isola di Calipso*.

[120] Reference to Goethe's vain attempt to engage the Berlin actress Auguste Düring for the Weimar Court Theatre.

[121] Zelter had recommended that Epimenides's song should be declaimed rather than sung; Goethe had suggested an off-stage chorus of spirits. Although Zelter wanted to reach agreement with Weber about it, the song was omitted in this performance – possibly because Weber's composition of this new section was not yet complete. In the 1816 edition it was treated as an off-stage chorus.

I will give this letter to Mendelssohn to take with him as he is leaving in the morning and he will arrive in Weimar sooner than the post.[122] The final rehearsal is next Saturday because Radziwill is travelling to Posen with his family.

### 193. Goethe

Weimar, 14 April 1816

Your letters, dearest Friend, surprised me most agreeably in my garden – gave me much to think about; they stimulated me to a wider-ranging conversation in the distance. Then came Mendelssohn, and as I was just in the humour, and he was recommended by you, I told him what I would probably have told you; this I think he deserved; he talked very intelligently, and in the course of his conversation discussed many important points in science, art, and life. Unfortunately I did not see his people. They stayed only one afternoon; I should have liked to invite them to breakfast today, and to have shown them all my things. […]

*Faust* may, in future months, afford you many a confused hour. If you go on being as rude as you were to the gloomy count, something will come of your endeavour [..]

Last Sunday we celebrated the grand homage celebration. The honours, distinctions, and compliments awarded to us told every sensible man among us very plainly that he must give himself up for the time being. However, the task allotted to me is the most pleasant one; I have nothing to do except what I thoroughly understand, and I have only to continue doing what I have done for the last 40 years, with ample means, great freedom, and without worry or hurry […]

My last empty page I shall fill with a few verses; you can use them if you feel inclined.

Enclosed: 'Das Publikum', 'Herr Ego'.[123]

### 194. Zelter

Berlin, 20 to 24 April 1816

My Passion Music was as profitable as last year. The room was so full that several hundred people had to be sent away. If I were a better mathematician than I am,

---

[122] Abraham Mendelssohn visited Goethe in Weimar on 10 April 1816.
[123] These poems were first published posthumously in Riemer's edition of the Goethe–Zelter correspondence (1833).

I would have presumed I could claim for a good part of my trip[124] from this loss or non-profit. [...]

I was to have seen the Wolffs at Prince Radziwill's on Sunday, but they didn't show up and instead sent the news that you were sick – critically ill![125] That was the 21st and your letter to me on the 14th mentioned nothing of the kind, and so I hope that you have recovered again. Don't leave me in uncertainty about it and if you don't want to write yourself, let me receive news from someone else. God! How could I live without you? Have I not suffered enough?

### 195. Goethe

Weimar, 3 May 1816

I answer your dear letter at once. [...] For what will you say now when I tell you that I, too, have had a severe blow lately? Pretty Berka on the Ilm, where we experienced so much in company with Wolf and Weber and Dunker![126] Imagine, first of all, that pretty Viennese piano, belonging to the organist Schütz,[127] with the music of Sebastian, Philip Emmanuel Bach, and so on.[128] Well, Berka was burnt to the ground, between 25 and 26 April.[129] By dint of extraordinary presence of mind, and the help of kind people, the piano was saved, as well as many other things in the house, in a maximum of seven minutes, which is astonishing; for a tremendous fire, which began at a baker's house, had, by half past eleven, spread its flames far and wide. All the organist's old pieces by the Bach family and Handel, which he had got from Kittel of Erfurt,[130] are burnt, and that merely owing to a mindless accident or chance: he had tidied them away into a rather remote room.

Of course, all these things are already engraved and in print; let me know how I could get them from Härtel's[131] in Leipzig, or elsewhere, for I should be glad to give him a little solace in this way. Heaven bless copper, print and every other means of multiplying things, so that a good work which has once existed can never

---

[124] To Wiesbaden, 14 July to 13 August, via Weimar, 5 to 8 July.

[125] Goethe's diary for 2 to 4 April records 'unwell these days', *WA* III/5, p .220.

[126] Goethe reminds Zelter of the days they spent together in Berka from 23 to 28 July 1814.

[127] Johann *Heinrich Friedrich* Schütz (1779–1829), spa inspector and organist in Berka on the Ilm.

[128] Goethe recalls Schütz's performances of the music of J.S. Bach and his sons when Goethe stayed with him in 1814.

[129] See Goethe's diary entry for 26 April: 'Sad news of the terrible fire which had broken out in Bad Berka at 1 a.m.', *WA* III/5, p. 226.

[130] The bequest of the organist and composer, Johann Christian Kittel (1732–1809), in Erfurt from 1756.

[131] Breitkopf und Härtel, Leipzig.

again be destroyed. If you should see Privy Councillor Wolf, give him my kindest regards, but tell him also that the accursed little trumpet piece[132] escaped being burnt by the strangest chance, as I happened to have it in the town; like a good many other things, it was saved by being housed in different places.

## 196. Zelter

Berlin, 8 to 12 May 1816

[...] I arrived back from Potsdam yesterday where I had spent a few days in the most beautiful burgeoning spring which only a soft continuous rain can open. A year and a half ago they started a Sing-Akademie there[133] and have long invited me to it, and it is only now that I could tear myself away from here. I would be amazed, even astonished, that in six months these people achieve what we have managed after 26 years of constant perseverance here in Berlin, if I did not realize that my wheelings and dealings have worked in far-off places and will continue to work if the model should fall apart after me.

You can imagine that these good people are really delighted with it and they were all the more pleased with my approval since the court, in Potsdam for communion on Good Friday, heard their Passion Music[134] afterwards and judged their performance on the unsuccessful details and considered it really bad.

The misfortune of that poor man [in] Berka has shaken me very badly because for a long time now I have imagined a [similar] disaster, a blazing fire among my lovely musical things, and I could not bear it any longer. It could happen so easily because I live between nests of fire: being a stables, the Sing-Akademie and the Kunstakademie contain so much hay and straw.

Therefore I send you fine manuscripts,[135] of which I have two, in the hope that they might give you comfort. They are yours and if you would like to give some to the organist, Schütz, then that is fine too.

---

[132] Presumably J.S. Bach's *Capriccio sopra la lontananza del suo fratello dilettissimo*, BWV 992. For an account of the performance of this piece for Goethe in Bad Berka; see Friedrich Wilhelm Riemer, *Mitteilungen über Goethe* (2 vols, Berlin: Duncker und Humblot, 1841), vol. 1, pp. 266–8.

[133] The Potsdam Institute, founded on 2 November 1814, was modelled on the Sing-Akademie. The director was Carl Bernhard Wessely (1768–1826); see Carl Wey, 'Zwei Briefe Karl Friedrich Zelters', *Die Musikpflege* 6 (1934): 91.

[134] Graun's *Der Tod Jesu*, which was performed in Potsdam and Berlin until towards the end of the nineteenth century.

[135] A page which is in the collection, 'Goethe, Eingegangene Briefe', in the fascicle of March 1831, could be identified as the contents pages for the dispatch to the spa inspector and organist in Berka, and containing: (1) J.S. Bach, *24 Preludes and Fugues* Part Two; (2) *Vom Himmel hoch da komm ich her* (with canonic variations for the organ); (3) *Aria*

I also send you two complete copies of my songs, which are finally available once more.[136] I am now able to provide what one person or another is missing.

I will forward the first book of Johann Sebastian Bach's *Preludes and Fugues*; I don't want to send the Leipzig edition[137] because I don't consider it a good edition. Part I is just as good as the second book but has no performative connection with Part II. They are really singular works.

For the past two weeks I have been really enjoying the first two volumes of the new edition of your works. The advance payment is so favourable and inexpensive that I have just paid for them in full and if I receive a copy from you, I will give it to my daughter. I have set to music the tiny poem with the title 'Gegenwart'[138] on page 59 for three soprano voices with piano accompaniment, as one would want to receive an honoured, beloved person in reserved circles; I would imagine it would work well, but I haven't heard it yet.

It is the same with me in the Sing-Akademie as it is for you with your actors. When I am among them, I have no judgement. If I heard them in a different place, I would have to pack them in. As a result I would like to have you here because you are the person whose opinion I most value in music. [...] Beethoven has composed a Battle Symphony that would make you as deaf as he is himself.[139] [...]

9 May: Yesterday evening the Battle Symphony was given in the theatre, and I heard it from the very farthest end of the parterre where all the deafening effect is lost, and yet I was gripped, even overwhelmed. The piece is a real whole, the parts of which can be intelligibly divided and connected. The English advance from afar, drums beating; as they get nearer, 'Rule Britannia' tells us what they are. Similarly, the opposing army moves forward, and is immediately recognized by 'Marlborough s'en va-t-en guerre'. The fire of canon and small arms is easily recognized on either side, the orchestral music, which consists of harmoniously connected thoughts and interests the ear of the listener, works like the storm and

---

with variations for two manual harpsichord; (4) A set of 15 pieces ['Symphonies'] for keyboard; (5) A set of 15 two-part keyboard inventions; (6) A volume (a long quarto) of keyboard works by J.S. Bach. The minuet with variations at the end of the book is probably by Friedemann Bach; (7) An organ fugue with an obbligato pedal by J.S. Bach; (8) Four collections of Keyboard sonatas by C.P. Bach, in one volume; (9) Eight suites by G.F. Handel; (10) Eight folios which together form two Lieder collections.

[136] Zelter, *Sämtliche Lieder, Balladen und Romanzen für das Piano-Forte* (4 vols, Berlin: Martin Schlesinger, 1816); a reprint of the 1815 volume.

[137] The edition published by Kühnel and Hoffmeister in Leipzig in 1801 was severely criticized by Johann Nikolaus Forkel and others, because it was edited from an inadequate copy.

[138] Zelter's setting of 'Gegenwart' has not been handed down.

[139] *Wellington's Victory*, also known as *The Battle of Vittoria* (op. 91); this short orchestral work composed by Beethoven in 1813 depicts British victory over Napoleon, and quotes various popular tunes including the British national anthem. It was conducted by B.A. Weber on 8 May 1816 in the Königliches Theater; a week earlier, on 1 May, Ignaz Schuppanzigh had conducted this work in Berlin.

chaos of battle. The armies seem to be engaged in hand-to-hand fighting; terrible onslaughts over wide stretches of land; the excitement mounting; one army yields, the other pursues, now vehemently and close at hand, now at a distance; at last there is respite. Then, as though issuing from the ground, muffled and mysterious, the 'Air de Marlborough' echoes sorrowfully in the minor key, interrupted by the dwindling accents of lament and sorrow. Then the victory of the conquerors is made known by the air of 'God save the King' and finally comes a complete, vivid, triumphal movement. All this hangs really well together, though it cannot be taken in at once, even by a good ear. Yesterday it brought me unusual enjoyment. The performance, too, was splendid, although 20 additional violins would not have been too many. *Vivat Genius*! And the devil take all criticism!

Privy Councillor Wolf sends his best greetings and takes a lively interest in that good man [in] Berka. He is now being punished for his dislike of the trumpet piece which, to make matters worse, was saved. [...]

When the first meeting about the idea of a performance of *Faust* was held, they formally invited me along. Princes, dukes, counts and lords were present. I restrained myself until it came to my turn. My first request was giving out the roles, which was soon finished. No one as yet had his own copy. We sent out for them. The majority of the book dealers had none themselves. [A copy] was lent to everyone. The poem was unknown to everyone [there] because it was also new to the artists. At another opportunity I made the observation that a prince of another country spoke better German than all of us and through so much diligence, perseverance and love made us acquainted with our own [artistic] treasures. [...]

## 197. Goethe

Jena, 21 May 1816

[...] I was very glad to get your report of Beethoven's Battle Symphony. That is the advantage of [living in] a large city, which we lack.

## 198. Goethe

Weimar, 8 June 1816

[...] At all events I hoped you would find and experience much to your taste in the first two volumes [of my works] and inspiration for many songs; thank you for affirming that for me.

Eberwein gave me your letter.[140] It, too, brought me great joy. You know the young man's talent. It is an inherited, surface [talent] which is nourished by

---

[140] Zelter's letter to Carl Eberwein, 13 May 1816.

nothing, neither character nor love, neither feeling nor taste. For that reason it remains stuck in the earth and cannot grasp why it cannot raise itself up from the ground. He composed the most miserable prose in a little opera with contentment and self-satisfaction. He was not going to grasp my intentions with *Faust*, but he should have taken my lead and done what I want; then he would have seen what it is about. This type of person, who, despite their good qualities, are lacking in what is really important, doesn't understand why it won't work out for them. They try to achieve it by intrigue and immediately offend the procured patron through arrogance and ineptitude, and so the fairy tale evaporates and they have gone backwards rather than forwards.

[...] When I tell you, you hardy and much-tried son of the earth, that my dear little wife has in these days left us, you will know what this means.[141]

### 199. Zelter

Berlin, 16 June 1816

One can be as frightened as a child: yesterday the black seal of your letter dated 8 June (which State Councillor Schulz gave me as he opened his parcel) stopped me short until I had opened it and recognized your own dear hand.

If only it were possible to be closer to you, to belong to you even more, it would be in what I have taken from your bereavement. But I am so long yours and no one else's that everything I do and don't do is in devotion to you and makes me more of a spirit. I would not be surprised if you had premonitions of this. [...]

I am glad that Eberwein showed my letter to you because I wanted to strangle him over a completely crazy argument in his letter where one fool responds to the other without having a clue. [...]

My departure to the spa[142] depends, taking the Cimmerian summer also into account, on the arrival of Madame Catalani,[143] because the professor must yield to the patient. We hope to have this singer with us within the next week. [...]

Next Monday we will have another rehearsal of *Faust*. My prophecy appears to be becoming true: we are making no progress. The good composer is so content with what is there and with what is incidental to it that the idea of the whole is lost in too much individual detail, where everyone is so happy that they occasionally

---

[141] On 6 June 1816, the day Christiane died, Goethe wrote the lines, 'O Sun, you strive in vain to cross dark clouds! It is my whole life's gain to weep her loss.' The news of Christiane's death, written in Goethe's hand on a small card with a black border, is enclosed with this letter in a letter to Christoph Ludwig Friedrich Schulz, with a stamp of receipt in Zelter's hand.

[142] Zelter left Berlin on 30 June 1816 to spend four days with Goethe in Weimar (5–8 June) and from there travelled to Wiesbaden, where he remained for four weeks.

[143] See *AMZ* 18 (1816), no. 29, 17 July, column 499; *MA* 20.3, p. 392.

believe they know what is needed only to continue the old with new enthusiasm; but I am not worried about getting help since Kotzebue is expected and Merkel is already here, and so on.

## 200. Zelter

Wiesbaden, 15 to 16 July 1816

[...] In Offenbach, I spent two afternoons with André,[144] whose father[145] I knew well. They have assembled a singing society here and naturally they have started the society with the freedom which amounts to leading the horse by the tail. Incidentally they understand everything so well that I really took care not to find it anything less than splendid, just as snuff from Offenbach and some very lively girls' faces cannot fail to be appreciated. [...]

When you come here, be so good as to bring the two complete editions of my songs[146] with you, if you still have them. André made me a present of his compositions and I should really give him something in return. I will replace them for you when I return to Berlin.

## 201. Goethe

Weimar, 22 July 1816

[...] Before leaving, I shall send a copy of your songs to Offenbach, for André. I am greatly pleased that my sombre Byzantine derivation could attract you;[147] without some such foundation and derivation, all criticism is tomfoolery, and even with it, nothing is done, for it still requires a whole lifetime of observation

---

[144] In his diary on 12 July 1816 Zelter records his visit to the Offenbach publisher Johann Anton André; see Johann-Wolfgang Schottländer (ed.), *Carl Friedrich Zelters Darstellungen seines Lebens. Zum ersten Male vollständig nach den Handschriften*, SchGG 44 (1931), p. 265. Hereafter referred to as *Carl Friedrich Zelters Darstellungen seines Lebens*. Goethe knew André from his trip to Frankfurt in 1815 the previous year (see Goethe's diary 31 August and 13 September 1815, WA III/5, pp. 179 and 181) and had also met him in Jena on 28 May 1816.

[145] Johann Christian André (1741-1799), composer and music publisher in Offenbach, Kapellmeister in Berlin, 1777–84. Zelter mentions him in his autobiography; see Schottländer, *Carl Friedrich Zelters Darstellungen seines Lebens*, p. iii.

[146] Zelter, *Sämtliche Lieder, Balladen und Romanzen für das Pianoforte* (4 vols, Berlin: Schlesinger, 1816). Zelter is referring to the copies he sent to Goethe in May 1816.

[147] Goethe, *Über Kunst und Altertum in den Rhein und Mayn Gegenden* (Stuttgart: Cotta, 1816).

and action; therefore, to no one would I more willingly hand over the surface of the earth, than to the bungler, who, with complacent cheerfulness demands indulgence, with apparent earnestness desires a candid criticism and with modest pretension wants to be thought a good deal of.[148] May my commentary show its gratitude to your text.

I have lately met with much kindness and affection. Friends from my youth, not seen for 25 years, and now elderly men, came to see me unexpectedly,[149] and were glad to find many things in their old places, and much that had progressed, progressing further. On the evening of 20 July I met Chladni, who is gaining great kudos by his thorough and formidable study of meteoric stones and figures of sound.[150] He is working for a time when men will once more rejoice to learn from others and gratefully make use of what they, by the sacrifice of their lives, have gained more for others than for themselves. Nowadays, when one speaks even to illustrious men of something that they ought to learn through tradition, they assure us that they have not yet had time to examine it. [...]

Things are looking quite cheerful in my household. August, as you know, enters very intelligently into everything, and we have, in a few hours, planned the programme for our next winter's entertainments.

### 202. Zelter

Wiesbaden, 26 to 27 July 1816

[...] I have just come back now at nine in the evening from a concert which Eberwein and the tenor Moltke[151] gave in the auditorium of the spa, which I only wish had had a larger audience. In particular I was really delighted with Eberwein's violin concerto. His tone was pure, mellow and flexible. It isn't lacking in skill and style and the Concerto in D minor, which is his own work, really surpassed all expectations in the last two movements. Moltke has a pure, sweet voice, with

---

[148] A reference to Zelter's previous letter to Goethe; it refers to the foundation of the Singing Society in Offenbach. The equivalent passage has been underlined (by Goethe) in Zelter's letter.

[149] In addition to Chladni, Goethe's diary entry on 17, 18 and 19 July 1816 mentions Friedrich von Laffert, court and chamber councillor in Celle, later Privy Councillor, *WA* III/5, pp. 254–5.

[150] The German physicist Ernst Florens Friedrich Chladni was already well known for his publication *Entdeckungen über die Theorie des Klanges* (Leipzig: Weidmanns Erben und Reich, 1787), in which he put forward the idea of sound figures (*Klangfiguren*), the forms of vibration made visible; he developed his ideas further in 1816 in *Nachrichten von zwei neuen musikalischen Instrumenten und einigen andern Entdeckungen*.

[151] Carl Melchior Jakob Moltke (1783–1831), singer and actor, in Weimar from 1809.

a range of two octaves and the delivery was good. But the good man sings arias by Paer and Generali which were expressly made for others, and to him are like a plank which does not want to come out of his mouth. I would like to bet that he has heard Brizzi[152] and believes now that he could follow suit: cool as you like but no chance! The granite is missing in his voice, the roundness – in short, schooling. If he were to sing German, as would be appropriate for a German and for his voice, he would, I think, have been pleasing, which at least today was not the case.

### 203. Zelter

Wiesbaden, 1 August 1816

[…] If the visual arts – even in their crudest form – are a religious affair by nature and depend on having an educational spirit, which is nothing other than the living breath which reveals itself though sound and music and, like an eternal source, sets tongues and lips in vibration, then we encounter a Paternoster, Credo, Te Deum, Kyrie, Gloria, Agnus Dei and so on which can well accompany the names of the saints which are in these pictures. The antiquated elements of the musical style also still fit perfectly with the fifteenth and sixteenth centuries. As a result the outer, melodic [elements], regular, serious, structured, stand there hollow, lifeless and sad and are in full accordance with the service of a church which only strives to preserve itself outwardly anymore.

Here in the history of music the bridge between the old and the new is missing. This was established afterwards through a harmony just as regulated, which Rousseau considered a gothic, barbaric invention,[153] as he saw it; and he saw nothing else in it other than an overfilled lower abdomen out of proportion to the general structure.

---

[152] The Italian tenor Brizzi gave guest performances in Weimar in November and December 1810.

[153] Jean-Jacques Rousseau supported the idea of a melodic centrism. He preferred vocal to instrumental music on the grounds that it was closer to nature; he enjoyed music which was light and pleasant and not dissonant, and he preferred harmony to polyphony. See Jean-Jacques Rousseau, *Lettre sur la musique français* (Paris, 1753).

## 204. Goethe

Tennstadt, 9 August 1816

[...] It really delights me that you have taken up my derivation of new art from the old. I am convinced myself of having laid a solid foundation. Your parallelism with music[154] is really welcome.

## 205. Zelter

Heidelberg, 20 August 1816

[...] I have once again made a detour from Darmstadt to Frankfurt in order to hear Catalani sing.[155] I enclose what I had cause to say publicly, so you can also get [something] from it.[156] I also enjoyed something of the way people from Frankfurt express themselves in such cases, which I found highly entertaining. The critics discussed her age as being between 32, 38 and 42, her pretensions about Frankfurt ducats and whether she was really the greatest of all singers, living or deceased, because if one were younger, one could also sing higher and lower and so on.

I got to know Grüner[157] in Darmstadt! [...] This director is hard to please and much had to be repeated and each time something different came out of it. Therefore I must treasure the honour I was granted because the Grand Duke (since he had invited me personally to this rehearsal) seemed determined to have my seal of approval on everything, which I was able to grant fully every time he asked for it. He cannot know that there is a difference between a Duke's Kapellmeister and a Kapellmeister who is a Duke[158] because he cannot experience it. The performance

---

[154] Zelter's remarks about the history of music, which are similar to Goethe's developed thesis in the plastic arts. Conversations on this subject seem to have already taken place during Zelter's visit to Weimar; see Goethe's diary of 7 July 1816: 'Went for an early walk with Zelter. About the similarities between composition in music and in the plastic arts', *WA* III/5, p. 250.

[155] Angelica Catalani gave a concert in Frankfurt on 14 August 1816; see Zelter's diary for this date (Schottländer, *Carl Friedrich Zelters Darstellungen seines Lebens*, p. 271) and also *AMZ* 18 (1816), no. 42, 16 October, column 717f.

[156] Zelter's article on Catalani was published in the 'Berlinische Nachrichten von Staats- und Gelehrten Sachen', *Spenersche Zeitung*, no. 95, 8 August 1816. It is also housed in the Goethe–Schiller Archive (GSA 28/71); *MA* 20.3, pp. 402–403.

[157] Franz Grüner, who – with Pius Alexander Wolff – studied acting with Goethe in 1803. He was engaged as director of the court theatre in Darmstadt for a short while; Zelter visited him on 18 August 1816.

[158] The Grand Duke Ludwig I von Hessen-Darmstadt conducted the orchestra in his own court theatre.

on Sunday was the most exact rendition one could hear. In particular, Grüner really had a favourable effect on the girl who sang Romeo's part.

### 206. Zelter

Heidelberg, 22 August 1816

I believe an anti-critic, Kanne,[159] recognized as the great man, tapped one of my reviews[160] written many years ago, saying that what is there is not in the work and that through deductions of this kind everyone could read into every work what one wanted. This work is Handel's famous *Messiah*, whose text, put together from purely word-for-word biblical passages, comprises a complete *Messiade*.

In the review I had divided the work into stages: 1. The Annunciation of the Messiah by the prophets; 2. The Birth [of the Messiah]; 3. The Life; 4. The Suffering and Death 5. The Resurrection and Ascension into Heaven; and noted that it derives from and returns to on High, and through this it distinguishes itself from early artworks of this kind, but especially through the way that in music and attitude the whole [work] is tied up with the complete concept of the redemption and salvation: suffering and death is temporary and passing. [...]

Paulus's daughter[161] has developed very well and plays Sebastian Bach quite advantageously, although (like us all) outwardly she still wanders all around the world, chewing the cud.

### 207. Goethe

Tennstedt, 28 August 1816

Your dear letter came yesterday in time for me to enjoy it today and have a chat with you. I am celebrating this birthday in special solitude. [...]

I have read with pleasure your article on Mesdames Catalani, Milder and Mara; people never understand that beautiful hours, like beautiful talents, must be enjoyed on the wing. You will already have seen from the newspapers how preposterously the people in Leipzig have behaved on this occasion.[162] I think we

---

[159] The Austrian composer and music critic Friedrich August Kanne (1778–1833).

[160] In: Johann Friedrich Reichardt (ed.), *Berlinische Musikalische Zeitung* (1805), no. 11, pp. 41–4 and no. 12, pp. 45–8.

[161] Sophie Paulus. Zelter's diary from 20 August 1816 contains the entry: 'Towards evening to Paulus with the Voßes. The daughter played the *Chromatic Fantasy* by Bach very well'; Schottländer, *Carl Friedrich Zelters Darstellungen seines Lebens*, p. 273.

[162] The scandalous criticism of Angelica Catalani, which appeared in the *Leipziger Allgemeine Musikalische Zeitung*.

shall have to keep God's higher gifts from such an obnoxious group of people, so that when an opportunity occurs, they may compare and elevate them. [...]

I have had reason lately to look into Teutonic poetry, and as usual I cannot resist taking some steps at once. If in doing this I can seize upon any ballads for you, that will be my greatest reward.

### 208. Zelter

Baden 30 August 1816

André from Offenbach writes to me[163] that he has not received my songs[164] and if they have still not been sent yet, I will have them sent to him from Berlin. I would like to know so that he doesn't unnecessarily receive them twice.

He offered to send me a detailed assessment of them,[165] which I am in fact looking forward to and hope they will be really methodically taken apart, as I know his songs[166] and his basic principles. He has fleeced Catalani, bitten, even torn her apart, like an unskilled butcher who doesn't know where the throat is.[167]

### 209. Zelter

Baden, Strasbourg, 5 to 12 September 1816

[...] Among other things which I fashion here, I wrote a new setting of the song 'Wer nie sein Brot' from *Wilhelm Meisters Lehrjahre*, which you will perhaps like better than the first rendition which is pretentious.[168] [...]

---

[163] J.A. André had written to Zelter on 20 August 1816; see Zelter's diary entry of 28 August; Schottländer, *Carl Friedrich Zelters Darstellungen seines Lebens*, p. 275.

[164] Zelter, *Sämtliche Lieder, Balladen und Romanzen*; Zelter had asked Goethe on 15 July 1816 to give his copies to André, which Zelter would then replace, and Goethe had announced sending these to André in his letter of 22 July.

[165] In Zelter's letter to André on 26 July 1816 he had, in fact, asked for André's opinion; whether this requested report was ever written cannot be determined.

[166] Johann Anton André, *48 Lieder und Gesänge*, op. 38–40 (1819).

[167] See Zelter's diary entry of 28 August: 'A letter from André in Offenbach of 20 August arrived with a bitter judgement about Madame Catalani'; Schottländer, *Carl Friedrich Zelters Darstellungen seines Lebens*, p. 275.

[168] Zelter's first setting dates from 1795; the revised setting is entitled 'Heidelberg, Sunday 25 August 1816' and at the end Zelter notes 'Completed [in] Baden, 2 September 1816' (SBB PK Mus. ms. autogr. Zelter 21, I, no. 13).

The judgement about Catalani in the Leipzig newspapers[169] is known to me only from what people say, but I can well imagine it, since I know the man,[170] who like a blind mail coach driver travels over the bad roads next to the good ones and curses the bad roads. What annoys me [most] about it is that these people prostitute German criticism and mislead the young generation, of which admittedly there is not much to ruin.

Your hunting for ballads delights me and if the right huntsman comes, I am not worried that there is game in the good German forests. I would love to see the faces of the well educated as you take something up, observe it and show it around, which they contemptuously let lie like Peter and the horseshoe.[171] I gave 'Totentanz'[172] to an educated woman, who is gladly counted as an admirer of yours, to read before it was published. I must confess she said that: I cannot get anything out of the poem and would not guess it was by Goethe if I hadn't [already] known, but let me hear your setting. [...] What gives me the most pleasure is the belief of many that I am carefully trained by you to set your poetry to music, because I don't value compositions until they please you. For of all ideas they could have, they are not content until they catch the densest.

At last I write to you, this time from Strasbourg where I arrived with Sulpiz[173] on the 9th of this month at six o'clock. [...] At nine o'clock this morning in loveliest sunlight we went back [to the cathedral]; first into the church, where for the first time I heard a commendable mass which is not a [concert] mass with orchestral accompaniment[174] but an ordinary service accompanied just by the organ, which was apparently a Silbermann, about which I will enquire.

11 September: Organs [built] by Silbermann from Strasbourg[175] have such a beautiful sound that they can easily be singled out from the best organs of other excellent masters. The cathedral organ is by the old Silbermann[176] and is now 102 years old. The most unusual thing about this organ is that no builder appears to have thought of a space for it. This space must have been assigned to it and accepted and it seems to me to be most dangerous in the church because of its proximity to the hollow place between the towers. Now my master didn't provide the work with pipes which are suitable for such a space. He put the whole work together, dressed it up in his old way like a shot in a rifle where no grain of power is idle.

---

[169] The essay, 'Ein Wort über Madame Catalani, nebst allgemeinen Bemerkungen über den Gesang, und die Verschiedenheit des italienischen und deutschen'. *AMZ* 18 (1816), no. 34, 21 August, column 569–92.

[170] Amadeus Wendt (1783–1836), philosopher and composer, professor in Leipzig.

[171] A reference to Goethe's poem 'Legende'.

[172] Zelter's setting of Goethe's ballad, enclosed in a letter to Goethe on 2 April 1814.

[173] Johann *Sulpiz* Boisserée (1783–1854), art collector.

[174] *Fiedelmesse* is slang for a concert mass with orchestral accompaniment.

[175] Johann Andreas Silbermann (1712–83) built the organ in the St Thomaskirche in Strasbourg (1737–40) and in the new St Thomaskirche in Strasbourg (1748–9).

[176] Andreas Silbermann (1678–1734).

Outwardly the rest of the work looks like new. [...] I cannot praise highly enough the song of the cantors in the mass. They let it be accompanied by two serpents,[177] which works exceptionally well. The cantus firmus is not without mistakes, but it is along the right lines and praiseworthy. Everything could easily be produced in the best form by anyone who understood it correctly.

Against that, how abhorrent is the *German* mass of the Abbot, the Electoral Palatinate Spiritual Councillor, the Court Kapellmeister and the state music teacher of Mannheim, Herr Vogler,[178] which he, to the shame of the Head of the Church of Heidelberg in whose presence it was performed, had published. It is pieced together from infamous popular songs and published by a reputable press, circulated and should be a sign to me. I purposely bought this 'masterpiece' in Offenbach and am bringing it with me. These gentlemen think that if you act commonly and unworthily, you are close to the people.

Thursday, 12 September: Yesterday someone showed me your dissertation[179] which I would gladly have copied, which, however, would never be permitted. I have come directly from mass where I had the opportunity to see inside the cathedral organ. I wanted to see the lungs which breathe into such a work and my wish was granted. Six bellows, which hold at least 600 cubic feet of air and which have 300 cubic feet always in reserve, and the strongest organist cannot exhaust them if they are worked by two people. The way in which it is put together can never fail, never embarrass and is a masterwork of mechanics. The weights are [made] of lead and fixed in place, which is very important. Everywhere one sees understanding, experience, thought and spirit: it is true to say the man [who

---

[177] A bass wind instrument, descended from the cornett and a distant ancestor of the tuba with a mouthpiece like a brass instrument but side holes like a woodwind; as the name suggests, it usually has a snakelike shape. The instrument was invented by Canon Edmé Guillaume in 1590 in Auxerre, France, and was first used to strengthen the sound of choirs in plainchant. Around the middle of the eighteenth century it began to be used in military bands and orchestras, but was replaced in the nineteenth century by a fully keyed brass instrument, the ophicleide, and later on by valved bass brass instruments such as the euphonium and tuba.

[178] Abbé Vogler, Deutsches Hochamt in A minor (1777, r.1807); first published as *Utile Dulci. Belehrende musikalische Herausgaben mit einer Zergliederung, die vorläufig die Inaugural-Frage beantwortet: Hat die Musik seit 30 Jahren gewonnen oder verloren?* (Munich: Senefelder, 1808).

[179] Goethe's treatise (written in Latin) *De legislatoribus*, which was not accepted by the faculty: 'The dean, a bright lively man, began praising my work, then proceeded to its questionable aspects, which he by degrees characterized as dangerous, and concluded by saying that it might not be advisable to publish this work as an academic dissertation. The candidate (he said) had demonstrated to the faculty that he was a young thinker of great promise; and in order to avoid delay, they would gladly permit me to defend some theses,' which Goethe did, and the doctorate was awarded, *Dichtung und Wahrheit*, Book 11, *MA* 16, p. 507. Zelter could hardly have seen the submitted thesis, which was not to be found in the faculty records, but rather an author's copy.

made it][180] was a son of the muses. [...] According to the inscription, which I read myself, the work began in 1713 and was finished in 1716, which is exactly 100 years ago. If I had been here, I would have arranged to celebrate the day. Some years ago it was renovated and the pipes were polished up. The organist who has to play it twice a day has 548 steps to climb up and down! That amounts to 200,020 steps per year and now he has to use the pedal as well! The two men who tread the pedals are strong men with good stomach muscles which the weights respect! In some German provinces one takes old, frail invalids there who are often so incapacitated that they send their wives and children, who corrupt the bellows and cause more damage than it costs to pay the organist. This misuse can never happen here because only one [person] can tread the bellows and controls the fixed weight. [...]

### 210. Goethe

Weimar, 27 or 28 September 1816

Last time you found me in a sorrowful state, and now I must sadden you. The enclosed letter contains the news of a great calamity,[181] and my only comfort is to know you are near me, and to feel that I am prepared to share your troubles with you.

### 211. Goethe

Weimar, 14 October 1816

The few days were too short. There was still much to discuss and to look at. Directly after your departure *Die heimliche Heirat*[182] was given a perfect performance; I would really like you to have been there.

---

[180] Andreas Silbermann.

[181] The death of Zelter's young daughter, Clara, which occurred during Zelter's absence at Weimar. Goethe wrote on the blue envelope: 'Pardon the grim news' with reference to the enclosed letter in which Lichtenstein informs Goethe of Clara's death, *WA* IV/27, p. 405. When Goethe wrote the lines is not known. The letter from Martin Heinrich Lichtenstein (1780–1857; Zoologist and Professor in Berlin), dated 19 September, must have arrived in Weimar between 21 and 23 September; the earliest Zelter could have received the news is 28 September, when he arrived in Weimar at midday; it is possible the message was not given to him until 29 September after he had a chance to rest, for he wrote to his daughter Doris that day (GSA 95/I, 8, 19).

[182] Domenico Cimarosa's *Il matrimonio segreto* was performed in Weimar on 5 and 7 October 1816; Goethe mentions both performances in his diary, which suggests he attended both.

## 212. Zelter

Berlin, 14 to 20 October 1816

Many people here are very fired up about and ridiculing Aubri's dog.[183] They say, to bring a dog on stage is simply to bring the theatre to the dogs and so on. But everyone is going to it and the house is always full. Yesterday I, too, was there and stayed to the end. The work has the most lovely music, which runs through the entire work without being sung. I would call the first two acts entertaining through the simplicity of the motif: that a murderer will be discovered through the victim's dog. There is hardly anything to criticize in the production. It is nicely done and fresh; true, the dog would have to be always on the stage and be continually around his master as long as he lives. I'd be surprised if this is not in the stage directions, since in this way the thing becomes natural and true to life. [...]

Today, Tuesday, *Der standhafte Prinz* is being performed. Unfortunately I cannot go and report something about the performance. Let's hope it will run for a while. [...]

Kapellmeister Winter has departed today. He put on a German opera, *Zaïra* here, which was well received. However, the libretto is so bad that it was called *Ça ira*,[184] though the music is considered good.

## 213. Zelter

Berlin, 25 October to 2 November 1816

[...] Our theatre offers some new things. Madame Seidler (née Wranitzky) plays and sings in *Johann von Paris*[185] to great acclaim. Wild, the tenor,[186] is here from Vienna and demands 5,000 thalers salary. Voice and style are good – very good.

---

[183] *Der Hund des Aubri de Mont-Didier oder Der Wald bey Bondy*, drama (from the French play) by René Charles Guilbert de Pixérécourt, translated by Ignaz Franz Castelli, with music by Ignaz Xaver von Seyfried; performed nine times in Berlin from 4 October to 27 November; see *AMZ* 18 (1816), no. 46, 13 November, column 792.

[184] 'That'll do'.

[185] This Singspiel by François Adrien Boieldieu, libretto from the French of Saint Just, translated by Carl Herklots, had been performed in Berlin since 25 March 1813. The performance Zelter mentions took place on 26 October 1816; for reviews see *AMZ* 18 (1816), no. 46, 13 November, column 795; Caroline Wranitzky-Seidler played the Princess of Navarra.

[186] The Viennese court opera singer Franz Wild (1792–1860) gave many guest performances in Berlin in October and November 1816, first as Tamino in Mozart's *Die Zauberflöte*; on 13 October he sang the title role in *Johann von Paris*; for reviews see *AMZ* 18 (1816), no. 46, 13 November, column 794.

Mademoiselle Brandt from Prague,[187] a good young girl, is supposed to be very nice. But all three seem to me planets that are too small to shine here for long – if we keep them. They are asking for money to match the weight of their bones. There is not much flesh in evidence!

### 214. Zelter

Berlin, 4 to 5 November 1816

For a while now I have carried around the idea of composing music for the Lutheran festival made up entirely of sayings by Luther. Please let me know your thoughts on this, if you are not, in fact, the only man equipped with the knowledge and ability to do this.[188] [...]

The day before yesterday I had a letter from Madame Mara,[189] who is staying in Reval at present. In it she reported that she had wanted to come to Berlin this autumn, but as this plan wasn't fulfilled, she would certainly come next summer. Furthermore she is 68 years old now and would be welcome here, as I am also getting closer and closer to my sixties.

---

[187] Caroline Brandt's first performance took place in Berlin on 30 October 1816 in the opera house where she played the title role of Nicolo Isouard's opera *Röschen genannt: Aescherling*, with Franz Wild as Prince Ramiro; on 31 October she performed Wilhelmine in Bretzner's comedy *Das Räuschchen*; for reviews of her guest performances see *AMZ* 18 (1816), no. 51, 18 December, column 877.

[188] In his letter to Zelter on 14 November 1816 Goethe answers Zelter's enquiry (first raised on 31 October) about the possibility of a collaborated project, a Reformation Cantata, and sends him a schematic plan and a detailed explanation of his ideas. In his following letter on 10 December he sends a further developed version, in which the dramatic framework and musical settings are indicated (Overture, choral passages). Despite such intensive collaboration at the beginning of the project – reinforced by Goethe's work on an essay to mark this celebration of the Reformation – work on the cantata came to a halt, was pushed aside by other projects, until Zelter finally notes with resignation on 3 March 1817 'that my Luther thereby loses his poor life'. The project was never realized.

[189] On 6 October 1816 the singer Gertrud Elizabeth Mara thanked Zelter for sending her the article on Catalani from the *Spenersche Zeitung*, 8 August 1816, in which Zelter had also praised Mara and named her 'Queen of female singers' (Königin der Sängerinnen). Mara assured him that 'no praise had never had made her so happy as this [did]'.

### 215. Goethe

Weimar, 7 November 1816

[…] There's not much happening in our theatre now. I treat it like a business, but if it succeeds, we want to expand again next winter […]. And so I say this to you as one who has seen the Sing-Akademie formed, has co-founded and preserved it.

### 216. Zelter

Berlin, 10 November 1816

The Federal anthem or Masonic song for the chamber council[190] has been finished for a long time but it is still fermenting. It takes time for me to work out a piece like this and if it is to please others, it has to please me too. Don't take it badly if I jot down in a quarter of an hour such a piece, which I cross out again after quarter of a year. I'm glad I am not a painter for I would be annoyed to the point of distraction if I painted something red which should be green. It is a very different thing for a composer to cope with a real poet than to infuse ideas into the work of a mere verse-maker. Naumann[191] was right to prefer bad operas with which one is happy when tailor and fiddler somehow bring a form to light.

### 217. Goethe

Weimar, 14 November 1816

The boatman melody[192] is in an edition of Rousseau's song compositions[193] which came out about 30 years ago. Like a thousand other things, it has gone astray on me, otherwise I would sent it to you. […]

To prevent our friendly and lively discussion coming to a halt, I send you a few words regarding your proposal to write a cantata for the Reformation Jubilee.

---

[190] Goethe's poem 'Wenn die Liebste zum Erwiedern', later published under the title 'Verschwiegenheit' in the *Ausgabe letzter Hand* (1827); Zelter's composition is entitled 'Männerkreis' in Goethe's version and 'Mauerlied' in the Berlin copy. The poem, with its freemasonry ideas, may have been connected the successful entry of August von Goethe in the lodge Amalia. Since 1812 Goethe had ceased to take an active role in the lodge.

[191] Johann Gottlieb Naumann (1741–1801), composer, Kapellmeister in Dresden.

[192] The song of the Venetian gondoliers.

[193] Jean-Jacques Rousseau's posthumous *Consolations des Misères de ma vie ou Recueil d'Airs, Romances et Duos* (Paris, 1781), p. 199.

It would, I suppose, best fashion itself on the lines of Handel's *Messiah*, a work which you have understood so deeply.

As the leading idea of Lutheranism rests on a very dignified foundation,[194] it gives a fine opportunity for poetical as well as musical treatment. Now this basis rests on the decided contrast between the Law and the Gospel, and second, upon the accommodation of such extremes. And now, if in order to attain a higher standpoint, we substitute for those two words the expressions 'necessity' and 'freedom', with their synonyms, their remoteness and proximity, you see clearly that in this circle is contained everything that can interest mankind. […]

To express these ideas in a poem adapted to music, I should begin with the thunder on Mount Sinai, with the 'Thou shalt', and should conclude with the Resurrection of Christ, and the 'Thou will!'

For the further development of my plan, I will add the successive order in which the piece should be arranged:

Part One
I   The giving of the Law on Mount Sinai.
II  The warlike pastoral life, as described in the Books of Judges, Ruth, etc.
III The consecration of Solomon's Temple.
IV  The dispersion of the worshippers, who are driven to the mountains and hilltops.
V   The destruction of Jerusalem followed by Babylonian captivity.
VI  Prophets and Sibyls announcing the Messiah.

Part Two
I   St John in the wilderness, taking up the Annunciation.
II  The recognition by the Three Kings.
III Christ appears as a Teacher and draws the multitude to Him. Entry into Jerusalem.
IV  At the approach of danger, the multitude disperses. Christ's friends fall asleep.
    His sufferings on the Mount of Olives.
V   The Resurrection.

On comparing these two parts, the first seems intentionally longer, and has a decided central point which, however, is not lacking in the second.

In Part One the first and fifth movements are parallel with each other; Sinai and the Destruction, the time of the Judges and the service of Baal; the second and

---

[194] The tension between 'law' and 'gospel', or as Goethe formulates it, 'necessity' and 'freedom'.

fourth movements are idyllic, energetic – the consecration of the temple constitutes the highest climax and so on.

In Part Two the first and fifth movements, the dawn preceding the sunrise, would be expressed with gathering intensity. The second and fourth movements form a contrast. The third movement, the entry into Jerusalem, might express the unrestrained and pious joy of the people. [...]

A thousand other relationships will occur to you at first glance. These things need not be historically but lyrically tied together. Everyone knows the whole and will let themselves be carried from one place to another on the wings of the poetry.

The text should consist of passages from the Bible, well-known evangelical hymns, bestrewn with new texts and whatever else can be found. Some words by Luther can hardly be used as the excellent man is absolutely dogmatically practical. So, too, is his enthusiasm. It is for you to look around in the Scriptures. Above all, read the completely invaluable preface to the psaltery. In addition read the prefaces and introductions to the remaining biblical books; you will probably come across useful passages. At the same time you yourself will be filled with the sense of the whole teaching whose gift we want to celebrate.

Perhaps this is the place to say a word about the Catholicism outlined above. Soon after its origin and development the Christian religion suffered. It lost its original purity through subtle and unsubtle heresies. But when they had to bring under control and rule very brutish people and corrupted civilians, strong measures were necessary. Not teaching but service was needed. The one mediator between the highest God in heaven was not enough, as we all know, and so a type of heathen Judaism was formed that is still with us to the present day. That had to be overthrown, which was why Lutherism drew solely on the bible. Luther's method is no secret and now that we are celebrating him, we only do it correctly if we acknowledge his service and show what he gave to his age and following ages. This feast should be celebrated in such a way that every well-meaning Catholic could join in celebration. More about that another time. [...]

### 218. Zelter

Berlin, 13 to 15 November 1816

Nieymeyer of Halle, with whom I am now in contact about the Hallean choir,[195] asked me whether I had handed over his parcel together with his letter to you.[196]

---

[195] The choir founded by Daniel Gottlob Türk (1750–1813) and later directed by August Hermann Niemeyer (1754–1828).

[196] Niemeyer's book *Religiöse Gedichte* (Halle and Berlin, 1814), which is dedicated to Goethe, and his letter to Goethe of 3 July 1816 were presumably both delivered to Goethe on the evening of Zelter's arrival in Weimar on 5 July. On his summer vacation Zelter had

Will you find a quarter of an hour to say a good word to him?[197] Probably on your account he gave me a friendly reception, for up to then I seem to have been unappreciative of him and have not answered two of his letters. [...]

## 219. Zelter

Berlin, 23 to 24 November 1816

[...] As yet I don't know the preface to the psalter at all, but will procure it immediately. Like you, I take 'sayings by Luther' to mean 'biblical sayings'. If one could use one or more of his church songs that would be good too. You have perfect freedom and I will follow your lead as closely as possible. [...]

Evening, 24 November: I have just seen Madame Tilly[198] perform Kotzebue's *Die Verwandtschaften*. Act One is very good. The other four are very ordinary. [...] The leading lady would please you.[199] [...] She performs with feeling and awareness.

Part One
I    Giving of the Law on Mount Sinai.
II    The warlike pastoral life.
III    The consecration of Solomon's Temple.
IV    The dispersion of the worshippers
V    The destruction of Jerusalem; Babylonian captivity.
VI    Prophets and Sibyls announce the Messiah.

Part Two
I    St John in the wilderness, taking up the Annunciation.
II    Recognition by the Three Kings.
III    Christ appears as teacher, drawing the multitude to Him. Entry into Jerusalem.
IV    At the approach of danger, the multitude disperses. Disciples sleep. Sufferings on Mount Olive.
V    The Resurrection.

---

passed through Halle and visited Niemeyer on 4 July; see Zelter's diary, 'With Niemeyer at noon', Schottländer, *Carl Friedrich Zelters Darstellungen seines Lebens*, p. 264.

[197]    The requested letter is not extant.
[198]    Karoline *Auguste* Tilly (1800–28), actress in Berlin, Magdeberg and Dresden.
[199]    Sophie *Auguste* Friederike Crelinger, née Düring (1795–1865), actress, from 1812 resident performer at the Königliches Theater, Berlin.

## 220. Zelter

Berlin, 2 to 3 December 1816

[...] The little song[200] is finally finished and I am also sending the poem back again with it because I have provided directions regarding the presentation of the melody in the different verses. It is in three parts – for two tenors and one bass. The middle voice can also be sung by a bass if there are not two tenors. The whole company[201] can repeat the last two lines of every verse, at which point the three soloists can take a breather. Admittedly I should know what singers you have. This time all will be well, but in the future I ask you to let me know how many singers are available in each part. [...]

The tone of the song is not easily hit and the singers must do their best in order to capture, in a flowing line, the contrasting elements: what is manifest and what is known in quiet contemplation.

In only making this observation now when the song is in its completed form in front of me, I wanted to tell you – for the reason that one doesn't know what one is doing and would be lost if God himself didn't know.

On the back I have written a canon[202] which would be suitable for that circle to perform. The main reason I did it many years ago, was to treat a whole poem with many stanzas in this way. The text should be the final stanza of a student song, which begins:

> My father was a rich man
> Who was lacking in money
> And were he not deceased
> He would still be in the world.

So the song moves through the various verses until the final one which is notated. It is the first clever student song which I have seen. I had long since striven to get it right before I finally arrived at the enclosed version. Most likely you have preferred to prop up an old song with a thought and there will undoubtedly be a happy moment for composing something enjoyable to this version, as the original nonsense is useless.

---

[200] Zelter's setting of Goethe's poem 'Wenn die Liebste zum Erwiedern', *WA* I/3, p. 392. The autograph manuscript of Zelter's three-part male voice setting, entitled 'Männerkreis', is in Goethe's music collection (GSA 32/23).

[201] Goethe's house choir.

[202] On the reverse side of Zelter's manuscript is a canon at the octave for 4 [male] voices.

## 221. Goethe

Weimar, 10 December 1816

Your little song has arrived;[203] we thank you heartily for what you have composed so well. If the melody is varied to suit the text as you have indicated, it cannot fail to be very effective. In return, I send you the scheme for the grand cantata,[204] developed further;[205] may it reach perfection with you! I have kept a copy of it [...]

I hardly remember whether I thanked you with regard to Tilly and have a question. 'She is not without a voice', you write. Does that mean that she can sing or that at the most she would be necessary as a chorister?

Part One:
Overture
At the end, thunder on Mount Sinai
Semi-chorus (the citizens) crowding around. It is bent on seeing closely what goes on
The Levites (a semi-chorus) restrain them. The people are forced back from Sinai and worship their God
Aaron inaugurates the scene. He mentions the defection to the golden calf
The people humble themselves and receive the Law
Speaker (Joshua)
March through the desert
Conquest of the land
Martial Shepherd Choruses, similar to those in my *Pandora*[206]
Speaker (Samuel) explains the wavering of the people between priesthood and monarchy
Loyalty of the king and the people to the idea of the one national God
Solomon's accession to the throne
Choruses of women
The Sulamite, the best beloved, is far off
Choruses of Priests
Consecration of the Temple

---

[203] Zelter's 'Männerkreis'.

[204] The sketch for the planned Reformation cantata – which was an extension of the first draft – was now divided into two parts. The text is based on Kräuter's copy (GSA 25 XX, 15, pp. 10–12).

[205] Goethe's second draft for a Reformation cantata is clearly structured with regard to the musical and scenic presentation: an overture, choirs (the people, different groups), soloists, a speaker; at the same time notion of juxtaposing the Old and New Testaments has been realized differently.

[206] *MA* 9, p. 159f.

Choruses of all kinds
Speaker (Elijah)
Preparing the way for the defection to Baal
Service on mountain tops and in the open air
Choruses of the people who are returning to the happiness of their former and freer heavenly life
Joyful, less religious celebrations
Choruses of the priests of Baal, imposing themselves with their clerical cruelty and coarseness
Speaker (Jonas). Threats, prophesying the coming of swarms of enemies
Approach of the enemy
State of fear
Downfall of the kingdom, with violence
Captivity. Gentle lamentation
Speaker (Isaiah) presages salvation and future happiness
Choruses, accepting the prophesy with gratitude but in an earthly sense
Choruses of Prophets and Sibyls, pointing to the spiritual and eternal
Triumphant Finale

Part Two:
Intermezzo
Sunrise
Beauty of the morning air
Rural, not pastoral
Expanse of solitude
Speaker (St John)
He receives the promise
He beholds the star of Bethlehem as the morning star
Ushering in the approach of the Three Kings
Procession of the Three Kings

There is nothing contradictory in Turkish music being used here, for it came to us from beyond the Oxus.[207] It would be especially appropriate on the arrival of the third king, who is always represented as something of a barbarian.

(This scene would have to be decidedly dramatic for the sake of variety.)

Departure of the kings into the distance
Speaker (Christ)
He appears as a teacher
Chorus attentive, but wavering
His teaching becomes more intense
The people crowd around Him and cheer, but always in an earthly sense

---

[207] The ancient name for the river Amu Darya in Central Asia.

Christ raises His teaching to the spiritual level
The people misunderstand Him more and more
Entry into Jerusalem
Speakers (Three Apostles)
Fear of danger
Christ consoling, strengthening; and admonishing
Alone in suffering of the soul
The intense affliction
Speaker (Evangelist)
Allusion to physical suffering
Death. Resurrection
Angelic Chorus
Chorus of terrified watchmen
Chorus of women
Chorus of disciples
Everything earthly dies away, and the spiritual soars higher and higher to the Ascension and Immortality

The composer will accurately weigh up the relationship between the different parts and in representing the thunder on Mount Sinai will insist on gradual intensification to be achieved through alternations.

Taking Handel's *Alexanderfest*[208] as my guide, instead of presenting the one speaker – Timotheus of that work – I have introduced several speakers, who may be imagined sometimes just reciting, sometimes singing, sometimes competing with the chorus, just as it suits the development of the piece.

The speakers are mostly men, but should it be necessary, women may be substituted. What I particularly wish to know is how the leading parts are to be allocated and at what points one should introduce regular arias, for which biblical and other pious sayings might then be adapted in such a way as to be recognizable, and yet at the same time would be rhythmically smoother.

## 222. Zelter

Berlin, 15 to 16 December 1816

[…] I have not heard Mademoiselle Tilly sing and if I said she is not without voice, I meant by it that her voice is resonant but it is still not rounded, which only can be attained by strict schooling.

I really like the plan for the cantata. You don't need to feel embarrassed by it and can give what comes easily to you. Arias, choruses, recitative and the like

---

[208] Zelter had expressed his enthusiasm for the choral writing in this oratorio during the Sing-Akademie's performance of this work in 1807.

form themselves. They must form themselves if the whole is to be clear without being ordinary.

The overture has been composed already, but I cannot put closure to it until I have the beginning of the [first] piece. The sense and spirit exists in the contrasts you yourself indicated: You should! You will! And for that I need the ordinary external means so that I am left with the (task of) broad development. [...] What will require the most work is the concrete, both within the narrow context and in the development. The mean between too short and too long is indefinable and to strike it once you would have to be a god.

I would create the difference between choir and semichorus by four single voices against the whole choir, if it is to be contrasting.

Besides, a female solo part is almost necessary in order to occupy a decent singer, and if need be two. Otherwise all voices – soprano, alto, tenor and bass – can be used as solo voices and the choir still exists separately.

I would imagine the whole work would be simple enough to stage so that one could comfortably perform the music even where only a small theatre with the necessary apparatus is available. One can also suggest Janissary music really well without [using] the instruments themselves. I find there is greater art in having something suggested, guessed, found, than in using people's backs for beating out the rhythm, which is really a disgrace.[209]

Of the arias, which should not be too long, one would be sufficient for the soprano, one for the tenor and a third for the bass. That which is really lyrical is arioso in style, even in recitative passages. Good biblical passages for the choir would work best to lend to the whole a respectable abode for the soul to dwell in.

The arias could be placed wherever is most suitable, as long as they do not come too near one another.

[Some] attractive songs are also finished: among them you would like 'Flieh, Täubchen flieh!'[210] and 'Wie sitzt mir das Liebchen'.[211] The word order of your verses is often so strange that at first glance I think that it could never be set. Yet

---

[209] Zelter is referring to the fifth poem ('Froh empfind ich mich nun auf klassischem Boden begeistert') in Goethe's *Roman Elegies*, II. 15–17: 'I have even many a time composed poetry in her arms, and softly, with fingering hand, counted out on her back the hexameters' measure.'

[210] Setting of Goethe's occasional poem from 1773 or 1774, which he had revised during his visit to the spa in Tennstadt. Goethe had given Zelter a fair copy (in the poet's hand) during his visit to Weimar at the end of September 1816. Zelter's manuscript, entitled 'Mädchens Held', is dated Berlin 3 October 1816 (SBB PK: Mus. Ms. Autogr. Zelter 21, 1, no. 20). The song was first published in *Sechs deutsche Lieder für die Altstimme* (1826). Whether Zelter sent a copy of the setting to Weimar is unknown; the copy in Goethe's music collection, by an unknown hand (GSA 32/54) can be dated from the first publication.

[211] Setting of Goethe's poem published under the title 'Gegenseitig' in 1816; Zelter's setting, which is entitled 'Der Entfernte' and dated 5 December 1816 (SBB PK: Mus. Autogr. Zelter 21, 1, no. 19) first appeared under a different title, 'Im Fernen', in Zelter's *Neue Liedersammlung* (1821).

when I have a look at it from all sides, I find within myself what I would not have searched for. Even I myself am surprised at 'Flieh, Täubchen'. However the verse, 'Und so soll mein deutsches Herz weich flöten', is a tricky one and won't settle. I myself can't get my tongue around it.

The day after tomorrow I am travelling to Stettin. I will need a whole week on this short journey because of the short days. Mendelssohn[212] is travelling with me, or rather I am going with him because I have nothing to do in Stettin and am using the opportunity to visit my daughter[213] in Bruchhagen[214] and my son[215] in Steckelin[216] [...]

### 223. Goethe

Weimar, 26 December 1816

I have received your letter in which you agree with my suggestions. For the time being I am leaving it lie with my other papers because I cannot see clearly how I can add anything. If we were together, then it would happen much more quickly. Now, however, the weather along with a lot of [minor] details are a burden to me, so that I don't know how I am to finish – even if I imagine a more fortunate year than the one gone by. [...]

### 224. Goethe

Weimar, 1 January 1817

[...] I must convey the important news to you, namely that the last two strophes of the unruly ballad 'Die Kinder sie hören es gerne'[217] have arrived. [...] I sent a song[218] for the artist's festival to Schadow, who gave me great pleasure through the medal.[219] May it help towards finally banishing the gloomy spirit which creeps through our art halls. [...]

---

[212] Abraham Mendelssohn.

[213] Juliane Huschka née Zelter (1791–1862), Zelter's second daughter from his first marriage to Johanna Sophia *Eleonora* Zelter.

[214] A place near Angermünde.

[215] Georg Friedrich Zelter (1789–1827), Zelter's eldest son from his first marriage.

[216] A place south of Stettin.

[217] Refrain in Goethe's poem 'Herein, O du Guter'.

[218] 'Zu erfinden, zu beschließen', first appeared in the *Gesellschafter* on 11 January 1817 under the title 'Dem edlen Künstler-Verein zu Berlin'.

[219] On his visit to Weimar on 8 February 1816 Gottfried Schadow had captured Goethe's profile and on 17 December he sent two wax records and ten bronze casts for a

## 225. Zelter

Berlin, 8 to 12 January 1817

[…] About the little ballad: that the children like to listen to it makes very me happy and that Paria's prayer is still not answered also delights me, because I thought it could only happen to me that something appears in the entertainment which I have to subvert. It is one thing to have an idea and another to represent it and so I often doubt the bit of talent I have. […]

Your poem[220] which you sent to our artistic society gave great joy. What architects, painters, sculptors and the rest of us musicians have endured for this year's celebration was not without gain.[221] If I make an exception of the presentation of *Phidias*,[222] then nothing produced was without spirit. […]

I mounted a little musical work for a group of living figures (Saul and David)[223] which would have sounded better if the room was not so narrow and [the ceiling] so low. However, the little work was well received because one cannot appear more pleasing to the general public than when one is not intellectual but gives oneself over to deep feeling. […]

I have read Luther's preface again, especially about the Old and New Testaments.

## 226. Zelter

Berlin, 11 to 14 February 1817

Prince Hardenberg has commissioned me to have a new organ[224] built for him in Neu-Hardenberg (formerly Quilitz) nine miles from here. This organ will be ready

---

display coin. Goethe thanked him on 27 December 1816 and requested further wax casts, which he received in February 1817.

[220] 'Zu erfinden, zu beschließen'.

[221] In his explanations for the commemorative programme containing Goethe's 'Künstlerlied', Schadow himself had described in detail the *Ephiphaniasfest* on 6 January 1817 in the hall of the Englisches Haus. After his speech, Schadow read out Goethe's poem. On an erected stage 'living tableaux' were shown against music by Zelter and Rungenhagen, including Zelter's *David and Saul*. The images bearing homage mentioned by Zelter and composed by Zelter are a homage to the art of sculpture and to the art of poetry; the conclusion was made up of the 'farcical dramatic duet in doggerel [*Knittelverse*]'.

[222] The actor August Wilhelm Mauer played the role of the Greek sculptor Phidias, who – in a poem written by Konrad Levezow – begged the father of the gods, Zeus, to make his image, as Homer describes it, arise in his imagination.

[223] Zelter, Gloria. Für den Künstlerverein Saul und David am H. drei K. Feste 1817 (SBB PK: Mus. ms. Autogr. Zelter 9).

[224] Built by Johann Simon Buchholz and his son, Carl August Buchholz in 1817. Karl Friedrich Schinkel designed the organ casing.

for the Reformation Jubilee and I would really like to have something ready for it.[225] One should hardly use an old piece for it, although the new is never overrated here.

### 227. Zelter

Berlin, 16 February 1817

Wild sang Orest for the last time today[226] – a role which I would prefer to hear [sung] by a natural baritone, so that here too both characters are distinguished from one another. Only their natural difference can form a beautiful ensemble. […]

### 228. Zelter

Berlin, 28 February 1817

[…] I just devoured a new opera: *Athalia* by Racine in a version by Gottfried Wohlbrück with music by Baron von Poißl.[227] In fact the music has more character than barons usually have, and has up to now been very successful through the great modesty with which it is presented. In fact one is happy once again to enjoy a work which is not abrasive to the ears. A bit more aria, in the strict sense of the word, would be of benefit. The German libretto would have some good passages if only the character of Athalia were elevated a little. Here she is a coarse and stupid woman, a real rascal; on the other hand little Joaschen is like a sausage stuffed with wisdom, piety and many fine expressions. The best thing about it are the sets, among which the interior of a temple and a landscape arranged by Schinkel are highly commendable. […]

---

[225] Zelter, Kirchenmusik zum Reformationsfeste für 4 Stimmen mit Orgel und Bleichinstrumenten (1817).

[226] The Viennese opera singer Franz Wild (1792–1860) performed Orest in Gluck's *Iphigenie in Tauris* in Berlin on 8 and 16 February 1817.

[227] Johann *Nepomuk* von Poißl (1783–1865). The opera was performed on 25 and 28 February; Zelter attended the second performance.

## 229. Zelter

Berlin, Evening, 7 March 1817

As I am in my theatre period, you must remain silent when I tell you something else about Antonin.[228] Today for the third time I saw him dance and playing the guitar at the same time. This person is not only a really perfect dancer; he plays this instrument masterfully. But this is not all: he combines both perfectly. He played the *Folie d'Espagne*[229] with variations and danced to it without any constraint. As the alterations become livelier, the liveliness of the dance also increases, so that there is no step, no leap, no movement that does not fit perfectly with the music. The orchestra was completely silent and even with the swiftest movements not a single note was lost. In short, I have never yet heard this imperfect instrument played so perfectly. I was completely amazed at the security and the strength to hold the instrument so firmly during the most energetic physical movements, and to play so purely and so beguilingly.

## 230. Goethe

Weimar, 9 March 1817

[...] *Athalia* hasn't been performed yet because of Stromeyer's illness.[230] We hope to perform it next Saturday, the 15th of this month.

## 231. Zelter

Berlin, 6 to 8 April 1817

[...] My Easter concert is over[231] and turned out very advantageously; I had a pretty little sum left over and the music was what I call good. [...]

---

[228] Parisian Dancer, based in St Petersburg from 1817 to 1827; for a review of his Berlin performance see *AMZ* 19 (1817), no. 16, 16 April, column 279f; *MA* 20.3, pp. 437–8.

[229] Popular seventeenth-century theme by Farinelli.

[230] Poißl's opera *Athalia* was due to be performed in celebration of Maria Pawlowna's birthday on 16 February. Due to illness of the leading singer, Heinrich Stromeyer, Bonini's *Drillinge* was performed and *Athalia* was rescheduled for 15 March 1817.

[231] The annual performance of Graun's *Der Tod Jesu*; for reviews see *AMZ* 18 (1817), no. 20, 14 May, column 348; *MA* 20.3, p. 439.

### 232. Zelter

Berlin, Middle of April 1817

We are expecting a new tragedy[232] by Oehlenschläger here. I have read it because I have to write some music for it, but I don't like it much. [...]

### 233. Zelter

Berlin, 21 June 1817

Madame Marianne Sessi (Baroness Natorp by marriage)[233] is here and proves herself a gifted singer. She must be between 30 and 40 and still has something of her former great beauty. The voice has a range of two and a half octaves counting down from the top F. It is not as versatile and as resonant as Catalani's but otherwise everything is just as genuine and more artistic. She has the loveliest theatrical head I have ever seen, just as the whole figure appears Roman, relaxed and grand, without being tall. But she is also a born Roman woman. When it comes to poses, she is second to none and there is a better sense of awareness than with Catalani. She also knows how to hold herself so that a lovely bust and perfectly beautiful arms play their part. You may think I have fallen in love again. I am also on good terms with her and again speak Italian, which is better than I have given myself credit for [...]

Finally, many thanks for the good reception of my Mendelssohns.[234] The little woman is of the very best and 20 years ago she really was exceptional, a true dove.

### 234. Goethe

Weimar, 20 August 1817

[...] State Councillor Schulz[235] very kindly invited me to Berlin and it sometimes seems to me that such a trip would be advisable and possible. Then, however, my

---

[232] *Axel und Walburg* by Adam Gottlieb Oehlenschläger performed in Berlin on 28 April and 5 May 1817.

[233] Maria *Theresia* Sessi, Viennese singer; Zelter refers to her concert on 13 June 1817 in the Königliches Opernhaus; for reviews of her performance see *AMZ* 19 (1817), no. 29, 16 July, column 494f; *MA* 20.3, p. 444.

[234] Contrary to Zelter's supposition, the meeting between Hinni Mendelssohn and her son never took place.

[235] Christoph Ludwig Friedrich Schultz (1781–1834).

opinion suddenly changes and in the end I don't see where the decision would come from. It is best not to think about it at all, but to let Holy Week come and wait to see whether in the end Graun's oratorio[236] tips the scales.

### 235. Goethe

Jena, 16 December 1817

[…] Unfortunately when I think of music, it seems strange to me that I am cut off from this highest and loveliest enjoyment. I find, at the same time, that still many a song succeeds for me and your good profoundly artistic intentions always hover around me […]

### 236. Zelter

Berlin, 21 December 1817

Your informative letter of the 16th of this month brightens the shortest and darkest day; at the same time it should abolish the long silence. I don't have much to report about my activities and strivings. I have moved into a comfortable, quiet, though expensive accommodation.[237] Happily the new organ in Neu Hardenberg is ready for the Reformation celebration and I have inaugurated it and the church itself (which has undergone much renovation) with a sizeable piece of music which had to be finished amongst much chaos. The best [news] is a little trip to Hamburg[238] from which I am back a week and which gave me a great deal of pleasure despite the wet weather. […] Some fine musical antiquities were passed on to me and with great delight I established them in our residence. In the Hamburg Theatre I heard a new opera, *Tancredi*, by Rossini[239] and found it quite pleasing and more impressive than Italian opera is generally perceived to be in Germany.

---

[236] *Der Tod Jesu.*

[237] Friedrichstraße 129.

[238] 16 November to 9 December 1817; for a detailed account of Zelter's activities there – which included a visit to the Hamburg Sing-Akademie led by Reichardt's daughter, Luise – see Zelter's correspondence with his daughter Doris on 20, 22–25, 26–28, 30 November (GSA 95/I, 8, 19).

[239] Performed in Hamburg on 21 November 1817; for a more detailed – and very critical account – see Zelter's letter to Doris on 22 November 1817 (GSA 95/I, 8, 19). Zelter attended further performances of *Tancredi* in Berlin on 5 January 1818 and in Kassel during the summer of 1818.

It was said here some days ago that Kapellmeister Müller in Weimar was dead.[240] Let me know whether it is true, because I am still indebted to him in artistic matters.[241] But what I am most concerned about is to know what is to happen to his bequest. He possessed an old musical work by Bodenschatz[242] which I would like to purchase unless more worthy hands in Weimar would like to possess it. If it is to be auctioned, be so kind as to let me know. I cannot spend too much on it; I have [already] bought much this autumn. [...]

Do you not have some poems lying about to offer something reasonable to the Liedertafel once more? Also don't forget to send me your report on Da Vinci's *Last Supper*, about which I am curious.

## 237. Goethe

Jena, 31 December 1817

First to your inquiry about Leonardo's *Last Supper*. Of this inestimable work, the first complete painted fugue,[243] which surpasses all that has gone before and is not to yield to any successors; there is not the slightest inkling how the figures approximately stood in relation to each other. [...]

At your suggestion I have been looking through the few scraps of poetry I have to hand and find only the enclosed that may perhaps come in useful for your society. It was an impromptu offering to my very old friend Knebel, on his seventy-third birthday.[244] Good luck to the society who will sing it at certain occasions. The musical movement recalls the popular 'Lasset heut im edlen Kreise'.[245] You will, however, find the character very different and you will perform it in line with your knowledge and conscience.

You shall hear about Müller's bequest next time.[246]

Enclosed: 'Lustrum ist ein fremdes Wort'

---

[240] August Eberhard Müller died on 3 December 1817.
[241] On his previous visit to Weimar Zelter had borrowed 15 song settings from Müller on 7 July 1816 and later had Franz Nicolovius settle the account.
[242] Presumably the famous motet collection, *Florilegium Portensee*, first published by Erhard Bodenschatz in 1603; a revised enlarged edition followed in 1618.
[243] Goethe also used this description, 'somewhat fugue-like', with reference to Carl Leybold's drawing *Charon*.
[244] See Goethe's diary entry on 30 November 1817, *WA* III/6, p. 142.
[245] The opening words of Goethe's poem 'Generalbeichte'.
[246] Goethe, in fact, never answered Zelter's request of 21 December.

## 238. Zelter

Berlin, 9 January 1818

Be so good as to pass on the enclosed letter. It contains a short little song[247] and guidelines, to give old Knebel something to listen to.

Along with Langermann I have learned a lot from what you said about Leonardo's *Last Supper*. [...]

## 239. Goethe

Jena, 20 January 1818

Since you have been quick to give us the benefit of your artistic skills,[248] so shall our thanks for it not be delayed but be paid instantly. [...] We will not discover what you have commemorated in this work, yet at the same time we know that it is necessary and customary for you composers to work spontaneously.

Furthermore, the question is whether you are in a good enough mood to look over the accompanying notes and give me your opinion.[249] The circle from which these songs arise is limited, but cheerful, brave and willing. I know full well that it is no work of art. It is up to you whether we should drop it and reject it.

[...] Rossini was once asked which of his operas pleased him best? His answer was *Il matrimonio segreto*.[250] [...]

---

[247] Zelter's setting of Goethe's 'Lustrum ist ein fremdes Wort', which bears Zelter's subtitle: 'Am 73 Geburtstag des 40jährigen Freundes' (GSA 32/19); the title 'Meinem Freunde von Knebel zum 30 November 1817' in Kräuter's hand is written on page one. Since the page handed down from Goethe's music collection was an autograph copy by Zelter, Goethe either had a copy made and had this sent to Jena or at a later stage received the copy back from Betty Wesselhöft.

[248] Zelter's setting of 'Lustrum ist ein fremdes Wort'.

[249] Settings, with guitar accompaniment, by the theologian Adalbert Schoepke of poems by Goethe. Goethe had received the settings on 1 January and replied in thanks on 16 February; Zelter, in turn, judged the settings favourably and passed them onto Prince Radziwill. Schöpke's settings have not been handed down.

[250] The source for this anecdote is Stendhal's *Rome, Naples and Florence in 1817*; Goethe's knowledge of this source is first mentioned in his diary on 18 January 1818, *WA*, III/6, p. 159. In this work Stendhal records a conversation with Rossini: 'I told him of my enthusiasm for *l'Italiana in Algeri* and I ask him what he loves best, whether *l'Italiana* or *Tancredi*. He replies '*Il matrimonio segreto* because it is forgotten as the tragedies of Marmontel are forgotten in Paris'. Zelter had missed the point of the anecdote, which is why Goethe – though himself in error – explained it to him in his next letter.

In Act Two of *Elena*, an opera by old Mayr of Bergamo,[251] there is said to be a very effective sextet; it is said to be based on a popular Bohemian melody, a sort of Notturno.[252] Would it be possible to get hold of the score of this sextet?

For several years past your Fasch[253] has been lying among a number of papers in Jena; I found it lately, and read it at one sitting, with great enlightenment. How it transports us into another world! [...]

## 240. Zelter

Berlin, 29 January 1818

I liked the little songs more than I had before.[254] They are singable and playable and not without truth. Their basis is midway between popular song forms of our time and the German words of an old melodic tradition which ring out. It is hard to describe: vocal composers have to work with the words of poets which they may need to discard. If all goes well and it blossoms, then it is no wonder that one is no longer conscious of the fruitful ground. Art demands that it is so. Now the words themselves are music, more or less. It is a question of showing or hiding them and there is no substitute for genius.

Furthermore one is embarrassed when one judges compositions whose texts are set by oneself. Ultimately a poem, seen in isolation, becomes something of its own right, like any other fragment of a whole, and yet at the same time something different.

I feel that especially in my better attempts, which emerge from the first impression and at the same time are the fruit of a passing mood which is bound up with particular circumstances. And if it is published and stands clearly before me, that is when I find the right sounds, and what is printed is painful to me.

I am not sending the manuscript with the letter because I was thinking of showing it to Prince Radziwill who should arrive any day. [...]

---

[251] Johann Simon Mayr, or Giovanni Simone Mayr (1763–1845), German–Italian composer, b.Bavaria. Pupils include Donizetti.

[252] A further reflection from Goethe's reading of Stendhal's book; on 20 November in Milan Stendhal wrote 'They are producing Mayr's opera, *Elena*, again which they had being playing before the *Testa di Bronzo*. What languishing! How ecstatic the sextet in Act 2! Here is music, like a nocturne, sweet, tender, real melancholy music, such as I have often heard it in Bohemia. This is a work of genius which Old Mayr has retained from his youth or which has been given to him; it has sustained the whole opera.' What is intended is Simon Mayr's opera *Elena e Costantino* (libretto by Leone Tottola), originally premiered in Naples in 1814.

[253] Zelter's Fasch biography.

[254] The Goethe settings by Adalbert Schöpke.

The opera *Il matrimonio segreto* may well prove to be the work of several composers²⁵⁵ [...] I will enquire after the opera *Elena*; if only [the manuscript] had not been burnt.²⁵⁶

The unfortunate fire also proved to be detrimental for me, for apparently next Good Friday will be the last one on which Graun's Passion will be performed officially. What I will lose thereby I won't carry away in my trouser pockets. I could have fully financed my trip to the spa with this income.

### 241. Goethe

Jena, 16 February 1818

You have, my dear man, lavished gifts of fine and good words from the depths of your musical talent so that I feel obliged to say something friendly in reply [...]

You didn't understand the joke which I told you. Someone named some of his works to that composer and asked him which he considered his best. He answered *Il matrimonio segreto*, meaning the composition by Paesiello.²⁵⁷ I don't need to explain for you how witty and charming the answer was. [...]

### 242. Zelter

Berlin, 1 March 1818

[...] It is 20 days to Good Friday and you are commanded to be here on the day to hear Graun's Passion. The King has even granted me the large opera house for it and I have no hope of ever getting it again. [...]

Mayr's opera *Elena* was destroyed by fire; worse still the music is unknown.²⁵⁸ In spite of that I commissioned them to get the piece you want.²⁵⁹ I suppose it is the well-known Simon Mayr.²⁶⁰ You did not write his Christian name, and here no one

---

²⁵⁵ Cimarosa's popular opera of the same title first performed in Vienna in 1792. Zelter's inaccurate statement can be explained by the large number of operas in the eighteenth and nineteenth centuries that dealt with the topos of marriage and characterized it with such words as 'scoperto' (discovery), 'per interesse' (intrigue), 'per inganno' (deception).

²⁵⁶ The manuscript was presumably lost in the fire in the Königliches Schauspielhaus on 29 July 1817; following the fire, theatrical performances took place in the Königliches Opernhaus until the new theatre opened in 1821.

²⁵⁷ Goethe is mistaken here: the opera is by Domenico Cimarosa.

²⁵⁸ The score was burnt in the fire in the Königliches Opernhaus in Berlin on 29 July 1817.

²⁵⁹ The sextet from the opera *Elena e Costantino*.

²⁶⁰ The Italian opera composer of German origin Johann *Simon* Mayr (1763–1845).

knows of any other Mayr among composers. No, no! One of my earlier disciples, Meyerbeer by name,[261] created a commotion in Padua last year with one of his operas[262] and he might be the younger, as you speak of the old Mayr.

## 243. Goethe

Weimar, 8 March 1818

My best thanks for 'Um Mitternacht'.[263] Here is something about old Mayr that will entertain you.[264] How I wish I could be raised up on Faust's cloak[265] and let myself down in the opera house at your grand soirée. Human methods will hardly bring me to Berlin.

## 244. Goethe

Jena, 19 March 1818

In these days you have done me a great favour, for 'Um Mitternacht' has been sung to me, fittingly and sympathetically, by a gentle, sweet creature,[266] whose energy failed her only in the final stanza. Once again, you have loyally and firmly set a seal on your love and regard for me. My son, who is not easily moved, was overjoyed and I fear that out of gratitude he will ask you to be godfather.[267] […]

If I am to be frank with you, then this composure is only on the surface for I have long wished to admire and enjoy precisely the musical character of your

---

[261] Giacomo Meyerbeer (1791–1864).

[262] *Romilda e Costanza*, performed in the Teatro Nuovo in Padua.

[263] Zelter's setting of 'Um Mitternacht'.

[264] A transcription of two passages about Simon Mayr from Stendhal's book *Rome, Naples et Florence en 1817* (Paris, 1817).

[265] The motif of the magic coat, which raises the magician and carries him wherever he wants: see Goethe, *Faust I*, v. 2065; *Faust II*, v. 6983–6 and v. 7039ff.

[266] Goethe's diary of 11 March 1818 states: 'Evening: Countess (Caroline) Egloffstein. Zelter's lied performed', *WA* III/6, p. 181.

[267] Goethe's prediction proved true: on the birth of his first son, Walther Wolfgang, on 9 April 1818, August asked Zelter to be godfather. In a letter to August von Goethe on 24 April 1818, Zelter thanked August for this offer but was unable not accept it since he had to provide for the wedding of his youngest daughter (GSA 37/XI, 6, 8).

Holy Week,[268] and now eye and mind are focused on political and social instability and anarchy.[269]

If I am to be perfectly honest, I take comfort in saying that if your feelings are true towards me, you will not invite me to come to Berlin; and on this point Schülz, Hirt, Schadow,[270] and all who really wish me well, agree. It would be all the same to our excellent friend Isegrimm[271] (please remember me to him); in me, he would merely have one more person to contradict. I have as much desire to hear about the hundred hexameters as about the hundred days of Bonaparte's last reign.[272] God preserve me from German metrics as from a change of government in France! The 6/8 time of your 'Um Mitternacht' does everything. Such quantities and qualities of tone; such variety of movement, of pauses, and intake of breath; this ever-changing sameness! Let the gentlemen with their long and short syllables work towards a consensus for a long time, but they will not produce such work as yours. [...]

### 245. Zelter

Berlin, 24 March to 7 April 1818

My Good Friday music went off so well[273] as to bring me in [...] 1,000 thalers profit, whereby I am able to supplement my earnings honestly because the entire takings amounted to 1,551 thalers, 12 groschen. [...]

The poem[274] looks strange on paper: like a workpiece, veined, grained and at the same time transparent. It is like a crown in water. [...]

Now I am keeping your description together with the music and I am really delighted by your ideas, as you recognize them as your own once more. [...]

Now, my Xenophon, I am sending a little work here once again. You will know that the poem was already set to music by me once before and was published.

---

[268] Goethe's desire to attend the Sing-Akademie's annual performance of Graun's *Der Tod Jesu*.

[269] In the foreground Goethe is referring to the issue of censorship, but beyond that also symbolically to the wider issue of the alternation between confusion and order in the world.

[270] State Councillor Christoph Ludwig Friedrich Schultz, Aloys Hirt and Gottfried Schadow had, like Zelter, repeatedly invited Goethe to Berlin.

[271] F. A. Wolf, philologist, author of *Prolegomena ad Homerum*.

[272] The reign of 100 days, namely Napoleon's rule from the time of his return journey from Elba to Paris on 20 March 1815 to the final abdication of his throne on 8 July 1815.

[273] See *AMZ* 20 (1818), no. 16, 22 April, column 298; *MA* 20.3, p. 468.

[274] 'Um Mitternacht'.

If only someone would say Handel composed music just as bad as I,[275] a cask of wine would not deter me from raising a toast to his health by drinking the lot. [...]

What beautiful soul then was German enough to sing you that song[276] without Italianisms and with such life that you could not help being pleased, since I needed your word to know whether it comes off and works? I have set for you 'Kennst du das Land' for the sixth time,[277] so as to do it once to my own satisfaction; I will send the best settings to Weimar [...]

The enclosed letter is from Boisserée. A young musician from Cologne,[278] who attends my classes here, thought he would be passing through Weimar, which he has not done and so he asks me to forward the letter to you.

## 246. Zelter

Berlin, 21 June 1818

You have here once again an industrious little song[279] to which I would gladly let you listen, although I have not yet heard it myself.

It became a little motet and I would like to know from you what you think about the rearrangement of the verse,[280] seeing that I had great fun working on the poem. I had to set it twice because the first rendition was polemical in nature and now it really should be more humorous.

Let me also know whether you are happy with the title or give me another,[281] because our Tafellieder would have to have a handle, otherwise they fumble about in the middle of the pot. [...]

---

[275] Zelter's answer to Goethe's claim: 'Xenophon wrote prose that was just as bad as mine.'

[276] Zelter's setting of Goethe's 'Um Mitternacht'.

[277] Mignon's song from Goethe's *Wilhelm Meisters Lehrjahre* which Zelter had set repeatedly in 1795, 1796, 1812, 1817, 1818.

[278] Bernhard Joseph Klein (1793–1832), Director of Music at the Instutute for Church Music in Berlin from 1818.

[279] Zelter's four-part setting of Goethe's 'Sänge sind des Lebens Bild'; the autograph entitled 'Apotheose', later altered by Goethe to 'Sängers Ermutigung', is in Goethe's music collection (GSA 32/9).

[280] Zelter had not only planned numerous repetitions of words and phrases, but had also repeated individual passages in different places of the poem.

[281] Goethe did not answer this request and the setting was first published as 'Apotheose' in the second edition of Zelter's *Liedertafel* (Berlin, 1820).

I would gladly undertake a journey to Göttingen: Forkel has died[282] and his artistic bequest is to be sold in its entirety. And so one would like to know what is there and what the things look like. [...]

I am not supposed to know that you are sick; whether the danger has passed I will hear from you. When you go, take me with you; take the true brother with you.

## 247. Goethe

Jena, 28 June 1818

I was delighted to receive your consignment of 21 June: it came at exactly the right time, as I finally pulled myself together after being in disarray two weeks. Actually it was only a cold, which is hard to avoid given the warm weather and the sharp wind from the north east. All is well again and I am back to normal, but don't know what to turn my attention to. [...]

Your motet[283] delighted and dismayed me: delighted me in so far as I can absorb it with the eye and could reasonably enjoy it; dismayed me as I must relinquish hope of hearing it. For I have not once been able, with Knebel, to have the fun of having the birthday song[284] performed. There are really lovely voices among the young people[285] here and they also perform well as a choir. However, whatever does not sound like 'Lützows wilde Jagd'[286] has no meaning for anyone. As things stand, it is also not advisable to close in on oneself: it is just as bad there

---

[282] Johann Nikolaus Forkel (1749–1818), musicologist and Bach biographer, died on 20 March 1818.

[283] Zelter's setting of Goethe's poem 'Sänge sind des Lebens Bild'.

[284] 'Lustrum ist ein fremdes Wort'. In a letter to Goethe on 9 January 1818 Zelter had enclosed a letter to Betty Wesselhöft and his setting of Goethe's occasional poem for Karl Ludwig von Knebel's birthday with instructions 'to give old Knebel something to listen to'; Betty Wesselhöft explained to Zelter on 4 October 1818 that the performance was too difficult to organize because it involved travelling to Knebel and also because of the unavailability of adequate singers (GSA 95/I, 7, 28).

[285] The students with whom Goethe often came into contact in the winter of 1817/early 1818, above all in Frommann's home. Without sympathizing with their ideas, Goethe had a very fatherly forbearance towards them. In the meaning, however, the escalation of conflict with political powers was foreseeable, as well as through the increasing politicization and partly also the radicalization of the students (presumably Goethe knew of the more-or-less revolutionary political programme of the student's duelling society in Jena and Giessen) and also through the intensified attacks and countermeasures on the other side.

[286] Poem by Theodor Körner set by Carl Maria von Weber. The Lützow Hunter was a famous volunteer corps in the War of Liberation 1813/1814; Theodor Körner had belonged to it and had died during the war. The song was very popular at that time, particularly among students, who inherited the liberal and national ideas of the War of Liberation.

in Weimar. Moltke[287] sings nothing other than his own songs, so that the society for whose pleasure one would invite would ultimately want to run from it. [...]

If it is not disagreeable to you, I should like to send a copy of your motet to Heidelberg for Thibaut;[288] although a lawyer, he has a sensitive musical temperament, and has, as I hear, gathered about him a circle of dedicated friends who perform the compositions of the older masters devotedly, passionately and precisely.[289] It is a reflection of what you have inspired; I cannot say, indeed, how good they were, but knowledgeable people were really pleased. [...]

In general it seems really miraculous when one watches people's activities with seriousness and good will. (I speak only about the fine arts of which I am best informed.) [...] If I am not mistaken, you composers have a great advantage in that at the very beginning you can urge your students to take up the established laws. I will also not investigate how it comes about that one individual after the other loses their way arbitrarily.

## 248. Zelter

Berlin, 27 August, 1818

As soon as I have recovered I am off to Darmstadt to wait upon my Grand Duke of the orchestra[290] who has coaxed a new opera from Spontini.[291] In Cassel I heard a first-rate performance of Rossini's world-famous opera, *Tancredi*.[292] The music is charming, which means it is of the genuine Italian kind, *chiaro, puro e sicuro*.[293]

---

[287] The Weimar tenor and actor Carl Moltke, who also composed, and was a founder member of Goethe's house choir.

[288] Goethe became acquainted with the lawyer and writer on music, Anton Friedrich Justus Thibaut during his Professorship in Jena (1802–6). Goethe resumed contact with him first when August von Goethe heard Thibaut lecture in 1808 and later again during Goethe's sojourn in Heidelberg in 1814/1815.

[289] The musical gatherings that Thibaut held in his home from 1810.

[290] Under the direction of the Grand Duke Ludwig I from Hessen-Darmstadt, the Krebs' Theatre-Society was taken over and reformed as the court theatre. Most of the rehearsals, which were organized as social events in the early evening, were directed by the Grand Duke himself.

[291] Spontini's revised version of his opera *Ferdinand Cortez oder die Eroberung von Mexico* (libretto by Joseph Alphonse Esménard and Victor Joseph Etienne de Jouy; German libretto by Ignaz Castelli) was premiered in Paris on 28 May 1817 and performed in Darmstadt on 7 November 1819.

[292] Zelter attended the performance on 20 August 1818 in the Kurfürstliches Hoftheater in Cassel.

[293] Clear, pure and assured.

Flowing melody, style and movement in every number; even the overture is nice, although it has nothing to do with the piece

I also found a small, sweet Italian Mademoiselle Marinoni in Cassel. She is 20, not too big, and teaches singing to the young princesses[294] of the Electoral Princess.[295] Admittedly she would be much too good for that, but she has a slight limp with her left foot and therefore will not take to the stage. She has a lovely full mezzo-soprano voice which would already sound exceptional in a church; vocal agility, taste and truth in all she does. I have induced her to learn to sing some German works and you would have really liked your 'Nur wer die Sehnsucht kennt' had you heard it.[296] She took it very favourably when I mentioned to her that the German people would not take it more amiss to hear good German from her beautiful mouth than Italians do when they hear their language badly sung by Germans [...]

## 249. Zelter

Berlin, 27 December 1818

[...] The imperial mother[297] arrived here between three and four o'clock on Christmas Eve, accompanied by my King,[298] who rode in front of her carriage. I thought I recognized the Grand Duchess in the Empress's carriage. It was known than the Empress would remain here until Sunday. The King had ordered the museum, the library, the university, the art gallery, the Akademie der Künste, the *Charité*, the maternity hospital, and everything else there is to see here, to be made ready to receive the noble guests and I didn't think I would see the Empress in the Sing-Akademie, since our present location[299] – on account of building the academy premises – is quite unsuitable to receive guests. It is so small that the society itself

---

[294] Caroline Friederike Wilhelmine (1799–1854) and Marie (1804–88) of Hessen-Kassel.

[295] Friederike Christiane *Auguste*, Princess of Prussia (1780–1841), daughter of Friedrich Wilhelm II of Prussia, married to Wilhelm II of Hessen-Kassel from 1797.

[296] Presumably Zelter's rendition rather than the 1795 setting by Reichardt published in Goethe's novel.

[297] Maria Fjodorowna (1759–1828), widow of Tzar Paul I of Russia, mother of Alexander I of Russia and Maria Pawlowna of Sachsen-Weimar-Eisenach, who, on this occasion, accompanied her mother from Weimar to Berlin.

[298] Friedrich Wilhelm III (1770–1840) of Prussia.

[299] During the reconstruction of the academy building and in lieu of the round room upstairs, the Sing-Akademie was assigned a room on the first floor of the new wing on Universitätstraße. In a letter of 19 May 1818, Zelter complained bitterly about the narrowness of the room; Schröder, *Carl Friedrich Zelter und die Akademie*, p. 23.

doesn't have room and since it is above a stable, the smell is unbearable, just like the cold because it cannot be heated.

However, completely unexpectedly Prince Radziwill sent [a message] to me to say that the Empress wanted to hear the Sing-Akademie; the whole court was looking forward to it and he wanted to give me his hall. It was the 11th day of Christmas. Everyone was scattered about the city and it was no bagatelle to call together 300 people in Berlin. On the second day of celebration around midday, they came together and it was decided to wait on the noble guest at two o'clock. Two hours later, around four o'clock, they assembled in Radziwill's palace[300] and around five o'clock the Empress arrived, led by the King, along with the whole entourage. When the Empress stepped into the hall, she was immediately greeted by the singing of a poem to the well-known melody: 'Heil Dir!'[301] The two poems were written and printed in two hours. Then a psalm by Fasch followed, 'Wohl dem Manne der rechtschaffen lebet – Der ist wie ein Baum der seine Frucht bringet zu seiner Zeit; und was er machet das gerät wohl.'[302] The whole thing closed with a fugue: 'Meine Zunge rühmt im Wettgesang Dein Lob!'[303] I had chosen this psalm in connection with the recently celebrated birthday of Kaiser Alexander.[304]

After [the performance of] these songs, which lasted less than half an hour, the Empress approached the choir, greeting them and thanking them. My answers to her questions about the foundation, progress, situation and age of the institution seemed to please her and she departed from us then because the theatre festivities, which the King had arranged, awaited her.

Whether this could have been a pleasure for a noble woman of such obvious understanding, for whom it was thrown together in haste and which almost passed by like a cool breeze, I cannot tell you. It was a day of celebration. Everyone was busy in his house to celebrate a public holiday in which everyone played his own part. Torn out here in a strange house, completely unprepared and so on. The music went off perfectly because I am always prepared for all instances of this kind with an existing repertoire. But to have an auditorium before you which one has no time to enjoy and is only waiting for the end, take from that what you can.

Recommend me to your excellent Grand Duchess. I thought about nothing else on the entire journey here from Weimar other than the enjoyment which I found

---

[300] The performance is reported in the *Vossische Zeitung*, 29 December 1818.

[301] The melody for 'Heil Dir im Siegerkranz' first occurred in the anonymous setting 'God save the King' in *Thesaurus Musicus* (1744); both text and music were attributed to Henry Carey.

[302] Based on Psalm 1, v. 1 and 3.

[303] The text is not word-for-word as in the biblical psalter; it is possibly one of the many poetic versions of psalms written by various authors in the seventeenth century. The fugue is also by Fasch.

[304] Alexander I of Russia, Aleksandr Pavlovich (1777–1825).

in her church service.³⁰⁵ It uplifted me greatly, and don't forget your promise to provide me with the mass of Saint Chrysostom.³⁰⁶

[...] If fish were not a dumb species,³⁰⁷ I would put the following setting of this ballad in their mouths.³⁰⁸ Therefore, have it sung for you by such beings who are not dumb but also not too restricted in sound and words. Some verses have driven me almost to despair. Many are mastered except for the poetic enjambment in the eighth strophe between verses three and four, which is lovely in itself but is very disturbing when sung: would it be possible to alter it?

### 250. Goethe

Weimar, 4 January 1819

[...] Since you left³⁰⁹ I have done next to nothing of what I had resolved to do. On the occasion of an imperial visit³¹⁰ I could not refuse to contribute to some festivities, so I undertook to furnish a masque. The programme is enclosed – the explanatory poems shall be sent to you later.³¹¹

The procession consisted of nearly 150 people. To dress them appropriately, to group them, to arrange them in rank and file, and when they finally appeared to explain what they were meant to represent, was no small task. It took me more than five weeks. However, in return we obtained universal applause, which certainly was well earned by the great outlay of imagination, time and expense. Those who

---

[305] Zelter had attended a service in the chapel erected for Maria Pawlowna and the Russian orthodox community in Weimar on 1 November 1818. See Goethe's diary entry: 'Ottilie with Zelter and Nicholovius in the Greek chapel', *WA* III/6, p. 260.

[306] Under the name of Saint John Chrysostom an early liturgy from the Middle Ages has been handed down, a small section of which can be attributed to Chrysostom. It is to this day the official mass of the orthodox service. Apparently Zelter had heard it on his visit to the Russian Orthodox Church in Weimar.

[307] Like Zelter, Goethe also uses the image of a foolish fish as a metaphor for unmusical people.

[308] Zelter's setting of Goethe's ballad 'Herein, o du Guter!' for solo voice and piano. Zelter's manuscript is in Goethe's music collection (GSA 32/25); a copy dated 20 October 1818 is found in Zelter's papers: (SBB PK: Mus. ms. Autogr. Zelter 29-2).

[309] Zelter was in Weimar from 25 October to 1 November 1818.

[310] The Russian Empress, Maria Fjodorowna, visited the Weimar Court from 25 October to 21 December 1818.

[311] The last and most important of all Goethe's masques, *Bei Allerhöchster Anwesenheit Ihre Majestät der Kaiserin Mutter Maria Fjodorowna in Weimar Maskenzug*, was completed during Goethe's visit to Berka, 17 November to 6 December. Although no longer Director of the Weimar theatre, Goethe directed rehearsals and a spectacular performance took place on 18 December 1818. The masque was published by Cotta in the *Morgenblatt*, no. 309 on Christmas Day 1818.

took part spared no expense in dressing themselves up. Yet ultimately all of this, vanishing in a few moments like a firework that explodes in the air, was costly enough.

I personally have little to complain of, for the poems, with which I took a great deal of trouble, exist, and an expensive present from the Empress,[312] enhanced by the friendly, gracious and confidential way she received me, repaid me beyond all expectation. [...]

Even the sight of your composition makes me happy again. I will endeavour to hear it now and see that I amend the awkward passages in the song.

I must tell you, by the way, that I spent three consecutive weeks in Berka writing the poems for the procession; the Inspector[313] played to me every day for from three to four hours and at my request, in historical order, selections from Sebastian Bach to Beethoven, including Philipp Emanuel, Handel, Mozart, Haydn, Dussek[314] too, and others like him. At the same time I studied Marperger's *Der vollkommene Capellmeister*[315] and could not help smiling as I learned. Yet how serious and conscientious those days were, and how such a man must have felt the trammel of a lack of culture that held him captive!

I have bought *Das Wohltemperirte Clavier*, as well as Bach's *Chorales*, and have presented them to the Inspector as a Christmas gift, with which he may refresh me when he comes here on a visit, and educate me when I go back to him again.

With your guidance I should indeed like to sink myself into the world of the chorale, into those depths where I do not know how to help myself unaided. The old intonations and basic musical practice are constantly applied to modern songs, and imitated by younger organists of more recent times; the ancient texts are set aside and inferior ones substituted, etc. How different is the sound of the prohibited song 'Wie schön leuchtet der Morgenstern' from that of the revised version now sung to the same melody; and yet the genuine and oldest version of all, probably a Latin one, would be still more suitable and appropriate.[316] You see I am again sniffing about on the borders of your territory, but where I am fishing, nothing can come of it.[317] This, however, is not the only point which would make one despair.

---

[312] A box with the portrait of the Russian empress on it, valued at 400 thaler.

[313] Johann *Heinrich Friedrich* Schütz (1779–1829).

[314] Johann Ludwig Dussek (1760–1812), Bohemian composer and pianist.

[315] Johann Mattheson, *Der vollkommene Capellmeister* (Hamburg, 1739). Goethe misnames the author as the music theoretician Friedrich Wilhelm Marpurg (1718–95); ZG 2 June 1819.

[316] 'Wie schön leuchtet der Morgenstern' is not in the revised edition of Herder's *Weimarisches Gesangbuch* (1795, r.1820) but the volume contains seven hymns which can be sung to the same melody. It is not clear to which of them Goethe's criticism is directed.

[317] Goethe uses Zelter's metaphor to illustrate the difficulties of hearing vocal music in Weimar; see Goethe's letter to Zelter on 4 May 1814. The house choir which Goethe founded in 1807, which ceased its music-making in 1811. From the end of 1812 the choir

## 251. Zelter

Berlin, 8 to 9 January 1819

Here I am sending the lament,[318] which I found easier than I originally thought as you will notice from the music. I would like a few comments from you. It is a very easy melody. It is really a death march: harps, trumpets and muted timpani drums are called for. The refrain is sung in unison by a choir of young voices and altos.

I have altered the second strophe because of a double syllable[319] and in the last line of the final strophe the words are changed around to suit the accentuation.[320] Let me know if it is not right and I will arrange it as it should go. [...]

We have had a rehearsal to mark our celebration of the Three Wise Men,[321] which, because of the bean feast[322] at the court, had to be postponed until tomorrow. I have composed some music for it;[323] however, on the whole I am not satisfied with it. Schadow or someone else will tell you what it should all mean. It is a mixture of many things and contains much good so that we don't all fall asleep. The worst thing is that no one does what he can; because if we did what we could, we would not be too bad.

---

only met occasionally as Goethe no longer had the same impetus to host a house choir on account of the type of music that its members wanted to perform.

[318] Zelter's setting of Goethe's 'Klaggesang. Irisch' ('So singet laut den Pillalu'), dated 6 January 1819, is in Goethe's music collection (GSA 32/22). The Berlin manuscript carries the same date and additional dedication: 'For Langermann' (SBB Mus ms. Autogr. Zelter 24, no. 7). The song was first published in Zelter's *Sechs Deutsche Lieder für die Bass-Stimme mit Begleitung des Pianoforte* (1826).

[319] In place of Goethe's 'Die Eule kam vorbei geschwingt [...] Ihr nun die Totensänge singt', Zelter wrote: 'die Eule kam herbei geschwirrt [...] Ihr nun in toter Wüste irrt'.

[320] Zelter replaced Goethe's 'Des Herrn einziger Sohn ist fort' with 'der einzige Sohn des Herrn ist fort'.

[321] The annual festival of the Berliner Künstlerverein (Society of Artists) which took place on 9 January 1819 rather than on its usual date, 6 January; see *Vossische Zeitung*, 12 January 1819; *MA* 20.3, p. 482.

[322] A custom on the day or previous evening of the Festival of the Three Wise Men: whoever from the society finds a bean baked in a cake is for that day the King of the Beans. There are other games and carnival entertainment built around this.

[323] Zelter, *Gloria*; a review of both work and performance is published in the *Vossische Zeitung*, 12 January 1819; *MA* 20.3, p. 482.

## 252. Zelter

Berlin, 11 January 1819

Writing in haste I will only remark of ['Klaggesang'], enclosed in the last [letter], that in the first and last four-line strophes, on the words 'Ochorro orro ollalu', the notes of the melody must be:

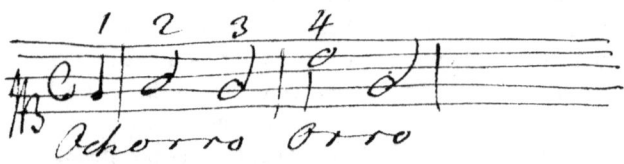

so that the note marked with 4, which is 'F' in the manuscript I sent, should be 'B', as can be seen here, and again in the final strophe. Everything else remains as is. [...]

Should you be willing to send me your elucidatory poems, please do so as soon as possible, as I am in the mood for composing right now; I always need more time for freeing myself from my usual surroundings than I do for the actual work. I could not help smiling, any more than you could, when I heard you had read Mattheson's *vollkommene Capellmeister*.[324] This man was Legation Secretary for Great Britain up to the time of his death and an eminently useful statesman at the same time. By the time he had reached his seventy-second year, he had written as many works, mainly musical, which make a strange impression nowadays. I am very fond of dipping into them, for they always give me ideas which I wouldn't come across otherwise.

Some time ago I sent you a good manuscript copy of *Das Wohltemperirte Clavier*, so you ought not to have been forced to buy it.[325]

The original Latin [text] of which our 'Wie schön leuchtet der Morgenstern' might be a translation is not known; in old songbooks they like to give the Latin beginning. It is attributed to Philipp Nicolai, Pastor of Hamburg, because it is printed in his *Freudenspiegel* published in Hamburg in 1598.[326] Wilhelm Ernst, Count and Lord of Waldeck (a name with is encoded in the opening letters of

---

[324] Johann Mattheson (1681–1764), theorist, composer, organist, singer.

[325] When Zelter sent Goethe a copy of J.S. Bach's *Das Wohltemperirte Clavier* is unknown. It is possible that Zelter is mistaking it for the copy of the 24 Preludes and Fugues which he had enclosed in a package to the inspector, Schütz, on 8 to 12 May 1816. Goethe's reaction would seem to confirm this.

[326] The well-known church song first appeared in Philipp Nicolai's *FrewdenSpiegel deß ewigen Lebens* (Frankfurt am Main, 1599). Zelter's information '1598 in Hamburg' is incorrect. Nicolai's song 'Wie schön leuchtet der Morgenstern' belongs to the most important Protestant hymns and has been firmly established in the evangelical liturgy since

the stanzas of the song),[327] could be the author and perhaps in that case it is also original. NB. It is in the Porst Songbook,[328] because more recent editions don't contain these facts.

### 253. Zelter

Berlin, 15 January 1819

Should an idea for a song for our artists' society occur to you,[329] then I would like you to write it. On festive occasions the women are brought along and there is singing at table. As I have, however, mostly composed male-voice settings, very little is suitable and you know our poets: you can't do anything with the woolliness.

On my last trip to Weimar we searched for 'Dir zu eröffnen mein Herz' and it was lost. I enclose it here once again.[330] It is better that you have two copies than none at all. The young bass[331] whom I admired on the occasion of the service for your Imperial Princess would certainly be able to sing it to your satisfaction with his touching, clear voice.

You would certainly have been delighted with your Hafiz 'Aus wie vielen Elementen'[332] at our Liedertafel last Tuesday. The piece has a quiet, certain and lively pathos, so I could hear it myself not without edification, and since I came across the first draft when rummaging about, I also enclose this, even though you might have it already.

Yesterday evening, Langermann sang ['Klaggesang'] for me for the first time. The piece is striking and touching and I would like to know what you think about

---

the first half of the seventeenth century. The song has received countless arrangements from Michael Praetorius and Samuel Scheidt down to the present day liturgical practice.

[327] From 1588 to 1596 Nicolai Pfarrer was court preacher and tutor of Wilhelm Ernst Graf von Waldeck in Altwildung.

[328] Anon., *Geistliche und Liebliche Lieder Welche Der Geist des Glaubens [...] in den vorigen und jetzigen Zeiten gedichtet [...] Nebst Einigen Gebeten*, rev. edition edited by Johann Porst (Berlin, 1708 r.1713).

[329] The Berliner Künstlerverein founded by Gottfried Schadow on 22 November 1814.

[330] The setting is no longer in Goethe's music collection.

[331] The name of the singer cannot be determined.

[332] A copy of a four-part setting by Zelter entitled 'Liederstoff' is in Goethe's music collection (GSA 32/36); as a fair copy with few corrections, it is unlikely that it is the 'first draft' enclosed here.

it. Writing it, my feeling was between Irish and Iroquois,[333] which is essentially all the same to me because I know neither: it will be human.

### 254. Goethe

Weimar, 18 January 1819

[...] Both the 'Ballade' and the 'Klaggesang' were performed to my greatest delight by Inspector Schütz, whom I deliberately employed. I find both very successful, as one discovers with repeated listening. [...]

*Das Wohltemperirte Clavier* would be doubly welcome, when it arrives, even as a second copy. I will keep it in the town and the good inspector will not always need to carry his here from Berka. The correction is also made to 'Klaggesang'.[334]

### 255. Zelter

Berlin, 20 May 1819

Your *Festgedichte* leaves me wanting more![335] If at first I read them through, one after another, in order to become acquainted with the whole [work], now I enjoy them for breakfast, before dinner, after dinner, in the evening and before going to sleep, one after the other [...]. It reminds me of a Haydn minuet, which I enjoy in a similar way.

### 256. Goethe

Weimar, 29 May 1819

It is a matter of course that you should like my *Festgedichte*, for while in Berka, where I wrote them – reading Marperger and listening to Schütz playing – I thought of you constantly and wished we were nearer one another. You have already got more than I can say out of this little series. Variety and freedom of metre came

---

[333] The Irish origins of the song (from Caroline Lamb's novel *Glenarvon*) and the exotic world of the north American Indians – a word play, perhaps, expressing something foreign, barbaric and yet human.

[334] Goethe's correction can be identified in the vocal line (bar 11) of Zelter's manuscript.

[335] A complete copy of Goethe's masque was published at the end of May 1819; presumably Zelter received his copy from August von Goethe, who visited Zelter at this time.

fortuitously while I was at work and contemplating the many different subjects. There is very little trace of modern artificiality; my main aim was the eight-line stanza and it is really curious that not one sonnet would fit into the cycle; even your instinct will hardly be able to suggest where it could have been introduced. [...]

### 257. Zelter

Berlin, 2 June 1819

[...] Your *Festgedichte* are being passed from me to Langermann and back again. I, at least, did not feel the lack of a sonnet because, despite my efforts, I have never been able to wrest from it a natural musical form.

You speak in your letter of having read Marperger. Do you not mean Marpurg or Kirnberger?[336] I don't know a Marperger. If it is Marpurg, he is one of the best, for his style of writing is the best, but here, too, as in the plastic arts, words fail to explain the essence and what one wants to know one can only learn by doing oneself. He has written much,[337] and was constantly at issue with Kirnberger about matters in which, in my judgement, Kirnberger was right; although the latter, when it came to writing, could not compare with the former, and consequently was always at a disadvantage before the world. I knew both of those men personally, and learnt from their conflicting opinions most of what I wished to know myself. [...]

The children will have plenty to tell you about the performance of the two scenes from *Faust*;[338] it was a start, anyhow, and there was no lack of goodwill.

---

[336] Zelter wrote about both in his autobiographies; Kirnberger comes across as a very angry person, although Zelter esteemed him as a critic of his early songs.

[337] Friedrich Wilhelm Marpurg, *Die Kunst das Clavier zu spielen* (Berlin, 1750, enh. ed. 1762; Hildesheim: G. Olms, reprint 1969); *Kritische Briefe über die Tonkunst* (Berlin, 1760–64; Hildesheim, New York: G. Olms, reprint 1974); *Abhandlung von der Fuge* 2 vols (Berlin: A. Haude and JC Spener, 1753–54; Hildesheim: G. Olms, reprint 1970).

[338] Radziwill's setting and production of two scenes from Goethe's *Faust* were rehearsed and performed in 1816. On 24 May 1819 the scenes were performed again for Radziwill's birthday; see August von Goethe's letter to his father (*GJb* 28, 1907, p. 36); the performance was repeated on 7 June 1817.

## 258. Zelter

Vienna, 20 July to 9 August 1819

I arrived here last Saturday, after a six-day boat journey down the Danube from Regensburg.[339] [...] After my arrival on Saturday evening I went directly to the Kärntnertortheater. The opera *Othello*, by Rossini,[340] is a fine new score which I heard performed really well here for the first time. The composer sacked the poet[341] and set some kind of libretto to music, which one can piece together really well from the score. He is, without doubt, a man of genius and knows how to use the means at his disposal, without, like Gluck, first having to think of the invention of the instruments needed to play his music. The music has *crescendi* which really mount, he can really let go and finally the idea emerges clearly. He plays with the notes and the notes play with him.

Sunday to the Marinelli Theatre. Three pieces were performed: (i) *Die Werber*[342] (ii) *Die Damenhüte im Theater*[343] (iii) a pantomime, *Schulmeister Beistrich*, otherwise known as *Das Donnerwetter*.[344] [...]

Wednesday, 21 July: A second work (*Der lustige Fritz*)[345] in the Marinelli Theatre, which was strongly recommended to me, was not a success. It is a popular work with audiences yet all the mutual good will was not enough to bring it off.

Thursday: Yesterday evening I heard Rossini's fourth Opera, *La Gazza Ladra*;[346] the subject is lovely and something very fine might have been made of it; properly speaking, there should be a comic figure – this, however, the poet[347] has forgotten; on the other hand, the emotional element preponderates, and of this again the composer has forgotten to make the most. On the whole, however, the music is witty and unrestrained, even to the point of licentiousness, and in this

---

[339] In Zelter's library there is a travelogue, *Donaureise von Regensburg bis Wien, mit Angabe aller Ortschaften an beiden Ufern, ihrer Merkwürdigkeiten, und der Flüsse, welche sich mit der Donau vereinigen* (Regensburg, 1802).

[340] The first German performance of this opera (in a libretto by Johann Christoph Grünbaum) took place in Vienna on 29 April 1819; Zelter attended the performance on 17 July 1819.

[341] A reference to the original Italian librettist, Francesco Berio di Salsa, who took a great deal of licence with Shakespeare's text.

[342] Anton Sartori's comedy *Die Werber oder Die belohnte Treue*.

[343] A local farce by Carl Meisl.

[344] Carl Meisl's pantomime *Das Donnerwetter*, with music by Franz Joseph Volkert.

[345] Carl Meisl's *Der lustige Fritz. Ein Märchen aus neuer Zeit* with music by Franz Volkert.

[346] First performed in Joseph von Seyfried's translation, *Die diebische Elster*, on 3 May 1819 in the Theater an der Wien. Zelter attended the ninth performance on 21 July; *AMZ* (1819), no. 38, 22 September, column 631.

[347] Giovanni Gherardini (1778–1861).

respect it borders on Mozart, who, however, is more daring and profound. The singing was not much to speak of, but the audience was content with everything as everyone obviously did his best. [...]

Salieri, who has written more than forty operas, is the most honest fellow in the world; he is as busy as ever in the most childlike way.[348] He is now 69 years old, and considers himself outdated; this he need not do, for his talent still flows, and none of his pupils surpasses him.[349]

Evening: I have just seen and heard a performance of Mozart's *Titus*,[350] which I think I am right in saying was done more successfully at Weimar.[351] All the ladies (there were four of them) were old enough to have been grandmothers, but are well trained. Campi[352] must have been excellent in her youth; now, however, she looks as if she had been old while still in the womb. Such a Titus has still to be born: he is to be in love with all young women, who all want to kill him.

Saturday evening, 24 July: Yesterday I bought myself an umbrella for 26 florins. With this in mind I went to the Prater after eating and got as wet as a drowned rat as I had left the umbrella at home, so I went to the Marinelli Theatre to laugh myself dry again. Now imagine my despair! *Der verlorne Sohn*[353] (as yesterday's play was called), I thought, would be able to laugh himself and make others laugh: wrong! The 'prodigal' [...] son is a moralistic melodrama, with choruses and dancing. The son, who is a scoundrel, has a wife, has learnt absolutely nothing; accordingly he loses everything and the piece ends after Act Four, in which the son becomes fortunate once again instead of getting his just deserts.

The poet Carpani[354] is one of my old acquaintances, whom I first got to know in Teplitz in 1810. As the good old gentleman does not speak a word of German, I am obliged to talk to him in Italian, which is getting better than I had expected after so many years of not speaking it. You will remember Carpani when I remind you of a little book of his, *Le Haydine*, which contains some very nice stories about old Hadyn.

---

[348] Antonio Salieri (1750–1825).

[349] An ill-informed statement, considering Salieri's students included Beethoven, Schubert, Liszt, Meyerbeer and Moscheles.

[350] Mozart's *opera seria*, *La Clemenza di Tito*, in German translation *Titus der Gütige*, had been in the repertoire of the Kärnthnerthortheater since 1817; Zelter attended the performance on 22 July 1819.

[351] In Christian August Vulpius's translation on 21 December 1799.

[352] The Italian singer Antonia Campi née Miklaszewicz (1773–1822) who played Vitellia.

[353] Melodrama by Ferdinand Rosenau with music by Joseph Drechsler.

[354] Giuseppi Antonio Carpani (1751/2–1825), Italian writer and librettist, known chiefly for his work *Le Haydine* (Milan, 1812), an enthusiastic eulogy on Haydn; the biography is written in the form of 17 long letters to an anonymous friend. He also published *Le Rossiniane*, a similar eulogy on Rossini.

Weigl[355] has told me a great many interesting things about Mozart's youth and last years. Weigl is a fine, stately man of the world; his works are pure, measured, natural, and full of character; he doesn't aim very high and what he achieves has an immediate effect.

The double bass is placed in a slanting position, so that the player sits beside it. I have not noticed any loss of quality and should like to see this method universally adopted. Those accursed goosenecks offend my eyes with their spikes; on the other hand, the prompter's boxes here are as large as in other parts of Germany and prevent the eye from finding a centre for itself, and in addition to this there is the ridiculously high seat of the conductor, so intrusive in all his movements. One can hardly understand why such vulgarity is allowed.

The Burg Theatre is in high repute here, but the actors are away on their holidays until next month. I intend now and then to slip over from Baden to Vienna and hope it will be worth it. The Theater an der Wien is an attractive house, big enough with five rows of boxes, exclusive of the parterre boxes. One can see and hear there very comfortably.

The Marinelli or Casperl Theatre (Leopoldstadt) is also a good one with three rows of boxes, but the seats are so extremely narrow that I can hardly find room for my knees. The Karntnerthor Theatre is the best; the music is attractive, appropriate and on the whole quite good, but the singers and players are dreadfully overworked and weary, for every day they have an opera and a rehearsal, and often two rehearsals on the same day. The instruments hold up even less than the men. The players in the orchestra are badly treated; several of them eat their dinner and supper in the theatre because they have no other time for it. Weigl, too, complained of the difficulty of his duties, and he has to compose as well.

Monday, 26 July. Yesterday was Sunday, and I saw the Prater in its Sunday dress. Four rows of sturdy old chestnut trees form three avenues that begin at the Leopoldstadt and continue for half a mile directly to the Danube. The middle one, 45 feet wide, is for carriages; the two side avenues, 24 feet wide, are for pedestrians. Several hundred carriages are to be seen on the move, some of them are very splendid; the small carriages turn out too; close at hand are the foot passengers, alone, in couples, or in groups. The variety is charming; it is delightful to see a promenade of so many men and women, beautifully dressed in every kind of costume, flitting about like shadows. On either side, cafes and resting areas are set up under the shade of noble groups of trees; everything is a picture of neatness and cleanliness. We sit down; music, issuing from the wood, echoes in our ears on all sides; now we are at the opera, now at the ball, or on parade. Coffee and cakes are served. A child presents me with a posy, a pretty girl offers me water as clear as crystal, an old woman hands me a toothpick; all this is paid for by copper kreutzers only, a good riddance for bad rubbish, for they are as heavy as one's conscience and drag your pockets down to your feet. This avenue, however, is not the only thing

---

[355] Joseph Weigl (1766–1846), Austrian composer, conductor and Kapellmeister at the Vienna Court Theatre; best known as the composer of *Die Schweizerfamilie*.

that forms the Prater. A second and third just like it fan out from the Leopoldstadt towards the Danube (that is, an arm of the Danube). Here we see, as it were, how the other half live, I mean the real people. The wider spaces of ground towards the Danube are occupied by refreshment stalls where you can get beer, wine, meat, ice-cream and drinks of all kinds, with the exception of coffee. The three single cafes in the great avenues have exclusive rights in selling coffee. These second-class bars so numerous, and so close to one another that the guests of one host are indistinguishable from those of another, and one is in danger of consuming what somebody else has paid for. This is Vienna proper; between these tables and chairs, and drinking booths, smokers, bands, and merry-go-rounds, a happy crowd moves backwards and forwards. People jog along, stop, meet a friend; it is a constant rest and bustle at the same time. Nothing is closed in, and there is no obstacle; for although the owners of houses are landlords, yet the ground and soil belong to the Emperor, and must not be enclosed in any way. The impression produced on the mind by the behaviour of the people – I will not call it the crowd – is one of careless oblivion. I don't remember thinking or observing anything, and what I now write, strictly speaking, I imagine, without being able to say: so it is, and so it was. What gives a really pleasant aspect to the whole is the large crowd of happy faces, belonging to all kinds of people, who, reconciled today with their God, see the world as they would like it to be. Neither men, nor women, nor old age, nor youth is here as it ought to be. There is an idea in existence, as there is an existence in the idea. The first day I went into the theatre a violinist was tuning his instrument. A waiter came into the pit, and sang in the same key as the violin:

Then another followed with:

And then the whole orchestra tuned upon this melody; I laughed so loud at this that everyone looked at me as if I were a madman. Let them think what they want of me; the things I don't like here I can get just as well at home and I hope to find them there again.

Tuesday. Yesterday evening there was a splendid display of fireworks in the Prater in honour of St Anne. The worthy pyrotechnist has, as a rule, the misfortune to have bad weather; all the spectators take the deepest interest in the matter, for the people like to see such a spectacle, just as much as the artist likes to produce it. Yesterday we had the finest weather imaginable. It had rained itself dry; there was no dust, no evening fog, no breeze, but a dark purple and blue evening sky. The rockets shot up straight as arrows, and everything went off successfully. There were two principal displays – the first in honour of beautiful women, and the last adorned with the name of St Anne. The thing had something magnificent about it that is not easily achieved with ordinary fireworks on account of the expanse of darkness at night. The scaffolding that is always erected for such occasions is from 80 to 90 feet high, and from 160 to a 180 feet in length. The three levels of boxes around the scaffolding, with the elevated Imperial box in the middle, easily accommodate 1,000 people. The parterre, which was completely crowded, held probably some 30,000 spectators; all the ladies were beautifully dressed, for it is normal for the fair sex here to be tastefully and beautifully attired. The charm of the scene is enhanced by the general satisfaction with everything, the way everyone quietly takes it to heart if there is a failure, and the way they all rejoice when it rights itself again.

This seems to me the only celebration in which the Austrians are willing to do without music, which for us here is so intrusive. I was assured by a musician in Carlsbad that music was a hard profession. I replied that the musicians are better off than the visitors. 'How come?', he asked. 'Why, surely', I answered, 'they can eat without music.' The good man went away abashed and I felt sorry for him, although my point was valid. It is really cruel to plague patients and convalescents in this manner. I can endure a good deal, but when I come away from the opera, sit down to supper and some harpist or balladmonger tries to rekindle what I have heard and enjoyed at the theatre – it is really too much – and I, poor fellow, quite forget that this scribbling is also a great deal too much; so farewell with kind regards and greetings to all your circle.

The Danube is now looking quite splendid. It has risen so high from the heavy rains and the melting of the snow upon the hills that it rushes by, like an arrow. I am just off for a drive with Salieri. God bless you!

Thursday, 29 July. The day before yesterday I had the most charming walk to Schönbrunn and back with Salieri. The old fellow is still so full of music and melody that he speaks as if he were singing and it seems as if he can only be understood in that way. It is the greatest enjoyment for me to observe this genuine character and to find him always truthful, always cheerful. I come back to this thought, now that I have obtained the score of the new Requiem by Cherubini.[356] This is a composition which, in these dislocated days, must certainly achieve widespread popularity and precisely because it contains no truth, and while everything is thought out and realized, there is not the faintest feeling of a *requiem aeternam*. The composer is only concerned to look up those passages in the poem where he can be boisterous – *dies irae-mors stupebit – rex tremendae majestatis – flammis acribus* – and to fill out the intervals with measured restlessness; in short, he highlights what is subordinate and it is as if one were constantly and passionately saying, 'No', and

---

[356] Cherubini, Requiem in C minor for four-part choir and orchestra.

at the same time nodding one's head. A review of this work, which I have before me, is just as bewildering and as disingenuous as the work itself; the composer is exalted into the seventh heaven, and then dragged down again, as one who has dared to enter the lists with Mozart and wishes to rival him, when Mozart has done it much better; as if nobody else were allowed to compose, or die, or find rest, after Mozart! All the newest books of instruction are based upon this opinion; the old perceptions are thrown aside; and that is the present form of art.

In the midst of all this, it is quite touching to observe the warm-hearted Salieri, who exalts this state of things without any sorrow and looks at it as an advance in Art that is necessary but unattainable by him. At the same time, he goes on writing in his usual manner in a style full of unconscious irony and humour and spins his own cocoon like a silkworm. He speaks with delight of a Requiem which he wrote under the impression that he would soon follow his wife[357] who died in 1807; but as this has not yet taken place, he has now written a much shorter one, thinking it was good enough for him. He has allowed me to copy a mass[358] and an offertory[359] he wrote in the year 1766. The latter is in no way inferior to the very best Italian works of the seventeenth century produced in this style. It is devotional, pure and elevating, composed in a manner that observes the practical requirements of art and the church. You should have seen his guileless gratification, when, at the very first glance at this music, I was able to make some meaningful remarks about it; he knows the whole thing from tradition, while I have only acquired it by observation and study and have had to get a picture of it for myself, for the theory of an ecclesiastical style of music has disappeared with the Church herself.

Beethoven, whom I should like to have seen once more in this life, is living in the country and no one can tell me where.[360] I was keen to write to him, but people told me he was almost incommunicado on account of his almost complete deafness. Perhaps it is better that we should remain as we are, since it might upset me to discover him in bad form.

[...] Among the local fortepiano virtuosi a Madame Cibbini (Kozeluch's daughter)[361] stands out. With regard to playing as such, she belongs to those who are not afraid to be heard. What one calls expression here is to me commonplace, and makes no impression on me. I would always prefer to hear swift, pure, sprightly, clear, rounded, clear playing than eternal pressing, pecking and nodding, as the expression of nothing to nothing, which they call feeling. These eternal sonatas (Grand Sonatas),[362] which are between heaven and earth, between the lowest bass

---

[357] Therese Salieri, née von Helfersdorfer (1755–1807).
[358] Presumably the *Missa capella* in C major (1767).
[359] This work cannot be identified: it is not in Zelter's bequest.
[360] Beethoven spent the summer in Mödling near Vienna.
[361] Katharina Cibbini, daughter of the composer Leopold Kozeluch. For reviews of her performance see *AMZ* 21 (1819), no. 8, 24 February, column 127; *MA* 20.3, p. 493.
[362] A term for large-scale sonatas for virtuoso performers (many of Beethoven's sonatas were originally given the title 'Große Sonaten').

C and A four octaves above middle C, float and wriggle like a thief in the gallows, put me in bad humour because at the end one is always supposed to cry 'Bravo', and thank God when the worst is over.

Friday. Yesterday I heard Madame Cibbini again. What she performs is, in fact, extraordinary: nice, secure, controlled and – to put it in a nutshell – masterly. Every finger appears to have five senses and all 50 together form an anarchy which could not be more agreeable. And yet even this Madame Cibbini is supposed to be surpassed by others. I listen to all this patiently for in fact I don't understand it. [...]

People know their music here and this is in direct contrast with Italy, which considers itself the gate of paradise. The people here, however, are really well educated. It is true they accept everything, but they only retain what is first-rate work. They are happy to listen to a mediocre opera if the performers are good, but a first-rate work, even if not performed in the best manner, remains popular with them. Beethoven is praised to the heavens because he works very hard and is still alive; but it is Haydn who presents their national humour to them, like a pure fountain which does not mingle with any other streams, and it is he who dwells within them, because he moves among them; they seem to forget him every day, and daily he rises to life again amongst them.

Baden, 2 August. How can I thank you enough for your Morphologie,[363] which I am devouring with the greatest interest, applying it to the Theory of Sound, and thereby arriving gradually at the Theory of Thought and Invention?[364] How naturally all this comes, and what will your honoured friend F.A. Wolf, say, when he comes to read the first lines in Hafis?[365] I am going continuously from one thing to another. I read something here, then something there – which gives me enormous pleasure, because with my distracted life here all sorts of ideas occur to me at once.

[...] Today – 3 August is the anniversary of the death of my noble friend, Fasch. Having lived with him for many years, without a cross word, I am delighted to be able to say, after a period of 19 years, 'Look, old friend and master, your work still lives! It is encouraged, it encourages others, they value it, and thank God that I existed and still exist to preserve for you, myself and art!' You recognize a sound idea years later.

9 August. To try something new, the day before yesterday I went to Ulrich's, the local bookseller, where I found a reprint of your works, and amongst them,

---

[363] Goethe's periodical *Zur Naturwissenschaft überhaupt, besonders zur Morophologie*. vol. 2, which Zelter had presumably received from Goethe during Zelter's visit to Weimar on 22–25 July 1819.

[364] Perhaps a reference to Goethe's essay *Meteore des literarischen Himmels*, with scientific-philosophic reflections.

[365] The first edition of the *Divan* opens with the last sentences of 'Verwahrung': 'Poetic works come into the hands of the literary person first as letters of the alphabet; then he sees them as books which he has to arrange and put in order'.

the biography of Philipp Hackert,[366] which forms the eighteenth volume of the 1811 edition. The way in which you have pieced together this little work out of mere fragments is so typical and so natural that it did my heart good to read it. It was as good as new to me, for in 1811, at Schweidnitz, I only had time to skim through it. If you should still have a copy, please be so good as to send it to me at your convenience, and address it to Berlin. Hackert's youngest brother, George,[367] the engraver, was my closest school friend at the Drawing Academy in Berlin, the Director of which in those days was the excellent Lesueur. Had I, at that time, been less obedient to my mother, I should have gone with George to Naples.[368] God knows how I envied him having a brother who could invite him there. Those times were quite different from the present and the awareness of my inferior talent lay so heavily on my youth that I did not understand how to work my way out of it. The book has vividly recalled that time to me and at this moment makes me feel 40 years younger.

If I compare the simple narration of a fruitful, artistic life with other pretentiously composed biographies in which the great appears small and the truth incredible, it is evident to me what it takes for one not to aim too high.

### 259. Zelter

Baden, Vienna, Prague, Dresden, 12 August to 1 October 1819

16 August. Yesterday, I heard some more vocal music; Italian, of course, for people here don't like speaking German let alone singing it. There is nothing but Rossini; he rules whether he chooses to or not; there's freedom for you! And the Italians are right. The voice will sing for its own sake, and whoever does what it wants has the edge. Now, however, criticism is beginning to form here too, and it will seize upon the nearest thing first; it might turn out badly for Rossini if he tries to do more than he can. A couple of 16-year-old girls sang the music very well and very securely; the craziest stuff sounds well as long as it is performed well.

Beethoven has retired to the country, but no one knows where;[369] he has just written a letter here from Baden to one of his lady friends[370] and [yet] he is not

---

[366] Jakob Phillipp Hackert (1737–1807), a landscape painter who Goethe met in Italy. The work Zelter is referring to is: Goethe, *Philipp Hackert. Biographische Skizze, meist nach dessen eigenen Aufsätzen entworfen*, vol. 18 (Cotta: 1811).

[367] Georg Abraham Hackert (1755–1805), Zelter frequently mentions him in his autobiography, Schottländer, *Carl Friedrich Zelters Darstellungen seines Lebens*, pp. 29, 46, 62, 80 and 221.

[368] Schottländer, *Carl Friedrich Zelters Darstellungen seines Lebens*, p. 22.

[369] Beethoven spent the summer in Mödling near Vienna.

[370] No letter exists in the Beethoven correspondence; the identity of the woman in unknown.

at Baden. He is said to be intolerably sulky; some say he is a fool. That's easy to say. God forgive us! They say the poor man is completely deaf. I know how I feel when I look at my fingers, for with me – poor devil – one finger after the other gets useless. Lately, Beethoven went to a restaurant, sat down at the table, and after an hour's meditation, called out to the waiter, 'How much do I owe you?' 'Why, your honour has not eaten anything! What shall I bring you?' 'Bring what you like, and leave me alone!'

His patron is said to be the Archduke Rudolf,[371] who allows him 1,500 gulden a year. With this he must try to manage like all other children of the muse. They are kept there like cats, and any one who does not understand the art of mousing will hardly save anything, and yet in spite of this, they are all as round and satisfied as weasels. [...]

In Vienna, and here I have in vain tried to find the opera *Elena e Costantino*.[372] Salieri and Weigl knew nothing about it. The opera is by Simon Mayr, and was performed at Milan during the month of August 1816.[373] The Baroness von Pereira has promised me that she will write to Milan and get the sextet; the opera itself is not popular – the sextet is said to give life to the whole work. [...]

31 August: I have now finished the music to a little poem 'Gleich und Gleich';[374] you may like to hear it and see whether I can breathe on yet another little flower that would give a tiny bee an appetite. I serve you as people offer sacrifices to the gods, by bringing to them their own gifts. Take, my old friend, what is yours [...]

14 September: The day before yesterday, I made a trip to Mödling to visit Beethoven. At the same time he was travelling to Vienna and, meeting each other on the road, we got out of our carriages and embraced each other most cordially. The poor man is as good as deaf, and I could hardly hold back my tears when I saw him. Then I continued on my journey to Mödling and he to Vienna.[375] [...]

I have found my old idea realized – that of making the orchestra [pit] so deep, that one does not see the woolly heads of the musicians; the music, too, which is not nearly as well organized here as in Weimar, comes out clear and distinct.

---

[371] Rudolph Johann Joseph Rainer (1788–1831), youngest son of Emperor Leopold II, half-brother of the reigning Austrian Emperor Franz I; he was both a student and patron of Beethoven's.

[372] On 20 January 1818 Goethe had asked Zelter about the score of the sextet from Act 2 of this opera.

[373] The first performance took place in Naples in 1814.

[374] Goethe sent this poem to Zelter on 22 April 1814. There is no autograph of the score in Goethe's music collection, only a copy of the published score (*Wiener Allegemeine musikalische Zeitung* (1820), GSA 32/1469). The Berlin manuscript bears the dedication: 'To Anton Salieri, [performed at] the Baden Fair, from Prof. Zelter from Berlin on 28 September 1819' (SBB PK: Mus. ms. Autogr. Zelter 31).

[375] Apart from this unexpected encounter on the road from Vienna to Mödling, Beethoven and Zelter saw each other briefly at the theatre the same evening. It was not possible for them to meet again because Zelter left Vienna on 20 September.

I cannot imagine anything less becoming on a stage, than to see the fine forms of well-dressed actors, and all that goes to make up a brilliant scene, fluttering between the confounded mops [of hair] of the fiddlers in front.

15 September. Yesterday I made the acquaintance of Grillparzer,[376] a well-built young man, 26 years of age, quiet, but rather sickly. He makes a very good impression. We drove through the country together and got on famously. [...]

I must admit comedy is cast very well here and the people are well rehearsed. I have seen two works which went off well. Since Liebich's death[377] it reeks of anarchy. The music is almost too bad. The first violinist does not appear idle and has the others tune up from him. He doesn't seem to notice that the men don't have proper strings: [they think] whoever plays well doesn't need to tune. The double basses hum and drone without having the proper number of cellos with them.

## 260. Goethe

Weimar, 30 January 1820

[...] No more for now in case the accompanying *Divan*[378] misses the post. May it inspire you anew to clothe musically these basically naked songs and send them out into the world! I am also busy in new ways and it bears fruit.

## 261. Zelter

Berlin, 11 to 26 February 1820

[...] Yesterday I set Suleika's little song (p. 166)[379] to music and after several days I will want to look at it again. Browsing through the *Divan* does bring something to light.

---

[376] *Franz* Seraphicus Grillparzer (1791–1872).

[377] Johann Karl Liebich (1773–1816) died on 21 December 1816; he had directed both corporative theatres in Prague since 4 August 1806.

[378] A special edition of Goethe's *West-östlicher Divan* which the poet had promised Zelter.

[379] Setting of Goethe's 'Suleika' ('Ach! Um deine feuchten Schwingen') on p. 166 in the first edition of Goethe's *Divan*; a Berlin autograph which bears the title 'Suleika. Divan 166', is dated Berlin 26 February 1820.

## 262. Zelter

Berlin, 1 to 7 April 1820

Yesterday afternoon, an hour before I wanted to go to the performance of my Good Friday music,[380] I received your precious letter of 23 March with the parcel.[381]

In the last few days I have only been preoccupied by this music, so I read the bound manuscript like a stranger[382] until, with the most cheerful astonishment, I finally worked out the most charming jest, which went from happiness to happiness, because my music went off well and the house was packed.

The Duchess of Cumberland[383] sent for me after the performance in order to say the loveliest words about you and to send her greetings to you a thousand times, whereupon I was able to say to her that I had just received your letter which had contained assurance of your well-being.

Our music was also crowned with applause. The Duke[384] had beat time in his box – an industry for which he paid three ducats. [...]

## 263. Goethe

Weimar, 12 April 1820

I want a genuine Zelterian composition for the enclosed hymn,[385] which might be sung in chorus every Sunday before my home. If such a thing could reach my daughter-in-law during the month of May, it would be rehearsed and give me a pious and friendly welcome on my return at the beginning of June.

---

[380] The annual performance of Graun's Passion, *Der Tod Jesu*, by the Sing-Akademie; for reviews of the performance see *AMZ* 20 (1820), no. 16, 19 April, column 262; *MA* 20.3, p. 506.

[381] The parcel contained a copy of Zelter's *Reisebriefe aus Wien* occasioned by Goethe, as well as Goethe's *Über Kunst und Altertum*, vol. 2, no. 2.

[382] Goethe had a book of Zelter's Viennese letters made to enable Zelter to remember and enjoy the trip. The 49 bound pages (in John's hand with corrections by Goethe), which bear the title 'Zelter's Summer Journey 1819', are in Zelter's estate (GSA 95/II, 3). Johannes August Friedrich John (1794–1854) was a copyist in Weimar and Goethe's secretary from 1814; hereafter referred to as John.

[383] Friederike Karoline Sophie Alexandrine of Great Britain and Hanover (1778–1841).

[384] Ernst August of Great Britain and Hanover (1771–1851).

[385] 'Veni Creator Spiritus': the enclosed manuscript (in John's Hand) with Goethe's translation, dated 10 April, is in the Kippenberg collection (GMD: KK 3877.7).

## 264. Zelter

Berlin, 19 April 1820

Our artists' society linked up with the Akademie der Künste for a celebration of Raphael's birth,[386] which in our way turned out very well. [...] Three large pictures, the *Madonna del Sisto*,[387] the *Madonna del Pesce*[388] and a picture of St Cecilia,[389] were erected near one another, high up at the end of a 110-foot-long hall. Among these Raphael's catafalque stood on a 7-foot-high dais. On both sides of the platform were statues of the hero's four favourite muses: Poetry, Painting, Architecture and Music, which stood 6-foot-high and beautifully draped by Tieck.[390] A burning candelabra was placed between every two muses rising up over the figures, which crowned them really well. Over the catafalque was the bust of Raphael, a good copy by Weitsch.[391] All spaces were well festooned with coloured cloth as well as the entire front area which was 40-foot deep.

A choir of 100 selected singers was [positioned] in this area: women clothed in white and the men behind them in black, arranged in a semi-circle. The programme was:

1. A Requiem by me.[392]
2. Raphael's life read by Professor Tölken.[393]
3. Antonio Lotti's [8-part] *Crucifixus*; noteworthy because of its grand style.
4. I read something to enhance understanding about this old work, in connection with
5. *Gloria in Excelsis Deo* by Joseph Haydn[394] in order to make the stylistic differences of the two eras perceptible.

---

[386] On the occasion of the three-hundredth anniversary of Raphael's death (6 April 1520) a 'Festival in memory of Raffael' was celebrated by the Berliner Künstlerverein and the Akademie der Künste.

[387] Friedrich Bury's copy of Raphael's *Sistine Madonna*.

[388] Karl von Steuben's copy of Raphael's *Madonna with the Fish*.

[389] Raphael's *St Cecilia with St Paul, John the Baptist, St Augustine and Mary Magdalene*: Karl Ludewig's copy from Dionysius Calvaert's copy in Dresden.

[390] The Berlin architect Christian *Friedrich* Tieck (1776–1851).

[391] Friedrich Weitsch's copy after a painting in Braunschweig, which today is believed to be a portrait of a youth by one of the Giorgione circle.

[392] Zelter's Requiem for Fasch (now lost).

[393] Ernst Heinrich Toelken's speech was later published; on behalf of the publisher Zelter sent the printed version to Goethe on 16 June 1820.

[394] Zelter's arrangement for eight voices of the *Gloria* from Haydn's Mass in B major.

The whole event took over an hour. What I read[395] I enclose for clarity, should you care to say something beneficial about it.

## 265. Goethe

Carlsbad, 2 May 1820

Let me congratulate you on your Raphael Festival; it was well thought out, and I feel certain that will have shown; it is hard for anyone to compete with you. [...]

I should like to have heard the music, though I am able to form some impression of it from what you say. The purest and highest style of word painting in music is that which you yourself also practise; the object is to transport the listener into that frame of mind which the poem itself suggests; the imagination will then form pictures from the text without knowing how it arrives at them. You have given examples of this in your 'Johanna Sebus', 'Um Mitternacht' 'Über allen Gipfeln ist Ruh'; where have you not realized it? Tell me anyone who has achieved this to the same degree as you! Painting in tones of thunder, crash, splash and splosh is detestable. A minimum amount of this, as you use it, merely dotting the i's, is effective. So I, deprived of sound and hearing, though a good listener, transform that great enjoyment into ideas and words. I know very well that on account of this, I lose one third of life, but one must be able to adapt [...]

## 266. Goethe

Carlsbad, 11 May 1820

Eberwein has composed several songs;[396] give me your opinion of them. I feel at once that your compositions are identical with my songs; the music, like the gas which is pumped into the balloon, merely raises them up. With other composers I must first see how they have understood the song and what they have made out of it. [...]

---

[395] A copy of Zelter's speech on Lotti's *Crucifixus* and Haydn's *Gloria* in Doris Zelter's hand, with corrections by Zelter, sent as an enclosure (GSA 28/1017, no. 183).

[396] See Goethe's diary 14 April 1820: 'Company in the evening. The Eberweins. Music, especially settings from the *Divan*,' *WA* III/7, p. 158; the songs were published under the title, *Lieder aus Goethes West-östlichem Divan in Musik gesetzt fürs Piano-Forte und der Frau Kapellmeisterin Hummel hochachtungsvoll gewidmet von C. Eberwein*, vol. 6 (Hamburg: Johann August Böhme, o.J, 1820).

Among those by Eberwein, 'Jussufs Reize möcht ich borgen'[397] went down well with me and with others. His wife sang really well, fluently and agreeably.

### 267. Zelter

Berlin, 13 to 16 May 1820

[…] As your letter speaks of word painting, should I say who else has done such things? Haydn in *The Creation* and *The Seasons*, Beethoven, in his character symphonies[398] and *The Battle Symphony*, have drawn the most curious pictures, and with distinction. What I have noticed is the following: if you take the words away and the thing remains coherent, it calms down. *The Battle Symphony*, which I have now heard four times, always puts me into a suitable hearty, fearful-fearless and spiritual mood. Only I mustn't think explicitly of the score, because straight away judgement, which is also biased, interferes. The English and French are recognizable by their music – one does not know whether that is a failing or an advantage.

The overture to Haydn's *Creation* is the most marvellous music in the world, for by the ordinary, methodical, conventional resources of art a chaos is produced which converts the feeling of deep disorder into one of delight.

In the overture which represents winter in *The Seasons* I freeze in comfort at my warm stove, and at that moment I do not know whether there is anything beautiful in the world apart from this.

What old Bach and Handel achieved has no limit, especially in terms of quantity, just as every passing occasion gives rise to an abyss of feeling which they note down with the familiar black dots. If human beings knew no limitations and the external resources were rich enough, one would recognize, in the belly of the earth and the bosom of the stars, the life of the All-Powerful […]

### 268. Zelter

Berlin, 21 May 1820

So, to begin with the first rehearsal of *Faust* yesterday,[399] about which I don't know what else to say other than that today's [rehearsal] will turn out better. The

---

[397] Verse 8 from Goethe's poem, 'Lieb' um Liebe, Stund' um Stunde', from the 'Buch Suleika'.
[398] Beethoven's Symphony no. 3 in E flat major, the Eroica Symphony (op. 55) and Symphony no. 6. in F, the Pastoral Symphony (op. 68).
[399] As in 1819, Radziwill's settings of scenes from Goethe's *Faust* were performed on his birthday on 24 May.

new choruses – 'Wird er schreiben?'[400] – and the final chorus didn't go too badly for a first rehearsal, despite the sparse style. The dilettante cannot deny himself, so he exaggerates everything and wants to express far too much. Nothing can be done to help him, because this has already cost him so much work that he is just happy to have it over. With a choir like ours he won't notice what's wrong, but if he eventually gets into a real theatre, they will show him.

Then the scene with the jewellery box in Gretchen's room[401] was performed for the first time and not without some affectation by Madame Stich,[402] who, to put it mildly, tried far too hard. That will be rectified, however, because she is a person with whom one can still discuss such things. [...]

The music runs through the whole scene, uninterrupted, and contains the loveliest passages, but for this very reason it is disturbing because too much was expressed, so that the rise and fall and fluency of delivery suffers.

The rat scene[403] is the most remarkable. It is, in fact, spooky and not at all a petty scene, just as it wasn't even played by Mephisto[404] as well as many other [scenes]. Incidentally the fun only lasted from six until after midnight. Today I think we should have it easier, if the enormous number of organizers don't drag it out.

The Duchess of Cumberland, with her two consorts,[405] was present and enjoyed it, and apparently for your sake put up with all the reprises of a first rehearsal. She says so much that is beautiful and good about you; in short, she is so much in love with you that instead of hands, fingers, mouth and eyes, I would need to be all ears in order to take everything in. [...]

I have set some [poems] from the *Divan* to music: (i) 'Suleika', p. 166; (ii) 'Wiederfinden', p. 168; (iii) 'Elemente', p. 14; (iv) 'Erschaffen und Beleben', p. 16; (v) 'Selige Sehnsucht', p. 30;[406] (vi) 'So lang man nüchter[n] ist', p. 187;

---

[400] Two short pieces from *Faust I*: the spirits' chorus, 'Wird er schreiben' (*WA* I/14, pp. 3181–9) as extended variations to verses 1739f., as well as the departure chorus, 'Hinaus! Hinauf', to be inserted after verse 2072. Goethe had written the choral pieces especially for Radziwill's *Faust* performance and sent them in a letter, dated 4 July 1819, to Pius Alexander Wolff, who had taken over the direction for this performance. See also Wolff's letter of thanks of 18 July 1819, *WA* IV/31, p. 381.

[401] *Faust I*, v. 2783ff.

[402] The actress Sophie *Auguste* Crelinger, née Düring, married to Wilhelm Stich.

[403] *Faust I*, v. 1512ff.

[404] Carl Friedrich August, Prince of Mecklenburg-Strelitz.

[405] Friederike von Mecklenburg-Strelitz, Duchess of Cumberland since 1815, with her husband Ernst August, Duke of Cumberland and Prince Wilhelm of Prussia, brother of King Friedrich Wilhelm III.

[406] Goethe's verse 'Sagt es niemand, nur den Weisen', published under the title 'Vollendung' in *Taschenbuch für Damen* (1817) before it appeared in Goethe's *West-östlicher Divan* (1819). Zelter's setting was published as no. 4 in his *Sechs Deutsche Lieder für die Bass-Stimme mit Begleitung des Pianoforte*.

(vii) 'Alle Menschen', p. 212;[407] (viii) 'In tausend Formen', p. 179.[408] Most of them need to be polished and are working themselves out in me. I still don't know Eberwein's settings. He used to send them to me and since I did not answer him directly, he eventually stopped doing it. [...]

## 269. Goethe

Carlsbad 24 May 1820

As a parting gift I send you a little song,[409] which you may lovingly interpret and compose. I have had a healthy, happy time. Now I am about to hurry home, where I hope to hear from you.

## 270. Zelter

Berlin, 25 May 1820

Yesterday was Princess Radziwill's birthday, and at last our *Faust* was smoothly and soundly launched.[410] The King[411] was so pleased with us that his praises seemed as sweet as honey to me, and I too can say I was pleased. [...]

The Duchess of Cumberland was full of your praises again, and regretted she had not been able to attend all the rehearsals, as the piece is really a rare thing, so that you cannot see it too often to probe its depth. 'Long live Goethe!' was shouted at supper by everyone. It came three times from a hundred voices.

Even if Radziwill's music had no merit at all, he would be entitled to great praise for having brought to light a poem up to now concealed in darkest shadow, which everyone, after reading and feeling, thought himself obliged to withhold from his neighbour. I, at all events, know no one else enthusiastic and innocent enough to put such a banquet before such people, which enables them for the first time to learn German.

---

[407] Goethe's poem 'Alle Menschen groß und klein' was published without a title in 'Buch der Parabeln', *West-östlicher Divan* (1819). Zelter's composition is not extant.

[408] 'In tausend Formen magst du dich verstecken'. On the evidence of two dated manuscripts, Zelter's composition was only completed in 1823 (SBB PK: Mus. ms. Autogr. Zelter 35: Berlin 2 March 1823 and GMD KK 832: 2 February 1823).

[409] *Sankt Nepomuks Vorabend* ('Lichtlein schwimmen auf dem Strome').

[410] For a detailed account of the performance see: Franz Ulbrich: 'Radziwills Privataufführungen von Goethes *Faust* in Berlin. Ein Abschnitt aus der Bühnengeschichte des Goetheschen *Faust*' in *Studien zur Literaturgeschichte* (1912): 213–18.

[411] Friedrich Wilhelm III (1770–1840).

Just think of the circle in which this goes on: a Prince is our Mephisto,[412] our first actor is Faust,[413] our first actress is our Gretchen,[414] a Prince is the composer,[415] a noble king is principal critic, with his youngest children and all the court about him, the finest orchestra that can be found,[416] and finally a chorus of the best voices,[417] the singers consisting of well-born ladies, beautiful girls (most of them) and men of high rank – amongst them a consistorial councillor, a clergyman, a consistorial councillor's daughter, court councillors and high officials. All this is managed by the general music director, acting as stage director, conductor and prompter; in the palace residence, in a royal castle;[418] – you cannot blame me for wishing we had had you amongst us.

## 271. Zelter

Berlin, 2 June 1820

[…] Our general music director[419] of the court ensemble has finally arrived and his long awaited arrival was celebrated by [a performance of] one of his operas,[420] which he received with great delight. […]

---

[412] Carl Friedrich August, Prince of Mecklenburg-Strelitz.
[413] Pius Alexander Wolff.
[414] Auguste Crelinger née Düring.
[415] Prince Anton Radziwill.
[416] Members of the Königliche Kapelle under the direction of Bernhard Anselm Weber.
[417] Members of the Sing-Akademie.
[418] Palais Monbijou.
[419] Gaspare Luigi Pacifico Spontini (1774–1851). Zelter used his influence for him in direct confrontation with the general manager and artistic director (from 1815), Brühl, [to secure] the French title for the position, 'Intendant général'. After years of negotiations with the Prussian king (behind Brühl's back), Spontini was, on 1 September 1819, bound by contract to ten years as the main Kapellmeister and General Director of Music, whereby *de jure* he was Brühl's subordinate but *de facto* from the very beginning became his most intense rival. On 20 February when he was due to take up his position, he requested an extension of his holiday in order to complete his opera *Olimpia*; he finally arrived in Berlin on 28 May 1820.
[420] *Die Vestalin*; for reviews of the performance; see *Vossische Zeitung*, 3 June 1820.

## 272. Goethe

Jena, 6 to 7 June 1820

[...] Now what am I to say in reply to your description of my *Faust*? The faithful account of it, which I owe to you, transports me quite clearly into the most wondrous region. After all, poetry is really a rattlesnake into the jaws of which one falls with reluctance. Certainly, if you stay together as you have up to now, it must be, become, and remain the most extraordinary work that the world has seen.

Many thanks for the singable returning Saints. The Holy Spirit will be developed in its own good time,[421] and so I want to announce the rest bit by bit, and some things should be left which will be best done when we meet face to face.

## 273. Zelter

Berlin, 7 to 9 June 1820

[...] Spontini, whose acquaintance I made yesterday, is having his last opera, *Olympia*, translated into German.[422] For this work he wants 40 violins in his orchestra (we have about half that number) and an extension of the space for the orchestra in the opera house. If the rest of the band is to be arranged in this area, the parterre may go and look for places outside. I, for my part, will learn from this experience, although I see clearly enough how and where it must end if we are to extract the kernel and get to the heart of the matter [...]

With the exception of the King and Crown Prince, who are not in Berlin, the court was again present at the second performance of *Faust*,[423] and they tried beforehand to make Spontini acquainted with the poem by means of Madame de Stael's explanations. What the Italian Frenchman will learn from Mephisto remains to be seen. He is treated by the whole court with the distinction he deserves, when one considers the hard work expended on his compositions and the readiness with which be submits to alterations, which can hardly benefit the form of the whole. [...]

Friday, 9 June. Yesterday evening I discovered Eberwein's fifth and sixth books of songs,[424] which had just arrived and are, in fact, better than his earlier volumes.

---

[421] The hymn 'Veni Creator Spiritus'.

[422] Translation by E.T.A. Hoffmann; the first performance of the German version took place on 14 May 1821.

[423] The *Faust* scenes were repeated in Spontini's honour in the Palais Monbijou on 7 June 1829.

[424] Eberwein, *Lieder in Musik gesetzt für Pianoforte* vol. 5 (Hamburg: Johann August Böhme, 1820) and *Lieder aus Goethes West-östlichem Divan* vol. 6 (Hamburg: Johann August Böhme, 1820). Eberwein sent both volumes to Zelter on 1 June 1820 (GSA 95/2).

The advantage of having a singer around[425] is invaluable since it is a question of making the melodies singable. This very seldom happens now, and though I associate with singers sufficiently and give many songs away, I rarely have the chance to hear one of them sung as I would wish, and in the end I hardly know why – whether [the reason] lies with me or with the singer. And in addition every song, like every poem, should be self-contained. So those who always want what is new continually acquire what they already have.

When I see a poem and restrict myself to its particular characteristics, then a complete feeling is established which I can't get rid of and often the correct tone is only discovered after a long time. This mood leads to a family of tone colours and if one goes to table before the best is ready, the whole mealtime will be incomplete. Then at last the limitations emerge which arise from the word order. All too often there is a syllable too many where the [central] meaning lies or where a keyword is conspicuously in a place to which the melody must be guided if the poem should remain as it is. That is something to be observed, especially in your poems, if the poem is to become music and not something else. By 'something else' I mean if the words should become a mere foundation, a kind of trap for some kind of melody or a crystallization thread, where one sings only to give movement to the voice and not to be elevated by feeling and thought.

### 274. Zelter

Berlin, 14 to 17 June 1820

[…] If I think how you stand there with the singers and don't let them off the hook until they have got to the crux of it, I enjoy your thanks like a fruit I have grown myself and – I understand myself if I may [presume to] think I understand you. […]

Price Radziwill resumes his governorship once again[426] and once more our *Faustiade*[427] is resting in order to come to the boil slowly. I myself have nothing to do with [the production], other than an odd word now and then – in the end I might need to step in and wave the red pen to remove some bits. Since the work comes into existence piecemeal, it is no surprise when some elements become isolated […]

---

Zelter's reply is published in Johann-Wolfgang Schottländer, 'Zelters Beziehungen zu den Komponisten seiner Zeit', *JbSK* 8 (1930): 223f.

[425] Eberwein's wife, Henriette Eberwein née Haßler (1790–1849).

[426] Since 1815 Radziwill had held office as Prussian Governor in the Grand Duchy of Posen.

[427] The readings, rehearsals and performances of scenes from Radziwill's setting of Goethe's *Faust*.

Tell me, how are Paul and Mary Magdalene connected with Saint Cecilia as they are depicted on Raphael's painting?[428] It is clear that they do not hear the music from Heaven because they should not hear it on earth. Saint Cecilia is the most important person in the picture for the very reason that she alone hears the music. Should Paul or Mary Magdalene be part of the good which lies around us on earth? [...]

### 275. Zelter

Berlin, 18 June to 8 July 1820

6 July. Lobe, the flautist from Weimar, performed at our theatre yesterday[429] to great applause, which he also completely deserved. A pure scale through the whole [range of] the instrument combined with the greatest skill is admirable. His own composition[430] was also rich in ideas, which are only lacking in the power which will come when the fingering has been sufficiently worked out.

### 276. Goethe

Jena, 9 July 1820

With regard to the picture of Saint Cecilia, I can only say that the saint stands in the centre, and the small organ she holds in her hands she lets droop in such a way that the pipes are slipping out, indicating that she is letting go of earthly music while she looks upwards listening to the heavenly. The other saints[431] do not stand in any relation to her. Besides these, there are patron saints of the city, the church and for whoever commissioned the painting. These have no connection with one another, except that which the painter's imagination contrived to give them. The *Madonna del Pesce* is composed in the same manner. The man who ordered the

---

[428] Raphael's painting *St Cecilia*, which Goethe had seen on his return journey from Italy in 1788 above the altar of the St Caecilia chapel in San Giovanni in Monte in Bologna; today it is housed in the Pinacoteca Nationale, Bologna.

[429] Johann Christian Lobe performed the intermezzi music for the play *Das letzte Mittel*. The Weimar flautist had already asked Goethe for a letter of recommendation to Zelter because he wanted to travel to Berlin during the theatre holidays. For a report of his conversation with Goethe, in which he gives a remarkable appraisal of Zelter's songs, *Gespräche*, vol. 3/1, pp. 154–63.

[430] *AMZ* 22 (1820), no. 33, 16 August 1820, column 564: 'Of the intermezzi, the Weimar court musician, Herr Christian Lobe, deserves a special mention for [his] allegro and variations for flute, which was received with applause'.

[431] St Paul, John the Baptist, St Augustine and Mary Magdalene.

picture was probably called Tobias.[432] Let us hear something of you and of your lively city. If I could be invisible or unidentified walking up and down by your side, it would give me great pleasure. For the moment I must make do with the wish frequently to hear something by you that gives me joy. In Weimar they are singing the 'Nepomukslied'[433] with great delight. I have still not heard it as I have not yet gone across; I can use my days here completely undisturbed and yet one does not make much progress. I am searching out what is decent from innumerable papers which I have written on thousands of subjects. Admittedly, I realize one cannot edit before one surveys the whole, and then the work does not progress so quickly, strength decreases and the problems increase.

### 277. Zelter

Berlin, 21 July 1820

[...] I have now heard Spontini's *Cortes*[434] twice. The text is by de Jouy, and not much better than the very bad German translation[435] performed here. I am inclined to prefer the music to that of *La Vestale*, but I need to hear it several times more, for I have only got a general impression, but as yet no firm grasp of it.

There are certainly admirable passages, and the ballets are really good and meaningful. What puzzles me most is that an aristocratic Italian, accomplished in high art, should clothe high heroic subjects with small melodious forms, which in themselves are problematic because challenged by the strength of the musical accompaniment. But we shall see if we can find a way to grasp it.

With regard to the rest, as an artist I am on very good terms with this composer; he approached me very personally of his own accord; and, what no Italian or Frenchman has ever done before, he has visited the Sing-Akademie four times and appears to take an interest in it, which I am glad to see.

What he has heard up to now were unrehearsed performances, for while I have some works in the repertoire of the institute, there is always something we know as well as something new throughout the year. And so we only prepare something when public performances of unknown works are given, where every individual, according to his capabilities, is formally required to have his voice ready.

---

[432] A reference to the Book of Tobias: Tobias was blinded by a bird; his son caught a fish from the Tigris river and on the advice of the angel Raphael, Tobias used its heart, gall and liver as medicine.

[433] Zelter's setting of Goethe's 'Sankt Nepomuks Vorabend'.

[434] Spontini's official inauguration as Kapellmeister was launched on 28 June 1820 with a performance of *Ferdinand Cortez oder die Eroberung Mexicos*; see *Spenersche Zeitung*, 1 July 1820. Further performances took place on 10 and 17 July.

[435] By Johann *Christoph* May (1757–1828), writer and translator in Berlin.

And so our ensemble appears to have attracted his attention, as we do not set out to turn out what one calls singers, but everyone is [required] to be or to become a master of his voice.

What is terrible about such an institute is precisely what is good. For a society of almost 300 regenerates itself by more than half every 10 to 15 years and since new blood comes in from time to time, we are always starting over again. Yet we remain eternally young and so we don't have an abundance of old women *feminini* and *masculini generis*,[436] and the choir doesn't look particularly bad even up close and in the light. The little women can do themselves up for the rehearsal twice a week, chat with one another, and through the pleasure which others get from it, the thing expands.

Admittedly it has no easy existence anywhere else because in the end gossiping becomes the main thing, which remains under control with us because every time I am the first on the spot and whoever comes then, be it man or woman, I can deal with appropriately. There is also the fact that now, after 30 years, the society has become a family of men, women, siblings, children and relations, and watches over itself very well so that no scandal of any kind has happened, other than what I myself sometimes cause through a flop and which then, of course, is the talk of the town for a week.

Only we now stand in a contradictory relationship with the singers who otherwise formed the Italian opera and although their authority is recognized by us, even regarded as a model, we were no professional Italian company kept for the court and the highest ranks. Of necessity we are lacking everything that protection [by the court] can give. Sharp eyes suspect they see a glimpse of envy and if we were a foreign company, we would boast about some Pharaoh-like oppression. Since, however, we didn't lose our position and only went forward where there was space, we retained our strength without power and, in short, there was nothing else to do but get on with it.

This alone is what we can be happy about, although today we still don't know where we are to lay down our head.[437] Spontini noticed this almost with shock. Since, like many good souls, he wants to discover the moon in the moon, he finds it inconceivable that a thing which the world knows by name but does not know, lodges in stinking stables and must live off scourings.[438]

---

[436] Literally: old women of both sexes.

[437] Zelter is referring to the ongoing need for rooms for the Sing-Akademie: at this time the rehearsals were still taking place in the round room of the Akademie der Künste, on the first floor of the royal stables on Unter den Linden. They had to wait until January 1827 for their own building.

[438] Zelter is referring to the parable of the Prodigal Son.

## 278. Zelter

Greifswald, Rügen, Berlin, 18 August to 16 September 1820

[…] Nevertheless a little joy is granted to me. The son[439] of the famous singer Margarethe Schick[440] is Music Director of a military band of the local garrison which is made up of almost 40 instruments. This young man, who lost his father and mother very young and whom I knew as a child, has brought this choir together so skilfully that it is a pleasure to hear symphonies and operatic pieces by Mozart, Mehul, Haydn, Cherubini, Beethoven and other such composers performed on nothing but wind instruments.

## 279. Goethe

Jena, 26 October 1820

I request [a copy of] your setting of Epimeleia's famous confession![441] Prometheus has turned up once again in Weimar.[442] People are delighted by the idea that you yourself once wrote music to it. Now I request only the individual piece. If you would like to send more, it would also be warmly welcome. […]

Towards New Year may you also shake your cornucopia so that 'Veni Creator Spiritus'[443] prepares a Whitsun feast in the middle of winter. […]

Just as I want to sign off, the accompanying revision pages have arrived.[444] You wanted the poem some years ago when I refused it. Now it has lost its sting and I hope retains its charm. I want to keep it secret at present. Compose it for the Liedertafel, keeping an eye on the voices and characters available. If a copy appears by Easter, you would immediately bring this poem to life along with [the Liedertafel]. May it crop up everywhere when appropriate.

---

[439] Friedrich Schick (1794–c.1858), clarinettist and composer, Prussian military Kapellmeister in Stralsund.

[440] Margarete Luise Schick née Hamel (1768/73–1809), court singer at the Königliche Oper, Berlin, married to the court violinist in Berlin, Ernst Schick.

[441] Epimeleia's monologue 'Einig, unverrückt, zusammenwandernd', from Goethe's *Pandora*. Zelter's setting, composed in Teplitz in 1810, is not extant.

[442] In Goethe's *Pandora*.

[443] Goethe is reminding Zelter of the promised setting which, however, was never finished.

[444] The proofs of Goethe's poem 'Die Weisen und die Leute'.

## 280. Goethe

Weimar, 18 February 1821

[…] The greatest charm of an author's otherwise hazardous life is that while one is personally silent to one's friends, one is meanwhile preparing a great conversation with them in all parts of the world.

It is the same with the musician, who, however, must act differently, like certain friends who do not allow their silent and absent acquaintances to benefit from the rueful songs of gentle Magdalenes[445] nor from the appeal to the Universal World Genius.[446] […]

## 281. Goethe

Weimar, 23 February 1821

I recommend a warm reception to Herr and Frau Boucher,[447] an admirable musical couple, and at their delightful performance I ask that you remember me with affection.

## 282. Zelter

Berlin, 24 February 1821

[…] At the moment we have a carnival consisting of opera, masquerades, balls, concerts, some significant bankruptcies, eats (as Wolf[448] is wont to say) and so on.

---

[445] Goethe, *Pandora*, Epimeleia, v. 491–568. 'Reuetöne' refers to v. 561: 'Und zur Sorge schleicht sich ein die Reue' (And in addition to worry remorse creeps in). The biblication term 'Magdalene', applied to Epimeleia, could apply to her compassionate role in the drama.

[446] The first draft of Goethe's version of 'Veni Creator Spiritus' bore the title 'Appel an Genie'; the setting Goethe sought was never finished.

[447] The violin virtuoso Alexandre Jean Boucher and his wife, the harpist Céleste Boucher, gave guest performances in Weimar in February 1821 and had visited Goethe often; see Goethe's diary 19 to 27 February 1821, *WA* III/8, pp. 20–23. Goethe's *Tag- und Jahres-Hefte* of 1821 gives an account of a 'private concert'.

[448] Friedrich August Wolf.

Schinkel's new concert hall[449] should be inaugurated next Tuesday with Dryden's *Alexanderfest* set to music by Handel.[450] I myself am involved.

The confession of our good Epimeleia is also to follow.[451] The score of it which was written in Teplitz is not to be sent, however, and I must make a new copy, which had been started when a really nasty eye infection held me back by five or six weeks. Even after it has gone I should not undertake any writing or reading on dark days, as a result of which ongoing work has gathered and I am still not able to get back into it with the same interest. Everything appears cold to me and unimportant. The next free hour should be well used.

## 283. Zelter

Berlin, 30 April 1821

Your Magnus or Alexander Boucher[452] played here yesterday to great applause.[453]

He reminds me of Baron Bagge,[454] with one exception that when the fool is subtracted from Boucher, a rare violinist is left.

Intonation; control of the fingerboard and bow; jaunty and earthy; sensitivity; audacity to take on the most daring things and to conquer are as natural to him as his dandyism. And so he can be praised for what he is. This is how one plays within

---

[449] According to the king's wishes, the new theatre built by Karl Friedrich Schinkel on Gendarmenmarkt included a separate concert hall in addition to an auditorium with a stage and all its equipment. The ceremonial opening of the hall took place on 27 February 1821; the opening of the theatre took place on 26 May 1821.

[450] For a review of the concert see *AMZ* 23 (1821), no. 12, 21 March, column 196.

[451] Goethe had enquired about the composition once again on 18 February 1821. The setting which was conceived in Teplitz is not extant; the new composition was never completed.

[452] A reference to Alexander the Great and Alexandre Jean Boucher (1763–1861). Spohr, who met this well-known French violin virtuoso at Brussels in 1819, spoke of his conscious resemblance to Napoleon. He traded on this resemblance and, on one occasion, advertised a concert in these terms: 'An unfortunate resemblance is forcing me to go into exile. Therefore, before leaving my beautiful fatherland, I will give a farewell concert.' He referred to himself as 'L'Alexandre des Violins'.

[453] The French violinist and his wife gave a series of six concerts in the Berlin theatre on 28 April, 9 May, 6, 17 and 25 June and 8 July, the success of which inspired three further concerts in the autumn on 11 September, and 5 and 18 October. At the concert mentioned by Zelter and in collaboration with the Königliche Kapelle and their leader, Friedrich Ludwig Seidel, Boucher performed a violin concerto by Viotti and a Capriccio which he himself had written.

[454] Baron Charles Ernst von Bagge (1722–91), Prussian Chamberlain, violinist and musical enthusiast. For reports of his playing see *AMZ* 21 (1819), no. 10, 10 March 1819, columns 152–62 and Zelter's letter to Johann Samuel Carl Possin (GSA 95/I, 8, 11).

one's four walls. When I wasn't looking at him, I imagined him in a nightshirt and slippers, and precisely this ability to stand alone on a three-foot-high stage before the general public – I admired it with amusement. His likeness to Napoleon, which was advertised beforehand,[455] attracted several people, although the room was not full.

I knew Baron Bagge very well. He was no chicken and in addition to his imaginary originality, he has the best heart for art and young artists. He set the rarest delicacies before the young people in order to teach us and some of us gave him money. We teased him [about] being the best, but he was not put off and the affection was mutual.

Madame Boucher[456] was applauded even more. Her simultaneous playing on the piano and harp[457] shows equal mastery of both instruments, a feat which demands long hours of practice, on account of the contrary motion of arms and fingers; though the whole thing is very odd in itself.

Her composition of the concerto[458] she played pleased me more than that of her husband.

Kapellmeister Hummel has had an extraordinary reception; today he gives his second concert,[459] and if he does not return to Weimar exhausted, the heat can't be blamed, for it is exceptional.

The King has been to hear my Passion Music this year,[460] and sent me 20 Friedrichs d'or, which were welcome as the little yellow discs are rare with me.

---

[455] See, for example, the review in the *Spenersche Zeitung*, no. 52, 1 May 1821 and also Eduard Devrient, *Meine Erinnerungen an Felix Mendelssohn-Bartholdy und seine Briefe an mich* (Leipzig: J.J. Weber, 1869), p. 23.

[456] Céleste Boucher, née Gallyot (d.1841), principal pianist and harpist at the court of King Karl IV of Spain and music teacher to the infanta of Spain.

[457] A Duett-Concertante by Céleste Boucher performed by her on both instruments at the same time [*sic*].

[458] Concerto for pedal harp composed and performed by Céleste Boucher; see the review in *AMZ* 23 (1821), no. 20, 16 May, column 349.

[459] Johann Nepomuk Hummel (1778–1837), Austrian composer and pianist, Court Kapellmeister to the Grand Duchy of Weimar from 1819, gave two concerts in April 1821 in Berlin, which included his own compositions. The first concert took place on 25 April and was reviewed in the *AMZ* 23 (1821), no. 20, 16 May, column 349. The second concert, on 30 April, included a Grand Trio by Hummel and a performance of Schiller's *Kassandra* given by Auguste [Crelinger] Stich.

[460] In a letter to the king on 13 March 1821, Count Brühl had recommended 'performing this music on Palm Sunday, 15 April' since 'His Majesty the King himself wanted to attend the Sing-Akademie's performance of the Passion Music' but he could not be present on Good Friday, the traditional day of performance of Graun's Passion (GSA 95/I, 7, 1). Zelter answered Count Brühl on 17 March that the proposal was to him 'all the more desirable because it makes me happy that for the first time in my life I am able to fulfil a wish of my King and Lord' (draft letter to Count Brühl). The postponed wish was realized on a different occasion: on 15 April 1821 Graun's Passion Cantata, *Der Tod Jesu*, was performed

Apart from this he has been so gracious as to give me a site near the University Garden upon which a hall for my Sing-Akademie is to be built.[461] [...]

### 284. Zelter

Berlin, 10 May 1821

[...] Yesterday Herr Boucher together and his wife were heard once again to greater applause[462] and in a fuller auditorium. His tone is in fact beautiful and his [technical] facility is really extraordinary. The way he played the *Capriciose* I believe to have recognized as almost innate, because it is without affectation and contains something romantic that one can respond to really well, though I would use this bundle of talents differently.

### 285. Zelter

Berlin, 8 July 1821

The day before yesterday Herr Lortzing came[463] and brought me your dear note of 30 June and awoke me from dreams of the distant past to modern conscience. I didn't want to refuse to give something to the son of a school friend and colleague,[464] so I

---

in the presence of the king in the new concert hall of the Königliches Schauspielhaus; see *AMZ* 23 (1821), no. 20, 16 May, column 349.

[461] After the completion of the opera trenches with the new guards, the designated place for a new building for the Sing-Akademie beside the Ministry for Finance was built. Schinkel was entrusted to draw up the plans, which were presented to the king on 27 March 1821 with a request for the handing-over of the plot in the chestnut woods. The king granted permission for this on 27 April and Zelter was able to produce the royal papers granting consent for the choir performing on 1 May. With that beginning – after decades of complaints about the Sing-Akademie's need for rooms – the history of its own house, the foundation stone, was laid on 30 June 1825 (ZG 1 to 2 July 1825) and the Sing-Akademie entered their new premises on 2 January 1827 (ZG end of October 1826 to 23 January 1827). Today the building is the Maxim Gorky Theatre on Unter den Linden, Berlin.

[462] For a review of the concert; see *AMZ* 23 (1821), no. 25, 20 June, column 438f.

[463] Johann *Friedrich* Lortzing (1782–1841), actor of the Weimar Court. Goethe had written a letter of introduction on 30 June 1821. See also Zelter's letter on 31 July 1821, where he relates: 'According to what I hear, Lortzing was not able to come [here] to play because his arrival was not prepared and Count Brühl is not present.'

[464] Heinrich Friedrich *Ludwig* Rellstab (1799–1860), son of the composer and music publisher Johann Carl *Friedrich* Rellstab (1759–1813), who published Zelter's early compositions (for example, his viola concerto in 1779, as well as songs and piano pieces in Rellstab's piano magazine, 1786/87).

am sending you a couple of copies of a song collection which Nägeli in Zurich has taken the trouble to bring to light, with a significant number of printing errors and smudges. No one will recognize my portrait, which doesn't matter. There should be an opportunity to observe the man himself with better eyes.

I am not sure if I have already thanked you for your prologue:[465] it has been staged here a thousand times, but what is special about this performance is that it is, without exception, only one voice; the good humour which this prologue generated on the very first day from the Most High down to the likes of me was so perceptible in the deepest silence; it rose from quiet reverence to the loudest jubilation in which the trumpets and timpani had joined in, as if under compulsion, at the very last moment. *Iphigenie* has never had the same effect as today – even on me. The Parzen's chorus shook everyone to the core – and it seemed as if they never knew it before. [...]

Yesterday Boucher gave his sixth concert[466] to a full house and he owes that to you.[467] The first time they wanted to laugh at him. I laughed so heartily at some pieces that I earned the honourable title of 'bulldog'. Boucher is, incidentally, a real musician; he knows how to shape his embouchure so that no air gets in. It is as pleasant to hear this couple together as to hear one of them on their own. The applause was extraordinary. We are on good terms with one another and I doubt that this will be his last concert.[468] In any case he will be here again in the winter. He also thinks that, with the exception of Paris, it's not easy to find so many good performers together. [...]

I almost forgot to say that the young man is called Rellstab and fought as Lieutenant in the last war. He is a born Berliner, son of the famous publisher and founder of a second Liedertafel here,[469] for which he endeavours to write verses.

---

[465] This passage refers to the official opening on 26 May 1821 of the new theatre which King Friedrich Wilhelm III had founded in place of Schinkel's old theatre, which had been destroyed by fire on 29 July 1817. Both Berlin daily newspapers gave extensive and glowing coverage – especially the *Spenersche Zeitung*. After an orchestral prologue Auguste Stich performed Goethe's *Prolog zu Eröffnung des Berliner Theaters im Mai 1821*. Then Goethe's *Iphigenie auf Tauris* was introduced by the overture from Gluck's *Iphigenie in Aulis*. The official opening was concluded with the ballet *Die Rosen-Fee*, and a public address by the architect [and master builder], Karl Friedrich Schinkel.

[466] The concert took place on Sunday 8 July in the concert hall of the Königliches Schauspielhaus.

[467] Goethe gave the couple a letter of recommendation to pursue performances in Berlin; GZ 23 February 1821.

[468] Zelter's supposition is correct: after their sojourn with Prince Radziwill in Posen, Alexandre and Céleste Boucher gave three further concerts in Berlin.

[469] The Jüngere Liedertafel founded in April 1819 by Ludwig Rellstab together with Ludwig Berger and Bernhard Klein, which included such members as E.T.A. Hoffmann.

He wants to meet you and is a fine young man. As he made me an honorary member of the Liedertafel without payment, I could not turn down his request. [...]

Enclosure: Songs from Zelter's New Song Collection.[470]

### 286. Zelter

Berlin, 8 to 13 August 1821

Boucher is still here and wants to follow the Radziwills to Posen where he will be really welcome. He may well return as he has won the [heart of the] general public. The chap is like an eel: he is easy to get on with. We are on good terms with one another. Last Sunday he listened to a couple of my students with whom he was not displeased. He asked for a violin concerto by Bach and acts as if he liked it. He has already played it twice in private and the amateurs enjoyed it to the full. We are learning from one another and he will give up the opinion that good old musical works need to be chopped up and thrown together. He knows that I treasure what's extraordinary in him and at the same time find what's ordinary extraordinary. He is, in fact, a reasonable person. He holds you in special affection. Have you heard him play?[471]

I have to praise Eberwein, who faithfully sends me his songs. In exchange I sent him one from the *Divan*, p. 26[472] which I prepared for the Liedertafel. As it stands I could not really use it because they don't sing it properly and ultimately the melody needs to be sung well. If this has been successfully realized, please temper your justice with mercy for I have attacked your verse and modelled [the setting] on it.

What I liked best from the *Divan* is 'Worauf kommt es überall an'.[473] You might like it because I like it, and it has also been successful

---

[470] The two reviews from the *Vossische Zeitung* and *Spenersche Zeitung* were also possibly enclosed as they are contained in the collection of letters received by Goethe (GSA 28/95, pp. 417–20).

[471] Boucher and his wife had given a concert in Goethe's house on 22 February 1821.

[472] Zelter's setting of 'Derb und Tüchtig': there are two copies in Goethe's music collection (GSA 32/35, 32/37), both by the same copyist; presumably one of these copies (GSA 32/35) was originally Eberwein's copy.

[473] Setting of Goethe's poem 'Dreistigkeit'; Zelter's setting, entitled 'Entschluß', is on the reverse side of 'Derb und Tüchtig' in Goethe's music collection (GSA 32/37).

## 287. Zelter

Berlin, Kunersdorf, Berlin, 20 August to 20 September 1821

I must communicate to you an old discovery that I am now making myself for the second time.

Flicking through my edition of my Lessing's works,[474] in volume 23 I came across the theatrical bequest, the *Hercules Furens* of Seneca, in which I found the most wonderful subject for an opera, and what is more, towards the end Lessing himself thinks the same [...]

I have a young pupil, now at work upon his third comic opera, to whom I should like to give a serious subject.[475] The boy's talent is solid; his work flows spontaneously and his love of the art ensures he is industrious. When the time is right, I think I will send him to Italy so that he can find his own way [...]

29 August: Yesterday evening your birthday was celebrated at the Sing-Akademie with Milton's *Morgengesang*.[476] I hardly know whether you are alive, so I must keep your memory alive in my own way. [...]

5 September: A new opera, *Der Freischütz*, by Maria von Weber, is causing a commotion.[477] A foolish huntsman, the hero of the opera, allows himself be enticed by equally stupid sorcerers into casting so-called magic bullets by means of black magic; if he fires the best shot, he will win the bride, who is already pledged to him. Does he finally kill her with this bullet? Not at all! He doesn't even manage to hit her. She faints when she hears the shot, springs immediately to her feet again, and marries him forthwith. Whether he hits it off in marriage any better, the story does not say.

The music is greatly acclaimed and is really so good that the audience tolerates all the smoke and steam. In all the huffing and puffing I can find but little genuine passion. The women and children are crazy about it; the devil is black, virtue white, theatre buzzing, orchestra lively, and that the composer is no Spinozist you

---

[474] Gotthold Ephraim Lessing, *Sämtliche Schriften* (30 vols, Berlin, 1771–94), complete in Zelter's library (Catalogue no. 462–91).

[475] Felix Mendelssohn. The three operas were *Soldatenliebschaft*, *Die beiden Pädagogen* and *Die wandernden Komödianten*.

[476] 'On the Morning of Christ's Nativity' from John Milton's *Paradise Lost* in German translation by Samuel Gottlob Bürde set to music by J.F. Reichardt.

[477] Five weeks after the first performance of Spontini's *Olympia*, Brühl produced the successful world premiere of Weber's *Der Freischütz* (18 June 1821) under the composer's direction in the new Schauspielhaus designed by K.F. Schinkel. Whereas Spontini's audience consisted mostly of royalty and nobility, Weber's was largely made up of wealthy citizens, including Heinrich Heine, Hoffmann and Mendelssohn, which was symptomatic of the rivalry between the two houses. For reports of the performance see *AMZ* 23 (1821), no. 29, 18 July, column 510.

may gather from the fact that he has created such a prodigious work out of the nothing suggested above.

17 September 1821: Last Tuesday Boucher gave his second last concert[478] and gained over 1,000 thaler profit.

Madame Campi[479] has arrived from Vienna and played twice in succession to an empty house. Yesterday a Mademoiselle Sessi[480] was also heard before empty benches. Both singers are important and are distinguished from one another in that the latter, with a Caesar's nose, is quite young and the former, with a polish nose – she is a Pole – is quite old. In comparison to Catalani both come out on top, which doesn't make them any richer, and one observes: nature can do what it likes and will always be victorious.

20 September 1821: There's no end to it: already another new singer. A Mademoiselle Kainz,[481] Viennese and a very capable girl, sang for me yesterday. Her figure and appearance are acceptable, though she could be a bit taller [...] but [with] a voice and a training, security, power and range which I have not come across for a long time: round, clear, soft and well placed – a good heart and willing.

I have now heard the little light-hearted work by Rossini as I wanted to.[482] [...] No, there is nothing better than a healthy human voice, and what I have known for a long time and what no one will believe from me is that the Italians alone know what opera is. Gluck took great pains with opera and he succeeded admirably in what he set out to do. But a voice made by God knocks over a whole armoury of artistic resources and whoever knows how to set it in motion is for me beyond criticism. Boucher is now giving a third 'final concert' at which Mademoiselle Kainz wants to sing.[483] He himself called it the second ['last concert'] in the paper. I believe, however, he has lost count.

---

[478] 11 September 1821.

[479] Antonia Campi, née Miklaszewicz, chamber and opera singer at the Viennese Court; Zelter had attended her performance in Mozart's *La Clemenza di Tito* in Vienna in 1819. Her Berlin concerts took place in the Königliches Schauspielhaus on 7 and 13 September 1821.

[480] Maria *Theresia* Sessi, singer in Vienna; performed in Southern Germany 1819–28.

[481] Marianne Katharina Theresia Kainz, married name Holland and later von Kosteloot (1800–66), singer in Prague, on guest performance tour from 1819. Her Berlin performance – in which she included an aria by Riccolini and Variations on a theme by Mozart – took place in the Königliches Schauspielhaus on 30 September.

[482] Presumably the scenes from Rossini's *Barbier von Sevilla*, which Marianne Kainz later performed in Italian and in costume with Röckel as a 'little intermezzo' at the Königliches Schauspielhaus on 6 and 11 October.

[483] 5 October 1821; Marianne Kainz sang arias by Mozart and Winter.

## 288. Goethe

Jena, 28 September 1821

[…] On arriving here, I find your dear letters and parcels, for which my best thanks; I have now got one of Streicher's multiple octave pianos[484] and I am told it is a success, so I hope my winter will become a little more musical because of it.

If you would like to visit and make you own judgement and enjoy our work here, decide when you would like to come, I suggest the second half of October,[485] but let me know, don't surprise me. I have still two weeks' work to do here, and there is neither time nor place, neither people nor the opportunity, to receive you. Let me know in your next letter what you think, what you have planned and what is possible for you. At this stage of my life, I can no longer improvise.

[…] Music is beginning to take effect at present and so once again may you work like a genuine musical friend. […]

I had written this much when I first received your welcome letter of 20 August to 20 September and, as you can easily imagine, it made me very happy. You will receive the present [letter] through a pianist Hartknoch,[486] a student of our Hummel, who would like to recommend himself to you on the grand piano. The best of thanks for everything communicated.

## 289. Zelter

Berlin, 13 to 21 October 1821

With regard to music, our sinful life[487] is, of course, as unnatural as possible and we shouldn't be too far away from it to learn what all have known for a long time; also it is fun to see my stupidity acknowledged. […]

This autumn our town is like a tree in full bloom to which the dearest, migrant songbirds fly to and fro. Singers, pipers, violinists form themselves naturally in

---

[484] A six-octave grand piano made by Nanette Streicher, Vienna; Friedrich Rochlitz had helped Goethe secure it. See Goethe's letter to Rochlitz on 21 June (*WA* IV/34, pp. 293–94) and 15 July, *WA* IV/35, p. 17. The grand piano was delivered by the music dealer Peters in Leipzig on 14 July 1821.

[485] Zelter, his daughter Doris, and Felix Mendelssohn visited Goethe on 4 November 1821.

[486] Karl Edward Hartknoch (1796–1834), pianist, composer, music teacher, student of Hummel's, from 1824 in St Petersburg, from 1828 in Moscow. Hartknoch had examined Goethe's Streicher grand piano and 'highly approved', Goethe to Rochlitz, 15 July 1821, *WA* IV/34, p. 409.

[487] Zelter is taking up Goethe's phraseology of the 'sinful life of musicians in Berlin'.

a queue like patient lambs with music, violins, flutes, clarinets under the arm in order not to surpass and, at best, outdo one another. Since we are wealthy people, we also act that way: paid much for little and vice versa. [...]

On Thursday Boucher played the last of his final concerts[488] to a full house once more. As a result, Berlin is his Athens. This could turn out to be all he has, as with Catalani, because what really pleases us, they find terrible in other places. [...]

Nägeli had really hoped that I would be extremely happy with his edition of my songs and is amazed at my impertinence in not improving the many errors and smudges in it. Regarding the picture, I have the satisfaction of knowing that people find me better looking. One can't take that amiss! [...]

Incidentally, something about the theatre [...] Boucher is the man of the moment. Whoever wants a full house at a concert must have Boucher there. [...] He knows the world and has feeling – even if it is French feeling! He has, in fact, done something moral to temper the acquired national hatred based on lies.

## 290. Goethe

Jena, 14 October 1821

[...] Eberwein is making arrangements for me to hear, instead of merely reading, some of the music you kindly wrote for me, but if in the Chorus 'Dichten ist ein Übermut' I restore the author contrary to your corrections without injuring the musical rhythm, you will perhaps forgive me. A poet feels strange when he discovers that he has been tricked, like the old gentleman fifteen hundred years ago[489] [...]

I am glad that Boucher and his wife are successful for there's continuous hard work backed by natural talent. I agree entirely with everything you say about the human voice. When I heard Catalani in Carlsbad,[490] I said, with originality, on the spur of the moment:

---

[488] On 18 October 1821 with the music director Carl Moeser; *AMZ* 23 (1821), no. 47, 21 November, column 796. This was, in fact, the last concert for 1821. The following year, in October 1822, Boucher performed in Berlin once again.

[489] Namely, like the editor of the *Iliad* and the *Odyssey*, two and a half centuries ago. The remark reveals Goethe's renewed interest in the Greek epics on account of his reading Schubarth's essay 'Ideen über Homer und sein Zeitalter'.

[490] Goethe had got to know the famous singer on 31 July 1818 in Prince Metternich's house. Metternich wrote to his wife afterwards, 'Goethe arrives at the first rehearsal for the concert. I introduce him to Madame Catalani and say to her that he is a man that Germany is proud of', *Gespräche*, vol. 3/1, p. 71.

In the drawing room as in the stately hall,
one never hears enough
One discovers for the first time
Why one has ears.

## 291. Zelter

Berlin, Leipzig, 21 to 31 October 1821[491]

It would have hardly occurred to me, at this stage, to pass judgement on our new theatre. Hopefully you are familiar enough with the plans to follow the points listed here.[492] [...] The latest hitches, since the house is now ready, are supposed to be in the following: [...] the orchestral members [complained] about uncomfortable entrances and steps to the orchestra. [...] The orchestra has stairs on both sides: a straight one in order to leave the house quietly and a winding one to the stage. [...]

Song, sound and speech can be heard well. As up to now I have heard all performances from seats in the front stalls or from the orchestra, I cannot report more about it.

23 October: About the concert hall[493] I could still say that it is generally acclaimed. It is true that musicians and singers complain about troublesome execution. I have no confidence in their judgement about this because in the hall itself, above and below and finally on the landings and on the stairs, music which is played well resounds clearly and freely.

One is much too accustomed to fingers and plucking to have an unbiased opinion, and this too, and the infinitely petty foolings, rough and mad antics of a Boucher, can be heard clearly from the remote staircases. I have just recently conducted Handel's *Alexanderfest*[494] and found it fine.

---

[491] Whether Zelter sent this letter from Leipzig or whether he delivered it himself and came unannounced to Weimar is unknown. The letter has no address and no postmark. At any rate, Goethe heard of Zelter's arrival on 3 November and travelled to Weimar the following day to greet his friend; see Goethe's diary, 3 November 1821, *WA* III/8, p. 132.

[492] Goethe had asked Zelter's opinion of the new Berlin theatre because after the initial enthusiasm for the new Königliches Schauspielhaus on 26 May 1821, complaints soon began.

[493] At the request of the Prussian King, Schinkel had included a concert hall as well as rehearsal rooms and storerooms. Accordingly the 1,600-seater was smaller than the previous theatre, which seated 2,000.

[494] On 27 February 1821, before the official opening of theatre (26 May), the concert hall was unofficially opened with a performance of Handel's *Alexanderfest*, under the direction of Spontini and Zelter.

26 October: Early tomorrow morning I, with my Doris and a pupil of mine,[495] Mendelssohn's son, a lively boy of 12 years old, will set out for Wittenberg to attend the festival. You shall hear from Wittenberg if all three of us are coming to Weimar. As your house is full enough, I shall book into the Hotel Elephant, where I have always been contented[496] once I can see you. I long for your company! I really want to introduce you to my Doris and to my best pupil, before I leave this world – in which, however, it is my intention to remain as long as possible! The pupil is a good and handsome youth, lively and well mannered. Admittedly, he is the son of a Jew, but no Jew himself.[497] The father, to his own disadvantage, has not had his sons[498] circumcised and educates them properly; it would really be curious if the son of a Jew turned out to be an artist.

## 292. Goethe

Weimar, 5 February 1822

[…] My kind greetings to Dorchen,[499] and thanks for her kindness to Ulrike;[500] remember me to Felix and his parents too. Since you left, my piano has been silent; one attempt to bring it back to life was almost a complete failure. However, I hear a great deal of talk about music, which is always a poor substitute.

Farewell! In your glorious Berlin, think of me who, in my sunny little back room,[501] thinks of you only too often.

## 293. Zelter

Berlin, 1 to 2 March 1822

Yesterday the King listened to our Liedertafel with obvious pleasure[502] and, contrary to what is customary, it kept going from nine o'clock until after midnight.

---

[495] Felix Mendelssohn (1809–47).

[496] Zelter mistakenly claims he has always been well looked after here, he had, in fact, stayed at a different hotel.

[497] Abraham Mendelssohn had his children baptized into the Evangelican church in the Berliner Neue Kirche; he himself converted to Christianity six years later.

[498] Felix and Paul Mendelssohn.

[499] Zelter's daughter Doris.

[500] Ulrike von Pogwosch, Otillie von Goethe's younger sister (sister-in-law to August von Goethe).

[501] Goethe's study.

[502] An account of King Friedrich Wilhelm III's visit to Zelter's Liedertafel on 28 February 1822 is in Wilhelm Bornemann, *Die Zeltersche Liedertafel in Berlin, ihre*

Prince Radziwill, who is a member of the Liedertafel, had summoned the plenary meeting to his home.

A long table for 30 singers was served in a spacious hall.

As hostess, Princess Radziwill[503] sat at the top section at a special round table with the King, Crown Prince[504] and the other princes and princesses of the royal family, the Grand Duke of Mecklenburg-Strelitz and his wife.[505]

The generals and chief civil servants [sat] with the women and girls at another three special round tables.

In between courses a series of 12 different songs were sung, among which 'Die heiligen drei Könige'[506] and 'Soldatentrost'[507] had a special effect on the audience.

At the meal the King asked for the large bronze wine goblet, which is also a pitched bell, and had me explain the meaning of it, along with the aims and organization of the whole foundation.

What delights me about it was that the thing has substance and has not gone out of fashion because we are almost ready to celebrate our third five-year anniversary. Since it spreads from here north- and southwards over Weichsel, Main and Rhine, one would readily find out that there are fish in the Spree. In Leipzig, where they know everything[508] and also have a Liedertafel,[509] they acted modestly as if their counterparts gave nothing away.[510]

Count Brühl has completely recovered and was also at our table where Prince Radziwill was the most attentive host. [...]

---

*Entstehung, Stiftung und Fortgang* (Berlin, 1851), p. xvf.

[503] Princess Friederike Dorothea *Luise* Philippine Radziwill, née Princess of Prussia (1770–1834), daughter of Prince [August] Ferdinand, niece of Friedrich II, the Great.

[504] Friedrich Wilhelm of Prussia (1795–1861).

[505] Georg Friedrich Karl Joseph von Mecklenburg-Strelitz (1779–1860) and Marie Wilhelmine Friederike von Mecklenburg-Strelitz, née Princess of Hessen-Kassel (1796–1880).

[506] Zelter's setting of Goethe's *Ephiphaniasfest*.

[507] 'Soldatentrost' ('Nein! Hier hat es keine Not ...'): the date of Zelter's setting of this poem written in 1792 and published in 1815 is unknown.

[508] A reference to Leipzig as the place of publication of Brockhaus' *Enzyklopädie*.

[509] The first Liedertafel in Leipzig was founded by Jakob Bernhard Limburger on 24 October 1815.

[510] Zelter's meaning here is that no one gives credit to the Liedertafel in Berlin.

### 294. Goethe

Weimar, 13 March 1822

First and foremost, congratulations on the celebrated Liedertafel! It is really nice that Prince Radziwill made it known to the King and let [him] enjoy the many qualities he has around him.

### 295. Zelter

Berlin, 17 March 1822

[...] Enclosed are six organ sonatas by Carl Philipp Emanuel Bach for our good spa-inspector[511] and two more recent sonatas[512] by my best students as [being] the most up-to-date of their kind. He brought me a music manuscript which at first glance I took for an original. Since he wanted to leave it, I offered him something in exchange for it. Among the Bach Sonatas there is also an original, a real rarity, which alone is worth more than the entire manuscript, which was composed by the former Kapellmeister Stölzel.[513]

Felix is good and working well. His third opera[514] is finished and scored out and will soon be performed by his friends. After his return from Weimar he also finished a Gloria;[515] besides writing more than half a piano concerto for his sister;[516] he has begun a Magnificat[517] too. Even if I fail to produce anything much myself, I keep my students focused and there are half-a-dozen I enjoy working with.

23 March: Thank our beautiful gracious one for me for her lovely gift. It was time that she went because I in fact began to be in love with her, as I of course was and still am. The whole of Berlin is also in love with her and I cannot compete with

---

[511] Which sonatas they are is unknown; Goethe sent the musical dispatch to the spa inspector and organist Schütz on 5 April 1822; see Goethe's diary *WA* III/8, p. 182.

[512] Again source unknown.

[513] An extract or handwritten passage from a theoretical work by Gottfried Heinrich Stölzel, possibly one of the manuscripts housed in the Berlin Staatsbibliothek today: *Anleitung zur musikalischen Setzkunst; Kurzer und gründlicher Unterricht, wie ein Liebhaber der Musik (...) einen Contrapunctum simplicem (...) erlernen kann.*

[514] Felix Mendelssohn, *Die wandernden Komödianten*, one-act Singspiel (1822); libretto by Johann Ludwig Casper.

[515] Gloria in E flat, for mixed choir, soloists and orchestra.

[516] Concerto in A minor for piano and string orchestra, written for Fanny Mendelssohn.

[517] Magnificat in D minor, completed on 31 May 1822. Both the Gloria and Magnificat were published towards the end of the twentieth century and are still relatively unknown. These compositions rank among Mendelssohn's most admirable achievements of 1822.

the whole of Berlin, because I am already sufficiently beaten by ailing fingers, so the misfortune is not greater than the stroke of good luck. Since she left everyone sings *Amynts Klagen über die Flucht der Lalage*.[518] The old cantata by Benda would perhaps never have been awoken again and because of it Lalaruk[519] is now completely forgotten.

Next Good Friday I am thinking about putting on Handel's *Messiah* instead of the favourite Graun setting of Ramler's Passion[520] and I shall take a step forward at my [own] risk, in so far as the choir is not completely happy with it. I am in agreement with Merkutio:[521] people have their freedom in order to renounce it and Handel's *Messiah* is without doubt a more poetic work than Ramler's *Tod Jesu*, which is founded on compassion. The *Messiah* contains nothing but the consolation of redemption which should certainly be the point of all suffering.

## 296. Zelter

Berlin, 29 March to 6 April 1822

[...] The ballet[522] is, in fact, praiseworthy because of the lively interventions which hold attention firmly through three not exactly short acts. There is an overflow of material [...]

Now, I have taken your advice and added the particular circumstances of my apprentice and journeyman years into my little autobiography[523] [...]

Easter Saturday evening: Yesterday evening our *Messiah*[524] was launched like a magnificent ship, and is now buried again for another year. The hall was packed

---

[518] Cantata by Georg Benda (1774).

[519] Spontini's setting of Thomas Moore's 'Lalla Rookh' (1817) composed for the court celebration of the Russian Grand Duke Nikolaus Pawlowitsch and Alexandra Fjodorowna née Princess Charlotte of Prussia, which took place after their wedding on 27 January 1821 in Berlin. The celebration was repeated on 11 February for a larger, educated audience.

[520] Zelter was not alone in his acclamation of Graun; Graun's recitatives were cited in J.G. Sulzer's *Allgemeine Theorie der schönen Künste* as exemplary pieces in the genre. So, too, Scheibe noted not only the technical quality of Graun's music but also its expressiveness.

[521] A relevant citation by Mercutio in Shakespeare's *Romeo and Juliet* could not be found.

[522] *Aline, Königin von Golkonda*, ballet by Jean Pierre Aumer, music by Carl Blum, adapted for the stage by François Michel Hoguet. Zelter attended the second performance on 29 March 1822; the Berlin premiere had taken place on 28 March.

[523] Zelter's revised version of his autobiography; see Schottländer, *Carl Friedrich Zelters Darstellungen seines Lebens*, pp. 215–19.

[524] Mozart's arrangement of Handel's *Messiah* was performed on 5 April 1822 in the concert hall of the royal theatre; the performance was given by the Königliche Kapelle,

full and I think I have earned around 1,000 thalers. My audience also appeared to be happy, which is also valuable when one plans to come again.

### 297. Zelter

Berlin, 7 to 11 April 1822

Yesterday, Saturday, Madame Mara[525] came to me of her own accord – and on foot – to help me count my well-deserved fee, or so she claimed. Just imagine this 72-year-old matron, this demon of a singer, being moved by our *Messiah*. She said the pain and the joy quite carried her away; those sitting near her must have thought she was daft. [She believed] the fugues flowed smoothly: an organ of living voices. She has sung this oratorio often enough in London[526]. She finished by confessing that our performance might compete with those in London, of which the English are proud enough. [...]

Now I must admit that after a single swift rehearsal (apart from a few mistakes made by the Königliche Kapelle who were well paid by me), I was really happy with it. That music lasting three hours can so continuously interest and satisfy a crowded audience shows that the work of 32 years[527] has borne fruit here and there. [...]

11 April: The day before yesterday they held the Liedertafel[528] without me; I am not supposed to go out. It is little wonder that no one understands the *Divan* because it is only [recently] known to me. I have quietly read the title a hundred times and thought nothing other than how anyone could be called Müller, Schulze, Noak. Now that I am setting to music one piece after another, I have discovered what the *Divan*, what Hafis means, and I am not going to reveal it to you. But, like the tongue of the Erfuhrt[529] bell, it will strike your ear when you come and hear 'Elemente',[530] p. 14 and 'Dreistigkeit', p. 25.[531] The effect of these pieces captures the universal. I hear it resound when I am sitting around at home. If one

---

directed by Moeser, and the Sing-Akademie; for reviews of the performance see *AMZ* 24 (1822), no. 21, 22 May, column 341.

[525] Gertrud Elizabeth Mara, née Schmeling (1749–1833) had undertaken her final English tour. On the return journey to her home in Reval, she visited Berlin.

[526] Mara first visited London in 1784, where she made her English debut in a Handelfest; she enjoyed enormous success for her role of Cleopatra in Handel's opera *Giulio Cesare*. She gave annual concert and stage performances in London until 1802.

[527] The Sing-Akademie was founded in 1791.

[528] In accordance with the statutes, the Liedertafel met once a month on the Tuesday nearest the full moon.

[529] The biggest bell of Erfuhrt Cathedral, named the 'Maria gloriosa'.

[530] Zelter's setting of 'Aus wie vielen Elementen' from Goethe's *Divan*.

[531] Zelter's setting of 'Worauf kommt es überall an' from Goethe's *Divan*.

has patience with people, then they have patience with themselves and will finally notice that a poem has something in its words which is transcendent. The devil can take me if these settings are not excellent; and if they are not, then he can have me for nothing.

## 298. Zelter

Herrnhut, Bautzen, Dresden, Dessau, 26 May to 26 June 1822

[…] On my arrival here in Bautzen I found the whole town in bustling activity. One local inhabitant,[532] who died many years ago, set up a trust to the effect that on every third day of Whitsun some 100 thaler in groschen would be shared among the poor. The action took place during organ playing and trumpet fanfares from the town hall tower. The organist (Berg), whom I wanted to catch at work and managed to get out of the inn, remarked, 'I get two thalers for which I must play 29 strophes. I accept that and give two thalers to a blind matron, and without moving a bone, I, poor devil, do much more good in life than that dead man who gives away what he doesn't need.'

Dresden, 29 May: A Herrnhut literary figure by the name of Peter Mortimer, a man of 72 years, five or six years ago sent an old manuscript to Berlin through old Körner,[533] in which he sets out various church music modes (which are also called Greek modes) very clearly.

As the material was important to me for a long time, because I had tried to assimilate much of it, as you have perhaps observed from many of my songs, for example, 'Mahadoh',[534] 'Der König in Thule',[535] so the manuscript has been published[536] with the help of our minister.[537] I myself wanted to correspond with the author, [and] send him new experiments as actual first fruits of his theory. The old fellow didn't answer and only once said to me what I had done was fine, which I found very irritating.

Therefore, nothing has been concluded and our minister has permitted me to track down Peter Mortimer in his Herrnhut community. […] The original reason for my journey was Peter; now I am here in Dresden and Peter hasn't eaten me;[538]

---

[532] Johann Christoph Prenzel (1718–94), senator and senior (town) treasurer.

[533] Christian Gottfried Körner (1796–1831), lawyer, father of Theodor Körner.

[534] Zelter's setting of Goethe's ballad 'Der Gott und die Bajadere'.

[535] Zelter's setting of Goethe's 'Der König in Thule' which was published in his *Sämtliche Lieder, Balladen und Romanzen*, vol. 3 (1812).

[536] Peter Mortimer, *Der Choral-Gesang zur Zeit der Reformation, oder Versuch, die Frage zu beantworten: Woher kommt es, daß in den Choral-Melodien der Alten etwas ist, was heut zu Tage nicht mehr erreicht wird?* (Berlin: Georg Andreas Reimer, 1821).

[537] Baron Carl von Stein zum Altstein (1770–1840), minister for finance and culture.

[538] A reference to the Acts of the Apostles, 10, 13: 'Rise up, Peter, slaughter and eat'.

rather, he is the best fellow in the world. Much is in his life that doesn't belong. His marriage is superfluous and at the end of day he is a Herrnhuter. He will not admit this, he has forgotten it and, in short, he is a scoundrel and your Hafis to a T.[539] [...] He has devoted his life to writing Latin verses on matters of brotherhood, which are praised, to translating missionary writing into different languages[540] and finally, for himself, to complete the above-named work on the Evangelical chorale[541] with the help of some old songbooks of the sixteenth century. [...]

Dresden, Monday, 2 June: I only wanted to spend two days in Dresden, but yesterday I heard a mass and am now in Pretzsch on the Elbe between Torgau and Wittenberg. The head preacher has founded a Singschule[542] which I am inspecting and everything is going well enough. I am very lucky to enjoy happiness in this life and to see shoots of my good Fasch's seed appearing.[543] In Frankfurt an der Oder and in other places I discovered a really good choral society and an almost better Liedertafel[544] where your songs are sung. In Görlitz[545] [it is] the same and likewise in Dresden.[546] In the latter the pupils of the Kreuz School up and down the streets sing the most contemptible stuff which they don't even enjoy themselves.

Dessau, 6 June: I haven't exactly gone away satisfied from Wittenberg. The music director[547] loves to read, to speak, to eat and most of all to drink, but he doesn't know how to behave. His organ is in decline;[548] his assistant who treads the

---

[539] The type of poetic figure portrayed in Goethe's 'Buch der Hafis', *West-östlicher Divan*.

[540] Peter Mortimer, *Geschichte der neuesten evangelischen Anstalten in England* (Barby, 1801–02) and *Missions-Societät in England. Geschichte ihres Ursprungs und ihrer ersten Unternehmungen* (Herrnhut, 1797).

[541] Peter Mortimer, *Der Choral-Gesang zur Zeit der Reformation, oder Versuch, die Frage zu beantworten: Woher kommt es, daß in den Choral-Melodien der Alten etwas ist, was heut zu Tage nicht mehr erreicht wird?* (Berlin: Georg Andreas Reimer, 1821).

[542] Ernst Clausnitzer (d.1759); there are no extant records of this Singschule.

[543] Fasch's foundation of the Berlin Sing-Akademie in 1791 inspired the formation of countless similar institutes throughout Germany.

[544] See Zelter's letter to the minister on 20 June 1822 in Georg Schünemann, *Carl Friedrich Zelter der Begründer der Preussischen Musikpflege* (Berlin, 1932), p. 49.

[545] Zelter is referring to the song society founded in 1813 and led by the organist Johann Schneider. A Liedertafel was not founded in Görlitz until 1828.

[546] Zelter is referring to the Dreyssing Sing-Akademie, which emerged from the music circle which gathered in Christian Gottfied Körner's home. The *AMZ* considered it a 'very praiseworthy imitation of the Berlin Sing-Akademie', *AMZ*, 14 (1812), no. 9, 26 February, column 144.

[547] Friedrich Philipp Christian Nothschiedler (dates unknown), active as music director in Wittenberg from 1822.

[548] The organ in the palace church, which had been built by Johann Ephraim Hübner; an application by Friedrich Ladegast for its restoration was not made until 18 November 1858.

bellows[549] endured a thunderclap in the accompaniment of an eight groschen work and I found the bellows room full of dust. The whole nest has got into a terrible state and the great bell is shattered and buzzes. I hurried to the fresh green Dessau, where a good organ builder[550] enticed me.

### 299. Goethe

Eger, 8 August 1822

[…] On 19 June I arrived at Marienbad[551] in very good weather to enjoy marvellous accommodation […] musical amateurs, pleasant evening entertainment […]

### 300. Goethe

Weimar, 14 December 1822

Your lovely parcel arrived on the first musical evening which I have enjoyed in years[552] and so immediately your rejuvenating settings of my poems were very happily and powerfully performed.

### 301. Goethe

Weimar, 18 January 1823

Warmest thanks for the little song:[553] I heard it first with my eyes and was pleased with the charming characteristic consistency [with which you have set it]. With your sympathetic mind you have grasped the other poems[554] really well. One would like to call it a duet cantata of direct farewell and movement with ever-receding distance, just as the rainbow joins near and far.

---

[549] Johann Ephraim Benjamin Schmidt (dates unknown).
[550] Christian *Adolph* Ludwig Zuberbier (*c.*1776–1856).
[551] Goethe was in Marienbad from 19 June to 24 July, followed by a month in Eger; he returned to Weimar on 29 August.
[552] See in Goethe's diary of 5 December 1822: 'Musical evening. *Graf Gleichen*, Act 1 (by Eberwein) rehearsed. Dispatch from Berlin, from both Zelter and Schultz', *WA* III/8, p. 269.
[553] Zelter's setting of Goethe's 'Das Sträußchen. Alt böhmisch'.
[554] 'Äolsharfe' ('Ich dacht ich habe keinen Schmerz').

Whether music, which is able to get close to the feeling of everything that eludes concepts and even imagination, can [or] should intervene here – that is a question for the master.

### 302. Zelter

Berlin, 24 to 25 January 1823

Our most wonderful boy has taken to versifying,[555] from which he sent me the enclosed little taste. If he doesn't cry for help himself, it won't be easy for anyone to get him out of it. It would be a shame if he were to drown in it. He began with hendecasyllables and with puzzles he is skating over water and floods which are so firmly frozen that even here we are beginning to suffer a lack of this element.[556]

### 303. Zelter

Berlin, 3 February to 11 March 1823

[...] Have you [ever written] anything better than the *Divan*? What is there? 'Lied und Gebilde'[557] [...] My setting is for male voices [...] yet these are only notes, seeds, which also take a living form [...] and I would never have known how to set something to music without imagining a vivid model for myself. Look over it once or twice, listen to it, you dear man, and let me know what you think – if not about the setting then in addition to it. One only knows how one appears through the mirror. [...]

11 February: Right now I am rummaging through *Neveu de Rameau*. It would be a shame if you hadn't kept a copy of the original.[558] Comparing details, I would share the opinion of Parisian friends that the person who translated it back would have done well to stay closer to the German. You will know that you have been

---

[555] Riemer identifies the poem by Friedrich August Wolf as 'Ultimatum', published in the *Morgenblatt für gebildete Stände*, 25 April 1823.

[556] Zelter implies a lack of water here, meaning Wolf is skating over the top and hasn't got the fundamentals sorted; in other words, Wolf is out of his depth.

[557] Zelter's through-composed setting of Goethe's poem 'Mag der Grieche seinen Ton'.

[558] The entire paragraph refers to Goethe's notes to his translation of Diderot's *Rameaus Neffe* in *Kunst und Altertum* IV, 1, pp. 159–61. Goethe had translated Diderot's *Le Neveu de Rameau* from a manuscript by the author which had landed in St Petersburg. Goethe had kept a copy of this manuscript, which he returned to the publisher Georg Joachim Göschen.

taken for Diderot himself. Without causing a big sensation, the German translation has been so influential that even I have noticed it. […]

11 March: My Felix has entered his fifteenth year; he is growing up before my very eyes. His astounding piano playing I may look upon as quite a secondary matter; he may just as easily become a virtuoso violinist. Act Two of his fourth opera is finished. All he does becomes more and more sound; he almost has the strength and power he needs; everything comes from within, external events remain external for him. Imagine my joy if we should have the experience of seeing the boy live and fulfil the promise of his youth. He is healthy. I would love his exquisite piano quartet to be dedicated to your Grand Princess. Tell me how we should set about it, and advise me soon. It is quite modern, and is even better than the one he performed in Weimar.

### 304. Goethe

Weimar, 23 March 1823

First sign of renewed life and love. Grateful. Affectionate.[559]

### 305. Zelter

Berlin, 29 March 1823

The first lines of your rebirth brightened more than a hundred eyes directly upon their arrival. They were brought to me shortly before the Liedertafel, where they were passed from hand to hand as an original signature to feast one's eyes on. […]

For the following days it gave me courage to dig in and work until I had my Good Friday music[560] behind me. […]

The public […] were delighted[561] that I put on my music again in the opera hall[562] and although I cannot accommodate so many people here and my costs

---

[559] The first lines which Goethe had written after a serious illness in February and March; during this time August von Goethe had looked after his father's correspondence.

[560] Graun's *Der Tod Jesu* was performed by the Sing-Akademie on Good Friday, 28 March 1823, in the Königliches Opernhaus with instrumentalists from the Hofkapelle, directed by Zelter; see: *AMZ* 25 (1823), no. 17, 23 April, column 273.

[561] For reviews of the performance; see *Vossische Zeitung*, 1 April 1823.

[562] Two years before, at the request of the king who wanted to attend the performance, Graun's Passion Music was performed on Palm Sunday in the concert hall of the new theatre; the previous year Zelter had performed Graun's Passion alongside Handel's *Messiah*, likewise at the new theatre. The 1823 performance took place in the Oratorio room of the opera house, which had just been reopened.

were doubled, the hall in the new comedy house[563] is more comfortable for the listeners and has a good acoustic.

So I go on with it and silently lament that the ignorant understand my work better than I do. Everyone wants to be in charge and conduct, and as soon as my students realize they could be helpful to me, they are sick and I am the only healthy one. [...]

Today is Saturday and for now I am free. Once more I have seen from my audience how a fundamentally natural presentation of a 70-year-old work which is well known and has been performed many hundreds of times[564] is capable of making a real impact. Ramler's libretto, be it what it may, and the same with Graun's music, have created for themselves a following, a belief, which everything created after it cannot destroy, no matter how much one is looking for something new, better, up-to-date. The Königliche Kapelle, a breathless group, performed *con anima, con amore*, this time taking pleasure in the work itself. The organizing and direction of yours truly played a part in this, and if I don't have to give them orders, nor do I have to say anything since I choose the best, pay them somewhat better and therefore am in the position to conduct the entire work with my forefinger. Yes, they almost see it as an honour to play with me.

The Königliche Kapelle had already performed this work to the best of their ability before a full audience in the garrison church.[565] One of them remarked to me that their own performance compared to mine was like a dull plaster cast compared to marble.

### 306. Goethe

Weimar, 2 April 1823

Here, my dear man, only hurried so as not to miss the post, is the warmest thanks for your Passion Week celebrations in which you let me take such a lively part.

### 307. Zelter

Berlin, 18 April 1823

As I have already written to you, [Wolf] responded favourably to our Good Friday music and at the same time picked up some mistakes. For example, Graun had the

---

[563] The concert hall of the new theatre on Gendarmenmarkt.

[564] From its premiere on 26 March 1755, Graun's Passion was performed annually until 1888.

[565] 26 March 1823 under the baton of Kapellmeister Seidl and the orchestral direction of Seidler.

following scansion: 'Und was er zu<u>sa</u>get⁵⁶⁶ das hält er gewiß'. He considered that such an obvious mistake could have been removed by the stroke of a pen, and the latter was my work if not my duty. To start with, I considered this mistake as being long forgiven and entered into the main book of common memory in which one recognizes the work from such signs – like the bump on Cicero's nose.

Then it would still have to be settled whether the mistake is also in the melody, which is acknowledged to be natural and expressing what is meant. The text demands its own place as well as the music. A verse which cannot be sung comfortably – which doesn't fit his thoughts like a light dress – could never be good verse that would justify ruining the melody on its account.

Finally it is questionable to rectify such minutiae in first-rate work, where there is often no end, if even an honourable poet like Homer[567] were to lose his great name because of the work of pedantic correctors.

The old orchestral member Mengis,[568] a student of Graun, once asserted that one could find no mistakes in his master's works because of the pure method of composition. A smart Alec (that was me) denounced a couple of consecutive fifths in the first chorale[569] of Graun's Passion Music. I'd like to see that, Mengis said. The published score was fetched and the fifths proven. After pondering a bit the old Mengis said: so it is when lesser people have the presumption to correct great men; these fifths are written with the best art and improve it in so far as they accentuate the word 'freveltat' […]

Now this approach to criticism is age-old, weighed down by the years and ready for the grave, but despite it I still think with affection of the true old man who was well disposed towards me until his death. […]

## 308. Zelter

Berlin, 22 April 1823

For five months I have a student[570] who makes the dreadful mistake of being rich. A 17-year-old bright blonde, with fine jet-black little ringlets over the bluest of eyes; firm flesh, lively movement and language; a voice like a glockenspiel and with the best manners [takes] the most innocent delight in herself. For every lesson

---

[566] A false stress on the 'stem' syllable; the line, a quotation of Psalm 33, 4, comes from the chorus, 'Freuet euch alle ihr Frommen'.

[567] Allusion to Friedrich August Wolf's *Prolegomena ad Homerum* in which the epics of Homer's were regarded as the work of several authors.

[568] Christian Mengis, horn player.

[569] 'Du, dessen Augen flossen'; an examination of this passage in the score confirms that these fifths were intended by the composer.

[570] Marianne Angelika von Almonde (1804–66).

I received a thaler and a kiss from the most beautiful lips which you yourself like to assess.

Since [her arrival] I have taken out old arias,[571] which I once composed in joy and in sorrow for my heavenly Julia,[572] and have found that singing alone makes the song because Almonde (as the most graceful little Danzig girl is called) sings me back 40 years.

At the end of June Doris goes to Ems with Mendelssohn's sister,[573] so I am expecting a quiet summer, which I intend to use to adapt my little art works to the new accommodation.

### 309. Zelter

Berlin, 7 to 9 August 1823

Hensel, the painter, has set out to meet you with the actor Wolff.[574] Has the young fellow given you both gifts with a letter? He is travelling to Italy and is a nimble sketcher; he travels at the King's expense and is royally commissioned to deliver copies.[575] […]

### 310. Goethe

Eger, 24 August 1823

In reply to your welcome letter, dearest friend, which reached me at a very fortunate moment, I shall, as I promised, write to you, before leaving the magic circle of Bohemia,[576] a letter you will warmly welcome because I have nothing but good news to communicate.

---

[571] Presumably the scenes by Metastasio which he mentions in his autobiography: 'Oh Dio, se in questo istante'; 'Vieni, audace nemio'; 'Barbaro, che a tuoi nodi'; 'Misero me! ah! che veggo!'

[572] Juliane Zelter née Pappritz, Zelter's second wife, who had died in 1806.

[573] On 16 June 1823 Zelter's daughter Doris travelled to a spa in Ems with Recha Meyer, Abraham Mendelssohn's sister and Hinni Mendelssohn, the wife of Joseph Mendelssohn, Abraham's brother.

[574] Zelter had mentioned this already in a letter to Goethe on 19 July 1823. Wilhelm Hensel (1794–1861), a portrait and historical painter, was later married to Fanny Mendelssohn.

[575] Hensel's main commission was to produce a full-scale copy of Raphael's *Transfiguration*.

[576] Poetic play on the special atmosphere of these weeks which Goethe spent in the company of Ulrike von Levetzow and her mother Amalie.

To start then, let me say that during the time spent recently in Marienbad, I met with nothing disagreeable; on the contrary, it was happy like returning to life again, and I am now feeling better than I have done for a long time.

Furthermore, I must tell you that after receiving that kiss, the bestower[577] of which you probably guessed, I was favoured by another splendid gift from Berlin; for I have heard Madame Milder sing four little songs, which she contrived to make so great that the memory of them still brings tears to my eyes.[578] So the praise I have heard bestowed upon her for so many years past is no longer a cold historical account but awakens true and deeply felt emotion. Give her my very best wishes. She asked me for something from my own hand and will receive through you this first page – not altogether unworthy of her.[579]

Madame Szymanowska,[580] an incredibly fine pianist, affected me just as powerfully, though in quite a different way. I imagine she might be compared to our Hummel, only that she is a beautiful and loveable Polish lady. When Hummel stops playing, a gnome rises up before us, who, by the help of powerful demons, has performed such wonders, that one scarcely dares thank him for them; but when she stops playing and comes and looks at us, we are not sure whether we should not consider ourselves fortunate that she has stopped. Welcome her warmly when she comes to Berlin, which will probably be not before very long; remember me to her and help her where you feel appropriate […]

This brings me to the painter Hensel, who delivered the gifts to me. He has, like so many others, an innate talent which could be developed, that's clear– not to God, who is hardly worried about such things – but I know it, having watched such misdirection for more than 20 years. He, too, is stuck in the shallow dilettantism of the time, which searches for a false foundation in the art of antiquity and the fatherland, seeks to find his element in a false piety, an atmosphere in which noble women, undiscerning patrons and incompetent amateurs so gladly meet one another; where an empty jargon one has created sounds so honeyed; a robe of maxims, which one had tailor-made to the puny body, dresses one in grand style; is everyday ailing with uncertainty, gnawed and consumed within, only to live and

---

[577] Elizabeth (Lili) Klein, née Parthey, later married to the composer Bernhard Klein, Director of Music, Institute for Church Music, Berlin.

[578] See Goethe's diary on 15 August 1823, *WA* III/ 9, pp. 93–4.

[579] This autograph page has not been handed down.

[580] Maria Agata Szymanowska, née Wolowska (1789–1831), Polish composer and pianist, based in St Petersburg from 1828. Goethe acknowledged his acquaintance with her in his diary on 14 to 20 August (*WA* III/9, pp. 93–6) and celebrated her musicality in the poem 'Aussöhnung' in *Trilogie der Leidenschaft*. The pianist and her sister, Casimira Wolowska, visited Goethe in Weimar from 24 October to 5 November, where they were daily guests at Goethe's table and Maria Szymanowska 'through her lively, accomplished, improvisatory piano playing soothed the love-sick heart of the divine poet and was able to ease the pain of loss of the lover', from Zelter's autobiographical report (GSA 25/II, 6,8Aa), *WA* I, 5/2, p. 21.

totter on and deceive oneself in the most ignominious way. Forgive and let me be silent. I have already said too much [...]

To free myself from such things as from aesthetic conversations and lectures, I devoted myself for six weeks to a very pretty child,[581] and by this I was perfectly secured against anything disagreeable.[582]

But now for the strangest thing of all! The immense power that music had over me in those days! Milder's voice, the rich sounds of Szymanowska, even the public performances of the local hunting corps untwisted me, just as one lets a clenched fist gently flatten itself out. By way of partially explaining this, I say to myself, 'For two years and more you have not heard any music at all, except Hummel, twice, and therefore this faculty – as far as it exists in you – has been lying imprisoned and isolated; now, all of a sudden, the divine art descends upon you, and through performances of great talent exercises her full power over you, claims all her rights and awakens all your latent recollections.' I am totally convinced that I would have to leave the hall at the first bar I might hear from your Sing-Akademie. And when I now consider what it is to hear an opera, as we perform them once a week (a *Don Juan*[583] or a *Il matrimonio segreto*[584]), renewing it within oneself and assimilating this feeling to the others that form part of an active life, then for the first time do I understand what it is to have relinquished such enjoyment, which, like all the higher enjoyments of life, takes a man out of and above himself, and lifts him, at the same time, out of the world and above it.

How good, how imperative then it would be for me to have an opportunity of spending some time with you. By gently guiding and directing me, you would cure my unhealthy irritability, which, after all, must be regarded as the cause of the above phenomenon, and you would, little by little, enable me to absorb into myself the whole wealth of God's glorious revelation. Now I must see how I can go through a silent and shapeless winter, which, to some degree, I look forward to with trepidation. However, we must endeavour, with good humour and courage, to use the dark days to the advantage of ourselves and our friends.

---

[581] Ulrike von Levetzow, daughter of Amalie von Levetzow, who inspired Goethe's Pandora. Ulrike was Goethe's Muse in the 'Elegie' of *Trilogie der Leidenschaft*.

[582] This refers to a previous paragraph where Goethe condemns contemporary dilettantism, including Fanny Hensel's husband, Wilhelm Hensel.

[583] Mozart's *Don Giovanni*, which had been in the repertoire of the Weimar Court Theatre since 1792.

[584] Cimarosa's *opera buffa*, *Il matrimonio segreto*, which had been regularly performed in Weimar from 1796.

### 311. Zelter

Berlin, 17 to 30 August 1823

29 August: Yesterday the Liedertafel gathered in celebration of your birthday,[585] as you will see in the *Spenersche Zeitung* on 30 August. To our delight, all elements came together like old friends. It was an indescribably beautiful day.

### 312. Goethe

Weimar, 9 January 1824

[...] That you gave me back so faithfully the message of the poem through inner sympathy was actually only a repetition of what you give to me through your compositions for a long time. But it was so characteristic that you wanted to read and read again.[586] You repeatedly let me hear what is dear to me through your gentle organ, full of feeling, to a degree which I don't like to admit to myself, and which no longer belongs to me anymore since I feel that you have made it your own. I would not like to let it out of my hands, but if we lived close by, you would have to recite it to me and sing it to me until you knew it by heart. [...]

I myself must admit that after my return journey this time I should have spared myself, and still have to spare myself because the enormous excitability, which, as you know, manifested itself through music, is really what put me in danger; although I cannot be hostile towards her since I have to thank her for every poem, through which feeling and imagination is so readily ignited from time to time.

[...] Do you know the following lines? I have become very attached to them; you really must set them free again by putting them to music:

> Yes, I would compare you to an Iris,
> A loving sign, a miracle
> Gliding with splendour, bright with harmony,
> Ever the same and ever new, as she.[587]

---

[585] The Liedertafel celebrated Goethe's birthday with a gondola trip to Treptow, festival songs and a celebratory lunch.

[586] Zelter's rereading of the Marienbad Elegy.

[587] The concluding verse of Goethe's 'Äolsharfe'. Goethe had sent the 'Cantata duet' to Zelter on 14 December 1822, asking for a setting, and he repeats the request here; it was, however, never set by Zelter.

## 313. Zelter

Ehrenbreitstein, Berlin, 19 November 1823 to 18 January 1824

[...] Early Wednesday, 17 December, departed from Naumberg and reached Weissenfels at noon. I have met a 19-year-old efficient music teacher who made the most charming progress with his choir. Healthy, cheerful, powerful, ready, willing, true-hearted; he is called Hentschel[588] and he deserves to be recommended. [...]

Thursday, 18 December, via Merseberg, where there is a lovely organ[589] in the cathedral[590] and on to Halle. [...] Here the local music director's position of the deceased Türk[591] is filled by one of my students[592] who is no sorcerer and usually prefers to see me going than coming. This time it was different. He had offered a collection of church liturgies and choral works to the King[593] and the King was so favourable to him as to grant him 3,000 thalers for it because the things were really good and are well preserved. As a result he is really delighted and since I have to accept them, he gave me a very good reception. In the evening in the Freemason's lodge he conducted a tolerable concert. I was there and was invited to a frugal meal after the music, where I had to be very well behaved because it was a table of over 200 people of high nobilities and professors with wives and daughters. A handsome choir of students, near me, sang really well. A bottle of champagne was placed in front of me, which I gave to the singers and I was already in bed asleep when I heard really lively singing on the street before my door, instead of which I would have expected earlier that one would break the windows on me. [...]

8 January: Maria Szymanowska has just departed. I have given her a recommendation for an old female acquaintance in Hanover that will certainly be useful for her. Yesterday she gave her second concerto[594] and to my delight she had

---

[588] Ernst Julius Hentschel (1804–75).

[589] In Merseburg Cathedral (in Zelter's day) there was an organ by Zacharias Thayssner hidden behind the Baroque screen; the organ was newly restored by Friedrich Ladegast and many of Liszt's large-scale organ works were premiered there.

[590] St John the Baptist and St Laurence Cathedral, founded in 1085, originally a cruciform Basilica, converted into a late gothic church with several naves.

[591] Daniel Gottlob Türk (1750–1813).

[592] Johann Friedrich Naue whose artistic work was especially aimed at improving the quality of church singing.

[593] Johann Friedrich Naue's work on liturgical music, publicized in the *Versuch einer musikalischen Agenda, oder Altargesänge zum Gebrauch im protestantischen Kirchen* (Halle, 1818), caught the attention of Friedrich Wilhelm III of Prussia, who purchased this publication as well as a large portion of Naue's personal library in 1824.

[594] Maria Szymanowska gave two guest performances in Berlin. The first performance took place on 10 December 1823 as part of the Königliche Kapelle concerts, in which she included a piano concert by Hummel. The second concert was given on 7 January 1824 at noon in the *Musikalishe Morgen-Unterhaltung* held in the newly built Alder Hall (Unter den

a full hall. Her playing rests on a mature talent and you have judged her really well. Had she experienced a happy hour, then everyone would have to share our opinion. She was exhausted from nerves and performance and yet always played like a true talent. The King was present with his entire court. She is madly in love with you and gave me a hundred kisses on the mouth for you. Her younger sister is also of a pleasant gentle nature and in her maturity still has a hint of blossom. [...]

Since you like to read letters from me, I enclose one here.[595] Doris is copying another to you. I am almost tormented by this kind of thing, yet I cannot help keeping an eye on the young men who leave my school to make their way in the world. The young man is Loewe, the music director in Stettin, and though neither without knowledge nor skill, he wishes to do exactly what God has not granted him. If he wanted to do what he could, what he knows, what he should do, he would not have to ask me. It would be difficult not to want to answer him at all. He will hardly show the letter to anyone; and so there is no harm in your seeing it.

### 314. Zelter

Berlin, 8 to 10 February 1824

[...] Yesterday evening, we had a private performance of Felix's fourth opera, complete with dialogue.[596] There are three acts, which, with two ballets, occupy some two-and-a-half hours; the work had its fair share of applause. The text, too, by Dr Casper, is clever enough, as the poet is musical.

From my inferior position I can hardly master my surprise at a youth just 15 years old, progressing so quickly. Everywhere I find novelty, beauty, real originality; there is intellect, movement, serenity, sonority, completeness, dramatic force. The handling of the ensemble is that of a master. The orchestration is interesting, not heavy or tedious, nor mere accompaniment. The musicians enjoy playing it, and yet it is not exactly easy. Familiar things come and pass by. They are not taken for granted but rather are welcome and appropriate, each in its own place. Liveliness, exultation without haste; tenderness, elegance, love, passion, innocence.

---

Linden 76). Here – in a very extensive concert programme – she took part in a performance of a piano quintet by Beethoven, performed a piano trio by Prince Louis of Prussia and concluded the concert with John Field's *Rondo alla Polacca*.

[595] Copy of Zelter's letter to Carl Loewe, 10 January 1824 (GSA 28/109, no. 233). The original letter is contained in Zelter's bequest (GSA 95/3).

[596] Felix Mendelssohn, *Die beiden Neffen* or *Der Onkel aus Boston*, comic opera, performed in Mendelssohn's family home, Neue Promenade no. 7. The rehearsals are described by Sebastien Hensel (ed.), *Die Familie Mendelssohn 1729 bis 1847. Nach Briefen und Tagebüchern* (Frankfurt am Main and Leipzig: Insel Verlag, r.1995), p. 175. Hereafter referred to as *Die Familie Mendelssohn*.

The overture is a strange thing. Imagine a painter, flinging a dab of colour on his canvas, spreads it out with finger and brush until at last, to our increasing astonishment, one finally looks around for the actual occasion of it, since what has happened must be true. Admittedly, I speak like a grandfather who spoils his grandchildren. Not to worry. I know what I am saying and insist that I have said nothing that I cannot prove.

First of all, by the lavish applause of the orchestra and singers; it is easy to see whether coldness and repugnance, or love and favour move their fingers and throats. You must know all about that. [...]

### 315. Goethe

Weimar, 8 March 1824

[...] Now I must tell you that the library here has purchased, at a Nuremberg auction, a manuscript bearing the title *Tabulatur-Buch geistlicher Gesänge Dr Martini Lutheri und anderer gottseliger Männer, samt beigefügten Choralfugen durchs ganze Jahr. Allen Liebhabern des Claviers componiert von Johann Pachelbeln, Organisten zu St. Sebald in Nürnberg*, 1704.[597] If it would interest you, I could send it to you at least to have a look at. It is bound in leather, gilt-edged, and looks exactly like an old piece of church furniture, although in a good state of preservation; it contains 247 melodies.

What you report about Felix is desirable, and touching when considered as text and commentary; I wish I could give you a similar account of one of my scholars, but unfortunately poetry and the fine arts have no recognized basis like yours. The most absurd empiricism is met with everywhere – artists and amateurs are equally inadequate; one creates, the other criticises without any reason, and as a result we have to wait till a man of unmistakable talent steps forward and is able to perceive the rational outside himself, because it lies concealed within him. [...]

I have again been strangely drawn to Handel; Rochlitz's essay 'Händels Messias' (in his first volume, *Für Freunde der Tonkunst*, p. 227)[598] has persuaded

---

[597] Anna Amalia Bibliothek in Weimar, Signatur Q 341. An undated prefatory note written by Carl Georg von Winterfeld (1784–1852) gives further clues to its contents: 'The tablature book only goes as far as no. 160 inclusive; apparently it is not in the author's hand, but rather a hurried copy by his son, Wilhelm Hieronymus, who was organist in Wöhrd, Nürnberg, around 1704.' Pachelbel had no connection with the remaining part. Nos 161–176 are from Freilinghausen's *Neues geistreiches Gesangbuch* (Halle, 1714); the rest is from the fifth edition of an older songbook by the same collector published in 1710. Johann Pachelbel had already died on 3 March 1706. A later owner of the book had included the other melodies and inserted them in the table of contents.

[598] Friedrich Rochlitz's essay, 'Händels Messias' in his *Für Freude der Tonkunst*, vol. 1 (Leipzig: Carl Cnobloch, 1868), pp. 227–80, sent to Goethe by the author

me to take up the Handel–Mozart score,[599] from which, it is true, I can only pick out the rhythmical motives; I hope soon to become better acquainted with the harmonic structures as well through Eberwein's performance.[600] This would have been an interesting topic for our meeting, which, compared with former ones, would have turned out badly had it not been for the good influence of the principal subject of our conversation. Here's to meeting soon!

### 316. Goethe

Weimar, 11 March 1824

After a short time, my dear friend, I come forward again, and this time with a wish and a suggestion. Listen then to my proposal.

I enclose a poem,[601] in explanation of which it may be necessary to state the following. State Councillor Thaer,[602] of whom you are sure to know something in general, as well as in particular, will be 73 on 14 May. On that day his pupils, from near and far, are going to meet at his house in Mögelin, where they intend to give him a wonderful party. Now they want to have some newly-composed drinking songs for the occasion, and so have addressed themselves in well-written and polite petitions to Weimar, to the actual agora of poetry in Germany. Our friends, too, are not averse to helping them.[603] With this in mind, the enclosed poem came into my head; for an initial understanding of it I attach the following commentary:

---

on 21 February 1824. Shortly afterwards, in a review of this book, Goethe wrote, the 'account of Handel's *Messiah* (...) aroused in me an irresistible desire to hear much of the work once again, which introduced me earlier to the serious study of music, with the result that the old feelings which had faded away could come to life again and the youthful pleasures, in spirit and soul, could be renewed once more.'

[599] Mozart had arranged Handel's oratorio in March 1789; the first edition of this score was published by Breitkopf & Härtel in 1803. Zelter's performance on 5 April 1822 used this edition.

[600] In his review of Rochlitz's essay, Goethe continued: 'I succeeded in this, under the direction of a decent music director with the participation of composers and amateurs. I can now appreciate the structure of this inestimable work, aided by this introduction.'

[601] Goethe's occasional poem 'Zum vierzehnten Mai 1824', written for the birthday and anniversary of 50 years of service of Albrecht Thaer. The original enclosure in lost. Zelter set the poem and sent it to Goethe on 4 April.

[602] Albrecht Daniel Thaer (1752–1828), farmer, doctor and educator of civil servants at Berlin University.

[603] At Goethe's request, Eckermann wrote an occasional poem which Eberwein set (see Goethe's letter to Eckermann, 8 March 1824, *WA* IV/38, p. 72) and Riemer contributed a festival ode (see Goethe's letter of thanks to Riemer on 24 March 1824, *WA* IV/38, pp. 87–8).

Strophe 1: Thaer, a physician, esteemed both as a practitioner and theorist, is searching about for a cheerful occupation in the field of Nature and becomes engrossed in gardening.

Strophe 2: But he soon finds his powers limited and longs for a wider range of activity; he turns his attention to agriculture.

Strophe 3: He learns of the English system of husbandry, and the very basic axiom: that with more activity and more intelligent farming a far greater advantage may be gained than by following the old familiar methods.

Strophe 4: And so he manages to persuade landowners to rotate their crops, gains students and disciples who find his teaching and directives excellent and propose now to give him, in his advanced years, a loud and public acknowledgment of their gratitude.

I hope that this poem, which is meant to be sung by a great number of landowners seated at a banquet, may incite you to set it to some bright music; it is a celebration that will not occur again, and I should like our two names to be joined together on this occasion. The man belongs first of all to Prussia, but after that to the world at large as well; his fame and reputation are completely genuine, and so one would be justified in undertaking something to celebrate with him and his friends.

I trust you will be able to send me a successful score soon, which I will then attend to further. Initially I should like to keep it to ourselves. If you know too little of the man, you need only ask those immediately around you; they will tell you enough to persuade you to undertake this project. Perhaps some one of his pupils, travelling here and there, will join your Liedertafel at a later date, in which case you could not entertain such a guest any better.

I carry on my usual routine as normal and am glad to say it keeps me going. [...] I am back on my feet again.

### 317. Zelter

Berlin, 20 to 23 March 1824

Your last letter from 11 March, which reached me a few hours after the earlier one dated 8 March, almost shocked me; I feared something sinister. The beginning of the letter expelled the worry. The poem to old Thaer contained in it is already set to music and that's enough; there is time for it to settle slightly, but if you would like to have it immediately, you only have to tell me. I knew Privy Councillor Thaer really well and have seen him often enough with Count Itzenplitz in Cunersdorf (near Möggelin). [...]

I anticipated that my accounts of Felix's progress would be of interest to you. You know the misery with most students longer than I: great intentions, little talent; enormous effort for nothing – that is the worst and so one is happy when he finds someone who does what he can and always has enough in reserve no matter what happens.

Send me the Pachelbel manuscript – the sooner the better – and how long can I hold onto it? Since I will be more and more preoccupied now with my Easter music,[604] I would also like to see it soon.

Your reference to Handel reminds me that I must still thank Rochlitz; he sent me his book too, in which he made plenty of complimentary remarks about Handel and me. Somewhere Herder calls Handel's *Messiah* a Christian Epic;[605] in this he has hit the nail on the head, for in fact in its fragmentary arrangement the work contains the complete complexity of Handel's Christianity, as truly and honourably as it is rationally poetical. I have always considered the intention of the whole, viewed as a work, as being accidental in origin, and I cannot get rid of that impression.

In Handel's time the main Christian festivals gave composers the opportunity to set biblical verses to music for all the gospels, from which the loveliest details had to come into being. Handel, who had taste and heart enough to cast aside the disgraceful church texts of Brokkes, Picander and others, at which he, Bach and Telemann[606] had to labour, finally gathered the choruses relating to the Passion into one group, had some clever man supply the connecting hooks and rings between them – if he didn't do it himself – and so a cyclical work followed, which I divide up into four or five parts:

1. The proclamation of the Messiah by the prophets [sent here] from above; the business of the redemption; secretive, morning; 'Comfort Zion! Speaks your God'. Breathing spring freshness.
2. The Birth on earth, first known to shepherds: Introduction (Siciliana) – an attractive pastoral piece would have to go before the chorus 'Unto us a child is born'. In Mozart's score the chorus, incorrectly, is first. The chorus begins, playfully and rocking, childlike, even childish and builds up to colossal proportions with the words 'Which ruler is at his shoulder.' Life and teaching: the good shepherd 'He feeds his flock'; 'Come, you who are burdened.'
3. Suffering and death: misunderstood, scorn, maltreatment. 'Come and see the Lamb'; He suffers our torment'; 'We are like sheep who have gone astray'; 'He calls on the Lord, who gave him safe keeping'; such shame breaks his heart;

---

[604] The Sing-Akademie's annual performance of Graun's *Tod Jesu* took place on Good Friday, 16 April 1824, *AMZ* 26 (1824), no. 20, 13 May, column 330; *MA* 20.3, p. 631.

[605] In Letter no. 46 of *Briefe, das Studium der Theologie betreffend* (1786): 'O friend! What a marvellous work is this *Messiah* – a true Christian epic in musical form', Johann Gottfried Herder, *Sämtliche Werke*, ed. Bernhard Suphan (vols. Berlin Weidmann 1891, repr. Hildesheim: Georg Olms, 1967), vol. 11, p. 72.

[606] Barthold Heinrich Brockes's Passion Oratorio *Der für die Sünde der Welt gemarterte und Sterbende Jesus* (1712) was set by Handel and Telemann, among others. Christian Friedrich Heinrici (pseudonym Picander) greatly benefited from Bach having used countless of Picander's spiritual poems in his compositions, for example, the *St Matthew Passion*, the *Christmas Oratorio*, as well as many cantatas.

'Behold and see' and so on. Suffering is completed through death and through this, victory [is gained]. The redemption is achieved. Now the consequence:
4. Resurrection and eternal life: as above, back to infinity. Prophecy steps forward, declaiming: 'Open the gates wide!' The King of Glory enters:
'The Lord gave the word!'
'Why do the heathens rage
'Rise Up! Break their bonds! Halleluja!'
'I know my Redeemer liveth!
'Since through one man came Death'
5. Apotheose: 'Worthy is the Lamb'
'Praise and worship'
'Amen!'

The expression of such work is to be appreciated as a whole, although everywhere there is no lack of good, even fine work.

The overture is only part of the work to the extent that it serves as a foreground or foil to set the blue radiant heavens of prophecy against it: the splendour of the Lord God is to be revealed. Clarity, power, truth govern all of part one.

In Part Two, a warm pleasant night; one feels the light of the stars. Pastoral-like, enticing, pure and benevolent.

In Part Three, suffering and death. Short without [being] condensed. Great, quiet, touching; no torment; no crucifixion or the like. The suffering of the righteous over humiliation of the good and beautiful is the foundation, the abyss through which a crystal spring hurries away. 'Behold and see! Who recognizes such torment'.

This final piece is a true cavatina[607] and leads us into the history of musical forms, about which the following is to be said:

I view the German chorale as a kind of original form, which makes the distinction between the Protestant and Catholic churches. Through the chorale as congregational song, which contains the gospel, the congregation becomes the conduit of the service.

The old cantus firmus had declined into something shapeless. The chorale, which developed out of it, presents a firm form: it is an image, the setting of strophe to voice, the idea to ear and memory.

Now, as usual, the thing goes further; song based on figured bass comes into being. In the beginning one would not tolerate it in the church. What does the composer do? He figures the chorale, gives it a colourful bass line and figured bass is smuggled into the church.

---

[607] Here, as in Handel, a lyrical solo song; however, also a two-part song, arioso in style, which developed out of the early eighteenth-century cavata and employed a simple lied-like form, an economical use of coloratura passages and textual repetition common to the aria.

The tenor, as the sustaining, principal and leading voice carried by the foundation, the bass voice, becomes thin in the great church. Three-part harmony is identified; a third voice becomes necessary. There is no foundation below the bass; one looks above it. The alto emerges as the upper voice and the tenor, who formerly ruled, is now covered above and below. Youngsters at school are brought into the choir; the alto line is too deep for them and above the alto the soprano emerges; four-part harmony is formed. Ground bass is discovered and now the theory of consonance becomes the theory of dissonance.

The new choir is established and wants to be employed. The chorus comes into being and finally the fugue [emerges], which always includes the chorale, if not as a theme, then as cantus firmus. Now a strict tempo becomes increasingly more important, the strict movement continues unabated and the motet is developed (from *motus* meaning movement) and the proud chorale, just like the powerful sea hardly wants to move in space, even less in time, dances to the tune of the piper.

From this point the vast possibilities [presented by] church style become more like a microcosm. The flexible voice becomes aware of itself, likes it sound and wants to please; the rigorous tenor has lost his fame and the soprano tyrannically rules the whole.

The church stirs, however, and will not endure it, so music seeks a place outside the church. The cantata, the oratorio, the opera appears: here the singer is a central person; the chorus is no fool and accompanies him.

In opera everything is centred round the action; passion, evolving, ripening to a turning point, which needs a point where it can let go, so the cavatina (aria) comes into being, in which a definite feeling is given full expression.

The singer is now the sole representative of the whole. He is pleasing to himself and others; therefore the *da capo* emerges. This *da capo* is finally taken up into the form and now no one knows any longer what all the talk is about: the *da capo* itself becomes a worthless residue, bad coins alone are valid and no one has a use for pure metal.

Now the composer does not want to be deprived of the original form; so the cavatina comes into being, and this is nothing other than an aria without its second section, which cannot be sung as a *da capo*, and we find such a true cavatina in the Messiah: 'Behold and see! He who knows such torment, heavy like his torment,' whereby the whole [notion of] suffering is summed up quietly and the business of atonement is perfected.

If you want to treat yourself to a particular pictorial pleasure, then look at the chorus once more: 'Unto us a child is born'.

After the pastoral folk have heard the message of the angel on the nightly plains and recovered from the fear, a part begins – 'Unto us a child is born' – and innocently dallies with the idea; then others follow in this manner, next the third [voice], then the fourth and finally with the words 'wonderful', 'mighty' and so on, everyone is in accord: the shepherds of the fields, the army of stars of the entire heavens, everyone wakes and is courageous and happy.

Now enough, ye muses, if not too much. When you have heard your *Messiah*, I would also like to hear about it from you. I always learn something when you speak about such matters.

The good Rochlitz deserves much thanks but his history of the development of the *Messiah* a priori appears to me like all history (which can be [justifiably] so called). The history of an artwork (and every artwork has his individual history) can't be so simple, if nature itself needs a millennium in order to make one such fellow, who is also only there by chance. Necessity itself cannot exist without chance.

So something occurs to me: that I already formulated the hypothesis outlined above about the fortuitous nature of Handel's *Messiah*, viewed as a complete work, 20 years ago in a review which, then as now, met with appropriate contradiction. The review is in the *Berliner Musikalische Zeitung* from 1805 or 1806,[608] which Reichardt brought out and it is definitely in your library.

Let everyone think about it in his own way; for me this accidental element is a necessary beauty in every work of a genius. It is easier for me in that I can enjoy it undisturbed and don't need to excuse anything. If I see all that in it, it is really there; if anyone wants to take it out, for him it is not there.

In Rochlitz's book (p. 76),[609] Mara [Mlle Schmeling] is said to have petitioned the King [Frederick the Great] three times for permission to marry Mara and to have obtained it the third time. That, I am sorry to point out, is not true. The King roundly refused.

When she ran away on the first occasion, and what is more, ran away from her engagement as first singer to the King, she was still Mademoiselle Schmeling. Mara was engaged on a good salary as a virtuoso in Prince Henry's orchestra,[610] so he was to be punished as a kidnapper.

The King wanted to keep Mara, but she had not wished to engage herself for life. Now, however, she offered herself to the King on a permanent contract for life providing the King would allow Mara, now advanced to the post of percussionist, to be relieved of his duties and give her permission to marry him. Consent was granted, and now, for the first time as a married couple, they absconded again. That was in 1778, after Mara had sung the part of Rodelinda[611] in January. When they arrested her again, the King ordered them to let her go.

The King hated Mara, who was much more than a member of Prince Henry's orchestra; but it was the noble prince who served his favourite [musician]. It must have been impossible to get at Mara's heart by a secret staircase and through thousands of favours. He was the commonest scamp and maltreated his master

---

[608] The article, signed 'Z', was published in the *Berlinische Musikalische Zeitung* (1805), nos. 11 and 12 (1805).

[609] Article on Gertrud Elizabeth Mara in Friedrich Rochlitz's essay collection *Für Freude der Tonkunst*, pp. 49–117.

[610] Friedrich Heinrich Ludwig of Prussia (1726–1802), Brother of Friedrich II.

[611] Title role in Carl Heinrich Graun's opera.

outrageously. He sulked at him for weeks on end and behaved impiously, disturbing the Sunday services and the sermon in Rheinsberg.[612] He would go to the kitchen and eat up the dishes ordered for the Prince, and he got really drunk when he should have been playing.

All was overlooked year after year. The King knew about it but was unwilling to spoil his brother's game. At last there was a catastrophe. Around the time of the carnival, Prince Henry was in Berlin with all his court and hosted masquerades which far surpassed the King's masked balls and all the other courtly entertainments. On one occasion the entire court had been invited to a concert given by Prince Henry to hear the admired Mara upon the violoncello. Everyone appeared including Mara, who was drunk and refused to play. Prince Henry, in despair at such a public affront, commanded, begged, entreated. Mara did not play and this formed the basis of the King's hatred.

I tell you this story based on authentic chronicles[613] because according to Rochlitz's book the King appears as a tyrant who practiced his revenge upon Mara and cruelly separated a married couple. At that time they were not yet engaged. Mara's relation to Reichardt, who had just become the King's Kapellmeister,[614] is also not clarified, much to the composer's disadvantage.

### 318. Goethe

Weimar, 27 March 1824

Your esteemed letter brought me more than an important gift and so I want to tell you first that the chorale book is going off by return of post. Tell me about its value, especially with regard to the epoch from which it emerged.

You have provided me with enlightenment by your analysis of Handel's *Messiah*. Moreover, your conviction of the unconscious origin of this work is quite in accordance with my own opinion: for it is quite possible for the mind to raise up out of fragmentary elements a funeral pyre and finally to point its flame like a pyramid to Heaven.

---

[612] Rheinsburg Palace was Prince Heinrich of Prussia's residence.

[613] Ernst Ludwig Gerber, *Historisch-biographisches Lexikon der Tonkünstler* (Leipzig, 1790–92).

[614] The 23-year-old Reichardt, who had just been appointed Court Kapellmeister to Frederick the Great at the end of 1775, had – through his determination to reform the Berlin Orchestra and to control the prima donnas – created many enemies, including the singer Gertrud Elizabeth Mara, who had been in Berlin since 1771. The incident is recorded in her autobiography. The dispute was settled at a later date.

One evening, recently, I was listening to the *Messiah*;[615] some day or other I shall say a few words on the subject myself, but meanwhile I will be following your guidance. I am grateful for the lead given by Rochlitz, though I find that here as elsewhere his honest intention and hard work are obvious, and one can only wish that he was capable of taking a firmer grasp of the subject and carrying through more decisively what he has recognized

Now I want to thank you that you lent a friendly ear to the request regarding Thaer and have already taken action. Admittedly they would like the announcement as soon as possible, since both poem and music should be printed before that deadline. But let the work remain with you. I will send you an address near to you where you can deliver it in good time.[616] Write both our names on it and though apart, we can still fondly celebrate the great festival. Send me a copy.[617]

The chronicle-like notices of the adventures of Schmeling-Mara certainly have the true character of an empirical world; so it is that everything historical is surrounded by a strange enigmatic character, and it really gets comical when we consider how determined we are to be certain about what is long past. […]

When you have had a look through the chorale book, hold onto it; I will enquire about it again at Easter.

### 319. Zelter

Berlin, 4 April 1824

I am returning the Pachelbel chorale book to you with my sincere thanks.[618] I almost believed I had made a real discovery in that I considered it to be an autograph manuscript. It is, however, a copy, admittedly by an unsteady hand, and contains quite a few transcription errors with which the published choir books of that time are also marred.

---

[615] 16 March 1824. A second evening took place on 14 April. Eckermann wrote: 'In the evening, I had a musical treat of a high order at Goethe's house, where some fine singers, under the direction of Eberwein, performed part of Handel's *Messiah*. Countess Caroline von Egloffstein, Fräulein von Froriep as well as Frau von Pogwisch and Frau von Goethe joined the female singers, and thereby kindly gratified a wish that Goethe had long since entertained', *Eckermann*, p. 118.

[616] Later Goethe asked the main organizer of the festival, Schultze from Heinrichsdorf, to collect the poem and setting from Zelter.

[617] Zelter enclosed a copy in his letter to Goethe on 4 April 1824. A copy is in Goethe's music collection (GSA 32/8).

[618] The chorale book was not enclosed with this letter, hand-delivered by Henriette Schwendler, but sent by post on 18 April.

This Pachelbel is a worthy man in his own way and has been praised by the best of his colleagues, for he lived in the midst of the best chorale writers, from Luther up to Sebastian Bach, in genuine possession of the traditional Church modes. [...]

|  |  | Born | Died |
|---|---|---|---|
| Conrad | Rupsch | 1475 | 1530 |
| Ludwig | Senfl | 1486 | 1542/3 |
| Ludwig | Johann Walter | 1496 | 1570 |
| Heinrich | Schütz | 1585 | 1672 |
| Johann Hermann | Schein | 1586 | 1630 |
| Samuel | Scheidt | 1587 | 1654 |
| Johann | Rosenmüller | c.1619 | 1684 |
| Kaspar | Kerll | 1627 | 1693 |
| Johann Jakob | Froberger | 1616 | 1667 |
| Wolfgang Caspar | Printz | 1641 | 1717 |
| Johann | Theile | 1646 | 1724 |
| Daniel | Vetter | 1657/58 | 1721 |
| Alessandro | Scarlatti | 1660 | 1725 |
| Johann | Pachelbel | 1653 | 1706 |
| Georg Philipp | Telemann | 1681 | 1767 |
| Johann Sebastian | Bach | 1685 | 1750 |

This may be an approximate, incomplete list of the names[619] which cannot be denied their historical place, and no doubt there are several more. The above-named Heinrich Schütz, Schein, and Scheidt are often called the Trinity of the Three Great S's.

There is plenty of confusion in this manuscript, especially from page 161 onwards, and one can see the transition of the strong, deep stream into the broad flat wilderness. The song 'Auf auf!', on page 61,[620] is a veritable and really fine minuet. There is a little Gavotte on page 184[621] and so everything moves really softly and pleasantly into the popular mode of songwriting in Halle.[622] What mainly contributes to this is the smuggling in of triple time which the large space spurns because it is not a natural metre, and so it takes flight to the narrow space between the walls of the living rooms and has brought about the whole great

---

[619] I have completed and corrected Zelter's list of dates.

[620] Johann Anastasius Freylinghausen's hymn, 'Auf, auf, weil er Tag erschienen'. no. 161 in Pachelbel's *Choralbuch*.

[621] No. 184 lists L.J Schlicht's hymn 'Ach mein Jesu sieh ich trette'.

[622] At the beginning of no. 161 in the *Tabulatur Buch*, the inclusion of Johann Anastasius Freylinghausen's *Neuem Geist-reichen Gesangbuch* (Halle, 1714) is indicated by the title 'Neu-Hallische Gesänge'.

general devotional movement. By comparison, read the *Divan*, p. 62, under the title 'Old Persian'.[623] 'Kennst du es wohl?'[624]

I intend to find a special use for your tablature book. By that I mean the little preludes which are called fugues here, which come before the chorale. They serve to pitch the chorale in its appropriate key, with the help of the organ, whereby soloists and congregation are able to enter securely. They are fugues in so far as the leading theme (theme, subject) and accompanying theme (countersubject and answer) should take turns with the art and modulation. This practice belongs – like the sacred modes – to the church, although it can and does produce really nice fugues and on the contrary gives rise to fugues which cannot be considered church-like for the very reason that they are outside this tradition.

In former times, when an organist or Kapellmeister was examined for official duty in the church, a subject was given to him (the *dux*) for which he himself was obliged to find the answer extempore. He had to work out a similar task on paper in a room by himself; once that was done, the exercise was judged by the Committee of Examiners and such a fugal work then received the name of *ricercar*. [...]

Since you have tasted a little of Handel's *Messiah*, I only want to say that on a similar occasion I met and spoke with our Crown Princess[625] for the first time last Wednesday. Our Crown Prince invited a choir of eight to ten members of the Sing-Akademie into his living room in the King's residence in Frederick the Great's music room and in the presence of his court had them sing many magnificent movements of the great work[626] to a mere piano accompaniment. I was invited less as a collaborator than as a guest among the audience. Much as I have to accept this as an honour, I was deeply saddened. I am used to rehearsing and realizing this divine work with the dignity due to it for the last 30 years, and with 180 fresh voices, in order to present what music is. Now I stand like a poor sinner and see the living work dead before me in a narrow coffin where it cannot move its limbs. I immediately drowned the deepest sorrow in a flood of champagne, which was no compensation. One would go mad if one were not mad already. They want to carry such a work in a knitted bag. *Messiah* wasn't up to it and they went off for a meal where things went much better.

Enclosed: Zelter's setting of Goethe's 'Zum vierzehnten Mai 1824'

---

[623] The section 'Ältere Perser', in the first edition of *Noten und Abhandlungen zu besserem Verständnis des West-östlichen Divans* (1819), p. 262, deals with the metamorphosis of the 'noble, pure nature religion' into a 'common cult'; Zelter recognizes a similarity in what is discussed here about the 'general religious devotion'.

[624] Zelter is playing on a line from Mignon's lied 'Kennst du das Land?' from *Wilhelm Meisters Lehrjahre*.

[625] Elizabeth Ludovike of Prussia, née Princess of Bavaria (1801–73), married to the Crown Prince, Friedrich Wilhelm (later King Friedrich Wilhelm IV of Prussia).

[626] Handel's *Messiah*.

## 320. Zelter

Berlin, 12 April 1824

[…] Today I am having rehearsal of the Passion Music which the Crown Prince will visit. I am almost expecting the King himself, who is eating with the Crown Prince at noon and could well stroll in with him after lunch, which would be very pleasant for me since he could always throw me a pair of Friedrichs d'or once again.

Privy Councillor Wolf, who wants to pass through Weimar,[627] insists on some kind of letter and so I am sending these lines with him. I still don't even know whether you have already received my last letter with the chorale book I returned. […]

## 321. Goethe

Weimar, 28 April 1824

[…] The chorale book is back again. I had hoped you would have been more excited about it. Admittedly this dispatch had the advantage that you were able to add such good words of praise.

As chief organizer of this festival in Möglin and Freyenwalde, Schultze […] will have collected the poem and composition from you. Warmest thanks that you have been willing to follow my wishes with this request. The melody and style are really delightful. I would really like to hear these country voices manage it. However, I hear they have brought some musicians into the circle.

I hope [Graun's] *Tod Jesu* has also prepared a happy Easter for you this year.[628] The most lamentable of all events has been turned to such profit by clerics, and painters have also become wealthy on it, so why should the musician not cash in?

My *Messiah* is of great benefit to me; not all of it, but the kernel of it.[629] At least the idea is becoming clearer and this is a good deal for someone like me. I am not

---

[627] Friedrich August Wolf had requested a year's sabbatical from the Prussian king in March 1824 so that he could act on his doctor's advice and travel to the south of France to recover his health, after a severe bout of pneumonia. Before receiving an affirmative reply, he left Berlin on 14 April and travelled to Weimar via Wittenberg, where he stayed from 18 to 25 April. He died in Marseille on 8 August 1824.

[628] The Sing-Akademie gave their annual performance of Graun's *Der Tod Jesu* on Friday, 16 April 1824. Zelter profited from the performance. In his letter of 18 April, which never reached Goethe, he wrote, 'Yesterday my Passion Music was well received again by a very full house. I took in much money and there could be no complaints about our music.'

[629] This refers to the performance of excerpts of Handel's *Messiah* with piano accompaniment which took place in Goethe's house on 16 March and 14 April 1824 at the

against the idea that it is a collection, a compilation garnered from a number of sources, for in reality it doesn't matter whether the unity forms itself at the beginning or at the end; it is always the mind that produces it, and moreover the unity was implied in the Christian Old and New Testaments. In the end this very thing may be relevant to Homer,[630] only one must not say so to Wolf, who, when people admit that he is in the right, assures them they do not understand the matter [...]

## 322. Zelter

Berlin, 5 to 27 May 1824

[...] Yesterday evening your *Tasso* was read at the Mendelssohn's.[631] Wolff, his wife[632] and house guests acquitted themselves well and approximately 30 friends got great pleasure from it. [...]

It delights me that you feel as I do about the *Messiah*. The artist took a lofty stance. He didn't try to work around the clerical positions; he simply flew above them, and the ideal of the redemption stands out clearly.

Perhaps you would like to look at the following little book[633] which is a translation by a contemporary art colleague here. Leaving aside some Philistines, he is not so slap-dash and fragmented as the contemporary critic who turns the man into a market doll and sees him as being no different from everyone else. Please return it to me sometime; it has become rare like any writings of Mattheson,[634] who has written some 80 books.

18 May: The festival[635] went well and the good old fellow earned the honourable title of the German *Woll-Thaer*.[636] One of my best students had taken over the choir. I feared the challenge was too much for him and I went along myself, accompanied

---

poet's request and directed by Carl Eberwein.

[630] Goethe is, of course, referring to Friedrich August Wolf's *Prolegomena ad Homerum*, in which he considered Homer's epics, the *Iliad* and the *Odyssey*, to be rhapsodies.

[631] From 1820 Abraham Mendelssohn held a salon in his home to which leading figures in Berlin society were invited, including, for example, the Humboldts, Hegel and Heinrich Heine.

[632] Goethe's favourite actor, Pius Alexander Wolff, and his wife, Amalie Wolff.

[633] Memoirs of Georg Friedrich Handel's life translated with critical commentary by Mattheson (Hamburg, 1761) from the original by John Mainwaring, *Memoirs of the Late Georg Friedrich Handel* (London, 1760).

[634] Significant works by Mattheson include: *Das Neu-Eröffnete Orchestre* (1713); *Critica Musica* (1722–25); *Der Musikalische Patriot* (1728) and *Der Vollkommene Kapellmeister* (1739).

[635] The birthday celebration also marking 50 years of service for Albrecht Thaer on 14 May 1824.

[636] Presumably a pun, Voltaire.

by eight capable singers. The people came from all directions: 250 people were at table and it must have been planned spontaneously. In short, the thing went well enough, although poet and composer had set it up for regular troupes. They had published your poem in the textbook[637] at the very end, keeping the best till last. One soon found it and it had to be sung at the beginning and once more at the end. What delighted me about it was that the refrain was sung by the whole table, farmers and nobility together; and I had set it up that way [...]

Ascension Thursday: On the day of repentance Spontini performed Handel's *Alexanderfest* for his charity performance.[638] He could have left it out, but he did no harm by it: what he didn't earn he has gained.

### 323. Goethe

Weimar, 26 June 1824

[...] Recently I heard a very charming performance of the Thaer cantata and once more was delighted with the music: with every strophe the meaning is deepened along with the feeling [...]

### 324. Zelter

Berlin, 1 to 14 July 1824

14 July: Eberwein has arrived in order to promote his opera,[639] since he will fight to see our shameful side. We are drowning in misery and expecting an explosion. As I have had nothing to do with such matters, I am equally close to both sides. Trojans and Greeks: one is the same as the other. An acquaintance of mine compiled a collection of documents about the quarrel over the opera *Euryanthe*[640] which is

---

[637] *Festgaben, dem Königlichen Preußischen Geheim-Ober-Regierungs-Rate Herrn Albrecht Thaer zur Feier seines funfzigjährigen Wirkens dargebracht von seinen Freunden und Schülern*, Freienwalde, 16 May 1824. A copy is held in the Staatsbibliothek in Berlin (SBB PK, Yf 2823-158).

[638] Spontini conducted Handel's *Alexanderfest* on 12 May 1824; for reviews of the performance see *AMZ* 26 (1824), no. 26, 24 June, column 421; *MA* 20.3, p. 633.

[639] *Der Graf von Gleichen* (libretto by Friedrich Schmidt) premiered in Weimar on 1 May 1824.

[640] For the reception history of this work, composed by Carl Maria von Weber 1822–23; see Friedrich Wilhelm Jähns, *Carl Maria von Weber in seinen Werken* (Berlin: Schlesinger, 1871, r.1967), pp. 366–75.

more interesting than the thing itself. Privy Councillor Schmidt[641] will take this letter with him. [...]

Three years ago for our second Liedertafel[642] I composed a drinking song by Förster,[643] to which one attaches a satirical, political connotation. Oddly enough Bierey from Breslau has set this poem to music and has had it published.[644] It is published under your name in the *Caecilia* which comes out in Mainz,[645] and was negatively reviewed.[646] The poem is spared criticism because your name is on it, but the music was written off. I mention this simply in case you hear of it.

Bierey is hardly likely to produce anything worthwhile. As long as the people write serious opera, they will find in the so-called passions an occasion and an excuse for all the rough and tumble with which they torment themselves and others. In humorous circumstances one recognizes the impoverished nature and so it is with the above-named composition. The critic was right – not that his review is any better.

## 325. Zelter

Berlin, 3 November 1824

[...] I would like to have given a report about the new theatre[647] but, to tell the truth, I have not been in it often enough. [...] Among the singers Spizeder[648] is excellent in comedy; a Madame Biedenfeld,[649] true Italian art and voice; Madame

---

[641] The Weimar Senior Civil Servant, Christian *Friedrich* Schmidt (1780–1850).

[642] Liedertafel founded by Ludwig Rellstab, Ludwig Berger and Bernhard Klein in April 1819.

[643] Friedrich Förster's 'Frühlingsmusikanten' ('Es wollt einmal in Königreich'), composed by Zelter on 25 May 1821.

[644] *Dämagogisch. Gedicht von Goethe, für eine Singstimme und vier Frösche, mit Begleitung des Pianoforte, in Musik gesetzt von G.M. Bierey* (Breslau: C.G. Förster, 1824).

[645] *Cäcilia, eine Zeitschrift für die musikalische Welt*, vol. 1 (Mainz 1824), pp. 133–9.

[646] Ibid., *MA* 20.3, p. 638.

[647] On 4 August 1824 the Königstädtisches Theater was opened; it was the first large-scale private theatre alongside the two court theatres. The need for a third theatre was to accommodate lighter entertainment; Carl Friedrich Cerf got concession from the court to run the theatre for 99 years on the condition that no serious operas or dramas would be performed and that there would be a two-year delay in taking up works which had been performed by the court. A directory of six bankers was founded and the first directorship was given to Carl Friedrich Kunowski; for an account of the opening see *AMZ* 26 (1824), no. 39, 23 September, column 633f.; *MA* 20.3, p. 644.

[648] Joseph Spitzeder (1795/96–1832), singer and actor.

[649] Eugenie Freifrau von Biedenfeld née Bonasegla (1788–1862), singer.

Spizeder[650] and Mademoiselle Eunike[651] [are] very good and almost no one is bad. A first-rate tenor seems to be lacking. Of the orchestra I will only say that it is developing; that is to say, it will be nothing if the Director of Music[652] remains a vain fool who, in spite of his merit, still doesn't know where the beginning is. He has fine young people under him, who see through him if they don't ignore him. [...]

### 326. Zelter

Berlin, 27 November 1824

As a counter-piece to the lovely things you inform me of, I am sending you a comedy leaflet,[653] from which you may well see that we are making progress while going backwards. For the first time in my life I saw *Die Mitschuldigen*[654] yesterday and in a quite good performance. The four principals[655] were well cast and well rehearsed. Schmelka and Mademoiselle Sutorius were outstanding, and it is worth remembering, well received. I was as amazed at the heartiness of the direction as at their knowledge of the local audience, which gladly attending every good play knew how to distinguish itself by it arousing applause, in contrast to the people in the first row, where I had my place today.

The impression the play made on us in the front row I would like to compare to the impact of *Die Wahlverwandtschaften*, which is intellectual without being beneficial. Yes, even Kotzebue's small-town dwellers[656] occurred to me because no one wants to be in the stocks: everyone wants to watch. A common theft carried out openly by a reckless person and all good or decent people are guilty; that made us feel so bitter that one would want to veil one's face before looking in the mirror.

---

[650] Henriette Spitzeder née Schüler (1800–28), singer.
[651] Katharina Friederike Dorothea Bernadine Eunike (1804–42), singer and actress.
[652] Carl Wilhelm Henning (1784–1867), composer and Kapellmeister, music director at the Königstädtisches Theater from 1824 to 1826.
[653] The theatre leaflet from the Königstädtisches Theater, 26 November 1824, with the announcement of Goethe's *Die Mitschuldigen* and the Singspiel *Der Sänger und der Schneider* (Text and Music by Friedrich von Dreiberg); the enclosed leaflet has not been handed down.
[654] Goethe's farce, a one-act comedy (in the first edition from 1768); rewritten in three acts in 1769; a second revision was completed in 1783 and published for the first time in the Göschen edition of Goethe's works; in this latter verse, committed to courtly propriety, the comedy was staged in 1805.
[655] Alcest was played by Ludwig Meyer; Sophie was played by Auguste Sutorius; the landlord by Heinrich Ludwig Schmelka; Söller by Wohlbruch.
[656] *Die deutschen Kleinstädter*, comedy by August von Kotzebue.

In short, good or not so good – it should dawn on us: the greater the theft, the more refined the public

[...] Once again we have been visited by a pair of virtuosi murderers: Madame Grünbaum (formerly Wenzel-Müller)[657] and Moscheles, the pianist.[658] The former sings our Milder and Seidler[659] clean off the earth, and Moscheles really plays in such a fashion that he makes one take a draught of Lethe and forget all who went before him. Why, the fellow has hands which he turns inside out like a shirt, and even his nails can play. Among the more recent composers, I like his style next to Hummel's. I had heard of him some time ago and in 1819 travelled through Prague to Vienna on his account; I missed him there because he was expected in both places. [...]

I heard Madame Grünbaum in 1810 in Prague when she was still single.[660] Her voice is quite mellow and has a good range, [but] has neither the metal nor the power of Milder and Catalani. Our Seidler has more brilliance in both tone and expression. Grünbaum is instructive to me because I find my preconceived opinion of Rossini confirmed by her. She makes his ornaments come to life so vividly that you believe you are hearing a song bird that is not yet known. She is also praised for her performance of Mozart's works, in which I have never heard her. Against that I have heard her three times in Rossini's *Barber of Seville*[661] – one [performance] after the other – where she made me delighted with the composer as well. [...]

---

[657] Therese Grünbaum née Müller, daughter of the composer, Wenzel Müller; engaged in Vienna from 1818. Guest appearances in Berlin from September 1824 included Donna Anna in Mozart's *Don Giovanni* (28 September, 2 and 26 November); the countess in Mozart's *Figaro* (1 and 24 October, 14 and 23 November); Rosine in Rossini's *Barbier von Sevilla*; Amazily in Spontini's *Ferdinand Cortez* (5 and 21 November); Julia in Spontini's *Vestalin* (3 and 10 October, 10 December). She concluded her visit with a performance of the title role in Spontini's *Olympia* on 28 December 1824. She won the acclaim not only of Berlin audiences but also the critics; see, for example, *Spenersche Zeitung* of 16 September and *AMZ* (1824), no. 52, 23 December, column 858.

[658] Ignaz (Isaac) Moscheles (1794–1870). Bohemian pianist and composer. On this visit Moscheles met the 15-year-old Mendelssohn and, at Lea's request, gave him some finishing lessons on the piano. In later years Moscheles appeared with Mendelssohn in his first Gewandhaus concerts in 1835 and was appointed principal professor of piano at the Leipzig Conservatory, founded by Mendelssohn. Following the composer's death in 1847, he resolved to maintain the high standard of teaching for which Mendelssohn strove.

[659] Berlin singers Anna Milder-Hauptmann (1785–1838), Caroline Wranitzky-Seidler (1790/4–1872).

[660] Therese Grünbaum (née Müller) was engaged in Prague from 1807 to 1816. On his visit to Prague in 1810, Zelter heard her in the Singspiel *Die Schweizerfamilie* and in the title role in Paer's opera *Sargines, oder Der Zögling der Liebe*.

[661] *Der Barbier von Sevilla*, opera by Gioachino Rossini, Libretto by Cesare Sterbini, *Il barbiere di Siviglia* from Beaumarchais' comedy.

## 327. Goethe

Weimar, 3 December 1824

[...] Your musical reports have been [...] of incredible value to me;[662] as far as it is possible to grasp music conceptually, you have enabled me to do so, and at all events, I now understand why of all Rossini's works, *Il Barbiere di Seviglia* is the one most generally praised. One evening recently I heard *Tancredi*;[663] it was a very commendable performance and I would have been really happy if only no helmets, armour, weapons and trophies had appeared upon the stage. However, I got past the difficulty immediately and transformed the performance into a *favola boscareccia*,[664] something like the *Pastor Fido*.[665] I also imagined the stage decorated by graceful Poussin landscapes; I peopled the scene with actors of my own so that there was no lack of ideal shepherds and shepherdesses as in *Daphnis und Chloe*,[666] and even fauns; and then there was nothing to criticize because the meaningless pretensions of a heroic opera fell away.

## 328. Zelter

Berlin, 10 to 11 December 1824

[...] You will have found in the *Wiener Theaterzeitung* a letter by Mozart[667] sent to a dear, good baron who had sent him compositions seeking advice and instruction but was actually wanting to learn the secret very briefly [of] how one manages

---

[662] Zelter's account of *Die Mitschuldigen* in the new Königstädtisches Theater on Alexanderplatz.

[663] Goethe went to the performance of *Tancredi* (in Italian) at the Weimar Court Theatre on 27 November 1824.

[664] A pastoral play.

[665] *Il pastor fido*, pastoral comedy by Giovanni Battista Guarini, who was also the librettist. The enduring popularity of his libretti spanned the seventeenth and eighteenth centuries.

[666] Longos's pastoral novel.

[667] An undated alleged letter of Mozart's to a Baron von T was published in the *Allgemeine Wiener Theaterzeitung*, no. 138 (1824). This letter, which had already been published by Rochlitz in *AMZ* 17 (1815), no. 34, 23 August, column, 561–6, was most likely a counterfeit. Goethe didn't respond to Zelter's hint but he did read the letter two years later through Chancellor von Müller, as Eckermann's record for 13 December shows: 'I read a letter by Mozart today, in reply to a baron, who had sent him his composition: "You dilettantes must be scolded because you are characterized by two faults: either you have no thoughts of your own and take those of others or, if you do have ideas of your own, you don't know what to do with them." Isn't that divine? And doesn't this fine remark which Mozart voiced about music, apply to all other arts?', *Eckermann*, p. 194.

to send something quite beautiful out into the world. The letter is a golden letter and reassures me about my old way of teaching: that one should not go to too much trouble with the young art enthusiasts. Whoever wants real knowledge will manage and whoever wants to win will invest. That's as much as I know and I keep on learning. [...]

To provide occasions for my enterprise in addition to the two Sing-Akademie days I have, for more than 20 years, a Friday collegium in my home,[668] where I am both master and servant. In addition to their formal studies, the most capable of my young students take part in the performance of excellent musical works from the past. Additionally I talk about my own experience and insights. Some days more is spoken and discussed than sung and played. [...]

Felix is still my best student. His admirable industry is the fruit of a healthy root, and his sister, Fanny, has completed her thirty-second fugue. The young people are wide awake, and when they have picked up anything that suits them, you see it in their work; they are as pleased as if they had conquered Mexico,[669] and they are fond of me, just as they find me, and come and go like bees about flowers [...]

### 329. Zelter

Berlin, 26 December 1824

[...] Today my Felix is to let us hear his latest double concerto.[670] The lad stems from a root that gives promise of a healthy tree. His individuality becomes more and more apparent and entwines so well with the spirit of the age that it seems to peep out of it like a bird from the egg. [...]

---

[668] Ripienschule founded by Zelter in 1807, one of the affiliated Collegium Musicum of the Sing-Akademie, established for the performance of ancient music.

[669] Zelter has in mind the constant dispute for power in the newly formed state of Mexico (independent of Spain), whose rich mineral resources were almost proverbial.

[670] Felix Mendelssohn, Piano Concerto for two pianos and orchestra in A major, composed in September and October 1824; the first public performance was organized by the composer in Stettin on 20 February 1827.

## 330. Zelter

Berlin, 29 January 1825

I had shared something from your letter with Madame Schulze,[671] who sings and acts *Tancredi*[672] better than anyone, and lo and behold she appeared as a well-built youth with a strong, full, clear voice and with only a suggestion of a helmet – whether it was to support what you said[673] or to avoid hiding her manly face with a strong Caesar's nose, big blue eyes, pearly teeth and ample lips so that the music meant more to me for its good qualities.

They had cut the opera, which can take a knock because a ballet in three acts still followed, but with the purpose of putting in something foreign – and that was good? It was a choral work from an Italian oratorio, *I pellegrini al sepolcro di N.S. Gesù Christo* by Naumann.[674] [...]

Our head chef and courtly train are trying to erect a memorial of the great minds by an evening meal at midday whereby the goblet must do its best.[675] The day before yesterday Mozart had to suffer,[676] and the thing was decent enough if one takes on board that approximately 300 heads were together with the same intention. They were, in fact, all cheerful and remained that way, for the effect of champagne is to transform the truth. The health of those celebrated[677] was spoken in German by our general music director, Spontini, and as nothing rhymes in German, one would expect the thing to have come out as awkward and unrhymed, and it was – exactly like that! [...]

---

[671] Josephine Schulze née Kilitzschky (*c*.1790–1880).

[672] Gioachino Rossini's heroic opera *Tancredi* was performed in Johann Christoph Grünbaum's German translation in the Königliches Opernhaus; Zelter attended the performance on 21 January 1825; for reviews see *AMZ* 27 (1825), no. 7, 7 February, column 116.

[673] Reference to Goethe's critique of the Weimar performance, where 'helmets, armour, weapons and trophies' were used on stage.

[674] Johann Gottlieb Naumann.

[675] Dinner party, essentially a celebratory evening meal, on this occasion brought forward to midday.

[676] Celebration of Mozart's birthday on 27 January.

[677] W.A. Mozart.

### 331. Goethe

Weimar, 4 February 1825

Everything which makes your circumstances clear to me and can bring me to your side is really welcome to me at any time: one moment I find you at the opera[678] and the next revelling in a big feast[679] in true Berlin style. [...]

### 332. Zelter

Berlin, 1 to 3 April 1825

[...] I am performing *Der Tod Jesu* today.[680] The seats are all sold and yesterday's rehearsal had around 800 listeners, many of whom had given up their purchased tickets in order not to roast the following day. Such a rehearsal provides a tolerable performance.

Easter Saturday: My hall[681] was packed full yesterday. In the evening, after the performance, I found a lovely big silver goblet on my table, with which 100 of my female students had honoured me. The inscription on it was: 'Drink, old man! The wine is good!' [...]

### 333. Zelter

Berlin, 12 April 1825

Chladni, who is here,[682] finds everything according to his taste and at the same time expresses his satistfaction with the acoustics at the Königstädter Theater.[683]

I repeat that the sound goes out, as I remarked, to the full house and thinner atmosphere by itself. At the same time the stage contains its own acoustic. Power

---

[678] Berlin performance of *Tancredi*.

[679] Celebratory performance marking Mozart's birthday.

[680] On Good Friday, 1 April 1825, Zelter conducted his annual performance of Graun's *Der Tod Jesu*.

[681] Concert hall in the Königliches Opernhaus, in which *Der Tod Jesu* had been performed.

[682] As reported in the *Vossische Zeitung* on 30 March 1825, Chladni was in Berlin to give lectures on acoustics in the house of chemist and Privy Councillor Sigismund Friedrich Hermbstädt (1760–1833).

[683] The new theatre, which had opened on 4 August 1824, was also used as a concert hall.

and beauty lie in the music and in the orchestra everything has its own part to play.

The entrance of the female singers as far as the footlights is a cheap trick with the audience to attract applause.

A voice, which is strained, doesn't know its limitations and is not the best. A beautiful voice sounds best from a proper distance. No one wants to hear a violin played too loudly or a flute overblown.

You are an old practitioner and so I am asking for my own sake, since an expert opinion about such effects demands understanding and experience.

If I could build a theatre with my money, I would try to cut off and retract the area between the curtains and the orchestra with a straight line, whereby perhaps the prompter's box, which I always hated, would be excluded.

The requested profile[684] is enclosed here and Ottmer asks for it back after you have made use of it.

Best of all, perhaps, would be if Coudray himself were to come to Berlin: blessed are those who see and also believe.[685]

In confidence I will still only say as a simple musician that a bad performance can seldom be attributed to the house, because with the cursed virtuoso musicians there is no thought given to the orchestral work. A proper orchestra can come about only where a concert master can build up a school around him. It doesn't matter if someone has the talent to tickle people here and there where they like it, as long as it does not have an influence on the students.

---

[684] The requested selection of architectural plans for the Königstädtisches Theater in Coudray's letter of 31 March 1825. According to Goethe's diary on 19 April 1825 (*WA* III/10, p. 45), there were two pages of plans, which he returned to Coudray on 7 June.

[685] A reference to Christ's words to the Apostles, 'Blessed are those who don't see and yet believe'.

## 334. Zelter

Berlin, 30 April 1825

That you remember me in your correspondence with Schiller really cheered me up again. Your support for Scutaris[686] and what you said about folksongs are both so close to my heart that I can substantiate them. It was exactly in this vein that I responded to a young man[687] who set Herder's folksongs and gave them to me for my assessment. [...]

## 335. Zelter

Berlin, 1 to 2 May 1825

Our building of the Sing-Akademie has started,[688] which means we are digging the foundations, finding water and should be grateful if a depth of 12 feet deep is enough. [...]

## 336. Goethe

Weimar, 21 May 1825

Mendelssohn stayed with us too short a time on his return journey from Paris;[689] Felix produced his last quartet[690] and astonished everyone. This personal musical dedication has done me a lot of good. I could only speak very fleetingly with his father, for I was prevented and distracted by the music and by a large concourse

---

[686] Two articles in a new edition of *Über Kunst und Altertum*, the first a translation of a Serbian song sent to Goethe on 8 May 1824 by Jacob Grimm; the second, Goethe's essay, *Serbische Lieder*, introduced by general observations on folksongs and their melodies.

[687] Presumably Carl Loewe; in a letter of 30 December 1823 Loewe had requested Zelter's opinion of his edition of three ballads, which included a setting of Herder's 'Edward'; Zelter replied on 10 January 1824 and outlined in his letter remarkable principles of nineteenth-century song aesthetics.

[688] The new building for the Sing-Akademie had finally been commenced after four years of planning.

[689] Abraham Mendelssohn and his son Felix stayed with Goethe on 20 May 1825. Goethe noted in his diary, 'The Mendelssohns, returning from Paris, payed a visit', *WA* III/10, p. 57.

[690] Piano Quartet in B minor, opus 3, dedicated to Goethe. Goethe noted in his diary, 'In the evening concert and company. Mendelssohn performed a quartet with Eberwein and some other musicians', *WA* III/10, p. 57.

of people. I would like to have heard something about Paris from him. Felix told the ladies something about the state of musical affairs there which is very characteristic of the time. Give my best wishes to the family and also keep me in the memory of that circle.

### 337. Zelter

Berlin, 28 May 1825

Felix has returned from Paris[691] and has made quite a name for himself in these few months. There he composed a Kyrie[692] for Cherubini that will stand up to performance and examination, all the more as that good fellow, following his clever instincts, has taken up the piece almost ironically, in a spirit which, if not the right one, is at any rate very much what Cherubini has always been on the look out for and, if I am not much mistaken, has never found.

I am amused that you study my letters! It must be a pretty awkward bundle that I wouldn't mind seeing myself! The letters may include academic matters, but they account for my life in the 25 years in which I first began to live.[693]

[Abraham] Mendelssohn has brought his younger sister[694] back with him from Paris; for some 20 years she lived there as governess to General Sebastiani's newly-wed daughter, and having realized a considerable pension, she now intends to reside in Berlin where she was born. The free and loveable disposition, which this girl has retained from childhood through the Parisian descent into hell, is to be commended. It is enough to reconcile one again to the Prophets: that the old, failing father should see the promise of Abraham fulfilled in all his children. Farewell, my dear friend! I am looking forward to your new complete edition with great anticipation.

---

[691] Abraham Mendelssohn had taken Felix with him on a business trip to Paris, from March to May 1825, in order to introduce him to Cherubini, whose opinion of his son's talent he sought.

[692] This work cannot be identified for certain; the most likely work is the Kyrie in C minor for choir and orchestra, housed in the Staatsbibliothek in Berlin.

[693] Zelter finds his identity at the beginning of his friendship with Goethe and here considers that he has really begun to live since then.

[694] Abraham Mendelssohn's sister Henriette had lived in Paris since 1802, first as headmistress of a boarding school for girls and from 1812 as governess to General Sebastiani's daughter Fanny, after whose wedding she returned to Paris in 1824.

You may receive more reliable reports from other sources about our celebrations.[695] As yet I haven't seen the new magic opera *Alcidor*;[696] I write 'seen', and I will have to wait until those, who have booked all the seats well in advance for the sole reason that they want to test the newly-created title for it – *All too Amazing: A Magic Opera* – have scolded it enough.[697] [...]

Our man from Heidelberg[698] chooses to be like someone who, astronomically speaking, knows only one pole. He thinks the most terrible tricks were played on Mozart with the words *Misericordias Domini cantabo in aeternum*,[699] in that he composed the opening words devoutly and the final words jubilantly.

The work appears to be very advanced and is an exercise in counterpoint to bind two contrasting themes with one another, taking the first words which occurred to the writer. [...]

## 338. Zelter

Berlin, 1 to 4 June 1825

[...] Our new massively heavy magic opera, *Alcidor*, which plays for four hours, has now survived two performances. Two quarrelling magic princes, of whom one rules a golden island with its residences keeps technical staff and decorators very busy. Choirs of gnomes and sylphs enact the magic work. A loving pair, plagued by the gnome folk and protected by the other side, is at last reunited and made human.

The libretto is written in French by Théolon and set to music in a French manner. So we finally possess a Berlin original – that is: changed into a new dress.

The music is an astonishing piece of work: one would have to be a really fine musician in order to admire it, let alone treasure it. It is a chaos of the rarest effects that want to wear one another down, like the singing princes, and presupposes

---

[695] Celebrations for the wedding ceremony of Prince Friedrich of Netherland to Princess Louise of Prussia on 21 May 1825, to which the *Vossische Zeitung* gave extensive coverage on 24 May.

[696] Spontini's opera (libretto by Carl Herklots, adapted from the French by Marie Emmanuel Guillaume Théaulon de Lambert) was first performed in a lavish production which cost 16,000 thalers on 23 May in the Königliches Opernhaus in Berlin; *AMZ* 27 (1825), no. 24, 15 June, column 404–406. Further performances were given on 26 and 31 May, and 3 June 1825.

[697] Spontini's high income was common knowledge; Zelter's comments also refer to the amount of money spent on the production of this *Zauberoper* opera, which lasted four hours.

[698] Anton Friedrich Justus Thibaut (1772–1840), lawyer and professor in Kiel (from 1798), in Jena (from 1803) and Heidelberg (from 1806), also a writer on music.

[699] Mozart's motet Misericordias Domini. Offertorium de tempore, KV 222 (1775).

immeasurable industry on the part of the composer. There must be ten years work in the piece. I could kill myself and would not bring forth anything like it.

In published and unpublished form the immediate critics here do the composition a disservice[700] insofar as what one throws away, the other deals with by coldly raising it up.

In what he set out to do, he succeeded only too well. He had wanted to excite surprise, wanted to shock, and with me he fully reached his objective. He seemed to me like his golden king who flings gold at the people, giving them holes in the head.

Since the performed music is based on excess, the great demands made by it are not unjustified and the complaints of the orchestra about the difficulties are nothing compared to what the ear has to withstand – to last so long in a thicket of sounds which is far too attractive, and, at the same time, too burdensome to be cast off. I know well what I can endure and I thought I would find it easier to cope with yesterday than the first time. But eyes and ears, even skin and bones are still sore today from watching, listening and sitting.

All of that is not just peculiar to me. It is characteristic of the period which leads to perdition everyone who is forced to let himself be carried away. Since I am reading the Winckelmann letters now, I see clearly that I, too, make undue concessions to the epoch. In short, the work is remarkable in all external respects because of the style, which is pushed to extremes, a style that expresses the strong and the lovely through travesty. With complete emptiness, it has a bewildering, even deadly effect.

What tries to be melodic seems to me like a contour drawing which always discontinues instead of flowing and loses itself in caricature.

Similar things of this period could be found in the completely extraordinary Beethoven, who could be compared with Michelangelo in the past and in the present with Spontini, for whom Cherubini paved the way.

What am I actually trying to say? Should one condemn that in which one is present? Should one suffer what is not to be endured? So (like Wieland) we need to live and let live.

### 339. Goethe

Weimar, 6 June 1825

[...] The Serbian folksongs have just been published at Halle in an attractive octavo volume.[701] The introduction, a short outline of the history of the fallen Serbian empire, is extremely good and exhibits [the author's] extensive knowledge;

---

[700] *Spenersche Zeitung*, no. 125, 2 June 1825 and no. 126, 3 June 1825.

[701] *Volkslieder der Serben, metrisch übersetzt und historisch eingeleitet von Talvj* (2 vols, Halle, 1825–26); volume one, which Goethe is referring to, contained a dedication to

a sufficient though uninteresting account. To have – just as I wished – all the national songs before you in one volume is extremely delightful and informative; you know at once what they are and what they are meant to be.

I cannot close without again recalling that overcharged music,[702] but, dear friend, everything nowadays is ultra, everything inexorably transcendent, in thought as in action. No one understands the element in which he moves and works; no one the subject that he is treating. There is no simplicity but plenty that is simplistic. [...]

### 340. Zelter

Berlin, 7 June 1825

Hauser,[703] a really fine bass, is travelling from Cassel to Dresden and then through Weimar with the sole purpose of meeting you and performing a song for you. He mentioned to me that he has already approached you once, but he was lost for words and so he asked me to put in a word with you on his behalf.

Just do whatever you would like and can manage. I owe him a favour. When he sang for me for the first time and had repeated for the umpteenth time all kinds of excuses which more or less all singers have learned, I came down on him probably harder than he had ever experienced before.

### 341. Zelter

Berlin, 19 to 21 June 1825

[...] I hope you are impressed that I guessed your riddle: it is the first which I ever unravelled in my whole life.[704] In Mendelssohn's house[705] where I am, as a

---

him. See Goethe's correspondence with Therese Albertine Louise von Jakob, who concealed her identity with the acronym, Talvj, *Gjb* 12 (1891), pp. 33–77.

[702] The recent Berlin performance of Spontini's *Alcidor*.

[703] Franz Hauser (1794–1870), singer and music teacher, in Prague from 1817, in Cassel (1821–25), engaged in Dresden in 1825 by Carl Maria von Weber. He announced himself at Goethe's house on 23 June 1825 and offered a recital which included performances by his wife and his sister-in-law (see Goethe's diary, *WA* III/10, p. 71). Goethe wrote to Meyer on 24 June 1825, 'A singer sent by our Zelter presented himself; my daughter, who had heard him perform, praised him highly, so once again I will hear some welcome music', *WA* IV/39, pp. 235–6.

[704] Zelter unravelled Goethe's *Rätsel nach dem Griechischen* (*MA* 20.1, p. 841) as 'sleep' which Goethe confirmed, *MA* 20.1, p. 850.

[705] Abraham Mendelssohn's house (since 1825), Leipziger Straße 3.

rule, twice a week, the same happens often enough. However, the children[706] are so superior to me at it that before long I could not completely unravel one of my own charades invented earlier: 'My first is feminine, my other one is masculine, my whole thing sour'. [...]

Count Brühl is thrown into confusion about the new opera.[707] The uninterrupted rehearsals for the past 8 to 12 weeks have – because of the numerous scene changes – held up the entire theatre so that nothing else of any consequence could be performed. Now this wonder work was launched at last and the house was so crammed that the audience was stifled and perspiring with the heat. Directly after the first performance Spontini demanded the regulation 1,050 thaler, which he gets for every new work; it was taken from the ticket sales and they have nothing left. People now say, 'Spontini takes the money which the others have to sweat.'

### 342. Zelter

Berlin, 26 June 1825

Our general music director, Spontini, asks me for a recommendation to the great Goethe, which should hardly be necessary between such kindred spirits in art. Yet, as I cannot help wishing that all my friends could be acquainted with each other, and I have discovered an opportunity of sending you one more warm greeting, may you not regret meeting the composer of the latest and greatest opera face to face. He is going to Paris [with his wife] and will return from there around the time of our next carnival.[708] [...]

### 343. Zelter

Berlin, 1 to 2 July 1825

We have progressed with the building of our Sing-Akademie as far as the road surface and early yesterday morning at five o'clock I lay the foundation stone in the company of the chairman and sub-directors.[709]

---

[706] Fanny and Felix Mendelssohn.
[707] Spontini's *Alcidor*, a Zauberoper. The opera never travelled beyond Berlin.
[708] The following day Zelter wrote a letter of recommendation to Goethe for the composer.
[709] Johann *Wilhelm* Bornemann (1766–1851), director of the Prussian State Lottery, Privy Councillor Christian Philip Köhler (1778–1842) and theologian Georg *Carl* Benjamin Ritschl (1783–1876).

Thirty apprentices, five teaching staff and twenty-two servants formed a semi-circle from two foremen; the other half consisted of the architect Ottmer,[710] the bricklayers, the carpenters, the stonemasons and the managers. The foundation stone was in the centre. I stood in front of the foundation stone and the following was spoken by me:

> 'Should it be my duty, today, in this place, before this gathering, to speak for the spirit [of this enterprise], so may honour be given above all to God who has sustained the Academy and through the grace of our great King who has allocated it its own building in this royal town.
>
> So look down on us favourably, Lord, let our work be directed to your glory and to the satisfaction of those who shall sing praises to Your Holy Name. Let it not lack what is necessary. May the spirit of Your peace protect every industrious hand. May the name of the Lord be praised!'

The chord was pulled and the square was drawn which the stone shall cover. I had the apron put around me, I took up the trowel, dipped it in water, took and laid the first trowel of quicklime. The women of the committee did likewise, the chairmen the same, the master and the other members did the same. The two foremen raised the stone and placed it in position. The masters levelled it.

> 'As leading conductor of the Sing-Akademie, I grasp this hammer and consecrate the foundation stone in honour of our great master, Carl Fasch,
> in the name of the Father, ○ ○ ○
> the Son ○ ○ ○
> and the Holy Spirit, amen. ○ ○ ○

Long live the King![711] Long live Fasch, our founder![712] Long live the members of the Sing-Akademie, the providers, the protectors, the patrons! Long live the architect! Long live the masters, apprentices and servants and may every hand be blessed that works for the good here. Amen! Those present took the hammer one after the other and tapped the stone. The business was concluded.

The morning stillness with the rich green surroundings of the site[713] was not without a festive effect. The weather could not have been nicer and I am now hoping to lay the first beams in four weeks. The building contains a large hall 84-foot long, 41-foot wide and 30-foot high and a smaller one. Downstairs there is a really nice living space[714] and a vaulted cellar in the basement. There is still a lot to do

---

[710] Carl Theodor Ottmer (1800–43), the Sing-Akademie Architect.
[711] Friedrich Wilhelm III.
[712] Carl Fasch (1736–1800), founder of the Sing-Akademie.
[713] The construction site for the Sing-Akademie lay in the so-called chestnut woods between the Department of Finance and the University Gardens.
[714] Later, Zelter's official rooms.

and I will have to keep at it. Please stay alive that I may live and at least leave behind this memorial to my art.

Spontini was in such a hurry and wanted to leave after the performance of *Alcidor* last Tuesday. I now hear that he is still here. People here make too little of him and begrudge his success which, to tell the truth, is in jeopardy. I would not swap places with him for twice the money. [...]

I end by thanking you for your beautiful love-letter to my Felix.[715] Any good that comes to him, I enjoy tenfold. He is almost finished composing his fifth opera,[716] and I rejoice to see that it sparkles with real life and does not rest upon mannerisms. He seizes the age with both hands and carries it along with him.

### 344. Goethe

Weimar, 5 July 1825

[...] Spontini passed through [Weimar] very quickly.[717] By chance, I was not at home and yet I managed to speak to him for quarter of an hour. How well we get on together you may guess from the fact that we ended the conversation with an embrace and it was the best acknowledgment of your introduction.

### 345. Goethe

Weimar, 5 August 1825

[...] You will not mind if I take great delight that the Königstädter Theater has turned out so well. I wish the same with your music hall,[718] of which I am hoping to hear the best news. [...]

---

[715] Goethe's letter to Felix on 18 June 1825, in which he thanked him for the dedication of the Piano Quartet in B minor, op. 3.

[716] *Die Hochzeit des Camacho*, comic opera in two acts. The libretto is variously attributed to Baron Karl von Lichtenstein, Karl Klingemann, or the elder August Klingemann (R. Larry Todd, *Mendelssohn: A Life in Music* (Oxford: Oxford University Press, 2003), p. 168. Rudolf Elvers has argued convincingly that Friedrich Voigt's contributed to Act 1 and parts of Act 2 in *'Nichts ist so schwer gut zu componiren als Strophen': Zur Entstehungsgeschichte des Librettos von Felix Mendelssohns Oper 'Die Hochzeit des Camacho'* (Berlin and Basel: Veröffentlichung der Mendelssohn-Gesellschaft e.V. 1976).

[717] On his travels from Berlin to Paris, Spontini visited Goethe on 4 July 1825.

[718] The new building for the Sing-Akademie.

### 346. Zelter

Berlin, 6 August 1825

Our director of music and concert master, Moeser,[719] a first-rate violinist who alone knows know to conduct Spontini's operas and also handle my large musical works, wants to leave soon and meet my old Goethe. So let him meet you and be nice to him.[720] [...]

### 347. Zelter

Berlin, 25 to 27 August 1825

The enclosed poems[721] relate to a silver jubilee of the Sing-Akademie and Liedertafel, and since it is permitted on such occasions to turn [wearing] a silly face into a good deed, I am saying nothing other than that I am happy with everything, and, in fact, have been very surprised because I want to celebrate this day in my own way, as you will see from the accompanying speech, no. 1. [Speech] no. 2 was spoken a week after the festival.[722] [...]

The little song[723] enclosed has been lying around for many years. At that time it was intended as a kind of exercise which I intended to tackle on good days. I am looking through it again now and I recognize the risks for that time and today. [...]

---

[719] Carl Moeser, who had written to Zelter on 29 July 1825 requesting a letter of recommendation to Goethe.

[720] The meeting never took place.

[721] *Festgesänge zum 4ten August*, a 16-page booklet with festival poems for the celebration of Zelter's 25 years of service as Director of the Sing-Akademie. The texts were written by Spiker, Körner, Köhler, Förster, Bornemann, Tscherning and Lange, with (unpublished) compositions by Rungenhagen, Ritschl, Wollank, Zelter and Flemming. The booklet sent by Zelter is no longer in Goethe's library. A copy in the bequest of Karoline Schulze, a student of Zelter, is held in the Staatsbibliothek (SBB PK: Mus. Ms. Theor. 1540).

[722] A manuscript of four pages (in Doris Zelter's hand) with amendments and additions added by Zelter has been preserved.

[723] Zelter's setting of Goethe's poem 'Blumengruß', set to music by Zelter in 1810; the autograph copy entitled 'Der 28. August 1749. Wilkommen', dated Berlin 3 September 1810, is held in Berlin (SBB PK: Mus. Ms. Zelter 7). There are several copies of this song in Zelter's estate: an undated copy entitled 'Zum Geburtstage'; a further autograph copy, dated Berlin, Monday 3 September 1810, entitled 'Der 28. August 1749' and a further manuscript in SBB PK) 1811, published in Zelter's *Sämtliche Lieder, Balladen und Romanzen*, under the title 'Willkommen dem 28. August 1749', vol. 2, no. 3. A copy of 'Blumengruß' is not in Goethe's music collection.

### 348. Zelter

Berlin, 8 September 1825

[…] I remember well when I performed your poems and Schiller's for you that [you accompanied them] with gestures. You acted as if you had to portray what you felt, and what could you feel naturally if it were not the basis on which your own ideal could be reproduced?

Since this time I have never again tried to invent a new melody, but rather to seek out much more that which you unconsciously have in mind if you wanted a certain sentiment revealed. You would best be able to teach me about this in so far as there must be some things among my songs which you have not disowned.

So that the grass would not grow under my feet, I set the enclosed song to music for your birthday,[724] and the local friends of Weimar celebrated the Jubilee of your Grand Duke[725] very devotedly. This group had me so fired up that the strength of my enthusiasm drove me in the early evening to undertake a difficult walk to Charlottenburg, after which I hit my bed completely fatigued and achieved a good night's sleep.

### 349. Goethe

Weimar, 19 September 1825

[…] The newspapers had already given me good reports of your very creditable festival and I could profoundly relate to the poems forwarded by post. I have assimilated your good and well-intentioned words. Of the three enclosed poems, if you would like to see the middle poem[726] as referring to you personally and to dedicate it to your Liedertafel, to fortify the belief of all well-disposed [persons], I will be very grateful to you.

That you celebrated my birthday in such a friendly, festive way is also much appreciated. […]

---

[724] Zelter's enclosed setting of Friedrich Förster's poem 'Am 28sten August 1825', for solo voices and choir, is published in facsimile in *Gedichte und Briefe, Glückwünsche zum 28. August 1825* with the title page signed 'Förster and Zelter' (GSA 28/115, p. 405f). A further autograph copy, dated Berlin, 1 September 1825, presented by Liepmanssohn (in collaboration with Thomas Richter) is in the archival catalogue, no. 174.

[725] The fiftieth anniversary of the day on which Carl August took office on 3 September (his birthday).

[726] Zelter's setting of Goethe's poem 'Laßt fahren hin das allzu Flüchtige!'

## 350. Zelter

Berlin, 5 November 1825

[…] On his return from Paris,[727] the King arranged for a very nice present to be delivered to me for the Sing-Akademie (the latest mass by Cherubini)[728] which he had brought with him. Such a present from the King is doubly welcome, or even more, since during its growth the Sing-Akademie had to console itself in the face of many secret insinuations: it is unnecessary to promote music that everyone else already devours; second, German song is a nothing; third, we are clinging to the past and hindering progress; fourth, we are leaning towards Catholicism; five, it is a marriage bureau. There is truth in all of them. To examine only the last: over the years the Sing-Akademie has consisted of nothing but parents and children, married couples, siblings. They are all mixed in together and watch over one another. Then it is also a place of blissfully happy freedom. From princes down to tradesmen an equality undeniably exists, through which every talent can be exalted.

## 351. Zelter

Berlin, 5 to 8 November 1825

6 November. […] My Felix is making progress and working hard. He has just finished an octet for eight obbligato instruments; it is very solid.[729] Apart from that, a few weeks ago he gave his worthy tutor, Heyse, a nice birthday present, – namely a metrical translation of a comedy by Terence (*The Girl from Andros*)[730] which he made of his own accord. They say it contains really good verses; I have not seen it yet. He plays the piano like the devil and he is not behind with stringed instruments; besides this, he is healthy and strong and swims quite well upstream!

---

[727] Friedrich Wilhelm III's journey through Magdeburg, Braunschweig, Lippstadt, Cologne, Coblenz, Aachen, Brussels, reaching Paris on 23 September where he visited museums, churches and state buildings, before returning to Potsdam on 18 September.

[728] Mass in A major for three-part choir and orchestra (1825); an autograph copy is in the Staatsbibliothek, Berlin.

[729] Felix Mendelssohn, Octet in E flat major, op. 20.

[730] Felix Mendelssohn, *Das Mädchen von Andros, eine Komödie des Terentius, in den Versmaßen des Originals übersetzt von F\*\*\*\* Mendelssohn*, edited with an introduction by K.W.L. Heyse (Berlin, 1826). Goethe received the work in a letter from Felix Mendelssohn on 30 April 1826 and sent thanks through Zelter on 11 October 1826.

In the *Berliner Musikalische Zeitung* they have given his quartets and symphonies a rather cold reception[731] which cannot hurt him, for these reviewers are also young fellows, looking for the hat which they hold in their hands. If one did not remember how Gluck's and Mozart's compositions were criticized 40 years ago, one might despair. These gentlemen move hastily over things that would never have occurred to them, and would assess the value of the house by a single brick. And I must give him credit for this, that he invariably works from the whole to the whole, finishing everything that he has begun, let it turn out whatever way it will; this accounts for his showing no special affection for what is completed. To be sure, there is no lack of heterogeneous material that gets swept away by the stream, and ordinary faults and weaknesses are rare.

### 352. Zelter

Berlin, 26 November 1825

Early yesterday our Sing-Akademie [building] was adorned with the most beautiful garlands[732] [..] A procession of almost a hundred masons and carpenters had brought it out of my house through the pleasure garden, past the front of the King's palace,[733] to the place it was destined for. On its arrival the song 'Gott segne den König'[734] resounded and an edifying carpenter's sermon was given from the balcony. […]

### 353. Zelter

Berlin, 27 November to 3 December 1825

[…] Forkel[735] was Doctor of Philosophy and Doctor of Music at the same time. His whole life long he came into immediate contact neither with the one nor the other and had a bad ending. He began a history of music and stopped at the point where a history of music is possible for us.

---

[731] This journal, founded by A.B. Marx with Heinrich Dorn and the poet Rellstab (1824–30), assumed a leading role in the city's music journalism. For the review of Mendelssohn's Piano Quartet, op. 3; see the *Berliner Allgemeine Musikalische Zeitung*, 1825, no. 44, 2 November, pp. 353–5 and no. 45, 9 November, pp. 361–3.
[732] In other words, the shell of the building was complete to the roof ridge.
[733] Beside the Königliches Oper, Unter den Linden.
[734] Prussian hymn, composed by Bernhard Klein.
[735] Johann Nikolaus Forkel (1749–1818), musicologist, Bach scholar.

He was really furious about Gluck's success and wanted to suppress his operas.[736] He was no more ready to acknowledge Mozart and would not have been alone in this. Sebastian Bach was his hero, who nevertheless drove him to despair, in so far as he didn't know how to marry his strictness, his petulance, his artistic licence and impertinence with a greatness and depth which certainly is not to be denied. In the end he wrote Bach's life[737] with this purpose in mind, without knowing anything about it but what is known to the world anyway.

### 354. Zelter

Berlin, 8 to 10 December 1825

[…] At midday yesterday I had good, almost naughty, fun. In company to which I am honoured to belong, a conversation came up about a symphony by Felix which was disparaged in the *Spenersche Zeitung* on 4 November.[738]

My neighbour,[739] sitting close to my right, repeated with pleasure the words of the reviewer. He, too, attacked the presumption of the young composer in performing a complete (so called 'Great') symphony in four movements, which offered more to complain about than real enjoyment. After he had spoken, I answered to the contrary that the review had always used the word 'we' in its assessment, which I, however, would not wish extended to me because I did not want to be the ass that would see an industrious orderly work dismissed so contemptuously.

I had hardly said this than the face of my neighbour turned as red as beetroot enough to turn the tablecloth red; in short, it was the reviewer himself, because he assured us that the review, while it was not by him, he would have to confess etc.

In fright – and you will forgive me being a little shocked – I grabbed my bottle of wine and missing my glass, poured it into his. He raised it to his lips and called my wine a potent full-bodied drink.

---

[736] See Forkel's article, 'Über die Musik des Ritters Christoph von Gluck' in *Musikalisch-kritische Bibliothek*, vol. 1 (1778), pp. 53–210.

[737] Forkel, *Über Johann Sebastien Bachs Leben, Kunst und Kunstwerke* (Leipzig: Hoffmeister & Kühnel, 1802), reproduced with an introduction by Walther Vetter (Kassel: Bärenreiter-Verlag, 1968).

[738] In the aforementioned excerpt from the *Spenersche Zeitung* (no. 258) there is an anonymous review of a concert on 25 October. Included, among other things, is a critique of a symphony by Felix Mendelssohn, conducted by the composer: 'We would prefer not to hear the symphony by the latter again because it is a chaotic mass, in which, while we cannot deny a diligent schooling, at the same time the listeners have more to complain about than enjoy. We had to admire the composure of the orchestra, led by Herr Seidler, under the hasty direction of the young virtuoso'.

[739] Samuel Heinrich Spiker, first honorary member of the Berliner Künstlerverein.

The whole affair is not painful to me but also not relished because the man is intelligent, astute, and well intentioned towards me. He wrote the flattering Latin poem for my Jubilee,[740] which I may well have sent you.

And what should a reviewer do? Especially one who edits all of the scientific articles of a political daily newspaper? If he is to praise what is good, he must have time at his disposal which he doesn't have; so he gets out it of it by condemning what is not to his taste and takes money for it.

On the other hand, a musician is worse off than painters and writers. I know only too well what I had to suffer and overcame in my attempts to bring an orchestra together, even when paid to perform religious works. Then there is the audience and above all the non-paying guests who expect nothing at all and demand the unattainable. They do not grasp how one can be so presumptuous as to want to hold their attention. One has to fight for oneself and others.

After dinner our reviewer persuaded me to go with him to the theatre and to see a work which was still unknown to me, *Die Lästerschule* (if I am not mistaken, after Sheridan). [...] I found the work very unpleasant. One finds oneself among bad folk; the best of whom are worth nothing. In such a frame of mind I forgot myself and said to him I wished this piece were by Felix and Felix's symphony by this author. With this I turned around expecting an answer and found a complete stranger sitting beside me, who looked at me wide-eyed. This second surprise in one day made me cheerful again and virtue itself would not make me attend a performance of *Die Lästerschule*[741] again [...]

### 355. Zelter

Berlin, 16 December 1825

[...] Yesterday a new translation of *Macbeth* by our state librarian, Spiker, was performed at our theatre[742] [...] The special novelty was a new incidental overture, with the witches' choruses and dances. The composer, Conductor Spohr of Cassel,

---

[740] This poem has not been identified. The *Festgesänge zum 4ten August 1825* contains only a single Latin poem, 'Integer vitae, scelerisque purus', an ode by Horace, composed by Flemming. Spiker's occasional poem for 4 August 1825, 'Willkommen! Tönen unsere Lieder', and a further festival poem by him, 'Blüten einen sich zu Kränzen', were both written in German.

[741] Comedy, adopted by Johann Leonhardi from Richard Brinsley Sheridan's *The School for Scandal*; Zelter attended the performance on 7 December 1825 in the Königliches Schauspielhaus.

[742] Shakespeare's tragedy *Macbeth*, in German translation by Samuel Heinrich Spiker, first published by Duncker & Humblot in 1826, first performed in Berlin in the opera house on 15 December 1825, with incidental music by Louis Spohr.

is a clever man, and were it not too much of a good thing, everything would perhaps be better.

I have nothing to say against the idea, for if the orchestra is present, it may just as well play what is appropriate. But what is appropriate is another matter. [...]

The play is coarse stuff and requires an earthy style. That was missing, and so one rejoiced when the murderers went to work again.

## 356. Zelter

Berlin, 24 to 26 December 1825

Yesterday, Maria von Weber's latest Opera, *Euryanthe*, got its first favourable reception in our grand theatre.[743] In Vienna, Dresden and elsewhere, the work failed to impress;[744] there are numerous reasons for this. The libretto itself is not suitable. Count Brühl has staged the work very impressively as is fitting to a friend and producer and in a style suitable to historical Romantic opera. At the curtain call everybody was applauded. The composer first was obliged to show himself after the first act, and deserves every encouragement for his intense industry, made twice as difficult by his feeble health.

Afterwards there was plenty of feasting and celebration;[745] such things bring enormous satisfaction and ultimately reconciliation. Several of his friends carried the composer away with them, choruses of singers and horns followed, and the celebrations continued into the early hours of the morning. You need not be surprised that an old fellow like myself must always be at hand on these occasions, for I am not such a fool as to go into a corner with begrudgers or to be put out by anyone's success

---

[743] A three-act opera (libretto by Helmine von Chézy), premiered on 25 October 1823 in Vienna. Weber conducted the Berlin premiere on 23 December 1825, followed by a second performance shortly after.

[744] After the Viennese premiere the work was performed in Dresden, Prague and Frankfurt am Main in 1824. The reception by the general public was not euphoric, as it had been with *Der Freischütz*.

[745] After the performance Zelter presided at the table of honour for Weber.

# Section III
# Later Years' Correspondence 1826–1832

**357. Zelter**

Berlin, 4 to 10 January 1826

Someone wrote a new setting of your *Jery und Bätely* and as I hear, in great style. However, it is supposed to have run its course and now they are asking for Reichardt's setting once again.[1] The new composer edits the local music paper.[2] In this there was much talk about the weakness of Reichardt's work which was once acclaimed. […]

**358. Zelter**

Berlin, 25 to 29 January 1826

27 January: The little piece by Director Struve[3] informs and delights me, since it contains nothing which contradicts my melodic handling of both ballads. August Schlegel, who was in Berlin at that time[4] when I set both pieces to music,[5] and for whom I performed them often enough, was also in agreement. Likewise Tieck, who is hard to please musically, was particularly pleased by my melody to 'Die Braut von Korinth'.

---

[1] The new setting, by A.B. Marx, was performed on 7 May 1825 in the Königliches Opernhaus, *AMZ* 27 (1825), no. 24, 15 June, column 404: 'On 7 May the royal company of actors performed a one-act comic opera by Goethe in a new setting by Adolph Bernhard Marx (editor of the *Berliner Allgemeine Musikalische Zeitung*). This pleasant Singspiel, which Reichardt originally set to music, had been forgotten for years. The reappearance of this setting gave rise to hopes which were not fulfilled, however, and even up to now there has been no repeat performance of the operetta. The composer [A.B. Marx] had the idea of creating a grand opera out of the Singspiel. Therein lies the indisputable reason why his excellent opulent music, original in concept, did not make the same impression which it would have under different circumstances.'

[2] Marx had founded the *Berliner Allgemeine Musikalische Zeitung* in 1824 and was prominent as editor.

[3] Carl Ludwig Struve (1785–1838), Director of the Gymnasium in Königsberg.

[4] August Wilhelm Schlegel was in Berlin from 1801 to 1804.

[5] *Die Zauberlehrling* (1799) and *Die Braut von Corinth* (1797).

## 359. Goethe

Weimar, 18 March 1826

I shall wait quietly to see how the enclosed page, by which I set great store, will appear to the connoisseurs and other kindred spirits.[6] The experts in musical harmony will be sure to find something fugue-like in it,[7] where manifold complications move, separate, meet, and answer one another. This page was distributed with the *Stuttgarter Kunstblatt*[8] but, folded as it is, it cannot be fully appreciated there. Take care of it and think it over. [...]

## 360. Zelter

Berlin, End of March to 4 April 1826

I received your lovely consignment of 18th March on Good Friday when I had completed arrangements for my Passion Music[9] and was just about to bring it to performance.

The first comfort from your *Charon* was that our art of fugue is still living, and that what we build will not fall to ruins. Certainly, without your explanation I should have had to reflect a long time, in order to get a clear picture of the beautiful contrasts (counterpoint), the way that here what is most serious stands in delightful conflict with the most innocent love of life. So, too, the poetry into which you have woven it will be his delight as well as mine.

I had a similar experience with old Haydn. In reviewing his *Creation*, and particularly the overture which has the heading 'Chaos', I had remarked that such a theme was not suitable for art;[10] but that genius everywhere has surmounted

---

[6] Johann Aloys Mayer's lithograph (after Carl Leybold's) *Charon* to Goethe's poem. A reproduction is published in *MA* 20.3, p. 732.

[7] Goethe's allusion to the interwoven lines, which, in a transferred sense, is comparable to the vocal lines in polyphony, or more specifically to fugue. Goethe often used the word 'fugue' with reference to painting and considered Leonardo's *The Last Supper* to be the first painted fugue.

[8] The lithograph was published as a supplement in the *Kunstblatt*, no. 10/11, 6 February 1826.

[9] Annual performance of Carl Heinrich Graun's *Der Tod Jesu*, which Zelter conducted each year on Good Friday; for reviews of the performances; see *AMZ* 28 (1826) no. 16, 19 April, column 265.

[10] There are two reviews of Haydn's *Creation* in the *AMZ*: the first following a performance on 5 January 1801 in Berlin ('Letters to a friend about music in Berlin, Sixth letter, Berlin 8 January' *AMZ* 3 (1800/01), no. 17, 21 January 1801, columns 289–96); the second following the appearance of the score in Vienna (*AMZ* 4 (1801/02), no. 24,

impossibilities, and therefore did so here – giving my reasons for this statement. Old Haydn let me know that, with regard to this matter, he had not thought about it beforehand at all but that my analysis concurred with his own conception, which he was only now aware of, and that he saw himself obliged to acknowledge the images I had referred to.[11] Other critics had hopelessly condemned the musical paintings in the work, but now I was justified. [...]

4 April: We are expecting your gnome-like virtuoso[12] who will grate on our ears once again. I will gladly listen to him once more because he is the best of his kind, and as Wolf is given to saying, 'The shepherd is also the ox'.

## 361. Zelter

Berlin, 11 April to 14 May 1826

[...] However often I have read these letters already, I still read almost every page two or three times and the clearest view comes to me through stone and rock into the belly of the deepest past. I am examining the genuine originals before me and I recognize the difference between them and a reproduction. It is much the same for me: I hear a good piece of music and then look at the score. Very often I find a thick wall between the two, if not the impossibility that both things are the same. Even what supports education serves the decline of art. [...]

All good singers are either sick, getting sick or are travelling abroad. Madame Schröder has arrived again,[13] who will help a lot, even if she is as corpulent as she was, and [if] we had half-a-dozen [like her] we could walk in the loveliest shade [they provide]!

---

10 March 1802, column 391). Zelter's authorship of both reviews is confirmed in his letter to the editor, Friedrich Rochlitz, on 23 February 1802, *MA* 20.3, p. 734.

[11] Haydn wrote to Zelter on 25 February 1804: 'You are a deeply perceptive musician; the correct analysis of my *Chaos* proves that you would have done the same as Haydn; I am grateful to you for your interest', Joseph Haydn, *Gesammelte Briefe und Aufzeichnungen*, ed. and enlarged from the collection of source materials by H.C. Robbins Landon, by Dénes Bartha (Kassel, Basel, Paris, London, New York: Bärenreiter-Verlag, 1965), p. 436.

[12] Johann Nepomuk Hummel.

[13] Antoine *Luise* Sophie Schröder, née Bürger (1781–1868) had been advertised but her arrival was, in fact, postponed.

## 362. Goethe

Weimar, 20 May 1826

First of all, my best thanks for the score of that truly enthusiastic song.[14] It is now a full 30 years old, and dates from the time when a rich, youthful spirit still identified itself with the universe, in the belief that it could fill it out and even reproduce it in its various parts. That audacious drive has bequeathed to us a pure and lasting influence upon life, and however much we may have progressed in philosophical knowledge and poetic treatment, still it was important at that time, and, as I can see on a daily basis, it inspired and guided many. [...]

We, too, had a fleeting visit from Matthisson;[15] our disciples of the Muses gave him a warm reception, sang his poems, presented him with laurel wreaths, and did all this at a celebratory dinner, which went off appropriately and well. [...]

When one thinks how many distinguished men finally float about like drops of oil on water, and at most come in contact only at one point, one can understand how one was so often in life thrust back into solitude. However, the fact of our having lived so long near one another, as we did with Wolf,[16] may have shaped and benefitted our endeavors more than we know or are aware of. [...]

It is evident from all of this that I was busy with your old letters again. I want to see now that I can catch up with some things for you. [...]

If you would like to tell me something about Hummel's performance in your own way, in my present state you would give me [double joy].

## 363. Zelter

Berlin, 22 to 23 May 1826

Tuesday, 23 May: Hummel has given two profitable concerts,[17] although the time of his arrival was not the most favourable. In my judgement, he is the epitome of contemporary pianoforte playing, for he combines what is genuine and new with feeling and virtuosity. One forgets fingers and keys, one hears the music;

---

[14] Zelter's setting of Goethe's poem 'Weltseele'.

[15] Friedrich von Matthisson (1761–1831), writer, theatre manager and librarian in Stuttgart from 1812, visted Weimar at the end of March.

[16] F.A. Wolf, who was in regular contact with Goethe from 1795 on the question of ancient literature.

[17] Hummel gave two concerts on 24 April and 4 May in the concert hall of the Königliches Schauspielhaus, in which his Concerto in E major, his Rondo brillant (op. 98) among other works, were very favourably received; *AMZ* 28 (1826), no. 19, 10 May, column 318f; see also no. 24, 14 June, column 392; *MA* 20.3, p. 741.

everything sounds as secure and easy as it is difficult. A pot made of the worst clay, filled with Pandora's treasures.

The Liedertafel takes place today and you will be remembered there. Count Sierakowski, whom Prince Radziwill of Posen recommended to me, is my guest.[18] My building progresses slowly and I have to drive myself mad with it, otherwise nothing at all would happen. I thought I would be out of here and Satan leads me back again. Soon I will have to take up residence, leave the lovely nest I have now and move again to a completely new house. The gods will decide what is to become of me.

### 364. Zelter

Berlin, 25 May to 27 May 1826

When he was ten years old, my Felix discovered with his lynx eyes, in the score of a splendid concerto by Sebastian Bach,[19] six pure consecutive fifths, which I doubt I should ever have found, as in the larger works I pay no heed to such things, and this passage is scored in six parts. But the handwriting on the manuscript is beautiful and clear, and the passage occurs twice. Now, is it an oversight or a licence? Either the composer has altered one part and forgotten to erase the other, or an accident, as I myself have experienced, could be the reason. I once maintained, when we were having a debate about harmony, that I could let them hear half a dozen pure fifths, one after the other, and they would never find it out, and I proved my point. It may have been so with old Bach, the purest, the finest, the most daring of all artists, *quo nihil sol majus optet*.[20] [...]

The enthusiastic song, as you yourself call it,[21] I myself don't know how to call it anything else other than: 'Aus der Luft' (Out of the Air). I read it, how often, and only certain durations of notes – spheres, planets and things of that nature – occurred to me as definite sounds, with which I had to do all the rest. And now, when you provide me with information, I am none the wiser, since you too have been driven to exhuberant expression by an infinite, indefinable idea. I have been asked about it more than once and I replied: it is my wedding song.

---

[18] As was customary every two months, guests could be invited to the Liedertafel; Zelter had originally planned to invite Charles and Selina Bracebridge on this occasion.

[19] Brandenburg Concerto no. 5; see Albert Schweitzer, *J.S.Bach* (Leipzig: Breitkopf & Härtel, 1908), p. 378; *Johann Sebastian Bach. Neue Ausgabe sämtliche Werke*, ed. Johann-Sebastian-Bach-Institut Göttingen and the Bach-Archiv Leipzig (Kassel, Bärenreiter, 1956), Kritischer Bericht, p. 111; Alfred Dürr, *Bach-Jahrbuch* 61 (1975): 65.

[20] Latin words in imitation of Horace's *Carmen saeculare*, v. 9–12: 'the sun may never choose [to shine on] anything greater'.

[21] Zelter's setting of Goethe's poem 'Weltseele'.

I have written to you about Hummel. For me he is more than a virtuoso, much more. I gladly listen to him improvising in spite of the presumption that he could wrest a fantasy from himself before a gaping crowd. And yet he manages to bring it off, although his facade plays a role with its rather abnormal sound figures. His playing has what one can hardly call expression, that is, free from affectation and inhibition. Whoever really understands would have to admire how innocently the most amazing things come to light.

The local music papers don't do justice to his playing.[22] They are all young, lively fellows, dilettantes, and their editor, a certain Marcus or Marx from Halle,[23] may have been baptized with gall, for his excrement has a grey-green-yellow colour.[24] They are like flies: they shit what tastes good to them. [...]

Enclosed: Zelter's essay on Haydn: Performance of *The Creation* on Joseph Haydn's birthday, 31 March 1826.[25]

### 365. Goethe

Weimar, 3 June 1826

[...] In the next few days our correspondence will be before me, neatly transcribed, bound in several volumes.[26] You should undertake a pilgrimage once in order to

---

[22] See, for example, 'Über das Konzert des Herrn Kapellmeister Hummel', *Berliner Allgemeine Musikalische Zeitung* 18 (1826), 3 May, p. 141. The review, signed '4', in which Hummel's reputation 'as a pianist equally outstanding in solid performance and admirable skill' was fully recognized, limited itself explicitly 'to an analysis of what the concert pianist offered the general public as composer', in particular Hummel's piano concerto in E major. The promised discussion of this work hardly goes further than the admission of the reviewer that 'it would always be difficult to judge a musical piece after one hearing'.

[23] Adolph Bernhard Marx (?1795–1866), music theorist, composer and editor.

[24] Zelter's anger, which Todd describes as Zelter's 'anti-Semitic spleen' (R. Larry Todd, *Mendelssohn: A Life in Music* (Oxford: Oxford University Press, 2003), p. 128), was ignited by Marx's public criticism of Zelter's early music performances. Marx rebuked Zelter for performing irrelevant eighteenth century repertoire, failing to add 'modern' wind instruments to Handel's orchestral scores, choosing improper tempos and altering composer's scores (e.g. smoothing out expressive leaps in Graun's recitatives).

[25] GSA, 25/XXXVIII, 1, 52a; *MA* 20.3, pp. 743–5.

[26] Goethe announces here the conclusion – for the time being – of a project begun in early May: namely the copy made by John of the correspondence between Goethe and Zelter up to and including 1825. Bringing together the letters and copying the correspondence was originally intended to jog Goethe's memory for his work on the *Tag- und Jahres Hefte*. The decision to publish the letters is not yet evident from Goethe's words, though his intention to ponder 'what might be done with it in the future' suggests that he had further plans for the correspondence.

pay due homage to such a work. I will go through it carefully in quiet evenings and see how it would best hold up in the future. It is a strange document, with real substance and baroque-like character.[27] Its like would hardly be found again. [...]

If, my dearest Zelter, you were to give me permission to score out your hymn for Mozart's birthday,[28] I would make an attempt at it as far as it is possible for me. We could come to some agreement about the employment. [...]

### 366. Zelter

Berlin, 6 to 10 June 1826

[...] The permission needed to score the hymn to Mozart's birthday is no less problematic to me. In case the little manuscript sent about Haydn is what what you meant, you have complete freedom with it, of course, since I have not committed it elsewhere. [...]

Old Madame Mara has written again from Reval[29] and recommends to me a student,[30] whom I have neither seen nor heard. She writes like a man, like a clever woman, and it is a joy to read her hand.

Felix has again finished another quintet[31] that we are soon to hear. I do everything I can to encourage him, as he drives himself on to experiment in the various new and more conventional forms. What really pleases me is that his music is really well paid by the publishers. In addition to this, he is very cheerful, and is very skilled at gymnastics, riding and swimming; I prefer to advise him not to fence because he really plays well. [...]

When you ask me to grant permission to knock my writing into shape, it weighs heavily on my conscience how I have sometimes dealt with your poems without asking you.

In order to admit my offence and to beg for absolution, I enclose a little experiment.[32] The piece is from the early stages of our Liedertafel, which will

---

[27] Perhaps Goethe is thinking of the polyhistoric diversity, lack of homogeneity of the themes and areas touched upon.

[28] Despite the erroneous title, Goethe is referring to Zelter's essay on Haydn's Creation. By the musical metaphor 'to score out your hymn', Goethe means the proofreading which Zelter had requested as well as his own editorial work.

[29] A letter of recommendation from the singer Gertrud Elizabeth Mara for one of her students, who, on an immanent journey to Berlin, 'wanted to meet the founder of the world-famous Sing-Akademie, GMD (1958), p. 31, no. 10.

[30] Frau von Baer.

[31] String Quintet no. 1 in A major, op. 18, first movement. The second movement was composed in 1832.

[32] Among the Goethe settings in *Gesänge der Liedertafel* (Berlin 1811), vol. 1, are some in which text alterations were made: in 'Generalbeichte', 3 strophe, v. 5–6: 'Manche

soon begin its twenty-first year.[33] If I had not kept after them, the thing would have turned into simple feasting. Now the other [Liedertafel] are there and if they do not collaborate, then each [society] suits itself; in short, it survives. Then it is also important with such songs to keep the plenary meeting light and cheerful. When one person sings solo for too long, the others cannot keep quiet and misbehave. Many a Liedertafel dies away over the Leipzig fair offerings because poet and composer don't have the real objective before their eyes.

### 367. Zelter

Berlin, 11 to 24 June 1826

I gave young Bohn,[34] lately married to one of Seebeck's daughters,[35] a short letter to the good Ernestine[36] and a little song, which Felix's sister has set very nicely to music.[37] It is a poem by Voß[38] on the death of our friend Schulz,[39] and I set it to music for him when I was in Heidelberg.[40] By chance Fanny happens to have set it

---

rasche Schäferstunde,/ Flücht'gen Kuß von lieben Munde' (G) to 'Manche rasche gute Stunde,/ Manches Lied vom lieben Munde' (Z); some slight alterations in 'Ergo bibamus!'; in *Ephiphaniasfest* Zelter repeats the final verses as a refrain but with alterations for the Liedertafel, for example in strophe 5, verses 4 and 5 are altered from: 'Ich esse gern, ich trinke gern,/ Ich esse, trinke und bedanke mich gern' (G) to 'So, so, Herr Gern, auch Sie Herr Gern./ Sie essen, trinken, und bedanken sich gern.' (Z); finally an alteration in verse 2 of 'Vers memorials' from '*Reminiscere* O wäre ich Braut' (G) to '*Reminiscere* mir juckt die Haut!' Which of the texts Zelter sent as an 'experiment' could not be determined; Goethe had received all of these compositions at an earlier stage, from which two copies are in his music collection.

[33] The constituent assembly of Zelter's Liedertafel was on 21 December 1808 (though the first rehearsal took place on 24 January 1809); the twentieth anniversary, beginning the fifth cycle of five years [the fifth lustrum], would begin in 1828.

[34] Friedrich Bohn (1775–1872), son of Sophia Bohn née Wesselhöft (sister of Johanna Frommann née Wesselhöft).

[35] Marie Therese Henriette Johanne *Rosalie* Bohn née Seebeck (1798–1888).

[36] Zelter's letter to Ernestine Voß has not been handed down.

[37] Fanny Mendelssohn, 'Begräbnislied', composed on 6 May 1826, WoO 26, 5; the manuscript is held in Berlin (SBB PK, Mendelssohn Archiv, MS 35, pp. 46–8).

[38] Johann Heinrich Voß, 'Begräbnislied' ('Ruhe sanft bestattet'), 1800, published in Voß's *Sämtliche Gedichte* (Königsberg: Nicolovius, 1802).

[39] Johann Abraham Peter Schulz (1747–1800), composer.

[40] Zelter was in Heidelberg from 19 to 26 August 1816; he sent the composition to the Voß family on 30 August. Zelter's diary entry of 1 September states: 'Wrote to Voß in Heidelberg on 30 August and sent him the lament for Schulz's death', Schottländer, *Carl Friedrich Zelters Darstellungen seines Lebens*, p. 275.

too and as she has captured the spirit of it better than I have, I have sent it to Voß's widow,[41] as it is equally applicable to his death[42] [...]

Our theatres limp along on all fours. It is summer. True the [financial] embarrassment affects the management, which must impose itself through money and becomes contemptible as soon as this energy is missing. So cliques and even artistic sects are forming. Opera and Schauspiel are quoted within the four walls of family societies and the artists take part in it themselves in order to forget their troublesome boards.

Just the day before yesterday people would have it that Carl Maria von Weber had died in London:[43] like Achilles at the height of his glory; but as the news is not confirmed, it is only believable because of his frail condition. Owing to his congenial manner, he has won widespread popularity and, considering the extent of his talent, he has certainly worked hard enough; all his works reveal strenuous effort and he had severe illnesses to fight against [...]

## 368. Zelter

Berlin, 26 July to 1 August 1826

28 July: Enclosed here is your little song,[44] which has been notated easily enough. Two tenors and a bass play their part and the women can also sing along in the *tutti* section.

The *Swarto*[45] has already been transcribed[46] and needs to be put aside a while in order to mature. [...]

---

[41] Marie Christiane Henriette *Ernestine* Voß née Boie (1756–1834).

[42] Voß died on 29 March 1826 in Heidelberg.

[43] Carl Maria von Weber died in London on 5 June 1826.

[44] Zelter's setting of Goethe's 'Wanderlied' ('Von dem Berge zu den Hügeln'). Three strophes, which are divided up differently, had already appeared in *Wilhelm Meisters Wanderjahre*. The second strophe from this early version is missing from Zelter's compositional text, where verse 3 replaces verse 2 and a new third strophe is added, which Zelter appears to have received especially for Goethe's birthday during his stay in Weimar on 8 July 1826. Goethe wrote in his diary on 8 July 1826: 'I adapted [my] "Wanderlied" for August' (*WA* III/10, p. 214) and the new version was published in an article, 'Zusammenfeier des Geburtsfestes von Hegel und Goethe' in the *Vossische Zeitung*, 203, 31 August 1826. Zelter read out this article at the joint festivities for friends and former students on 27/28 August; his manuscript setting is in Goethe's music collection (GSA 32/7), dated B. 25 July 1826.

[45] Goethe's translation of Swarto's monologue ('Vom Franken ein Gesandter!') from Manzoni's tragedy.

[46] Zelter mentions his setting again on 2 to 3 February 1827, but he never signed off on it and never sent it to Weimar.

Since sheet music still has its place, a [single] key canon will be put to regular use.[47] The artistry consists in the way each of the four voices starts from the same note of the scale and every voice sings from its own clef. The canon is very strict in the first five bars and the arrangement will be repeated three, four or five times, whereupon the piece comes to an end. [...]

Minister von Humboldt sends his warm greetings. He enquired after your well-being yesterday and we spoke a lot about you. He, too, has begun to read Schiller's correspondence[48] [...] and considers [it] a welcome gift to the world since the genesis of [Schiller's] best works become clear in it and how his development was dependent on you. It is certain that since Schiller's ascension to a higher sphere, the desire to understand your works has increased constantly. With Schiller everything works from without to within; with you everything comes from within to without; people want to understand what they feel. This gives rise to deductions which are Schiller's forte and this turns our minds in the same direction.

I notice that it is the same in music. It is only since Mozart that there has arisen a greater inclination to understand Sebastian Bach, for the latter appears thoroughly mystic, where the former impresses us clearly from without and there is a lighter air about him, seeing that he is inspired by life around him. I myself felt no pure pleasure in Mozart's works because I had known Bach much earlier. Compared with him, Mozart seemed like the Flemish painters are to Italian and Greek artists, and it is only since I gradually began to gain more clarity on these points that I esteem both at the highest value, without demanding of one what the other achieves. The mystical must and will remain what it is, otherwise it would not be mystical; I can sleep quietly on that, while the whole throng is after me, screaming for a verbal explanation while it stumbles over the sense.

Mozart stands much nearer to Sebastian Bach than Emanuel Bach and Haydn, who, both original, stand between the first two. *Don Juan* and *Die Zauberflöte* show plainly enough that Mozart had something mystical within him, and that he is all the more sure of an easy effect, the more he works from without to within, where it is still bright and only becomes dark very gradually.

1 August: Tell me something about Madame Sontag.[49] She will be here tomorrow because she has to sing on 3 [August].

---

[47] Canon on the toast 'Dieses Glas dem guten Geist' on the same manscript as 'Wanderlied' (GSA 32/7). Zelter explains the title 'key-canon' in the following passage.

[48] From the beginning Wilhelm von Humboldt was in on Goethe's plans to publish his correspondence with Schiller (see Goethe's diary 13 and 14 November 1823) and often acted as mediator and advisor between Goethe and Schiller's heirs. A public report of the planned publication was still not circulated; the contract with the publisher, Cotta, was drawn up in September 1826 and certified the following December.

[49] Gertrud Walpurgis *Henriette* Sontag (1806–54), German soprano, who had made her debút at the Berlin Königstädter Theater as Isabella (*L'italiana in Algeri*) on 3 August 1825.

### 369. Goethe

Weimar, 5 August 1826

You dear musical hieroglyphs[50] shall soon dissolve into music for my ears and I will certainly be delighted and refreshed by it. [...]

### 370. Goethe

Weimar, 8 August 1826

When I surveyed the catalogue of your multiple settings from the *Divan*,[51] it occurred to me in general that we treat the good and the noble which we encounter every day far too carelessly and let go of it as easily as the usual commonplace [things]. I regretted that so many lovely compositions by you had passed through my hands without my knowing where they went. My discontentment was assuaged as I opened the music cabinet and discovered it like an old archive: unused but unspoilt.

The catalogue,[52] which I made immediately, is enclosed here for which an additional song or two might perhaps turn up. See what else you can comfortably pass on to me. Some settings have already been given to Eberwein.[53] He wants to have them performed for me by the choristers and seminarians. [...]

I have heard nothing further of Madame Sontag other than what is common knowledge: that she concluded with *Die heimliche Heirat* to great applause.[54] Developments next time.

---

[50] The compositions sent with Zelter's last letter: Goethe's 'Wanderlied' and accompanying canon. By solving the musical hieroglyph, Goethe means the performance of Zelter's musical text. The day before he wrote to Zelter, Goethe had given 'some Zelter compositions' to Eberwein, director of his house choir; see Goethe's diary 4 August 1826, (*WA* III/ 10, pp. 225–6).

[51] Assembled in Goethe's diary on 7 August 1826, *WA* III/10, p. 227.

[52] A catalogue of Zelter's compositions to poems from Goethe's *West-östlicher Divan* is neither preserved in the version sent to Zelter nor in the copy retained by Goethe. In Goethe's music collection a copy *Zeltersche Kompositionen Goethescher Gedichte* in Kräuter's hand (GSA 32/1509) includes settings of poems not included in the *Divan* and also copies of settings which were sent to Goethe after August 1826, for example 'Kriegsglück'.

[53] In his role as director of Goethe's house concerts.

[54] See, for example, *Spenersche Zeitung*, no. 177, 1 August 1826.

## 371. Goethe

Weimar, 12 August 1826

[…] Your nightingale is still fluttering around. They say she has gone to the sea[55] and will come to us at the end of next month at the earliest, since we too are hoping to admire her. […]

On taking up Streckfuß's translation of Dante a few days ago, I admired the ease with which it moved within the given metre, and when I compared it to the original and tried to make some of the passages clearer and more flowing in my own way, I soon found out that this had already been achieved and that nothing would come of tinkering with the work. Meantime it gave rise to a little poem[56] which I wrote in the accompanying book.

Let Streckfuß keep Manzoni's tragedy *Adelchi* as a remembrance from me. If he doesn't know it already, he will be pleased with it. If he feels inclined to translate it, he would render a service to German iambics as well as to the trimeter if he would in a similar way follow the Italian style of writing, which would be all the easier as the rhyme does not hinder him. What I think about this is clearly seen from the monologue of Swarto and it would in any case be immediately apparent to such a clear-sighted man. The whole tragedy may be resolved into recitative. I am anxious to have your composition.[57]

---

[55] It had been reported that her health had suffered from sheer exhaustion and she had gone to recover at a seaside resort: *Spenersche Zeitung*, 11 August 1826.

[56] The verse, 'Von Gott dem Vater stammt Natur', written as a dedication for Streckfuß in a copy of Manzoni's *Adelchi*.

[57] Setting of Swarto's verses. Directly after his return from Weimar (where he had received the text from Goethe) Zelter recorded on 26 July 1826 that the composition was 'already written down'. Even after a reminder from Goethe, Zelter never signed off on the setting. Whether Goethe ever received this composition is, at least, in question. There is a volume in his music collection entitled *Gesänge verschiedener Meister. Ottilie von Goethe* (GSA 32/168), which contains a setting of Swarto's verses but in another hand and without any details. Goethe's Italian diary on 4 November 1825, which records that he discussed the monologue with Eberwein, suggests Eberwein as the likely composer.

## 372. Zelter

Berlin, 10 to 19 August 1826

[…] You have added fine improvements to our Haydn,[58] for which I send the best of thanks. I didn't name the Handel [work] as I would have had to name many pieces, because the same applies to Hasse, Graun, Mozart, Gluck, Mayer and others.

Of Mademoiselle Sontag we know as much as you. She still hasn't come back and the supreme court misses the old wigged gentlemen who have run to Paris with her because court cases are held up.

11 August: Your dear letter of 8 August has just arrived and I will set about copying a new piece[59] for you immediately. It is far too serious, even curt, although good work. It is designed for a church[60] during a long anniversary sermon at which I had to function without understanding a word. Then I thought of the poem[61] and it was thought out very quickly. See how you get on with it. […]

19 August: This page should have arrived with you last week if the music transcriber had not taken so long over the musical score.[62] Keep in touch because I have a long list of questions. Yesterday afternoon my former students,[63] all of them now music directors, drove me by coach to Stralow, where they organized an enjoyable evening for themselves and me. They are able to do that because they are with me very often. One such occasion is a seminar at which they discover things with all kinds of merriment, for which they search in vain in the textbooks and I learn the most in the process.

---

[58] Zelter's essay on Haydn was edited by Goethe and published in Goethe, *Über Kunst und Altertum*, vol. 1 (Stuttgart, 1812–32; reprint Bern, 1970), v 3 (hereafter referred to as *KuA*). A new copy dating from the time this letter was written has still not been found. However, Zelter received an advance copy on 5 August.

[59] Zelter's setting of Goethe's 'Zwischengesang'. There is a part-song (for four solo voices and four-part choir) based on this poem in Goethe's music collection (GSA 32/95), with the parts written in a different hand, for which the authorship can be validly accepted as Zelter, as Goethe wrote to Zelter on 26 August 1826 'the score which I received thankfully is being written out'. Johann Nepomuk Hummel was asked by Goethe for a setting of the song on 3 September 1825 and so he, too, would be considered a possible author; however, his setting (published in *SchGG* 31, p. 149) is not identical with the one named.

[60] Zelter mentions this context again years later in a letter to Ottilie von Goethe on 11 April 1832, in which he thanks her for using his setting, 'Laßt fahren hin', at Goethe's funeral, *SchGG* 28, p. 28.

[61] 'Zwischengesang', from the poetic trilogy *Zur Logenfeier des dritten Septembers 1825*, sent to Zelter on 19 September 1825.

[62] Zelter's setting of Goethe's 'Zwischengesang'.

[63] The identity of the student has not yet been established.

### 373. Goethe

Weimar, 26 August 1826

With Riemer I am reading through the correspondence,[64] which we find informative and entertaining. I still have not found a single word which one should take back. On the contrary, we sound very charming in our limited day-to-day discourse.

The score, which I received thankfully, is being written out;[65] when the holidays are over, when the songbirds have all flown, I can surely expect to receive this and other dear works by you.


### 374. Zelter

Berlin, 30 August to 2 September 1826

A song which for a long time wasn't to the taste of our Tafel members, because they can't take a good joke, is starting to find favour now.[66] I don't see it in your catalogue and so I enclose it here.

It makes itself a clear favourite: light, cheerful, playful the way they sing it at the second Liedertafel.[67] All the drummers play the drums like tambourines and end suddenly together, which has a delightful effect.

On your birthday, which fell on an academy day,[68] we first sang your poem 'Laßt fahren hin das Allzuflüchtige', three times, one after the other – the third time it went exquisitely – followed by Handel's *Te Deum*.[69] Since they all knew what was meant (there were about two hundred singing), they roused themselves and it wouldn't surprise me if you had heard it!

The *Te Deum* contains passages which could move a child in its mother's womb. The 'Omnis terra veneratur'; the 'Sanctus'; the 'Te ergo quaesumus'; the 'Te patrem immensae Majestatis' – one could say the heavens opened up so

---

[64] The complete copy of the Goethe–Zelter letters up to 1826.

[65] Namely, the individual choral parts for Zelter's setting of Goethe's 'Zwischengesang' are being transcribed from Zelter's score.

[66] Zelter's setting of Goethe's 'Kriegsglück' ('Verwünschter weiß ich nichts im Krieg'); an undated autograph copy (with the text in another hand) is contained in Goethe's music collection (GSA 32/27) for solo voices and choir. Goethe's poem was written in February 1814 and published the following year.

[67] The Liedertafel founded by Ludwig Berger and Bernhard Klein in 1819.

[68] 28 August 1826 fell on a Monday, the traditional *Akademietag*, yet the celebration took place on the Tuesday. Either Zelter changed this or he meant the rehearsal on the Monday, at which all singers were not present, however.

[69] Handel, *Te Deum*, HWV 283, written for the victory of Dettingen, was one of the most frequently performed pieces in the repertoire of the Sing-Akademie.

that you could see the world of holiness and adoration with your own eyes. And it's clear that the musician in particular doesn't produce something genuine that doesn't dwell within him as image; at the same time Chladni's sound figures really occur to me everytime. [...]

2 September: Last Sunday I was called to a special conference in the consistory. A spiritual counsellor gave the lecture:

1. The churches shall have choirs again.
2. Whether the still existing choirs can be used for this? And if they are not suitable because not good enough or morally unfit, then
3. How to abolish them and replace them with completely new ones?

The matter was discussed backwards and forwards at great length, so that the first point was completely overshadowed. I myself could hardly get a word in. The city councillor doesn't want to contribute to it and he may be right. He advocates closure. From my early years I am used to building; let him who can and will tear down and throw away.

### 375. Goethe

Weimar, 6 to 9 September 1826

The table of the Theory of Sound,[70] which is the result of many years' study, was written, as you may remember, somewhere around 1810, after discussion with you. It was not my intention to meet the demands of a discourse upon physics in any way,[71] but to make the scope and substance of the subject clear to myself, and to point them out to others. I was undertaking to give an outline of all the various branches of physics in this way. I found this table when clearing out the music cupboard; I had not quite forgotten it, but did not know where to look for it. I do not know whether I have ever shown it to you. In the same way I have also lost several essays, which some chance occurrence may obligingly deliver into my hands again. [...]

---

[70] Goethe's *Tonlehre* was sketched when he concluded his *Farbenlehre*. The attempt to carry reflections on his theory of colour into the area of acoustics was the result of conversations between Goethe and Zelter in Carlsbad in 1810. See Goethe's draft letter to Sartorius on 19 July 1810, *WA* IV/21, pp. 251–4. At Goethe's request Zelter returned the table on 10 July 1827. Whether the copy sent between Weimar and Berlin is the same as the copy in Goethe's bequest (GSA 26/LIX 14, I) cannot be ascertained.

[71] The corresponding report is not extant. A similar attempt found in Goethe's bequest is the sketch *In Sachen Physik contra Physik*; an engagement with physics is also mentioned in Goethe's *Tag- und Jahres-Hefte* of 1810, *MA* 14, p. 216.

The composition of the little song really delighted me.[72] Even here no one wanted to see the joke. The dear women of the society found it all too close to home and had to make admissions that annoyed them. The patriotic veil[73] served to cover up much; one slipped in behind it in the usual way – as happens in lover's intrigues.

That Mademoiselle Sontag has passed through here with her wealth of sounds and tones was certainly a unique event. Everyone says, of course, that one should hear such singers regularly and the majority would like to go to the Königstädter Theater again today. So would I. For in reality, first of all one ought to think of her and understand her as an individual, to know her in a contemporary context, to assimilate and accustom oneself to her; then she would remain a lovely pleasure. When heard in an impromptu performance, her talent confused rather than delighted me. The good that passes by without returning leaves behind it an impression that may be compared to a void and is felt like a deficiency.

Enclosure 3: Goethe's Table: Theory of Sound

**The Science of Music**

Develops the laws of the audible. This arises from the vibrations of bodies, and for us more particularly from the vibration of the air.

In the broad sense the audible is infinite. But from this we set aside: noise, sound and speech.

There remains that with which we have immediately to do, the musically audible (musical sound).

This comes from the purity of material and the measure of the body that vibrates or causes vibrations.

To come to this measure, let us first take the sounding body as a whole.

---

[72] Zelter's setting of Goethe's 'Kriegsglück'.

[73] Goethe's poem is a light-hearted satire on war experiences in 1806 and 1813. Eckermann reports a conversation which took place over dinner in Goethe's house during Zelter's visit to Weimar on 4 December 1823: 'Goethe's social song, 'Kriegsglück', was then cheerfully discussed. Zelter was inexhaustible in his anecdotes of wounded soldiers and beautiful women and they all tended to show the truthfulness of the poem. Goethe himself admitted that he had no need to go far for such realities; he had witnessed them all in Weimar. Frau von Goethe maintained a lively opposition saying that she would not admit women were so bad as that "nasty" poem represented them to be.'

The definite sound given by the whole of itself is called the 'basic sound'.

The whole, diminished, gives a higher note, enlarged, a lower note.

We may diminish the whole gradually and continuously. This produces no proportional parts.

We can divide the whole; this gives proportions.

The chief proportional parts are at some distance from each other (chords).

The space between these is filled by intermediate relationships, resulting in a kind of gradual progression (scale).

By these steps the basic sound proceeds upwards and downwards, until it finds itself again (octave).

More than this is not necessary at the beginning. The rest must be developed, modified and explained by performance. The theory is founded on the whole experience, and is presented in three sections. The musically audible appears to us: (1) Organically (subjectively); (2) Mechanically (partly subjectively, partly objectively); and (3) Mathematically (objectively). All three are ultimately united: naturally by the power of the musician, and in a more complex manner by scientific demonstration.

## I Organic (Subjective) [Music]

As the world of sound is revealed out of and through mankind, it appears in the voice, is received again by the ear, exciting the whole body to respond, and providing a mental and moral inspiration, and a development of the inner and outer senses.

### Science of Singing

Song is perfectly productive in itself. The natural gift of the outer sense and the genius of the inner spirit are absolutely required.

### The Chest Voice

The voices, varying in height and depth, are as follows, from the lowest to the highest: bass, tenor, alto and treble. Each is to be considered complete. Each comprises over an octave. They overlap one another, and together make up about three octaves. They are divided between the two sexes. Hence the significance of puberty and subsequent change of voice that can be prevented by castration.

*Register*

That means the limit of the chest voice.

*The Head Voice*

Transition into the mechanical. Union of both voices. Detailed explanation of the organization of chest and throat. Adding in the voices of animals, especially of birds.

*Acoustics*

Receptiveness of the ear. Its apparent passivity and indifference (adiaphoria). Compared to [vision], hearing is a less-perceptive sense – only part of a sense. Yet we must ascribe to the ear, as to something highly organized, both reaction and demand, whereby that sense is by itself capable of taking up and grasping that which is presented to it from without. But in the case of the ear, special attention has always to be given to the medium of the sound, which actively produces the effect. The productivity of the voice is thereby generated, aroused, elevated and multiplied. The whole body is stimulated.

*Rhythm*

The whole body is incited to move in step (march), or in skips (dance and gesture).

All organic movements are manifested by means of systole and diastole.

It is one thing to lift the foot, another to put it down.

Hence arise rhythmic weight and counterpoise.

Arsis, the upbeat.

Thesis, the downbeat.

Kinds of time: even, and uneven. These movements can be considered alone; but soon they are necessarily combined with modulation.

## II Mechancial [Music] (Mixed)

Tones produced by various means, in accordance with musical laws.

*Instruments*

*Material.* Its tone quality, purity and elasticity.

*Form.* Natural, organic and artificial, metal, wood, glass. Reeds, length and area.

*Method of exciting vibrations.* Stroking. Blowing. Horizontally or vertically.

*Striking.* Relation to mathematics. The instruments result from knowledge of the proportions of measure and number, and increase this knowledge by means of multiplicity.

Discovery of natural relations of tones other than those shown by the monochord. Relation to the human voice. These are a substitute for that, and inferior to it, but are raised on a level with it, by treatment that is expressive and spiritual.

## III Mathematical [Music] (Objective)

How the elements of music are revealed in the simplest bodies outside us and are reduced to relationships of number and measure.

*The Monochord*

Sounding together of the harmonic tones. Different ways of describing how it happens. Sympathetic vibrations. Mechanical vibrations. Organic demand for and subjective excitement of complementary sounds.

Objective converse proof through sympathetic vibrations of strings in tune with one another.

Foundation of the simplest tone proportions. Diatonic scales. The demands of nature [are] not to be satisfied in this way. Practical exemplifications [are] not to be accounted for or shown in this way.

Reference to the minor mode. It does not originate in the first series of harmonic tones. It is manifested by means of less obvious relationships of number and measure, and yet is perfectly suited to the nature of mankind, even more perfectly than the major mode.

Objective proof through the sound of tuned strings, which is discovered by practical experiment. (Thus the basic key of C gives the harmony of C major when ascending, and the tonality of F minor descending.)

The major and minor modes are the polarities of musical theory. The first principle of both: the major is generated from rising, the tendency to ascend, and to extend all intervals upwards; the minor, from falling, its tendency is to descend, and to extend its intervals downwards. (The minor scale raised becomes major.) Working out of this contrast as the basis of all music.

Origin and necessity of the leading note. The semitone rising and the minor third falling.

Connection of the two modes by dominant and tonic. (The first must always be major. Question as to whether the latter must always be minor?)

Origin of Arsis and Thesis in all movement of this type, as also of the cooperation of material bodies and of rhythm.

*Artistic Treatment*

| | | |
|---|---|---|
| Limitation of the octave. Identical transpositions of the octave. Definition of tone proportions. With and against nature. | The art of rendering tones nebulous and rounding tones in order to make different keys accessible to one another and to make it possible to use one as well as the other | Instruction in singing. Exercises, to acquire insight into what is easy and what is difficult in the fundamental and derivative elements of singing. Application of genius and talent, and the employment of all that has been said before as material and tool. |

Limitation of the octave. Identical transpositions of the octave. Definition of tone proportions. With and against nature.

The art of rendering tones nebulous and rounding tones in order to make different keys accessible to one another and to make it possible to use one as well as the other.

Instruction in singing. Exercises, to acquire insight into what is easy and what is difficult in the fundamental and derivative elements of singing. Application of genius and talent, and the employment of all that has been said before as material and tool.

Union of speech with song, particularly with *canto fermo,* recitative, and *quasi parlando.*

Distinction (of song) from speech by a kind of register, and transition to this and therefore to meaning.

Sound (noise). Transition into the formless and the accidental.

### 376. Goethe

Weimar, 15 September 1826

Here, dearest friend, the latest thing of the day (or more precisely) of the hour![74] The poem has just been recited, but now we should like to sing it too.[75]

The rhythm is similar to Thaer's song. Admittedly the more important subject matter deserves a more serious treatment; this will be up to you.

### 377. Zelter

Berlin, 1 October 1826

Schiller's son, who is taking leave of me now, is leaving tomorrow, and wants to take something with him. So I am hurrying to make a fair copy of this little song. The music transcriber can fill in the following verses in the parts which are scored out. In performance it would be nice if every second verse were to be sung by a soloist so as to create some variety. It is really written for your choristers to be sung before your house. This little piece, in the squares in Weimar, might also be on the lookout for other friends.

---

[74] Goethe's poem, marking the return of the youngest son of Carl August from America: 'Dem glücklich-bereicherten, Ihrem Durchlauchtigsten Bruder Herren Carl Bernhard, Herzog von Sachen-Weimar-Eisenach Hoheit die verbundenen Brüder der Loge Amalia zu Weimar'. The poem was performed on the occasion of a celebration of Goethe's son, August, in the freemasons lodge in Weimar. Goethe presumably sent Zelter the once-off publication of the poem for this occasion.

[75] Goethe's request remained unfulfilled.

## 378. Goethe

Weimar, 11 October 1826

[…] The little songbook[76] is really curious and there should be no niggly criticism of your judgement. I find it really appropriate and I imagine friends will also find it so. I thought the introduction was fine and good. Who does not want to look at himself in a favourable mirror? Let me know the author and the best of thanks. […]

Do not delay in writing your reaction to the table I sent you.[77] You will see from it how serious my endeavour was to define at least for science the boundaries of that limitless realm. Every chapter, every paragraph points to something meaningful; the method of arrangement may be allowed to pass; I chose it, because I thought of making it somewhat similar in form to my *Farbenlehre*. I intended to have done a good deal more, but it had to be set aside, owing to the frantic pace of my life.

One ought to say to oneself at times that it is advisable to avoid everything one cannot assimilate with enjoyment or do productively for one's own pleasure and that of others […]

Now, in haste, let me ask you kindly to thank most warmly the excellent and energetic Felix for that splendid copy of his careful aesthetic studies;[78] his work, as well as that of his master, is to provide educational entertainment for our Weimar art lovers during the long winter evenings, which are now drawing near. These friends have just examined the festival songs very closely and your claim remains completely unchallenged. They also want to try to say something about the character and value of other unnamed songs. Warmest thanks for the song sent through Schiller.[79] I hope that with such help my surroundings will gradually be blessed by the sound of songs. […]

---

[76] The published booklet, *Das Goethe-Fest in Berlin. Gefeiert von der Mittwochs-Gesellschaft am 28. August 1826*, with an address and 12 festival poems, presumably brought back from Berlin by Ulrike von Pogwisch; see Goethe's diary 4 October 1826, *WA* III/10, p. 252.

[77] Goethe's *Tonlehre*, GZ 6 to 9 September 1826.

[78] At the end of September 1826 Felix Mendelssohn had sent a copy of his translation of the Terence comedy *Das Mädchen aus Andros* to Goethe, who had organized a reading of it in Weimar.

[79] Zelter's setting of Goethe's poem welcoming Duke Carl Bernhard.

## 379. Goethe

Weimar, 9 January 1827

[…] Incidentally I understand well that you are extremely busy at the moment, but let the present arouse you to cast a glance and send a word in my direction. I will ask you especially that you don't lose the musical table[80] in the confusion of relocating. I was led to some very nice thoughts by which the matter was rounded off very nicely for me. Whether they are also appropriate for others the final communication will show.

## 380. Zelter

Berlin, End of October 1826 to January 1827

I don't see that there is anything to criticize with regard to your table and the way it is laid out. I am in complete agreement with it.

Art is infinite. If it is to become a science, if it is to be taught, it must be limited, made finite. That is what has happened up to now since one cannot do anything else. We have accepted the tonic, but the concept of it was confused enough in both old and new manuals. One called the sounds intervals (relationships), but the root (the tonic) was not to be an interval, as if the ratio 2:1 could not just as easily be 1:2.

Türk himself didn't want to admit this.[81] He stayed with the idea that the relationships (the numbers) were derived from the division of the whole and he could not understand that the whole (the first note to be divided) was a finite entity separated off from the infinite. And as I said to him: like must come from like; sound from sound; man from man; a cat could eat as many mice as she wanted, she would never produce a mouse herself. He appeared to take it badly. The more recent theorists are all much more inferior to Türk, but Chladni[82] is not to be confused with them.

---

[80] Goethe's *Tonlehre*, which was enclosed in his letter of 6 September 1826.

[81] In *Anweisung zum Generalbaßspielen* (Halle & Leipzig, 1791) Daniel Gottlob Türk, in his overview of the intervals, also cites the unison on account of its completeness; for him the question of whether the unison is an interval is a linguistic problem: 'One would only have, I think, instead of the invented interval, a different word or introduced one afterwards, if, thereby, the relationship of two tones to each other could be considered without [any] regard to the notional or non-existence space between them'.

[82] Through his textbook, *Die Akustik*, Ernst Florens Friedrich Chladni became the creator of experimental acoustics.

[...] The table[83] is safe and sound and placed where I can see it everyday. The teaching room stands on good columns but will have to be examined carefully, since with regard to architecture it is more or less necessary to to forget oneself, especially in days when science and art (which, when separated, are nothing at all) suffer more and more from critical indifference.

Since 2 January our Sing-Akademie has quietly entered the new building[84] and is trying out the most suitable positions. The acoustics are good; Chladni who was here recently considers them first-rate. At the same time nothing is completely finished. Today the doors were still not hanging, the seats are still not finished and the smell of the different paints in a completely new building will not disappear until everyone has smelt his share of it. [...] My move should take place at the end of March and there is much to do, since once again I must begin to learn a new trade, which no one seems interested in learning.

23 January: The Crown Prince with his wife[85] and the other royal princes[86] want to visit the Sing-Akademie today.[87] If one were in the main prepared, one would want to examine the building and its advantages, but so much is still lacking, the completion of which has been hindered by the short, cold days.

### 381. Zelter

Berlin, 2 to 3 February 1827

So that the correspondence begins to flow again, I want to say first that Privy Governing Councillor Streckfuß had me read his letter from you and I have given him *Swarto* (written in your hand) to copy. My music to it is long finished and I have not had a chance to glance through it again. It is entirely suitable as a sung recitation. I already made the same remark about theatrical works by Calderon. In reading *Die Tochter der Luft* again and twice in succession I find recitatives, arias, duets, trios and every kind of ensemble given very clearly. If anyone wanted to set it to music, he would just have to take hold of it.

---

[83] Goethe's *Tonlehre*; Zelter is answering Goethe's request to keep an eye out for it during the move.

[84] The Sing-Akademie building was so far finished at the beginning of January 1827 that the concert hall could be used. The ceremonial opening took place on 8 April 1827.

[85] Friedrich Wilhelm of Prussia (later King Friedrich Wilhelm IV) and Elizabeth née Princess of Bavaria.

[86] Friedrich Wilhelm Ludwig, Friedrich Carl Alexander and Friedrich Heinrich Albert of Prussia.

[87] See the letter from the major-domo, Julius Eberhard Wilhelm Ernst von Massow, to Zelter on 22 January 1827 (GSA 143/13); *MA* 20.3, p. 785.

### 382. Goethe

Weimar, 6 February 1827

As usual, I had almost forgotten an important point that his Royal Highness, the Crown Prince, had said to me about your musical performance in the new hall.[88] He seemed to be satisfied with the new building, spoke about your institution with interest and remarked that there was a very large audience. Tell me something from your side about this blessed official opening. [...]

### 383. Zelter

Berlin, 7 to 10 February 1827

[...] It was almost the same with me when I read the appendix which is found on the last page of your letter for the first time. Certainly these noblemen[89] were in the Sing-Akademie on 23 January and spoke about everything most graciously, even though the building is still not finished enough to greet such guests with due honour. Since they wanted to travel to Weimar and could assume they would find you interested in this now well-known institution, they must at least have seen it and heard its acoustic shortly before. Apart from these members of our royal family, there is nothing much to say about our other listeners, for they were made up entirely of members of the Sing-Akademie. On the day there were 209 people (apart from me), which I can be certain of since every Tuesday the names of those present are written down. [...] If I have to admit it (and I would prefer not to), the thing has wound itself around me since I worked with Fasch from my own financial resources; now there is a shortage of money through which the whole thing becomes more widely resepected in the world.

### 384. Zelter

Berlin, 20 February 1827

[...] My Felix has accepted an invitation to Stettin, to conduct his latest works there;[90] he left Berlin on the 16th. The boy reached his nineteenth year on the third

---

[88] The (unofficial) opening of the concert hall of the Sing-Akademie, officially opened on 8 April 1827.

[89] The Prussian Crown Prince, his wife and brothers.

[90] In February 1827 Felix Mendelssohn undertook a journey to Stettin, where he was able to conduct a performance of his overture to Shakespeare's *A Midsummer Night's Dream* (op. 21) to great acclaim.

of this month and his art grows in maturity and individuality. His last opera,[91] which takes a whole evening to perform, has now been waiting for more than a year to be granted a performance at the Königliches Theater and never sees the light of day, while all manner of French rubbish and nonsense is on the stage and hardly survives a second performance. When we are young, and all other advantages are on our side for which many others have to wear away the best part of their life, it cannot do us very much damage – if I did not wish that with his industry he might as soon as possible outgrow our time, which we have to accommodate, whether we like it or not. I dare say I might still be of some use to him, by making him fall back upon himself more and more.

## 385. Zelter

Berlin, 11 to 12 March 1827

A true fragment to the restauration of Phaethon was found, to which I wish success.[92] [...] From my youth I had a great interest in the fable. It was the first opera which I saw and heard when I was 12, performed by the Italian theatre here. I remember the liveliest, youthful shock of the marionette crashing down to the accompaniment of thunderclaps. I still have Graun's music to it[93] and it surely makes a strange impression alongside the text of Euripides, although the libretto is not the worst compared to its time, even though the meaning of the fable is completely ignored. Because of the throne, Phaeton wants to marry a princess who has been promised to a son of Jupiter (Epaphus). This Epaphus cries to his father for revenge, [his plea] is heard, and Phaeton is thrown out down of his carriage.

---

[91] *Die Hochzeit des Camacho.*

[92] Zelter is referring to the article 'Euripides Phaethon', which had recently appeared in *KuA* IV 1, and was an expanded version of the article 'Phaethon, Tragödie des Euripedes' which had appeared earlier. Goethe discovered this work in *Diogenes Laertios* through William Göttling; see Goethe's letter to Zelter, 12 August 1826, *MA* 20.1, p. 940.

[93] Carl Heinrich Graun's opera *Fetonte* (1750), which Zelter had heard in the Königliches Opernhaus and which he discussed in his autobiography; Schottländer, *Carl Friedrich Zelters Darstellungen seines Lebens*, p. 16.

## 386. Zelter

Berlin, 17 March 1827

[...] I read in Aristotle's *Politics* (in Garve's translation)[94] what was written about music[95] with respect to education. Here, too, you have completely enlightened me.[96] Who knows what music is and was and where it is heading. It is strange enough how everything is demanded from the arts, especially from music, since everyone can see in himself what he achieves and what he gains from it.

I am just as delighted with your remarks about Handel's music,[97] which you consider rich in material. Handel has created a master work without further ado simply by handling it dramatically. I am venturing to bring the whole thing onto the stage just as it is and to full theatrical effect. The poem,[98] on the whole, is epic in proportions and Dryden (as an Englishman) thought that as long as the material is musical, the composer will also find welcome material. That must be what our deceased philologist[99] meant when he said to me after the performance that the music was neither really antique nor modern, which would be exactly right because it is dramatic and therefore contains everything.

Regarding an epic treatment in a musical context: right from the beginning I could not have thought of 'Der Gott und die Bajadere' as being anything other than rhapsodic.[100] I believe I noticed the same about the general effect: when I performed the work to you and to Schiller,[101] you both mimed it.[102]

---

[94] *Aristotle. Die Politik. Übersetzt von Christian Garve*, ed. Georg Gustav Fülleborn. (2 vols, Breslau: Korn, 1799–1802). Volume 1 is listed in the register for Zelter's library (no. 138).

[95] Aristotle, like Plato, allocated a place to music in the section on education; but he also considered music to be the object of pleasure and distinguished between music which is morally good and morally beautiful.

[96] Namely, by introducing him to Aristotle's writing on music.

[97] 'The effects of music are [more] material, like what Handel has produced in his *Alexanderfest*', Goethe, *Nachlese zu Aristoteles' Poetik*, MA 13.1, p. 342.

[98] John Dryden, 'Alexander's Feast or The Power of Music. An Ode in honour of St. Cecilia's Day'.

[99] Friedrich August Wolf.

[100] Zelter set Goethe's ballad 'Der Gott und die Bajadere' as a simple strophic song, with a change of time in the refrain so that it followed the metrical patterns of the text. The syllabic vocal setting, the indication *Romanzenton*, Zelter's insistence on a harp accompaniment for the singer, are all features of the 'epic' treatment of the ballad throughout the composition which are mentioned in the letter. By 'rhapsodic' rendering, Zelter means the kind of performance by a Greek singer with kithara accompaniment.

[101] During Zelter's first visit to Weimar from 24 to 28 February 1802. Schiller's visits are recorded in Goethe's diary on 24, 25 and 26 February 1802, WA III/3, pp. 51–2.

[102] Zelter recalls it in GZ 8 September 1825.

### 387. Goethe

Berlin, 19 March 1827

How should a friend answer his friend in such a case?[103] A similar crisis[104] drew us so close to each other, that the bond between us could not be more intimate. The present misfortune leaves us as we are, and that of itself is so much.

The fates are never weary of relating to one another the old myth of the night descending thousands of times and always once more. To live long means to outlive many;[105] such is the pitiful chorus of our vaudeville-like listless life; it comes round again and again, troubling us and at the same time goading us to new and serious ventures.[…]

### 388. Goethe

Weimar, 23 to 29 March 1827

It still remains to be reported briefly that the revision of our correspondence[106] always gives myself and Riemer opportunities for discussion and provides the most engaging entertainment you could want.

### 389. Zelter

Berlin, 5 to 14 April 1827

8 April: On the occasion of this first edition of Shakespeare[107] I am reminded of Dr Forkel,[108] who in his judgement of the prolific Sebastian Bach insists that it would be better to put aside the youthful works of such men of such genius than

---

[103] Goethe's question refers to the death of Zelter's eldest son from his first marriage to Johanna Sophia Eleonora: Georg Friedrich Zelter (1789–1827) who was Zelter's only remaining son.

[104] The suicide of Zelter's stepson, Carl Flöricke; in his letter of consolation of 3 February 1812, Goethe had changed over to the 'du' form of address.

[105] See GZ 26 March 1816 on the death of Zelter's son, Adolf: 'Unfortunately it is the old cliché that to live long is to outlive many.'

[106] The editorial check through the copy of the Goethe–Zelter correspondence which had been made on Goethe's orders.

[107] Reference to Goethe's review of *The first edition of the Tragedy of Hamlet*, KuA VI, 1.

[108] Johann Nikolaus Forkel, *Über Johann Sebastien Bachs Leben, Kunst und Kunstwerke* (Leipzig: Hoffmeister & Kühnel, 1802).

to preserve them to the disadvantage of a purified taste. The Gods have graciously preserved me from such a purification principle up to now. Familiar with every single pen stroke of my hero who belongs to the unfathomable, I collect what I can and constantly purchase the most important thing at a ridiculously low price, for what flows from this source into our era could remain secret for a long time, since it cannot be compared with what exists today. Sometimes it seems to me as if I saw a cross-section of the universe and the connection of one half with the other, and it is all nothing but music: no German or Italian music – just music.

To gain this intimacy with him, I had acted more or less as you and Schiller did with Shakespeare's *Macbeth*.[109] Old Bach, with all his originality, is a son of his country and of his age, and could not escape French influence, and in particular that of Couperin. One wants to please and thus something is created which does not endure. One can, however, dissociate him from this foreign element like [removing] a thin froth, and the brilliant substance lies immediately beneath. Consequently, I have arranged much of his religious music,[110] purely for myself, and my heart tells me that old Bach gives me the nod of approval, just as honest Haydn used to say, 'Yes, yes, that was what I intended!' [...]

The greatest stumbling block in our time is easily discovered in those entirely damnable German church texts which serve the polemical seriousness of the Reformation. Through the thick fumes of confessional belief they stir up unbelief that no one wants. The extraordinary thing about Bach is that a genius, in whom taste is innate, should from such a soil have revealed a spirit that must have very deep roots. He is most marvellous when he is in a hurry and is not in the mood. I possess manuscripts of his where he has thrice begun and then crossed it out again. It wasn't working, but next Sunday there was a wedding or funeral to prepare for. Even the very worst rough draft seems to have been scarce sometimes, but the work had to be done, now it begins to flow, and at last the great artist is there to a T. He makes his improvements, quite as an afterthought, and with the tight writing it becomes dark, unclear and learned. He uses his own signs, which not everyone can decipher, so that I have to refrain almost entirely from tampering with his manuscripts, because I find it no easy matter to put them down again. [...]

---

[109] In the early months of 1800 Schiller realized his old plan for a translation and adaptation of Shakespeare's *Macbeth*. Zelter is stressing here Schiller's high-handedness in dealing with the original.

[110] Georg Schünemann goes as far as stating that Zelter rearranged the aria 'Ich folge dir gleichfalls' from *St John's Passion* according to the taste of the Berlin Liederschule. See Georg Schünemann, 'Die Bachpflege der Berliner Singakademie', *Bach-Jahrbuch* (1928): 138–71. Apart from Zelter's many alterations to the music text of Bach's manuscript, there is such marginalia as the following: 'I have put together this score from the collected fragments which were, in part, in the author's hand, and out of an old devotion to the great master I have wanted to make much of this material accessible for the ability of my students who are a hundred years younger [than Bach]. In doing this my intent is to be in agreement with him should I come ever meet the good Bach'.

Chladni's death hit me very badly.[111] He was still with me a few weeks ago. He wanted to come to Berlin again, and now one must follow him. [...]

Easter Saturday. Today my weeks of torture come to an end.[112] Yesterday my Passion Music was performed for the first time in the new hall[113] and I had the honour of seeing the King among my audience. Your letter of 10 April arrived yesterday and really cheered me up, for the burden of the last few days was very heavy.

### 390. Zelter

Berlin, 15 April 1827

Madame Catalani has sniffed out a few extra groschen, which I begrudge her.[114] Too much is too much! She still makes no preparation for her departure, for she has a couple of rehashed, transformed airs which she would like to churn out gratis. After all, what are a few thousand of our thalers when we get 'God save the King'[115] as an encore!

It really is a pity! What a voice! A golden bowl with common mushrooms in it! And we – one could almost curse oneself for admiring what is so contemptible! It is unbelievable. An irrational animal would despair. What an impossible state of affairs! An Italian turkey comes to Germany – Germany with her academies and high schools, and old students and young professors sit to listen, while she sings in English – yes, English – Handel's German arias.[116] What a disgrace, when it is meant as an honour! In the heart of Germany too! [...]

---

[111] 3 April 1827.

[112] The pressure Zelter felt on account of the many annual musical performamces during Holy Week.

[113] For a glowing report of the performance; see *AMZ* 29 (1827), no. 20, 16 May, column 338; *MA* 20.3, p. 816.

[114] The singer Angelika Catalani, whom Zelter had long admired, could – despite her advancing age – set up numerous concerts during her visit to Berlin in April 1827 on account of her earlier success. She gave a concert of spiritual music on 6 April 1827 at the Königliches Opernhaus, where 'despite being double the standard price for the opera, the beautiful, spacious house was completely full'; *Spenersche Zeitung*, 9 April; see also *AMZ* 29 (1827), no. 20, 16 May, columns 338–40.

[115] Catalani usually closed her concerts with the British national anthem; see Zelter's account of the concert in Frankfurt am Main on 14 August 1816; Schottländer, *Carl Friedrich Zelters Darstellungen seines Lebens*, p. 271.

[116] Handel had, of course, composed the arias of the oratorio using the English texts. It was customary to perform the operas and oratorios in translation; Zelter himself had made a singing translation of Handel's *Alexanderfest*.

### 391. Goethe

Weimar, 21 to 22 April 1827

I was very much struck by your significant remark that Bach, who was basically so original, had allowed himself to be affected by a foreign influence; I immediately looked up Franz Couperin in the biographical dictionary,[117] and understand how, given the great activity of the arts and sciences at that time, a Gallic influence[118] may have been blown over here [...]

But to return to Couperin and Bach, I do entreat you to let me hear some important remarks from you about what you call French froth and which you distinguish from what is fundamental in German music; and so, in one way or another, clarify for me this enlightening relationship [...]

[...] It is a shame about Chladni. He was an active and good man who remained true to his subject, to which he had devoted himself and so could work effectively on the most disparate things. You can see that he could be entirely disinterested, so the meteor stones, after the sound figures, extracted from him the love and desire to give them constant scientific treatment.

Now I must tell you how yesterday evening, when revising our correspondence with Riemer, I was really delighted with your splendid letter of 20 March 1824, where, while tracing the development of Handel's *Messiah*, you so admirably show how the chorale, which grew out of the *canto fermo*, gradually developed into four parts. This leads me to the hope that you will continue to think me worthy of instruction on similar subjects, and therefore that you will soon, as a friend, converse with me by letter about Couperin and Bach.

### 392. Zelter

Berlin, 22 to 28 April 1827

24 April: This week Felix's most recent opera is to be performed[119] – if it ever does come off we have yet to see. He has had to alter a great deal, the libretto is not worth talking about and so even the improvements are unlikely to be brilliant.

My Good Friday music was received fairly well. I cleared several hundred thalers and can be satisfied with that. [...]

---

[117] Johann Gottfried Walters, *Musicalisches Lexicon oder Musicalische Bibliothec* (Leipzig 1732) in Goethe's library (Ruppert, no. 2602).

[118] Zelter had mentioned the French influence – in particular, the influence of Couperin – on J.S. Bach.

[119] *Die Hochzeit des Camacho*. The Berlin premiere took place on 29 April 1827.

### 393. Zelter

Berlin, 2 June 1827

You will get the best report of our opening celebrations[120] from the newspapers. I greeted the noble couple with my people along with many thousand others and saw the gracious little head nodding towards us. At the new opera in the evening,[121] the celebrated couple were greeted with prolonged welcoming signs that were repeated just as continuously at the close of the performance. The special thing about it, which has never happened before, was that all our best singers and dancers,[122] who gladly dispute their ranking, were all able to give of their best.

### 394. Zelter

Berlin, 8 to 9 June 1827

What I called Sebastian Bach's French froth[123] is not so easily skimmed off that you can grasp it in your hand. It is like the air, everywhere but intangible. Bach passes for the greatest of harmonists, and rightly so. One can scarcely dare to call him a poet of the highest order, although he belongs to those who, like your Shakespeare, are far above childish theatre. As a servant of the church he composed only for the church, though his music is not church-like. His style is Bach-like, like everything about him. That he is necessarily obliged to use such common signs and names as Toccata, Sonata, Concerto is like saying a man is called Joseph, or Christopher. Bach's original element is seclusion, as you actually admitted when you once

---

[120] The arrival of Princess Maria of Sachsen-Weimar-Eisenach and Prince Carl of Prussia in Potsdam on 24 May 1827 and in Charlottenburg on 25 May on the occasion of their marriage on 26 May, as well as the celebrated arrival of the couple in their Berlin residence on 28 May; see *Spenersche Zeitung*, no. 121, 26 May, no. 122, 28 May 1827.

[121] Premiere of Act 1 of Spontini's opera *Agnes von Hohenstaufen*, libretto by Ernst Raupach, on 28 May in the Königliches Opernhaus. The opera was 'only half-composed by the knight Spontini without a new overture', *AMZ* 29 (1827), no. 28, 11 July, column 483–5; the first performance of the complete opera took place on 12 June 1829.

[122] The performance of the opera was preceeded by a ballet, *Amphion, anakreontisches Divertissement*, by the royal choreographer, Titus.

[123] In the explantion requested by Goethe, Zelter names historical facts which manifest themselves in Bach's works in many dimensions: Bach remains unaffected by the discussion, which was sparked off by the ideal of the *gallant homme*. Above all, however, he assimilated the heterogeneous stylistic features of French music, be it in his orchestral suites (BWV 1066–1070), composed after the model of French ballet, be it in his suites for piano (among others the French Suites BWV 812–817), solo violin and solo cello. In particular, French harpsichord practice, in the form of François Couperin's textbook *L'art de toucher le clavecin* (Paris, 1716) had a lasting influence on Bach.

said, 'I lie down in bed[124] and make our organist, the mayor of Berka,[125] play me Sebastian.' That's what he is; you have to eavesdrop on him.

Well, besides that he was a man, a father, a godfather, a cantor in Leipzig, and, as such, no more than anyone else, even if not much less than a Couperin, who served two kings of France for over 40 years.[126] In the year 1713 Couperin published and dedicated to his king[127] this first bit of fundamental advice: do not strike the piano but play it.

A king of France playing the piano, perhaps even the organ, pedals and all! Who would not immediately have imitated him? Couperin's new method consisted mainly in the introduction of the thumb, which makes even and sure execution possible. (If I am not mistaken, in Carlo Dolce's picture of Saint Cecilia,[128] the thumbs, if not hanging down, are not in use!) The more advanced Germans and Bach had long since practised this method as the obvious one and yet it was still limited to the right hand, the left hand being evidently spared.[129] The Bach method makes use of all ten fingers, which, with their different length and power, are meant to perform every kind of service; to this method we are indebted for the incredible performances of the latest *toucheurs*. Now as all men must be French, if they mean to live, Bach made his sons practice the small, delicate, graceful Couperin notes with their ornaments; he himself even made highly successful efforts as a composer in this manner, and so the French decorations wove themselves into his style.

Bach's compositions are partly vocal, partly instrumental, or both. In the vocal pieces there is often much more than the words imply, and often enough he has been taken to task for this. Nor is he strict in the observance of the rules of harmony and melody, and he breaks the rules with great audacity. But when biblical texts, such as:

---

[124] This phrase is not from this correspondence but dates back to the time in early summer 1814, which Goethe and Zelter spent together in the house of the spa inspector and organist Schütz. In a letter written there Zelter told Christoph Ludwig Friedrich Schultz that Goethe had 'Schütz play Bach's work to him for an hour every evening, laid down in bed beforehand, as he maintained it shouldn't be obvious that one is listening to Bach's music, since the music is being performed for itself', *Gespräche*, vol. 2, p. 914. The content is similar to Goethe's remarks about Schütz in GZ 4 January 1819 and 29 May 1819.

[125] Johann Heinrich Schütz, spa inspector and organist in Berka.

[126] From 1693 until his death in 1733 Couperin was organist and harpsichordist at the Court of Louis XIV and Louis XV.

[127] The work was dedicated to Louis XV.

[128] This picture by the Florentine painter Carlo Dolce has not been identified.

[129] I have interpreted this passage to make musical sense of: 'auf rechte und linke Hand beschränkt wobei die letztere sichtbar geschont ist'.

'Break thy bread for the hungry,' and so on, [130]
'Ye shall cry and lament,' and so on,[131]
'Jesus took the twelve unto himself,' and so on, [132]
'Let our mouths be filled with laughter,' and so on[133]

are composed as choruses, I am often inclined to marvel at the sacred freedom in these passages, the apostolic irony with which some quite unexpected effect is produced, without raising a doubt about the sense and taste inherent in it. A 'passus et sepultus' introduces the last pulsations of the silent powers; a 'resurrexit' or a 'gloria Dei patris',[134] the eternal regions of sanctified suffering, in contrast with the hollowness of earthly desires. This feeling, however, is, as it were, impervious to analysis, and it would be difficult to extract from it a melody or anything of a material nature. It only renews itself, strengthens itself, continually gathers up its strength again through repetition of the whole.

In all this, Bach is to that point still dependent on some kind of theme. One should follow him to the organ. This is his own peculiar soul into which he immediately inspires living breath. His theme is the newly born feeling, which, like the spark from the stone, invariably springs forth from the first chance pressure of the foot on the pedal. So by degrees he gets into it until he isolates himself and feels alone, and then an inexhaustible stream flows into the infinite ocean. His eldest son, Friedemann (of Halle),[135] who died here, referred to the same quality when he admitted, 'Compared with him, we all remain children.'[136] Not a few of his grander compositions for the organ come to an end somehow, but they are never over; there is no end to them.

Here I must stop, however, though much remains to be said. Weighing every possible testimony against him, this Leipzig cantor is one of God's phenomena; clear, but inexplicable. I might cry out to him, 'You've made me work and I've brought you to light again.'[137]

---

[130] Opening chorus to Cantata BWV 39.

[131] Opening chorus to Cantata BWV 103.

[132] Opening chorus to Cantata BWV 22.

[133] Opening chorus to Cantata BWV 110.

[134] Sections of the Credo from the Catholic mass.

[135] Friedemann Bach was active as a composer in Halle from 1764; he died in Berlin on 1 July 1784.

[136] This expression presumably dates back to Johann Nikolaus Forkel, who, at the beginning of chapter four in his Bach biography (1802), wrote, 'W. Friedemann was also a child in this respect compared to his father, and declared himself to be so in all honesty'.

[137] This saying is presumably Zelter's own.

## 395. Goethe

Weimar, 9 June 1827

In the periodical *Cäcilia*, volume 24, you will find an important essay on 'The Condition of Music in Naples' written by a F.S. Kandler,[138] a man whom I would like to know more about. I found everything very pleasing in this little treatise, as one may call it: a calm mind, true knowledge, overview, interest in detail, serious established beliefs, casualness towards the living, and moderation. His honesty is so pure that – allowing for the praiseworthy and the reprehensible existing side by side as a consequence of the past and as indispensable to the present and it makes sense of many a moment – it still seems a worthy quality.

This little book made this impression on me as a layman. It speaks purely to my historical understanding but doesn't contradict what I already know and understand. So then I may trust that artistic colleague who as a person thinks very meaningfully, honestly and logically, and also, in so far as one also considers him as a sociable musician, appears really charming. I would hope that your judgement would confirm my impression.

[...] On this occasion some of my old observations surfaced again and I will voice them here. The musician, if in other areas of his life he lives with his senses and is sensible, is moral and decorous, enjoys great advantages in the course of his life, because he can assimilate himself better than others to the course of life and to all kinds of pleasures. For this reason, your descriptions of your travels[139] have a distinct and double charm: the architect and musician are combined with the man of sterling value, and the extent of this society can hardly be appraised [...]

If you come across my musical table[140] when unpacking, do send it to me. I would like to have a look at it once again, for I think I have gained new insights into this area. [...]

---

[138] Franz Sales Kandler, 'Musikstand von Neapel' in *Cäcilia, eine Zeitschrift für die musikalische Welt* 6/24 (1827): 235–96; the article was published with an accompanying manuscript of a Neopolitan Tarantella melody and *La Monacella*. Goethe knew the journal for a long time and possessed a copy himself (Ruppert, no. 2549); he started a review of Kandler's treatise which, unfortunately, remained a fragment.

[139] Zelter's travelogue in letters from his journey to Vienna in 1819.

[140] Goethe's *Tonlehre*, which he had sent to Zelter in a letter of 6 to 9 September 1826; Zelter returned it to him on 10 July 1827.

## 396. Zelter

Berlin, 16 June 1827

At last we have in our hands the much-disputed score of Mozart's Requiem,[141] corrected from manuscripts, and we know what we knew.[142] Since you are familiar with the periodical *Cäcilia*, you must have become acquainted with the bitter, sour jabbering of Gottfried Weber[143] of Darmstadt against the authenticity of this posthumous work. There he affirms that the Requiem is as good as not Mozart's at all, and that if were, it is the weakest, nay, the wickedest thing, that ever came from the pen of that illustrious man. So he says Mozart left the work incomplete, but after his death Süßmeyer[144] came along and suppressed Mozart's thoughts, so that the work, through his completion of it, was corrupted, if not poisoned – and since Mozart's death, the world has been living in an astonished and astonishing state of deception about this legacy – a deception based on a fanciful origin of the work – and no one hitherto has had the courage to bring to light the blunders, spots and faults of a spurious work of art. So much for Weber's humour.

But we, too, have been in the world since childhood; Mozart was born two years before me (1756) and we remember, only too well, the circumstances of his death.

Mozart, I say, who had been so soundly taught that he could compose very easily and have time left for hundreds of things besides – dallying with women and the like – had thereby run his good natural disposition too close. In this way he comes to have a wife and children and falls into the extreme of poverty in which his basis for existence is lost. Lying on his sickbed, wretched in his home, worried,

---

[141] In a rough draft of this letter, Zelter wrote: 'At last I have the latest long-awaited score of Mozart's Requiem. The score also includes indications of the passages which are known to be genuine.' The score was published by Johann André in Offenbach in 1827.

[142] The corresponding passage in Zelter's draft letter, again clearly differentiated from the letter sent, states, 'This Requiem is a posthumous work of the composer, to which, on its first appearance, a mysterious genesis was attributed and this was due to the death of the composer at this time. Because of this, it initially received great recognition, which it has retained up to now in its own right' (GSA 95/I, 8, 4).

[143] Gottfried Weber had published two comprehensive articles on the question of the authenticity of Mozart's Requiem: 'Über die Echtheit des Mozarts Requiem' in the periodical, *Cäcilia* 3/11 (1825): 205–29, and 'Weitere Nachtrichten über die Echtheit des Mozartschen Requiem', *Cäcilia* 4/16 (1826): 257–352. In the first essay Weber wrote, 'After all these considerations the authenticity of the work, to say the very least, is highly suspect, and the truth, that the greater part of it is not by Mozart but by Süssmayer, is highly plausible', p. 211. Mozart's Requiem, 'as we now possess it, is vastly different from what Mozart wanted to have given us – and the worst thing about it is that he had already given it to us, but up to now it has still not been passed down to us.' Ibid.

[144] Franz Xaver Süßmeyer came to Mozart in 1790 in order to take composition lessons. He was decisively influential in the completion of Mozart's Requiem.

decried, with no helpful friends, in the end he is without even the commonest necessities of life.

An honest fellow orders any work Mozart may choose, so as to give him a little money in the most delicate way. A libretto is not forthcoming at the moment and Mozart says, 'I have a mind to write a Requiem which you may use for my funeral.'[145] The weakness increases; he begins to care for his soul, and in solemn, solitary self-introspection, certain beginnings of single parts of the Requiem are unfolded, (as once, with so much truth, you placed them in the mouth of your Gretchen)[146] Dies irae – Tuba mirum – Rex tremendæ – Confutatis – Lacrimosa[147] – and it is precisely these pieces which reveal the deepest contrition of a religious mind, showing at the same time, on one side, the last remains of a great school, and on the other, the passionate feeling of a dramatic composer. Consequently the style is a medley – uneven, nay, fragmentary – and so arises like that confusion, in which the criticism of today takes such delight. Tradition ran like that at the time, but no honest man would repeat it out loud.

After Mozart's death, worthy Süßmeyer comes forward as the true friend, puts the Requiem together, and completes what is wanting, so that the suffering family gains some money to meet its basic needs. The work is sold and printed;[148] Süßmeyer makes as good an explanation as he can of his share in the work, and soon afterwards follows his friend into Eternity.

Now comes the aforesaid Hans Taps,[149] accuses the friend of adulteration and lying, and talks in the most contemptuous tone about a well-meaning friend,

---

[145] This unverified remark of Mozart's goes back to reports and memoirs which were in circulation after the death of the composer in 1791. In connection with the first public mention of the Requiem, the *Salzburger Intelligenzblatt* wrote in the form of an anecdotal report: 'Now Mozart had to write, which he often did with tears in his eyes, and said: "I fear that I am writing a Requiem for myself"; he completed it a few days before his death. When his death was common knowledge, the servant came back and brought the other 30 ducats, didn't ask for the Requiem and there was never any enquiry about it. It was also true that it [...] was performed in his memory in St Michael's church.' So, too, in Franz Xaver Niemeczek's Mozart Biography, which is based on information from Mozart's wife, Constanze, it states: 'On the evening of his death he had the score brought to his bed. "Have I never mentioned before that I wrote this Requiem for myself?"' Two years later a report by Friedrich Rochlitz in the *AMZ* 1 (1798) states Mozart believed, 'that he worked on this piece for his own funeral. He never gave up on this idea; he worked like Raphael on his transfiguration, always with a feeling of his impending death, and like [Raphael] produced this transfiguration of himself', Christoph Wolff, *Mozarts Requiem. Geschichte, Musik, Dokumente, Partitur des Fragments* (Munich, Kassel, Basel: dtv and Bärenreiter, 1991), pp. 122, 124 and 15.

[146] *Faust 1*, Cathedral scene.

[147] Parts of the Latin Requiem Mass.

[148] *Mozarts Requiem*. The first edition was published by Breitkopf and Härtel (Leipzig) in 1800.

[149] Gottfried Weber in his essays published in the journal *Cäcilia*.

without suggesting any safe criterion as to what is Mozart and what is Süßmeyer, ascribing to Süßmeyer what he cannot possibly have written, and vice versa; without reflecting that if a clever man like Süßmeyer puts his mind to it, he can quite well avoid the *Dormitat Homerus* himself.[150] And this really happened. The Benedictus is as good as it can be and cannot be Mozart; the school decides as much. Süßmeyer knew Mozart's school but he had not been in it; he had not been through it in his youth, and here and there traces of this are found in the beautiful Benedictus. On the other hand, whatever is found fault with in Mozart's work, Süßmeyer is said to have done. Thus the critic explains that the first number in the Requiem has been borrowed from Handel,[151] and consequently cannot be by Mozart – who often and unquestionably attempted to write in the Handelian manner, in order to convince himself that he, too, could do that kind of thing. In this piece we have besides the choral music, a cantus firmus, and an old melody too; guess what? It is the simple melody – (how does the 'Magnificat anima mea'[152] come into a Requiem?) in a word, it is the old cantus firmus to be found in the Luther Chorale Book up to this very day, 'Meine Seele erhebt den Herrn'.[153] Just now I called the work fragmentary and uneven, by which I mean that the movements collectively are like a mosaic and he who insists on considering them as a whole is mistaken, as are several excellent composers. The whole Requiem consists of such pieces, and in spite of that, it is the very best I know of in the last century.

Before Mozart had taken a look round north Germany,[154] Handel may have shone out for him as the most powerful talent in Germany; some of his compositions bear the superscription 'Nel Stilo di Haendel'. Then Mozart arrives in Leipzig, while Hiller is yet alive, and pricks his ears up at Sebastian Bach, to the great astonishment of Hiller, who is trying to fill the St Thomas choirboys with horror at the crudities of that Sebastian. What does Mozart do? He tries his hand at this style with a dexterity that only such a school can give. Just listen to the music of

---

[150] Reference to Horace, *Ars Poetica*, v. 359. Literally, 'Homer nods', meaning the slips one can make.

[151] The musical material of the Introitus is, to a large extent, derived from the opening chorus of Handel's *Funeral Anthem for Queen Caroline*, HWV 264.

[152] The opening words of Mary's hymn of praise ('My soul glorifies the Lord') Luke 1, 46–55.

[153] For the 'Te decet hymnus Deus in Sion', in Part One of the Requiem Mozart chose the 'tonus peregrinus', occasionally called Psalm no. 9, to which the German Magnificat of the Lutheran Liturgy is sung ('Meine Seele erhebt den Herrn'). Luther's German translation of the text of the Latin Magnificat found its way into the Porst songbooks used in Berlin.

[154] In 1789 Mozart undertook a journey with Prince Karl von Lichnowsky to Berlin, where he received a commission for a string quartet from King Friedrich Wilhelm II. On his return journey through Leipzig he sought out Johann Friedrich Doles, a student of Bach, who, on account of quarrels with the rector, had retired from his position of Cantor at the St Thomas Kirche. Doles arranged for the Thomaskirche choir to demonstrate Bach's motet *Singet dem Herrn* for Mozart, who performed and improvised on the organ at the Thomaskirche.

the black men in *Die Zauberflöte* (before the ordeal by fire). It is inlaid; it is the Luther Chorale 'Wenn wir in höchsten Nöthen',[155] interwoven with the orchestra in Bach's style – and so on.

I can help with your desire to discover more about Kandler through the enclosure, where you will see that once again we are of the same opinion about the same subject. The report on the condition of music in Naples also pleases me. I have also never regretted seeing the contemporary nature of my art with favourable eyes in comparison with the earlier cherished conditions of art in Italy. One can do the art lovers of the last century too much honour if one wanted to attribute too much artistic integrity to them. The beautiful and the great are often found isolated, floating on a sea of Mannerism. Admittedly it is still to be admired that Italian commonness still has a certain greatness founded, as it were, itself on their right of ownership. Whoever, with a healthy sense, wants to convince himself of this should come to us and see and listen to how a beautiful feminine creature with a magnificent voice of a rich nature fills our opera house, innocently, naturally with buck-trills, hackneyed mannerisms, chromatic botched-up work, and discredits the nobler attributes we really have. One sees it with disapproval, criticizes, goes back again. So it was and is.

The best of the Italians have – everyone knows – been surpassed by Handel and Hasse here and also by the more flawed Graun. But [the Italians] were on home [territory] [...] the foreigner has to take care and at least wins back his stake.

Your table[156] is firmly fixed on my wall. I thought you would have kept a copy. Now you will have it copied first, which I would not be able to do in the next few days.

Nineteen letters from 1826 are enclosed here.[157] It will be a strong collection. [...]

The 'Altschottish' is an excellent work;[158] the metre is very manageable. The tone of the whole piece is not so easily found. In a peculiar way your own handwritten copy is at the same time very significant to me. Something similar happened me with the 'Pillalu',[159] which, if I am not mistaken, is completely successful in that I was really lucky to capture the right mourning tone of the funeral march, the metre of which was going round in my head. We have no concept of such work afterwards and yet how would we know whether it hits the right tone when we have no image of it? In 'Pillalu' I see the entire procession marching by me. [...]

---

[155] Zelter means the song of the two men in armour, 'Der, welcher wandert diese Straße voll Beschwerden'; this does not hark back to the chorale melody mentioned by Zelter but uses the melody for 'Ach Gott von Himmel, sieh darein'.

[156] Goethe's *Tonlehre* which Zelter returned on 16 July.

[157] Seventeen letters from 1826 have been handed down; possibly Zelter included Goethe's letter of 30 December (which arrived on 3 January) and counted one of the long correspondences, for example 6–9 September, as two letters

[158] Enclosed GZ 9 June 1827.

[159] Zelter's setting of Goethe's poem 'Klaggesang. Irisch'.

## 397. Zelter

Berlin, 16 to 19 June 1827

[…] Monday. Yesterday there was a pleasant festival in our new music hall.[160] The local horticultural society[161] celebrated the anniversary of its foundation […] The King was invited but didn't appear. […]

Tuesday. According to the agreement this lovely garden kingdom was to have been cleared away by yesterday morning. I asked them to stay till this evening so that all the members of the Sing-Akademie, which meets on Mondays and Tuesdays, could enjoy it, whereby I had also invited the horticultural society as audience. I had also suspected something which, in fact, came true. Yesterday evening around six o'clock the Sing-Akademie was still there and the King asked whether the exhibition was still there and if he could see it in private. I replied, 'After seven', and released the members around this time. Then he appeared with his entourage to find only me, looked through everything attentively, named many of the plants saying, 'I have that too'. (They were all out of his gardens.) He praised the hall: lovely proportions, tasteful and so on […] From this noble gathering of approximately 12 people, Princess Marie remained behind with her husband, Prince Carl.[162] Her first question was how you are […] She had me show her the remaining rooms of the hall, sat down on a chair here or there […] asked about this thing or that in the most gracious manner and finally enquired about little Felix who is now an 18-year-old student at the university,[163] almost an adult, and whom I could praise from the heart on account of his continuous industry in everything which is worthy of being known, about which she showed her appreciation and delight.

Imagine now your gruff old fish in the presence of a quiet, intelligent, very young, newly-wed, royal princess, who is listening graciously and patiently to what the spur of the moment places on the lips of an old man. At the same time imagine a calm pleasant coolness of the evening after surviving Catalani in an oppressive opera house. There is nothing more to report other than that an approaching rainstorm perhaps robbed me of such a sweet presence[164] somewhat earlier [than expected]. I was on my own home territory where one may speak

---

[160] To cover the building costs the concert hall of the new Sing-Akademie building was hired out to other organizers. See, for example, the review of an exhibition in the Sing-Akademie hall on 17 June, *Vossische Zeitung*, 193, 18 June 1827.

[161] Berliner Verein zur Beförderung des Gartenbaues in den Königl. Preußischen Staaten (The Berlin Horticultural Society).

[162] Maria Luise Alexandrine of Prussia, née Princess of Sachsen-Weimar-Eisenach (1808–77) married Prince Carl Alexander of Prussia (1801–83), third son of King Friedrich Wilhelm III, on 26 May 1827.

[163] Felix Mendelssohn registered at Berlin University in the Autumn of 1827. The publication of the Terenz translation was accepted as proof of his qualifications.

[164] Princess Maria, wife of Prince Carl of Prussia.

freely otherwise perhaps many words would have been spared. In the course of the conversation I had named Felix as the best performer. The Prince asked hastily, 'Better than Hummel?' I no longer remember exactly what I answered; let's say: the best person which one can be in every situation.

### 398. Goethe

Weimar, 21 June 1827

It is clear from your invaluable writings,[165] my dear Zelter, that you have developed the gift of teaching perfectly and thereby are very thorough with your students in every case. You have answered my question in such a way that – as difficult and as remote as it is – I can approach it feeling some relief. It is really strange that music, as it emerges from its first simple depths, soon belongs to the fleeting moment and must caress frivolous ears. No wonder that after so many years it finally runs off on the course we now see it following.

### 399. Goethe

End of June 1827[166]

[...] At this juncture I thought of the worthy organist of Berka; for it was there, when my mind was in a state of perfect composure and free from external distraction, that I first obtained some idea of your Grand Master (Sebastian Bach). I said to myself, it is as if the eternal harmony were conversing with itself, as it may have done in the bosom of God just before the creation of world. So likewise did it move in my inmost soul, and it seemed as if I neither possessed nor needed ears nor any other sense – least of all the eyes.

As soon as music makes the first vigorous advance towards having an outward expression, it powerfully excites our inborn sense of rhythm, of step and dance, of song and rejoicing by degrees, it runs off into the transoxanic, (*vulgo* Janissary music) or into the yodel, into the love-cooing of birds.

Now, however, a higher culture steps in; the pure Cantilena flatters and charms us; gradually, the harmonic Chorus is developed, and thus developed, the whole strives to return again to its divine origin.

---

[165] ZG 8–9 June 1827.

[166] This letter is from *MA* 20.3, p. 833; the letter is marked 'Cassiertes Mundum', meaning an invalid fair copy.

### 400. Zelter

Berlin, 6 to 10 July 1827

[...] The Theory of Sound [table] is copied and is included here[167] with a request for forgiveness if it should have suffered through being pinned. My ideas for some parts still have to be developed. [...]

### 401. Goethe

Weimar, 17 July 1827

[...] The high pressure of musical, prosaic, dramatic, literary, scientific and other performances [in Berlin], which the newspapers thrust on us, could almost disconcert and overpower a distant recluse. However, I like to believe that, in the midst of all this activity, one may remain true to oneself, just as it is possible to find inspiration on the shores of a raging ocean. [...]

### 402. Zelter

Berlin, 13 July to 8 August 1827

I have finally seen, heard and tasted your La Roche and in *Il matrimonio segreto*.[168] The roles of the absent Spizeder have fallen to him; Spizeder[169] is rightly a favourite [actor], and so, as people were saying, La Roche was not likely to appeal, and so he really surprised me. He sang the Privy Trade Councillor in this opera well and acted excellently. Besides being a vain half-deaf fool, he is also a father. The whole thing is very funny.

---

[167] Goethe sent his *Tonlehre* to Zelter in September 1826 and requested it back on 9 June 1827; Zelter retained a copy.

[168] Johann *Carl August* La Roche (1794–1884), actor, singer, director in Weimar 1823–33, sang the part of the Privy Trade Councillor in Cimarosa's opera *Die heimliche Ehe* in the Königstädtisches Theater on 13 July. In a draft of this letter, Zelter had given his opinion of both actor and opera: 'But La Roche is a true actor. Disposition, feeling, spirit, bearing, tone and voice are so well fused, that no particular apect stands out and it is good to find a practitioner who doesn't want more than he should or can [be]. Here we have only one such actor (Beschort), who nonetheless is not without characteristics which reveal his individual personality. The whole opera, which, on the whole, I would gladly listen to, went well but (as is usual during the summer months) the house was packed.'

[169] Joseph Spizeder (1795/96–1832), singer and actor, engaged by the Königstädisches Theater from its establishment in 1824.

## 403. Zelter

Berlin, 10 to 23 August 1827

19 August: Our friend Nägeli produced a musical work which was philosophically, theosophically, pedagogically, historically and critically prophetic; claiming that the new instrumental music, which is raised up to the highest point and is to be intensified to an infinite degree, as ideally the highest[170] – finally combined with a choir of a hundred voices[171] – will end by representing transfigured humanity in a transfigured sound creation.

There is something attractive about his ideas which I would envy him, if one had not also had such notions 50 years ago, and now – I am still groping around in your songs. He claims such choirs of 100 voices were already in existence in his Swiss and southern German towns: 'I can, with full certainly, and with an eye on the previous course of development, predict how and through what main means instrumental music will and must reach a boundless idealization'[172] and so on. Mozart suffers rather badly; Pleyel is always treated with esteem;[173] old Bach and Beethoven come out the best. Since you hardly ever read such things you might like to accept a private note about it and this will be a good way for me to get rid of it.

With regard to your Theory of Sound[174] I have something that will make you happy. It is still not ready, although I have already carried it around with me for years. It concerns the minor scale. It is as if it were nailed into me, but one is torn this way and that. When the opportunity is there to talk about it, it abandons me. Then if I hear others speaking about it again, I want to laugh out loud at my own ideas.

---

[170] 'Once a principle of such a transfigured and transfiguring music has taken root, if the artists as such are able, in this way, to honour truth in beauty, then a time comes about when instrumental and vocal music is to a large extent linked. Then superb folk choirs will be formed and the artists will be able create the true and the genuine for them in a grandiose style so that instrumental music, with all its effusive splendour serving as a background to a hundred voice choirs, *will represent a transfigured humanity in a transfigured music creation*'; Hans Georg Nägeli, *Vorlesungen über Musik mit Berücksichtigung der Dilettanten* (Stuttgart, Tübingen, 1826), p. 282.

[171] 'Such choirs of a hundred voices are already in existence in our Swiss towns and those of Southern Germany', Nägeli, p. 282.

[172] Nägeli, p. 278.

[173] The Austrian composer Ignaz Joseph Pleyel (1757–1831) is favourably presented; Nägeli, p. 181.

[174] Zelter didn't follow this up in the letters which follow, but may have discussed it with Goethe on his visit to Weimar on 12 to 18 October 1827.

## 404. Goethe

### Weimar, Middle of August to 6 September 1827

[…] Put on paper what you have in mind about the minor scale: it would arrive exactly at the right time. I have also thought out something with Riemer about it.[175] I want to dictate it, seal it and wait for your consignment rather than send it straight away. It would be really nice if we reached the same conclusion in different ways. […]

I would like to have your *O Jemine*[176] […] as a text forming the basis of a long, serious sermon. I suspect a sense for music should accompany each and every artistic sense. I would like to support my claim through theory and experience. […]

## 405. Zelter

### Berlin, Munich, Coburg, Weimar, 5 September to 13 October 1827

7 September: If I could give you on a good day (because it is suitable to that time) one of Bach's motets to listen to, you would feel yourself at the centre of the world, where someone like you belongs. I am listening to the work for the hundredth time and am still not finished with it and never will be. 'Compared to him we are all children', his son Philipp Emanuel remarked. Yes, children! I feel myself raised up and destroyed. He is terrible but divine. The majority of us are also not hawfinches, so it is amusing how they act at the beginning and do not come to themselves until they have left Rossini behind.

Munich, 22 September: Today they are expecting the King[177] at the assembly and so I also want to go. I saw him and his beautiful wife[178] at the opera[179] yesterday evening. I was with Spontini in the artistic director's box, but I only enjoyed Act One because I was also invited with Cornelius and Bertram to the von Cotta's. […] They have not settled in yet and could not entertain properly, which suits me fine. The evening was really pleasant and no one else was there other than Cornelius and Bertram. […]

---

[175] There is no hint of what this might be in the diaries of Goethe or Riemer.

[176] Zelter's 'O gemini!', suggestive of twins and of a general cry of terror, is directed at the Humboldt brothers.

[177] Ludwig I of Bavaria (1786–1868).

[178] Therese Charlotte Luise Friederkike Amalia of Bavaria, née Princess of Sachsen-Hildburghausen (1792–1854).

[179] Ferdinando Paer, *Sargines, oder Der Triumph der Liebe* (libretto by Giuseppe Maria Foppa, in the German adaptation by Cäsar Max Heigel) performed on 21 September.

A good part of the evening conversation here is concerned with the theatre. They complained generally about plays and operas: everything should have been much better, even incomparable, and until yesterday evening I listened to everything quietly. They demanded a comparison with Berlin: [...] As a guest I cannot know how it is here. With us the audience is divided. One demands Italian opera, the other German opera. Typical Italian opera really exists; individual attempts can turn out one way or another. Even one successful performance is enough for reconciliation. A German opera (of this kind) does not exist at all. They want to call good works from earlier times obsolete and the very latest works are never new. The composers complain about the poets, the singers about the composers, and vice versa. You'd get the impression that the poet, the composer, the singer – no one understands his profession and knows what he wants. A lady offered me her arm to let me lead her to table: 'Why have you not spoken about it with the scientists?' The evening was incidentally very cheerful and pleasant. [...]

26 September: I have been to the Königliche Bibliothek[180] three times. It is really well stocked and contains rare musical codices and manuscripts from the sixteenth century which are splendidly produced and well preserved. I myself am mainly interested in the majority of works from the second half of the seventeenth century and the first half of the eighteenth century in order to enrich my Sing-Akademie even more, because we have assembled a really good collection in Berlin. The earlier works belong to the Catholic Church as the mass vestments belong to the priests. In the Altschneider, formerly the Frauenhofer Institute,[181] I had to admire the largest telescope and smaller instruments as well. The institution itself is in full swing and appears to be bombarded with work.

Thursday. There was an opera yesterday evening: *Die Prinzessin von Provence*, an original magic opera in three acts. The libretto and the music are by von Poißl,[182] artistic director of the local Nationaltheater.

The poet and composer has been my very good friend for some years and right now an especially dear friend. Recently he lost the mother of his children[183] and his eldest grown daughter. We sat beside each other in the box and here I fully realized what it means to speak the truth to such a kind friend and double author, when he gladly listens and compares it to accepted judgements. The house was full: theatre and orchestra equipped as an author would want who has the power in his hands. Loud applause does not happen here in the presence of the nobility and so sitting next to a friend I was able to be honest about every single passage

---

[180] In the former Jesuit college Neuhauserstraße; the building for the Bayerische Staatsbibliothek was built by Friedrich Gärtner between 1832 and 1842.

[181] The Mathematisch-mechanische Institut founded by Joseph von Utzschneider, Georg von Reichenbach and Joseph Liebherr in 1804 was, in 1819, united with the Institute founded in Benedicktbeuren by Joseph von Fraunhofer in 1807.

[182] Baron Johann *Nepomuk* von Poißl (1783–1865), composer.

[183] Baroness Maria Walpurga von Poißl, née Countess von Hegnenberg-Dux (1778–1826).

which could be praised and pass over in silence what he himself considered to be successful. But it is and remains a hopeless situation, all the more since it can easily be observed that the author does not lack public favour. So I left the box quietly, mixed among the people (the faithful followers) who will always be there, gently pressing forward and holding back and discovered what all the wisdom in me could only have discovered late: the opera is a masterpiece of a musical amateur and not one among many thousands will match the author in what he has achieved here. I would have been able to sleep peacefully if before going to bed I had not drunk an inordinate amount of Bavarian beer, which a stranger has to respect. [...]

27 September: I got into a conversation about the origins of language with Professor Martius who spent four years in India.[184] If I understood him correctly, he believed he had discovered there the infancy of humanity. He sets against our music their way of communicating with one another through pure sound and physical movement and thereby seems to conclude that language is older than singing. He also was able to offer many examples, which I don't remember but which would be opposed to anything that could be deemed lyrical. [...]

Sunday: Today Spontini is conducting his *Die Vestalin* in the Königliches Theater.[185] The orchestra are enchanted by the opera and also with his direction. That's a recipe for success.

Nuremberg, 4 October. [...] Yesterday I got to know the 82-year-old von Imhof,[186] former senior civil servant at the royal castle, who at the same time was willing, at the request of the ladies, to perform old arias from his era for me on the fortepiano for half an hour, and to improvise. The good old fellow became highly animated as he told me about Hasse, Gluck, Emanuel Bach and Haydn, whom he had known personally, and was able to make me green with envy. I was able to praise his playing honestly; it was not too bad.

8 October: We arrive at the [St] Sebald basilica to the sound of the loveliest bells. Trumpets play the chorale *Jesus meine Zuversicht* from the tower and then finally, as we passed other churches, all the bells came together. We arrived at the door of the graveyard gates. Here a coffin was uncovered [...] A choir of brass instruments played the funeral music softly [...] The coffin was put into the tomb

---

[184] The botanist Carl Friedrich Philipp von Martius had taken part in an expedition to Brazil (not India), after which he published a three-volume work and an atlas with Johann Baptist von Spix, *Reise in Brasilien auf Befehl Sr. Majestät Maximilian Joseph I. Königs von Baiern in den Jahren 1817 bis 1820 gemacht und beschrieben* (Munich, 1823, 1828 and 1831). As Spix died in 1826, only volume one and three chapters of volume two are by both authors); see exhibition catalogue, *Brasilianische Reise 1817–1820. Carl Friedrich Philipp von Martius zum 200. Geburtstag*, ed. Jörg Helbig (Munich: Hirmer Verlag, 1994).

[185] On 30 September 1827 in the Munich Nationaltheater; a second performance took place on 11 October; *AMZ* 29 (1827), no. 52, 26 December, column 888f.

[186] Johann Siegmund Georg Imhof von und zu Ziegelstein (1745–1831).

to the accompaniment of Klopstock's Lied 'Auferstehen wirst du'.[187] I also saw Dürer's grave in this atmosphere, and went for something to eat and only got my appetite back by eating.

Coburg, 11 October: Here again I discovered Kapellmeister Schneider,[188] whom I have known for 30 years. His brother took lessons with me with Fasch in Berlin: an odd fellow who called himself 'Seneiders' because the name 'Schneider' sounded too common to him. [...] I have just come from an opera rehearsal where they were rehearsing, and not badly, the opera *Euryanthe* by Carl Maria von Weber,[189] which is to be performed tomorrow. What one seldom finds can be found here: all the singers on the stage are better than the orchestra, who admittedly are badly directed. A bass by the name of Schmitt[190] is even first-rate: voice, physique, and range of performance, age – everything comes together; at the same time he is also valued as an actor here. Of all the others I could not call one bad. The first soprano[191] and first tenor[192] are even good and everyone is very musical. Even the choruses were good and stood out. I am not in a position to judge the production. I place the music to *Euryanthe* above *Der Freischütz* (which I admittedly cannot stand). As in all of Weber's compositions there is also much in it that is striven after, so many bits and pieces, a combination of fine morsels; difficult and foreign passages together; forced liveliness, and, amid all this, certainly good passages and a diligence which I admire with horror because all the junk doesn't deserve it. The Germans, who begrudge the Italians their fame, nonetheless want to reproduce the *parlare cantando* or *cantare parlando* and don't grasp that the Germans don't learn to speak. Whoever can speak like the Italians will sing automatically. Everything else is irritating. To drum, blow and bow is still not singing – not by a long shot.

---

[187] 'Die Auferstehung', first published in Klopstock's *Geistliche Lieder*, vol. 1 (Kopenhagen und Leipzig, 1758); set by Carl Heinrich Graun in 1758, by C.P.E. Bach in 1787, later composed by Friedrich Heinrich Himmel and Bernhard Klein, well known as a funeral hymn from the beginning of the nineteenth century.

[188] Georg *Laurenz* Schneider (1766–1855), composer, music director and organist at Coburg.

[189] The premiere of Carl Maria von Weber's *Euryanthe* took place on 11 October 1827, a few months after the ducal theatre of Sachsen-Koburg-Gotha had been set up on 1 June. See Rudolf Potyra and Jürgen Erdmann, *Die Theatermusikalien der Landesbibliothek Coburg* (2 vols, Munich: G. Henle Verlag, 1995).

[190] Johann Adam Schmitt (*c.*1790–1827/28), singer and actor.

[191] Either Anna Posch or Auguste Weinkauf, née Amberg (1796–1833), both of whom were singers at the Coburg Theatre at this time.

[192] Julius Rochow (d.1863).

## 406. Zelter

Weimar, 16 October 1827

Admittedly our correspondence over many years has not been lacking in material. You have really taken an interest in my bit of musical knowledge, where the rest of us [musicians] stagger around. Who was to tell us?

## 407. Goethe

Weimar, 11 March/17 October 1827[193]

Admittedly, my dear Zelter, it is a difficult task if we expect the average fellow to sing such poems[194] and to see any meaning in them. If someone demanded a commentary[195] from me, I would offer to write another poem with the same content and meaning but comprehensible and more accessible. If I were successful, I would also ask you likewise to compose it for the Liedertafel and to get it going without revealing the purpose, and then announce the task: they are to elucidate the abstruse text and assimilate it. We could indulge in such cheerful and basically useful and meaningful exchanges. With distance such actions are hardly conceivable.

I don't recall having a conversation about Serbian poetry.[196] Don't neglect to introduce yourself to these remarkable products of our southern neighbours, which, for us, are also gradually sprouting, blossoming and bearing fruit. If one or other of the little songs speaks to you, don't begrudge them your penetrating harmonic expression. In general, the achievements of the eastern languages, which take in such an enormous area, are gradually becoming of interest to us.

---

[193] This letter was dictated at the earliest on 12 or 13 March 1827 and answers Zelter's letter of 26 February to 10 March which arrived in Weimar on 12 March. Presumably the letter was not sent due to the news of the death of Zelter's son, Georg, on 15 March. Goethe handed the letter to Zelter on 17 October during his stay in Weimar from 12 to 18 October.

[194] Namely, 'Dreistigkeit'.

[195] On 26 February Zelter mentioned that he had been asked for an explanation of Goethe's poem.

[196] Goethe's first reference to the Serbian poems published in *KuA* VI, 1. See also GZ 23–29 March 1827.

### 408. Zelter

18 October 1827[197]

Old Voß once said to me, when I had merely altered the position of a single word in his 'Friedensreigen', 'You may leave that alone!' – and of course I might have done so, but it would have been all bound up with my love of the poem. I must be allowed to appropriate a part of it, in order to make it completely my own; what do I care about the poet? His word is a stone, hurled into space, which I pick up, and how I pick it up, and how I look at it, know and interpret it is my affair; and if he wants to be just, and if he has understood me, as I have understood him, he will remember that his word is printed, and remains his own. [...] Naumann of Dresden[198] had not altered a single word in Schiller's 'Die Ideal', and Schiller scolded like a fishwife at that famous man's composition, because it turned a beautiful poem into a throat exercise for a prima donna. But with no words am I more cautious, more pure, than with yours. The very first time I read your poems, I grasp the sense, the feeling of the whole, and the melody comes at once; I only stop short at a word, a phrase; then I let it lie, until – Heaven knows how long afterwards – my word comes of itself and then I finish. A number of your poems have been lying thus for years. [...]

### 409. Zelter

Berlin, 28 to 30 October 1827

[...] I have had the pleasure of seeing Mademoiselle Sontag twice at the Königliches Theater, as Myrha in the *Opferfest*, and Susanna in Mozart's *Figaro*.[199] Though I cannot particularize any special quality in her, her entire being is suited to the stage. She knows how to look well on the larger stage, whether as third, fourth or fifth and so on, surrounded by so much that is strange, and her ability to vocalize and articulate perfectly raises her above much stronger voices like a bright star. Her face moves with the melody, as do her arms and hands, and all that without repetition; it is always the same, and yet it is new. One duet was called for

---

[197] This letter is from *MA* 20.3, p. 867, where it is entitled: 'Draft to a letter that was never written or was never sent'.

[198] Johann Gottlieb Naumann.

[199] Henriette Sontag appeared in Peter von Winter's opera *Das unterbrochene Opferfest* (libretto by Xaver Huber) on 25 October 1827 and in Mozart's *Die Hochzeit des Figaro* on 27 October 1827; see *AMZ* 29 (1827), no. 47, 21 November, column 794; *MA* 20.3, p. 874–5.

again; the two singers came back[200] as they had gone off; first she had stood on the right side, now she stood on the left and the whole duet seemed like a new piece, which I, at all events, could have heard for the third time. Some people also called out 'da capo' again. [...]

### 410. Goethe

End of October to 6 November 1827

6 November: Thank you for your delightful account, which helped me to realize the gracefulness of that dainty singer;[201] my ear is long unaccustomed to the pleasures of such music, but my spirit is still receptive. The recent performance of *Die Zauberflöte*[202] had an ill effect upon me; in the past I was more susceptible to such things, even though the performances were not any better. Now two imperfections had to do with this, one external, the other internal, and the sensations produced were such as one experiences when striking a bell with a crack in it. It is very strange; for even the repetition of your much-loved songs was not going to succeed. It is better to put up with such a state of affairs than to continually talk or even write much about it.

### 411. Zelter

Berlin, 7 to 17 November 1827

What I wrote to you about Madame Sontag was meant as an explanation of the general impression. One can imagine that such a person, who can put aside an honorarium of 11,000 thalers in a few weeks (not counting significant presents) will arouse envy among those around them. Those performing with her admit to her that they enjoy acting and singing with her and that the effect is good.

A composition of one of my students[203] may reach you. The girl was sent to me for lessons from the Friedrich Society in Danzig. Pretty, healthy, 20 years old, a lovely voice, talent and invincible desire. She is the third one who comes back from Danzig already well trained. If she remains so and her talent is not wasted, she could turn out very well. She has already gone far enough on the piano for it to be useful to her. [...]

---

[200] Henriette Sontag and Carl Adam Bader in Myrrha and Murney's Duet, 'Wenn mir Dein Auge strahlet', from Winter's *Das unterbrochene Opferfest*; see *Spenersche Zeitung* no. 252, 27 October 1827.

[201] Zelter's account of Henriette Sontag's performances, ZG 28 October 1827.

[202] On 20 October 1827 at the Weimar Court Theatre.

[203] The identity of the student has not been established.

### 412. Goethe

Weimar, 21 November 1827

I must report to you that our wandering nightingale[204] arrived on Sunday, 11 November, but owing to some unsuperable confusion, the result of misapprehension, neglect, ill-will and intrigue, she has not appeared in public.[205] On Monday she sang at a breakfast arranged by the Dowager Grand Duchess,[206] and was greatly applauded; afterwards, she paid me a visit, and gave us some little examples of her extraordinary talent; these were enough for me, in so far as the impression I had of her was confirmed and reaffirmed. [...]

### 413. Zelter

Berlin, 23 to 27 November 1827

[...] Our King[207] occasionally has his own quirk: for example, he refuses to have any virtuoso as his Kapellmeister. Bernhard Romberg, who is a composer as well, is clearly ahead of all virtuosi. He got there with patronage and great effort when he discovered that the King had engaged Spontini in Paris. At this time I pointed out to him that a king should in any case be allowed to do what the most ordinary person would do – namely to spend his money and buy a conductor wherever he liked. So Romberg still bears me a grudge, although he wishes to become once more what he didn't want to remain – and could still be if he had followed my friendly advice.

[...] Privy Councillor Bunsen arrived from Rome with treasures,[208] some of which the Sing-Akademie will enjoy. The Crown Prince wants to attend a

---

[204] Henriette Sontag. From the time of her first performance in Berlin she was continually referred to by the press as a nightingale; see, for example, the *Spenersche Zeitung* of 5 August 1825 and 9 September 1825.

[205] See, for example, *AMZ* 30 (1828), no. 5, 30 January, column 74: 'Sontag, who we had hoped to hear at the theatre on her journey through [Weimar], sang only at the court for a royal audience, accompanied on the piano.'

[206] Maria Pawlowna, wife of the future Grand Duke, Carl Friedrich of Sachsen-Weimar-Eisenach.

[207] King Wilhelm Friedrich III.

[208] Bunsen's official commission was to accompany the Raphael painting *Madonna della famiglia di Lante* from Rome to the Berlin museum, where it was to be housed. The Sing-Akademie treasures Zelter refers to concern the church music from the Vatican collection. See the chapter 'Reise nach Berlin 1827–1828' in Christian Carl Josias von Bunsen, *Aus seinen Briefen und nach eigener Erinnerung geschildert von seiner Witwe* (3 vols, Leipzig: F.A. Brockhaus 1868–71), vol.1, pp. 275–334.

performance of 'O Roma Nobilis'[209] from the seventeenth century with us today. I have never been to Rome and don't know anything about it. The melody from the seventh century is modern enough; the current papal Kapellmeister Baini arranged it in four-part harmony.[210]

### 414. Goethe

Weimar, 24 January 1828

[...] When I think of all the things happening above your head whose influence you cannot completely fend off, I am not surprised that, caught up in a whirlpool of musical, aesthetic, physical and natural-philosophical exhibitions, you could hardly ever have time to yourself, even if you did not have to play such an important role yourself. Cast a glance around you once again and report some things so that the year 1828 will not be turn out to be too thin. Send me my letters from 1827 so that I can lay out the codices. Also enclose the little book by Kandler again: the way this man lives musically and lets live made a particular impression on me.

### 415. Zelter

Berlin, 28 January 1828 to 3 February 1828

28 January. [...] Our building has cost money, more than we have,[211] so *Judas* had to be called in – not the one with the purse.[212] It was not in the budget, however, and – scraping money together becomes more difficult as I grow older. [...]

Breidenstein, whom the ministry sent to Bonn five years ago as Professor and Director of Music so that he might learn from the students there, has come back to Berlin because he couldn't make any headway there. He read a lecture about

---

[209] A paean in three strophes from the six verses in the form of an Asclepiadian ode, presumably stemming from Verona (tenth century); it celebrates in song Rome as the scene of the martyrdom of the Apostles, in particular St Peter and St Paul, whose feast day it celebrates. The text is an amalgam of early church songs dedicated to the Apostles. For further information; see Ludwig Traube, 'O Roma nobilis', *Abhandlung der Bayerischen Akademie der Wissenschaften* 19/2 (1891): 299–395.

[210] A score in Zelter's own hand for solo voice and piano is entitled 'O Roma nobilis aus dem VII Jahrhunderte (spätestens) Harmonie v. Baini, korrigiert von Zelter' (SBB PK: Mus. Ms. Autogr. Zelter 34).

[211] The new building was estimated at 28,000 thaler.

[212] *Judas Maccabaeus* not Judas Iscariot. The Sing-Akademie performance of Handel's oratorio took place on 17 January 1828; see *AMZ* 30 (1828), no. 9, 27 February, column 146; *MA* 20.3, p. 890.

musical theory[213] here for men and women, specialists and laity. I was also present at the first lecture. He then expatiated on those who live from hand to mouth and since I am one of these and know it, I left him to his theories. [...]

The letters from the year 1827 are enclosed.[214] The little Kandler book is also enclosed.[215] Of the latter I will only remark that the information about Hasse is taken from Gerber's musical dictionary,[216] which the French Lexicon[217] and also the latest Italian Lexicon of Pietro Lichtenthal[218] have regurgitated with all its imperfections. [...]

Next Wednesday we will perform *Judas Maccabaeus*[219] for the general public once more. If only you could hear it. The way people talk and write about it, neither Handel nor anyone else would recognize his work.

### 416. Zelter

Berlin, 7 to 9 February 1828

[...] Our *Judas Maccabaeus* was set to sea with a favouring wind and to our advantage. The King found us worthy enough to listen to and paid 20 Friedrichs d'or for his box and in person showed his approval of me. This is of infinite value to me, just as his pieces of gold are necessary to us because we have to raise

---

[213] Zelter had already been highly critical of Heinrich Carl Breidenstein (1796–1876) as Director of Music at the University of Bonn when Zelter had visited Bonn in November 1823. Breidenstein, who had been made Professor of Music in Bonn in 1826 (and holder of the first chair of musicology in Germany), spent his sabbatical in Berlin in 1827/28. On 9 November he gave the first of a series of 12 lectures on the Theory of Music; these events were intended for those connected with the opera and the orchestra, but they were open to all who were interested.

[214] Goethe's letters to Zelter from 1827 which were being sent to Weimar to be copied.

[215] Kandler's biography of the composer Hasse, which Zelter had requested again on 24 January; Goethe returned the book on 8 January 1829.

[216] The article 'Johann Adolf Hasse' in Ernst Ludwig Gerbers, *Neues historisch-biographisches Lexikon der Tonkünstler* (4 vols, Leipzig: Breitkopf, 1790–92), pp. 590–601, or in the revised version of the dictionary, *Neues historisch-biographisches Lexikon* (Leipzig: Kuhnel, 1812–14), pp. 517–19. Zelter had both editions. Further editions were published in 1835, 1860 and 1873, the most recent edited by Othmar Wessley 4 vols in 3 (Graz: Akademische-Druck und Verlaganstalt, 1966).

[217] *Dictionnaire historique des musiciens* (2 vols, Paris 1810–11, r.1817).

[218] In his preface to his *Dizionario e bibliographia della musica* (2 vols, Milan: A. Fontana, 1826), Peter Lichtenthal acknowledged the use of Gerber's lexikon; he didn't include a biographical article on Hasse.

[219] The Sing-Akademie's second performance of Handel's *Judas Maccabaeus* took place on 6 February 1828.

over 3,000 thalers per annum. Otherwise we are quite enjoying ourself as already reported: carnival, German opera, French comedy, masked balls and balls. [...]

I hear yesterday's perfomance of our music praised from all sides. That comes from a clever Italian Prince (Lucchese),[220] who said that if one wants to hear good music, one has to come to Germany. [...]

The post is leaving. I still want to report that the Gesellschaft der Musikfreude of the Imperial Austrian State[221] unexpectedly appointed me an honorary member and sent me their diploma certifying it.

### 417. Goethe

Weimar, 20 February 1828

[...] Our dear Crown Grand Duchess has now arrived in Berlin.[222] I have asked her to make sure she doesn't miss your Sing-Akademie.

### 418. Zelter

Berlin, 10 to 23 February 1828

A review of my *Tafellieder*[223] said that the absolute value of my songs was not as great as the aesthetic value – which I would gladly take as praise except that it wasn't meant as such. The aesthetic value of a song is the umbrella concept

---

[220] His identity has not been ascertained.

[221] The Gesellschaft der Musikfreunde, established in 1812, was known for its lavish performances of Handel's oratorios; the man who was responsible for this was Ignaz Franz Edler von Mosel, who, next to Zelter, was one of the leading figures in the Handel Renaissance brought about by amateur choirs.

[222] After she had called on Goethe on 14 February, Maria Pawlowna had travelled to Berlin mid-February for the confinement of her daughter, Maria of Prussia, who had married Prince Carl of Prussia in 1827. Goethe had asked Varnhagen von Ense 'to wait upon' the future Grand Duchess.

[223] Ludwig Rellstab's review series in the *Berliner Allegemeine Musikalische Zeitung* 4 (1827), no. 7, 14 February, p. 51f. and no. 8, 21 February, pp. 59–62: *Tafellieder für Männerstimmen*, vol. 1 by Friedrich Wollanck, vol. 2 by C.F. Rungenhagen, vol. 3 by C.L. Hellwig, vol. 4 by F.F. Fleming, vol. 5 by C.F. Zelter, vol. 6 by Fr. Lauska. The correct title was *Gesänge der Zelterschen Liedertafel in Berlin für Männerstimmen* (Berlin: T. Trautwein o.J, 1827). The passage Zelter refers to in vol. 5 reads: 'It is, however, not to be denied that the absolute musical value of his songs is, in general, not as great as the aesthetic value in that, from time to time, melody and harmony are not of the same high quality. Against that, however, he never writes a song that is not original from any perspective; indeed highly distinctive features are offered in the conception and reproduction.'

and embraces the musical, which would otherwise not be aesthetic. So the review wants to set me up, itself devoid of understanding, and ultimately criticizes me without understanding me, in that it misses many songs in the collection which are already well known. The collection also contains my latest Lieder, which are still unknown because I don't want the public to buy what it already has free of charge. [...]

Telemann (of Hamburg) said, 'One must be able to set a custom's document to music'. Here is a joke about it. A member of our Liedertafel,[224] who we aren't glad to see missing on account of his lovely voice, excuses himself more often than he should. So I set his last letter of excuse to music and now we will see whether the chap improves himself or wants to be left in prose.[225]

## 419. Zelter

Berlin, 5 to 8 March 1828

I waited on your Grand Duchess[226] last Saturday. She recognized me immediately in von Humbold's lecture and made an appointment around ten o'clock today through His Excellency von Henkel.[227]

Yesterday evening after five, just as the Sing-Akademie gathered together, Her Highness quietly announced her presence through Chamberlain von Oelsen and immediately refused any fuss. Our lighting is very rudimentary when we are without noble guests; but we just about managed to light up the court box. Reichardt's 'Morgengesang'[228] (in Bürde's translation of Thomson),[229] which has

---

[224] Staberoh, a merchant and member of Zelter's Liedertafel from 1817 to 1840.

[225] The note had the following wording: 'My dear friend! Since I am feeling slightly off-colour, I cannot enjoy the pleasure of attending the Liedertafel today. As far as the choice of the new Table Officials, I gladly submit to the majority voice. Your humble Staberoh'. Zelter composed a witty amusing little song to be sung by the soloists Hellwig and Gern, accompanied by the Liedertafel chorus. Despite Goethe's request, Zelter did not sent a copy to him; the autograph copy, entitled 'Indisposition' and signed 'Poetry by Staberoh. Music by Zelter' is in Zelter's estate (SBB PK: Mus. Ms. Autogr. Zelter).

[226] Maria Pawlowna of Sachsen-Weimar-Eisenach.

[227] Countess Ottilie Henckel of Donnersmarck, grandmother to Ottilie and Ulrike von Pogwisch, senior stewardess to Maria Pawlowna since 1804.

[228] Reichardt had composed the hymn *Miltons Morgengesang* 'for the Berlin Sing-Akademie of the noble master, Fasch' and it was published in Kassel in 1808. The date of composition is unknown, but it was certainly composed during Fasch's lifetime because Zelter mentions it in his Fasch biography of 1801.

[229] The text, which comes from Milton's *Paradise Lost*, was translated into German by Gottlob Bürde (Berlin 1793). It is not clear which Thomson Zelter is referring to, presumably the English poet James Thomson. His 'Hymn to the Seasons', widely used in Germany, does not show any similarities to the given text. Since Gottfried von Swieten's

long been cast aside, was performed once more to complete the annual repertoire and because the work is not easy, it is now time to load the guns. Now that is the advantage, even the privilege of the Sing-Akademie that I can let the choir go on at an easy pace without much lecturing from one week to the next, but when it is essential and they know that I mean it, no one messes about and I myself am more likely to make a mistake, which they all notice very readily and are clear about.

The psalm lasts almost an hour. After the music her Highness called me to her box and revealed herself to be someone who has a proper understanding of music, although she seemed surprised that Reichardt would be capable of such style and such a work. It truly delighted me to hear that from a noble connoisseur, the likes of which one is not used to here because Reichardt was no mere kitten. His talent was genuinely musical; but there wasn't enough for him to do here. And his political striving drowned him.[230] Water has no beams. He wanted to climb: how? Where? And he drowned.

Doris has just returned from the palace. Her Highness really enjoyed herself with us and in the evening spoke of an enjoyment which is not usual for her. In particular the tenor Stümer appealed to her and he is my student.[231] I have brought him up from the Currende[232], taught him for three years; now he is on the payroll of the Königliches Theater,[233] has taken for his wife a pretty woman[234] – the daughter of one of my friends[235] – who is also not poor. What's it got to do with you? Enough! That's the way it is. [...]

The Sing-Akademie, an ensemble of 150 to 180 trained voices, must have an undreamed of effect on someone who hears it for the first time. I put the thing together like so many small pieces of a mosaic and keep it in shape. [...] What distinguishes our choir completely are the inner voices: the crux of a true

---

libretto for Haydn's *Creation* is based on Milton, it is possible that it is confused with *The Seasons*, which is based on Thomson.

[230] Reichardt's open sympathy with the aims of the French Revolution; his sans-culottism reinforced the hostile attitude towards him and this was shared by the king, who had become mistrustful of him.

[231] Johann Daniel Heinrich Stümer (1789–1856), who 'joined the Sing-Akademie in 1804, where he sang as male alto and had the opportunity to hear classical church works, which was a major influence on his artistic development in later years (...) From 5 April 1814, he was a member of the oldest Liedertafel established by Zelter', Carl von Ledebur, *Tonkünstlerlexikon Berlins. Von den ältesten Zeiten bis auf die Gegenwart* (Berlin: L. Rauh, 1861), p. 80f.

[232] Literally 'runners'. From *currere*, to run. A choir of needy schoolchildren who ran singing through the street; this tradition of busking, which extended into the eighteenth century, could still be encountered in the nineteenth century, at which time it began to peter out.

[233] Heinrich Stümer was engaged as a tenor by the Königliches Theater from 1811 until his retirement in March 1831.

[234] Anna Christina Henriette Stümer, née Weltz (1794–1865).

[235] Johann Gottlob Weltz (b.1757), court official in Berlin.

choir. Nowhere else in the world is there such a choir of beautiful female alto voices, and that is no small feat because everyone wants to sing high and boys voices break, whereas the female voices increase in fullness and character with the years.

The day before yesterday (Thursday) Hummel gave a delightful new public performance of his concerto (in A flat major) in the royal concert hall.[236] The applause was unanimous, although the work was not found to be of the same standard as his previous ones. That comes down to the people again, who want to have the first impression repeated like a da capo of an eclipse of the moon.

## 420. Zelter

Berlin, 31 March 1828

For the last 25 years our good singer Milder has been a credit to our opera and has deserved the favour of all well-disposed people.

A number of friends, among whom I am one of the most favoured, will, on 9 April, present a porcelain vase with her portrait to the lovely heroine[237] and would love a few favourable words from you.[238] If you can you find a free moment since you also belong to the circle of friends, your Zelter would be very grateful to you.

---

[236] On his way to Breslau and Warsaw, the Weimar Court Kapellmeister Johann Nepomuk Hummel gave a concert in the Königliches Schauspielhaus in Berlin; his programme included his latest Piano Concerto in A Major; see *AMZ* 30 (1828) and *Spenersche Zeitung*, 12 March 1828.

[237] The vase is still in the possession of the Sing-Akademie; a picture of it is in Werner Bollert (ed.), *Sing-Akademie zu Berlin. Festschrift zum 175jährigen Bestehen* (Berlin: Rembrandt Verlag, 1966), p. 24.

[238] Goethe had already dedicated a verse (on 12 June 1826) to the famous singer whom he had met in Marienbad. The autograph – enclosed in the letter from Zelter in thanks for the songs which she had performed in Marienbad on 24 August 1823 – may have contained [additional] verses which have not been handed down. Due to time constraints, Goethe was not able to fulfil Zelter's request for a poem in celebration of Milder's 25 years on stage.

## 421. Goethe

Weimar, 22 April 1828

How gladly I would have fulfilled, your request, dear Zelter, and write a few friendly poetic words for the celebration of our valiant and well-deserving Milder.[239] I was intending to do it right until the last minute, but it just wasn't going to happen because it's a long time since I have been so hard-pressed as in recent weeks. If I were to say how [pressurized], you would hear the most wonderful quodlibet.

Your Easter concert went off well.[240] You have really won favour with our Crown Grand Duchess and it earned for me the really special consolation that this splendid lady has become aware of your endeavours and achievements. The effect was as good as you could have wished for. May the means to such lovely ends not turn out too sour for you. […]

My surroundings remain tuneless and unmelodious. Recently I sought solace in the opera,[241] but the bass drum, which made our whole wooden house shake to the rafters, frightened me off any further attempt. […]

Our 1827 correspondence increases in the number of transcribed sheets. The little volume for this year is still far too thin.[242]

## 422. Zelter

Berlin, 26 April 1828

[…] Our fete in honour of Milder, held at my house on the 9th [April],[243] as well as the Dürer fete on the 18th [April], surpassed all expectation.[244] For the latter

---

[239] Milder's anniversary of 25 years on stage.

[240] Zelter had conducted the traditional performance of Graun's *Der Tod Jesu* on Good Friday, 4 April 1828.

[241] There is no operatic performance mentioned in Goethe's diary in March or April 1828. Possibilities at this time include Rossini's *Die Belagerung von Corinth* and *Tancredi*, as well as Mozart's *Hochzeit des Figaro*; it is also possible that he attended a rehearsal of Carl Maria von Weber's *Oberon* (premiered on 28 May 1828).

[242] The copy of the letters made in 1827 with a view to posthumous publication.

[243] The anniversary celebration of Milder's 25 years on stage.

[244] A celebration to mark the 300-year anniversary of Dürer's death, organized by Gottfried Schadow, had taken place in the Sing-Akademie on 18 April 1828. In addition to a Mendelssohn symphony and an address by the Sing-Akademie secretary, Toelken, a specially commissioned cantata by Mendelssohn (to Konrad Levezow's text, 'Abrecht Dürer') was premiered. Apart from the limited complaint that the music had lasted two hours, the reaction in the press was positive and a repeat performance of *Dürers Festmusik* was scheduled for 8 May.

occasion Felix wrote music,[245] which, in spite of the words, contains beautiful passages; the technical work is masterly throughout.

### 423. Zelter

Berlin, 27 April 1828

[…] If you could only spend four weeks with me here in my corner room.[246] […] At midday when the guards change [one hears] the best military music[247] – the loveliest works by Beethoven, Mozart, Cherubini, Spontini, Rossini – without putting a foot outside the door. If I don't want to listen, I go back into my corner room. […]

### 424. Zelter

Berlin, 30 April to 11 May 1828

That should have counted as a day of repentance[248] – and I count it as one. All theatres were closed; there has to be a day when the bewitched actors themselves can get drunk undisturbed.

To keep such a day holy our general music director set up a charitable foundation for musicians,[249] since spiritual works are being performed in the theatre by orchestra and singers.

---

[245] Ibid.

[246] Zelter's new accommodation in the Sing-Akademie building on Dorotheenstraße since March 1827.

[247] Harmoniemusik – arrangements of operas, overtures and symphonies for wind instruments – were extremely popular and through which audiences became acquainted with many works. Military music played a special role in promoting opera. In Berlin, Georg Abraham Schneider, music director, Kapellmeister and director of the army band, arranged Spontini's *Olympia*, for example, and Friedrich Weller arranged Weber's *Oberon* before its Berlin premiere. In addition to their official engagements, this military band gave countless garden and promenade performances, and their contribution to the musical life of Berlin cannot be overrated.

[248] Annual official day of repentence, at that time in Prussia on the Wednesday following the third Sunday after Easter.

[249] The *Spontini-Fonds* was established in 1826 to support the theatre personnel and, above all, members of the orchestra and choir; an annual benefit concert took place every year.

Today's choice consisted of the most exquisite rare works: two powerful symphonies by Beethoven,[250] half of a mass by the same,[251] half of a Credo[252] by Sebastian Bach and a German Sanctus by Emanuel Bach.[253]

The critical public[254] found this combination rather too much like a miscellany and scattered, rather than clever and appropriate – even if at other times it is inclined to find that an entire work is nearly always too complete for them. Neither one nor the other composer was going to make a complete work which hung together, but the intention was much more to achieve a great variety of individual pieces. The good intention was obvious here: to offer the ears the most entertaining piquant [music] of today's and yesterday's world of art, which also became so substantial to me that I could never forget it, as long as similar things are not on offer too frequently. Since they recognized no enemies among themselves, commanders and generals, officers and the general public argued with such zeal as if they had the new manifesto in the bag. The dear audience (nearly all connoisseurs who don't pay) were beside themselves with pleasure over the most noticeable oversights. I myself was surprised how they dispersed all bright and comforted at the end as if nothing had happened to them. I was almost beaten because I didn't join in the abuse, but I was beaten and tortured for their sins![255] I had a glass of wine; the general music director,[256] however, was sick.

8 May: Today our Albrecht Dürer Celebration Music was to have been repeated on account of many requests. We cancelled it.[257] Musical life moves here like a

---

[250] Beethoven, Symphony no. 5 in C minor, op. 67 and the Coriolan Overture, op. 62.

[251] Kyrie and Gloria from Beethoven's Mass in D Major, op. 123.

[252] Six lines of the Credo from J.S. Bach's Mass in B minor, BWV 232.

[253] C.P.E. Bach's *Heilig* for double choir, Wq 217.

[254] In an announcement of the concert in the *Berliner Allgemeine Musikalische Zeitung*, no. 18, 30 April 1828, column 146. A.B. Marx criticized the programme: 'the compilation of so many different works and mere fragments of works, which are very worthy of a complete performance, makes a highly unfavourable impression; a later review, in the *Berliner Allgemeine Musikalische Zeitung* (1828), no. 19, 7 May, columns 152–4, uses the latter criticism as a reproach aimed at Zelter, namely that J.S. Bach's works had not yet been performed in Berlin.

[255] Isaiah, 54, v. 4. The text 'I was beaten and tortured for their sins' is a reference to the suffering servant of God: 'We considered him, namely the suffering servant of God, who was tormented and beaten and martyred by God, but he has been wounded for our misdeeds and bruised for our sins.'

[256] Spontini.

[257] Mendelssohn's Cantata for mixed choir, soloists and orchestra, which was premiered at the Dürerfest marking the 300th anniversary of Dürer's death, should have been repeated on 8 May 1828 in the Sing-Akademie hall and the profits given to the building fund. The day before the scheduled performance a notice in the Berlin newspapers announced that the advertised concert had been postponed; the reasons for this cancellation have not been determined.

crab in a kettle. Everyone is critical [of the theatre], makes negative comments about it, and no one can get enough. They keep on going there and come away unchallenged.

### 425. Goethe

Weimar, 21 May 1828

Regarding the missing letters, I have the following to report for the present: in my copy the letters have not been numbered, but on close examination the copy is complete. On the other hand a gap remains in your original letters as I have them. The last letter from you is from 14 June and announces Frau von Zschokke. The next letter is from 5 September and discusses the Begas portrait. Such [a gap] has to be explained in the following way: when he was finished, the copyist put the originals into order again. One must have been moved from this pile, as can happen with even the best of organization. The original version will certainly turn up and your letters will follow immediately. In any case the copies are there and the gap could be filled in different ways. [...]

### 426. Goethe

Weimar, 2 June 1828

So much for now, as this is essentially a letter of recommendation for a young man, von Schwendler,[258] who is presently studying in Berlin. Welcome him for my sake because we owe a great deal to his parents.[259] He will report to you with a page from me.[260] He is supposed to have a musical bent and some experience in it, which I would like you to assess and foster accordingly.

---

[258] See Goethe's diary for 25 May 1828: 'President von Schwendler's thanks in advance for the provisional recommendation of his son to Zelter', *WA* III/11, p. 223. Reinhold von Schwendler studied law in Berlin; the planned visit to Zelter had still not taken place on 5 June.

[259] Friedrich Christian August von Schwendler (*c.*1772–1844), president of regional administration, and his wife, Henriette August Sophie Schwendler née Mützschefahl, divorced Countess von Schlabrendorff (1773–1853).

[260] A letter of recommendation, GZ 2 June.

### 427. Zelter

Berlin, 26 May to 3 June 1828

[...] The day before yesterday our good Weitsch[261] the painter died [...] He was musical and liked to lecture me about it, much to the amusement of my friends – I listened quietly to him and they knew quite well what I am like with professional musicians. He will be buried tomorrow: we will all follow the coffin, apart from me. I have the desire still to wait a little and he should not take that badly; I will follow in my own time. [...]

### 428. Zelter

Berlin, 9 to 12 June 1828

11 June: Yesterday our Grand Duke was in the Sing-Akademie accompanied by Major von Germar[262] and Major von Staff.[263] Prince Carl[264] came afterwards. The old fellow endured some short pieces by me, by Fasch and von Stölzel very nicely. He came shortly after six and we were finished at seven. For a delicate unspoilt ear we view such things exactly the same as an operation. I hardly know myself how I would endure it if it were offered to me for the first time. Our performance room seemed to please the Duke. The music, in fact, sounded very good and the pieces went without a hitch, as is almost always the case when such esteemed guests honour us.

### 429. Zelter

17 to 24 June 1828

23 June: The music director Rungenhagen (second conductor of the Sing-Akademie), the music director Bach (not belonging to the old family), the Supreme Court Councillor Gedike (son of the famous Biestergedike), all the students and participants of the Sing-Akademie are on tour southwards through Thüringen and

---

[261] *Friedrich* Georg Weitsch (1758–1828), painter; member of the Akademie der Künste in Berlin.

[262] Friedrich von Germar, Sachsen-Weimar officer in Carl August's entourage during his Berlin visit.

[263] Hermann von Staff, Prussian general who had been on duty in Sachsen-Weimar from 1807 to 1814.

[264] Prince Carl of Prussia, son of King Friedrich Wilhelm III, since 1827 married to Princess Maria of Sachsen-Weimar, a granddaughter of Carl August.

will bring these lines with them.²⁶⁵ Should your current chaos and physical health allow you to see these good people briefly, they will tell you that they have left me in good health. I will be busy through their two-month absence and have lighter work to do. One gets things done best without so-called help. [...]

### 430. Zelter

Berlin, 19 to 20 July 1828

A lady in Königsberg²⁶⁶ said, 'In our songs the music is to the poetry as stone is to steel.' Saemann, who has undertaken a Liedertafel in Königsberg,²⁶⁷ told me that and I have given him a number of contributions for it. Admittedly one cannot live off such comfort from a distance. However, one feels that one lives and only giving means living. [...]

Weber's new opera, *Oberon*,²⁶⁸ is still new here and friends of the departed won't be neglected. Unfortunately I still have not seen the opera because it has only been performed when I myself am working. Whoever on these occasions doesn't drop everything and join the throng is not looked on favourably. I see them coming back and hear them as they slave away trying to be funny and lay claim to singers, actors, painters and everything else. At the end of it all the most important thing is the conversation, to which one never comes too late.

### 431. Goethe

Dornburg, 27 July 1828

[...] It would be great if you could tell me of an author from whom I could gain information as to what kind of musical system was used during the first half of the seventeenth century, and how it could have been so expressed that a Hamburg

---

[265] Carl Friedrich Rungenhagen, August Wilhelm Bach and Wilhelm Gedike. The meeting (and handing-over of the letter) did not take place on account of Carl August's death. See Goethe's letter to Rungenhagen on 21 October 1828 in response to this 'cancellation' and also to Rungenhagen's request for poems for Zelter's birthday which he, Mendelssohn and Hellwig might set.

[266] Her identity has not been established.

[267] A choral society founded by Karl Heinrich Saemann in Königsberg in 1818.

[268] Carl Maria von Weber, *Oberon, Königin der Elfen*, a three-act romantic opera (libretto by James Robinson Planché after Wieland's *Oberon*, translated by Theodor Hell); premiered in London in 1826. The Berlin premiere took place on 2 July 1828 with repeat performances on 4 and 9 July.

Rector[269] of that day was able to pass it down to his pupils on three printed pages? Right now I am engaged in studying that important epoch to which we owe so much.

### 432. Zelter

Berlin, Beginning [of August] to 4 August 1828

You ask me – what kind of musical system was used during the first half of the seventeenth century, and how it could have been so expressed that a Hamburg Rector of that day could pass it down to his pupils on three printed sheets? In the first place – so far as I can tell you – there were many such treatises, partly transcribed by students of music, partly dictated by teachers; these take up very little room, inasmuch as they contain only isolated examples, or none at all. In Vienna I saw another such volume, the work of Wolfgang Amadeus Mozart;[270] I myself have dictated several to many of my pupils – possibly Eberwein, your musical director, may have kept one of them. [...] A relic of that time, still in great demand, containing a collection of musical theories is David Kellner's *Instruction in Ground Bass*,[271] a little tract consisting of less than a hundred pages, printed at Hamburg, in quarto, in 1732; this has been reprinted many times. [...]

If one wanted to undertake a basic investigation of the first teachings of melody and harmony, one would have to realize that they were all built on the foundations of singing schools.[272] But who still thinks of the invaluable discovery

---

[269] As his diary shows, Goethe occupied himself from 30 June 1828 with the works of Joachim Jungius, for whom he had intended to create a 'thorough memorial' in his essay *Leben und Verdienste des Doktor Joachim Jungius, Rektors zu Hamburg*. (See Goethe's letter to Soret on 2 July 1828, *WA* IV/43, p. 1.) The desire to study Jungius's writing came about through Goethe's preoccupation with De Candolles' botanical work, in which Goethe saw a forerunner to the Theory of Metamorphosis. Goethe was awaiting information from Zelter on Jungius's *Harmonie*.

[270] Zelter presumably meant the textbook for Barbara [Babette] Ployer, KV 453 b, in the possession of Abbé Maximilian Stadler, whom Zelter had met in Vienna on 14 September 1819, although Zelter could also have meant the *Kurzgefaßte Generalbaßlehre* which was falsely attributed to Mozart in the publication in Vienna in 1817 and in Berlin in 1822.

[271] A draft letter deals with this more fully: 'This is not just a book on ground bass for the use of a keyboard player but for all other players and singers. If it is not found in your library, we have it here for your use. The trouble with all these works and large compendia is the lack of sufficient examples which an experienced teacher can give, although a real talent doesn't need much guidance since the best part always has to be intuitive' (GSA 28/1028).

[272] Perhaps Zelter is referring to Johann Josef Fux, *Singfundament*, which was praised in the *AMZ* 30 (1828), no. 3, 16 January, columns 35–41.

of nine numbers and the 24 [German] letters of the alphabet? I am happy to refer you to your own words in *Über Kunst und Altertum*, Volume VI, Book 24, p. 29.[273] What is said there about the old Greek style of painting I am inclined to apply here: what is called light and shadow in the new painting can be thought of as chromatic (dissonant) in new music,[274] in that the music from this point onwards takes on a dramatic character which it didn't have up to now. So the seventeenth century separates art written in servitude from governing art which stands by itself.[275] Rhyme that as well as you can and say something about it.

Pietro della Valle,[276] whom you know better than I do,[277] places the music of his time high above that of the fifteenth and sixteenth centuries; the chromatic scale had crept in, and had given to the music character, flexibility and freedom. Here expanded rules were now necessary in order not to lose the old foundation: melodic progressions into larger than big and smaller than small intervals should be avoided. One called them augmented and diminished in so far as they were not comfortable enough to sing, and since the notation itself was also lacking there, they were not [used] as a rule. Against that an aesthetic foundation was not lacking because they were supposed to introduce the passionate, the luxuriant. To the finer types still belonged: the cautious use of the minor third at cadences; the progressions through parallel movement between voices, in octaves, sixths, fifths, fourths, and thirds, whereby the teaching of double counterpoint already announced itself because this would also have been practised, [as would] the handling of dissonance and so on.

These finer innovations, by which mastery was supposed to be recognized, were already systematized at the end of the seventeenth century, although they were handed down only by tradition to favoured musicians. The product of that time appeared in a work by John Joseph Fux, *Gradus ad Parnassum, sive manuductio ad compositionem musicæ regularem, nova ac certa nondum ante tam*

---

[273] Review of *Peintures de Polygnote dans la Lesche de Delphe par Riepenhausen*, most likely written by Johann Heinrich Meyer, *KuA* VI, 2, p. 289.

[274] In the following passage Zelter describes the change in musical style around 1600. The 'stil antico', which in the nineteenth century was primarily associated with Palestrina, is set against contemporary performance practice in which the music primarily expresses the dramatic intention of the text.

[275] With the controversy between Claudio Monteverdi and Giovanni Maria Artusi over the relationship between words and music at the beginning of the seventeenth century, a new epoch in the writing of music history was ushered in. The dramatic expression of the spoken word in Monteverdi was known as *seconda practica* and was set against the older style of polyphony.

[276] Pietro della Valle, known as il Pellegrino, (1586–1652), Italian composer and music theorist.

[277] See Goethe's treatise on Pietro della Valle in the *Noten und Abhandlung zu besserem Verständnis des West-östlichen Divans* (*MA* 11.1.2, p. 236ff).

*exacta ordine in lucem edita*.[278] In accordance with this theory, the author had for years trained his illustrious pupil, Carl VI,[279] who became a master in the art; and the cost of publishing the work in the Latin language, in a splendid folio edition, was defrayed by the Emperor in the year 1725. The work has been translated into German;[280] the Latin edition is getting scarce, although I have two copies in my possession.

The work is written, as all the educational works of Germany were in those days, in question and answer between master and pupil and, for that reason, it is often laughed at today. The master was unwilling to appear publicly as superior to his illustrious pupil, and names the pupil Joseph (the author himself), but [he names] the master Aloysius, namely *Praenestinus*,[281] whose principles are here preserved for posterity as unsurpassable. These principles form the groundwork of all great and beautiful masterpieces of music up to the present day; they are the techniques of composition, and they leave to anyone who has mastered them plenty of scope to write what is beautiful correctly.[282]

---

[278] Johann Josef Fux, *Steps to Parnassus, or introduction to the standard composition of music. This introduction is new and established and, to date, has never been published in such an organized form* (Vienna: Johann Peter van Ghelen, 1725, reprint New York: Broude Brothers, 1966).

[279] Joseph Franz *Carl* VI, King of Spain (as Carl III) from 1703 and Holy Roman Emperor of the German nation from 1711.

[280] By Lorenz Christoph Mizler von Kolof (1711–78), musicologist.

[281] Franz Sales Kandler records the Latin name for Palestrina as written on his gravestone: 'Johannes Petrus Aloysius Praenestinus Musicae Princeps'; Franz Sales Kandler, 'Memorabilien aus G. Pierluigis da Palestrina Leben'. In: *AMZ* 31 (1829), no. 49, 9 December, column 803.

[282] In a rough draft of this letter Zelter wrote: 'This work is, actually, the connection of the old teaching with the new, the old style with the new, because Beethoven, Mozart, Haydn, Handel, Sebastian Bach, Graun and whoever else has worked according to these principles like men of genius. Approximately 40 years before Fux, the work of Prinz Wolfgang Caspar of Waldthurn *Musikalische Wissenschaft de concordantiis singulis* appeared, which only deals with the unison, the octave, fifth, major and minor third, fourths, major and minor sixths, and it is is unmistakable how far the theory lags behind the practice because [Johann] Sebastian Bach, born in Eisenach in 1685, who, through a continual series of spiritual works which nothing could withstand, paralysed the concordance method in such a way that it cannot recover even up to the present day, although the foundation of it all is the old style. Reichardt and many others after him believed they made exception to the rules and all have been left behind: art has progressed. Because, as in the plastic arts, all definitions of the elements are based on a type that is in Nature, so also in melody and harmony, everything dissonant has to rest on the consonant; from there the theory of ground bass re-emerges' (GSA 28/1028).

### 433. Goethe

Dornburg, 9 August 1828

[…] I am twice as delighted with my old friend, Joachim Jungius, for having inspired you to write so kindly that instructive page; it is just what I needed, and something more: just as much as I understand, and in addition to that, something that I have a presentiment of. This may well be enough since you yourself give your communication a symbolic turn.

If we want to get even half way to the proper understanding of a man, we must, above all things, study the age in which he lived, perhaps completely ignoring him for a while; but discover, when we return to him, the greatest satisfaction with his discourse. Therefore, I made it my business to learn, if only imperfectly, what this extremely thorough man might have dictated to his pupils in the first half of the seventeenth century. Even at a very early age, he was Professor of Mathematics and Physics at Gießen,[283] where later on what was normally known of the Theory of Sound could not have been an undiscovered or unfamiliar study to him.

### 434. Zelter

Berlin, 11 to 17 August 1828

[…] Your derivation of the new Greek education jumped out at me. What I have long treasured in my heart I was able to add here. Music has only old natural laws. Today's theorists want to have new rules for sham music or for what is more than music. Let them get on with it. The genius will discover the new through the old and the philistines need no rules to go to the devil.

### 435. Goethe

Dornburg, 26 August 1828

I am asked to announce and recommend to you Chélard, Maître de la Chapelle de S. M. Le Roi de Bavière.[284] He brings me this request from Weimar, whither he

---

[283] At the age of 22, Joachim Jungius was made Professor of Mathematics in Gießen in 1609; he took up the study of medicine in 1616 and was Professor of Mathematics and Medicine in Rostock and Helmstedt from 1624 to 1626; from 1626 until his death he was rector of the academic grammar school and (until 1640) of the Johanneum in Hamburg.

[284] The French composer Hippolyte André Jean Baptiste Chélard visited Goethe in Dornburg on 25 August 1828. Goethe mentioned this meeting in his diary: 'I had a pleasant conversation with him about the current state of music and literature in Paris.

came with good letters of introduction; you will recognize him from his works. I am not quite clear on his position; in Paris he wrote an opera, *Macbeth*,[285] with which he probably expected to open up a new path for himself; it appears to me it was never performed there; anyhow, I have never read anything about it in the Parisian papers. I suppose it was either rejected or it was a failure; he took his score, travelled to Germany, and came to Munich, where a German translation was used[286] and the work was performed to great applause.[287] The King conferred on him the above title.[288]

He is now going to Berlin,[289] presumably to make arrangements for a performance there, and if possible to double the good name he has gained and re-establish his fame in his own country. In addition to this, he may be looking about for other opportunities in German music to further his own ends. All this you will soon see and be able to judge for yourself and assist him, as you think fit. […]

If you will add a few notes to the enclosed verses,[290] I would be delighted to receive them and see them live anew.

Enclosed: 'Dem aufgehenden Vollmonde'

### 436. Zelter

Berlin, 30 August 1828

[…] Your Kapellmeister[291] has still not arrived here and he shall be made welcome. Hopefully with respect to music he will encounter the most brilliant things we

---

When questioned, he named the musical reviewer for *The Globe*, Vitet. He didn't seem to be too happy with him but admitted that he was an enthusiastic musical amateur', *WA* III/11, p. 268.

[285] Chélard's first tragic opera, *Macbeth* (libretto by Rouget de l'Isle and Auguste Hix), was premiered in Paris on 29 June 1827, but the critical reception was rather indifferent and he was granted only five performances.

[286] As indicated on the programme, 'freely adapted' by Cäsar Max Heigel.

[287] On 20 June 1828 in the Königliches Hof-und Nationaltheater in Munich; a second performance took place on 24 June 'in an abridged version by the composer' (programme note).

[288] After the successful German premiere of Chélard's *Macbeth*, Ludwig I of Bavaria appointed him Königlicher Bayerischer Kapellmeister 'without service', as the reporter in the *Berliner Allegemeine Musikalische Zeitung* remarked on 24 September 1824.

[289] Zelter never mentions a visit by Chélard, who possibly altered his plans.

[290] Goethe enclosed a copy of his poem 'Dem aufgehenden Vollmonde' in this letter. Zelter's intention to set the poem to music (ZG 30 August 1828) was, in fact, never realized.

[291] Hippolyte André Jean Baptiste Chélard; GZ 26 August 1828.

have to offer [...] for apparently all our magnificent operas are to appear one after the other. Von Humbold and Lichtenstein are constantly preoccupied with the reception of such esteemed guests. Time will tell, since one wants to show that good hosts are worthy of good guests. [...]

Bach has gone back to Teplitz and Rungenhagen is the only one completely unharmed. He, however, grieves all the more that he has to miss you since he did not want to leave his travel companions.[292] I can't console him.

The strange cloud formations which pass in front of and by the moon have awoken the Ossian in me and I have a desire to set your verses to music, although I am completely out of my routine.[293] I had to promise Madame Milder an aria, which is started but unfortunately it is not going to get finished of its own accord.

## 437. Zelter

Berlin, Middle of October to 19 October 1828

Your dear didactic pages of 5 October came just in time to preserve me from the unpleasant after-effects of an annoying conference.[294] How much there would have been to report if one had been able to enjoy, hear, understand and assimilate from so many long scholarly presentations. [...] For my part I wanted to do something for the amusement of the guests. The day before the opening of the meeting, the Sing-Akademie had performed Handel's *Alexanderfest*,[295] although with a pretty incomplete rehearsal as two of the soloists were missing. Despite this the choir was in flying form and I didn't have to find fault with them. When they are effective, they sing as one voice. Then, for our money, we served a lunch for our foreign and local guests for our Liedertafel.[296] There were seven to eight hundred participants gathered. Both Berlin Liedertafel had got together[297] and since the restaurant is wide and high enough in its new parade house, the thing went off much better than

---

[292] Carl Friedrich Rungenhagen, August Wilhlem Bach and Wilhelm Gedike were supposed to bring a letter to Goethe from Zelter on their journey through Thüringen. As the visit never happened, Rungenhagen had posted the letter in Dresden.

[293] The composition – or even a fragment– is neither in Zelter's bequest nor in Goethe's music collection; it was obviously never set to music.

[294] The septennial conference of the Gesellschaft deutscher Naturforscher und Ärzte (Society of German Scientists and Doctors) in Berlin from 18 to 26 September 1828. The first session, opened by Alexander von Humboldt, took place in the Sing-Akademie hall, as did the other public sessions.

[295] Handel's oratorio was performed in the Sing-Akademie hall on 17 September 1828; see *AMZ* 30 (1828), no. 44, 29 October, column 741; *MA* 20.3, pp. 953–4.

[296] *AMZ* 30 (1828), no. 44, 29 October, column 742; *MA* 20.3, pp. 954.

[297] Zelter's Liedertafel as well as the Jüngere Liedertafel (modeled on Zelter's) which had been founded by Ludwig Berger, Bernhard Klein and Ludwig Rellstab in 1819.

I expected. Seventy male voices, all in good voice, made themselves so powerful that one could hear the words clearly from outside and many of our guests swore that they had never heard the likes of it, where no flattering remark was needed in so far as it is an ensemble. I have one last wish that you had heard the material performed ('Aus wie vielen Elementen').[298] One must not imagine the poem; one must hear it, which does the job and awakens the unnameable everytime.

19 October: Yesterday evening out of despair I went to the theatre – *Preciosa*.[299] [...] The story is illustrated by dance and choral music – with recitatives spoken to music, so that you understand neither the one nor the other – they call it melodrama, and it is described on the programme as a play with incidental music and dance, which means neither one thing nor the other through four short acts; even these are much too long as really there is no action and everyone is bored. The actors do not understand themselves why they are so done up; one is always waiting for the other to do something. The composer has taken the greatest pains, by strange modulation and all kinds of tempi, to produce a sad but humoristic work that will characterize a group of bandits. The audience and orchestral members do not know what they are listening to, or what they are playing, and the public sits as quiet as a mouse until it is all over.

A pretty stranger[300] appeared for the first time as Preciosa. She is said to be the intimate friend of her prince. Who would like to see the object of his affections running around on the street like that? Were she mine, she should remain nicely at home.

It now occurs to me, for the first time, that poet and composer are no longer alive. *De mortuis nil.*[301] You can see what kind of humour I am in. Throw away the page and forgive your

Zelter

---

[298] Zelter's setting of Goethe's poem 'Elemente'.

[299] Pius Alexander Wolff. Romantic play in four acts with song and dance, overture and incidental music by Carl Maria von Weber, part of the theatre repertoire in Berlin from 1821. Zelter is referring to the performance in the Schauspielhaus on 18 October 1828, in which the actress Lina Kuhn gave a guest performance of the title role.

[300] The actress Lina Kuhn, from the Grand Ducal Court Theatre in Baden, Karlsruhe. Her guest appearance in Berlin was, in fact, this single performance as Preciosa on 18 October 1828.

[301] *De mortuis nil nisi bene.* 'Nothing but good about the dead.'

### 438. Zelter

Berlin, 23 to 26 October 1828

[...] Von Cotta's wife[302] sent me through Doris two delightful arabesque illustrations[303] of Bavarian folksongs by a young artist from Munich. The melodies are also so charming and unsophisticated. I would not want be able to do the same; it is characteristic of the area.

### 439. Goethe

Weimar, 30 October 1828

If I may announce to you, my good Zelter, that I also possess the two charming pages of the illustrated songs from Tyrol[304], I can also add that the same young artist called Neureuther has also decorated many of my ballads with similar charming glossy borders.[305] This news will be very pleasant to you, but more pleasant some day will be your contemplation of those works, which are the most spiritual and most proper which have come to me in a long time. [...]

---

[302] Elizabeth von Cotta, née Baroness von Gemmingen-Guttenberg (1789–1859), Cotta's second wife from 1824, who was interested in publishing and was editor of the *Taschenbuch für Damen*, for which she could even count Ludwig I of Bavaria among its authors.

[303] Like Goethe, Zelter also received two lithograph pages of pen-and-ink drawings by Eugen Neureuther, a young artist from Munich. These are clearly sketches for the work *Baierische Gebirgslieder mit Bildern, gezeichnet von Eugen Neureuther* (Munich: Cotta, 1831); Zelter later praised these pages as 'really charming and fresh'.

[304] In Dornburg Goethe had received Neureuther's lithographs along with drawings for his own ballads and romances, with accompanying letters from Neureuther's teacher, Peter von Cornelius, and from Neureuther himself on 30 August 1828. Of Neureuther's pictures Goethe noted in his diary the following day, 'carefully observed'.

[305] Cornelius's dispatch contained two drawings by Neureuther, where Goethe's poems were illustrated in arabesque borders. Shortly afterwards Goethe spoke very highly of them in letters to Councillor von Müller (1 September) and Heinrich Meyer (6 September).

## 440. Zelter

Berlin, 14 November 1828

Yesterday evening we treated the public to Handel's *Samson*.[306] With real power Handel has set to music the essence and last hours of a strong man who succumbs to a woman. The ear becomes the eye: one thinks one distinguishes colours, forms, sexes.

We had just received the tragic news of the death of the Russian Dowager Empress.[307] That brought us a double loss in that the King[308] could not come. Otherwise it was an attentive, responsive audience. The Duke of Cumberland,[309] who usually thinks we are lacking an organ, declared himself very gratified this time.

Handel, who was a distinguished organist,[310] did not write an organ part for any of his oratorios,[311] though he treated the chorus carefully and artistically. Were he still alive, he would have to say, 'With such a chorus as that, I don't need an organ!' Even if he did not say it, he did it. An organ may be necessary, either to mask or to compensate for the weakness of a chorus. On the other hand, played neither wisely nor well, it may weaken and ruin the best choir. I was obliged to say as much to Cramer,[312] the English king's Kapellmeister,[313] who was here a short time ago, for I know from the best source (Handel himself) what choirs are like throughout England and it is still the same now. People might confuse us if we

---

[306] The performance of Handel's oratorio on 13 November 1828; the performance was very favourably reviewed in the *Spenersche Zeitung*, no. 269, 15 November 1828 and the *AMZ* 30 (1828), no. 51, 17 December, column 857f.; *MA* 20.3, pp. 958.

[307] The mother of the Russian Tsar Alexander, Tsarina Maria Fjodorowna, died on 3 October 1828.

[308] King Friedrich Wilhelm III.

[309] Duke Ernst August of Cumberland, King of Hannover from 1837.

[310] As a budding musician Handel had already taken organ lessons with Friedrich Wilhelm Zachow, the organist of the Liebfrauenkirche in Halle. In 1702 Handel was appointed organist at the castle and cathedral in Halle. In Italy Handel continued to play the organ and he composed organ concerti for the first time in England, which were used as intermezzi for the oratorios *Esther* and *Deborah* (1732/33). Handel's fame as an organ virtuoso was founded on his own performances of these concerti. Through printing the three collections of organ concerti, each containing six concerti, were widely known in the eighteenth century by virtue of being printed.

[311] For the performance practice of Handel's oratorio with organ as a continuo instrument; see Friedrich Rochlitz's revised edition of his essay on Handel's *Messiah*, first published in 1824, in *Für Freunde der Tonkunst* (Leipzig, r.1830), vol. 1, p. 260f.

[312] Franz Cramer (1772–1848), violinist and leader of the orchestra, member of the Königliche Kapelle in London, promoted to Master of the King's Music in 1837.

[313] Kapellmeister to George IV.

hadn't lived too. If they are in love with themselves and their pitmines, who shall blame *us* for loving what we are able to have? What do *they* know about Handel?

Our knight, Spontini, was full of admiration and said, 'Laissez moi vos Chœurs'.[314] It is true: youth and beauty of every rank, trained, brought into order, with great energy and properly balanced, should make an impression upon anyone, unless, like me, he has for years had to work from the centre of the organization outwards and, all through the varying seasons of success and failure, continue showing things up energetically and untiringly.

The cost of training the Chorus for the Königliches Theater amounts to 6,000 thalers per annum; for that sum they ought to be better, if the teachers fulfilled even the most basic duties. Many of the chorus do not know their parts, and have them drummed into them by a violin, badly played. Our choruses are sung by all at sight and the most difficult music often goes as well as possible at the third rehearsal, for they work together and talking is not tolerated. The late King of Saxony[315] was the first and last who conversed with me on the subject like a man who understood it – and he gave me the loveliest gold snuffbox.

### 441. Zelter

Berlin, 15 to 16 December 1828

[...] Rungenhagen's music to your words has been very successfully received,[316] to which I must add my praise.

---

[314] 'Let me have your choirs!'

[315] After his visit to the Sing-Akademie in 1814, King Friedrich August I of Saxony had made Zelter a present of a golden snuffbox.

[316] Rungenhagen's cantata for three choirs ('Dichtende', 'Singende' and 'Bauende') and *fundamento* (continuo). *Zelters siebzigster Geburtstag, gefeiert von Bauernden, Dichtenden, Singenden am 11ten Dezember 1828*, a hand-written score of 82 pages is in Goethe's music collection (GSA 32/70). The performance was reviewed in the *AMZ*: 'On the same evening the Sing-Akademie celebrated the 70th birthday of (...) Professor Zelter, with a celebratory performance of a cantata to poems by Goethe, which the Director of Music, Rungenhagen, the real assistant to Zelter [sic], had set to music with considered order [of form], clarity and warmth of feeling, simple and melodic, as appropriate', *AMZ* 31 (1829), no. 1, 7 January, column 18.

## 442. Goethe

Weimar, 16 December 1828

Enclosed herewith you have at last a transcription of the excellent Jungius's *Harmonie*;[317] it was difficult enough to get this done, – the type of translation you desired could not be managed. Amongst your musical colleagues and students there must be someone who understands Latin and who would go through the work with you; afterwards I should like a solid account of it, for I am anxious to erect a substantial memorial to that worthy man.

I enclose a copy of the letter you sent at my request; what you say has special relevance to the close of the seventeenth and the beginning of the eighteenth century; but with regard to the state of music in 1650, the most reliable information is probably to be got from the pamphlet in question, for though the man was first and foremost a mathematician and logician, he had spontaneously devoted himself to living nature and had written works that were ahead of his time. Amongst the things that interested me was that he was a contemporary of Bacon,[318] Descartes,[319] and Galileo,[320] and yet he managed to retain his originality both in his studies and his teaching.

---

[317] The copy of *Joachimi Jungii Lubecensis Harmonica* (Hamburg, 1679), which Goethe had requested from Zelter on 24 October. The 23-page copy in John's hand is in the Sammlung Kippenberg in Dusseldorf (GMD: KK 3877.3, Kat. der Musikalien, no. 2596). Goethe had borrowed the printed publication, which had been bound with another work by Jungius (*Praecipuae opiniones physicae*) from the library in Jena on 10 July 1828. He sent the book, together with other works by Jungius, to Friedrich Siegmund Voigt emphasizing: 'The middle blue signs indicate a representation of harmonic relations in music.' Voigt returned it to Goethe on 23 August and it was returned to the library on 8 September, shortly before Goethe's return to Weimar. It was borrowed by Goethe once again on 15 October, presumably for making a copy. The title Riemer gave in the first edition of these letters (*Harmonica Theoretica, compendiosissime et optima methodo sonorum et sonorum proportiones et distinguendorum instrumentorum musicorum rationem exhibens et demonstrans. E Ms Auctoris edita a Joh. Vagetio. Prof. Hamb.* (Hamburg 1768)) never existed as an edition; see Hans Kangro, *Joachim Jungius' Experiemente und Gedanken zur Begründung der Chemie als Wissenschaft* (Wiesbasden: Franz Steiner, 1968), p. 351.

[318] The English philosopher and statesman Francis Bacon (1561–1626).

[319] René Descartes (1596–1650), French philosopher and natural scientist.

[320] Galileo Galilei (1564–1642), Italian physicist and astronomer.

## 443. Zelter

Berlin, 22 to 29 December 1828

[...] You did well not to spare my lazy modesty; I can read the little book fairly well myself. Because of the musical content, I could spell out what is problematic in it more easily than many a Latin scholar could put it into German for me; for many a mistake has arisen from coining Greek and Latin artistic terms in German. The basic principles of harmony, as outlined here, were carried out in practice by Hans Leo Hassler, Palestrina and others as early as the beginning of the sixteenth century, and they are still applicable, though the most modern theorists will try to convince us that it is all quite different now. This is so little the case, that even the old mistaken definitions, quite as mistakenly Germanized, are still valid: for example 'Soni dissoni sunt, quorum mixtura auditui ingrata est'[321] – which to this day still means: 'A dissonance is a cacophony'. But a dissonance (if you do not mean by that something absolutely unmusical) is no cacophony. It is in its origin as well as its resolution consonant, and is to be looked on as the consonance into which it must resolve itself. Similarly, major and minor are neither 'hard' nor 'soft', yet everyone knows what is meant by the terms as long as people do not translate them into German!

29 December: On account of the feast days in the next few weeks, I hardly know what day it is. We wanted to perform Handel's *Messiah* on 4 January since they have laid another foundation stone again. Then jubilee anniversaries, weddings, operas, balls, carnival follow and everything I don't need. My choirs are very well rehearsed. Everything is running like clockwork; and with meaning and sense.

## 444. Goethe

Weimar, 2 January 1829

[...] My mother was often wont to say when she was overrun with visitors, 'They did not allow me to blow my nose'. It amuses me to think of you in a similar predicament.

[...] No one understands how I value a succession of hours, for the interrupted ones are, in my opinion, not only completely lost, but must be considered as harmful and destructive. It is the same with strangers, who do not understand what exactly I am robbed of by an interruption. And yet it is always disagreeable to me when, in self-protection, I have to refuse seeing people who have travelled a long way. You might complain of something similar, but as musician you are forced

---

[321] 'Sounds are dissonant when their mixture is unpleasing to the ear.' This sentence is from Jungius, *Harmonica*, no. 9.

to keep up with the world; the world has nothing of me, except what it can see in black and white.

### 445. Zelter

Berlin, 16 to 17 January 1829

[…] It surprised me to know the time and place of your verses for the Jubilee celebration of your immortalized master,[322] 'Laßt fahren hin das Allzuflüchtige'. I believe I conceived the melody in the church of St Nicolas during a Jubilee sermon which I had to sit through and couldn't understand anything. I regarded it as being too serious, even pedantic, and now I see that I would do it the same way again, now that I know more about it. […]

### 446. Zelter

Berlin, 31 January 1829

[…] Our *Messiah* was launched smoothly enough, after it had rocked long enough at anchor.[323] On this occasion I again learnt what you and I already know. In the end the music had to be performed without the help of the court musicians.[324]

---

[322] Goethe's 'Zwischengesang', one of the poems from the poetic trilogy written for the celebration of Carl August's 50 years as ruler, which took place at the Weimar Lodge 'Amalia'. On 19 September 1825 Goethe had recommended Zelter set them for the Liedertafel when he sent him a copy of the first publication, *Zur Logenfeier des dritten Septembers 1825*, which didn't contain the details of the celebration on 13 September. Zelter first discovered the details of the first performance of Goethe's 'Zwischengesang' through vol. 4 of the *Freimauer-Analecten* with a report on the memorial ceremony of Carl August: 'This moment (in memory of Carl August) could not have had a better introduction than through the deeply moving poem, and yet very ennobling poem, which lifts up heart and mind, by the venerable brother, von Goethe, the elder, which he had made a present to us three years ago for the celebration of his sublime royal friend, not realizing how we would soon seek and would find comfort for the most troubled hours. The last sound died away, this song so energetically composed by our brother, Hummel, splendidly performed by brother Moltke and in the solemn silence, the deputy master von Müller spoke', *Freimauer-Analecten* 4 (1829): 28f.

[323] The performance on 29 January 1829 was favourably reviewed by the local papers; see *AMZ* 31 (1829), no. 8, 25 February, column 130 and the *Spenersche Zeitung* no. 26, 31 January 1829; *MA* 20.3, p. 980.

[324] The soloists, Anna Milder (soprano), Heinrich Stümer (tenor) and Eduard Devrient (bass), singers at the Königliches Theater, had appeared as soloists at earlier performances given by the Sing-Akademie.

There is no lack of skill in my choir, but they are afraid to be on show [as a group] and individually. In the end that was overcome and lo and behold! If they were unwilling at first and timid, it finally changed. They became lord and lady, they proved themselves to be independent; they expressed themselves, which is precisely the wrong thing, and out of the fully convinced, sincere and heartfelt 'Ich weiß daß mein Erlöser lebt'[325] we got a sad, whining thing like – a fart.[326] Meanwhile one must not knock three times. You have to attack sometimes!

### 447. Goethe

Weimar, 12 February 1829

[…] I think I understand your complaints, or more exactly your invectives against limited performances of music prepared long beforehand. The tendency of the day to drag down everything into weakness and wretchedness is becoming more widespread. I could show you half a dozen poems which have been written to praise and honour me and yet treat me as is if I am already one of the blessed departed. In the end, according to the latest system of philosophy, everything will disintegrate into nothing before it has yet begun to be. […]

### 448. Zelter

Berlin, 31 January to 14 February 1829

Make sure that I have my own copy of your correspondence with Schiller.[327] I have to give back the copy I am reading. What extraordinary people you both are. The correspondence is splendid.

12 February: You have another wedding[328] and we have the carnival without Spontini's operas. Our Princes, who left the day before yesterday, will fill you in

---

[325] Soprano aria, no. 40 in part three of *The Messiah*.

[326] Goethe explained the passage on *The Messiah* in Zelter's letter to Eckermann, who, in turn, tones Zelter's words down, saying 'this weakness is characteristic of our century … where an aria is sung in too mellow, too delicately [or] too sentimental a way'.

[327] Of the six volumes of *Briefwechsel zwischen Schiller und Goethe in den Jahren 1794–1805* (Stuttgart and Tübingen: Cotta, 1828–29), vols 1 and 2 (November 1828) were available at the time of this letter; the remaining four volumes were issued throughout 1829.

[328] Prince Wilhelm of Prussia, the second son of King Friedrich Wilhelm III, had travelled to Weimar for his engagement to Augusta von Sachsen-Weimar-Eisenach, daughter of the Grand Duke Carl Friedrich; he arrived on 14 February, on the day after his brother, the Crown Prince Friedrich Wilhelm. The engagement party took place on

on it. It is boring, irksome and is known around the town in its various versions. From Paris they had described Spontini as a schemer. Now that I can see it is about to affect me in my situation, I neither have to complain nor to take sides. He, however, appears to have offended everyone so much at the theatre itself, the court, the general public, that his best, even his highest patrons are compromised. I was mistaken in him in so far as I took him for a man of the world and regarded him as being more clever than – dense. For example, he persuaded Kapellmeister Schneider (in the director's room) before the general rehearsal to go into the theatre and to ask the orchestra in open forum whether they would prefer to see the opera *La Muette de Portici* conducted by Spontini[329] than by Kapellmeister Schneider.[330] That took place and the orchestra played *La Muette de Portici*. Schneider asks loudly one more time and repeatedly, but there is still no answer. And all that in the presence of the King who doesn't know anything about it and should not and would not, and with all his power is not in a position to lend his support to such stupidity. They say Prince Carl asked the King very graciously to spare his wedding celebration from Spontini's latest opera[331] because half an opera was not sufficient for a whole wedding. As is well known, this opera *Agnes* was to have been performed at the wedding of Prince Wilhelm, but only Act One was performed because the whole thing was not finished. Now it is still not ready and they are worried that the wedding might have to be postponed for that reason.

14 February 1829: [...] Yesterday, for the first time, I heard [Auber's] *Muette von Portici*.[332] One may look upon the work as the beginning of a new genre, for it is neither an opera proper, nor a play, but a true melodrama which is not spoken but sung. It hangs together well, and the interest is sufficiently sustained throughout the five acts to give them real unity. Scribe's text is nothing special. The leading character, a Neapolitan fisherwoman, has been seduced by the son of the Viceroy, who then gets married to a princess. But why, and from what cause the lady is dumb, never emerges. Running through all this is a conspiracy of the Neapolitans

---

16 February; on 19 the Crown Prince set out for Berlin after visiting Goethe on 16 February. The engaged couple were with Goethe on 11 March before Prince Wilhelm returned to Berlin on 28 March.

[329] General director at the Königliche Oper in Berlin.

[330] Georg Abraham Schneider (1770–1839), hornist, cellist, Kapellmeister and leader of the court opera.

[331] *Agnes von Hohenstaufen*. The opera had been commissioned for the marriage ceremony of Prince Carl with Princess Maria, at which Act 1 had been performed on 28 May 1827. The complete opera in three acts was premiered on 12 June 1829, with stage set designed by Schinkel.

[332] Daniel François Espirit Auber, *La Muette de Portici*, grand opera in 5 acts (libretto by Eugène Scribe, adapted for the German stage, under the title *Die Stumme von Portici* by Baron Karl August von Lichtenstein); performed for the first time in the Königliches Opernhaus on 12 August 1829; see *AMZ* 31 (1829), no. 8, 25 February, column 128f. and no. 10, 11 March, columns 166–9. Zelter attended the performance on 13 February 1829.

against the Viceroy, who is rebuked as a tyrant. The staging of this music drama is regal.[333] Whoever has not witnessed Vesuvius in action[334] should come to Naples-Berlin and be astonished!

### 449. Zelter

Berlin, 26 to 28 February 1829

One of the 13 dramatists, our Willibald Alexis, has cast his shadow over the muse of the King's suburb with a melodrama,[335] discussed in the enclosed.[336] It is called a melodrama because by virtue of its serious content it would not have been allowed to be performed at this theatre.[337] So a famous unnamed composer[338] (the editorial staff of the local musical paper) made a completely homogenous setting of it, which I heard yesterday. If the composer didn't know where he was going, he showed clearly enough from where he was coming because his painstaking botched-up job only exists in bones and droppings from Beethoven's table,[339] wrapped in such terrible noise that children in the womb would get goosepimples. I thought I was hearing the standard examples from all the musical textbooks reeled off one after the other in their different keys. Afterwards the orchestral members looked as if they had escaped from their graves. Actually the opus uplifted me – as this brother Marcus (now Marx)[340] tormented himself and mounted his fortepiano. There I don't begrudge the joker anything and the King's suburbian audience showed no sign of

---

[333] See the review in the *Spenersche Zeitung*, no. 11, 14 January 1829.

[334] The flaming Vesuvius, into which the mute protagonist throws himself at the end of the opera, had impressed the critics; *AMZ* 31 (1829), no. 5, 4 February, column 73; *MA* 20.3, p. 985.

[335] *Die Rache wartet*, melodrama in three acts by Wilhelm Alexis (namely Wilhelm Häring) on 22 February 1829, performed for the first time at the Königstädtisches Theater; Zelter attended the second performance on 25 February.

[336] A critical review of *Die Rache wartet* in the *Berliner Courier*, no. 622, 23 February 1829.

[337] In accordance with the articles of association, neither serious dramas nor heroic operas were permitted to be performed at the Königstädtisches Theater to avoid rivalry with the court theatre.

[338] A.B. Marx, founder and editor of the *Berliner Allgemeine Musikalische Zeitung*. Marx included a passage on Wilhelm Alexis's *Melodrama* in his autography; see A.B. Marx, *Aus meinen Leben* (2 vols, Berlin: Otto Janke, 1865), vol. 2, p. 42.

[339] Marx was a founder of the Romantic image of Beethoven which reached a pinnacle in his two-volume Beethoven biography (1859).

[340] With reference to Mark the Evangelist, who is often represented at the scriptorium or at a desk; it could also be a reference to the journalistic activities of the composer.

curiosity about the identity of the perpetractor of the confused murder rumpus. We won't talk about it any further.

### 450. Zelter

Berlin, 9 March 1829

You will already have seen from the paper that we are going to perform Bach's Passion.[341] Felix has studied it under me, and is going to conduct it, so I will give up my desk to him. I will send you the text shortly, to which I have written a preface. Felix has been invited to London by Moscheles;[342] after that he may go to Italy.[343] The lad brings great comfort to me and it is good for him to get away from the parental home. All that he needs intellectually he can take with him, and soon I hope to hear more of him.

---

[341] For an account of the *St Matthew Passion* conducted by Mendelssohn; see Todd, *Mendelssohn: A Life in Music*, pp. 193–8.

[342] Felix Mendelssohn's English journey from April to December 1829 was part of a grand educational and concert tour throughout Europe. On 12 December 1828 Abraham Mendelssohn had written to Moscheles, asking his advice about the course Felix's tour should take. Among other performances, Mendelssohn had conducted his Symphony no. 1 in C minor (op. 11) and his *Midsummer Night's Dream Overture* (op. 21). He found the English a benevolent, later even an enthusiastic audience, and travelled to England ten times as a conductor and performer.

[343] Mendelssohn's journey to Italy began mid-May 1830 and lasted until July 1832.

## 451. Zelter

Berlin 12 to 22 (?) March 1829

Our Bach performance came off successfully yesterday,[344] and Felix proved to be a calm, competent director. The King[345] and the entire court witnessed a closely packed house before them; I sat with my score in a little corner near the orchestra, from where I could survey my students and the public equally well. About the work itself, I scarcely know what to say. It is a wonderful, sentimental mixture of music in general. [...]

If the melody did not bear occasional resemblance to the more modern German operatic composers, such as Gluck and Mozart, bringing us back again for a moment to our own time, we should feel ourselves between heaven and earth and at the same time 30 years older! And it may be this that makes the music difficult to perform. But if only old Bach could have heard our performance! That was my feeling at every successful passage, and here I cannot praise highly enough the whole body of my pupils at the Sing-Akademie, as well as the solo singers, and the double orchestra.[346] You might describe the whole as an organ, in which every pipe was gifted with reason, power and will, nothing forced, no mannerism. There is no duet, no fugue, no beginning, no end, and yet all is as one, and everything in its place with its singularity and connection to the whole. A wonderful dramatic truth is created: one hears the false witnesses – that is, one sees them step forth;

---

[344] The first performance since Bach's death of the *St Matthew Passion* was given by the Sing-Akademie, conducted by Felix Mendelssohn, on 11 March 1829. The soloists were the sopranos Anna Milder-Hauptmann (who had left Berlin over a quarrel with Spontini), 17-year-old Pauline von Schätzel, alto Auguste Türrschmidt, tenors Heinrich Stümer (Evangelist) and Carl Adam Bader (Peter), baritone Eduard Devrient (Christ), and basses J.E. Busolt (High Priest and Governor) and Weppler (Judas). The chorus was 158 strong (47 sopranos, 36 altos, 34 tenors and 41 basses), nowhere near the 300 to 400 mentioned in Devrient's account (See Martin Geck, *Die Wiederentdeckung der Matthäuspassion im 19. Jahrhundert* (Regensburg: Gustav Bosse, 1967), p, 34, based on Georg Schünemann, *Die Singakademie zu Berlin: 1791–1941* (Regensburg: Gustav Bosse, 1941), p. 54). Most of the orchestral personnel were amateurs from the Philharmonische Gesellschaft founded by Eduard Rietz in 1826 (the first chairs of the strings and the winds were members of the Königliche Kapelle). Using a baton, Felix conducted from a piano placed diagonally on the stage, with the first chorus behind and second chorus and orchestra before him. The performance was an enormous success; see *AMZ*, 31 (1829), no. 16, 22 August, column 258f.; *MA* 20.3, p. 993.

[345] Friedrich Wilhelm III of Prussia.

[346] The total conception of the *St Matthew Passion* is documented on the title page and in the heading of Bach's autograph manuscript (SBB PK): *a due cori*. By *coro* Bach intended the choir, instrumental voices including soloists.

one sees the high priests with their 'Es taugt nicht' and so on, 'es ist Blutgeld',[347] and the crowd, 'Ja nicht auf das Fest' and so on, and the disciples, true, honourable followers, ruffians, 'Wozu dienet dieser Unrat'.[348] They seem to be very original tones which we did not know but are now compelled to recognize. Then, in the middle of it all, the heartfelt lament for the glorious Son of Man, the Friend, the Counsellor, the Helper, the Judge, and so on. That that is all new now and natural is noticeable in this, that it is not so much gladly received and grasped afterwards as that one immediately wants to hear it again and again and again and finally would like to understand it. It is all of a piece, no matter how scattered the plot is in the text.

The Evangelist, Stümer of the Königliches Theater,[349] one of my former pupils, sang the narrative part so admirably (especially in the execution of it) that you heard the repetition of the Gospel words with delight. Before the performance I had advised him not to hinder the progress of the story by sentimentality, and he did it excellently.

In response to many requests we repeated the Passion Music once again before a full house. The old audience returned, and new listeners came as well. The opinions are justifiably different; and amongst many, one only shall be named, who has the right to judge – a right as great as that of any other, and greater. Philosophers, who divide the real from the ideal, and throw away the tree in order to recognize the fruit, are to us musicians as we are to their philosophy, of which we understand nothing further than that we bring before their door the treasure which we have found. Take Hegel, for example! He is currently giving lectures on music; Felix takes very good notes[350] and with the freedom of a bird with extreme naivety and all his personal idiosyncrasies he understands how to reproduce them. In Hegel's opinion Bach is not the right kind of music;[351] we have advanced further, although

---

[347] Bach, *St Matthew Passion*, Part II, High Priests' Chorus (Matthew 27, 6), no. 41c.

[348] High Priests' Chorus, 4b (Matthew 26, 5) and the Disciples, 4d (Matthew 26, 8f). Zelter had already rehearsed both choruses with the Sing-Akademie on 8 June 1815; see Georg Schünemann, *Bach Jahrbuch* 25 (1928): 138–71.

[349] See review in the *Spenersche Zeitung*, no. 61, 13 March 1829; *MA* 20.3, p. 994.

[350] Felix Mendelssohn's notes from Hegel's course of lectures, *Ästhetik oder Philosophie der Kunst*, in the winter semester 1828/29 are in private possession; see Rudolf Elvers, 'Felix Mendelssohn Bartholdys Nachlaß' in Carl Dahlhaus, *Das Problem Mendelssohn* (Regensburg: Gustav Bosse Verlag, 1974), p. 43. Mendelssohn discussed Hegel's lectures in a letter to his parents from Weimar in May 1830; *Gespräche*, vol. III/2, p. 625. Passages on musical logic from an unpublished letter from Hegel to Mendelssohn on 30 June 1829 are cited in Eric Werner, *Mendelssohn: Leben und Werk in neuer Sicht* (Zurich: Atlantis, 1980), p. 102.

[351] What Zelter is explaining here is in contradiction with Hegel's view in his *Ästhetik*, where the philosopher offers a much more positive view of Bach's music: 'Protestants also have produced musicians of great depth as well as of religious sensibility, solid musicianship and variety of invention and style. A prime example is Sebastian Bach, a master whose

we are still a long way from the right thing. Well, that we know or don't know as well as he, if he could only explain to us musically whether he has discovered the right thing. We all don't know what we should pray for and still carry on and so let the others do the same.

The biography of Mozart[352] which I am reading gives me the greatest joy owing to the original things it contains. The letters are invaluable[353] as they confirm to me every opinion about this wonderful man and coincide perfectly with my artistic outlook on the whole. If one looks at the mass of contemporary artist rabble by way of comparison one hardly knows whether one should laugh at the young people or weep for Jerusalem.[354] Mozart's love for his parents[355] and for his sister[356] is really admirable. His father was an excellent musician; his violin tutor[357] is a work which is very useful as long as a violin remains a violin. It is so well written. How this family must have dragged themselves around. I envy their misery and think: nothing more agreeable could have happened me than to have the opportunity to imbibe the wide world. Eating hay and straw would not have prevented me if, out of obedience to my father and mother, I enjoyed the best with loathing. I wrote to my son Carl at the border of Italy where he had no desire to go,[358] that I would gladly pull a waggon to Italy and France if I could still be in his position. I had prepared the loveliest opportunities for him though Minister Humboldt.[359] He could have gone where he wanted. And I have to be grateful and am. Forgive my tears. Bye for now.

Zelter

---

magnificent, genuinely Protestant, strong and yet learned genius we have recently learned to value again completely'; Hegel, *Ästhetik*, ed. Friedrich Bassenge (Berlin: Aufbau, 1955), p. 859.

[352] Most likely Georg Nikolaus Nissen's *Biographie W.A. Mozarts nach Originalbriefen* (Leipzig: Breitkopf und Härtel, 1828). In the list of subscribers at the beginning of the original edition, Zelter is cited as a customer who has ordered a printed copy.

[353] Available today in *Mozart. Briefe und Aufzeichnungen*, collected and annotated by Wilhelm A. Bauer and Otto Erich Deutsch (Kassel: Bärenreiter, 1971).

[354] Reference to Luke 19, v. 41.

[355] Johann Georg *Leopold* Mozart (1719–87) and Anna Maria Walpurga Mozart née Pertl (1720–78).

[356] Maria Anna ('Nannerl') Mozart (1749–1829), pianist and ultimately piano teacher in Strassburg.

[357] Leopold Mozart, *Versuch einer gründlichen Violinschule* (Augsburg: J.J. Lotter, 1756).

[358] See Zelter's letter to his stepson in Karlsruhe; Max Hecker, 'Vater und Sohn. Briefe Carl Friedrich Zelters an seinen Stiefsohn Carl Flöricke' in *Funde und Forschungen. Eine Festgabe für Julius Wahle* (Leipzig: Insel, 1921), p. 18f. According to the letters, Carl Flöricke's plans to set out on his years of travel from Karlsruhe to France and Italy were unrealized because of his tragic suicide.

[359] Wilhelm von Humboldt.

## 452. Goethe

Weimar, 28 March 1829

Your last letters, my dearest friend, serious and lighthearted, arrived at the right time to do me good. The most recent, bringing news of the successful performance of that grand old musical work[360] has set me thinking. I seem to hear the distant roar of the sea. Consequently, I must congratulate you on such a perfectly successful rendering of that which it is almost impossible to represent. I imagine the connoisseur and witness of such an art, when listening to such works, has the same mental experience that I myself had lately when I set the legacy of Mantegna[361] before my eyes again. It is already complete art, its possibilities and impossibilities are fully alive, yet are still not developed; were it mature it would not be what it is here, not so illustrious, not so rich in hope and in essence. I heartily rejoice with you about Felix; I have hardly been as fortunate with even a few of my students [...]

## 453. Zelter

Berlin, 28 March 1829

[...] A Madame Müller from Brunswick, a beautiful 25-year-old woman, performed here the day before yesterday.[362] Her husband[363] is a violinist in the Brunswick band and is supposed to be excellent. The woman has an alto voice of the loveliest range: clear, even, pure; one could mistake it for an Italian voice. She is looking for employment here, which she will find hard because – you know the way things are here. She lacks nothing other than experience because she is very shy. If you

---

[360] Bach, *St Matthew Passion*, performed by the Sing-Akademie on 11 March.

[361] At noon Eckermann showed Goethe a copy of Mantegna's original copper plate engraving *Triumphal Procession with the Elephant* and Andriani's woodcut; see Goethe's diary 20 March 1829, *WA* III/12, p. 41. Goethe and Eckermann's preoccupation with Mantegna's triumphal procession is almost documented daily from 20 to 27 March. Goethe, who was already acquainted with Mantegna's work from his Italian journey, possessed an extensive collection of prints in the style of Mantegna. In *Über Kunst und Altertum* (1823) he published an extensive study of Mantegna's *Julius Caesar's Triumphal Procession*, which were available to him on single pages and above all in Andrea Andriani's woodcuts.

[362] Minna Müller née Gerson (c.1804–47), singer at the Ducal Court Theatre in Brunswick, shared a concert with the actress Auguste Crelinger and the singer Carl Adam Bader (1789–1870), directed by Moeser, in the hall of the Königliches Schauspielhaus in Berlin; see *AMZ* 31 (1829), no. 16, 22 April, column 260.

[363] Franz Ferdinand *Georg* Müller (1808–55), violinist in the Hofkapelle in Brunswick.

can use someone like her in Weimar let me know, but soon, because I don't believe that they will be able to stay here long. They would perhaps be able to make do with a reasonable salary. On top of that the woman is very musical, a pianist and is very attractive-looking. A kiss from her is no mean thing.[364] Her husband has fallen out with his family on account of his marriage to her. That is all I know and maybe that's why they decided to leave Brunswick. A tall, thin figure like our Crelinger[365] but with more natural charm, she sang arias by Rossini really well,[366] pure and supple, although self-conscious. Her voice is also full, bright and not straining like many Italians; she would have to learn such mistakes from the great Divas. Since you wrote to me a few weeks ago that your theatre is beginning to pick up, I mention her. Perhaps it would be also possible to use the young woman as an actress. The husband is Müller's younger brother, who is leader of the orchestra in Brunswick.[367] As an orchestral violinist he is better than his brother, who is more a virtuoso.

## 454. Zelter

Berlin, 31 March 1829

Our theatre is a nest of anarchy. All the singers are against Spontini.[368] The singer, Bader, complained to the King about him and asked for the satisfaction of never singing in one of his operas again. Madame Wolff can tell you in person.[369] It's tedious to me.

---

[364] *kein Katzendreck!*

[365] The Berlin actress, Sophie *Auguste* Crelinger née Düring.

[366] In the programme the two Rossini arias are unnamed; she also sang an aria by Anschütz and a duet with Carl Adam Bader; again more exact programme details are unknown.

[367] Karl Friedrich Müller (1797–1873).

[368] The conflict between the theatre manager and artistic director, Count Brühl, and the general director of music, Spontini, which lasted for years, was only seemingly resolved by Brühl's resignation in December 1828. A difference of opinion soon arose with the successor in office, Count Wilhelm von Redern, appointed on 13 December, ultimately over the rejuvination of the ensemble demanded by Spontini. Spontini's plan to replace a personnel that was exhausted by age and sickness – and not least by the constant demands put on them by the composer – by younger forces to be signed on from all parts of Germany caused great opposition to him from established singers, male and female.

[369] At the end of April Amalie Wolff traveled to Weimar for a long engagement as guest performer.

### 455. Goethe

Weimar, 2 April 1829

I immediately passed on to Kapellmeister Hummel your friendly news of a first-rate [female] singer. After consultation with colleagues and superiors he brought me an appreciative but negative reply. In their constrained circumstances an alto would be no help to them. If you could allocate such a soprano to them, they would be grateful. And the way things stand, this is the most pressing requirement of our theatre. [...]

### 456. Zelter

Berlin, 6 to 11 April 1829

[...] I enclose you an account of a similar little dispute[370] going on at the moment; it will allow you to see what one has to contend with. In return, I present my adversary with a snare for so-called connoisseurs, and if he falls into it, he shall have it hotter this time. He is a serious admirer of the compositions of Wilhelm Friedemann Bach, (eldest son of Sebastian Bach), which I am not, for which he finds fault with me. Apropos of this, he sent me an Organ Concerto by Friedemann Bach,[371] and copied for me the saying of Quintilian[372] referred to in the letter. To save you the trouble of looking up chapter and page for yourself, here it is:

> Modeste tamen et circumspecto judicio de tantis viris judicandum est, ne, quod plerisque accidit, damnent quae non intelligunt.[373]

---

[370] Goethe had returned Bendavid's note with the extract from Franklin's writing in his letter to Zelter on 2 April; Goethe had written his reply to Bendavid's note on the same sheet of writing paper. Zelter made a copy of this note and forwarded it to Bendavid. Lazarus Bendavid (Ben David) (1762–1832), philosopher and mathematician, director of the public Jewish school in Berlin.

[371] Wilhelm Friedemann Bach had passed off his father's, Johann Sebastian Bach's organ arrangement of Antonio Vivaldi's Concerto in D minor for two violins and orchestra (RV 565) as his own work, writing on the top of his father's manuscript 'di W.F. Bach, manu mei Patris descript' (by Wilhelm Friedemann Bach in the hand of my father). See Zelter's discussion of this work in his letter to Griepenkerl (GSA 28/1024, no. 378).

[372] A quotation from Quintilian's *Institutio oratoria*, Book 10, chapter 7: 'One should, however, be moderate in one's judgements of such great men, so that one doesn't dismiss (like the majority of people) what one doesn't understand', Quintilian, on misinterpretation of the great orators and writers. The passage was well known to Goethe, who had already referenced it in *Ephemeriden*; see Otto Seel, 'Quintilian bei Goethe' in *Quintilian oder Die Kunst des Redens und Schweigens* (Stuttgart: Klett-Cotta, 1977), pp. 288–313.

[373] 'Judgement, however, about such men should be modest and careful, lest, as happens to many people, they condemn what they don't understand.'

This Friedemann Bach of Halle[374] was the most consummate organist[375] I have ever known. He died here in 1784, when I was already a citizen and stonemason. He was considered obstinate because he would not play for everybody; he was not arrogant towards us young people and he would play for hours. As a composer he had the odd characteristic of being original, of distancing himself from father and brothers, and consequently he sank into affectation, pettiness, barrenness whereby he was as easily recognized as one who shuts his eyes to become invisible. We were continually arguing about this and as to this very day my æsthetic companion still holds such original views, I cannot help confronting him [...]

### 457. Zelter

Berlin, 17 to 18 April 1829

Good Friday, 17 April: Today, instead of Graun's Passion Music, which is customary, I mean, by special request, to give another performance of Bach's Passion[376] in defiance of my old bent fingers, for my assistant, Felix, is swimming on the seas past Helioland to England, where he has been invited. As he plays the organ well, and there the organs are better than the organists, I think he may try his luck there too. [...]

Saturday evening: My hall was full yesterday. The King,[377] Prince and Princess Wilhelm,[378] the Duchess of Cumberland[379] and several people from the court were there. The others complained about the terrible heat and you can imagine how dear it is to me if they all sweat through and through as I did, too. I am happy to sweat. The cool grave will put me right again. One can take one's time. One has the whole of eternity before one.

Paganini with his damned violin concertos is driving men and women mad here[380] and will carry off from Berlin 10,000 thalers once more, if he does not first

---

[374] Wilhelm *Friedemann* Bach (1710–84), eldest son of J.S. Bach, worked in Halle from 1746 to 1770 before taking up residence in Berlin after a four-year sojourn in Brunswick.

[375] See Zelter's draft letter to Griepenkerl (GSA 28/1024, no. 378).

[376] Third performance of Bach's *St Matthew Passion* in the Sing-Akademie hall.

[377] Friedrich Wilhelm III.

[378] The king's brother, Prince Wilhelm, and his wife, Marianne.

[379] Friederike, Duchess of Cumberland, was the Prussian king's sister-in-law and sister to the late Queen Luise.

[380] Although originally only four concerts by the violin virtuoso Niccolò Paganini, were planned (on 4, 13, 19 and 28 which was postponed to 30 March), he gave a further ten concerts between March and May 1829 mainly in the opera house, but also occasionally in the hall of the new theatre (6, 16, 25, 29 April, 5, 9, 13 May). In these concerts he played mainly his own compositions, above all his Violin Concerto and Variations for solo

lose them again at Faro. I have not enough funds to give him two thalars for each performance and have heard nothing of him, beyond seeing his portrait in which he resembles the son of a witch. The real misfortune he brings upon us is that he is the complete ruin of the young violinists in our orchestra.

**458. Goethe**

Weimar, 28 April 1829

A Frenchman has set eight passages of my *Faust* to music, and sends me the score which is very beautifully typeset.[381] I should like to forward it to you and hear your favourable opinion.

This reminds me that you still have a score of my Cantata *Rinaldo*, composed by Winter for Prince Frederick of Gotha.[382] I still have the vocal parts, and many memories are associated with this opus. So let me have it back again if you can find it. […]

---

violin, but also virtuoso works by other composers. Two such works played by Paganini on his German tour were the sets of variations on *Il Carnevale di Venezia* and 'God save the King', the main feature of the latter being an intermingling of left-hand pizzicato with bowed notes, probably the first example of such a complicated technique. The reviews were extremely positive; see, for example, *AMZ* 31 (1829), no. 16, 22 April, column 215ff and no. 22, 3 June, column 364f; *MA* 20.3, p. 1005.

[381] On 10 April 1829 Hector Berlioz sent Goethe two copies of the score of his setting of eight scenes from *Faust*, based on Gérard de Nerval's translation, and an accompanying letter (*HA Briefe an Goethe*, vol. 2, p. 506). The composer, Ferdinand Hiller, wrote to Eckermann about it on 23 March 1829: 'A good friend of mine, a young talented composer by the name of Berlioz, has set eight scenes from Faust, unfortunately in the French translation. He is going to send Goethe a copy. You would do a good turn if you could get Goethe to write a few lines to him. It would make the young man very happy as he is besotted by Goethe' (GMD: KK 3700). Eckermann answered: 'Goethe showed me the copy and tried to sight-read the score. He had the deepest desire to hear it performed. A very well-written letter from Hector Berlioz was enclosed, which Goethe also gave me to read, and whose educated, very polite tone pleased us both. He will definitely answer Berlioz, if he has not done so already.' Goethe never replied to Berlioz, presumably on the basis of Zelter's crushing judgment.

[382] Goethe's cantata *Rinaldo* was set to music by the Munich Kapellmeister Peter von Winter in 1822. It was composed for Prince Friedrich of Sachsen-Gotha (Duke Friedrich IV from 1822). When Goethe handed over this score to Zelter is unknown (perhaps on Zelter's visit to Weimar in October 1827). Zelter had it returned to Weimar through Philipp Christian Weyland and received from Goethe the fair copy he requested on 11 June 1829.

## 459. Zelter

Berlin, 1 to 5 May 1829

Last Tuesday Paganini visited me at the academy and listened to our performance; and the following day I finally heard him play.[383] It is extraordinary what the man has achieved, and I must say this, that his technical mastery, which everyone would be glad to possess, quite surpasses the comprehension of other virtuosi upon his instrument. His being is therefore more than music, without being higher music, and I expect I would have the same opinion if I heard him more often. I was positioned where I could see every movement of his hand and arm, which – as his figure is rather small – must possess some rare flexibility, strength, and elasticity, for he is never tired of mastering difficult passages in an ascending scale, with the same regularity as a clock which contains a soul. The hundred techniques of his bow and fingers, to each one of which he has devoted thought and practice, follow each other in good taste and order, and also distinguish him as a composer. But in any case, he is, in the highest degree, a perfect master of his instrument; that which, with the best will in the world, he does not succeed in, is heard as a bold variation. [...]

The score of *Rinaldo* is returned here with thanks. I wanted to copy it myself, even improve it. The willing mind at first thought it had eyes and time for the work. But if you have a reasonable music copyist, I would like to have a copy.

Please send your Frenchman's *Faust* one of these days; the subject is attractive to composers. [...]

Sunday 3 May: Water and rain and the cold: the swallows have gone away again and von Praun,[384] a new violinist, is here and I heard him yesterday. The boy is 18 years old and plays better than a Baron.[385] He would be finished with technique if he could master material and limbs, which cloak the music in finger execution that one notices nothing other than hands and feet. What you have too little of one must tire of here. We drown in patchwork music and Grünberg champagne. One is like a hen on a tremendous heap of rubbish and scratches and picks a few seeds out which the high-spirited suitors have overlooked. Laborious work but one learns from it. [...]

---

[383] On 29 April 1829 in the Berlin opera house.

[384] Baron Sigismund Otto von Praun gave a concert in the Königstädtisches Theater on 2 May 1829 following a free adaptation of Gellert von Holbein's play *Die Witwe und der Witwer* or *Treue bis in den Tod*. He performed, among other works, a violin concerto by Lafontaine, variations by de Beriot, a caprice by Paganini and a polonaise by Mayseder.

[385] Most likely a reference to the violinist and amateur musician Baron Bagge.

## 460. Zelter

Berlin, 14 May 1829

In the table of your Theory of Sound, which I look at daily,[386] line ten states: 'Key relationships are distant from one another./ Chords.' I recommend putting 'tonic chords' or 'primary chords' because they develop first of all from the home key, then modulate into less remote relationships until the root finds itself in the second octave and the series comes to an end by itself. A primary chord is therefore one which is composed of thirds, placed one on top of the other:

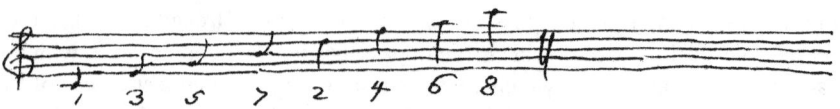

From this the intervals of the diatonic scale were built and even closer interrelationships, which from the ascent of diatonic intervals or their descent call forth a melody (gently progressing), which ultimately brings about the theory of dissonance through which music becomes art.

Take note of this: the intervals of the triad in root position show no tendency to change or movement. Such a tendency comes about with the 'third third' (the seventh of the scale), which longs for resolution at the octave, through which it forms a dissonance against the root, and so on with the ninth or the second, eleventh or perfect fourth, and third or sixth. Here the theory of consonance and dissonance comes into being in relation to the root through which music becomes the art of artists. Through the tendency of dissonance to impetus, modulation comes about; the exception [being] the demand of one key to move from its tonal centre in order to establish a new tonality without which no context could come about and at the same time provide the answer to the old question: whether melody or harmony comes first, since a series of tones unrelated to the tonic could not appeal to the ear. Through this consideration of dissonance we are led to the key with respect to high and low (smaller or greater vibrations). A single chord, whether it is consonant or dissonant is still not a key: the latter is first established through the dominant chord (the major chord on the fifth). In these two chords following one after the other, the dominant and tonic, or tonic and dominant, my individual feeling finds the original elements of metre: arsis and thesis or thesis and arsis, which my ear hears on the stroke of the hour and in the beat of the pulse, even in the quiet movement of the

---

[386] Goethe had sent Zelter the table of his *Tonlehre* in September 1826, but requested it back the following year as new ideas had occurred to him. Zelter had returned it to Weimar on 10 July 1827, after he had taken a copy of it. Goethe's request for Zelter's opinion of the *Tonlehre* in October 1826 is eventually answered here.

pendulum just as the latter is already metre which relates to rhythm in the same way as narrow to wide, as restriction to freedom:

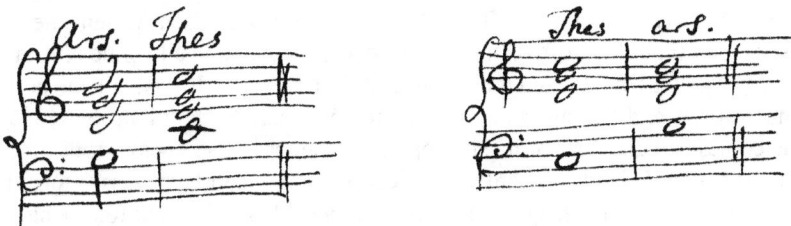

I find here the foundations of the rule against consecutive fifths in so far as they, according to the basic laws of both chords of the dominant and tonic, are not modulatory and therefore are offensive.

They are offensive because they don't relate to the tonic key and don't form a key, in that every chord is in itself a foreign primary chord and therefore is also unrhythmic. They become completely offensive when they occur on consecutive strong beats.

However, at the same time they cease to be offensive if they appear rhythmically (from arsis and thesis) in a manner which is well thought-out, that is when they are prepared through a dominant triad:

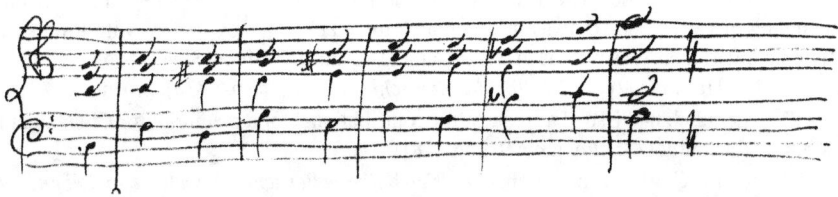

This rule soon led to the expansion of a fine phrase and melodic progressions so that it had to be treated with extreme rigour; it gave genius an opening to creations of great beauty.

Since you are so good as to keep my scribblings, I ask your permission to send numerous letters sometimes which contain scientific responses and as they turn out to be negative, they are not well received and are even hidden away by the recipients. One of my former students,[387] who became a schoolmaster in Breslau and is an active young man, had the idea of writing a joint Festschrift for our Chladni and the deceased organist Berner.[388] He is gathering together contributions and has written a biography of Berner[389] for this purpose. Then he sent me 50 copies which I should sell off. At first I wanted to answer him that I would give one Friedrichs d'or for Chladni and took another back for Berner. But what's the point of long quarrels and talking with such people? So I am sending him the money for the copies and am clear of it. The copy of the letter is also enclosed; use it as you wish. I should also lay a copy at the feet of the Russian Emperess[390] for this purpose; the Russian messenger Count von Alopeus[391] is doing that for me since the Empress is passing through Breslau.

Yesterday I heard Paganini again;[392] the man is a rarity – he is the violin. One is amazed, one laughs, one is in despair at the most daring escapades; the difficulty is clear to all, for the effect is experienced by all. Grace and spirit are not wanting, and even that which is not perfectly successful, is still new and interesting.

---

[387] Johann Gottfried Hientzsch was in Berlin from the end of February until the beginning of December. He 'was lucky enough to be able to enjoy lessons with Professor Zelter in music theory, as well as in singing and to be able to visit his Sing-Akademie', Carl Julius Adolf Hoffmann (ed.), *Die Tonkünstler Schlesiens* (Breslau, 1830), p. 198.

[388] Hientzsch had issued a 'request for contributions' for a memorial for Chladni and Berner in the journal *Cäcilia*, issue 9, 35 p. 181ff.

[389] Johann Gottfried Hientzsch, *Friedrich Wilhelm Berner (...) nach seinen Leben und Wirken in der Musik dargestellt. Zugleich ein Beitrag zur Geschichte des Musikwesens von Breslau während der letzten 20–30 Jahre; besonders abgedruckt aus der Eutonia* (Breslau, 1829) with an announcement on the title page: 'The proceeds from the purchased copies are intended as a contribution towards erecting a memorial for Chladni and Berner'.

[390] Alexandra Fjodorowna née Princess Charlotte of Prussia, daughter of Friedrich Wilhelm III, married to Emperor Nikolaus I Pawlowitsch of Russia.

[391] David Maximowitsch, Russian envoy in Berlin from 1813.

[392] On 13 May 1829 Paganini gave his last concert in Berlin: a benefit concert for the Spontini Foundation in the opera house. The orchestra along with many well-known singers took part in the concert with Paganini, who entertained the audience with three violin concerti, among them a work of his own.

### 461. Zelter

Berlin, Middle of May 1829

[...] In Letter 345 [of your Correspondence with Schiller][393] he writes that the melody for the 'Bajadere'[394] does not fit all the strophes equally well. Perhaps you will remember, when I sang it for Anna Amalie,[395] that Wieland told the Duchess he had thought it impossible for the same melody to be repeated so often without becoming wearisome and on the contrary to became more effective. Admittedly my singing is not much to speak of, but against that, many a singer cannot declaim [a poem]. Besides, Schiller was quite satisfied with my music to 'Der Taucher',[396] and he complained vehemently to Naumann, who had just set 'Die Ideale'.[397] I had won a similar wager with 'Der Taucher'. One of our friends was dissatisfied with the ballad forms used by the poets, and exclaimed, 'Who could think of setting such verses, such a diver to music?' Several of us were there, and I, who had been listening silently to the whole conversation, called out, 'I could! and Schiller himself shall praise it!' There and then I wrote down the notes, and so they have remained, however clumsy they may appear. When I presented them immediately afterwards (for I knew the poem by heart), an anything-but-musical matron planted herself by my side and made the movement of a metronome with her knitting needle. Hardly was the last word over when she exclaimed amidst floods of tears, 'Well, that was an infamous king!'[398]

---

[393] Schiller's letter to Goethe, 7 August 1797: 'Recently Zelter sent me the melody for your Bajadere and the song to Mignon. The latter especially pleased me. The melody for the ballad doesn't fit all verses so well, but for some, as in the third last verse, the choir for 'Wir tragen die Jugend' works particularly well; *MA* 8.1, p. 382.

[394] Zelter's setting of Goethe's ballad 'Der Gott und die Bajadere'.

[395] During Zelter's first visit to Weimar, on 25 or 26 February 1802; see Goethe's diary, 'To a concert in the palace. At the palace in the evening.' *WA* III/3, p. 52.

[396] Zelter's setting of Schiller's ballad 'Der Taucher'.

[397] Johann Gottlieb Naumann's setting of Schiller's poem 'Die Ideale', first published in the *Musen-Almanach für das Jahr 1796*.

[398] The infamous king (in Schiller's *Der Taucher*), who sends the diver down a second time to retrieve the golden chalice and thereby has him drowned.

## 462. Goethe

Weimar, 17 May 1829

First of all, let me thank you heartily for your description of Paganini. When I compare it to what is to be read in the Berlin newspapers,[399] my reason and imagination give me what seems a comprehensible picture. What one must have actually heard becomes to some extent clear to the intellect. I am glad he had such a listener, and you such a virtuoso.

You also deserve gratitude for explaining the important musical principles in your last letter. Resolve to do the same from time to time and you yourself will be storing up a treasure in my books. I am happy with my table[400] as a naked but well-stuctured skeleton to which a genuine artist might add the necessary flesh, skin and entrails and bring it to life through practice and thought. By this means I look across in a wonderful way to a region in which I was not supposed to find enjoyment, let alone find joy in reflecting on it. [...]

## 463. Zelter

Berlin, 21 May 1829

I am gradually making my way through Part Two of the Schiller letters, about the first appearance of *Wilhelm Meister*, which took place just when I made my first contact with you.[401] A new phase in my life had emerged out of the deepest affliction.[402] I had just been happily married to my second wife, whom I had known from her childhood, for I had attended the same Gymnasium as her brothers.[403]

---

[399] *Spenersche Zeitung*, no. 55, 6 March; no. 64, 13 March; no. 68, 21 March; no. 83, 8 April; no. 98, 28 April; no. 101, 1 May; no. 107, 8 May.

[400] Goethe's *Tonlehre* of 1810.

[401] Zelter, who had three of the six volumes of Goethe and Schiller's correspondence by May 1829, was rereading the letters of 1796 in volume two. Of the principal themes discussed mid-year, Zelter is preoccupied with the discussion of the final book of *Wilhelm Meisters Lehrjahre* as well as the appearance of Part IV of the novel in October 1796, but also the earliest documentation of Goethe's contact with Zelter on the occasion of the settings for Schiller's *Musenalmanach*. Zelter himself remembers this fateful year of 1796, which not only was the year of his remarriage (to Juliane Pappritz) but of his first published settings of Goethe's poems in his collection *Zwölf Lieder am Klavier zu singen* and in Schiller's *Musen-Almanach für das Jahr 1797* which met with Goethe's approval; see Goethe's letter to Helene Unger of 3 May 1796.

[402] Zelter's first wife died on 24 October 1795; he married Juliane Pappritz, a friend from his youth, on 1 May 1796.

[403] Ludwig Friedrich Pappritz (1755–1829) and Georg *Carl* Albecht Pappritz (1763–1846).

Before this I had given her lessons in singing, or rather through her crystal voice and clarity of delivery, I had experienced for the first time what no teaching can give. I could not help being pleased with my own arias when she performed them. People held their breath, so as not to miss even the smallest nuance. At that time I had already written down my first impressions of your poems on a series of sheets[404] which unfortunately have been lost, for they marked the transition from life as a civilian to my natural vocation.

I had so many children, so many mouths to feed, so much work, such delight in my strength, and then, I had another gentle wife, who took the children in hand – and when the father came home, we had great fun. I built houses for people, who to this day owe me the money which I laid out. When others worried about what it would all come to, I was as cheerful as possible. Clearly there were difficulties; I spoiled my customers, who had too much of a good time and wanted to have what I myself did not possess. That was what was amusing. Then *Wilhelm Meister* enters my household[405] with his lively company of rational and irrational beasts. People said I had lost my wits. I saw only green fields and the sky full of fiddles. [...]

### 464. Goethe

Weimar, 11 June 1829

Although I cannot believe, dear Zelter, that you could ever take notice again of my crazed unsteady hero in Winter's score,[406] I will send a clean copy, according to your early request, with the wish and hope that it will be alright with you.

---

[404] That Zelter is thinking of his handwritten *Sammlung von kleinen Liedern zum Singen beim Klaviere gesammlet und komponiert von C.F. Zelter* (Berlin, 1780) must be questioned, for he says the pages are 'unfortunately lost'; this collection was still held by the Bibliothek des Berliner Grauen Klosters in 1936; it was lost or destroyed during the Second World War.

[405] *Wilhelm Meisters Lehrjahre* was published by Unger in *Goethe's neue Schriften* in 1795 (vols 3–5) and 1796 (vol. 6).

[406] Goethe's cantata *Rinaldo* had already been produced in Winter's setting in 1812; however, the score was not in Goethe's possession at that time. When Goethe received it and when he gave it to Zelter is unknown. Goethe requested it back from Zelter on 28 April 1829, and Zelter had Philipp Christian Weyland return it to Weimar for him after he had made a copy of it.

## 465. Zelter

Berlin, 19 June 1829

This page, my dear Goethe, is to recommend you the most agreeable fat little Blondine,[407] who is the best contralto we have in the Sing-Akademie and is travelling through Weimar to meet you. She is travelling all alone to Holland, without her husband and the loveliest children, to see her mother again.

I have recommended her to Ulrike whom she knows and if Ulrike is in good health, she will oblige by introducing Madame Türrschmidt to you.

## 466. Zelter

Berlin, 12 June to 16 July 1829

Our friend Madame Szymanowska recommends a talented Polish compatriot and poet, especially to you as Prince of poets.[408] He is called Mickiewicz and wants to travel through Germany on his way to Italy. Madame Szymanowska is now in St Petersburg, is giving lessons, has separated from her husband,[409] has two daughters and a son.[410] The young man already speaks fairly good German and is especially recommended. You can discover the rest from him himself. [...]

21 June: Certain people can only show their awareness and appreciation by means of loud coughing, snorting, croaking and spitting; Berlioz seems to be one of these.[411] The sulphur smell of Mephisto attracts him, and so he must sneeze and puff, until all the instruments in the orchestra get the jumps – only not a hair of Faust's head moves. However, thank you for sending me the music; the opportunity will turn up to make use of it in a lecture as an abscess, an aborted work, which arises from the most terrible incest.

---

[407] Auguste Türrschmidt née Braun (1800–66), singer based in Berlin; whether the planned visit took place is unknown.

[408] Maria Szymanowska, the Polish pianist whom Goethe had met in Marienbad in 1823 and who settled in St Petersburg with her three children after touring as a concert pianist, had recommended the Polish poet Adam Mickiewicz, presumably in a letter to Zelter which has not been handed down. Szymanowska had come to know Mickiewicz in St Petersburg where he lived after he had been banished from Poland as politically suspect in 1824; he later married her eldest daughter, Celina.

[409] Józef Szymanowski.

[410] Celina, Helena and Romuald.

[411] Zelter's devastating critique of Hector Berlioz's *Huit Scènes de Faust*; Goethe had sent him the second copy of the printed score on 11 June 1829.

Worthy Winter's *Rinaldo* has, on the contrary, a human form of some kind, which is suitable for a tenor; but now we are as far removed from that, as that so-called artificiality of tones is from music. [...]

16 July: The Polish poet recommended by Madame Szymanowska asked for a letter for you and has not collected it!

### 467. Zelter

Berlin, 16 August 1829

[...] Since I can well imagine now you will be in demand in the next few days,[412] I will say nothing further other that that I am as well, for apart from my relationship to the Sing-Akademie I am now committed to 42 lessons a week[413] and to the teaching of rudiments of singing to boys and lads, who (long taught) discover for the first time and to everyone's surprise that while singing one has to open the mouth, have an expression, and must be able to walk [out] and stand [correctly]. It begins to give me real joy to start from the beginning once more, and to let myself be laughed at by the bunglers who reveal the secret attractions of vocally demanding grand operas to the young girls of Berlin.

### 468. Zelter

Berlin, 11 to 20 August 1829

Naue, the Director of Music,[414] has me (in the papers) coming to Halle to his festival of music and then he invites me afterwards. You needn't lose sleep over it: I have to sweep before my door and also know to be busy!

20 August: Naue does not know how to occupy himself in his position. He once went through my school and, with the help of all kinds of patrons, took over the position of the deceased Türk and in addition Professor Maaß's daughter.[415] May he serve her better because she is the first of those he needs to bring in to

---

[412] Goethe's 80th birthday was on 28 August 1829.

[413] The musical seminars for students at the University of Berlin, initially organized by Bernard Klein, were taken over by Zelter in 1829. In the early months of 1830 Zelter formed a *Collegium musicum vocale* from the most gifted singers. The musical seminars, which were originally intended for theological students, were very popular with the student community in general.

[414] Johann *Friedrich* Naue (1787–1858), Director of Music at the University of Halle.

[415] Naue's wife, a foster-daugher of Johann Gebhard Ehrenreich Maaß, Professor of Philosophy in Halle.

do his work for him. Now he comes and asks to be able to place my name beside the names Spontini, Moeser and so on, in what is for him a completely unfruitful undertaking. I didn't say no only because I would not allow myself any rejection of these men and will give no opportunity for importunity to the indiscretion of a vain music director – that's [the end of] the story. Afterwards he wants to send a carriage for me and my household – good accommodation and catering at a desirable location is to be made ready – which I can honourably decline and not be under a compliment. [...]

Felix is in Scotland[416] and has already written down to us from the Highlands.[417] I have commissioned him to transcribe the national songs and dances[418] more accurately than those travelling amateurs and untutored copyists from whom we have derived our knowledge up to now. The dear rascal has the luck of finding and making friends everywhere; he has even met Walter Scott.[419] Then in London he met a young Hanoverian[420] who was attached to the English Embassy here and who is now his companion on this instructive journey, whether they travel by foot, by horse, or by water. From there, via Ireland and Holland, he will come home in

---

[416] At the end of July Felix undertook a one-month tour of Scotland and the Hebrides with Karl Klingemann. Their journey is documented in Mendelssohn's letters to his family, the first of which was written to his father from Edinburgh; see Rudolf Elvers (ed.), *Felix Mendelssohn Bartholdy. Briefe* (Frankfurt am Main: Fischer, 1984), p. 79ff. Hereafter referred to as *Mendelssohn Briefe*.

[417] Perhaps Zelter means the letter of 28 July to his father, or those written to his family on 3 and 7 August; *Mendelssohn Briefe*, pp. 79–85; a letter from Felix to Zelter from this time in unknown.

[418] Scottish folk music was very popular, as illustrated by the arrangements of Haydn and Beethoven. In unpublished letters of 5 July and 6 August 1829 (Werner, *Mendelssohn*, p. 184), Zelter tells Mendelssohn to pay attention to folk music but Mendelssohn wrote to his father from Llangollen on 25 August, half in earnest, 'Anything but folk music! May 10,000 devils take all national traditions. Here I am in Wales, and oh, how lovely! A harpist sits in the lobby of every respectable inn playing so-called folk melodies to you – dreadful, vulgar, fake, and simultaneously a hurdy-gurdy is tooting out melodies – it's enough to drive you insane!'

[419] In a letter to the Mendelssohn's from Abbotsford on 31 July, Karl Klingemann described the visit effusively but ironically and in a postscript to the letter, Mendelssohn added, 'Klingemann is lying above; we found Walter Scott about to leave Abbotsford, we looked at him as we would at a new gate, we travelled 80 miles and lost a day in order to have half an hour of insignificant conversation'; Sebastien Hensel (ed.), *Die Familie Mendelssohn 1729 bis 1847. Nach Briefen und Tagebüchern* (Frankfurt am Main and Leipzig: Insel Verlag, r.1995), p. 274.

[420] Karl Klingemann (1798–1862), Hanoverian Legate in London.

the autumn for his sister's marriage with the court painter Hensel,[421] and then set out for Italy.[422] He is hard at it, building his career, and there is no lack of stone.

### 469. Goethe

Weimar, 20 August 1829

[...] Our Polish poet has just announced himself;[423] had he come a few days earlier he would have been welcome to join our circle, but now I have to receive him alone, and that is very difficult, almost impossible [...]

### 470. Zelter

Berlin, 23 to 25 August 1829

[...] Felix sent me a young Scotsman from Edinburgh,[424] who unfortunately doesn't speak anything apart from English. He is, however, very musical and so we will have to deal with each other through music. Since these islanders set great value by what they have, he was all ears last Friday when he could listen to a piece of music by old Bach *prima vista* with a score in hand, which at least went off smoothly. If I placed my Scotsman against your Polish poet and Englishman,[425] we would have a trio, the like of which you don't find everyday, in order to crack open a piece by Klopstock. [...]

---

[421] On 3 October 1829 Fanny Mendelssohn married the court painter Wilhelm Hensel, whose work embraced historical and church pictures as well as numerous portraits of the Mendelssohn family. Felix's attendance at the ceremony was prevented by a coach accident.

[422] Felix's two-year journey through Italy, Switzerland and France began in May 1830.

[423] Adam Mickiewicz, recommended by Zelter on 11 June 1829.

[424] Mendelssohn had written to his family from Edinburgh on 30 July 1829: 'The young man, J. Thompson, who brings you the letter speaks neither German nor French; you must act as if you were in Edinburgh and go on speaking English through thick and thin. He really loves music; I know an attractive trio he composed and also some songs which I really like', Hensel, *Die Familie Mendelssohn*, p. 270. The Scottish composer John Thomson had befriended Mendelssohn on his tour of Scotland; returning to Edinburgh after a sojourn in Germany, he became best known for his music for Scott's *The House of Aspen*.

[425] John Thomson, Adam Mickiewicz and Henry Crabb Robinson.

## 471. Zelter

Berlin, 28 to 29 September 1829

In Halle 4,000 thalers in excess of the takings is to be paid.[426] To achieve this, willing hearts are being sought. They have the courage to continue with such festivals,[427] even to move to Berlin and Potsdam, which is why we want to see a similar festival nearby. No one fails to applaud the performance of major works since such works were rehearsed by our best people well in advance. If one doesn't want to be too strict, such festivals are a means for making some thousands of thalers circulate, which, of course, would be everything. [...]

Will you be so good as to have the enclosed canon[428] delivered to the Chief County Councillor Töpfer?[429] They were so nice in the shooting society as to repeat, for our sake, the shooting which had already taken place before noon. I don't know any other way of showing my appreciation since they presented a copy of their songbook to me which was partly decorated by your poems. As they couldn't stop singing, the simple canon may go down well with them and travel to foreign parts.

---

[426] Zelter had Naue report to him on the last days of the music festival and found out 'that the takings had still not reached 3,000 thaler, leaving a deficit of over 1,000 thaler'; Schottländer, *Carl Friedrich Zelters Darstellungen seines Lebens*, p. 294. 'The festival accounts' were also discussed with Naue's wife the following day. Ibid., p. 295. Whether the different information about the amout of the deficit is based on a mistake by Zelter or on new information is unknown.

[427] As a result of the postive reception of the festival in Halle – see, for example, the *Spenersche Zeitung* of 23 September (*MA* 20.3, p. 1040) – the idea of continuing this event soon arose; see Zelter's conversation with Naue recorded in his diary on 25 September, 'and so he still has the courage to uproot and move his Thuringian music festival to Potsdam and to offer me the direction. So I could become a Pots-doctor to the Potsdamers – let's think about it between now and then?' Schottländer, *Carl Friedrich Zelters Darstellungen seines Lebens*, p. 295. Despite the financial fiasco in Halle, Naue announced a 'Big Music Festival in Potsdam'; *Berliner Allgemeine Musikalische Zeitung* (1830), column 270.

[428] 'Der Schütze sang mit Freuden', probably by Christian Philip Köhler, composed by Zelter for the Weimar Crossbow Society.

[429] On 2 October 1829 Goethe had given Zelter's composition to Martin Christian Victor Töpfer with an accompanying note, written by one hand, and with Goethe's seal 'To Councillor Töpfer, passed on for further safe keeping' (GSA 29/512a). On 4 October Töpfer paid a visit to Goethe to thank him, on behalf of the society, for the consignment from Zelter.

## 472. Goethe

Weimar, 19 October 1829

[…] Now here is the greatest wonder of antiquity for those that have eyes to see the good of the moment and what this is worth. For although by the most terrible misfortune these pictures were buried among ruins for nearly two thousand years, they are still just as fresh, as outstanding, as successful, as they were in the hour of fame and contentment which preceded their fearful entombment. If we were asked what they represent, one would find it rather difficult to find an answer; meantime I should say that these forms give us the feeling that the moment must be pregnant and sufficient to itself if it is to become a worthy segment of time and eternity.

What is said here about plastic art applies in reality even better to music, and when you, old fellow, reflect upon your own work and your own institution, you will accept this opinion as being valid. Indeed, from this point of view, music fills up the present moment more decisively than anything else, whether it awakens in the tranquil mind reverence and worship, or whether it summons the active senses to dance and celebration – leaving the rest to devout and true feelings and to discerning thoughts.

## 473. Zelter

Berlin, 26 to 27 October 1829

26 October: In London my Felix has met with an accident;[430] he has been thrown out of a carriage and is unable to attend his sister's wedding in Berlin. I am afraid he may have broken something for it is a long delay and he cannot write; still, they say he is getting better. As he is expected to return through Calais, he will, I am sure, travel via France to Weimar[431] and pay you a visit […]

---

[430] On 18 September 1829 Mendelssohn wrote to his father, 'what happened is that yesterday a stupid little gig I was travelling in tipped over and robbed me of a nice bit of skin with accompanying flesh, black trouser cloth, etc, and Dr Kind gave me strict orders to remain quietly in bed for four to five days'; Elvers, *Mendelssohns Briefe*, p. 94. Mendelssohn's knee injury was worse than it at first appeared, and delayed his departure from England until the end of November.

[431] Mendelssohn's return journey was from Calais (29 November) to Brussels (1 December), Maastricht (2 December), Cologne (3 December) to Berlin, without passing through Weimar.

## 474. Goethe

Weimar, 1 November 1829

I will say this much about the most immediate concerns: one of the four English people in Ulrike's care is quite distraught that he has not heard your musical achievements. He is – I don't know whether by talent and profession – passionately dedicated to music. Every day he plays the cello for three hours with our Haase[432] and never goes anywhere except where there is playing and singing. This is the one Ulrike thought was worthy of you receiving him, in so far as circumstances allowed. They had firmly resolved and promised to be here again on Wednesday evening and on Thursday evening to attend a ball, which has had to be cancelled now because of the death of the Grand Duchess of Darmstadt.[433] […]

## 475. Zelter

Berlin, 5 November 1829

Yesterday on 4th of this month we gave a public academy concert for the benefit of the unfortunate Silesians who were victims of the flood and we are able to donate around 250 thalers.[434] That is the reason no listeners were let into the rehearsals.[435] The young fogies have to be addressed in German sometimes and that cannot be edifying for foreigners. Now I have worries for us because our creditors are demanding interest which has to be earned by the poor Sing-Akademie, and at the same time one still has to be charitable as if one had something to give. Those are the current people. Their successors will take double the amount to no purpose and will be no cleverer than their forefathers.

---

[432] Johann Michael Haase (d.1854), chamber musician, cellist in Weimar.

[433] Luise von Hessen-Darmstadt, sister-in-law of Duchess Louise of Sachsen-Weimar-Eisenach.

[434] A Sing-Akademie benefit concert for the victims of the Silesian flood took place on Wednesday 4 November 1829 (originally advertised for 3 November); it was an a cappella concert made up exclusively from their own forces. The programme included a motet by Zelter (to a poem by Count Leopold von Stolberg), Antonio Lotti's *Crucifixus*, J.S. Bach's motet ('Ich lasse Dich nicht') and a composition by Mendelssohn for 16 voices.

[435] Zelter's explanation as to why the English guests recommended by Ulrike von Pogwisch could not be let into the Sing-Akademie rehearsals.

## 476. Goethe

Weimar, 9 November 1829

[…] I, too, have now heard Paganini[436] and immediately afterwards, on the very same evening, I opened your letter,[437] which allowed me to imagine that my estimate of these marvels was fairly accurate. I thought something was lacking to make up what we call enjoyment, something which for me is always hovering between sense and understanding – a base to this pillar of flame and cloud.[438]

Were I in Berlin, I should seldom miss the Moeser quartet evenings.[439] I have always found performances of this kind more intelligible than other instrumental music: one hears four rational persons conversing together, and imagines one gains something from their discourse and becomes acquainted with the peculiarities of their different instruments. This time I felt such a foundation was lacking – both mentally and orally; I only heard something meteoric, and could not interpret it further for myself. Yet it is strange to hear people, and especially women, talk about it: their opinions are essentially confessions which they express with great confidentiality.

And now I want to know whether you have received good news from the worthy Felix;[440] I take the greatest interest in him; it is very painful to see an individual who has made such great strides held back by an unfortunate accident. Let me have a few comforting words about him […]

---

[436] Paganini gave a guest performance in Weimar on 30 October 1829; *AMZ* 32 (1830), no. 7, 17 February, column 109. Goethe mentions his performance in an earlier letter on 1 November 1829.

[437] Presumably Zelter's letter of 1–5 May 1829, in which he reported meeting Paganini and praised his virtuosity.

[438] See Exodus, Book 2, 13, 21. The meaning of the Old Testament image used here can be found in the essay *Israel in der Wüste, Noten und Abhandlungen zu besserem Verständnis des West-östlichen Divans*; *MA* 11, 1.2, p. 215. Applied to Paganini, the divine presence can be seen as a pillar of cloud by day and as a fire meteor by night; in other words as a leading light, an example to be followed.

[439] Carl Moeser's Quartet-Soirées, set up in 1813, 'the true refuge of classical music' which had to accept the reproach that it neglected contemporary composition.

[440] About the accident, Zelter could now report that Felix Mendelssohn's arrival in London was now immanent.

### 477. Zelter

Berlin, 10 November 1829

[...] Some time ago I wrote to you about Berlioz's music to your *Faust*.[441] Now I am sending the Berlin musical newspaper,[442] which in general is always half and half except that the editor[443] is more than that: half a Christian and a total Jew. This paper affects me like damp cloud passing by the moon; it blocks the light which I receive and reflect because I don't fly their flag. I am better off and although I have not forgotten how to fence, why should I slave away for nothing?

I would also like to send you a later page in the newspaper.[444] It contains a critique of our Wednesday music, which went off quite smoothly. I had placed my student, the organist Grell,[445] at the grand piano. To my delight the critic praised his direction[446] and happily didn't notice who conducted it. That tickled me!

### 478. Zelter

Berlin, 13 to 16 November 1829

Your letter of 9 November has just arrived. What you say about Paganni[447] is pure reason and exactly the way I see it. The first time he seemed to me like Moses who

---

[441] ZG 21 June 1829.

[442] *Berliner Allgemeine Musikalische Zeitung* no. 39, 26 September 1829, review of Berlioz *Huit Scènes de Faust*, by A.B. Marx; the enclosed copy has not been recorded. In contrast to Zelter's scathing criticism, the critic here calmly weighs up praise and criticism and also includes a consideration of the problems of the French translation. 'Should a French composer feel the need to give his native land a new music, then he will be led astray by French translations of German poems, if he himself has not learnt the German language in Germany, doesn't assimilate it according to its full meaning and spirit and then with an educated German artistic spirit makes his mother tongue into a poetic musical language.' What the reviewer overlooks is that in his translation of *Faust I* (1828) Gérard de Nerval (1808–55) succeeded in presenting a 'French Faust' which inspired Berlioz's setting and which Goethe, in fact, preferred to his own: see my introductory essay to this volume: A Musical Odyssey: Thirty-Five Years of Correspondence between Goethe and Zelter, p. XX.

[443] Adolph Martin (formerly Abraham Moses) Schlesinger (1767/69–1838).

[444] *Vossische Zeitung*, no. 260, 6 November 1829, with Rellstab's praise for the concert on 4 November.

[445] Grell, August *Edward* (1800–1886), composer and organist in Berlin.

[446] Ibid.

[447] A draft letter of Zelter's contains further remarks about the Paganini phenomenon: 'I have just read in the paper that Paganini has also paraded in Halberstadt. The report is quite intelligently and freely written; I would bet [written by] a woman, perhaps Madame Körte.

displayed his arts to the Eygptians.⁴⁴⁸ I was spoiling for a fight. It was the same the second time and I want to see whether that impression lasts when he comes again. In general it is like the woman who, with her nose in the air, punishes the non-believers like aetheists as if they were all Eves giving away paradise for an almond. What focuses attention on these virtuosi is essentially a mingling of what's fashionable with a desire not be rooted in anything. It is a mania but without manners: a special individual but without anything unique because, like a thread that always becomes thinner, it leads to nothing. It makes music desirable in the same way as an imitation oyster, peppered, pickled, is swallowed.

According to the latest news: Felix is leaving London on 17 November and could be in Germany sometime this month.⁴⁴⁹

What I must envy you and at the same don't begrudge you is your desire to read and ability to do so. [...] What distresses me most is that I am beginning to find it hard to read music. The more this ability is taken away, the more I need it since I am becoming more and more alone. When a young bird is fully fledged, it will throw itself into everything. If I no longer knew how to do this, I would be long gone.

Your sharing of literary news from Paris is highly pleasant to me since I am normally not up to date with the latest thing and a word from you teaches me more than my own reading. [...] The French are the other species on the continent. They dance around everything and consider themselves blessed to come into the suburbs. Their mannered music is still what it was: they drive everything forward and drag everything with them. Only the Italians appear to let the spectre pass by calmly until such time as the next genius will arrive to settle among them. Until then they at least hold onto their caricature, which at least suits them even if it is botched up.

14 November: That fine word Faustus, Fauste, Faust,⁴⁵⁰ has been imbued by you with such ominous meaning that it is only right that you ought to become acutely aware of its further consequences. So listen: yesterday evening, for the

---

Then your words about women came back to me – "it is actually a complete confession which is pronounced with complete confidence" – absolutely! One could agree because he scratches where he is itchy and that can be honestly admitted. But he is an Italian, by nature a person of good taste. One must hear him without the accompaniment of other people and [one must hear] his own compositions as pieces where a sound hand obeys the dictates of a sound mind. Under his bow other people's music seem to me like fluids of a different nature; the field of his art is limited, which is why he needs to include other people's music [in his programme] in order to add musical variety' (GSA 95/I, 8, 4, no. 54).

⁴⁴⁸ In other words, to put on a show of deception.

⁴⁴⁹ It is not known where Zelter received this news. In the last published letter to his family from London on 6 November 1829, Felix was afraid that he would have to wait two weeks for departure.

⁴⁵⁰ What Zelter presents in the rhetorical figure of detractio is the derivation of the name 'Faust' from the Latin adjective 'faustus' (meaning 'lucky, happy'), whereby he also plays on the ominous nuance which the name has aquired through Goethe's poetic figure.

first time, I heard and saw, from beginning to end, *Faust*, the Grand Opera by J.C. Bernard and Spohr.[451] If I am not mistaken, the composer got together a Sanedrin, or whatever they call it,[452] in order that they might jointly sanction laws that are valid for grand and light opera, which are made clear from the above monumental work. Whether an understanding was arrived at, I don't know, nor have I asked.

Yesterday's performance of this full, highly developed work, received my greatest praise, and the full house did not fail to applaud it. The orchestra, the highest faculty of an opera, sounded like one voice; the singers were as perfect as possible; supernumeraries, machinery, decorations, witches, ghosts, and other monsters – all received recognition and the best reception [...] Now, with regard to the work of the composer, who certainly merits more recognition for his artistry than as a musician and melodist. Everything is astonishingly well worked out, down out to the smallest detail, so as to outwit, to outbid even the most attentive ear. Compared to it the finest Brabant lace is coarse work. You can't do without the book at the performance because the expression of words, high and low, bright and dark, firm and loose is razor-sharp, worked like a beehive [...] With regards to the composer and the orchestra, the performance can't be praised highly enough.

### 479. Zelter

Berlin, 17 November 1829

The way you speak of Moeser's quartets, it seems you must have heard them even as far as Weimar. I must say, although I rarely go to hear them, they are the things I like best of their kind. I don't know whether I ever wrote to you upon this subject, but I doubt if Haydn, Mozart and Beethoven ever enjoyed such a pure, healthy and secure rendering of their quartets as is given here when Moeser is at his best; for

---

[451] The Berlin premiere of Louis Spohr's *Faust* (with libretto by Joseph Carl Bernard) – first performed in Prague in 1816 – took place on 14 November in the Königliches Opernhaus. A second performance took place on 17 November; a third with new scenery took place on 22 November. The original two-act Romantic opera was reworked as a three-act grand opera. It is unclear why Zelter speaks of a grand opera as early as 1829. It is most likely bound up with the decision of the Berlin opera to stage the opera in five acts – much to Spohr's displeasure – and to use Spohr's overture to *Macbeth* before Act 5. The libretto is primarily based on Friedrich Maximilian Klinger's *Faust Leben, Taten und Höllenfahrt* of 1791.

[452] Sanhedrin: during the Roman occupation, the top Jewish authority, the high council of Jerusalem, correctly quoted by Zelter, bringing the article into line with the German translation. With 'Sanedrin' Zelter is probably referring to Spohr's 'Call to German Composers' which had appeared in the *AMZ* 25 (1823), columns 457–64. The article calls upon composers to create through-composed German grand opera, and Spohr's *Faust* was not yet at this stage, and it formulated the conditions for their success. Spohr announces his own *Jessonda* as a model of grand opera without spoken dialogue.

it would be too much to ask that he could produce that every day. He knows how to electrify his fellow players. The listeners also don't know what is happening to them. They feel as if they are playing along, they understand the incomprehensible. They are gripped and don't know from what. At the same time he doesn't look as if he is even there. Unfortunately he is not lucky in love and is doing a lot of penance to which two divorced ladies (the third is dead) contribute, and apart from them the one who has him now makes her contribution. Anyway, he is also an excellent leader of an orchestra. It would be presumptious of me, standing in the aisle of the Opera House, to say whether Moeser or another was playing first violin. I gladly have him in the performances of my oratorios. He does not contradict and if I turn my eyes towards, him he understands and is secure like a God. He is the only one with whom I can be completely at ease, since I cannot abide the damned baton. Now the dreadful nonsense is rampant in the Königliches Theater: that of making the first violin musical director. The court orchesta has four of them.[453] Three don't function at all, since no one will play under the other. At comedies (apart from the opera) a fifth person joins the first violins[454] and then the other four do nothing at all. You can well imagine it, since you are familiar with how it goes. Whether the newly appointed intendant[455] (about whom nothing is still clear) will want to agree to this institution, since it happens under the direction of the general music director,[456] time will tell. At the same time that a performance is still possible, such as I heard a few days ago and reported to you, is no surprise with an orchestra of 30 violins and the amount of rehearsals which are held because of the singers who don't learn their parts at home but in rehearsal. [...]

---

[453] Presumably Friedrich Ludwig Seidel (1765–1831), Georg Abraham Schneider (1770–1839), Director of Music from 1820, Carl Moeser (1774–1851), Director of Music from 1825 and promoted to first leader of the orchestra, and Karl Heinrich Blum (c.1786–1844).

[454] Perhaps Carl Wilhelm Henning, who had given up his position as Director of Music at the Königstädtisches Theater in 1826 and had gone back to being leader of the orchestra at the Königliches Oper, where he was eventually made Director of Music in 1836.

[455] Count Wilhelm von Redern; following Brühl's resignation at the beginning of December 1828, Redern was made acting manager and artistic director; his postion was made permanent in 1831.

[456] Spontini.

### 480. Goethe

Weimar, 12 to 16 December 1829

I may not refrain from speaking out: that you agree about the mental enjoyment of music does me good because I must content myself with that.[457] It is always constructive to convince onself that in old age, intellectual reason or, if you like, reasonable understanding, can be a legitimate substitute for the senses.[458] You will never be in this category, on account of your fortunate profession, to need this serious surrogate.

Your account of Spohr's opera gives further proof that although the poetry dissolves into nothing, the musician can at the same time have his chance, give a satisfactory interpretation and even partly delight [his audience].

Tonight *Die Stumme von Portici* is being performed for the third time[459] and I am hearing much that is good about the way the whole thing has been introduced and carried out. I have already heard elaborate accounts from my grandsons, and further up the scale[460] from the well-disposed audience. In terms of progress and coherence, it would seem to be an attractive lively work. [...]

### 481. Zelter

Berlin, 17 to 18 December 1829

Small causes and great effects! A mute fishermaiden, seduced by the son of the Viceroy of Naples, is the heroine of a famous French Opera, *La muette de Portici*.[461]

---

[457] Zelter had written to Goethe on 17 November 1829: 'The way you speak of Moeser's quartets, it seems you must have heard them even as far away as Weimar.'

[458] This could be read as a critical reflection on Kant, who, in *Kritik der reinen Vernunft*, sees 'reason' as distinguished by the tendency to transcend the realm of experience.

[459] Daniel François Espirit Auber's opera *Die Stumme von Portici* (libretto by Eugène Scribe's *La Muette de Portici*, translated by Theodor von Haupt) was performed in Weimar for the first time on 21 November 1829; a second performance took place on 28 November and a third performance took place on 12 December.

[460] Goethe had received reports from his son August, who wrote a critique on the opening night of the Weimar premiere; on 22 January Coudray followed and in the afternoon Eckermann and his grandson, Wolfgang. Eckermann's diary on 23 January records the lasting success of the work: '*Die Stumme von Portici* was played for the sixth time to a packed house. In front of the Sonne [hotel] I counted 60 sleighs, Privy Councillor counted 70 before the Swan, Elephant, and the Erbprince [hotels]', Houben, vol. 1, p. 451. About the same time as Goethe's letter, Zelter, too, writes about the opera.

[461] Staged in Lichtenstein's German translation from 12 January 1829.

The maiden is mute as a fish, but all the others, Herr Auber[462] at their head, make such a horrible commotion, five acts long, that at last even Vesuvius awakes and, grumbling and roaring, spits its furious inside at the sky. Our public revels in this dinner of the Titans, which it has now devoured for the twenty-seventh time and never has enough! The singers and players are half roasted afterwards and I came away really well done myself. However, there is no lack of wit [..]

This evening our *Samson* by Milton and Handel[463] will add to the atmosphere. The quality of the singing is properly prepared with full orchestra. May the Gods be merciful. I was only able to hold one full rehearsal and must watch out like a shooting snipe. Pray for me! I have no time to do it myself. [...]

18 December: I have just heard Auber's opera *Die Braut*.[464] When you speak of a man, you should at least recall two of his actions. The lady wants to and is supposed to marry an upholsterer and gets a cavalry officer in his place; a great commotion arises from this, which the orchestra has to make, and does make, alone, because on this occasion thunder and lightning are missing or are somewhere else. Wit and entertainment, fullness and force are not wanting, although everything revolves around itself. – They have just brought me your letter of the 16th, in which you speak of the *Muette* by this same composer. You have formed your own opinion and I agree with you. All true music can only be and work mentally; what is beyond that has been already forbidden by Lycurgus[465] and rightly so, for it is bad! But in spite of that severe lawgiver, I must make an exception in favour of the organ, because from my youth that [instrument] has stirred my deepest conscience, like a serious confessor, as you showed quite involuntarily in *Faust*.[466] That scene, in its place, is crushing in effect, and if no one knows how, I know it, for I have the whole church before my eyes [...]

---

[462] Daniel François Espirit Auber (1782–1871), composer of the opera.

[463] Handel's oratorio *Samson*, performed by the Sing-Akademie on 17 December 1829; see *AMZ* 32 (1830), no. 3, 20 January, column 46.

[464] Daniel François Espirit Auber, *Die Braut* (libretto by Eugène Scribe, *La fiancée*), performed in Berlin for the first time in Karl August Lichtenstein's adaptation on 3 August 1829; Zelter attended the performance on 18 December.

[465] The legendary Spartan legislator had also defined the function of music in the state: already an important component of education (Agoge), above all it served to stimulate the war-like virtues of mental armament; see Plutarch's *Vergleichende Lebensbeschreibungen* (Lykurg, chapter 21).

[466] *Faust 1*, The Cathedral scene, Gretchen's words 'Mir ist als ob die Orgel mir/ Den Atem versetzte', v. 3809f.; *MA* 6.1, p. 647.

## 482. Goethe

Weimar, New Year's Eve 1829

I gather from your letter, dear friend, that it was Milton's tragedy that induced Handel to write his *Samson*. However, I should be curious to know how he treated that glorious poetic work, and how he epitomized it. I read Milton's *Samson* last summer, with an English man of letters[467] who was staying with us, and my admiration of it was boundless. I could not mention any work that expressed so closely the meaning and style of ancient Greek tragedy, nor one whose text and performance deserved equal recognition. Handel has probably dealt with it, as with the Bible, extracting – in accordance with dramatic rules – the most expressive, the most important and, at the same time, the parts of the story which are most singable. If a short programme was printed for your performance,[468] pray let me see it, or tell me how I can find the information I desire.

## 483. Zelter

Berlin, 5 to 7 January 1830

I enclose a copy of our *Samson*.[469] It is wonderful what Handel has made of it. The lament of the loss of sight (p. 6)[470] can only be composed by a man who (the same as Samson), with a premonition of terrible emptiness, must end the most active of lives, for Handel was blind when he died. When I heard this aria for the first time, my eyes closed involuntarily. In the second section (p. 10) the aria which is performed with the choir has a shattering yet positive effect.[471] I have never experienced the like of it. If I don't open my eyes, the whole work is like a dramatic performance for me: I see and feel it with the ears. Since after all one must himself enjoy what is supposed to be appetizing, I immediately sent to the Königliche Bibliothek for a good translation of Milton's tragedy and happily discovered my

---

[467] Goethe had already written to Zelter on 20 August a detailed account of the reading the first part of Milton's *Samson Agonistes* with the English lawyer and writer Henry Crabb Robinson on 18 August 1829. On that occasion Goethe had not praised Milton [to Robinson] with the warmth with which he eulogized Byron; *Gespräche*, vol. III/2, p. 458.

[468] *Samson. Ein Oratorium aus dem Englischen des Milton zu Händels Musik frei übersetzt (...) von I.F. Mosel* (Berlin, 1828); Zelter sent the libretto to Goethe on 7 January 1830.

[469] Ibid. The libretto is no longer in Goethe's library.

[470] Samson's aria 'Total eclipse' from Act 1.

[471] Micah's Aria 'Hear my plea O mighty God!', answered by the Chorus of Israelites 'They are trampling your servant into the dust and count him among the dead'.

Handel as Samson and Milton once again. I would not have understood either so well if I did not understand you.

### 484. Zelter

Berlin, 9 January 1830

Back again with our *Samson*. If it is too much, it is partly your fault. You will remember that earlier I found this subject useful for a tragic opera[472] and that it would be able to fit comfortably into three acts. Admittedly the cast are Jews, but they are characters from antiquity: a hero, a beautiful woman, an uncommon relationship between the two; tribal factions, a brilliant catastrophe – what more can one want!

In his tragedy[473] Milton has Delila run off; they don't know where she is. Samson can never forgive her; the misfortune is too great and he himself carries the greater half of the guilt. Before the world she is to be excused: she is a woman, from an enemy tribe; she really loves, is jealous not without cause; besieged by priests and relations but she is not bought. In short she is a Dejanira. Samson didn't want to go to the temple and is compelled; Delila must also not want it; she is persuaded and hopes to do some good, if not to obtain forgiveness. She is the keystone of the catastrophe. As she approaches to offer her hand in reconciliation, he seizes the pillars and pulls them back and forth; so she must also be destroyed. The collapse of the temple would not have to happen at the same time. On all sides people try to escape; whereever they flee is to their death.

### 485. Goethe

Weimar, 12 January 1830

[…] Your letters from the years 1828 and 1829 lie before me ordered very neatly;[474] for that reason send mine now from both years so that the older codices, which were

---

[472] ZG 25 April to 8 May 1812.
[473] John Milton, *Samson Agonistes*.
[474] There were regular dispatches of Goethe's earlier letters exchanged between Berlin and Weimar from the time Goethe first requested an occasional handing-over of his letters written to Zelter in order to have a complete copy made of the letters. The last exchange took place in February 1828, when Zelter sent Goethe's letters from 1827 to be copied; they were returned to Zelter in May 1828. On 18 January 1830 Zelter sent Goethe's letters from 1828 to Weimar to be copied; the letters of 1829 were sent as soon as Goethe's 1828 letters were returned to him on 12 April 1828.

drawn up, do not remain incomplete. Even with that the copyist[475] will have three months work to do. On the other hand we can also see from the correspondence with Schiller how the day always brings the best to serious friends through which the year, when the days are added up, guarantees an incalculable advantage. The individual details are actually the life; the results should be treasured, but they astonish people more than they are of use to them.

[…] In Milton, according to classical style the woman wasn't able to come on stage again after that scene of hatred and violence.[476] I understand that the musician would have further need of her, all the more so because an audience of more recent times demands a complete resolution, whether for good or for evil. I will enquire whether the score is perhaps still in the Chamberlain's office from long ago and then delight myself with further comparisons. […]

### 486. Zelter

Berlin, 13 to 14 January 1830

[…] 13 January: Today we have our third subscription concert.[477] I will rest today in order to appear relaxed for the performance. […]

### 487. Zelter

Berlin, 17 to 18 January 1830

A curious thing happened yesterday evening. I went to a concert to hear Chélard's overture to *Macbeth*.[478] The orchestral leader[479] had placed it at the end, directly

---

[475] Johann John (see Goethe's diary of 25 January 1830, *WA* III/12, p. 186).

[476] Goethe's reply to Zelter's reproach, 'In his tragedy Milton has Delila run off; they don't know where she is', ZG 9 January 1830.

[477] On 14 January 1830; the programme included works by Leonardo Leo, Johann Sebastian Bach, Joseph Haydn, Wolfgang Amadeus Mozart, Karl Friedrich Fasch, Felix Mendelssohn and Zelter's motet *Der Mensch lebt und besteht*; the concert was very favourably received; see *Spenersche Zeitung*, 16 January 1830 and *AMZ* 32 (1830), no. 9, 3 March, column 139f. and the *Berliner Allgemeine musikalische Zeitung* 7 (1830), no. 3, 16 January, columns 20f. and 23f.

[478] Carl Moeser organized a big concert on 16 January 1830 in the hall of the Königliches Schauspielhaus; the last item on the programme was the overture from André Chélard's opera *Macbeth*.

[479] Carl Moeser.

after a long, heavy church scene from Spontini's last opera[480] where church, organ and nun's chorus are all muddled up. The scene seemed to be unending – something at which our Spontini is a master. Finally the close came and everyone got up to go. I, poor devil, had listened to the whole muddle and swallowed down the overture to *Macbeth* along with the scene, organ and nuns [...] If I were a critic,[481] I would receive such things badly. [...]

### 488. Zelter

Berlin, 26 to 27 January 1830

Yesterday we had our first carnival opera, *The Siege of Corinth*,[482] music by Rossini, whom the German critics,[483] for the last 15 years, have worn themselves out writing against. The libretto is a strange melange [...] The music to this sad story has a fresh, jaunty character with powerful passages which explode like fireworks. That one with such rich talent could make the most perfect music which is also only tolerated is undoubtedly true, however, and is its own excuse. I like the continual praying least of all and after that the hand-clapping. Our performance is really splendid; but since one is also used to that here, I heard this opera referred to, on many sides, as the weakest by this composer. We hardly know how to recognize what one person has, and what he doesn't have he cannot give. He cannot be worse off than when he writes for his own time and its people. It would have to be so easy for him as for one who like an impatient horse would prefer to run around the same circle 20 times and so feels free, rather than let himself be seized and held. Nevertheless you can imagine that the whole thing was entertaining because the

---

[480] The penultimate item on the programme read: 'Dramatic scene, consising of the nun's chorus, followed by an aria and duet from Act 2 of the opera *Agnes von Hohenstaufen* by Spontini, performed by Fräulein von Schätzel, the royal singer, Zschiesche and the choir of the Königliches Theater'.

[481] The critic of the *Spenersche Zeitung*, no. 15, 19 January 1830, praised the rendition of Spontini's work but criticized the concluding overture.

[482] Opera by Gioachino Rossini (libretto by Guiseppe Luigi Balocchi and Alexandre Soumet, *Le siege de Corinthe*); the Berlin premiere of the German version (by Joseph Kupelwieser) took place on 25 January 1830. See the review in the *AMZ* 32 (1830), no. 7, 17 February, column 115.

[483] In contrast to the enthusiasm for Rossini among the general public, the reception of the critics was changeable and split. The centre of rejection of Rossini was in Berlin; above all the violation of 'dramatic truth', 'failure of characterization' and the lack of sensitivity to the meaning of the words were reprimanded (essentially by advocates of German national opera) in the *Berliner Allgemeine Musikalische Zeitung*. For Rossini's reception in the *Leipziger Allgemeine Musikalische Zeitung* see J. Loschfelder, 'Rossinis Bild und Zerbild in der Allgemeine Musikalische Zeitung Leipzig' in *Bolletino del centro Rossiniano di studi* (Pesaro, 1973), vols. 1 and 2, pp. 23–42.

music also holds my interest in its derivative shapes. So I find myself compelled to confess that he could not put it down and will not leave it [alone]. The dance music is so lovely, lively and exciting that it makes one want to dance to it. [...]

### 489. Goethe

Weimar, 26 to 27 January 1830

The letters sent here from 1828 have arrived and will be written out carefully with mine to the end. I am looking forward to these years and to seeing the whole thing bound. This 30-year correspondence gains such an attractive appearance that a royal Egyptian booklover would hardly fail to take it into his collection. [...]

### 490. Zelter

Berlin, 2 February 1830

[...] The enjoyment which I by nature and habit have in works of art is, in general, indefinite until I take pen in hand and as it were lay out an equation mathematically, through which an image of the object appears to me, which, like the artist with his model on a moveable tripod, I can then turn over and change, [and judge] whether the parts fit the whole. I also really like to listen to a piece of music when the throng has expressed itself loudly or through its silence, through which I gain a certain self-confidence and external recognition. In the end my view is also sometimes finally called for and seen as valid. [...]

The two psalms and the organ work deserve praise – if they are only beginnings. The best which the world knows also began somewhere.

In my humble opinion the musical working of a psalm, for example, is like a sermon to a text, which should always become clearer, more powerful through the sermon. If the sermon doesn't do that, it shatters the text into incomprehensibility; so it is no better than if a stone were attached to it and it sank into the sea; because it is work lost and no one pays attention to it.

Applying this theory to musical composition, we know that even the great masters were not always successful in their application and the same could be expected from their students. The student can expect, demand that it would be explained to him what art is and what it has to achieve; that even the best only do what they can is self-evident.

### 491. Zelter

Berlin, 11 February 1830

[…] This evening at seven you might keep your fingers crossed for me. We are launching our *Judas Maccabaeus* (by Handel).[484] Our orchestra is 200 strong. A single long rehearsal was granted to us on account of the carnival and terribly stormy weather.

### 492. Zelter

Berlin, 21 to 23 February 1830

[…] When I wrote my [biography of] Fasch, who I admittedly loved dearly, I read the manuscript in the Sing-Akademie directly after his death before more than one hundred members, more or less all of whom had known the good man during his life. I asked that if someone or other did not recognize our man in the one described, or found him different, to share it with me since I would gratefully take up every memory and make corrections accordingly before publication. When the manuscript appeared in print, I found before me Fasch's oldest friends, who had drunk with him, smoked and had associated with him politically, surprised to discover their cheerful everyday journeyman as a serious, deep, highly educated artist; but it seemed unbelievable how I, as a modest citizen, should become the biographer of such a man. If someone stepped forward to say he helped me, he would hardly have been without support.

My first word to the society after Fasch's death was, 'Fasch's place with us remains open and I retain my position at the grand piano.' This speech gave the directors at that time (to which I didn't belong) the courage to see me as an ordinary member, as a subordinate until the opportunity appeared through which the leading chairman suddenly resigned from his office and handed over the monitory affairs. I immediately made the third chairman into the first, ordered him to take over the money and to make some kind of arrangement according to which every contributing member can see for himself the condition of the economy, since the box office is visibly increasing in size.

---

[484] Handel's oratorio, performed as the fourth and final subscription concert of the Sing-Akademie on 11 February 1830 with the soloists Pauline von Schätzel, Auguste Türrschmidt and Eduard Mantius, was well received by the critics; see *Spenersche Zeitung*, no. 37, 13 February 1830 and *AMZ* 32 (1830), no. 11, 17 March, column 170 and *Berliner Allgemeine Musikalische Zeitung* 7 (1830), 13 February, p. 56.

## 493. Zelter

Berlin, 4 to 11 March 1830

[…] Tomorrow we are to perform Mozart's Requiem in public.[485] It is happening in honour of your deceased Princess. They wanted to hear Bach's Passion once again and thought that no one was dead. Against that it was argued that the Requiem was made in full health for the living. […] So may Mozart's Requiem and God grant us a pleasant hour, because we had to get by with one long rehearsal on account of the wretched opera.[486] Your Princesses and mine are invited.[487] I'll be surprised if they respond and whether their situation permits them to attend.

Last Sunday I endured Spontini's opera *Olympia*;[488] from beginning to end it lasts almost four hours. It is a shame to put up with so much in the enjoyment of such a commendable work of art; I cannot approve of it, nor can I let it alone. What I learn from it is that I cannot live without music. Your metaphor about the silkworm in *Tasso* struck a chord with me every time I heard it.[489] One recognizes oneself […]

## 494. Zelter

Berlin, 15 to 23 March 1830

[…] Felix has undertaken to deliver the facade of the Count Redern's house to you. The drawing is by Schinkel and you will be familiar with the design already from Florence. The Count asked me to send you the page myself and if you care to

---

[485] Performance of Mozart's Requiem and Handel's Psalm 'O preiset den Herrn mit einem Munde' on 11 March 1830 by the Sing-Akademie, conducted by Zelter; see *AMZ* 32 (1830), no. 16, 21 April, p. 252.

[486] Since Zelter brought in musicians from the Königliches Orchester for his Sing-Akademie performances, this had a knock-on effect at the opera: the coordination of organizing rehearsals and performances was not only made more difficult but also meant limited rehearsal time with the orchestral musicians who were brought in.

[487] Princess Maria Luisa Alexandrine of Prussia (1808–77), eldest daughter of Maria Pawlowna of Sachsen-Weimar-Eisenach and Prince Karl of Prussia's wife, and Maria Luise *Augusta* von Prussia (1811–90), second daughter of Maria Pawlowna of Sachsen-Weimar-Eisenach and Prince William's wife.

[488] See ZG 7 to 9 June 1820; Zelter attended the performance on Sunday, 7 March 1830 in the Königliches Opernhaus.

[489] Go tell the silkworm, he should cease to spin,/ Whenever nearer death he spins himself!/ From his most secret being he unfolds/ The costly wool, and never doth he rest,/ Till in his coffin he himself hath sealed. *Torquato Tasso*, Act 2, v. 2453–7.

send a favourable reply through me, it would be to my advantage since I frequently need to seek his favour. [...]

Our Requiem was very effective. I myself was very moved despite the careful concentration which was needed. Every time Spontini is astonished by what we can achieve with one rehearsal, when he works away and gets annoyed 20 to 25 times and still does not come away from it without mistakes, although his direction is calm and intelligent. There is no greater mistake in rehearsing than to upset the good will of decent people through dissatisfaction over secondary matters. Those who are capable don't make the same mistake twice; they trust me as I trust them and so I come away better than with many repetitions which bore the best people because they are sympathetic. The worst thing for us are the distracting social conditions, since there is hardly a house is in Berlin which could not produce a quartet itself and no evening during the week at which all kinds of musical desirables and undesirables would be assembled. Now one cannot expect anything of amateurs at public performances (which the Sing-Akademie undertake) because they don't understand how to listen. As a result one must have good professionals and then again that is expensive. Then these would also have to be doubly skilful in order to handle older works well, which always go down best under my direction. Two years ago Spontini included a Credo by old Bach[490] in a benefit concert for the widows of musical directors.[491] It was a disaster: out of sheer fear no one knew what he was to play.

There are now at least four song societies here in Berlin, of which mine is not the best. I and several of my age are not to be killed off and those new on the scene are not even as good as we were. Against that the second Liedertafel[492] is in fact the best. It consists of young people with good voices. They write the songs themselves and there is no shortage of good old songs. I can honestly say that I prefer to be here than with our group. I only know of the existence of the other two, and there are perhaps a couple of others.

From Easter onwards I intend to conduct an experiment with students from our university[493] and I will see how I get on with the young people. Perhaps I will prefer them to the old wigs, with whom nothing can be done because they have to be in bed by ten o'clock. It will, however, cost me money again. Whoever wants to

---

[490]   From Bach's B Minor Mass, BWV 232.

[491]   On 30 April 1828.

[492]   The 'Jüngere Liedertafel' founded by Ludwig Rellstab, Ludwig Berger and Bernhard Klein.

[493]   Zelter took over the direction of the university choir for church music formerly directed by Bernhard Klein, who had to step down from this position on account of his planned studies in Italy. The register for lectures in Berlin University during the summer semester 1830 announced: 'The academic choir, in which students may participate free of charge, is led by Herr Zelter', quoted by Wilhelm Röntz, 'C.F. Zelter und die Zeit seines akademischen Singkollegiums. 1830–32' in *Sonderabdruck aus der Deutschen Sängerbundeszeitung* 22 (1930), no. 30, 26 July 1930, p. 4.

feast with students must learn to borrow. The minister[494] will give me 200 thalers and we will decide in what way it should be spent.

On the day of our Requiem our honest to God bass singer, Gern,[495] died shortly before the performance. His voice had the ease, power and beauty of a god. Madame Mara was enchanted by his sound. He was also a good actor. His [roles as] Friar Laurence in *Romeo and Juliet*, his water-carrier and so on, were incomparable. When he sang 'Generalbeichte' at the Liedertafel and spoke the absolution, we were all free of sin. He was 70.

## 495. Zelter

Berlin, 26 March 1830

[…] What flourishes most now are the complaints about the new songbook.[496] The enlightened don't want to sing the mouldy German anymore and the old faithfuls don't want to let the reformers be considered poets. Bunsen is said to have written to the King of Rome and have interceded for the old songbook.[497] One of his

---

[494] Baron Carl von Stein zum Altenstein (1770–1840).

[495] Johann Georg Gern died on 11 March 1830; Johann Philipp Schmidt praised him in his obituary in the *Spenersche Zeitung* as 'a real gem and a pillar of German opera, always active, undaunted, without a trace of artist temperament and demands, free from envy and *amore proper*. [Gern] dedicated his talent to the truly good and beautiful of every genre, whole-heartedly and with all his strength'; *Spenersche Zeitung*, no. 64, 17 March 1830; see also *AMZ* 32 (1830), no. 16, 21 April, column 250.

[496] For a detailed account of the revision of the Berlin evangelical songbook, which was inspired in the years after 1806 but only completed in 1827 (through a commission set up 1818), and [finally] established by a royal decree in 1830; see 'Das neue Berliner Gesangbuch von Jahre 1829' in Johann Friedrich Bachmann, *Zur Geschichte der Berliner Gesangbücher. Ein hymnologischer Beitrag* (Berlin: Wilhelm Schultze Verlag, 1856; reprint Hildesheim/New York: Georg Olms Verlag, 1970), pp. 218–31. The public controversy starting immediately about the reform found expression in the following publications: Friedrich Schleiermacher, *Über das Berliner Gesangbuch. Ein Sendschreiben an Dr. Ritschl* (Berlin: Riemer, 1830); Schleiermacher, *Unparteiisches Gutachten über das neue Berliner Gesangbuch* (Leipzig: Tauchnitz, 1830); Klaus Harms, *Beleuchtung des vielseitigen Tadels* (Berlin, 1830); the *Evangelische Kirchen-Zeitung*, February 1830 and the *Homiletisch-literarischen Korrespondenz-Blatte* (1830).

[497] Bunsen, who had put together an *Allgemeines Evangelisches Gesangbuch in der deutschen Kirche*, 'drawing on established canons', stated his critical opinion of the new Berlin songbook in a letter to Niebuhr from Rome on 19 June 1830: 'The appearance of the Berlin hymn book has induced me to write a series of letters about it, which, for the time being, I concluded with the presentation of my canons. The first letter was written in the hope that it would not be too late to warn the King and the congregrations against such untenable work. Friends of mine had it published in church papers and I gather that

arguments is that many songs of the old songbook were written by royal ancestors and women. [...]

Felix, who departs from here in the next few days, will bring this page to you and the facade of the house of Count Redern.[498]

### 496. Goethe

Weimar, 27 March 1830

[...] It really delighted me that you expressed your need for music: what pours out of you, you also want to hear outside. One demands the other and true enjoyment only exists in such exchange. [...]

Invaluable, on a smaller scale, but nicely brought off within this context, are the two volumes of Neureuther's pictorial musical compositions alongside my ballads.[499] They have been in the shops for a long time and should have already arrived with you. [...]

The correspondence from 1828 is transcribed; you will receive your originals first;[500] then send 1829[501] and take care that the current year, 1830, will be very rich,

---

it found favour beyond its immediate readership. It is in good company with some essays by Raumer on the same subject'; Baron Christian Carl Josias von Bunsen, *Aus seinen Briefen und nach eigener Erinnerung geschildert von seiner Witwe* (3 vols, Leipzig: F. A. Brockhaus 1868–71), vol. 1 p. 376.

[498] Felix Mendelssohn, who had planned to stay with Goethe on his way down to Italy, had to postpone the journey because he was ill with measles. Abraham Mendelssohn posted Zelter's letter to Goethe with Julius Schoppe's lithograph of von Redern's palace (after a drawing by Karl Friedrich Schinkel).

[499] Eugen Neureuther's series of lithographs *Randzeichnungen zu Goethes Balladen und Romanzen* (Stuttgart: Cotta, 1829). Volume one (dedicated to Goethe) contained: 'Heidenröslein'; 'Der König in Thule'; 'Legende'; 'Mignons Sehnsucht'; 'Das Blümlein Wunderschön' and 'Der Totentanz'. Volume two contained: 'Der Gott und die Bajadere'; 'Der Sänger'; 'Vor Gerricht'; 'Schäfers Klagelied'; 'Erlkönig' and 'Der untreue Knabe'. Volume 3, dated 1829, became available with volume 4 in 1830; vols1–4 are in Goethe's library (Ruppert, no. 2463). Goethe praises the 'figurative, musical' effect of the arabesques time and time again. On 23 September 1828 he described them to Neureuther as a pictorial expression 'which accompanies every single poem like a kind of melody' and on 12 December Goethe considered them 'a new form of art (...) a progressive poem accompanied by a moving image as in a melody'. On 24 April 1831 he described them to Sulpiz Boisserée as: 'a large sheet (...) with commentary or much more, a musical performance of the *Parabel*.'

[500] Goethe posted them on 7 April; Zelter received them on 12 April.

[501] Zelter announced the new dispatch on 12 April 'in the course of next week'; as he already enquired about Goethe's receipt of them in the next letter, they must have been

whereby our exchange of letters will not end someday like those with Schiller, like the Rhine lost in the general run of the day.[502]

My kindest remembrances to Felix, whose arrival you inform me of.[503] I am not mentioning it here so that the pleasure of seeing him again may be increased by the surprise.

### 497. Zelter

Berlin, 24 to 30 March 1830

I have seen a born-again adaptation of Shakespeare's *Julius Caesar* by Dr Förster twice [...] During the victory procession the people sing my melody to the words 'Gallias Caesar subegit, Nicomedes Caesarem'.[504] At the same time the vermin who shortly before made herself so lousy-mousy, looked so pious as if she was on a pilgrimage. I could not guess what the orchestra piped and fiddled in between. I also don't know whether I should be annoyed or delighted that I understand my Suetonius better than these Romans. [...]

Your letter of 27 March has arrived just now [...] Felix sent a letter to you over a week ago and the drawing of Count Redern's house. Now Felix is laid up and has the measles.

### 498. Zelter

Berlin, 11 to 12 April 1830

Increasingly it seems to me that I have nothing to apologize to Rossini for, because he gradually insinuates himself here against all opposition so that one hardly listens if he is criticized. The accusations against one or another of his works are

---

sent in a separate dispatch without an accompanying letter. (Their return was confirmed by Zelter on 15 July 1830.)

[502] With similar resignation about the published correspondence, Goethe expressed his opinion in a letter to Caroline von Wolzogen on 29 September: 'it gives me a sad feeling, which, if I understand as follows: in our advanced years, when we have to be economical with our time, we become extremely annoyed with ourselves and others because of wasted days.'

[503] Goethe could not have known of Felix Mendelssohn's illness which delayed his arrival; Mendelssohn finally reached Weimar (for his last visit to Goethe) on 21 May 1830.

[504] The verse 'Caesar subdued the Gauls and Nicomedes' is in Gaius Suetonius Tranquillus's biography on Caesar, chapter 49.

admittedly not without [justification]. People don't need to make allowances for him. He wouldn't thank them for it. [...]

Last week Mademoiselle Sontag made her first appearance as Desdemona[505] in Rossini's *Othello*[506] at the grand opera. I have already spoken highly of her to you and I don't need to take anything back. [...] In short everything about her from head to foot – even her very dress – is song.

This is Eastertide, and since in the meantime I have conducted two versions of the Passion Music[507] on Palm Sunday (for the benefit of our mortgage) and Good Friday (for my cellar which is full of water), I have had plenty to do. By this, I wished to satisfy, as far as I could, two sections of my good Berlin, by putting on one after the other in the one week, two genuine German religious composers: Johann Sebastian Bach, whom people here compare to Calderón, and Carl Heinrich Graun, whom his friends like to compare to Tasso. Each performance attracted its own audience. *Der Tod Jesu* is especially valued by those who have received Communion on Good Friday and Bach's Passion attracts persons, who understand something more than the general public. I wanted to show the latter the mutual relationship of two original German geniuses – the second of whom formed himself entirely upon Italian models and generally worked upon Italian texts, while the other never went out of Germany, and (to my knowledge) never set any Italian piece. They are distinguished by nature from each other, one by depth, another by clarity, while in terms of productivity they are equal; with regard to the Cantilena where they speak to us in general, however, both are genuinely Italian, which means they are natural.

Yesterday, after accompanying to the grave my oldest friend, who died at the age of 90,[508] I went straight to Mozart's *Figaro*, and found the charming Sontag as brilliant and delightful a Susanna as possible.[509] [...] In this role she delighted me because her natural gift reveals how this opera, as I feel it, differs from Mozart's other works: by the style of intrigue in the music. One finds this style perhaps in

---

[505] Henriette Sontag, engaged at the Königstädtisches Theater from 1825 to 1827, had gone to Paris at the beginning of 1828 and after triumphant success at the opera and in England, had returned to Berlin as a guest artist in 1830. Her first appearance as Desdemona in the Königliches Opernhaus on 3 April, as well as her performance as Rosina in Rossini's *Barbier von Sevilla* on 6 April, were both enthusiastically received; see *Spenersche Zeitung*, no. 80, 5 April 1830 and no. 83, 8 April 1830; *MA* 20.3, p. 1103.

[506] Rossini's opera *Othello* was performed in Johann Christoph Grünbaum's German version from 1821. The performance, *Othello, der Mohr in Venedig*, which Zelter speaks of here, was performed on 3 April 1830; see *AMZ* 32 (1830), no. 21, 26 May, column 342f.

[507] Bach's *St Matthew Passion* was performed in the hall of the Sing-Akademie on Palm Sunday, 4 April and Graun's *Der Tod Jesu* was performed on Good Friday, 9 April 1830; see *AMZ* 32 (1830), no. 22, 3 June, column 357f.

[508] The man's identity has not yet been discovered.

[509] On 10 April 1830 in the Königliches Opernhaus; see *AMZ* 32 (1830), no. 21, 26 May, column 343.

the individual pieces of any other Italian composer (Cimarosa, Grétry too, and others) but here it starts suddenly with the overture pervading the whole action and this seems to me to be original.

Felix had a letter from me to you and has stayed here because of ill-health;[510] I had instructed him to send the letter to you and I hope it has happened. They say here that your son August is going to Italy with Eckermann;[511] I wish him a safe arrival, lovely weather, and an eruption of Vesuvius.

### 499. Zelter

Berlin, 16 to 17 April 1830

I have just come back again from Rossini's *Othello*;[512] Spontini collected me in his carriage. He, too, (like all the critics)[513] is totally against this opera. He affirms that there are hardly six bars suitable to the action: a Charivari, a Galimathias without dignity,[514] strength, sense, and so on. For his justification, I had again read right through Shakespeare's *Othello* to discover the cruel effect of jealousy in a moral depolarization – true, I cannot refute Rossini's enemies and I observe an obedient silence. The work is quite strange […] Basically, I cannot find anything wrong with it, even if I were forced to go yet again; if that most senseless play, opera with its songs and dances, light-heartedness and significance, is to have its own place, then to me Rossini is a born opera composer, so I have been delighted – and so have all the others against their will. The clapping, shouting and calling went on and on and the house was full and beside itself with enthusiasm. Finally, I agree with Rossini himself that he is a man of genius, and besides that he knows his trade […]

---

[510] Zelter's letter of 26 March 1830; on account of his son's illness, Abraham Mendelssohn posted the letter (and accompanying lithograph) on 1 April 1830.

[511] August von Goethe set out on his Italian journey accompanied by Eckermann on 22 April 1830.

[512] The performance Zelter mentions took place on 16 April 1830 in the Königliches Opernhaus, with Henriette Sontag in the role of Desdemona; it was the same production as Zelter had attended on 3 April.

[513] See, for example, Rossini's reception in the *Spenersche Zeitung*, no. 16, 6 February 1821.

[514] A hotch potch; a mixum-gatherum.

18 to 19 April: [...] Madame Milder, on her journey to St Petersburg,[515] passed by Reval and helped celebrate the eightieth birthday of our Elizabeth Mara.[516] That ancient nightingale still sings, and cannot give it up; she gives singing lessons, and is true to the confession she made to me, 'I shall die, when I no longer sing.'

### 500. Zelter

Berlin, 24 April 1830

[...] Haydn's *Creation* is to be performed next Wednesday in the Garnison church for charity[517] and that has to be ready at the right time as if one had nothing at all to do. No one asks then whether the wheels and horses will hold out! [...]

### 501. Zelter

Berlin, 28 April to 6 May 1830

Once again we have finished a performance of Haydn's *Creation*,[518] and again we have not exhausted it. Everyone who calls himself a musical director in name, status and dignity – assembled upon this occasion to celebrate the work, under Spontini's direction.[519] To me it was as if I were to enjoy it for the first time today

---

[515] 'Anna Milder was engaged in the Berliner Königliches Theater from 1816. On account of a dispute with Spontini, whose operas she had brought to prominence through endless performances, she left Berlin and indeed Germany for many years. She travelled to Russia first; in St Petersburg she celebrated her last triumphs as a dramatic singer'; Gustav Schilling (ed.), *Encyclopädie der gesamten musikalischen Wissenschaften* (6 vols. Stuttgart: Franz Heinrich Köhler, 1836–38), article on Milder.

[516] After her stage and concert career, the famous singer had lived in Moscow from 1802 to 1812, where she lost all her possessions in the fire of 1812. She first moved to Reval and at 70 moved to London for two years; she returned to Reval in 1822 and celebrated her eightieth birthday there on 23 February 1829.

[517] The performance in aid of the 'patriotic society in support of destitute soldiers of the Berlin Garrison' took place on 28 April in the Garrison church before an audience of 4,000; see *Berliner Allgemeine Musikalische Zeitung* 7 (1830), no. 18, 1 May and *AMZ* 32 (1830), no. 22, 3 June, column 358.

[518] Ibid.

[519] The Königliche Kapelle, the choir of the Sing-Akademie under Zelter's direction, the singers Henriette Sontag, Mlle Hoffmann, Carl Adam Bader, Carl (or Heinrich) Blum and Eduard Devrient were involved in the benefit concert; Spontini was General Director of Music for the event.

since I pursued it publicly it 30 years ago[520] against the accusations of inadmissible descriptions of external objects. What my predecessors had failed to see was the simple fact that the text took on the task of outlining the story of creation and it comes down to this: how to do it and afterwards throw away the words like a scaffolding and have an architectonic work before you, which one takes up like a significant symphony or sonata, which at the same time it is not, in which it is raised up from imaginable negativity to large quantities of unimaginably good material. The nothingness; the emptiness; the wilderness; the depths; the darkness was granted; the chaos.[521] – May God grant that this be so – let there be light; let there be sun, moon and stars; children of the light should become the eyes of that which does not exist and that which will arise from the chaos. Now the Music; beginning; initially monsterous unison between unrecognizable heights and depths; the space between the poles – 'the world in its deepest foundations', hard and wide, not major, not minor – 'With longing, without sound' – one sound and no sound, heavy, thick, pea-soup fog. Resounding with electric power – 'a painful sigh!'[522] It rises, moves, differentiates itself distinguishing one thing from another; it starts to flow; forms itself into groups, attracts and repels; life makes room for itself, the pulse beats, seeks a rhythm, the shape, the measured appears, takes shape; a planet which is just completed rises up, moves, climbs, runs through its course and stands as nailed to its place in the firmament: and so it continues until final order. What more can I say? Put your ideas of 'God and Word' on this image of chaos and so it fits as if the lid of the pot.

Since this chaos, even without the words, is artistically comprehensible, healthy, intensely enjoyable; so I envisage, leaving the words out of the whole work. Then to consider what the amateur judges as brushwork – from the growling

---

[520] Zelter had expressed publicly his opinion of Haydn's *Creation* on at least two occasions. Neither review took issue with the discussion about tone-painting in music which had started up again in relation to Haydn's *Creation*, having originated in Johann Jacob Engel's theoretical writing and Sulzer's *Allgemeine Theorie der schönen Kunste*. The first review handles the question in the background, while the second review goes into it only indirectly through a preliminary appreciation of Haydn's instrumental music. The most significant criticism levelled against Haydn was published after Zelter's first review in Triest's 'Bemerkungen über die Ausbildung der Tonkunst in Deutschland im achtzehnten Jahrhundert', *AMZ* 3 (1800/01), nos.14–26; see in particular no. 24, column 408. See also Friedrich Ludwig Aemilius Kunzen in the *Zeitung für die elegante Welt*, 1 (1801), no. 153, 22 December 1801, columns 1228–32. In his remarks Triest announced a fundamental 'attempt at limiting the representational possibilities of music, especially with regard to tone painting' (column 409, footnote). In reponse to this debate over *The Creation*, Zelter took up his firm position of support once again in his review of Haydn's *Creation*, *AMZ* 6 (1804), columns 513–29 and validated Haydn's particular form of tone-painting.

[521] Zelter takes up the wording from his first review of Haydn's *Creation*; *AMZ* 3 (1800/01), column 291f.; *MA* 20.3, p. 1111.

[522] The quotations are from Goethe's poem 'Wiederfinden', from his *West-östlicher Divan*, published in the section, 'Gott und die Welt'; Zelter quotes verses 9, 24 and 14.

and bellows of Behemot[523] and the lion to the sound of the nightingale – to be a suite of delightful phenomenon which the sensitive ear decodes. And that was good! Admittedly, towards the end, since no poet can ever stop chattering, there must be a Part Three;[524] man appears, the philistine, the word is hardly out: be fruitful and multiply! And so it goes with kisses and marriages; you can almost see with your eyes old Haydn with his Marzebille live in the music,[525] waltzing and courting, so that saliva gathers in my mouth: this hound of poets[526] who corrupts man's nature.

1 May: I have left others to read the newspapers, since I have the advantage over you to discover the latest news from conversationalists in the Monday Club[527] who are avid readers[528] and to spare my eyes […]

As you will hardly read as far as page 208 of Dr Lautier's *System of Figured Bass*, let me recommend you read the last 14 lines of that page,[529] for they say what the whole book means and what of course is self-evident.

---

[523] The giant described in the Book of Job 40, 15–21; Trio no. 19 from Haydn's *Creation* describes the leviathan (40, 25–26).

[524] Part Three of Haydn's *Creation* deals with God's praise through Adam and Eve, the apotheosis of marriage and the warning to the first man and woman: 'Do not know more than you should!' Again this passage is echoed in Zelter's review of the score; *AMZ* 4 (1801/2), no. 24, 10 March 1802, column 395; *MA* 20.3, p. 1111.

[525] A reference to Haydn's long-standing lover, the singer Luigia Polzelli; 'Marzebille' is generally used as a synonym for 'beloved' in imitation of Tieck's comedy *Kaiser Octavianus* (after the adventure novel *Florens* from the late Middle Ages), in which Florens, the Christian hero, loved and conquered Marzebille, daughter of the Sultan of Babylon).

[526] Adaptation of Goethe's poem 'Musen und Grazien in der Mark', v. 7–8.

[527] A society of the religious elite of Berlin, founded in 1749 by Georg Schultheß and Johann Georg Sulzer, originally with only eight members and strict statutes for entry. The statutes of the Berlin Monday Club were newly formulated, as a result of which the number of members increased.

[528] Zelter's answer to Goethe's remark that he has 'done away with reading all newspapers'.

[529] 'As a result anyone can accurately state: there are essentially no rules because every conceivable harmonic step – and, in general, breaking every rule – is possible; it can also be stated just as validly: everything holds or there are no rules. Whoever has overlooked the rules must then follow this path through and in particular establish no new rules. Even so it must be added: all rules are valid because breaking a rule is only correct in so far as it is a rule and follows the system. The opposition of this compositional method is not a mere protest but an understandable and recognized opposition, which the contradiction and its solution is', Gustav Andreas Lautier, *Praktisch-theoretisches System des Grundbasses der Musik und Philosophie, als erste Abteilung eines Grundrisses des Systems der Tonwissenschaft* (Berlin, 1827), p. 208.

To say a word about the performance of the *Creation* last Wednesday: I hear it praised and am in agreement. They praise the personal strength of our choir,[530] as above all Spontini did himself. There were 230 of us; that is philisitinism, however. In total we are over 400, since we have to be so strong as to support ourselves economically. One has to make sure that not everyone comes because everyone would like to take part. The effect is produced by half of them and we have to be careful that what is over and above that is not harmful. One would have to be much stricter if one were to be strong enough to resist the fairer sex. There is, however, a good attitude in general. The breeder is prepared to be criticized if only the stock is good!

### 502. Goethe

Weimar, 21 April 1830

[...] How are things with Felix? Has he recovered in order to delight us soon?

### 503. Zelter

Berlin, 10 May 1830

With regard to my singing colloquium at the university, 50 lads have not got off to a bad start for a first time, and if they want to keep up the pace, I think it will turn out well for them. The ones among them who started out cheeky and boisterous became flexible, even charming in the course of my instruction, since they had to represent themselves through their own element (the voice). They endeavoured [to do] what I recommended and lo and behold they seemed to be pleased with themselves. We will wait and see what happens. The little library and collection of musical materials of the institution,[531] which I am now taking over, needs to be reordered, for which I have requested money from the minister. [...]

---

[530] See, for example, the *Spenersche Zeitung*, no. 100, 30 April 1830, and the *Berliner Courier*, 30 April 1830, enclosed with Zelter's letter to Goethe (GSA 28/1025, no. 432); *MA* 20.3, p. 1113.

[531] The music library, founded in 1818, was initiated by Zelter among others. It contained collections of books and manuscripts from Forkel's bequest, purchased through Zelter by the ministry, and was expanded by the purchase of Naue's library in Halle. Together with Georg Poelchaus's important music collection, acquired after 1836 and which contains among other things C.P.E. Bach's bequest, this library formed the basis of the music section of the Königliche Bibliothek, today's Staatsbibliothek in Berlin.

I have now heard Mademoiselle Sontag three times in *Othello*.[532] I wanted to see if she was always mistress of the situation. She was different on each occasion and yet she was always Desdemona. [...] Unfortunately the sweet creature is about to become a countess![533]

Felix, to whom I have given a letter for you, has, day after day, been on the point of setting out.[534] On Friday he played another concerto of old Bach's at my house, like a true master because the concerto is as difficult as it is beautiful, and it would have been worth old Bach himself hearing it. I can hardly wait for the time when the lad will leave the wild jingling of Berlin behind and go to Italy; in my opinion, he ought to have gone there at the beginning. [...]

Today is already 10 May and I don't know whether Felix is still here; he wanted to leave today. If he calls by before the post leaves, he can take this letter with him.

### 504. Goethe

Weimar, 3 June 1830

A few minutes ago, at half past nine this morning the first-rate Felix left for Jena[535] with Ottilie, Ulrike and the children, accompanied by the clearest weather and the brightest sunshine, after having spent a cheerful fortnight with us[536] and delighting

---

[532] Performances of Rossini's *Othello* with the Königliche Kammersängerin ['royal chamber singer', a title awarded to a singer of outstanding merit] as a guest artist in the role of Desdemona, were given on 3 April (to a full house), and on 16 and 7 May; see *AMZ* 32 (1830), no. 21, 26 May, column 342f. During April and May 1830 Henriette Sontag appeared as guest artist in the following operas: as Rosina in *Der Barbier von Sevilla* on 6 April; as Susanna in *Die Hochzeit des Figaro* on 10 April; as Hannchen in *Joconde* on 14 April, 23 and 24 April in Potsdam; as Donna Anna in *Don Juan* on 20 April and 17 May; as Pamyra in *Die Belagerung von Corinth* on 26 and 30 April; as Anna in *Die Dame auf Schloß Avenel* on 11 and 13 May; and the title role in the premiere of *Semiramis* on 15, 19 and 21 May.

[533] Already before her return to Berlin (probably in 1828) Henriette Sontag had married Count Carlo Rossi, diplomat from Sardinia; in 1830 she was elevated to the nobility by the Prussian King and called herself Countess Rossi Sontag von Lauenstein from then on.

[534] Having fully recovered from his illness, Felix Mendelssohn arrived at Goethe's home on 21 May 1830 (see Goethe's diary *WA* III/12, p. 245) and delivered Zelter's letter of 10 May.

[535] The Fromann family; see Mendelssohn's letter of 6 June 1830, *Gespräche*, vol. III/2, p. 632.

[536] At Goethe's request, Felix stayed with the poet for two weeks, from 21 May to 3 June. From Weimar he travelled to Munich en route to Italy.

everyone with his accomplished, lovable art;[537] there, too, he will enthral our well-disposed friends and will leave behind a memory which will always be treasured in our neighbourhood.

To me his presence was especially beneficial, for I found that my relation to music is still the same as ever; I listen to it with pleasure, interest and reflection, and I love the historical part of it. Who can understand any kind of occurrence if he is not thoroughly acquainted with its development down to the present time? What was great for me was that Felix understood this progressive advancement admirably and luckily his excellent memory enables him to call before him at will every kind of example. Beginning with the Bach epoch, he brought Haydn, Mozart and Gluck to life again for me,[538] gave me a fairly good impression of the great masters of technique in more modern times, and finally led me to experience and contemplate his own compositions; so he parted from me with my fervent blessing.

All this I have written off to you very hastily that I may challenge you to a new letter. Give the best most serious praise you can to the parents of this outstanding young artist; give an eager botanical friend the enclosed note,[539] and think of me as of a friend who is not indeed always easy, but is passionately active, aspiring and keen to learn from the examples you send him.

### 505. Zelter

Berlin, 13 to 15 June 1830

The tender, paternal affection with which you have honoured our Felix has raised his parents and siblings into the seventh heaven. I give you every thanks I can; it will be a lifelong joy to him. At times I get rather worried when I look at the course

---

[537] As recorded in Goethe's diary, Mendelssohn gave daily recitals at the piano, explaining the historical progession of music (24 May 1830) and in the evening he played 'significant works, old, new, including his own compositions'; (31 May 1830), *WA* III/12, pp. 246 and 249–50.

[538] In a letter dated 25 May 1830 Felix wrote to his parents, 'I have to play to him for an hour in the morning all the great composers in historical sequence and explain to him what each has done to further the art, while he sits there in a dark corner, his old eyes flashing fire like a thundering Jupiter. He didn't want to hear anything by Beethoven – but I said to him I can't help that and performed the first movement of the C minor Symphony. That had a very strange effect on him. He said at first, that does not move one at all; it only causes astonishment. It is grandiose [...] completely mad. You'd be afraid the house might cave in. And what if everyone played together!'

[539] Goethe's note to Heinrich Friedrich Link (1767–1851), Professor of the Botanical Gardens, Berlin; Goethe's note, which has not been handed down, contained a request for plant seeds, to which Link replied on 10 or 11 June 1830; GZ 13 to 15 June 1830, enclosure.

of the boy's life. Up to now he has met hardly any opposition. As a pupil I neither overestimated him nor found it necessary to praise him, although I can only view with pleasure his natural docility and the drive to busy himself mentally when he is not forced to do anything. I can think of myself as having taught him the truth, as I recognize it fulfilled in him to the second and third degree. He takes away with him from here a complete system, upon which he can build what genius inspires him with, and if he continues to develop in this way, he will have reason to think of his teacher. [...]

I am busy enough at the moment. Apart from my other functions I now have 76 students,[540] lads and lasses, twice a week at my house and I would like to see who can criticize me. We are preparing to sing a first-rate work (in the great University Concert Hall on 25 December), for a festival of the Augsburg Confession[541] which we ourselves are planning, to tug the fur of the frosty academics. No one thought that it would come off and look, it's happening! As I live and work at the university, the boys are at hand every minute. As I begin directly with the first one, they race to be first in the queue. And I, poor fool, am delighted about it and for that reason would swap a pair of our professors if you could see me among my fellows and hear the German power that lives in a willing generation who doesn't want to give less than the best. If it comes off, I am thinking of preparing a party for them so that they will also remember me afterwards. They still can't do anything, but they should learn something and at the same time not know how they managed it.

15 June: A letter from Felix to his parents has just arrived from Munich,[542] where he has had first-rate introductions. The lad still basks in the happiness that he experienced in Weimar and in Jena.

---

[540] The university choir had expanded so much that in a petition to the minister on 30 May, Zelter had asked for permission to copy the available music materials and requested 50 thalers for new acquisitions, because four to five men had to sing from one part; see Wilhelm Röntz, 'C.F. Zelter und die Zeit seines akademischen Singkollegiums 1830–32', *Sonderabdruck aus der Deutschen Sängerbundeszeitung* 22 (1930), no. 30, 26 July, p. 4.

[541] To mark the third centenary of the handing-over of the Augsburg Confessions (confession of faith of the Lutheran Church, in the version by Melanchton and Luther, and presented on 25 June 1530), a solemn service was held in the cathedral on 25 June 1830 in the presence of the king and all members of the university. After it a celebration was held in the university lecture hall. The varied programme – which included festival speeches by Hegel and Marheineke and doctoral degree ceremonies – began and ended with music from Zelter's university choir, including the performance of *Eine feste Burg ist unser Gott* see *Spenersche Zeitung*, no. 146, 28 June 1830; *MA* 20.3, p. 1116.

[542] In a letter from Munich on 6 June 1830, Felix Mendelssohn told his parents about his visit to Goethe. In: *Reisebriefe von Felix Mendelssohn Bartholdy aus den Jahren 1830 bis 1832*, ed. Paul Mendelssohn Bartholdy, 3rd edn (Leipzig: Hermann Mendelssohn, 1862, reprint Bonn: H.C. Schaack, o.J., 1947), pp. 11–14; hereafter referred to as *Reisebriefe* (1862); excerpts in *Gespräche*, III//2, p. 631f.

## 506. Goethe

Weimar, 8 July 1830

[…] I must tell you that Felix has recalled his amiable presence to our minds by a very charming letter from Munich,[543] in which he discusses that marvellous place with great judgement. He made friends there especially with the court painter Stieler,[544] who, when painting my portrait during a stay of more than eight weeks here, became quite one of ourselves. It is pleasant to learn what such a man, at such a time, and under such circumstances, thought he found and was prepared to assimilate.[545] Furthermore, I am sure I must have mentioned to you before, that my son and Dr Eckermann started for the south at the end of April. My son's journals[546] on the way as far as Milan, and from there to Venice, testify to his clear views of worldly matters, his thoughtful activity in learning to know and make himself familiar with men and circumstances. The great advantage that this will be to him, and to us, is that he will get to know himself and will discover what is in him, which in our simple and limited surroundings cannot be discovered with any great clarity. In all this you will give him your blessing. […]

I just want to find out, to hear in your words and in your own way, how the singing went off with the newly formed and newly taught choir,[547] of which the papers only report the general [impression].

## 507. Zelter

Berlin, 11 to 15 July 1830

[…] My students, 81 in total, have, on the occasion of the centenary celebration, performed a piece of music the likes of which the Pope himself doesn't have. Our *Te Deum* and Lutheran chorale, 'Ein' feste Burg ist unser Gott',[548] sung and

---

[543] Felix Mendelssohn's letter to Goethe from Munich on 16 June 1830; see *GJb* 12, 1891, pp. 82–5.

[544] Joseph Karl Stieler (1791–1858), portrait painter; court painter in Munich.

[545] Mendelssohn had written about Stieler, 'the way he spoke to me about you and yours, the warmth and joy which radiated from his whole being, the more he recalled his time spent with you, the more I was won over by him'; *GJb* 12, 1891, p. 83.

[546] Since his departure in April, August von Goethe had kept a diary through regular correspondence and had sent it in sections to Weimar; see Goethe's diary, 1–4 May, 12 May, 2 June and 4 July 1830, *WA* III/12, pp. 235–6, 241, 250–51 and 268–9.

[547] The university choir's performance at the 300th anniversary festival of the Augsburg Confessions.

[548] Luther's chorale *Ein feste Burg* was performed in Philip Buttmann's Latin translation; two strophes were sung before the doctoral proclamations and the third verse

declaimed in good Lutheran tradition by vigorous, capable, lively lads, raised the roof of the university building and made the whole area resound. A senator asked whether it had to be so strong. Yes (was the answer) [...].

Now it is all go for 3 August (the King's[549] birthday). A new Latin ode is being rehearsed and my boys are as I want to have them. Last week they really delighted me in the evening with some of your songs. The university garden in front of my window is as if designed for it; they are also able to serenade me very comfortably from there and I hope I deserve it!

### 508. Goethe

Weimar, 18 July 1830

It has been absolutely impossible to contribute anything to the brothers' worthy *Taschenbuch*. Should you care to give them the cantata and song[550] written for your birthday, I would not object. While it is well known to a certain circle, it is also well forgotten. Enough said! All I mean is: do just as you like and as are fitting to the circumstances. [...]

Every success to your student chorus! I can quite imagine that a contemporary audience, who care for nothing but sentimental droning and humming, should find a powerful style of song, which lifts the heart and splits the roof, horrendous; their choral singing is never anything else but 'Ein laues Bad ist unser Tee'[551] and then they imagine nevertheless that they have something of a sure stronghold and that some kind of deity is troubling himself about them. [...]

---

was sung after the announcement of the competition by Hegel. After the *Te deum laudamus*, which, according to the *Vossische Zeitung*, was a setting by Eduard Grell, Marheineke's speech brought the academic ceremony to a close.

[549] King Friedrich Wilhelm III of Prussia.

[550] Goethe's cantata *Zelters Siebzigste Geburtstag, gefeiert von Bauenden, Dichtenden, Singenden am 11ten December 1828* ('Schmückt die priestlichen Hallen', *MA* 18, 1, p. 29) and Goethe's *Tischlied, Zelters siebzigstem Geburtstage* ('Lasset heut am edlen Ort', *MA* 18, 1, p. 34). Goethe's cantata was actually printed under the title *Zwei Festgedichte von Goethe* in the *Berliner Musenalmanach für 1831*: 3–7. A facsimile of the published poem was published in *Dem würdigen Bruderfeste Johanni 1830* ('Funfzig Jahre sind vorüber', *MA* 18, 1, p. 42).

[551] 'Our tea is all a lukewarm bath': Goethe's word play here is a parody on the Lutheran chorale *Ein feste Burg ist unser Gott*, with reference to the Singtees.

## 509. Zelter

Berlin, 27 August 1830

[...] Yesterday, for the first time for several months, I went to the theatre. Deinhardstein's *Hans Sachs*[552] is rather well staged here; the poet has very cleverly contrasted the position of a craftsman who has also acquired intellectual distinction over that of other citizens and artisans. In general the everyday citizen is quite right, and in particular instances it is just the same with them as with the higher and the highest classes. You, too, have had enough to say on the subject and experience this more and more every day. But you must feel glad that you suggested this pretty play by your honourable mention of the ancient father of German poets.[553] The house was not full, but the play had a good effect – on me at any rate, if not to such an extent on any other of the audience as with me.

One of our young musicians in the orchestra had composed music for the Entr'acte,[554] which seemed to me quite charming, if only because it does not attempt to say what it cannot. Many composers of this class will repeat after the end of an act the very thing we are glad to be rid of, or else they betray beforehand what is to come, tormenting the ear which doesn't know what they are at. Consequently, the value of a suitable piece of music, which falls into its right place and fills up the given time successfully, is immense.

## 510. Zelter

Berlin, 29 to 31 August 1830

[...] Yesterday, on your birthday, my students began their holidays very ceremoniously. They had written poems in praise of you and set them to music and surprised me with them. Von Seckendorff[555] produced the best and in your name I thanked them for their love. I must confess that the young people become dearer to me every day. If I attribute part of it to my way of teaching, admittedly

---

[552] Two years before Count Brühl had asked Goethe's permission to use his poem 'Hans Sachsens poetische Sendung' as a prologue to Johann Ludwig Deinhardstein's libretto *Hans Sachs*; it was first performed on 13 February 1828 in the Königliches Schauspielhaus in Berlin. Zelter had attended the performance on 26 August 1830, at which the one-act melodrama by Friedrich Wilhelm Gotter with music by Georg Benda was also performed.

[553] Goethe's poem 'Dein Ehrenandenken des Altvaters der deutschen Dichter', published earlier in the *Teutschen Merkur* (1776).

[554] The identity has not been discovered; there is no information on the theatre programme.

[555] Baron Veit Bernhard *Emil* von Seckendorff-Gudent (1804–90), law student at the universities of Leipzig and Berlin (1828–30).

long-enough practised, you can imagine that the work itself becomes a vacation on which I feast because it is material that I am already familiar with.

## 511. Zelter

Berlin, 4 to 7 September 1830

For over a week now I am obsessed with a lively song[556] that I drafted in freely when I was reading. Like [a hen] with an egg I cannot lay it and cannot manage to make it round. The poem is insignificant, but it has something that offered me a particular structural form.

Another by Förster is completely successful – metrically I would even consider it a masterwork. He sent it to you himself because he wrote it in Rome for your birthday. It is called 'Die Campanelle'[557] and it is really good. It is also valuable to me because I composed it a week ago for your birthday. Hegel was with us that evening and since then he is laid up with a fever. [...] One of my students, Baron Emil von Seckendorf, had also written two poems and set them to music.[558] I promised to send you a fair copy. It is the basic conviction that I revere and recognize. Words are water and water doesn't do it. I am already working on a supply for the winter semester in order to make them worthy of my audience. It would amaze me if someone were so smart as to write down what I tell them. I confess that I myself would like to read it. As soon as I lift the pen, I am blank and write only what I already know. [...]

A guest singer, Mademoiselle Heinefetter, has just arrived. I have to praise her; she is capable of a lot and doesn't do too much. That is rare! She really pleased me as Desdemona[559] without reminding me of Madamoiselle Sontag, and that tells me something!

---

[556] Undiscovered source.

[557] Friedrich Förster's poem 'Die Campanelle', set to music by Zelter in 1830; the text was published (without any acknowledgement of the author) in Ottilie von Goethe's journal *Chaos*, in 1830. A year later Zelter's setting appeared in the same journal.

[558] There are no settings by Emil von Seckendorff in Goethe's music collection.

[559] Sabine Heinefetter (1809–72), the prima donna of Italian opera in Paris, gave guest performances in the Berlin opera house during August and September 1830. The performance of Rossini's *Othello* mentioned by Zelter had taken place on 31 August 1830; the performance scheduled for 27 August had to be cancelled on account of the singer's hoarseness. Further guest appearances given by Heinefetter in Berlin were: the title role in *Fidelio* on 20 August; Sextus in *Titus* on 25 August; Agathe in *Der Freischütz* on 5 and 17 September; the title role in *Semiramis* on 9 and 12 September; *Susanna* in *Die Hochzeit des Figaro* on 15 and 21 September; and Amazili in *Ferdinand Cortez* on 24 September.

## 512. Zelter

Berlin, 26 September to 5 October 1830

[...] I have no comfort to give you about musical matters; I carry on in my old way and let the rest of the world get on with it. Marx or Markus,[560] not the Evangelist – although in the *Musikalische Zeitung* he preaches the doctrine of bunglers – brought me greetings from Felix who is in Munich;[561] the message is fine, though there is no good understanding between me and the bearer. This Marx has just published in quarto a *Kunst des Gesanges*,[562] at which, by his own account, he has worked for nine years – finally to make Italian music a grief to the Germans. The work begins thus: 'We now find ourselves at the end of a period in the art of music in which Italian music fills all countries, Germany included, almost making us forget what German art and German music are.'[563] If that were true, undoubtedly the best thing the Germans could do would be to compose music that would make us glad to forego the Italian. But the attack on the excesses of the Italian style, as exemplified in the once *salv. ven.* castrati and other forgotten horrors,[564] is as stale as the whole doctrine of Marx. Have but talent, my worthy Germans, and with that go where you will find ears, eyes, joy and meaning; foreign countries will do you no harm. Dürer, Hackert, Goethe, and many others besides, strengthened and confirmed their talent in Italy, and he who takes nothing there will bring nothing back. Handel, Graun, Hasse, Mozart made music wherever they were; whether Scottish, Italian, Evangelical, it was all the same to them – and the world is filled with what they did and did well. All honour to your German science – ye professorial gentlemen – if you will only let music be music still!

The quarrels over the new Berlin hymn book[565] are still going on; the truth may lie in the middle, though each faction may be far from it. The Porst hymn book[566] is, of course, useless, unless one venerates the sentiment, the earnestness, and the truth contained in it. The new book, on the contrary, is neither a new one nor the old one – even the very necessity of a new one just now could be contested when the inability to make a new one is so candidly confessed. The soling and peeling

---

[560] A.B. Marx was editor of the *Berliner Allgemeine Musikalische Zeitung* from 1824.

[561] During his stay in Munich Felix Mendelssohn had, in fact, met Marx, who subsequently wrote to Fanny Hensel about her brother's activities in Munich.

[562] A.B. Marx, *Die Kunst des Gesanges, theoretisch-praktisch* (Berlin: Adolph Martin Schlesinger, 1826); Marx's preface is largely directed against the degeneration of Italian singing (namely, unintelligible words, exaggerated ornamentation). The main body of the text is, however, a factual, elementary introduction to the art of singing.

[563] Ibid., preface, p. iii.

[564] Ibid.

[565] ZG 26 March 1830.

[566] ZG 11 January 1819.

of the old ox-hide verses is – however brave a name one may attach to it – at best a green fig-leaf to the original sin. […]

Would you be so kind as to hand over the enclosed to Madame Milder when she reaches you?[567]

### 513. Zelter

Berlin, 9 to 21 October 1830

[…] I will gladly publish the music to 'Campanelle' in *Chaos*[568] – I just want to hear it first [to see] whether it shows what I put into it. Let me know the final deadline when you must have it. May I also ask for a complete copy at the end of the year? I have some individual pieces which are doing the rounds amongst my art-loving Francophile and Anglophile ladies.

It would mean a great deal to me if my music to 'Generalbeichte' had contributed to making your Taunus-hearted Frankfurt people[569] to do penance. The music has 30 years around its neck. We still sing it and I am the one who gladly hears it again. […]

In the evening the Liedertafel took place; the second (of which I am an honorary member) made me happy because it endeavours to outdo the first (of which I am chairman).[570] When they got together at the beginning, they wanted our songs.

---

[567] Presumably a letter from Zelter to Anna Milder. The singer had been engaged at the Königliches Theater in Berlin from 1816 to 1829; she had resigned after a disagreement with Spontini and now gave guest performances in different opera houses across Europe. She was guest performer at the Weimar Court Theatre in October 1830 and visited Goethe on 7 October (see Goethe's diary, *WA* III/12, pp. 313–14). She returned to Berlin at the beginning of November.

[568] ZG 4–7 September 1830 and GZ 12 September 1830, where he wrote, 'They have accepted *Die Campanella* in *Chaos*; if you were to send your setting of it, we could also see the music in print'; Zelter sent Goethe the requested composition on 10 May 1831.

[569] For Goethe's 81st birthday 13 citizens of Frankurt had sent Goethe a silver goblet and two cases of wine, with an accompanying letter which concluded with verse 5 of Goethe's poem 'Generalbeichte'; see Wolfgang Hecht, *Allerlei freundliche Dinge. Geburtstagsgeschenke für Goethe* (Weimar: Neue Folge (GSA), 1985), p. 65f; an image of the goblet is included on p. 67.

[570] The Jüngere Liedertafel had been founded by Ludwig Berger and Bernhard Klein in Berlin; they distinguished themselves from the first Liedertafel founded by Zelter by not having a cap on the number of members and because they 'represented the new political tendencies'; see Peter Nitsche, 'Die Liedertafel im System der Zelterschen Gründungen' in Carl Dahlhaus (ed.), *Studien zur Musikgeschichte Berlins im frühen 19. Jahrhundert*, (Regensburg: Bosse, 1980), p. 11–26, quote 21. Zelter had been an honorary member of the Jüngere Liedertafel since January 1830; he always spoke well of the society, even ranked it higher than his own – despite the natural suspicion that he perceived them as rivals.

I said then, 'If you want to be a mere shadow of us, you are no good at all. Instead you should consider your society as a good sequel to a good thing, so write some songs or steal them as you can.' They did this. I myself wrote some completely new songs for them and some of their members have supplied such good settings that one would have to praise them. 'In allen guten Stunden'[571] I like better than my own composition, which admittedly is orginal, and if they gradually get rid of 'Sandwirt'[572] and other lugubrious patriotic songs, they could compete with everyone. They are vigorous young people, somewhat inclined to anarchy, but really decent and well disposed towards all that is good, though they are like my barometer which is always dancing up and down to good weather without ever becoming settled.

### 514. Zelter

Berlin, 26 October 1830

[...] As a wind-up to the royal wedding festivities (of Prince Albrecht), they gave us a grand performance of *Wilhelm Tell en masque* at the opera. The real *Wilhelm Tell* was composed by Rossini for Paris; it gave offence, however, on account of its revolutionary tendency, so they offered us a completely new text, and the opera is now called *Andreas Hofer*.[573] No one is supposed to notice this. Essentially they are just like little children, who imagine that no one can scent them out if they keep their eyes shut.

What kind of a man Rossini is will now be revealed. My reputation is at stake. If, however, the work pleases, I have won; because I affirm that no poet can fault him, nor write him off. One of these days some one will venture to fit a *Figaro* into

---

[571] Setting of Goethe's poem 'Bundeslied' by Gustav Reichardt (1797–1884), published as no. 1 of *6 Tafelgesängen für vier Männerstimmen*, op. 5, full score and parts (Berlin, 1825).

[572] Also known as 'Sandwirt Hofer' and 'Andreas Hofer', set to music by Ludwig Berger, no. 5 in *Tafelgesänge*, vol. 1, op. 20 (Berlin, 1825).

[573] Rossini's grand (and final) opera, *Guillaume Tell* (libretto by Victor Joseph Etienne, alias De Jouy and Hippolyte Louis Florent Bis; premiere on 3 August 1829 in Paris) was – on account of its seemingly revolutionary content – only allowed to be performed in a completely distorted German version: 'Andreas Hofer, Grand Opera with ballet in 4 acts, after the contents of the English opera of the same name by (James Robinson) Planché, with accompanying music by Rossini, freely adapted for the German stage and organized into scences by Baron Karl August von Lichtenstein'; *Spenersche Zeitung*, no. 245, 21 October 1830. The Berlin premiere took place on 18 October 1830, with two further performances on 22 and 31 October.

his *Semiramis*.[574] I haven't even heard the work yet. I don't like to say that I am sick because no one would believe it, but I can't really not say it. [...]

Tell me something about Madame Milder's stay with you.[575] She is so quiet with me and I can't really get anything out of her.

### 515. Goethe

Weimar, 29 October 1830

[...] I saw the dear Milder briefly here, but unfortunately I didn't hear her. I no longer go to the theatre and it wasn't possible to arrange a concert in my home. I also could not speak with Frau von Wahl whom you recommended earlier, who, according to Ottilie, is back from Italy cheerful and well. To think of other people's situations no longer suits me. I have to direct and settle my own affairs. [...]

### 516. Zelter

Berlin, 29 October to 2 November 1830

Yesterday, I, at length, saw and heard the much-abused *soi-disant* Andreas Hofer *ci-devant* Wilhelm Tell[576] – and I think I have won my game.

This time the composer has written an opera for Paris,[577] which has a capital orchestra and screamers for singers. I recognized the man himself in his complete individuality; still, his work is a novelty as his ground is new. Actually I consider this opera actually unfeasible in Italy, as the singers will decline to sing it, and the orchestra cannot play it. The work is in four acts, and throughout all is spirit and life. Although in Rossini's Italian operas we may have many a dreary moment, here there is nothing but continuous animation, fire and variety. The libretto is a ridiculous falsification of the history of our time, and reminds one of the countless

---

[574] German title of Rossini's opera *Semiramide* (libretto by Gaetano Rossi) with a quite different protagonist, distorted in the same way as Rossini's *William Tell*.

[575] Anna Milder appeared as guest artist of the Weimar Court Theatre on 9 October in the role of Elvira in Mozart's *Don Juan* (in the German adaptation by Friedrich Rochlitz); on 13 October she sang Clytamnestra in Gluck's *Iphigenie in Aulis*; her final guest appearance was given on 16 October in the title role of Gluck's *Iphigenie in Tauris*. Goethe mentioned her visit on 7 October in GZ 29 October 1830.

[576] The title of the politically correct German adaptation of Rossini's *William Tell*; Zelter attended the third (and final) performance in the Königliches Opernhaus on 31 October 1830; see *AMZ* 32 (1830), no. 51, 22 December, column 829.

[577] Since 1824 Rossini had lived in Paris, where he was director of the Théâtre Italien; his *William Tell* was premiered there on 3 August 1829.

defeats of the triumphant party, nay, of the disgraceful fall of a brave patriot, about whom no one has troubled himself, except the enemy of the Fatherland.[578] [...] The music excited me so much that I could not sleep that night; perhaps I will send you more details about the second performance. [...]

Frau von Wahl arrived here yesterday and I have still not seen her; I was rehearsing our music which we intend to put on this week for the general public.[579]

Felix will, I expect, be in Rome now,[580] whereat I greatly rejoice, as his mother was always opposed to Italy. I dreaded seeing him here, and in the country too, dissolving like a jelly under the corrupting influence of family gossip, for I consider him really a first-rate player because he plays everything and is a master of all styles. Let him go forth, therefore, into the world and discover his masters, and awake them, and begin where the beginning is; the materials for that he brings with him. [...]

## 517. Goethe

Weimar, 6 November 1830

As to that branch of your Liedertafel,[581] you are not dissatisfied with it and I should say that these excellent young people, in accordance with the advancing age, naturally also want to go forward; but where to? That is the question! The rest of us, as all our songs prove, required birth within the bounds of sociability, and placed ourselves in innocent opposition to the Philistines. They, it is true, are neither conquered nor exterminated, but no longer come into consideration. The more modern boon companions seek their opponents on a higher stage and it would surprise me if your pupils did not follow in Béranger's footsteps.[582] That certainly is a field where there is still something to be done, and where they can outbid us, provided they have as much talent as the aforesaid. However, let us commend this, with much besides, to those demons who have their fingers in every pie of this kind.

---

[578] Napoleon.

[579] The first subscription concert of Handel's oratorio *Alexanderfest* was performed on 4 November 1830; see *Spenersche Zeitung*, no. 259, 6 November 1830.

[580] Felix Mendelssohn had set out on his Italian journey in May 1830; after staying in Weimar and Munich, he travelled on through Salzburg, Bratislava (then Pressburg), Venice and reached Rome on 1 November 1830.

[581] The Jüngere Liedertafel, Berlin.

[582] Goethe's initial enthusiasm for the song poet Jean Pierre de Béranger changed when Béranger's anti-government attacks – for which he was often held in custody – become increasingly intense; see Eckermann, 2 April 1829, p. 343.

## 518. Zelter

Berlin, 12 to 13 November 1830

[...] The day before yesterday I heard *Il matrimonio segreto*[583] once more at the Königstädter Theater. One sits there calmly on the chair without further ado, hears the hundred thousandth story of all the days that were and will be. One is at ease with the sorrow. I am fanned by the lightest, cheekiest, most innocent eternally relevant musical play, despite all the trouble they go to up there to turn white into black or something else. I have heard the music often enough and went back to hear a Mademoiselle Vio[584] who has to replace Madame Sontag[585] and seems to have been well tolerated in her place. In concentrating on the music I have forgotten the rest: I have to be able to do that once in my life! [...]

## 519. Zelter

Berlin, 13 to 18 November 1830

[...] *Die Räuber*[586] was a play which wounded me as deeply as it delighted me greatly. [...] Then appeared *Kabale und Liebe*, in which a musician was represented,[587] in whom I recognized the exact counterpart of our Stadtpfeifer, George.[588] This man was a first-rate hand at various instruments, a well-intentioned fellow, though of rough manners, and entirely devoted to me. Then there appeared a review of *Kabale und Liebe*, which made me angry – I think Moritz was the author of it.

---

[583] Domenico Cimarosa's comic opera (libretto by Giovanni Bertati) was performed in the Königstädtisches Theater in the German adaptation entitled *Die heimliche Ehe*; Zelter attended the performance on 10 November 1830.

[584] The singer and actress Elizabeth (Betty) Spitzeder née Vio (1806/08–72), engaged at the Josephstädter Theater in Vienna, employed at the Königstädtisches Theater in Berlin from 1830.

[585] Henriette Sontag was employed by the Königstädter Theater Berlin from 1825 and by the Paris opera from the beginning of 1828; she returned to Berlin in 1830 but had to give up her operatic career according to the orders of King Karl Albert of Sardinia on account of her marriage to the Sardinian diplomat Carl Graf Rossi.

[586] Schiller's *Die Räuber* was published in 1781; Franz and Karl Moor were contrasting brothers, sons of the principal protagonist, Count von Moor.

[587] The Berlin premiere of Schiller's tragedy *Kabale und Liebe* took place on 22 November 1784; one of the characters in this play is Miller, 'local musician or professional piper'.

[588] As a young man Zelter had taken lessons with Johann Friedrich Georg, the town musician who lived in the Königstädter suburb of Berlin; Zelter mentions him many times as a friend and teacher in his autobiography; Schottländer, *Carl Friedrich Zelters Darstellungen seines Lebens*, pp. 40–45; 122–6; 226f and 240.

I could have killed the reviewer; I declared so often and so loudly against him, that my father[589] once said to me, 'You seem to me like one who washes himself with dirty water, for you take pleasure in that which displeases you, you love going on about what vexes you; I think you can do something better than what you have never learnt to do, nor do I myself understand it.' This – like everything that my father used to say – made me reflect; and when *Fiesco*[590] appeared and was played here by Fleck with great applause, there arose a coolness in me which almost passed into coldness – so that now, what I liked best was to take my part as a player in old Döbbelin's Orchestra,[591] let the operas be what they may. This second epoch extended itself up to the time of Wallenstein.[592] I had then become more intimately acquainted with Engel, Nicolai, Zöllner, Moritz, and others.[593] When I heard the faults of the play discussed – it was not in harmony with history; it had cost eight years' work and was still so incomplete and so on – I was obliged to hold my tongue, though I could not agree with them. Fleck's acting of *Wallenstein* was masterly; the more I saw him, the more I was attracted. I summed up to myself all that I had heard about Schiller up to that point, and a deep desire arose within me to make the personal acquaintance of the poet. Speaking sincerely, the chief inducement in coming to you people in the first instance was that I might get to know Schiller, and therefore I came by way of Jena, because I did not know that Schiller had already settled in Weimar.

Schiller was not long back from Dresden.[594] Naumann had composed music for his 'Ideale',[595] and made a pupil of his, a Mdlle Schäfer,[596] sing it to the poet. The

---

[589] Georg Zelter (1723–87), master bricklayer in Berlin.

[590] The Berlin premiere of Schiller's *Die Verschwörung des Fiesco zu Genua* (1783/84) took place on 2 January 1787.

[591] In his autobiography Zelter has written about his involvement in the orchestra at Doebbelin's theatre; see Schottländer, *Carl Friedrich Zelters Darstellungen seines Lebens*, p. 111. Carl Theophilus Doebbelin had taken over many actors and the orchestra of the Koch troupe, and as a private entrepeneur had founded a theatre with them in the Komödienhaus on Behrenstraße.

[592] The three plays of Schiller's Wallenstein Trilogy received their Berlin premiere at different times: *Die Piccolomini* was first performed on 18 February 1799, *Wallensteins Tod* was first staged on 17 May 1799 and *Wallensteins Lager* was premiered on 28 November 1803.

[593] Zelter was introduced to the writer Johann Jacob Engel (1741–1802), in Bejamin Veitel Ephraim's house in 1783. Zelter formed a long acquaintance with the writer and publisher Christoph *Friedrich* Nicolai (1733–1811), and rebuilt his home, Brüderstr.13, in 1788. Johann Friedrich Zöllner was chief councillor of the consistory in Berlin. Zelter mentions his friendship with the writer Karl Philip Moritz (1756–93) in his autobiography; see Schottländer, *Carl Friedrich Zelters Darstellungen seines Lebens*, pp. 51 and 120.

[594] Schiller had stayed in Dresden from 9 August to 15 September 1801.

[595] Johann Gottlieb Naumann's setting of Schiller's poem 'Die Ideale' was first published in the *Musen-Almanach für das Jahr 1796*.

[596] Her identity cannot be established.

first thing that Schiller talked to me about was this composition, over which he got quite angry – that so illustrious a man could so belabour a poem, as to tear its soul to tatters with his vile tweedle-dee – and so he launched out against composers as a body!

I need not describe the effect of so comforting an oration. I had brought Schiller's and your poems in my bag, and in one moment lost all desire to unpack them. This was before dinner. Schiller and I were to dine with you.

His wife came and said, 'Schiller, you must go and dress – time's up.' So Schiller goes into the next room and leaves me alone. I seat myself at the piano, play a few chords, and hum 'Der Taucher' quite quietly to myself. Towards the end of the strophe, the door opens, and Schiller – only half-dressed – steals in. 'Yes, that's right, that's as it ought to be,' and so on. Then the wife begins again; 'Dear Schiller, it is past two o'clock; do just dress first, you know Goethe does not like waiting too long.'– And so it all came right.

You will remember how often in those days I showed off my musical divertissements before him and you and all the rest, and how you used to send Ehlers[597] to my room to practise the little pieces with me, and how well he performed several of them.

Forgive me for being such a gossip. Today is Sunday, when one has an hour's peace, though I have already attended a stiff three-hour musical rehearsal. I pretty well agree with what I find in Thomas Carlyle about Schubart,[598] I, too, felt strongly about the violent treatment he met with, for he was a musician, though his music gave me no pleasure; nor did his *Æsthetik der Tonkunst*, wherein he taught what I was just on the point of abjuring – how to break through the wall, so as to penetrate into the sanctuary when the door is close by. He had learnt nothing and is gone to the place from where he came.

This letter was not intended to go until I knew some more particulars about you, but today is 18 [November], so I shall send it. Felix arrived in Rome on 1 November and has written to his parents from there.[599] Let me have a word from you; I cannot set foot in the street, without being asked how you are.[600]

---

[597] Johann Wilhelm Ehlers (1774–1845), singer, actor, composer of songs with guitar accompaniment.

[598] Christian Friedrich Daniel Schubart (1739–1816), court music director in Stuttgart. Carylyle's biography *Leben Schillers* concludes with a 20-page highly critical appendix on Christian Schubart; *MA* 20.2, pp. 1143–44.

[599] Felix Mendelssohn reported his arrival in Rome in a letter to his parents on 2 November 1829.

[600] Goethe was, in fact, seriously ill in late November 1830, which strengthened his resolve to complete the remaining parts of *Faust, Dichtung und Wahrheit* and this correspondence with Zelter.

## 520. Zelter

Berlin, 21 November 1830

Yesterday Prince Radziwill let me hear three new scenes from his *Faust*.[601] I cannot sufficiently praise the care with which everything is thought out, right down to the smallest details. The first of the scenes is the Requiem mass for the mother.[602] It opens in front of the church. Gretchen already hears the sound of the organ from a distance, goes into the pew, the Requiem begins and the mass gets under way. During the choral song of the Dies irae and so on, Mephisto, in person, as it were, steps behind the sinner in the place of conscience and loudly declaims the well-known lamentations. Though everything is skilfully and industriously woven and fitted into the course of the action, nevertheless it doesn't work because not only the prayers of the sinner but also the church service itself, namely the choral song, is disturbed through the spoken interruptions. It is also not Catholic. As I said, one would have to praise the work; I would not like to complain about the [artistic] intention or the effect because the work is there and the critics have come too late.

The second scene is 'Spaziergang vor dem Tor'[603] with Wagner, in particular the conversation about the poodle. Metrically the verses are opportunely inserted into the on-going instrumental music as if the action could seem real and the orchestra could not go along with it.

The third scene pleased me most of all, although it is also set melodramatically as they say. 'Spaziergang im Garten':[604] Faust with Gretchen, and Mephisto with Martha, move in a circle around a broad grass area so that the couple who speaks is seen while the other couple walks among the bushes. Here the music moves forward really well, one minute delightful, the next ironic; with tasteful continuity. Verse and rhyme are so delicately and metrically interwoven in the course of the music that I would consider it the best which has been ventured of its kind. Admittedly it would also be required that the declaimers are musically good and that all the musicians together provide such a feast to the ears that they slow the tempo and increase it again. Here the accursed baton has to do its duty, for without it one would never be able to stand up again and go to bed.

The concert given by our Madame Milder[605] went off successfully enough last Thursday, in spite of opposition from all quarters. In accordance with her wish and the first announcement, I was to conduct the music, though I only did so as a mediator, for without my presence it would have been difficult to avoid a complete

---

[601] ZG 14–20 March 1810.
[602] The Cathedral scene in *Faust 1*.
[603] 'Vor dem Tor', v. 903–1177.
[604] 'Garten', v. 3073–3205.
[605] On 18 November 1830 in the Sing-Akademie hall; works performed included passages from Handel's *Messiah* and scenes from Gluck's *Alceste* with chorus; see *Iris im Gebiete der Tonkunst* (1830), nos. 43 and 44.

breach with friends and those opposed to her moods, caprice, bad behaviour and so on. She appears to like giving orders. Even then her voice is a work of God.

Nothing is announced yet about the forthcoming carnival. Spontini is being sought after,[606] if not hoped for. In Paris he is said to have praised Berlin, just as he praised Paris when he was here. No new operas have been heard of,[607] and *Andreas Hofer*[608] has not yet been performed again. The ballet is in vogue now and little Elßner[609] really dances, or rather I should say twists and pirouettes marvellously. Madame Birch-Pfeiffer has not appeared again;[610] she did not go down well. She could not get into the running, and tried to with tragedies which are not popular here. Also the critics did not exactly express themselves in her favour, and that counts for something; now and then they, too, are right. [...]

### 521. Zelter

Berlin, 25 November 1830

[...] The Sing-Akademie will find it difficult to train and support an administrator. I have spoilt them. They live and operate to please me and I have lived through two generations of them, and I still like them. But where do I get it from and what do I draw on? Our bank manager, now deceased, once asked me innocently what I get from it, and that is a long time ago. But I have lived and live and must treasure it if the least of our 400 members abroad refers to himself as a member of the Sing-Akademie in Berlin. [...]

---

[606] Spontini, whose ten-year fixed contract as General Director of Music at the Königliches Theater had expired, had gone to Paris in the autumn of 1830 before any decision could be made about extending his contract. He resumed his post in Berlin at the beginning of April 1831.

[607] Spontini was bound by his contract to produce two large-scale works every three years.

[608] After its third performance on 31 October 1830, *Andreas Hofer* was not performed again in Berlin.

[609] Franziska (Fanny) Elßler (1810–84), leading dancer at the K.K. Hoftheater, Kärntnertor, Vienna, gave guest performances – mostly with her sister, Theresia Elßler (1808–78) – from October 1830 to January 1831 in Berlin.

[610] Charlotte Birch-Pfeiffer (1799/1800–68) gave five guest appearances at the Königliches Schauspielhaus in October and November 1830; the final performance took place on 11 November. Her acting abilities were strongly criticized in the *Spenersche Zeitung*, no. 260, 8 November 1830.

## 522. Zelter

Berlin, 2 to 4 December 1830

My concert yesterday (*The Seasons* by Joseph Haydn) had a good and joyful reception.[611] Apart from an obvious mistake which I myself made, I hardly noticed anything else and I can be happy since the accursed theatre-ballets and wretched opera nonsense prevent even one prolonged, continuous rehearsal because there is always one or other important individual missing. If my primary singer, Fräulein von Schätzel, were not the most pleasant girl with the loveliest voice, irrepressible good spirits, docility and impertinence, one could not trust the public performance of such a great, difficult work to good luck. Although you are older than I, you probably haven't seen the like of it. At the same time she sightreads and has a natural ability to sustain, tackling the most difficult [music] on the spot. I also had to be on top of the situation. Apart from that she does nothing but laugh and concentrate like someone shooting woodcocks. May God grant that the theatre doesn't corrupt her. While the others are at one another's throats, she is laughing.

## 523. Zelter

Berlin, 6 December 1830

[...] Just for so long as opera has been drawing plays and tragedy along in its wake, now the ballet exercises its sovereignty over the theatre, which can thus find it difficult to survive on account of the significant money for itinerant virtuosi. Yesterday's completely new opera[612] must have been so well supported merely because of the ballet that followed it. Two Viennese dancers[613] show themselves to their advantage through well-proportioned bodies, lightness and grace in the most wonderful jumps and positions; the light clothing which displays the outline of the whole body keeps lustful eyes busy. The girls are very young, very pretty, not too thin and since both act well, it is a shame that there is no choreographer to

---

[611] Performance of Haydn's *The Four Seasons* on 2 December 1830; it was the Sing-Akademie's second subsription concert; see *AMZ* 33 (1831), no. 3, 19 January, column 42f.

[612] The Berlin premiere of *Alfred der Große König von England* took place on 28 November 1830; Zelter attended the second performance on 5 December.

[613] The sisters Fanny and Theresa Elßler made their Berlin debut in the ballet *Das Schweizer Milchmädchen* on 8 October 1830 (with further performances on 21 October). They appeared in *Die neue Amazone* (29 October, 4, 9 and 17 November) and *Oberon, König der Elfen* (7 November) and the Berlin audiences were delighted by their extraordinary dancing; see *Spenersche Zeitung*, 1 November 1830 and *AMZ* 33 (1831), no. 4, 26 January, column 54; *MA* 20.3, p. 1150.

occupy such talents more worthily. Our ballet is called *Die Nachtwandlerin*[614] – who through her sleepwalking is found by her fiancé in bed with a cavalier, from which discord, sorrow and joy then ensue.

The new opera by Theodor Körner and J.P. Schmidt[615] is called *Alfred der Große*;[616] in the war against the Danes, the king loses his bride, but wins her back again intact. The libretto may be a weak one, but the composer broadcasted his own weakness so loudly, that I should gladly have gone to sleep, if the devil had not led me into the midst of the batteries, for I was in the orchestra, having given up my reserved seat to my daughter Rosamunde. [...]

## 524. Zelter

Berlin, 17 to 18 December 1830

[...] I think I told you that we had a performance of Haydn's *Seasons*,[617] with Thomson's words; this music ought to be esteemed [as] one of our lost treasures, sung as it is by rustics, vine-dressers and tillers of the soil – countrified, yet with a brilliancy of its own – so realistic that I am always transported by it to a condition of innocence and perfect mental equilibrium. Two factions emerged in the rehearsals. The special people didn't want to join in singing the 'Heida! Hopsa! Juche!'[618] of the grape harvest with the simple country folk. And bearing in mind the time, I was inclined to leave these pieces out because, performed without enthusiasm, they couldn't be received with enthusiasm. Now, since I didn't show any real aversion to it, I have the satisfaction of knowing the best of the people on my side and the others remained reasonable, since they were not treated as automatons, and are now critical amongst themselves. The performance went down extraordinarily well[619] and now they want to hear the whole thing again. They can come to me about it. I added an introduction to the text in order to give connoisseurs an overview, which, as I hear, was appreciated. I am enclosing it here[620] [...]

---

[614] *Therese, die Nachtwanderlin*, ballet with mime by A. Titus, after the French *La Somnambule ou l'Arrivée d'un nouveau seigneur* by Eugène Scribe and Jean Pierre Aumer with music by Louis Joseph Ferdinand Hérold.

[615] Johann Philipp Samuel Schmidt (1779–1853).

[616] The opera *Alfred der Große, König von England* was performed twice in Berlin: on 28 November and 5 December 1830; see *AMZ* 33 (1831), no. 1, 5 January, column 13.

[617] On 2 December; ZG 2 December 1830 and ZG 2 to 4 December 1830.

[618] No. 16, Choral song, 'Juhe, juhe! der Wein ist da!' (from 'Autumn').

[619] See Ludwig Rellstab's review in the *Vossische Zeitung*, no. 283, 4 Decemmber 1830; *Spenersche Zeitung*, no. 284, 6 December 1830, enclosure and *AMZ* 33 (1831), no. 3, 19 January, column 42f.; *MA* 20.3, p. 1154–5.

[620] In the libretto *The Seasons. After Thomson. Set to Music by Joseph Haydn* (Berlin 1830); Zelter signed the first three pages 'Z'; the enclosure has not been handed down. In the

## 525. Zelter

Berlin, Second half of December to 30 December 1830

[...] A letter from Felix, dated Rome, 1 December, tells me of the Pope's death,[621] which occurred the evening before at the Quirinal.[622] That lad came into the world at a happy hour. In Hungary he sees an Imperial head crowned, in Rome he finds a Conclave, and Vesuvius is getting itself ready for a performance. In Rome I gave him an introduction to the Maestro di Capella, del Sommo Pontefice, Baini, and to the Abbate Santini.[623] The latter, a musical antiquary and collector, writes to me, 'Oh, what a brilliant youth that is! With what pleasure do I call him my friend; one may well say of him, as Scaliger used to say, when speaking of Pico della Mirandola, 'He is a monster without vice.'

Santini has written an Italian version of Ramler's words to Graun's Passion Music, and they write to him from Naples about it, 'All our connoisseurs nowadays will listen to nothing else but the music of Graun and Handel; how true it is that the truly beautiful can never be lost.'[624]

## 526. Goethe

Weimar, 4 January 1831

Felix, whose successful visit to Rome you report on, cannot but be favourably received wherever he goes: such great gifts, so young, so charming! [...]

---

foreword Zelter comparison of Haydn's two oratorios, *The Creation* and *The Seasons*, is followed by a general appreciation of Haydn's work before concluding with a short commentary on the musical programme for *The Seasons*. Zelter closes with a short note justifying the reduced version of the oratorio, thereby subtly answering the dispute before the Sing-Akademie's first performance of Haydn's oratorio: 'So we have also left out some passages here in order not to run over time. May such licence be forgiven if for no other reason that that we have had to endure all kinds of derision over the past year.'

[621] In a letter written on 1 December 1830, Felix Mendelssohn describes his impressions of Rome and the performances of the Capella del sommo pontifice (in the papal chapel) and in the Sistine Chapel which Mendelssohn had visited four times. Apart from that he reported, 'I have come directly from the Quirinal, where the Pope (Pius VIII) died yesterday evening.'

[622] The Quirinale Palace was, until 1870, the second papal palace.

[623] Fortunato Santini (1778–1861) was one of the great nineteenth-century music collectors. Through his translation of German religious works into Latin, he contributed greatly to the distribution of the music of Handel, Graun and Bach throughout Italy. Today his library is held by the Cathedral of the Bishopric.

[624] Spontini's letter to Zelter has not been handed down.

In the evenings Ottilie is reading me our correspondence.[625] There is in both of us a calm, constant, serious-passionate activity, always going in the same direction. Outwardly little is asked, everyone goes his way and lets the rest happen. [...] And now a pregnant little word in conclusion: Ottilie says that our correspondence is more entertaining for the reader that the one with Schiller. What she means by this and how she explains it you shall, if possible, hear some day soon.[626]

### 527. Zelter

Berlin, 7 January 1831

The day before yesterday I was again at the opera to hear *Die Vestalin*,[627] which was very well performed. The work itself is incredibly lightweight, and at the same time provides a perfectly valid criterion for the current state of art in Europe; for this opera is considered on every account as one of the better ones – a work in the grand style. It is the most ungraceful bagatelle I can imagine. The audience were delighted and the overture had to be repeated, which one may take as a sign of the hopes which are entertained for the piece.

### 528. Zelter

Berlin, 8 to 20 January 1831

In rereading your letter, I again come across your view of Niebuhr's work in relation to the individuality of the writer,[628] and I enclose the programme with the words of Handel's *Te Deum* which was performed here last week to show the preface I wrote for the work.[629] Strictly speaking, no one knows what a Te Deum

---

[625] Goethe's diary on 29 October 1830 records for the first time: 'With Ottilie later. We began to read the Zelter correspondence'; *WA* III/12, p. 323.

[626] Ottilie's comparison between Goethe's correspondence with Schiller and his correspondence with Zelter was never communicated, despite Zelter's request; ZG 7 January 1831.

[627] Spontini's opera was performed for the first time in Berlin on 18 January 1831. Wilhelmine Schröder-Devrient made a guest appearance as Julia on 5 January 1831; see *AMZ* 33 (1831), no. 8, 23 February, column 122.

[628] Niebuhr was a member of the Berliner Akademie der Wissenschaften; in this capacity he held lectures in ancient history at the university until his departure to Rome in 1816.

[629] *Das Dettingensche Tedeum von Georg Friedrich Handel. Voher: Hymnus zur Feier des Confessionsfestes. Nach aufgegebenen Worten des 119ten Psalms von Eduard Grell. Darauf: Das Göttliche. Hymnus von Goethe and Rungenhagen* (Berlin, 1831), Ruppert,

ought to be, although thousands have written more than one. Here I wanted to explain how Handel treated it in this one case, namely as a German in England, as a Lutheran German Christian, and as none other than Handel. Of course I have been acquainted with the work for the last 50 years.

Rungenhagen set your poem 'Das Göttliche' to music.[630] He shouldn't have bothered. The music is to be praised in itself: only the devil took the divine, which is perhaps all he is interested in.

### 529. Goethe

Weimar, 29 January 1831

[...] Your introduction to Handel's *Te Deum* is splendid and quite worthy of you. That beloved contemporary audience of ours thinks that one must always serve up fresh cakes hot from the pan. They have no idea that first one has to be educated up to anything new or any really antique novelty. But how could they know this? Why, they are always being born anew. [...]

Ottilie continues to read the correspondence to me in the evenings, where there is the most delightful contrast of a man who lives, enjoys travels and is continually active in the world as an artist with a friend who is more or less stationary, contemplative, sacrificing the present, and devoting himself to the future.

The manuscript that you know is neatly written out, but it is full of particular defects which we are finding and noting as we read through it.[631] Professor Riemer is taking on the future publication for a fair honorarium. In my lifetime I will try to see the manuscript is cleaned up as far as possible and confer with him about it. I can easily correct omissions and mistakes for which one would have to carry out many futile investigations later on. [...]

---

no. 2586. Zelter had not only written an extensive four-page preface but had also provided a translation of the *Dettinger Te Deum*. Handel's *Te Deum* and the two hymns were performed at a Sing-Akademie subscription concert on 13 January 1831.

[630] Carl Friedrich Rungenhagen's hymn on Goethe's poem 'Das Göttliche' was performed on 13 January 1831; see *AMZ* 33 (1831), no. 8, 23 February, column 123; *MA* 20.3, p. 1166.

[631] There is an interesting passage about the future publication of the correspondence in Goethe's will, section 6, paragraph 4: 'Correspondence with Professor Zelter in Berlin. Of this we can say for the present, that after the death of both men, the [correspondence] should be printed in full and offered for sale. One half of the profits is for my grandchildren, the other half to both daughters of my friend Zelter, Doris and Rosamunde, as yet unmarried. I hereby decree that one half shall and must be paid to both [women] – or to their heirs – since their father has granted me exclusive ownership of the correspondence under this condition.'

## 530. Zelter

Berlin, 1 February 1831

I have to thank you very much for the trouble you have taken to bring the manuscript of our correspondence into respectable order for posterity. Although I am not worried but am instead convinced that the topical subjects of the moment which are suitable to communication by letters cannot appear to the world in the same form, I am amazed by your work in editing such a copious correspondence, for which I would not have the patience. It runs like an independent thread through a portentous age. [...]

I am delighted that you praise my introduction to Handel's *Te Deum*, since it was received very nicely here. Someone said, one knows what one is hearing when one sees so many mouths open at the same time. If I think now how it has often been for me, the wonderful secret play of characters in me, as on Chladni's glass table,[632] I know no more than anyone else and even from the writings of good old Rochlitz on the *Messiah*[633] one should conclude the wheel of fate is still spinning, since the world, and he with it, have long been profited by it and continue to enjoy their winnings. One mystifies oneself and that's the true name of the child.

## 531. Goethe

Weimar, 1 February 1831

[...] Now don't forget to send the letters from the previous year, 1830, as soon as possible, so that they can be taken up in the series of folio volumes. A precaution occurs to me. Your travel diaries brighten up the correspondence in places.[634] You have copies of them;[635] hold on to them and keep them secret; and take care that neither now nor in the future any copies will be made. The publishers are all the more dangerous since they want to be considered honourable, even generous people and always want to be in the right because no law prevails in this anarchy. [...]

---

[632] In his autobiography, which was published as an obituary in *Cäcilia* 6/24 (1827): 297ff, Chladni describes his discovery of his so-called 'sound-figures'; see *MA* 20.3, p. 1169.

[633] Friedrich Rochlitz, 'Handels Messias' in *Für Freude der Tonkunst*, vol. 1, pp. 227–80.

[634] Zelter's travel diary written in letters of his journeys to Vienna, the Baltic Sea, Herrnhut, Holland and Munich during the years 1819 to 1827.

[635] Goethe had copies made of Zelter's travel diaries, four of which are included in this correspondence: Vienna (and Prague), Herrnhut, Holland and Munich.

**532. Goethe**

Weimar, 3 February 1831

[...] The dear Mara, justifiably loved and admired by you, celebrates way up in Thule, I think Reval, a very advanced birthday.[636] They want to arrange something pleasant for her there. They have asked Hummel for music and through him, me for something poetic.[637] It was pleasant for me to remember that in 1771, as an excitable little student, I had furiously applauded Mademoiselle Schmeling.[638] This gave a good counter image and so a couple of verses were easily produced.[639]

Admittedly, with ingenious musical collaboration this lady could have been given the most boundless joy of remembering, it if were to fit the first verse to the [musical] motifs of *Santa Elana al Calvario* so celebrated at that time, through which she would have been painfully yet charmingly drawn back to her youth. I had already thought out the programme, but it remained closed in my breast. I don't know what happened. I am sending off the two verses to you. Most likely they will be revealed either from there or elsewhere; but I don't want to anticipate.

What I have written so far can be sent as a way of receiving warm memories.

---

[636] The singer Gertrud Elizabeth Mara, née Schmeling, impoverished since 1822, had returned to live in Reval, where she celebrated her 82nd birthday on 23 February 1831; see *AMZ* 33 (1831), no. 24, 15 June, column 396.

[637] See Goethe's diary on 17 January 1831: 'Privy Councillor von Müller soliciting an occasional poem for Madam Mara. I wrote one before going to sleep since a happy theme was found in the past'; *WA* III/13, pp. 12–13. The following day Goethe sent the poem to Chancellor von Müller: 'The memory that in the course of my apprenticeship years I belonged to the enthusiastic admirers of Mademoiselle Schmeling made it possible for me to fulfil the request made of me. May the modest enclosure please distant friends – Kapellmeister Hummel will be free in his musical treatment and will handle the verses as he pleases.'

[638] Goethe had attended a performance of Johann Adolf Hasse's oratorio *Santa Elena al Calvario* given by Corona Schröter and Gertrud Elizabeth Schmeling in December 1767 (not 1771); he recalled the performance in his review of Rochlitz's book *Für Freude der Tonkunst* in 1824: 'I was amazed by Mademoiselle Schmeling, at that time a developing singer and, for us inexperienced boys, a highly-polished one. I can still recall the arias, 'Sul terren piagata a morte' etc. and 'par che di giubilo' etc., from Hasse's *Helena auf dem Calvariberg*.

[639] GZ 19 February 1831, enclosure.

### 533. Zelter

Weimar, 4 to 9 February 1831

6 February: Last Friday I was at Beethoven's *Fidelio*[640] and wanted to describe the charming, lucrative music to you, but when I went out, deep snow, water and ice had gathered and I fell so heavily on my old back that suddenly it cast out every thought that I had pieced together so well. The house was full (even without the court) and if the opera is given again, you won't be allowed to miss it. [...]

If Hummel has set your verses to music for Mara, he will hardly be slow to have them printed. I would love to know them and would not let them out of my hands.[641] I myself am no longer so quick and certain of producing something successful. With knowledge comes doubt. I have a number of works which started out well. If I were in control of my good hours it wouldn't take much, and of course that would be the ideal.

### 534. Zelter

Berlin, 12 February 1831

Yesterday a new opera by Ferdinand Ries[642] was given for the second time, with the applause of his friends, myself included. The technical part is admirable; the orchestra, though it worked hard, kept an artistic fete-day and covered itself with glory. The piece is called *Die Räuberbraut*[643] [...] Madame Schröder-Devrient[644] made a very dainty bride, and her singing left nothing to be desired. In my

---

[640] Performance of Beethoven's opera on 4 February 1831 in the Königliches Opernhaus with Wilhelmine Schröder-Devrient in the title role; see *AMZ* 33 (1831), no. 13, 30 March, column 207.

[641] A publication by Hummel has not been discovered.

[642] *Die Räuberbraut* by Ferdinand Ries (libretto by Christian Wilhelm Häser) was first performed in Berlin on 8 February 1831; it received three further performances on 11 and 20 February and 13 March 1831; see *AMZ* 33 (1831), no. 13, 30 March, columns 207–209. Ferdinand Ries is the pupil of whom Beethoven said, 'He imitates me too much. His works are learned, but they have no vitality or real genius in them'; he is best remembered for his *Biographical Notices of Ludwig van Beethoven*, parts of which were translated into English by Moscheles.

[643] In conversation with Felix Mendelssohn on 24 May 1830, Goethe made the following judgement: 'Then the conversation embraced anything and everything; he believed *Die Räuberbraut* by Ries contained everything which an artist needs today in order to be a success – a robber, a bride – and then he criticized the prevalent feeling among the younger generation who were so melancholic'; Felix Mendelssohn to his parents, 21 to 24 May 1830, *Reisebriefe* (1862), p. 4.

[644] The actress and singer Wilhelmine Schröder-Devrient.

judgement, she is superior to her illustrious mother, inasmuch as she combines this gift with smooth acting, dignity, and womanliness [...]

### 535. Zelter

Berlin, 19 February 1831

To accompany the enclosure I will only add that our music from the day before yesterday[645] was launched smoothly enough and met with approval.[646] That surely means something, with masses gathered together of more than two hundred Berliners, one from every corner of the town, with and without trousers, since it is impossible to hold even one rehearsal of an entire work. The completely different dependencies of the performers, solo singers and instrumentalists from family and servant relationships that leave no time at present, become like a lottery ticket, which if it comes out and wins, helps the old director to a sleepless but enjoyable night. Only afterwards he realizes he doesn't understand, since we all don't know how we do it.

Our Scotsman Müller[647] still didn't want to perform. However, yesterday he had to play the viola to a mass by old Bach.[648] He thought it was strange but gradually he got the hang of it!

### 536. Goethe

Weimar, 19 February 1831

[...] As I can refuse you nothing, the stanzas on Mara's festival are enclosed.[649] I do not know whether Hummel has set them.[650] According to my idea, the first verse

---

[645] Performance of Haydn's *The Seasons*.

[646] See, for example, *Iris im Gebiete der Tonkunst*, 2 (1831), p. 32.

[647] Robert Müller (*c.* 1804–55), piano virtuoso and composer of German descent, living in Edinburgh; Ottilie von Goethe's describes him in a letter to Zelter (GSA 95/I, 75, 5).

[648] Performance of Bach's B minor mass.

[649] GZ 3 February 1831.

[650] Hummel set the first poem 'clear, powerful and in the old style'; the second he set 'gently, quiet and modern' as fitting for a work composed in 1831 (E. von Rosen, *Revaler Theater-Chronik. Festschrift des Revaler Deutschen Theater-Vereins* (Reval, 1910). In a letter to the composer on 18 March 1831, Gertrud Elizabeth Mara thanked Hummel for 'the lovely composition' and reported that 'the meaningful music with which he had set the words of the great poet had been suitably performed by her students; see *GJb* 21, 1900, p. 256.

would have to be reminiscent of Hasse's *Santa Elana al Calvario*; the second can be as original and modern as one wants.

And now for something really commendable! I have now gradually come to realize that I must become accustomed to living without my son and the enforced attempt at acting as head of the family again is not succeeding at all badly;[651] but that the echo of that sincere nature may not subside so suddenly for his patrons, I have recorded, primarily for his Italian friends, a very short sketch of his travels,[652] a copy of which I shall send you some day soon.[653] There is always something: his diaries are certainly most interesting,[654] but due to the recurring evidence of those traits to which you were no stranger, they cannot be made public in their own energetic and penetrating style. They would be good reading for us some day, if things could be so happily arranged that you could visit us again; the swan would spread out its wings for you.[655] [...]

Enclosure: To Madamoiselle Schmeling. After a Performance of Hasse's *Sta Elan al Calvario*. Leipzig, 1771

> With clearest voice, with cheerful heart
> Purest gift of youth
> You visited the Holy Sepulchre
> With the Empress.
> There, where all was well
> You transported me
> With your commanding song,
> Ecstatic among the blessed.

To Madame Mara: On the Happy Occasion of the Anniversary of her Birthday, Weimar, 1831.

---

[651] This theme recurs in Goethe's letters around this time; see GZ 21 November 1830 and also Goethe's letter to Count Sternberg on 4 January 1831; *WA* IV/48, pp .69–71.

[652] Enclosed in Goethe's letter to Kestner on 27 December 1830; Goethe picked up the report of August's Italian journey in a draft letter to Mylius on 3 February 1831; *WA* IV/48, pp. 107–10; he also sent a copy to Zelter.

[653] GZ 23 February 1831.

[654] In a draft letter to his son written around 8 to 10 November 1830 Goethe wrote, 'Your diaries have reached us continually and made us very happy.' In the same letter he quotes a report in an English newspaper: 'Goethe, Father and Son – the son of the great German poet, Goethe, the Chamberlain Goethe, has just drawn up a diary of his journey through Italy, which Goethe, the father, is about to publish', which Goethe commented on as follows, 'the above (...) we can let stand; it is my wish that you would edit your diaries and would bring them to completion; it would make a pleasant occupation for you'; *WA* IV/48, p. 275.

[655] A figurative allusion to the inn, Zum weißen Schwan, where Zelter often stayed on his visits to the poet; GZ 17 June 1826 and GZ 18 February 1827.

Your journey full of song and honour
Expanded every heart
I too sang up hill, down dale
To lighten toilsome journeys
Now when I am near the end
Recalling distant joys
May you feel my soul
Greet you with a blessing!

## 537. Goethe

Weimar, 23 February 1831

*In Memoriam – in Friendship and Sympathy*

My son was travelling to recover his health.[656] His first letters from beyond the Alps[657] were a great comfort and a delight to me; he had seen and visited with real, living sympathy Milan and Lombardy with its fertile fields and glorious lakes,[658] returning there after he had been to Venice. The unbroken narrative of his diary bore witness to his open, unclouded views of nature and of art, and he was happy in applying and increasing the wide-ranging knowledge he had formerly acquired. So it continued up to Genoa where, to his delight, he met up with an old friend Sterling,[659] through whom I had been made acquainted with Lord Byron. At that

---

[656] August von Goethe left Weimar on 22 April 1830, accompanied by Eckermann; in his first letter to Ottilie from Milan on 13 May he gave a frank account of his desolate, physical and psychological condition: 'I was so ill leaving Weimar that I didn't believe I would reach Frankfurt alive (…) it was a choice between an outing (…) to the cemetery or into the wide world.' In his letters to August, Goethe himself expressed the hope 'that your physical and mental health will greatly improve'; 5 July 1830, *WA* IV/47, pp. 130–32; after the news of August von Goethe's death reached Weimar, Goethe's comment spread that he had already despaired for his son when August left Weimar; *Gespräche*, vol. III/2, p. 676.

[657] On 11 May following his arrival in Milan on the evening of 10 May; from Milan on 30 May and 2 June; from Venice on 10 and 21 June.

[658] Chancellor von Müller reported on 8 June 1831, 'communication of the travel route of his son to Lake Como and Lake Maggiore'; Renate Grumach (ed.), *Kanzler Friedrich von Müller: Unterhaltungen mit Goethe* (Munich: Beck, reprint 1982), p. 194.

[659] Charles Sterling (1804–80), son of James Sterling, the English consul in Genoa, had, as bearer of Goethe's panegyric *An Lord Byron*, 'forced a way to a closer relationship with the highly acclaimed Lord Byron'; Goethe to Sterling, 13 March 1824, *WA* IV/38, p. 79. Sterling, whose friendship with August had not been destroyed by his open love affair with Ottilie von Goethe in 1824, looked after August following his accident in La Spezia and during his fatal illness in Rome.

point he parted with Dr Eckermann, who had accompanied him so far and now returned to Germany.[660]

The fracture of his collarbone, which unhappily occurred when he was on his way from Genoa to Spezzia,[661] kept him there nearly four weeks, but even this accident, and a skin disease that attacked him at the same time and was also very troublesome in the great heat, he endured manfully and with good humour. He continued writing his diary and did not leave the place until he had seen all the surrounding countryside and even visited the quarantine buildings.[662] He knew how to make the very best of his short stay in Carrara[663] and his longer visit to Florence,[664] always paying logical attention to things. His diary might serve as a guide to any like-minded person.

After leaving Livorno by steamboat and encountering a heavy storm, he landed in Naples on a day of festivities. There he found the able artist Zahn,[665] who developed a warm relationship with us during his stay in Germany. He received

---

[660] Eckermann reported from Genoa on 12 September 1830, 'It was Sunday morning 25 July at 4 a.m. when we embraced each other in farewell on the streets of Genoa.' For Eckermann's reasons for cutting short the journey, completely explained only to Goethe himself; see *Gespräche*, pp. 496–509. Eduard Castle records the most important travel dates (also for August's winter journey) in the volume of commentary for his edition of the *Gespräche* (Berlin, 1916), p. 202f.

[661] On 27 July August wrote to Goethe from La Spezia, 'Monday 26 July we left at 2 a.m. in order to benefit from the coolness; I dozed a little, and then [the carriage] overturned and unfortunately I felt that I had broken my left collar bone (...) naturally I developed a fever from the wound and I have to be patient'; *WA* IV/47, pp. 204–205.

[662] There were isolation wards for the protection from epidemics in Italian ports and in the most important borders even in the sixteenth century and also in La Spezia, in one of Italy's largest natural ports; see Goethe's father's account about his internment in Palmanova in the preface to his *Viaggio per Italia* (1740; reproduced as Johann Caspar Goethe, *Reise durch Italien im Jahre 1740*, trans. Albert Meier (Munich: Deutscher Taschenbuch Verlag, 1986, reprint 1999) and Ludwig Schudt, *Italienreisende im 17. und 18. Jahrhundert* (Vienna & Munich, 1958), p. 159. The quarantine practice, which was already reduced in the nineteenth century, was revived again in La Spezia in 1829 when the Prussian General Carl von Müffling was interned there on his return journey after the peace talks at Adrianopolis, which was a reason for August von Goethe to explore the area; see Goethe's letter to Ernst August von Gersdorff, 3 September 1830, *WA* IV/47, pp .451–2.

[663] On 19 August.

[664] From 23 August to 3 September.

[665] The archaeologist Wilhelm Zahn, professor at the Berliner Kunstakademie from 1829, was in Weimar from 7 to 15 September after one of his many Italian journeys and had brought Goethe drawings and copies of the excavations in Pompeii. Goethe had remained in correspondence with him since that time, occupied himself with this information and following Zahn's most recent visit (from 13 to 16 March 1830), Goethe published an extensive review of the wall decorations, *Die schönsten Ornamente und merkwürdigsten Gemälde aus Pompeii, Herculaneum and Stabiae*; *MA* 18.2, p. 297. August met Zahn in Pompeii on 7 October at the uncovering of a villa which he named *Casa di Goethe* after

him in the most friendly way and now proved himself to be a most desirable guide and assistant.

His letters from this place, however, I must confess did not altogether satisfy me; they showed me a certain haste, an unhealthy state of exaltation, although, with a view to recording his careful observations, he retained a certain equilibrium in himself. He felt quite at home in Pompeii; his thoughts, observations, and activities in that city show that he was cheerful, even in high spirits.

A quick journey to Rome[666] did not calm his already overwrought disposition, and he only seems to have enjoyed, with a kind a feverish haste, the honourable and friendly reception given him by the German people and distinguished artists residing here.[667] After a few days he was carried to his rest near the Pyramid of Cestius,[668] in the place his father used to long for in poetic dreams before he was born.[669] Perhaps in future days his diaries will give us an opportunity of reviving

---

August's death (today: Casa del Fauno), and in which he discovered the so-called Alexander mosaic.

[666] From 15 to 16 October

[667] Named in Goethe's letter of thanks to Georg August Christian Kestner on 27 December 1830: the Prussian diplomat and archaeologist Carl von Bunsen, the Saxon legate, painter and art historian Ernst Zacharias Platner, the Danish sculptor Bertel Thorvaldsen and the Weimar painter Friedrich Preller. In his letter to Kestner on 16 November 1830, Chancellor von Müller extended Goethe's thanks to the painter Rudoph Meyer from Dresden 'for heartfelt sympathy and care'.

[668] On the night of 26/27 October 1830 in Kestner's house (Via di Porta Pinciana 17) August von Goethe died of a stroke as the result of pox which didn't break out visibly; see Kestner's letter to Weimar on 28 October, following the post-mortem; *GJb* 1956, pp. 180–89. August was buried on 29 October in the Protestant cemetery beside the Cestius Pyramid in Rome. The grave is marked with the words: 'Son of Goethe, preceding the father, died at the age of 40/1830' and with a bronze relief by Thorvaldsen (a circular relief containing a profile of August's head).

[669] Goethe is referring to the closing verse of the seventh poem in his Roman Elegies: 'Let me stay here, Jupiter, and let Hermes lead me quickly down, past Cestius' pyramid, to the underworld'; see also Goethe's letter to Fritz von Stein from Rome on 16 February 1788: 'You wrote recently of the grave of Miss Gore in Rome. Some evenings ago when I was melancholic I drew mine by Cestius's pyramid'; see Goethe's drawings, Gerhard Femmel (ed.), *Corpus der Goethezeichnungen* vols 1–7 (Leipzig: E.A. Seemann, 1958–73; Munich, reprint 1972–81). See also his second Roman visit in the *Italian journey* on 22 February, where he writes, 'If in the meantime I am laid to rest next to the pyramid, these two poems ['Hans Sachsens poetische Sendung' and 'Auf Miedings Tod'] can serve as my biographical data and funeral oration.'

and recommending to sympathetic friends the memory of this special young man.[670]

And so, over graves and onwards!<br>Goethe

### 538. Zelter

Berlin, End of February to 5 March 1831

Thank you for sending those two glorious little poems, which, across a gap of 60 years, carry a double meaning, revealing two active living individuals. Our lady is about a year younger than you and throughout her long career as an artist has retained her special characteristics, independence and individuality. She wrote to me two years ago to tell me that she was thinking of writing her biography, as people knew one side of her and by no means the right side – which we now await. To the very end she proved capable of nobly ignoring the original source of her many sorrows, and that was her husband, the most promiscuous of all Greeks.

She came to us from Leipzig, as Mdlle Schmeling, in the year 1771 and made her debut in Hasse's *Piramo e Tisbo* with Concialini, to the admiration of the king, who would hardly listen to her before, because presumably her paternal name sounded so typically German to him. From that time until 1773 she sang here in the festival operas: *Britannico, Ifigenia, Merope*. Then she fell in love with Mara, a violoncello player and Ganymed to Prince Henry (the brother of the king), and as neither of these gentlemen would permit a marriage between Berlin and Rheinsberg, the lovers eloped without permission. They were caught and Mara was transferred to a regiment at Cüstrin, where he was obliged to play a fife in the band. Mdlle Schmeling was reappointed for life. Mara came back to Berlin and was allowed to marry her. From December 1773 onwards she sang in the following festival operas as Madame Mara: 1. *Arminio*; 2. *Demofoonte*; 3. *Europa galante*; 4. *Parthenope*; 5. *Attilio Regolo*; 6. *Orfeo*; 7. *Angelica e Medoro*; 8. *Cleofide*; 9. *Artemisia*; 10. *Rodelinda*.

In 1779 there was no festival on account of the Bavarian War of Succession and in the following year 1780, after a relaunch of the opera *Rodelinda*, man and wife secretly took flight for the second time. Once again they were taken into custody, but the king ordered them to be let go because, even at a high price to himself, he wanted to dismiss the husband. We have written records of this, but our friend declines to recognize it and it is quite conceivable that she could complain

---

[670] August's travel record, collected in two folio-fascicles, entitled 'August von Goethe. Tagebuch einer Reise nach Süden (1830)' and 'Separat-Faszikel zu dem Tagebuch auf einer Reise Augusts von Goethe nach Süden (1830)' (GSA 28/354), were published by Gabriele Radecke and Andreas Bayer (eds), *August von Goethes Tagebuch auf einer Reise nach Süden 1830* (Munich: Carl Hanser Verlag, 1999, r. dtv 2003).

of force. The widespread acclaim she received began with her appearance in the opera of *Britannico* as Agrippina, where she sang the aria 'Mi paventi il figlio indegno!', addressing someone behind the scenes with a voice of thunder transposed into maternal femininity. I cried floods of bitter tears every time I heard her perform. The aria is a true bravura aria of those days; it was as if a thousand nightingales cried for vengeance. In all tragic parts she looked a foot taller. I have heard nothing grander than her Queen Rodelinda. Connoisseurs blamed her for being too composed in passionate roles. 'What!' she exclaimed, 'am I to sing with my hands and legs? I am a singer; what I can't do with my voice, I will not perform.' The relations between such a person and her husband were a subject of general concern.[671] [...]

I don't say this for the pleasure of being unkind, although Mara was no great friend of mine, but in defence of the great king, who got as little praise for this as for the Müller-Arnold trial, since one does not praise the right thing, and, indeed, would rather not know what the right thing is. There was a good deal besides: beautiful Rheinsberg, close to the Mecklenburg country, was a nest of smugglers, whom, since they were under the favourite's protection, one who valued his life dared to disturb. However, the king knew exactly where the smuggler's thread began, which through the Court carriages of Rheinsberg it unraveled itself as far as Berlin. Mara ended his days here in complete depravity, although his wife never really left him. I once confessed to her my admiration of her noble behaviour towards him, whereupon she remarked, 'But you must own, he was the most handsome man you could behold.' Reichardt, too, had constant arguments with him because Mara wanted to get involved in the Königliche Kapelle. Once the king let him sleep all through the entire festival in the guardhouse on the plank beds, where the ordinary soldiers were allowed to have their fun with him. That made Reichardt feel in a strong position, and now as a young patronized Kapellmeister he wrote many letters of complaint to the king about the senior musicians. Thereupon the king said, 'I thought I had freed myself from the opera but now I have the same problem as well as another fool.' Had Reichardt thrown Mara into the river Spree, he would have been punished, but it would have been better for him in the end. Such was the king whom he had vexed. I have begun to gossip. Forgive me, these are common topics, but I cannot forget them [...]

I do not know whether I told you that it was the eldest Schmeling who denounced me as a composer to my father. In the evening my father used to join a select circle of citizens –clergymen, musicians, and so on – to converse over beer and tobacco. On one occasion, when they were reading the newspaper, they came across the announcement for one of my compositions – I think it was the Pianoforte Variations on an air of Cherubino's in Beaumarchais' *Figaro*. My father said it was the first time he had ever found mention of his own name unconnected with himself, at which point Schmeling replied, 'It is your son, too, whom I know.'

---

[671] The story of Herr Mara's refusal to play which follows is already related in ZG 20 to 23 March 1824.

The following day at dinner my father asked me what that meant and whether I knew the man. 'Oh, yes,' I answered, 'and you, dear father, also know him.' 'Then it is you they are acclaiming. Take care that they praise your drawing and geometry', which as far as I know, never happened.

It would surprise me if Hummel is familiar with Hasse's *Santa Elana al Calvario*.[672] These spiritual dramas (which gave rise to the opera) are now overshadowed by the cantata. The cantata belongs to chamber music but the oratorio, even if it is not part of the liturgy, belongs to the church, like the musical vespers and so on. Hasse composed two settings of this oratorio by Metastasio – one for Dresden and the second for Vienna. Possibly what you heard in Leipzig in 1771 was the first setting. I was lucky enough to come across the arrangement for Vienna just as you discovered your [Annibale] Caracci;[673] I got it from distinguished connoisseurs, for people imagine one is better than the other, because it is the other. Hasse wrote about a hundred operas, if not more, quite apart from his sacred compositions. Each of his works contains powerful passages, such as only a German genius educated in the better times of Italy could compose. In spirit, energy, grace and productivity he surpassed people such as Leo, Durante, Vinci, and Pergolosi, as well as the master, Alexander Scarlatti, whom he acclaimed. If you cast aside the Italian mannerisms universally adopted in those days, you have an original work in all its German power and glory. Besides that, he was a universal favourite, so that, having full confidence, both in the world and in himself, he could give the world what it wished and at the same time slip in what is really his own; the result being that, too easily accepted, he is not properly appreciated himself [...]

What you write about our August is lovely for me to read, for in answer to repeated questions, I boldly ventured, as is my wont, to give the same answer, founded on your earlier letters, and daily and yearly records; Felix's letters from home, too, agree beautifully with your account.[674] That fine fellow has always given me pleasure. Art goes on crutches in Italy. Outsiders dominate it intentionally or unintentionally; still the Italians are industrious and if they stay at sea, there will be good sailing weather again. [...]

Our Scotsman Müller keeps me busy. First I must prepare myself in the basics. He has already composed a large sonata and other such works but knows neither the ABC nor the ten commandments of music, and since he wants to, we have almost started from the beginning and he is always surprised at the basics. However, he doesn't play badly, is with me daily and appears to be at ease with my family. Since there is music here every day and he lives relatively close by, it is also easy

---

[672] This refers to Goethe's idea that Hummel might use a motif from Hasse's oratorio *Santa Elena al Calvario* in Hummel's setting of stanza one of Goethe's occasional poem for Gertrud Elizabeth Mara, to evoke the memory of the performance in Leipzig in 1767 which Goethe's verse commemorates.

[673] Annibale Caracci (1560–1609).

[674] Zelter is referring to Goethe's *Italienische Reise*; a letter from Felix to Zelter from Rome from January or February 1831 has not been handed down.

enough for him. I will close for now; I hear my students coming. [...] At midday I will be with Prince Radziwill, who is probably preoccupied with his *Faust*.

### 539. Goethe

Weimar, 9 March 1831

[...] Commend me to His Highness Prince Radziwill most warmly.[675] Do let me know also whether *Faust* gradually proves to be more harmonious in these discordant times.[676] [...]

### 540. Zelter

Berlin, 13 to 14 March 1831

[...] Princess Amalia once let me see her collection of music manuscripts[677] – the titles – through a glass cabinet. Then she took out a work, held it in her hands, turned over the pages and let me look through it. As I took hold of it, I took the folio volume out of her hands. She stepped back and made eyes as big as carriage wheels: they were the eyes of her great brother. If I had already known Homer at the time, she would have been my oxen-eyed goddess. In short, whoever wanted to learn something here at that time was not allowed if he refused to clean stalls, to wait on children and to chew the rinds which the Lords were not able to bite. If I look at the striving of the contemporary young art world which, with all its money and facilities, only political jokes are produced in turbulent times – which the Sultan, the prince of all believers and Rothschild, the believer of all princes are – there is little hope of the precious collection having an educational function for our time.

Prince Radziwill's *Faust* moves forward slowly. [...] I want to go quietly about my Easter music and see what I can do well with my people. Let time bring what it has and what it costs must be paid, and with that – it is not much but enough for today.

---

[675] Radziwill had enquired about the latest edition of Diderot's works, presumably *Mémoires, correspondance et ouvrages inédits de Diderot, publiés d'après les manuscripts confiés, en mourant, par l'auteur a Grimm*, which appeared in 1830 and 1831 but did not contain Diderot's *Neveu de Rameau*.

[676] The completion of Radziwill's setting of Goethe's *Faust*.

[677] For a description of the music collection of Princess Anna Amalia of Prussia; see Eva Renate Blechschmidt, *Die Amalienbibliothek. Musikbibliothek der Prinzessin Anna Amalie von Preußen (1723–1787). Historische Einordnung und Katalog mit Hinweisen auf die Schreiber der Handschriften* (Berlin: Berlin Studien zur Musikwissenschaft, 1965).

## 541. Goethe

Weimar, 31 March 1831

First of all I must tell you that I have received a delightful, detailed letter from Felix, dated Rome, 5 March, which portrays a clear picture of that exceptional young man.[678] His parents and friends in Berlin will no doubt receive similar accounts, reported with the same controlled freedom. There is nothing to be concerned about there; the fine swimming-jacket of his talent will carry him safely through the waves and breakers of the dreaded barbarism.

Now, you will remember well that I have always passionately adopted the cause of the minor third,[679] and was angry that you theoretical music fellows would not allow it to be a given of nature. Of course a string made of gut or wire is not so precious that nature should exclusively confide her harmonies to it alone. Man is worth more and nature has awarded him the minor third to enable him to express an undefinable yearning with intimate pleasure. Man belongs to nature, and he is the one who can take up into himself, control and modify the most subtle connections of all the elementary phenomena. Chemists need the animal organism as a reagent and shall we continue to hold onto mechanically definable relations of sound, while we are driving the noblest of gifts out of nature into the realm of arbitrary and artificial laws? Forgive me. My interest in the subject has been excited lately and above all I would like to let you know where I wilfully remain and why [...]

## 542. Zelter

Berlin, 6 April 1831

Spontini, who is singing your praises, let me know immediately that you are in good form. He is going to send you his *Athéniennes*;[680] you have promised him

---

[678] Felix Mendelssohn's letter to Goethe from Rome on 5 March 1831 predominantly describes the impression which the plastic arts – especially Titian – made on him; he also records the election of the pope and the carnival which followed immediately after it but was suppressed by military for fear of revolutionary activies in the wake of the Paris July revolution (*GJb* 12, 1891, pp. 85–93். The arrival of Felix's letter is recorded in Goethe's diary on 22 March 1831; *WA* III/3, pp.50–51; on the same day Eckermann records Goethe reading Felix's letter to him and paraphrases the contents; Eckermann, p. 503.

[679] GZ 22 June 1808.

[680] On the occasion of Spontini's third visit to Weimar, Goethe recorded in his diary: 'Coming from Paris, Spontini reports on his new opera which he is planning with Jouy. Promised to send the libretto'; Spontini sent Goethe Jouy's libretto – through Doris Zelter – for the planned opera *Les Athéniennes* at the beginning of January 1832.

good advice, which I hope will meet with an equally good reception. My Easter performances[681] are behind me and it is curious that I know nothing at all to write in a time when the world is in such flux and many must be in the same position. [...] My Scotsman, Müller,[682] is a good, true soul and very industrious because I have him working flat out. He gradually sees the virtuoso phenomenon for what it is and is working at becoming a very thorough teacher. [...] he is often in my house and so he can visit freely all the good concerts.

[...] I have heard Beethoven's *Fidelio* again, with great pleasure.[683] The composer has been admirably successful, precisely in those parts where the poem is far too weak; he has breathed such life into one sad, dreary scene in particular, that I marvel again and again when I hear it. This is the advantage that distinguishes genius: it insults and reconciles, it wounds and heals; one must go along with it; there is no use stopping and loitering.

### 543. Zelter

Berlin, 14 April 1831

Recently I attended a performance of *Der Gott und die Bajadere*, a new opera by Scribe, with music, songs and ballet by Auber[684] [...] The music is not to be despised, and contains many good passages though it is much criticized, and so am I, for trying to discover a good thread which runs through it. On the other hand, Madame Romain,[685] the Bajadere elect, was, despite some disapproval, incessantly applauded. She bared her not altogether attractive body for groping hands.

Your enthusiasm in defending the minor third is admirable.[686] At some point I must have expressed myself ineptly if not incorrectly. The minor third is contained

---

[681] Bach's *St Matthew Passion* was performed by the Sing-Akademie on Palm Sunday, 27 March 1831 and Graun's *Der Tod Jesu* was performed on Good Friday, 1 April 1831; see *AMZ* 33 (1831), no 17, 27 April, column 280f.

[682] ZG 19 February 1831.

[683] On 26 March 1831 in the Königliches Opernhaus with Wilhelmine Schroeder-Devrient as Leonore; *AMZ* 33 (1831), no. 17, 27 April, column 279.

[684] Opera with ballet and mime by Daniel François Espirit Auber (libretto by Eugène Scribe, German adaptation by Karl August von Lichtenstein); Berlin premiere on 8 April 1831; see *AMZ* 33 (1831), no. 22, 1 June, columns 359–61. Whether Zelter attended the premiere or the second performance on 12 April is unclear from this letter.

[685] Angélique Robert née Mees-Saint Romain danced the role of Zoloé, one of the three Bajaderes.

[686] For the following very condensed and unclear summary of the case of the minor third, Zelter gives various derivative ideas which had been discussed in his day: 1. The minor third can appear as the upper third of the major chord between the 5th and 6th partials of the overtone series. The term 'mediant' is used here in a broad sense to indicate the third

even in the upper part of the harmonic triad, although not as the third of the fundamental tone but rather [as the third] of the mediant. Against this the minor third as such lives and sounds along in the fifth below[687] of the harmonic triad, from which it can be deduced that nature itself demands that the minor key be in command and that the triad with a major third [with a minor third above it] is the dominant harmony, the true leading chord for the minor key. That the lowest note of a triad *lies in the middle* and above it that of the major third, while under it the minor third sounds along[688] was observed by Rameau and became the basis of his theory of [musical] sound, which admittedly did not go unchallenged. Meanwhile we must all follow nature, whether we want to or not.

Your honest, sympathetic interest in my music is ever present with me, so that I think of you as one of our audience, especially when everything is well rehearsed and comes off well. Our late cathedral organist, Schale,[689] Graun's most devoted worshipper, told me as far back as 36 years ago, that he wished his departed friend, Graun, could have heard our performances of his music. I need not feel ashamed of

---

of the tonic key, which in the harmonic series does not produce a minor third. 2. In the fictitious 'undertone' series, which was not derived from Rameau's ideas but developed through contemporary discussions, the minor chord is symmetrical to the major chord of the overtone series [if you consider the major chord as rising and the minor chord as descending from the same note. Starting from the same note, 'C', for example, the major chord would ascend by a major third (C–E) followed by a minor third (E–G) giving the chord of C major, whereas the minor chord would descend by a major third (C–A flat) followed by a minor third (A flat–F) giving the chord of F minor]. Since the sense of cadence is given by the descending fifth [in the bass], the major triad of the overtone series would be on the fifth degree of the minor key. 3. The contradictory remark that 'the lowest note of a triad lies in the middle' presumably arises from the double derivation of the minor chord from the keynote in the middle, which is, in this configuration, the source of the major chord (rising) and the minor chord (descending). These three derivations have their roots in Rameau, though not only in his groundbreaking theory of sound, *Traité d l'harmonie réduite à ses principes naturels* (Paris, 1722). It is debatable whether or not Zelter knew this work in the original. His brief summary points to d'Alembert's synopsis of Rameau's ideas in *Systematische Einleitung in die Musikalische Setzkunst nach den Lehrsätzen des Herrn Rameau* which had been translated into German by Friedrich Wilhelm Marpurg (Leipzig: Breitkopf, 1757) and which had been responsible for the dissemination of Rameau's ideas throughout Germany.

[687] Zelter probably means that when the major triad is considered from the top down, for example in a C major triad read as G, E, C, the minor third G to E would come first and consequently be in command.

[688] Zelter appears to mean that the fundamental of the harmonic series that is related to the triad is in the middle, for example C in the middle, with E above (a major third higher) and A below (a minor third lower).

[689] Christian Friedrich Schale (1713–1800), composer, cellist, member of the Königliche Kapelle in Berlin from 1763 and cathedral organist; Zelter mentions him in his autobiography; see Schottländer, *Carl Friedrich Zelters Darstellungen seines Lebens*, p. 110f.

that, when I have already earned nearly twenty thousand thalers from this work,[690] which have been gobbled up. Who knows how else I would have been forced to earn the money? [...]

Yesterday I visited Prince Radziwill, who warmly returns your greetings. [...] Dr Seebeck has sent me your two poems for the birthday celebration of our old friend Mara;[691] they were printed in Reval with another verse by a local poet. I suppose you have received a copy.

### 544. Zelter

Berlin, 19 April 1831

The good Dr Müller from Bremen, who in 1814 introduced us to his dear little daughter, who you wanted to pair off with one of our theologians, has just sent me his *Einleitungen in die Wissenschaft der Tonkunst*[692] in two sizable octavo volumes and complains bitterly that, despite his request, I shared nothing historical with him about my artistic life. Obviously I should have answered him. The truth is that I forgot to and now when I see his book I don't regret it, since I must consider his introduction a shambles. He finds the current state of music to be of the highest standards. His knowledge of the history of music is inept and his criticisms risible: salon gossip that we hear everyday after sitting through an opera or concert. The men he sets store by are Rochlitz, the two Webers,[693] Nägeli,[694] and all those who have a lot to say. But it is a book for which I will always have a certain respect because I am not capable of writing such a book. Probably he has sent it to you and so you yourself might like to look into it.[695]

Yesterday we heard an extraordinarily good performance here of Beethoven's oratorio *Christus am Ölberge*, conducted by Moeser.[696] The work appears to be

---

[690] Graun's Passion *Der Tod Jesu*.

[691] A letter from Thomas Johann Seebeck to Zelter has not been handed down; the poems were published for the first time in *WA* I 5/2, p. 190.

[692] A letter from the music writer Wilhelm Christian Müller has not been handed down; the enclosed work is *Ästhetisch-historische Einleitungen in die Wissenschaft der Tonkunst. Versuch einer Ästhetik der Tonkunst* (2 vols, Leipzig, 1830).

[693] Jacob *Gottfried* Weber (1779–1839) and probably Friedrich *Dionys* Weber (1766–1842), both of whom were known for their music theoretical works.

[694] Hans Georg Nägeli (1773–1836), Swiss composer and music educationalist.

[695] Müller's book is not in Goethe's library.

[696] The work was performed on 18 April 1831 as part of a Beethoven (memorial) festival in the hall of the English house organized by Carl Moeser.

a fragment and it seems as if the composer had adapted the text[697] for his own purpose. Here is a sample:

1. In the introduction, a deep, sorrowful, heartfelt prayer of a soul in the keen agony of a fresh grief gradually emerges. The full orchestra is like an overflowing heart, a pulse of superhuman power. I was entranced. After the introduction, Christ sings (upon the Mount of Olives):

> Jehovah, you my Father, O send
> Comfort, power, and strength to me!
> It approaches now, the hour of my sufferings,
> Chosen by me already, before the world
> At your behest, from Chaos did emerge, and so on.

The underlined words, skillfully connected by tremendous artistry, emerge as strong picturesque motifs – something like an exercise in drawing, when between five or more given points chosen at random a beautiful form, or group, has to be limned by the hand of a master. The nonsense contained in the words vanishes, familiar tones appear as if they had never been heard before – it is captivating.

No. 4. The soldiers, who are to seize Jesus, march like regular troops to the attack, and sing, first softly and then louder:

> We have seen Him
> Going to the mountain,
> He cannot escape,
> He awaits Judgement.

The music for the march cannot be commended too highly, and if the Russians have anything like it, God have mercy on their enemies! At last the disciples are aroused, and sing, still half asleep:

> What means the noise?
> How will it fare with us? and so on.

And so a trio begins: Peter wants to attack, Jesus calms him, and a Seraph, who at an early stage sounded like Saul among the prophets, now joins them, each

---

[697] The libretto for Beethoven's oratorio, by Franz Xaver Huber, was possibly influenced by Beethoven and was heavily criticized from the start – a opinion which Beethoven himself later endorsed. The fragmentary nature Zelter notices is probably due to the incomplete presentation in the biblical text. Through the absence of an evangelist, the action was portrayed through the eyes of a sentimentalized Christ-figure; the epic form – on which the whole tradition of oratorio is based – was replaced in favour of the operatic scene.

retaining their own distinct style. Meanwhile, the soldiers, not idle and rather coarse, [sing]:

> Up! Seize the betrayer
> Await here no longer!
> Drag him swiftly to judgement!' And so on.

At that point a concluding chorus of angels resounds, 'Worlds shall sing thanks and praise', and so on.

Even if the work has no style as a whole, everything is dissolved into the most pleasing forms, with such a humane and ethereal effect, that it is like a pleasant summer night's dream. Viewed critically, the work is a fragment, parts of which are missing, and one could dispense with the text. Still one must have it close at hand, if only to convince oneself with surprise of the truth of what Ramler tells me about Graun, connected with *Der Tod Jesu*:[698] 'Only words, my dear Ramler! Only give me words, I will do the rest.' The rest! – isn't that great? [...]


### 545. Goethe

Weimar, 24 April 1831

[...] I have received a very charming handwritten letter from Madame Mara[699] to the effect that the poet deserves all the praise for the beautiful clear way in which he perceived and clearly expressed a connection which spun its invisible threads through many years[700] [...]

A passage in one of your earlier letters, which I came across when rereading them, cast my mind back to the minor third; your last explanation has completely satisfied me, for what exists in nature must after all one day be avowedly taken up in theory and practice.

---

[698] The libretto for Graun's Passion *Der Tod Jesu* was written by Carl Wilhelm Ramler.

[699] The singer Gertrud Elizabeth Mara sent a letter from Reval on 18 March 1831 thanking Goethe for the poem he sent for her birthday: 'My birthday celebration was one, celebrated in a way which was inwardly very pleasing, among dear and benevolent people and marvellously crowned by your friendly acclamation (...) May you, my honoured friend, please accept from me the blessed greetings which you sent and which I so happily received' (GSA 28/598).

[700] Mara had written, 'I gladly recall the time when I was granted [the ability] to delight many people through my singing and with gratitude I recognize that the benevolence of the noblest people accompanies me to the end of my life' (GSA 28/595).

Your friend Ramler,[701] who only requires words in order to make music, reminds me of Telemann with his playbill.[702] Those good people respect neither the value of words, nor the powerful possibilities of their art. Bad thoughts, bad verses they can make use of, and perhaps they prefer these because it enables them to take poetic licence. You have even an admirable sketch of the opportunities, which significant words, even in an absurd connection, afford the musician. [...]

*The Vampyr*[703] has been repeated here; the subject is detestable, but, from what I am told, the piece is very well received as an opera. There we have it: significant situations arranged in an artful succession, and the musician can win great applause. Words, in a coherent, balanced relationship, offer the same result, as you have so often proved in the case of my poems.

## 546. Zelter

Berlin, 10 May 1831

Our Königliches Theater now approaches its so-called 'sour-gherkin time'. Not less than nine important individuals are sick and have left. Madame Milder appeared as Armide and Alceste again;[704] on the day of repentance Spontini performed Handel's *Alexanderfest*[705] and I saw or heard not one of them. [...]

According to his father Felix has arrived in Naples;[706] he has not yet written to me.

I suppose you would like to have my setting of 'Campanella',[707] which I enclose for you in score. The solo singer must set the tempo according to how he feels it

---

[701] Goethe confuses the librettist (Ramler) with the composer (Graun).

[702] Georg Philipp Telemann; this anecdote runs through the correspondence; see ZG 6 April to 7 May 1808; GZ 15 January 1813; ZG 10 to 23 February 1828.

[703] Romantic opera by Heinrich August Marschner (1795–1861), composer, Director of Music in Dresden, Kapellmeister in Hanover. The opera (libretto freely adapted from Byron's tale by Wilhelm August Wohlbrück) was performed in Weimar on 23 April 1831 (see Goethe's diary, WA III/13, pp. 66–7).

[704] The performance of Gluck's opera *Armide* (libretto by Philippe Quinault after Torquato Tasso's *La Gierulsalemme liberata*) was reviewed in *AMZ* 33 (1831), no. 23, 8 June, column 376. Gluck's opera *Alceste* was performed in the Königliches Oper on 1 May 1831 with Anna Milder in the title role; *MA* 20.3, p. 1196.

[705] For reviews of the performance; see the *Spenersche Zeitung* on 26 April 1831 and *AMZ* 33 (1831), no. 23, 8 June, column 378f.; *MA* 20.3, p. 1196.

[706] Felix Mendelssohn had left Rome in April 1831 with the painters Bendemann, Hildebrandt and Karl Sohn, and travelled south to Naples and Pompeii; see the letters from Naples to his sister Rebecca of 13 April, to his family on 20 and 27 April and 17 May, and to his sisters on 28 May 1831.

[707] Goethe had asked Zelter to send his setting of Förster's 'Die Campanelle' for publication in *Chaos*. Zelter, who, as usual, had wanted to play through the work before

and the movement must then be retained to the end. I hate the *chronomètre*[708] and even more the man who is dependent on it. The theorists would drive me wild; they even misled Beethoven into scoring his works with metronome markings, which do not suit the music at all.[709] What can't exist on its own two feet can go to hell. [...]

### 547. Zelter

Berlin, 17 to 21 May 1831

Old Körner[710] died last Friday, and yesterday evening his body was taken to Wöbbelin to be buried alongside his children.[711] There was a great gathering in the house of mourners, tributes were made and sung; he was an active member of the Sing-Akademie.[712] I was not present, and at my time of life I must avoid such emotions. We shall follow soon enough if not via Wöbbelin. [...]

Our opera is rather unhealthy; they are obliged to re-engage retired members and consent to their rather arrogant demands. In addition to her pension Madame Milder is paid 150 thalers for every opera, and for an opera by Spontini she demands 50 Louis d'or because he is responsible for her being pensioned off.[713] Spontini himself told me this.

---

sending it to Goethe, now encloses the score; the enclosed copy has not been handed down; the autograph setting is in Zelter's bequest. Zelter's setting of Förster's poem was published in the second year of *Chaos*, as a supplement to no. 1.

[708] *Chronomètre*; metronome invented by Johann Nepomuk Mälzel of Vienna in 1816.

[709] Beethoven had begun to give metronome markings for his works from 1817. In the *AMZ* 19 (1817), no. 51, 17 December, column 873f, he published additional metronome markings for 'the movements of all Ludwig van Beethoven's symphonies, by the author himself, using Mälzel's metronome markings'. Although Zelter's remarks are typical of attitudes to metronome markings of nineteenth-century composers, later Rudolph Kolisch campaigned to have Beethoven's metronome markings taken seriously.

[710] Christian Gottfried Körner, father of the poet Theodor Körner, died in Berlin on 13 May 1831.

[711] Körner's son, Theodor, died in Rosenow near Gadebusch in Mecklenburg on 26 August 1813 and was buried in Wöbbelin (near Gadebusch); Körner's daughter, the painter Emma Körner, died in 1815.

[712] Körner joined the Sing-Akademie in 1815 – the year of his appointment to the Berlin Ministry of Culture – and remained a member until his death.

[713] Anna Milder, engaged by the Königliches Oper Berlin from 1816, went into retirement in 12 May 1831 – evidently at the instigation of Spontini. For a long time the General Music Director had complained about the number of older singers in the ensemble; according to the minutes for the theatre conference on 22 July 1829, Spontini had stated 'how fundamentally important it is to improve the opera personel, which for the most

Demoiselle Schechner of Munich[714] demands 5,000 thalers per annum, 2,500 as a pension for life and three month's leave every year; in addition she also insists on her own choice of parts and full pay on sick leave. So claims Count Redern,[715] our present Director [...]

Friday. At Prince Radziwill's Quartet yesterday evening and afterwards pleasant conversation. Count Redern and Spontini were also there. They like to talk in this house and I listen. I am much more at home with music. [...]

## 548. Goethe

Weimar, 1 June 1831

Do not fail, my dear friend, to continue sending me from time time a few sheafs from the rich harvest of the outer world to which you are sent,[716] unlike myself who am completely confined to the inner life of my garden hermitage.[717] Let me tell you in one word that I submit to this in order to finish the second part of my *Faust*.[718] It is not easy in the eighty-second year of one's life to represent objectively that which was conceived at the age of 20[719] and to furnish a living skeleton like this with sinews, flesh and skin and cast over the finished work some

---

part, consists of people who are unwell and how absolutely desirable an early replacement for Milder is'; he recommended touring Germany in order to hear singers who had been recommended to him 'who would be able to replace Milder when she was pensioned off'.

[714] Nanette Schechner (1806–60), singer at the Munich Court Theatre; Zelter had heard her when she was in Berlin giving guest performances in 1827.

[715] Count Wilhelm von Redern (1802–83), theatre manager and artistic director of the Königliche Schauspiele in Berlin as successor to Count von Brühl.

[716] Reference to the biblical words of the great harvest, Matthew 9, v. 37–38; Luke 10, v. 2.

[717] In his late years Goethe often uses the image of a hermitage with reference to his own walled garden; see his letters to Reinhard on 28 January 1828 (*WA* IV/43, pp. 265–9) and to Willemer of 2 March 1831 (*WA* IV/48, pp.136–7), to Zelter on 26–29 January 1830 (*WA* IV/46, pp. 221–6) and to Wilhelm von Humboldt on 1 December 1831 (*WA* IV/49, p. 164–7). Mostly this image stands for Goethe's loneliness and seclusion from the world; here it refers to Goethe's endeavour to bring *Faust II* to completion.

[718] Act 5 was 'as good as finished' at the beginning of May and was passed on to Eckermann to read. Work on Act 4 was resumed on 26 June and the fair copy was already complete by 20 July, as reported in a letter to Heinrich Meyer and in his diary on 21 and 22 July.

[719] When Goethe had sketched a plan for *Faust II* cannot be ascertained with any certainty. In *Dichtung und Wahrheit*, Part 2, Book 10, he himself places it in his Strasbourg years: 'I took great care to conceal from him [Herder] my interest in certain subjects which had rooted themselves in me and seemed to be developing gradually. These were *Götz von Berlichingen* and *Faust*.'

additional folds of drapery, so that the whole may be an open riddle to delight mankind forevermore and also to give them something to think about.

Bless you in your musical life, rich in sound. Lately I have had some thoughts about the Cantilena[720] which are very fruitful for me. Perhaps they would be of no use to others; they have had a really beneficial effect on me since they occured to me. I won't say anything to you about it because you have it, have used it and enjoyed it.

## 549. Zelter

Berlin, 29 May to 7 June 1831

3 June: A former student, Teschner of Mageburg, wrote to me from Milan[721] a very satisfactory report about the opera and the ballet and hears the things like a native. That is so comforting as so many don't know what they should be looking for if they are not to be lost in admiration in a country which is so rich in music.

5 June: In Paris a female composer has set *Faust* to music and to complete applause.[722] There's no denying it: the Germans are cruel but compared with the monsters Paris conjures up from the abyss, we are minors, children! [...]

The little pages of drawings to your folksongs,[723] which I still have on my wall before me, are as delightful and fresh as if they lived and moved.

If you can let out some of your thoughts about the Cantilena, then share them with me. They would be well preserved because they, too, belong to the illustrative arts which demand a skilful hand.

---

[720] In a passage of a letter intended for Zelter but never sent, Goethe had already occupied himself with the Cantilena in June 1827. It is conspicuous that he both withholds his plans from Zelter at that time and also informs him this time 'I won't say anything to you about it'.

[721] This letter from Gustav Wilhelm Teschner (1800–1883), a former singing student of Zelter's, has not been handed down.

[722] The opera *Fausto* by Louise Angélique Bertin, which was performed in the Parisian Théâtre Italien on 7 March 1831; the libretto, which had been written in Italian verse in 1830, was performed in French translation without any acknowledgement of the author's name; see Andreas Maier, *Faustlibretti. Geschichte des Fauststoffs auf der europäischen Musikbühne nebst einer lexikalischen Bibliographie der Faustverordnungen* (Frankfurt am Main: Peter Lang, 1990).

[723] ZG 23 to 26 October 1828.

## 550. Goethe

Weimar, 9 June 1831

[...] In the *Revue de Paris*, No. 1, 1 May, in the third issue, there is an extraordinary article on Paganini.[724] It is written by a doctor who knew and treated him for many years; he argues, in a very convincing manner, that the musical talent of that unique man was assisted by the conformation of his body, and by the proportions of his limbs, which helped and even required him to perform what seemed incredible – almost impossible. This leads the rest of us back to our conviction that organic functions bring about the peculiar manifestations of living beings.

## 551. Zelter

Berlin, 10 to 15 June 1831

Have you seen the lithograph of my portrait by Begas in the Leipzig *Musikalische Zeitung* of 1830?[725] Chance gave a hint of sorrow to the left corner of the mouth, which I don't acknowledge [as mine]. On this occasion the editors expressed fine praise of my achievements, which I am glad to hear, and they express the wish that I would erect for the world a worthy memorial to myself through a selection of my best songs. They could have had that long ago, but I could have been looking for it for a long time. I have never been criticized for destroying myself by working on your poems. What they like they can keep and what can't be saved can rest in the bosom of Abraham.

The main topic of conversation is now: *cholera morbus*. [...] I must escape in my own way.[726] There is no other way. I would need a substantial amount of time before I dared to say whether *Sargines* is a good opera or not.[727] Up to this point I had heard it without knowing the libretto and could not enter into it. Paer, productive and instructive as he is, has for a long time been a favourite of singers. He himself is said to have sung his own songs with so much grace that Napoleon, for instance, whom I consider very frank, as he was not in the habit of restraining himself, was delighted with the performance; this kind of thing can often surprise me. So now I have got my hands on the text and am beginning to get some insight.

---

[724] Francesco Bennati, 'Notice physiologique sur Paganini', *Revue de Paris* 26 (1831): 52–60.

[725] Lithograph by Friedrich Krätzschmer with the subtitle 'Dr C.F. Zelter' after the painting by Carl Begas (1830); it was published as the title page of *AMZ* 32 (1830).

[726] Here Zelter means to escape through art.

[727] Zelter's negative appraisal of the opera *Sargines, oder Der Zögling der Liebe* by the Italian composer Ferdinando Paer (1771–1839) was already expressed in his letter of 28 to 30 July from Prague.

15 June: Yesterday when I returned from Potsdam your two letters of 9 June arrived at the same time [...] My Potsdam expedition[728] did not go off too badly and even received more applause than is usual. The mess was execrable. First, in the rehearsal I let them stand where they were used to. Nothing was in its place; everything was muddled up: geese, hens, cows, pigs as they came from pasture in the evening. The best stood apart at the back, the upper-class amateurs in the front. I had a couple from Berlin with me who had to be fitted in. Faces were made at that. The overture had to be repeated three times. 'And there was evening and morning one day'.[729] Then everything went much more smoothly and in the end they were all delighted with themselves. The following day the performance was as sleek as possible, at least without mistakes, and I should not forget to praise the docility and good humour. As many asked whether I was pleased with them, the question followed as to whether they were happy with me. The whole thing was, nevertheless, mysterious. Here and in Potsdam there are perhaps a dozen directors who seldom forget to refer to themselves as such and they are all younger, more skilful and more powerful that I who never bore that title. And people, who are used to giving orders, let themselves be tormented by such a fellow![730] *jam satis!*[731] [...]

I enclose a passage of a letter from Felix,[732] who I imagine is back in Rome right now. His father would not allow him to see Sicily. He may have his reasons, but the father of an obedient son should recognize the limitations of his power. I have gently pointed this out to the old gentleman.

Enclosure

7 May 1831

'Sterne has become a great favourite with me. I remembered that Goethe, when talking about *A Sentimental Journey*, once said that the defiance and despondency of the human heart could not possibly be better expressed, and when I chanced upon the volume accidentally, I thought I should like to make myself acquainted with it. I was delighted the way everything is so clearly and finely observed and expressed. Here I get very little German to read, so I am limited to Goethe's poems which Hauser presented me with, and, by Heaven, there is enough food there for reflection; they are always new. The poems that specially interest me here are those which he evidently wrote in or near Naples, for example 'Alexis and Dora', for I see almost daily before my window how that marvellous poem came into

---

[728] The performance of Haydn's *Creation* by the local Sing-Akademie.
[729] Genesis 1, v. 5; here a passage from Haydn's *Creation*.
[730] Zelter is, of course, referring to himself.
[731] 'Now that's enough!'
[732] Enclosed excerpt (in an unknown hand) from Felix Mendelssohn's letter of 7 May 1831 from Naples to his father in Berlin (GSA 28/1026, no. 470).

being; as happens with all masterpieces, I often think involuntarily and suddenly that it is as if the same thing must have struck me, too, under similar circumstances and that it was only an accident that he expressed it. I maintain that I have actually found the locality of the poem 'Gott segne Dich, junge Frau'.[733] I maintain that I have actually dined with the woman, though naturally she must by this time have become quite an old woman, and the babe at her breast a lusty vine-dresser; there they were both of them. Between Pozzuoli and Bajae lies her house, 'the ruins of a temple', and to Cumæ it is a good three miles. So you can imagine how the poems are renewed for one and how differently and freshly they affect one [on closer acquaintance]. I really cannot speak of Mignon's Song. But seeing that Goethe and Thorwaldsten are alive and Beethoven died only a few years ago – what madness for H to maintain that German art is as dead as a doornail. *Quod non ...*'

## 552. Zelter

Berlin, 18 June 1831

I could support your conviction about the effect of the organism upon man's intellectual nature with an example of my own. Morally, too, it is confirmed by the most remarkable individuals of my personal acquaintance. One might say of old Bach that the pedal was the basic element of the development of his unfathomable intellect, and that without feet he would never have fully reached those intellectual heights. So I fail to understand the strange question which Lessing makes his painter ask, whether Raphael would have been just as great a genius if he had been born without hands?[734] Here is a man (our painter Begas) who can sniff a pinch of tobacco with his arm stretched round the back of his neck. Perhaps such elasticity belongs to a painter; but had I been so endowed, my talent, eagerness, and industry would have made me the best of violin players, for all my instincts drove me to that instrument which I practised unremittingly – and by so doing, brought about the gout in my hand. In spite of that, in earlier days I performed significant music on the violin, both in drawing rooms and churches, and I was able to give successful public performances of Tartini, Benda, Celli, and Corelli's concerti.[735] In a word, in the human organism there dwells a soul which seeks its companion, as you long ago expressed it: to one talent belongs another.

---

[733] Goethe's poem 'Der Wanderer'.

[734] Lessing, *Emilia Galotti*, dialogue between the Prince Hettore Gonzaga and the painter, Conti, Act 1, scene 4.

[735] Violin and viola concerti by Giuseppe Tartini, probably Franz Benda, Antonio Lolli and Arcangelo Corelli.

Finally, after the twentieth performance in the Königsstadtisches Theater, I survived the highly acclaimed magic opera *Lindane* (by Bäuerle).[736] Again, typically Viennese: fantastic, good, even very decent enough to put a serious man in good humour. A slipper-maker celebrated his engagement among close relatives. Before the marriage the bridegroom has to make a journey to a dying relative, who decided to make a bequest to him only in person. The journey passes through an enchanted forest which is governed by a fairy in love and so the bride is worried about the fidelity of her beloved (Spizeder) who in respectable naievity is subjected to all kinds of temptations by the fairies. The charm of the story is genuinely bourgeois, with delightful puns and innocent meetings of a coincidental nature. The music is also good. It is a pastiche of tirades from the best-known operas which are so well unified so as to put many genuine operas to shame. Technical equipment and transformations surpass the expensive Königliche Kapelle by far. What I referred to as decent above is that in this fairy tale the philistinism of the slippered Christian, who consciously remains true to his honour, contains nothing humiliating for his trade. The company work so well together that the comedy is also well played, just as when I saw, with pleasure, your *Die Mitschuldigen* performed here.[737] The director of all this was a Jew and a typical Jew in every way. And that was good! […]

## 553. Zelter

Berlin, 22 to 25 June 1831

Yesterday your letter of the 18th of this month arrived and found me in the best of form. It was the weekly big assembly of the Sing-Akademie.[738] Around half past six the King[739] was announced unexpectedly, not to hear us but rather to see the exhibition of flowers in our big hall. It was not easy to rearrange the society immediately. They positioned themselves in the small hall behind the orangery trees fairly invisibly so that the large hall could appear completely free in the evening sunlight and the King and his wife[740] – surrounded by groups of flowers –

---

[736] *Lindane, oder Der Pantoffelmacher im Feenreich*, a large-scale romantic Zauberspiel in two acts by Adolf Bäuerle, adapted for the Berlin stage by Leopold Bartsch with music arranged by Vinzenz Kugler, premiered on 20 April 1831. Zelter would have presumably attended the performance on 15 June; for reviews see *AMZ* 33 (1831), no. 23, 8 June, column 377f.

[737] On 26 November 1824.

[738] On Tuesday 21 June; at that time all members of the Sing-Akademie gathered to rehearse on Tuesdays.

[739] Friedrich Wilhelm III of Prussia.

[740] Countess Auguste von Harrach, since 1824 Princess Liegnitz, morganatic marriage to Friedrich Wilhelm III.

found themselves alone in a 200-foot circle, to cast a glance over the very rich collection of flowers. The King, who as a rule does not show his favour to social clubs and our Sing-Akademie, couldn't help noticing that our society had vacated the room for him. I mentioned that today was our usual day of gathering and, if he would care to command it, every member of the Sing-Akademie would be prepared to offer him a pleasant performance which would not last more than ten minutes. He was in a hurry as he still wanted to go to Schönhausen[741] in order to wish happy birthday to one of the princesses, the daughter-in-law of Prince Albrecht[742] today, but he wanted to stay to hear it. So I presented the text of a 'Hymnus auf die Sonne'[743] to him and to his wife. At the nod I let the invisible choir be heard which – including soft solo passages – lasted nine minutes. After that I paid my respects, the King rose up, thanked, praised, enquired about the soloists who were outstanding and took leave calmly as if he had time to stay on longer with us.

The thing was so successful for this occassion that I would have to praise the music itself if it had not by chance been mine, because everything was a decision of the moment which turned out well. The King must have felt that I arranged it for him alone, but in truth everything was unprepared – like a gift from God. The members gathered didn't know what happened to them; obedient to a nod without one asking how? why? and the effect brought about general good humour. The King had hardly gone when your letter was brought to me letting me know you are alive and well.

## 554. Goethe

Weimar, 28 June 1831

Your Postdam expedition[744] gives the rest of us reflective people a good opportunity to focus on egoistical anarchy which allows a person to force his way in, where he has no business, to some agreeable post which he cannot properly fill. But after all, this much can be said in praise of anarchy, that once it has a fixed goal in mind, it looks about it for a dictator, and then sees that things are in order.

The advantage that you musicians have over all other artists is that a general universally accepted basis exists for the whole, as well as for the parts, so that

---

[741] Village near Berlin, summer residence of the royal family.

[742] Marianne of Prussia (1810–83), wife of King Friedrich Wilhelm III's son Albrecht, gave birth to a daughter, Charlotte, on 21 June 1831.

[743] Presumably Zelter's setting of 'Hymnus an die Sonne' by Christoph August Tiedge.

[744] Zelter had been summoned to Potsdam to take the place of a conductor who was too ill to lead a performance of Haydn's oratorio *The Creation*; see ZG 10 to 15 June 1830.

anyone can write a score with the full certainty of getting it performed, whatever it may be. You have your field, your laws, your symbolic language, which everybody must understand. Every musician, even if he had to perform the work of his deadly enemy, would necessarily, on this occasion, give a good rendition. There is no art, scarcely any handicraft even, that can claim it does the same. You can continually celebrate the oldest masters without pedantry, you can delight in the latest composition without heresy and obstruction and even if an individual of your circle produces something avant-garde, ultimately it must relate to the orchestral forces.

And now a word or two about the worthy Felix. Papa was wrong not to allow him to travel to Sicily; the young man will feel dissatisfied and that could have been avoided. In my last letters from Sicily, or the following ones from Naples, there must be some traces of the unpleasant impression I had of that idolized island; I don't wish to dwell on the subject by repeating myself.

The second thing I must tell you, which you must not betray me on, is that the poem 'Der Wanderer' was written in the year 1771, many years before my Italian journey.[745] But this is the advantage of the poet, that he can feel beforehand the value of a thing, which the person who seeks it out in reality loves and enjoys twice as much when he discovers and recognizes it in real life.

### 555. Zelter

Berlin, 27 to 30 June 1831

Your lovely dear letter of 28 June, which I had started to answer, reminds me of a joke during the Potsdam expedition. They had started the only day's rehearsal so late that dusk fell and no one could read anymore. I, too, could no longer make out the score and really we should have stopped. They all pulled themselves together and persevered until the work was finished. On the way out of the church one of them said of me, 'The old fellow must have cat's eyes because I couldn't see a thing!'

---

[745] Goethe's reference to his poem 'Der Wanderer', which had already been written before his Italian journey, namely in 1772. He picks up on a passage in Felix Mendelssohn's letter from Naples on 7 May 1831, passed on by Zelter, where Felix had written that he believed the poem originated 'between Pozzuoli and Bajae'.

## 556. Zelter

Berlin, 29 June to 7 July 1831

[…] Today, 29 June, I have received a letter from Felix, written in Rome on the 16th of this month;[746] I expect it is the last one from there.[747] It contains an account of the Easter ceremonies in the Sistine Chapel during Holy Week. The lad did not let a single note escape him; he looks at the whole historically, without betraying the foreigner and the heretic. It says something for him, that he can grasp the whole in its original form which is now in tatters, and that he can recognize the empty body behind the outward pomp and ceremony.

Your annoyance about idyllic Sicily can only be right; also, nothing is to be garnered there for the musician and I myself would not give up the opportunity to be in Naples and to have seen Palermo […]

In setting your poems to music, I have been inspired to seek out how and where they arose, and as many of my melodies have pleased you, the apple cannot have fallen so very far from the tree. I have had similar good fortune with many different poets. Schiller, Voß, Matthisson, Tieck, Tiedge, and even Klopstock have praised my melodies. When Naumaun's eldest son was born, Countess Eliza commissioned settings, from Himmel, myself and others, of a cradle-song she had written.[748] Naumaun, the child's father, was to choose the song that pleased him most without knowing who had composed it. He said that in the melody that he liked best, he recognized Himmel,[749] his favourite pupil – but that melody was in fact mine.

---

[746] The long letter from Felix Mendelssohn Bartholdy to Zelter is published in *Reisebriefe* (1862), pp. 171–88.

[747] Felix left Rome on 19 June 1831; he travelled through Florence, Genoa, Milan, Switzerland, Munich, Stuttgart, Heidelberg, Frankfurt, Bonn, Liège to Paris, where he remained until April 1832.

[748] The poem 'Wiegenlied für Mutter Naumann' by Elisa von der Recke, composed to mark the birth of Johann Gottlieb Naumann's son, Carl Friedrich (1797); Zelter's setting appeared in volume one of the *Musikalisches Museum* (1800).

[749] The composer Friedrich Heinrich Himmel (1765–1814), composer and pianist, Court Kapellmeister in Berlin.

### 557. Zelter

Berlin, 18 July to 6 or 7 August 1831

[...] Prince Radziwill has just buried his second grown-up son.[750] I have just come from the Catholic church where Mozart's Requiem was sung for him. That [work] does not allow itself to be buried, neither by a bad review[751] nor a moderate performance. What moved me so deeply (besides this Requiem) was the old unison singing of the 'Libera me de morte aeterna' sung by priests around the coffin. I had to kneel down to conceal bitter tears and was afraid to stand up. What is man! What strength does he have!

### 558. Zelter

Berlin, 26 to 27 August 1831

My good students, who have still not got over Riemer's applause and discovered from him that you still have not heard a song powerfully sung from the *Divan*, had made a pact to use the holidays and to serenade you in your garden, until I had to confide in them that you are not in Weimar for your birthday and, in general, would not want to be met anywhere. They wanted to seek you out since they travel and some have to go away. However, I think they should be sensible enough from now on to be satisfied with their signs of good will. [...]

### 559. Zelter

Berlin, 28 to 30 August 1831

[...] A 72-year-old pious (unbaptized) Jewess[752] has just sent me a bottle of Rhine wine from 1873 with the task of consuming it in honour of your well-being. I immediately discovered the effect it had on devout activity because I had just read my morning prayer: as the grey, rising phoenix warns his pupil Achilles to be lenient towards his fellow people and to show forgiveness towards the hated

---

[750] Friedrich Wilhelm Ferdinand August Heinrich Anton *Wladislaus* Radziwill (1811–31).

[751] Zelter is alluding to Gottfried Weber's two published articles in which he contested the authenticity of Mozart's Requiem and which were published in *Cäcilia* in 1825 and 1826.

[752] Her identity has not been established.

Atreids.[753] I found myself suitably moved by it and, after I revived, a canon occurred to me and one gets back into one's stride:

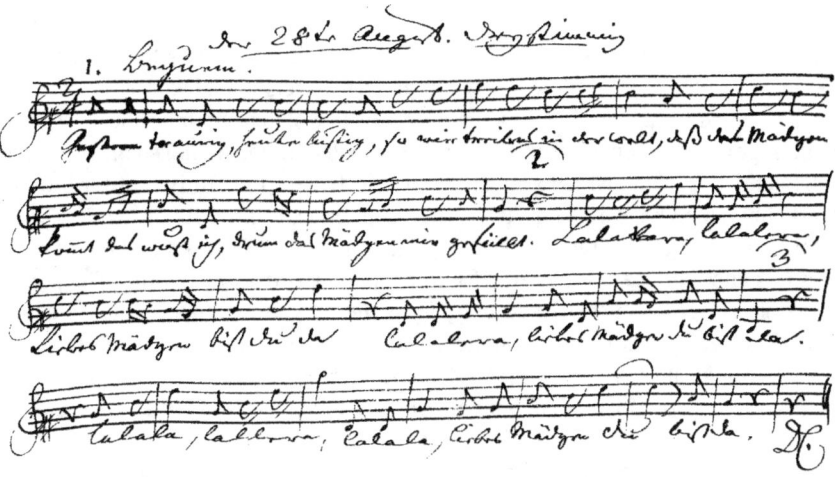

*Nulla dies sine linea.*[754] Given the day it is, it had to be so. The little work could disappear into the new *Chaos*.[755] I couldn't find any other words. If you don't like them, you might like to write new ones to it.

[...] At the Sing-Akademie yesterday evening we began with Fasch's grand 'Gloria in Excelsis Deo', followed by the chorus in 16 parts, 'Laudamus Te, benedicimus Te, adoramus',[756] and so on. Afterwards, as a secret tribute to you,[757] we had old Bach's melodious Motet, 'Singet dem Herrn ein neues Lied, die Gemeine der Heiligen soll Ihn loben'.[758] I knew by the performance that they knew what I meant, and they asked for that great masterpiece over again, and sang it with such reverential joy, in accordance with my previous instruction that old Bach (who was still living when you were born) must have stirred in his grave [...]

---

[753] Homer, *Iliad*, 9.
[754] 'No day without a line.'
[755] By 'the new *Chaos*', Zelter means the second year of the journal beginning in August 1831; Zelter's composition was not printed in this edition.
[756] Presumably from Fasch's *Missa a 16 voci in quattro Cori* (1783–88).
[757] 28 August is Goethe's birthday.
[758] Motet by J.S. Bach, BWV 225.

## 560. Goethe

Weimar, 4 September 1831

For six days, and the best days of the entire summer, I was away from Weimar,[759] having taken the road to Illmenau, where in former years I had worked a lot[760] and hadn't visited for a long time.[761] On a lonely little wooden summer-house,[762] at the highest point of the pine forest, I recognized the inscription of that song, written on 7 September 1783,[763] which you have so tenderly and peacefully sent forth to the world upon the wings of song, 'Über allen Gipfeln ist Ruh'.[764] After so many years I could recognize what remains and what has vanished. Success stood out in relief and was cheering, misfortune was forgotten and its sorrow overcome. The people lived on as before in their own way, from the charcoal-burner to the porcelain manufacturer. Iron was being smelted, and brown coal was brought up from the mines, though it is not in as much demand as before. They were boiling pitch, and collecting soot in small containers that were most artistically and elaborately finished. Hard toilers were bringing up coals to the pit's mouth. Gigantic, primæval trunks of trees had been discovered in the pit, whilst the men were at work; one of these I forgot to show you – it stands in the garden house. [...]

---

[759] From 26 to 31 August 1831; see Goethe's notes to his diary for his sojourn in Illmenau.

[760] For an account of Goethe's work in Illmenau; see Kurt Steenbuck: *Silber und Kupfer aus Illmenau. Ein Bergwerk unter Goethes Leitung, Schriften der Goethe-Gesellschaft* 65 (1995). Hereafter referred to as *SchrGG*.

[761] Goethe's previous visit to Weimar was from 26 August to 2 September 1813, with an excursion to the Gickelhahn.

[762] On the wooden wall of a hunting box on the Gickelhahn near Illmenau; an image is published in: Wolf Segebrecht, *Johann Wolfgang Goethes Gedicht 'Über allen Gipfeln ist Ruh'* (Munich and Vienna: Carl Hanser Verlag, 1978), p. 192.

[763] According to Goethe's diary, the correct date of inception was 6 September 1780.

[764] Zelter's setting of Goethe's poem 'Über allen Gipfeln ist Ruh', entitled 'Ruhe', was composed in February 1814 in Carl Friedrich Zelter, *Fünfzig Lieder für eine Singstimme mit Klavier* ed. Ludwig Landshoff (Mainz, London, New York, Paris and Tokyo: Schott, 1932), p. 9.

The Försters[765] have probably told you of the celebration in Weimar on my birthday;[766] it went off very successfully. The pretty little person[767] whom I was so glad to see at my table made a considerable effect. The ladies declared that her exquisitely tasteful bonnet had much to do with it. [...]

You inquire about *Faust*; Part Two is now complete in itself.[768] For many years I have known perfectly well what I wanted, but only worked out those particular passages that interested me at that time. As a result gaps became evident and these had to be filled in. I firmly resolved to do this before my birthday and so I did. The whole work now lies before me and I only have to correct a few little things. So I shall put a seal on it and then it can add to the weight of the volumes that are to follow, whatever might come of it.[769]

You have seen a wonderful scene or much more a wonderful part of the whole work. Whatever you will have assigned for yourself will appear more entertaining in the context.

Now that these demands are satisfied, new ones immediately press forward from behind *à la queue* as in a baker's shop. I know well what is needed; the future will show what can be done. I have planned far too many projects and in the end I have neither means nor strength to finish them. I dare not even think of *Die Natürliche Tochter*: how could I call to mind the enormity of the task there?

---

[765] Friedrich Förster and his family visited Weimar in August 1831 (see Goethe's diary on 25 August 1831, *WA* III/3, p. 128) and had apparently taken part in the festivities for Goethe's birthday on 28 August 1831.

[766] The Weimar festivities, organized by the citizens of Weimar on 28 August 1831, commenced with the unveiling of David d'Anger's colossal marble bust of Goethe in the Duke's library, the celebrations were framed by the performance of a cantata to a text by Chancellor von Müller, set to music by Hummel, and an address by Riemer. Over two hundred people attended the meal in the town hall held afterwards where Ottilie von Goethe received the various good wishes and honours on behalf of her father-in-law. Though Goethe had escaped from the Weimar festivities, the people of Illmenau would not let his birthday pass unnoticed. Early in the morning they assembled in front of the Lion Inn where he was staying and sang the chorale *Nun danket alle Gott!* In the evening, they performed the miners' comedy mentioned in *Wilhelm Meisters Lehrjahre*.

[767] Laura Förster, who had already visited Goethe in Jena on 27 September 1820; at that time Goethe had described her as 'very pretty' and later described her as Zelter's 'beautiful student' in a letter written on 14 October 1821.

[768] See Goethe's diary on 22 July 1831, where he notes 'Managed to complete the main part. Final draft. Everything filed for fair copy'; it was the same day on which Zelter arrived unexpectedly in Weimar. Any final work on the manuscript must have been completed after Zelter's visit. On 7 September 1831 Goethe wrote to Reinhard, 'I must confirm – but confidentially – that I have succeeded in finishing *Faust. Part Two*'.

[769] Published by Riemer and Eckermann after Goethe's death as *Ausgabe letzter Hand. Nachlaßbände* (final edition. Posthumous volumes).

## 561. Zelter

Berlin, 4 to 5 September 1831

[…] Förster tells me that you were in Illmenau on the day of your birthday.[770] One embarrasses people and afterwards one will still always be grateful. Someone asked me why I didn't go to Weimar for the celebration. I answered, because I would not have wanted to travel any further. You know I am living on good terms with many people. Many have what suits me and what doesn't suit me, and I myself don't exactly make it my profession to please. What I find repulsive I cast aside; what I find attractive I treasure. […] With you it is very different. The friendship is ingrained in me and comfortable and I like everything about you. […] To me you are the one who will live on after his death and if I saw you in person, I would then consider myself departed.

## 562. Zelter

Berlin, 7 to 8 September 1831

Yesterday evening I saw a couple of acts of *Götz von Berlichingen* which were chosen for your birthday.[771] The play remains the same: there isn't a wrong word in it. […] I also know through music: the nearer to perfection, the more painful the wrong note. A young girl with a magnificent voice brazenly carried off the role of George and pleased me most of all. […]

Your experience of the lovely autumn days in Illmenau[772] compensated you sufficiently for the celebration that you were happy for everyone else to enjoy[773] and Förster gave me a good account of it.

What I had imagined, however, to my relief came true. I thought that your contentment with a completed work[774] would bring back the cheerfulness of earlier times for you and inspire you to new production. Your letter is like a garden in blossom through which I frequently wander since yesterday and never have enough. Since I have never seen your wooden hut on the heights of Illmenau, I must be happy to have entered so surely into your loneliness and like a born minor to see the quiet words brought to light from the devices in the rock where they

---

[770] Zelter had not yet received Goethe's letter describing his time in Illmenau; it arrived in Berlin on 7 September.

[771] Goethe's *Götz von Berlichingen* was performed in the Königliches Opernhaus in Berlin on 6 September 1831. The new production was performed for the first time on Goethe's birthday on 28 August 1831.

[772] GZ 4 September 1831.

[773] The Weimar festivities for Goethe's birthday.

[774] Goethe's completion of *Faust II*.

finally rested. Your recognition gives the few notes a value which time cannot take away again, because they recapture the unfathomable – time, place, heart and mind – after so many years. Should I not feel praised when you praise me because, from my anti-polar circumstances[775] to your mountain heights, I am capable of casting a glance in your depths like a miner's light? How fortunate we are that we are doing things of our own when so many thousands, out of sheer boredom, are very busy breaking one another's necks while at the same time talking of peace.

### 563. Zelter

11 to 13 September 1831

[…] The days rush by towards shorter [days], which should also have their good points. Our Sing-Akademie have had to survive two consecutive Requiems in their own ranks. Two members died suddenly;[776] the last of them, Minister of Justice Wollank, diagnosed with Asian cholera, died very suddenly in a few hours. No one within these walls has fallen ill. Public buidings are being fumigated until one is nauseous and weary of it. Here in the house we are just taking care that there is fresh healthy air. Some sensible people follow suit.

[…] One of my young students, Otto Nicolai[777] – this time no relation to that average man[778] – has trained himself to be a very cultivated singer and has set several of your poems to music.[779] I have given him a recommendation to our dear Ottilie,[780] begging her to introduce the little fellow to you. Out of gratitude to me he performs my bagatelles. I acknowledge his efforts because they show me it is not my fault if the songs are not to everyone's taste. Now, if you could find a leisure hour in which to listen to this youth, it would give him joy for rest of his life. […]

---

[775] In his account of Illmenau, Goethe had written he wished 'for nothing more than to see you appreciating the enormous contrast between your external circumstances and this'.

[776] On 27 June 1831 the bass soloist Otto Grell had died and on 5 September Friedrich Wollank, a member of the Sing-Akademie since 1799, died.

[777] Karl *Otto* Ehrenfried Nicolai (1810–49), composer, who studied with Zelter and at the Königliches Institute für Kirchenmusik from 1828 to 1830, later Kapellmeister in Vienna and Berlin. As a member of the Sing-Akademie he sang the part of Jesus in the revival of the *St Matthew Passion* on 27 March 1831.

[778] The Berlin publisher and writer Friedrich Nicolai.

[779] There are very few settings of Goethe's poems by Nicolai before 1831: the four-part choral setting of Goethe's 'Mailied' from the op. 6 Lieder; the duet setting of Goethe's 'Rastlose Liebe', op. 23 and a vocal quartet, op. 9, 'respectfully dedicated to the poet'.

[780] See Ottilie von Goethe's letter to Zelter on 13 September 1831 (GSA 95/I, 8, 5).

## 564. Goethe

Weimar, 17 September 1831

[...] The fools of the day[781] would like to see the nobility abolished, as though it were possible for a man of worth to lose anything by possessing worthy ancestors! Why, I suppose next they will be taking your great-uncle away from you and your descendants. Instead of that they ought to ask God daily and hourly to let all that has stood the test of time be recognized as being legitimate, and that from time to time a creature may be born who shall stamp entire centuries with his name.

One quiet evening I remembered that Cicero had left us a little work called *De Senectute*. For the first time I felt inclined to take it up myself[782] and I found it most charming. As these ancient authors, for the most part, write discursively, it is as if what one understands as a matter of course were rattled off in conversation.[783] He makes the elder Cato speak,[784] and he – if you look into it closely – only gives a list of the excellent people in history 'who have grown old', and describes how well old age worked to their advantage. Then comes, as an example, how unreasonable it is to want to recall anything – even the immediate past. Much else that does not concern me I leave aside, but I must mention how highly he esteems the value, the

---

[781] Presumably Goethe is referring to Saint-Simon, among others, whose protests brought about the abolition of nobility by birth.

[782] Possibly Goethe is referring to works he had read earlier: following a conversation with Riemer on 12 February 1825 about Lucilius, Cicero's *Cato maior de senectute liber*, Marcus Aurelius, among others, Goethe had already borrowed from the Weimar library Cicero's philosophical work *Cato maior de senectute liber* in the German translation by Friedrich Samuel Gottfried Sack (Elise von Keudell, *Goethe als Benutzer der Weimarer Bibliothek. Ein Verzeichnis der von ihm entliehenen Werke* (Weimar: H. Böhlau, 1931, reprint 1982), no. 1597. Hereafter referred to as Keudell.). On the other hand Goethe had as late as 1826 refused to read the treatise, 'About Old Age and its Condition': 'I have read nothing from this treatise (...) because I was of a mind to experience and to know an inevitable human fate when it affected me'.

[783] Goethe is referring to the popular practice of the ancient philosophical writers, who (following Plato's model) presented their themes in fictional conversations, wherby the popular moral philosophy (of Epictetus, Seneca etc.) made use of the discussion through an individual who dealt with a fictitious opponent or, as Cicero preferred (in the manner of Aristotle), the juxtapostition of different opinions in related speeches of the participants; the strict method and abstract language of the tract was consciously avoided and the interests of a wider public was kept alive by way of rhetorical means, quotations, examples and anecdotes.

[784] The main person in the conversation is Marcus Porcius Cato the Elder with the epithet 'Censorius', whom Cicero had presented as an 84-year old. His rigorous stoicism, his strictness and obduracy is tempered in the dialogues; his younger partners in the conversation are Publius Cornelius Scipio Aemilianus 'Africanus' the Younger (185–129 BC) and Gaius Laelius (*c.*190 to 129 BC).

respect, the honour that are bestowed on old age after a life's achievement. This comes freely out of the mouth of a first-rate Roman, who both thinks and speaks so admirably about his ancestors that we cannot amount to much if we remain unaffected by it. [...]

I have decided to bring Felix's most charming letter[785] to light through the *Chaos* when a fitting opportunity presents itself.

Your protégé shall be kindly received.[786] Ottilie knows how to handle the situation so that a stranger, who may not happen to interest me at a particular time, is brought to me in a happy hour. I must take this opportunity to tell [you] that she and the children behave most charmingly; I could elaborate but really there is nothing to report, because something so tender cannot be expressed in words.

I myself have been renewing my friendship with the 24-year-old manuscript[787] from which you have read some passages.[788] I hope one day it will give you a cheerful, and even at your advanced age, an informative hour. In this I am confirmed by the words of the ancient sage, the truth of which I have recently discovered: 'I am ever learning; and only thus do I notice my increasing years.'[789] [...]

---

[785] Felix Mendelssohn Bartholdy's letter to Goethe from Lucerne on 28 August 1831, in which he described his arrival in Switzerland following his Italian journey, a storm in the Bernese Oberland, his visit to a monatery in Engelberg, a performance of Schiller's *Wilhelm Tell* and the completion of his choral setting of Goethe's 'Die erste Walpurgisnacht'; *GJb* 12 (1891): 93–8.

[786] Zelter's student, Otto Nicolai. Nicolai's planned visit to Goethe never took place. In his diary on 18 May 1832, after Zelter's burial, Nicolai writes about his last meeting with his teacher: 'He spoke of Goethe and still said to me, "You see what a stupid thing you did by not going to Weimar in the summer!" (At the time he had given me a letter of introduction to Goethe's daughter-in-law, through which I would have made the acquaintance of the prince among poets). "But the young always believe they have plenty of time." How gladly I would have gone to Weimar in the summer, but money, which had completely run out in Leipzig, did not allow it. I explained to Zelter that it caused me unspeakable regret but I had had no more money for the journey. In keeping with his usual bluntness, he replied, "Alright, then you should have begged!"'; B. Schröder (ed.) *Otto Nicholais Tagebücher* (Leipzig, 1892), p.6.

[787] Goethe alludes to the beginning of the fourth part of his autobiography, *Dichtung und Wahrheit*.

[788] On 23 July 1831, during Zelter's visit to Weimar.

[789] Plutarch, Solon, 31, 7; Goethe was familiar with this through Cicero's *Cato maior*.

### 565. Goethe

Weimar, 4 October 1831

[…] Music, which is your life, is almost completely vanishing from my unpractised senses. […]


### 566. Goethe

Weimar, 5 October 1831

[…] Yesterday I experienced a strange phenomenon. A father who was travelling to Paris brought to me his pianist daughter, who performed contemporary Parisian compositions; the type [of music] was new to me; it demanded great skill of the performer, but is always entertaining; it is a pleasure to follow it and you accept. Since you will certainly know such music, please enlighten me.[790]

---

[790] Friedrich Wieck and his 12-year-old daughter Clara, later wife of Robert Schumann. Of her visit, Goethe wrote in his diary on 1 October 1831: 'A very dexterous little lady, playing piano, led by her father, played for me. They were new Parisian compositions, demanding great skill of the performer, but always entertaining, so you gladly followed [the music]'; *WA* III/13, pp. 148–9. Friedrich Wieck wrote of the visit in his diary, 'On 1 October at 12 noon we had an audience with his Excellency, the 83–year-old Minister Goethe. We found him reading and the servant led us in without further announcement because the day before he had asked us to come and see him at this time. He gave us a friendly reception; Clara had to sit on the sofa next to him. Soon after, his daughter-in-law arrived with her two very precocious-looking children, ages 10 to 12. Clara was then called upon to play, and since the piano stool was too low, Goethe himself fetched a cushion from the anteroom and put it in place for her. She played *La Violetta* by Herz. During her performace, more visitors came and she then played Herz's *Bravour-Variationen*, op. 20. Goethe pronounced very accurately on the compositions and on Clara's playing; he considered the pieces entertaining and piquant in the French manner, and he praised Clara's [ability to] capture this character'; Berthold Litzmann, *Clara Schumann. Ein Künstlerleben. Nach Tagebüchern und Briefen* (3 vols, Leipzig: Breitkopf & Härtel, 1902–8), vol. 1, p. 28f.

## 567. Zelter

Berlin, 9 to 11 October 1831

[...] After the destruction of Troy – I mean the conquest of Paris[791] – the victorious Blücher was received by us at the Sing-Akademie with this song,[792] and he complimented me as a good general, whereby he admitted that he never yet ventured an action with such a mass of attractive women, and that he doubted whether he would succeed; at which point I replied that his good sword was at home everywhere and that he should be certain of his victory over our hearts.

[...] We are far advanced in the perfection of our pianofortes.[793] When comparing our fortepiano with the first made by Silbermann of Strasbourg, we should be convinced that he laid the foundation of a Babylonian building that is the confusion of tongues, the despair of musical sages, who fight like dogs to take it all into their theory. French music may be compared to their politics: it is such a mixture of feminine rambling; their best writers cannot shake themselves free of it. A short time ago I heard *Der Wasserträger*[794] again, a reputable work which I would not criticize. And yet the music in itself, in those parts where it aims at personifying the real earnestness of the libretto, is about as good as a drum covered with human skin – and this is the best work by one of their best composers. I will say nothing about this composer's setting of *Medea*.[795] Punching the air and fights with the mirror; all too much to amount to anything. Whoever finds the confusion of sensations uninspiring should clearly stay away. Grétry[796] is forgotten too quickly; he does not overreach himself but his strength is growing. He lets himself down gently and keeps his wings moving so that he can raise himself again immediately.

---

[791] In March 1814.

[792] Goethe's 'Vorwärts', from *Epimenides*. It will be remembered that Blücher was nicknamed 'General Vorwärts' by his soldiers; ZG 8 to 12 November 1814.

[793] Reflections in connection with Goethe's report of Clara Wieck's virtuoso performance on his Streicher piano.

[794] Opera by Luigi Cherubini performed in Berlin in an adaptation by Gottlieb Heinrich Schmieder after the libretto by Jean Nicholas Bouilly, *Les deux journées, ou le porteur d'eau* (Paris, 1800).

[795] Opera by Luigi Cherubini; libretto by Carl Herklots after François Benoît Hoffmann's *Médée* (Paris 1797).

[796] The French composer André Ernest Modeste Grétry (1741–1813).

## 568. Zelter

Berlin, 15 October 1831

Our Liedertafel is suspended[797] and the money we would have spent is to be given to widows and orphans. The Sing-Akademie also wants to put on a public performance for such a cause in its hall on the 23rd of the month.[798] The cost of official measures [to cope with the cholera outbreak] should amount to 12 million. The King is supposed to have indignantly rejected the suggestion of fencing off the courts in Sansousi and Charlottenburg with the words: you want to turn me into a wren king. You may be more respectful than the cholera, but you are expensive enough.

## 569. Zelter

Berlin, 27 October 1831

The Hamburg Bach[799] had allowed a fugue to be published. Agricola asked him, 'Have you read Marpurg's criticism[800] of your new fugue? He has criticized you

---

[797] On account of the cholera epidemic.

[798] A subscription concert 'for the local poor who have been placed in misery and in desperate straits by the cholera epidemic'. The concert, which included works by Fasch, J.S. Bach, C.P.E Bach, Spohr and Zelter, was held 'at 12 noon so that whole amount without deduction of costs could be used for the intended purpose (...) without hereby wanting to set a limit to the well-known generosity of the Berlin public, the price of an entrance ticket will be fixed at 20 Sgr.'; Announcement in the *Spenersche Zeitung* on 1 October 1831; the *AMZ* reported on the concert, which was not terribly well attended, *AMZ* (1831), no. 46, 16 November, column 762.

[799] Carl Philipp Emanuel Bach (1714–88).

[800] In a fragmentary essay about a letter of C.P.E. Bach's and the polemics between Kirnberger on the one hand and Reichardt and Marpurg on the other side, Zelter wrote: 'Since Bach was both industrious and liked to have his excellent pieces printed, then the broadcasting and recommendation by recognized artists pleased him more that the criticism, which could be no more help to him. Marpurg had strongly criticized Bach's two-part fugue in D minor, at which Bach had said to his former student, 'Shame! Shame! Why hadn't Marpurg written his lovely review before I had finished my fugue? Now I know what it is lacking. As long as I live I intend to write fugues, but none better than I can'; quoted by Heinrich Bellermann, 'Nachtrag zu Kirnbergers Briefen'. In: *AMZ* 7 (1872), pp. 441–4, quote page 443. Bach's only two-part fugue in D minor (H 99) is published in *Friedrich Wilhelm Marpurgs Fugensammlung* (Berlin, 1758), but without criticism. Also in Marpurg's *Abhandlung von der Fuge* (Berlin, 1753/54) there is a very positive analysis of a *Duos in A minor* (H 76). Possibly the the criticism arose from Marpurg's fugal war with Kirnberger, in his *Kritischen Briefen zur Tonkunst*.

very severely.' 'No', said Bach; 'had he told me of his criticism beforehand, I might perhaps have been directed by him; but if he likes his own fugues so much, I cannot see how one of mine could please him.'[...]

A new opera by Scribe and Auber, *Die Liebestrank*,[801] is so desperately weak and empty that the house, on the occasion of the second performance, seemed like a morgue.

On the other hand, the people at the Königstädter Theater have staged another new opera by Rossini, *Das Fräulein am See*,[802] *La donna del lago*, and very nicely too; it is certain to be a success. A Scottish knight named Douglas has promised his beautiful daughter to a Herr Roderick; James V, King of Scotland, is also interested in her, but she, no matter what, is determined to marry a Herr Malcolm Grame. And that could happen anywhere. The text is a wonderful medley of continually repeated, worn-out, recognizable Italian operatic conventions;[803] yet the whole thing is as feasible and agreeable as willing girls. So there you have the opera.

What drew me to it immediately was that you didn't miss having a long, broad, pathetic overture.[804] The opera commences with the action; it has all the distinctive characteristics that enable us immediately to recognize the well-known composer, while at the same time there are very clear signs that he is still developing as a composer. The singers have more that enough to do, and yet they are assisted by the orchestra which Rossini handles as easily as if he were holding a bell in his hand – weaving his instrumentation in as ingeniously as if it were a natural growth. There is much to find fault with too, but he who concentrates on that is in danger of missing the most daring and delicate passages, as they fly by very quickly. The chorus often enters with such brilliance and force that for a moment one feels older by a few thousand years. The scene is, as I said before, in Scotland, and at times it felt as if I was transported from the King's Bridge in Berlin to a solemn Highland region, although the composer has not bothered to search out a single national Scottish song.

I mentioned to you before that I had taken another turn at the Schiller correspondence. Two letters, numbered 389 and 390,[805] have set me thinking again.

---

[801] Opera by Daniel François Espirit Auber (libretto by Eugène Scribe, *La philtre*, German adaptation by Karl August von Lichtenstein), premiered in Berlin on 15 October 1831 in the Königliches Opernhaus; see *AMZ* 33 (1831), no. 46, 16 November, column 760.

[802] Goethe lightly edited Zelter's remarks on Rossini's opera *Das Fräulein am See* and on the Königstädtisches Theater and had them published in Ottilie von Goethe's journal *Chaos*.

[803] Gems from the text of this opera are to be found in a very humorous article, 'With Some Librettists' in the *Cornhill Magazine* for November 1885.

[804] Like all his Neapolitan operas, Rossini begins *La donna del lago* without an overture.

[805] Schiller's letter to Goethe on 12 December 1797, in which he, prompted by work on *Wallenstein*, speaks about 'the tragic' in literature; Goethe's replied on 13 December.

Schiller writes, 'Can it really be that tragedy doesn't suit your nature because of its pathetic force?' And later, 'A certain reckoning on the spectators is a hindrance to you and perhaps for that very reason you are less suited to being a writer of tragedy because you are completely created to be a poet in the generic sense. Anyhow I see in you all the poetic specialities of a writer of tragedy in fullest measure and if, bearing this in mind, you are really unable to write a perfectly genuine tragedy,[806] the reason must lie in the non-poetical requirements.' For my part, I do not understand this chiaroscuro even though I know quite well what writing a tragedy means and whether such things can be written, since poetry bears about the same relation to writing as music does to the notes.

### 570. Goethe

Weimar, 31 October 1831

I am glad to hear you sometimes go back to the Schiller correspondence. There you find two men of serious intent at a fairly high level, you are inspired to the same intellectual activity, you strive to place yourself beside them and if possible above them; that is all to the benefit of the next generation. […] As regards tragedy, that is more difficult.[807] I was not born to be a tragic poet because my nature is conciliatory. As a result a purely tragic tale cannot interest me for it has to be, by its nature, irreconcilable and to me, in the exceeding flatness of this world, the irreconcilable seems an utter absurdity. I must not continue for in the course of conversation one can go off the point – something I would prefer to avoid.

### 571. Zelter

Berlin, 30 October to 7 November 1831

The cholera creeps through the streets like the dragon which a priest of Apollo had prayed for and needs to eat more or less from one day to the next. People have also got used to it: it is discussed in pulpits, cathedrals, over a drink and a smoke.

3 November: Yesterday I was at Molière's *Médecin malgré lui* in the French theatre.[808] The three acts unfolded all right and even with musical intermezzi the whole thing was over within an hour.

---

[806] Reference to Schiller's words in the above letter to Goethe: 'if you really are unable to write a real tragedy, then the reason must lie in the unpoetical demands [of tragedy].'

[807] Reference to Zelter's remarks on Goethe as a tragic poet; ZG 27 October 1831.

[808] The Berlin premiere of Molière's three-act comedy took place in the Königliches Schauspielhaus on 2 November 1831, performed by French actors and followed by Scribe's *Une Faunt*.

6 November: You know already that I relate everything to music and so I think tragedy relates to the tragic like the fugue to fugal counterpoint. [If] the poet wants to rise high up, lay a hand on the unfathomable, he becomes like the Titans and he can consider himself lucky if he has to turn back unhumiliated.

### 572. Goethe

Weimar, 15 November 1831

[...] You see that things are the same with me as always. Among the hundred things that interest me one always asserts itself the central planet and the remainder of the quodlibet of my life revolves around it variously, like the many shapes of the moon, until one or other of the satellites succeeds in moving to the centre.

Next I should like to hear what news you have of our excellent Felix. I had a highly interesting letter from Switzerland,[809] part of which I reported in the *Chaos*; I wrote to him in Munich but have not heard from him since then. [...]

### 573. Zelter

Berlin, 16 to 26 November 1831

[...] The youngest daughter of Moses Mendelssohn was buried yesterday.[810] Of all the family, she was most like her father, petite and not well formed – a woman of a refined, sharp intelligence, and above all very amiable. She inherited only a small sum of money from her father and travelled to Paris, where she made the acquaintance of General Sebastiani and became governess to his only daughter. She educated this child up to the time of her marriage and received a pension of nearly 3,000 francs for the rest of her life, which allowed her to return to live in her native Berlin. It was a remarkable thing, to find no difference in language, manners, or way of life in the Jewish maiden of Berlin, who, without the aid of an imposing presence, had become a lady in one of the foremost Parisian houses. Since she came back to Berlin ten years ago, though I have seen her frequently (and always with pleasure), I have hardly heard her utter a word of French, English, or Italian; on the contrary, she spoke the most transparent, flowing German with a liveliness which reminded me of your *schöne Seele*. Her vocation as a governess in Paris had made her convert to Roman Catholicism, but apart from her daily attendance at Mass, no appearance of positive religiosity was discernible. Felix was her particular favourite; she liked to have my letters to him and transcribe

---

[809] Goethe had already written to Zelter about this letter on 17 September 1831.
[810] Henriette Mendelssohn (1775–1831) died on 9 November 1831.

them for herself. She was at my house very recently and now all that remains with me is a very pleasant memory of her.

### 574. Zelter

Berlin, 3 December 1831

A Madame Fischer, who had appeared as a guest here as surrogate for the leading lady in the Königliche Oper, did not perform again.[811] No one will say what [...] is wrong with her. Young, pretty, flexible, healthy, a reliable voice but immature. If they let the dear woman play 20 times, they could make a judgement. I only heard her once and she was very good in places, though admittedly she appeared to me to be much too good to be drowning 30 violins in the new large-scale operas.[812] They want one false thing after another and in the meantime I am trying to calm down and I have not tried to get to know her personally. I really liked her.

### 575. Zelter

Berlin, Middle of December to 31 December 1831

Your dear present,[813] so well prepared for me from a distance, which reached me on the 11th of this month, more than marked my birthday in the most pleasant and

---

[811] Beatrix Fischer-Schwarzböck from Karlsruhe appeared in Berlin from 7 October 1831. Her first guest role was as Donna Anna in Mozart's *Don Giovanni* with the Königliche Oper. Further roles included: Agathe in Weber's *Der Freischütz* on 9 October; Emeline in Weigl's *Die Schweizerfamilie*; the title role in *Fidelio* on 21 October; Julia in Spontini's *Die Vestalin* on 4, 13 and 16 November, and Donna Anna again on 8 November. Although her guest appearances should have ended on 18 November with a further appearance in Weigl's *Die Schweizerfamilie* on 18 November, she sang the title role in *Fidelio* on 25 November and the part of Julia in Spontini's *Die Vestalin* on 11 and 18 December – which Zelter could not have known when writing this letter.

[812] On his return journey from Berlin, the Weimar flautist Johann Christian Lobe wrote, 'But the numerical strength of the Berlin orchestra, coupled with the excellent performance under Spontini, who conducted his work himself, really inspired me. The orchestra was made up of 30 violins, 10 cellos, 7 double basses, 6 clarinets etc.'; Johann Christian Lobe, *Aus dem Leben eines Musikers*, quoted in *Gespräche*, vol. III/1, p. 183.

[813] Goethe's poem 'Ein Füllhorn von Blüten', written for Zelter's birthday on 11 December. The turn of phrase 'in der Entfernung so wohl bereitetes' (what is prepared from afar) refers to its content: the desire to bring the present, the cornucopia, to the celebration was prevented by the wild snow storm; the symbolic images on the medal – and in the poem itself – are the gifts prepared from afar.

enduring way. [...] On that morning 40 of my students[814] were the first to arrive with some poems, specially written and set to music, which they had rehearsed completely by themselves although I only began my colloquium this month.

Then 24 trumpet players of the Guards Uhlan regiment arrived with completely new works by them, well prepared, and blasted out the house as if to bend it and were not a little delighted when I stepped among them in order to grate my ears and test my nerves. The fellows blew as if [it were] the Day of Judgement.

Then a choir of young women, youths, men and matrons of the Sing-Akademie [arrived] who were also not shy in letting themselves be heard.

At twelve noon the violinists arrived and so it was lunchtime and children and grandchildren, friends and companions enjoyed a prepared table[815] and greeted the wine cellar. That was a day which, 73 years ago, created for my mother painful joy.[816] [...]

### 576. Goethe

Weimar, 2 to 3 January 1832

[...] The correspondence from 1830 is revised as far as slips of the pen are concerned. I leave it to Riemer's judgement regarding which passages are to be left out and which modified. Hopefully, given the torrent of words that comes with the all-powerful freedom of the press, he won't be too meticulous and succinct. Leave this to future generations! [...]

### 577. Zelter

Berlin, 4 to 7 January 1832

I had hardly put down the pen when a new *Opus operandum* appears published by Oels in Schlesien. Lindau, Vice Chancellor of the Gymnasium there, sends his German translation of Pindar's first Pythian Song of Victory[817] with the innocent instructions to set it to music, Greek in style. The good man doesn't consider that

---

[814] The Sing Collegium (university choir) led by Zelter.

[815] Reference to Psalm 23, v. 5.

[816] Another reference to Genesis I, 5.

[817] On 6 September 1831 August Ferdinand Lindau sent Zelter his translation of the first ode from Pindar's *Pythischen Epinikia*; in the extensive accompanying writings he explained his discoveries on verse metre and music in Pindar's odes and asked Zelter for a setting of translation in the style of Greek music. He believed 'that the totality would have a lovely effect and would be a suitable piece for the Sing-Akademie, which is flourishing under your direction'.

we have fitted our own 'Heil dir im Siegerkranz'[818] to the old English national anthem (God save the King) and that half of our poets have worn themselves out paraphrasing and setting the Lutheran Lord's prayer without anyone paying attention to the melody. Now I am embarrassed about answering the man who praises me highly and almost calls me his godfather. Or should I wait until the honourable Pindar beyond the Styx should let music sound around my ears? I enclose the correspondence to give our friend Riemer something to mull over, because it's not the kind of thing I do. Please return it to me sometime.

[Doris] is bringing you your letters from last year[819] which I don't have time to read beforehand. The total is 32. Let me know how many of mine are in your possession from this year. [...]

Next Thursday, 12 January, is [the performance of] our second oratorio, *Judas Maccabaeus*[820] by Handel, which is causing me concern. My first violinist[821] with the orchestra, a reliable (finally) attentive violinist, is coughing up blood and so I have to break in another [first violinist] in three days who, admittedly, is good and from the Königliche Kapelle [..]

### 578. Zelter

Berlin, 8 January 1832

[...] For the sake of convenience I enclose the text for our next oratorio,[822] which we performed three years ago.[823] One of our directors of music and royal court organist[824] (from my school) has had a piano reduction of this oratorio published[825] with a preface to which he has signed his own name[826] and sent me a copy. Wouldn't it be amazing if I liked this introduction? [...]

---

[818] Prussian hymn, sung to the melody of 'God save the King'.

[819] Doris travelled with Angelika Facius to Weimar, where she was a guest in Goethe's home from 10 January to 18 February.

[820] For reviews see *AMZ* 34 (1832), no. 10, 7 March, column 156; *MA* 20.3, p. 1281.

[821] Eduard Rietz died on 22 January 1832.

[822] In Goethe's library there is a copy of *Judas Maccabäus, ein geistliches Oratorium, in Musik gesetzt von Georg Friedrich Händel* (Berlin: Dieterici, 1828), with a two-page unsigned preface.

[823] It was performed four years earlier on 17 January and 6 February; Handel's *Judas Maccabaeus* was in the Sing-Akademie's repertoire from 1811.

[824] Karl Friedrich *Ludwig* Hellwig (1773–1838).

[825] *Händel's Oratorium Judas Maccabäus nach Mozarts Bearbeitung im Clavier-Auszuge von Ludwig Hellwig, Musikdirektor und Hoforganist in Berlin* (Hamburg: Johann August Böhme o.J, 1832).

[826] The preface is signed 'Berlin, September 1820. Ludwig Hellwig'. It gives, with little alteration, the wording of the unsigned preface (by Zelter) in the libretti, which had

Spontini wanted to send the manuscript of his new opera *Les Athéniennes*[827] [with the letter] today; but nothing has arrived yet. According to him, you promised him some comments on the text.[828] When returning it, you might let it pass through my hands. Since I am at the moment reading Greek,[829] it will be doubly interesting. [...]

### 579. Zelter

Berlin, 9 to 10 January 1832

Sunday evening after the children set off [830] and everyone with them, the whole house was like an empty bird's nest. So I decided to see and listen to a brand new opera: *Der Orakelspruch* by Contessa, with music by Baron von Lauer.[831]

A magic fairy, who was unlucky in love, decided upon raging hatred of the male sex. At the same time she enclosed herself in a solitary area with a high wall (as one now says). In order to bring up a tender delightful daughter with an abhorance of love, she turned her male servants into hunchbacks. But an oracle spoke out against it: if a dumb man could win the love of the girl, the spell would be broken. A young prince, who, during the hunt, strayed across the wall mentioned, was struck dumb and there you have the whole story, which apart from not unpleasant verses has no lack of evenness and breadth. The music appeared to please friends of the composer more than other people and after the second or third performance had to be laid to rest. The opera has only one act, which I find bearable since I have still encountered no one who can do it better than he can. [...]

---

been published by the Sing-Akademie for the performances of the oratorio (Dieterici 1814, 1820, 1828).

[827] Referring to his announcement of the opera on 31 March 1831, Spontini gave Doris Zelter the libretto by Etienne Jouy for the planned opera *Les Athéniennes* as well as a politely written letter to Goethe. Shortly afterwards Goethe praised Jouy's text in a letter to Zelter and equally in his letter to Spontini on 19 January 1832; *WA* IV/49, p. 208.

[828] See Spontini's letter to Goethe, where he writes, 'You also deigned to promise me to write commentary in your own hand on the empty page of the manuscript or beside the text'; perhaps here the desire for a highly valuable document in Goethe's own hand was more important that his literary judgement. On 19 September 1832 Goethe thanked Spontini for the manuscript and with full appreciation gave him his impressions based on a first reading and asked for some time for a more thorough reading.

[829] Reading the dramas of Euripides and Socrates.

[830] Departure of Doris Zelter and Angelika Facius for Weimar.

[831] One-act opera by Adolf Lauer von Münchhofen (1795/96–1874), libretto by Wilhelm Contessa, first performed on 8 January 1832 in the Königliches Opernhaus, Berlin.

Tuesday, 10 January: Yesterday evening was my first rehearsal of the oratorio[832] mentioned and my new first violinist[833] conducted himself courageously and attentively. In the second rehearsal this evening I hope to see everything go off smoothly. The soloists, Madame Milder, Madame Türschmidt,[834] Mantius and Riese, are superb and the choruses are rehearsed in the usual way. What is still missing for me now is that you and Handel are those I would gladly learn from, even if the various kinds of quacking of the female soloists are driving me to despair. Even that can be dealt with, since it results in two hours of happiness. [...]

Spontini sent me a letter for you with the manuscript of his opera[835] very late and strongly sealed. Doris dutifully removed the seal and hopefully read nothing. Would you allow Doris to copy his letter to you and send it to me as well?[836] I would in fact be very interested in what it might contain. Let me look through the libretto[837] with your remarks on it; I can vouch for the most discrete use.

## 580. Zelter

Berlin, 14 January 1832

A word from you or from our friend, Riemer, about Pindar's Song of Victory[838] would be very helpful to me since I really want to answer the good Lindau, although I have to guard against translating his translation into music. He points me to our linguist, Wilhelm von Humboldt. He might as well have directed me to his brother Alexander, because neither are in Berlin and I won't be going either to Tegel[839] or Paris.[840] [...]

The day before yesterday our second oratorio[841] finally went off not too badly. Choirs and orchestras [performed] smoothly and decently; one can guarantee that

---

[832] Handel's *Judas Maccabaeus*.

[833] Hubert Ries (1802–86), violinist and music educationalist, brother of the composer Ferdinand Ries.

[834] Anna Milder (soprano) and Auguste Türrschmidt (alto).

[835] See ZG 8 January 1832.

[836] Goethe could no more accede to this request than to Zelter's request to have a look at the libretto.

[837] The libretto for *Les Athéniennes* by Etienne Jouy.

[838] ZG 4 to 7 January 1832; in Goethe's letters to Zelter Lindau's translation is no longer mentioned.

[839] Wilhelm von Humboldt lived in the Tegel residence.

[840] Alexander von Humboldt was on a diplomatic mission in Paris from January 1831 to April 1832.

[841] Handel's *Judas Maccabaeus* was performed by the Sing-Akademie on 12 January 1832.

at any rate and be acknowledged. The bass arias were excellent and powerful, all sung by a superb student.[842] The female singers of higher social rank are of the opinion that they have been given everything by nature and if they are not happy with themselves, the fault lies with the composer, or at least not with them. Since they don't ask, I keep my opinion and my wine to myself. The whole thing was marvellous, however, and great, and gave that impression. What more could one want! [...]

I must listen. My students[843] want to rehearse some night music for their Professor Neander[844] with me today, and I am glad to encourage them since they are usually so good that I envy them their youth and the opportunities I give them.

### 581. Goethe

Weimar, 14 January 1832

Through the arrival of the good Doris we are really drawn so much closer to you.[845] [...] She brought so many things with her that I cannot understand how they put such luggage in the express carriage. First and foremost my letters, which have already been inserted between yours.[846] The sum of the latter amounts to 41, compared to 32 of mine. You are that many steps ahead of me. Don't neglect to outdo me again this year. In all honesty, my circumstances were pieced together from so many little parts that one would almost fear the whole thing would crumble. With you there are still large undertakings, from which you derive intense joy through which the inevitable annoyances are compensated for and cancelled out. [...]

The libretto of *Judas Maccabaeus* looks good.[847] The old tale: the conquered, the oppressed, first patient, then rebellious after varying success, finally achieved liberation – this is a good theme especially suited to music. [...]

Jouy's libretto for Spontini's opera *Les Athéniennes* is truly admirable.[848] I have read it through once; there is great understanding of dramatic effects, an assured and fresh treatment of such situations from which there is no escape; there are pleasant resting places which interrupt the movement, which is partly solemn, partly passionate, where unsophisticated arias can be introduced; the finales are lively, well grouped and full of movement. Let anyone who has to sit through Act

---

[842] Friedrich Riese (d.1859), a member of the Sing-Akademie since 1828, appeared as bass soloist from 1829 to 1851.

[843] Zelter's Sing Collegium.

[844] August Neander, Professor of Theology at Berlin University.

[845] Doris Zelter and Angelika Facius arrived in Weimar on 10 January 1832.

[846] Goethe's letters to Zelter from 1831.

[847] ZG 8 January 1832.

[848] See Goethe's letter to Spontini on 20 February 1832 and Spontini's reply on 29 February (GSA 28/872).

Three have something to strengthen the heart and senses. Still, I do not know of any passage that I would cut or alter, I can only praise, and give sound reasons for my favourable opinion [...]

I hear about the particular aspects of your world of music more precisely through your good Doris. How many have an idea of the power of understanding which is required in order to hold together such a body!

### 582. Zelter

Berlin, 16 to 17 January 1832

Yesterday, Sunday, after I had already worked with my students,[849] like the King of France with his Ministers,[850] the musical entertainment took place according to the instructions on the enclosure, which is intended for a quartet. Since there is no joy without variations, new art forms have to be invented like No. 1 double quartet for which eight people are required.[851] Then No. 2 in the morning before breakfast one is served up a serenade. Also the different feelings all in one place with 500 people are more than different enough. Finally a military septet could belong to such designations. The military aspect is a single trumpet which tries to get along with six other players in the best possible way and which for that reason gave me the most pleasure, since all of Hummel's works of this nature are the best that our time has to offer. Wit, lightness, perfection, calm singability and flow: superb! It always does me good.

Apart from that, the four-part vocal quartet with grand piano was the most delightful thing. I would have gladly listened to a repeat; our people are happiest when they omit them. [...] The effect of the serenade for four cellos,[852] towards evening on the lawn – only not today and before dinner – would certainly have been very pleasant. My own feeling was not very clear. It was mythological, a conversation amongst Ovid figures, at the same time Indian, bajaderian, gentle, delighted without being delightful, and so on.

Someone who plays the double bass found the combination of four cellos very ingenious and wondered whether it would also work four double basses in their own way? I was of the same opinion since a group of four bulls in harmony would have to astonish all the cows!

---

[849] Zelter's Sing Collegium.
[850] Louis XIV, who, at the beginning of his day, gathered his ministers around him.
[851] Louis Spohr, Double Quartet in D minor, op. 65.
[852] Franz Lachner (1803–1890), Serenade in G major for four cellos, op. 29.

## 583. Zelter

Berlin, 18 to 24 January 1832

[...] You need not trouble yourself about Jouy's operatic text;[853] you only have to send it back to Spontini, who will certainly lay it before me with whatever comments you make. I, too, will let him know your enthusiasm for the text. I am on good artistic terms with him, and he understands this very well for we both make no pretences. We have often conducted important concerts back to back and on such occasions I have found myself between two forces. The last time this happened, in our largest church,[854] and in the presence of the whole of the court orchestra and chorus, he launched out very loudly in my praises; while I, in my turn, could only admire his potential discretion in letting that with which he was basically unfamiliar take its own course. The most agreeable part of it was the universal acknowledgement; I had not moved but everybody knew what was meant. [...]

I enclose another programme.[855] Until recently the Italian composer Bellini was unknown to me; God only knows whether I know him now. A duke has forcibly stolen the count's beloved and made her his wife. The count returns six years later as a pirate, kills the duke and thereby destroys himself; the wife goes mad, and all that is left is a little five-year-old boy. The score is a musical melange which deliberately contradicts everything that happens on stage. One is tossed and turned between eye and ear, feeling and reason, all of which clash with each other. Having said all this, the fellow has talent and audacity, and lords it over the orchestra and singers in the most impertinent fashion. Such stuff is now being performed with a kind of virtuosity at the Königsstädter Theater. Now and then I was in such despair that I was on the point of running away, but before I could quite get up from my chair, something always caught my attention again. In the end I was exhausted by it. [...]

22 January: My excellent leader, Rietz,[856] died the day before yesterday. It's all very sad – and we'll cope with it. Now I shall have to roll the new stone

---

[853] Out of consideration for Spontini, Goethe could not grant Zelter's wish to see Jouy's unpublished libretto for their new opera.

[854] Zelter is referring to the performance of Haydn's *Creation* by the Sing-Akademie and the Königliche Kapelle directed by Spontini on 28 April 1830 in the Garisonkirche, Berlin, attended by over 4,000 people

[855] A theatre programme for a performance of Vincenzo Bellini's opera *Der Pirat* (libretto by Felici Romani, *Il Pirata*) on 20 January 1832 in the Königstädter Theater.

[856] Eduard Theodor Ludwig Rietz (1802–32) violin virtuoso and Kapellmeister, who in 1826 founded a Philharmonische Gesellschaft, an amateur orchestra that participated in the Sing-Akademie concerts. His early death deeply affected his intimate friend Mendelssohn, who inscribed the Andante in the String Quintet, op. 18, with the words 'In memory of

uphill again.[857] There are some left to pick from still; they are all keen to have the position; expertise and strength will come in time. Rietz had all those qualities and was also dutiful.

### 584. Goethe

Weimar, 27 January 1832

[...] The excellent Doris seems to be quite happy and at home here; she has come just at the right time, when everything is in full swing and things are a little crazy even in my house. A few days ago they performed a quodlibet of dramatic fragments[858] at a private home[859] under the direction of Ottilie, who understands that sort of thing very well and is, therefore, in great demand and is listened to. [...]

Inwardly and outwardly one lives in a perpetual state of conflict because of the young people whose ways and activities one cannot sanction and at the same time cannot completely avoid. I often pity them for having made their appearance in times that are so out of joint, when a rigid unyielding egotism hardens itself in ways that are partly or completely false and presents the true self from working out its own development. The result is that when a free spirit perceives and expresses what can allow itself to be clearly seen and expressed, everyone falls into despair. Then they lead one another by the hand into the old, conventional labyrinths, without noticing what they will encounter on the way. I shall guard against expressing myself more concretely, but I know best what it is that keeps me young in old age, and more especially in the practical and productive sense of the word, which, after all, is what matters.

---

E. Rietz'. The autograph is dated 'Jan. 23, 1832,' and entitled 'Obituary'. An obituary is published in the *AMZ* 34 (1832), no. 10, 7 March, column 158.

[857] Zelter compares training up a new first violinist to the work of Sisyphus.

[858] Goethe's diary on 24 January 1832 states: 'At Schwendlers. Large-scale entertainment under Ottilie's direction until midnight.' As detailed in Goethe's diary entry of 8 January, these 'living tableaux', representing the 12 months of the year, were performed: 'Later Ottilie (...) She explained to me the presentation of the 12 months of the year at Schwendlers as being more sensible than in the form of charades. The result was rather paradoxical, but well thought out for social entertainment.' *WA* III/13, p.203.

[859] In the house of the Weimar government official Friedrich Christian August von Schwendler.

## 585. Zelter

Berlin, 25 to 28 January 1832

The Royal Academy of Science had announced an official gathering in celebration of the birthday of Friedrich II,[860] and Moeser, the music director, likewise arranged a similar celebration for Mozart's birthday[861] with music and a meal. So I was between two tempters and didn't know whether I should put myself in bad humour or give myself an upset stomach. Rosamunde[862] must have noticed this as she had prepared a small evening meal in our home among friends, so we let the dead rest and the living live. [...]

## 586. Zelter

Berlin, 1 to 2 February 1832

I will not be able to write much this week and next because I have an official production[863] ahead of me a week from now. [...] A couple of new operas[864] invite little comment. Everything endeavours to cultivate barren deserts and shifting sands and there is a rich harvest of dead grass and chaff. At the market there are buyers for everything and one enjoys criticizing: everything will be discussed, written, read up and down, and so one wiles away tedious hours.

[...] Felix is now in Paris,[865] and is causing a sensation both as composer and performer. I enclose a short extract from his letter,[866] from which you can see for yourself what else he is occupying himself with.

---

[860] On 24 January.

[861] One the evening before Mozart's birthday, a concert of Mozart's vocal and instrumental works under the direction of Carl Moeser took place in the Jagor Hall on 26 January 1832.

[862] Zelter's daughter.

[863] The third subscription concert took place on 9 February; apart from an aria and a motet by J.S. Bach, the programme consisted of Mozart's Requiem. The performance was dedicated to the memory of the deceased leader of the orchestra, Eduard Rietz; see *AMZ* 34 (1832), no. 13, 28 March, column 218.

[864] Wilhelm Taubert's Singspiel *Die Kirmes*, libretto by Eduard Devrient, premiered on 23 January 1832 at the Königliches Schauspielhaus (with further performances at the opera house on 25 and 29 January, and 1 February). Also the opera *Zampa oder die Marmorbraut* by Louis Joseph Ferdinand Hérold, libretto by Carl Ludwig Blum after Mélesville's *Zampa, ou La fiancée de marbre*, premiered at the opera house on 31 January 1832; see *AMZ* 34 (1832), no. 9, 29 February, column 140ff.

[865] Felix Mendelssohn was in Paris from December 1831 until the end of April 1832.

[866] Felix to Abraham Mendelssohn, 21 January 1832 (GSA 28/1027, no. 503).

## 587. Zelter

Berlin, 7 February 1832

[…] Right now I am reading Italian and happen to be looking up a passage in Benvenuto Cellini.[867] […] I still remember the first impression it made on me 30 years ago when you first brought the book to my study. I have now started it from the beginning again and one chapter leads to another. The naivety with which that young fellow describes his justified hatred of that accursed music attracted me very powerfully, as I myself had experienced the same thing except the other way round. How often have I, with tears and faithful prayers,[868] called out to God to change that dreadful taste of mine for the beloved music that I loved into a talent more suitable to my condition and more rewarding to my father. All that was so vividly present to me as if the former agony of my soul at that time was for the first time brought before my eyes in a vision. I dare say I have written to you about this ten times already, but the effect is always the same.

[…] I mentioned to you that I was reading Italian, which reminds me that the Italian Spontini has just been dissolving your little Mignon[869] like a pearl in the river of German instrumentation. The little piece is pretty and effective and Mignon plays there like a child among children; if it continued in this way to the end, it would be fine. However, the main focus is placed on very long-drawn, everlasting repetitions of 'Kennst du es wohl?'[870] and I should like to see the man who would say, 'I suppose that means Italy'. It was performed at yesterday's concert with full orchestra (drums excepted) to great applause. As the people were going out, someone called out quite clearly, 'Away. Be gone and leave us unscathed.'[871]

---

[867] Goethe's translation of Cellini's autobiography, *Leben des Benvenuto Cellini, Florentinischen Goldschmieds und Bildhauers, von ihm selbst geschrieben* (1803, reprinted, Frankfurt: Insel, 2004).

[868] In Cellini's account of his father's wish to educate his son in music and Cellini's own determination to become a goldsmith, Zelter recognizes the converse of his own youthful years: namely the conflict between his father's desire for Zelter to become a builder and his own musical inclinations.

[869] On 6 February 1832 a concert was given in the hall of the Königliches Schauspielhaus; the programme included Spontini's setting of 'Mignons Gesang', which was performed with orchestral accompaniment.

[870] Refrain from Mignon's song 'Kennst du das Land?'

[871] A parody of the opening line of the refrain from Mignon's song 'Kennst du das Land'. In other words, 'Be off with you, Spontini, to Italy, – you and your high prices' – There is a similar play on the word *wohl* in the sentence above.

## 588. Zelter

Berlin, 10 to 11 February 1832

Yesterday's public performance went off smoothly enough and with a single rehearsal of one and a half hours for a performance of two and a half hours. Two rehearsals were arranged but on the day of the second rehearsal a grand opera was performed, the court orchestra were not to be had, and so we had to do what we could. Even this one rehearsal was raced through because the musicians still had to play a public concert.

I must recognize it as a particular grace of God that, with my orchestra consisting for the most part of voluntary amateurs, there has never been a scandal such as I have seen with other orchestras. A hearty [impromptu] address to my people (who are 300 strong) produced the effect once again [...] All ran and came and stood like the walls and joyfully got down to it. They appreciated my encouraging glance and were delighted like children over a couple of mistakes that I made. They don't know how to play down such things. My new concert master[872] is a good boy and concentrates like a snipe shooter.

I also have a couple of new complicated operas behind me again: [...] *Die Marmorbraut*[873] and [...] *Der Templer und die Jüdin*[874] [...] The two composers are of the same breed more or less. They bombard people's ears with their music as if they were tanning leather! A rogue gives more than he has! Now the time has come to refute the adage. God knows how it comes about that I can't say anything from deep down within me that you haven't said better. So I think I should be able to withhold my wisdom and refer to what you expressed at length under the title 'Music' in the appendix to *Rameus Neffe*.[875] Be it confirmation of a true belief and of a similar feeling or fruit of a healthy seed. It is there and wants to remain.

---

[872] Hubert Ries.

[873] *Zampa, oder die Marmorbraut*; ZG 1 to 2 February 1832.

[874] Opera by Heinrich Marschner (libretto after Walter Scott's novel, *Ivanhoe*, freely adapted by Wilhelm August Wohlbrück) premiered in Berlin on 3 August 1831; Zelter attended the performance in the opera house on 10 February 1832.

[875] In the chapter entitled 'Music' in Goethe's 'Commentary' in his translation of Diderot's *Le Neveu de Rameau*, 'something general about the art' is said, 'so that every reader will be able to form some sort of opinion about the ideas which are often enough strangely expressed.'

## 589. Zelter

Berlin, 14 to 18 February 1832

16 February: I have written to you about Auber's opera *Der Gott und die Bajadere*.[876] Yesterday's performance[877] was so remarkable in every respect that I really quite revelled in the music. There is something Indian about it, quite different from anything we have had before. Wit, novelty, easy flow – and our guest performer, Mdlle Elßner,[878] (the Bajadere) not only dances but acts more perfectly than anyone I have seen since Vigano.[879] The whole theatre was delighted with her. [...] Every part of her face is a keyboard of colour played upon with marvellous charm [...] The vocal parts are admirably cast. Mantius[880] (the God) is a beginner, and rather undersized, but his tenor voice is of great beauty and even throughout. He has made excellent progress in a very short time. [...]

The day before yesterday we commemorated, with a Requiem mass, the memory of a 21-year-old charming girl of obvious talent, who died of nerve fever. When I took her on she sang high soprano arias and handled them with all the power of a youthful physique. I advised her not to strain her lovely mezzo-soprano voice. But her friends and whatever such vermin are called knew better and I cannot get rid of the impression that my dear Ulrike Peters[881] sang herself to death.

## 590. Goethe

Weimar, 23 February 1832

I will slot in here what I had occasion to jot down a few days ago:

> The consciousness of having effected the artistic development of an important natural talent lives in us as one of our finest feelings, but presently it is of greater value that before when every beginner still believed in schooling, rules and mastery, and modestly subjected himself to the fundamentals of his particular subject about which most young people of today don't want to know.
>
> For the last 30 years German plastic artists have been under the delusion that natural talent can develop itself and a profusion of enthusiastic amateurs who have no fundamental training strengthen them in their belief. A hundred times I

---

[876] ZG 14 April 1831.

[877] On 15 February 1832 in the Königliches Opernhaus together with Johanna Weißenthurn's comedy; both works were performed with ballet interludes.

[878] Fanny Elßner in the role of Zoloé, one of the three Bajaderes.

[879] The famous Italian dancer Maria Viganó (?1756–1833).

[880] An unknown singer, Jakob Eduard Mantius (1806–74), played the part of the god.

[881] Ulrike Peters (1807–32), member of the Sing-Akademie from 1828.

hear an artist boast that he owes everything to himself! I generally listen to this patiently, but sometimes I reply in annoyance, 'It looks like it too!'

For what is man in and through himself? When he opens his eyes and ears he cannot avoid objectivity, example, tradition; he educates himself through these for a while as well as he can, according to what is enjoyable and comfortable. But just when he reaches the highest point, he finds this fragmentary existence is not enough; the malaise which is the particular problem of the [purely] practical man sets in. Happy is he who is quick to grasp what art means!

Much as I have accomplished in general and much as I have set in motion, I can still only name one man who has cultivated himself from beginning to end in accordance with my ideas. This was the actor Wolff, who is still honourably remembered in Berlin.[882]

### 591. Zelter

Berlin, 19 to 27 February 1832

[…] Now for another opera, *Fra Diavolo*![883] […] This Diavolo is a handsome, young, long, thin, pale bandit and sings tenor like all tenors after the voice change, continually singing in falsetto, for that is the current fashion. […] Now about the action!

> The dragoons booze and sing;
> The bandits steal and sing.
> My lord is sulky and sings, how he will not endure that damned singing.
> The lovers torture each other and sing, and make up and sing again.

It takes a man like Auber (whose talent the critics are not agreed upon) to compose music to three such acts, which will prevent anyone dying of ennui, and for this an orchestra as good as the Parisian orchestra is required, and not worse than ours; for the difficult passages given to singers and orchestra are the best thing about it, if it all goes off well.

---

[882] Pius Alexander Wolff, for whom Goethe had made the notes that form the basis of *Regeln für Schauspieler*, was acknowledged by Goethe to be his most faithful disciple in artistic matters. Wolff was in Weimar from 1803 to 1816; it was a blow for Goethe and the Weimar theatre when he and his wife, Amalia, left for the Königliches Schauspielhaus in Berlin in 1816, but he took the Weimar [acting] style with him.

[883] *Fra Diavolo oder Das Gasthaus bei Terracina*, comic opera in three acts by Daniel François Espirit Auber (libretto by Carl Blum after Eugène Scribe's *Fra Diavolo, ou l'Hôntellerie de Terracine*) in the repertoire of the Königliches Theater from 3 August 1830. Zelter attended the performance on 24 February 1824 in the Königliches Opernhaus.

I have received from Paris a letter from Felix, dated the 15th of this month.[884] As he has often been there, new acquaintances have been made continually, and apparently, the political, no less than the artistic life there rekindles his love for Germany. In respect of his artistic life, his experience is as I expected – though I have never been to Paris – and businessmen or merchants, with whom he has been acquainted from childhood, direct him to the best opportunities [...]

### 592. Zelter

Berlin, 4 to 6 March 1832

Yesterday at noon Prince Radziwill finally performed new and old passages from *Faust*,[885] for which I provided some 40 accomplices. The noble composer has gone very deeply into the text, one could say fallen into it. One can notice the effect the libretto had on him rather than how the music responds to the text. An oyster-like clinging to the situations is paralysing, since no art is more transient than music. The Dies irae seems unsuccessful to me because to clothe matters related to the conscience in music is a task which contains an evil spirit in itself. In the libretto it is placed perfectly through the words: Cathedral. Mass, Organ and Song.[886] That makes everything very clear. Gretchen says, 'That's not right. You must believe in it'[887] – and you can't. You hit the nail on the head through the simple title as if the organ had tackled you itself. To me it has always been a strong confessor; it contains something accusatory, something satanic in itself. Against that the stroll through Martha's Garden is very charming: like the scornful irony which weighs itself against genuine love and prevails. We only had a grand piano without orchestra and an audience of nobility: our Crown Prince,[888] Duke Carl of Mecklenburg (Mephisto),[889] the Grand Duke Strelitz,[890] [who] was delighted as

---

[884] After his return from Italy Felix Mendelssohn reported in his letter to Zelter on 15 February 1832 his musical experiences and impressions on his travels from Munich to Düsseldorf via Stuttgart and Frankfurt. After that he writes a detailed criticism of Parisian musical life.

[885] Prince Radziwill was preoccupied with the setting of individual scences from Goethe's *Faust* from 1808; Zelter had often reported on the progress of the work, which was always interrupted by work, and on the performances in Prince Radziwill's home, most recently in March 1831. In March 1830 three more scenes had been completed: 'Spaziergang mit Wagner'; 'Marthens Garten' and the cathedral scene.

[886] Title of the cathedral scene in Goethe's *Faust*.

[887] Gretchen's reaction to Faust's evasive answer to her questions about his religion in the scene 'Marthens Garten'.

[888] Friedrich Wilhelm, later King Friedrich Wilhelm IV.

[889] Duke Carl von Mecklenburg-Strelitz, in the role of Mephisto from the beginning.

[890] The Grand Duke Georg von Mecklenburg-Strelitz.

always and whether he would have been if he could hear better, I don't want to know! A spark ignites some receptive places here and there. Quietly the libretto has borne fruit, amazing but frightening. You could see a different expression on everyone's face in the audience and no one can conceal the devil. They read it the way Catholics read the Bible.

I hardly know what to say about the performance of our *Messiah* last Thursday.[891] Whoever stands on the sun doesn't see it and the tongue doesn't hear the bell. The reviewers are sympathetic, touched on things of an accidental nature,[892] and prefer to remain popular among the young folk who also consist of reviewers and visibly show a genuine seriousness. So we deal with one another best when I know how things stand. But we must earn interest on 60,000 thaler per year[893] and be happy if musical professionals and popular virtuosi do not begrudge us the thalers which we try to earn for them. Our hall was full this time and the professionals and judges also had to pay.

### 593. Zelter

Berlin, 11 to 13 March 1832

A music director from Stettin,[894] whom I helped to be promoted there ten years ago, came here a week ago, announced a concert[895] in which he would have his own compositions performed, rented our hall, hired a large orchestra and since he was certain of his stuff and didn't want to wait for a more suitable day, the concert took place yesterday after I had removed some major obstacles.

---

[891] Handel's *Messiah* was performed in the context of the fourth subscription concert by the Sing-Akademie on 1 March 1832.

[892] Ludwig Rellstab wrote in the *Vossische Zeitung* on 3 March 1832: 'As far as the whole thing is concerned, we can't remember such a successful performance of the work as this: details such the incorrect tempo form the aria 'Das Volk das in Dunkeln wandelt' and prominence of the string instruments, which were too loud for the unusually delicate colours which Mozart added in the wind instruments, furthermore the wavering of the beat in some places, for example in the introduction to part two, and other minor matters, hardly come into consideration against the magnificent, noble conception of the entire work, which was specially expressed by the performance of the choir.'

[893] The building cost of 60,000 thalers was three times the original cost estimated by Ottmer for the construction of the Sing-Akademie. The subscription concerts were established as a means of repaying the debt.

[894] Thanks to Zelter's recommendation and references, Carl Loewe had been music director in Stettin since 1821.

[895] For Loewe's account; see C.H. Bitter (ed.) *Dr Carl Loewes Selbstbibliographie* (Berlin: Müller, 1870, reprint Hildesheim: Germanistische Texte und Studien vol. 20, 1976), p. 124f.

An overture and a piano concerto were really very good. In between he sang ballads by Uhland and Herder[896] and called upon me to give him a poem by Goethe to improvise at the piano, which I modestly declined. Prince Radziwill set him the challenge of 'Der Zauberlehrling'[897] and the improvisor didn't come out of the wager badly, since it is no small feat even to read the poem publically without any preparation.

After the concert the virtuoso stayed back for a glass of wine and [to eat] fish with us in order to digest the applause of the grateful public, which unfortunately consisted of connoisseurs (free tickets). Since one didn't let the reverberations die off over the meal, he found the opportunity to lament the meagre takings, which for him hardly covered a third of the outlay. I then said, my dear man, you have discovered 'Der Zauberlehrling', now learn what it means. One doesn't sweep in a paying audience with the broom and one will not get rid of the philistines. Your concert is worth a thousand thalers; 300 cover the costs, the sum of 700 thalers worth of fame and glory are left over for you. Take these with you to Stettin; they will bear interest. That's how people with ability start. For only the master conjures up the spirits; but Berliners are not Stettiners. This cleared the air. But he left and is off today to invest his capital. And am I the better for it? The waters are rising over my head and I would drown if I didn't take an occasional glass of wine. The day before yesterday I listened to no less than 11 hours of music, one after the other, and hardly had any time to eat. A bell will crack if it is struck long enough.

Tuesday 13 March: And you would have to ponder how priests and sextons, goldsmiths and blacksmiths – each lives for his work and is supposed to be happy in the fullness of his work. So it should be reported that along with essential daily rehearsals over three days, four three- and four-hour rehearsals were dedicated to the worthy Doctor Faust. Yesterday evening was the fourth, in the Prince's hotel[898] in the presence of the court. The very best members of the Königliche Kapelle under their Kapellmeister[899] and a specially chosen vocal choir with my accompaniment were, of course, not yet able to satisfy the princely master. The strictest obedience and goodwill towards an honourable general is at the same time not everything. I have already reported to you once on the matter from Darmstadt,[900] I believe. You, too, witnessed something similar in 1806.[901] But everything could still be enjoyed

---

[896] See the review in the *AMZ* 34 (1832), no. 19, 9 May, column 318f.; *MA* 20.3, p. 1303.

[897] Ibid.

[898] Rehearsals for Prince Radizwill's setting of scenes from *Faust*, in his palace at Wilhelmstraße, 77.

[899] Georg Abraham Schneider (1770–1839), horn player, cellist, conductor and composer.

[900] ZG 20 August 1816.

[901] Perhaps Zelter is thinking of the episode with Colonel von Massenbach described in the *Tag und Jahres-Heften* of 1806, where Goethe wrote, 'Also the inclintion to [be a ] writer of political acumen and military activity got in his way.'

(since under such hands a complete failure is hardly imaginable) if the failure consists in external details which could go wrong even for the best of people, where the audience notices nothing unless it is expressly pointed out to them. If they are fortunately brought off and recognized, they don't appear as an improper rendition.

For years the noble composer[902] has spun himself into that work of the poet like a silkworm: every thread holds him firmly. He has wedded the modernity of the text which dwells in antiquity (eternal truth) with contemporary music which sways back and forth in itself. What can be born naturally of this is jealousy of the highest kind. One kills the other like the moor kills his beautiful white wife and himself.[903] The music in itself is good and so well thought-out that a basic opinion of it is perhaps impossible; especially since we all don't understand what we sing and play with enjoyment. So you, too, may construct your gods, men and beasts,[904] their duties and desires as suits you.

### 594. Goethe

Weimar, 11 March 1832

That's right! After having built and established your citadel through dedication of your whole life, and not being without a trustworthy bodyguard and warlike federation, you are manfully taking steps to preserve what you have won, to promote your chief aim, and to lessen the burdens which must necessarily accompany a position like yours.[905]

Here all kinds of examples from ancient history pass through my mind. I cast these aside, however, for as a general rule one does not find any comfort in the thought that the greatest of our ancestors must have fared much worse than ourselves.

Fortunately, your individual gift is bound up with sound, namely with the moment. Now, as a series of consecutive moments is always a kind of eternity in itself, you have been allowed to remain constant in the midst of what is transitory and so to satisfy fully both me and Hegel's spirit, in so far as I understand it.

Look at me on the other hand – living mainly in the past, less in the future and for the time being in the distance – and remember that in my own way I am quite content.

I have received from Naples a very pleasant communication from Zahn, that good, energetic young fellow whom I dare say you still remember. I am really

---

[902] Radziwill.

[903] Shakespeare's *Othello*.

[904] A reference to Goethe's *Götter, Helden und Wieland*.

[905] Here Goethe uses the word 'citadel to refer to the building of the new Sing-Akademie (the institution as well as the building); by 'efficient guards' he refers the student Sing Collegium which was under Zelter's direction and which was always praised by him.

pleased to discover that they have given my name to that house[906] which has been recently discovered, though they have not completely unearthed it. I am happy with this. This is an echo from the past meant to temper the loss of my son.[907] The house is considered to be one of the most beautiful discovered so far and remarkable for a mosaic such as we have not yet met with from antiquity.[908] This was all announced in the newspapers long ago, so perhaps you have already heard something about it.

They are sending me a detailed drawing of the vast enclosed space, columns and all,[909] as well as a miniature copy of the famous painting.[910] We must be careful that we don't behave like Wieland,[911] who, with his delicate flexibility, allowed what he last read to wipe out all that went before, for we might be quite tempted to say that nothing has as yet come down to us from antiquity which matches this in beauty of compositon and execution.

What would you say were they to lay before you an intelligible page of a musical score belonging to a time in which you were forced to recognize a master of the fugue, by its inner and outer criteria? I refer to a time suggestive of earlier Grecian models.

The few but really serious connoisseurs you know[912] will find ample material for conversation and edification in this subject for some days to come. Besides this, some perfectly different, yet equally interesting things have found their way to me – namely, several specimens of an organic world that disappeared before all historic times. Fossils of animals and plants[913] are gathering around me, but it is essential to refrain from thinking of anything but the origin and position of the place of discovery, because to absorb oneself further in the contemplation of the ages could only lead to madness. I should really like one day, as a joke, when you,

---

[906] 'Casa di Goethe' in memory of August von Goethe who had been present at the excavation of the house in Pompeii. Today it is called 'Casa del Fauno'.

[907] August von Goethe had died in Rome on the night of 26/27 October 1830.

[908] Floor mosaic after the Hellenic painting from 300 BC; it shows Alexander the Great's victory over Darius III. Wilhelm Zahn, under whose direction the mosaic was uncovered, describes the mosaic in a letter to Goethe on 18 February 1832; *HA*, Briefe an Goethe, vol. 2, p. 612. See also Bernard Andreae, 'Goethes Interpretation des Alexander-Mosaiks', *JbSK* 3 (1974): 41–9.

[909] Ground plan of the 'Casa di Goethe in Pompeii by Wilhelm Zahn', *MA* 20.2, p. 1676.

[910] Drawing of the Alexander Mosaic by Wilhelm Zahn.

[911] In conversation with Eckermann on 11 April 1827, Goethe remarked of Wieland: 'He was like a reed, moved hither and thither by the wind of opinion, yet always adhering firmly to the root'; Eckermann, p. 250.

[912] Riemer (see Goethe's diary on 6, 8 and 9 March) and Coudray (see Goethe's diary on 11 and 12 March; *WA* III/13, pp. 232–3).

[913] This idea is expanded in a letter to Count Caspar von Sternberg some days later.

with your lively disciples[914] are rehearsing live choruses, to place before you a primeval elephant's molar dug out of our gravel pits; you would feel the vivid and charming contrast.[915]

So be it, then!<br>J. W. von Goethe[916]

## 595. Zelter to Privy Councillor und Chancellor von Müller at Weimar

31 March 1832

I could not thank you until today, honourable sir, for your most friendly consideration notwithstanding the present occasion.[917]

What was to be expected, what was to be feared, inevitably came. The hour has struck. The hand of the clock stands still like the sun at Gideon; for behold, the man who bestrode the universe on pillars of Hercules lies overthrown, while under him the powers of the earth contended for the dust beneath their feet.

What can I say of myself – to you, to all there? And everywhere? As he is gone before me, so daily do I draw nearer to him, and I shall catch up with him again and perpetuate that lovely peace which for so many successive years cheered and enlivened the space of 36 [German] miles[918] that lay between us.

Now I have a request: continue to honour me with your kindly letters. You will be able to judge how far I can be trusted, as the undisturbed relations between two close friends who were always one – though judged by their capacities, far apart – are well known to you. I am like a widow who has lost her husband, her lord and provider, and yet I should not grieve. I am astonished at the riches he brought me. It is my duty to preserve that treasure, and to turn the interest into capital.

Pardon me, noble friend! I should not complain and yet my old eyes don't want to obey and they let me down. But once I saw him weep – and that must justify my tears.

---

[914] Zelter's Sing Collegium.

[915] Reference to Luke 21, v. 22.

[916] This is Goethe's last letter. Zelter wrote to Goethe for the last time, on the day of the poet's death, 22 March 1832; the letter reached Weimar on the day of the funeral.

[917] This letter is from *JbSK* (1927/28).

[918] The German mile was much longer than a western European mile. It was 24,000 German feet as opposed to the English statute mile of 5,280 feet.

# Appendix

**Goethe and Zelter: Encounters**

| Year | Dates | Place |
|---|---|---|
| 1802 | 24 to 28 February | Weimar |
| 1803 | Early Summer (End of May to 11 June?) | Weimar |
| 1805 | 9 to (presumably) 12 August | Lauchstädt |
| 1810 | 15 to 20 July | Carlsbad |
|  | 7 to 23 August | Teplitz |
| 1814 | 24 to 28 June | Berka |
|  | 28 June to 7 July | Weimar |
|  | 29 July to 31 August | Wiesbaden |
|  | 1 September | Winkel |
| 1816 | 5 to 8 July | Weimar |
|  | 28 September to 2 October | Weimar |
| 1818 | 25 October to 1 November | Weimar |
| 1819 | 22 to 25 June | Weimar |
|  | 26 to 27 June | Jena |
|  |  | Dornburg |
| 1821 | 4 to 12 November | Weimar |
|  | 15 to 19 November | Weimar |
| 1823 | 24 November to 13 December | Weimar |
| 1826 | 7 to 19 July | Weimar |
| 1827 | 12 to 18 October | Weimar |
| 1829 | 14 to 17 September | Weimar |
|  |  | Dornburg |
|  |  | Jena |
|  | 19 to 21 September | Weimar |
| 1831 | 22 to 26 July | Weimar |

# Bibliography

**Primary Sources**

*Berliner Allgemeine Musikalische Zeitung*
*Berlinische Musikalische Zeitung*, (ed.) Johann Friedrich Reichardt, vol. 1 (1805) and vol. 2 (1806).
Eckermann, Johann Peter, *Gespräche mit Goethe in den letzten Jahren seines Lebens*, (ed.) Heinrich Hubert Houben, 26th edn (Wiesbaden: Insel Verlag, 1975).
Goethe, Johann Wolfgang von, *Werke. Weimarer Ausgabe*, (eds) Gustav von Loeper, Erich Schmidt, Hermann Grimm et al. on the instructions of the Grand Duchess Sophie von Sachsen-Weimar-Eisenach (143 vols, Weimar: Hermann Böhlau, 1887–1919; reprint Munich, 1987).
—— *Goethes Werke Hamburger Ausgabe*, (ed.) Erich Trunz (14 vols, Hamburg: C.H. Beck, reprint 1994).
—— *J.W.V. Goethe. Sämtliche Werke nach Epochen seines Schaffens. Münchner Ausgabe*, (eds) Karl Richter et al. (21 vols, Munich: Carl Hanser Verlag, 1985–98).
*Briefwechsel zwischen Goethe und Zelter in den Jahren 1796 bis 1832*, (ed.) Friedrich Wilhelm Riemer (6 vols, Berlin: Hermann Böhlau, 1833–34).
Briefwechsel zwischen Goethe und Zelter in den Jahren 1799 bis 1832, (ed.) Ludwig Geiger (3 vols, Leipzig: Reclam, o.J.).
*Briefwechsel zwischen Goethe und Zelter*, (ed.) Max Hecker (Frankfurt am Main: Insel Verlag, reprint 1987).
*Briefwechsel mit Zelter*, (eds) Hans-Günter Ottenberg, Sabine Schäfer and Edith Zehm in Karl Richter (ed.) *Goethe Sämtliche Werke nach Epochen seines Schaffens. Münchner Ausgabe*, vols 20.1, 20.2 and 20.3 (Munich: Hanser Verlag, 1985–98).
*Goethe-Zelter Briefwechsel*, (ed.) Werner Pfister (Zurich and Munich: Artemis, 1987).
*Briefwechsel zwischen Goethe und Zelter. Eine Auswahl*, (ed.) Hans-Günter Ottenberg. (Leipzig: Reclam, 1987).
*Goethe Handbuch*, (eds) Bernd Witte, Theo Buck, Hans-Dietrich Dahnke, Regine Otto and Peter Schmidt (4 vols, Stuttgart and Weimar: Metzler Verlag, 1996–99).
Goethe im Urteil seiner Kritiker. Dokumente zur Wirkungsgeschichte Goethes in Deutschland, (ed.) Karl Robert Mandelkow (4 vols, Munich: C. H. Beck, 1975ff).

Goethe über seine Dichtungen. Versuch einer Sammlung aller Äußerungen des Dichters über seine poetischen Werke, (ed.) Hans Gerhard Gräf (9 vols, Frankfurt am Main: Literarische Anstalt Rütten & Loening, 1901–14).

*Goethe und die Romantik. Briefe mit Erläuterungen*, (eds) Carl Schüddekopf and Oskar Walzel, *SchGG* 13 (1898) and *SchGG* 14 (1899).

Mendelssohn-Bartholdy, Felix, *Briefe aus den Jahren 1830–1847*, (eds) Paul and Karl Mendelssohn Bartholdy (2 vols, Leipzig: Hermann Mendelssohn, 1861–63).

—— *Reisebriefe von Felix Mendelssohn Bartholdy aus den Jahren 180 bis 1832*, (ed.) Paul Mendelssohn Bartholdy, 3rd edn (Leipzig: Hermann Mendelssohn 1862, reprint 1947).

Mendelssohn Bartholdy, Karl, *Goethe und Mendelssohn* (Leipzig: Hirzel Verlag, 1872).

Reichardt, Johann Friedrich, *Lyceum der schönen Künste* 1 (Berlin: F.J. Unger, 1797).

Schiller, Friedrich von, *Schillers Werke. Nationalausgabe*, edited in collaboration with the Goethe and Schiller Archive, Weimar, and the Schiller National Museum, Marbach (46 vols, Weimar: Verlag Hermann Böhlaus Nachfolger Weimar GmbH & Co., 1943ff).

Zelter, Carl Friedrich, *Die Liedertafel* (Berlin: Zelter's Manuscript Copy GMD Catalogue no. 1931, 1818).

—— *Karl Friedrich Christian Fasch* (Berlin: J. F. Unger, 1801).

—— *Carl Friedrich Zelter. Eine Lebensbeschreibung. Nach autobiographischen Manuscripten bearbeitet von Wilhelm Rintel* (Berlin: Otto Janke, 1861).

—— *Lieder. Faksimile der wichtigsten gedruckten Sammlungen nebst Kritischem Bericht*, (eds) Reinhold Kubrik and Andreas Meier, *Das Erbe deutscher Musik*, vol. 106 (Munich: C. Henle Verlag, 1995).

**Secondary Literature**

Abert, Hermann, *Goethe und die Musik* (Stuttgart: J. Engelhorns, 1922).

Adrio, Adam, 'Wirkungen Goethes im Berliner Musikleben seiner Zeit' in Fritz Moser (ed.) *Goethe in Berlin* (Berlin: Wedding-Verlag 1949).

Albertsen, Leif Ludwig, 'Kritik an Schuberts Umgang mit Goethe-Texten mit einem Anhang über Zelter', *GJb* 102 (1985): 226–37.

Anonymous, 'Rezension des Briefwechsels zwischen Goethe und Zelter', *The Foreign Quarterly Review* 32 (1836): 328–60.

Anonymous, 'Der Zeltersche Briefwechsel und die preußische Censur', *GJb* 22 (1901): 107–109.

Arnheim, Amalie, 'Zur Geschichte der Liebhaberkonzerte in Berlin im 18. Jahrhundert', *Mitteilungen des Vereins für die Geschichte Berlins* 30 (1913): 166.

Auerbach-Schröder, Cornelia, 'Frauen in der Geschichte der Sing-Akademie' in Werner Bollert (ed.) *Sing-Akademie zu Berlin. Festschrift zum 175-jährigen Bestehen* (Berlin: Rembrandt Verlag, 1966), pp. 97–105.

Bandtz, Hans-Joachim, *Die Beziehungen Zelters zu Potsdam und zur Potsdamer Liedertafel*. Typescript (Potsdam, 1934).

Barr, R.A., *Carl Friedrich Zelter. The Study of the 'Lied' in Berlin* (Wisconsin: Unpublished Doctoral Dissertation, 1968).

Baser, Friedrich, 'Goethes Freund in Heidelberg', *Alt-Heidelberg. Wochenbeilage zum Heidelberger Tageblatt* 42 (1931), 17 October.

—— 'Der Liedkomponist Zelter in Heidelberg', Die Heimat. Beilage der Heidelberger Nachrichten/ Heidelberger Anzeiger 21 (1932), 21 May.

Bauman, Thomas, *North German Opera in the Age of Goethe* (Cambridge, New York: Cambridge University Press, 1985).

Baumberg, E. von and Weizsäcker, P., 'Zum Goethe-Zelterschen Briefwechsel ed. Ludwig Geiger', *GJb* 22 (1901): 91–109.

Becker-Cantarino, Barbara, 'Leben als Text. Brief als Ausdrucks- und Verständigungsmittel in der Briefkultur und Literatur des 18 Jahrhunderts' in Hiltrud Gnüg and Renate Möhrmann (eds), *Frauen. Literatur. Geschichte.* (Stuttgart: Metzler Verlag, 1985), pp. 83–103 and 515–17.

Béringuier, R., 'Carl Friedrich Zelter', Vermischte Schriften im Anschlusse an die Berlinische Chronik und an das Urkundenbuch 1 (1888): 1–8.

Birnbaum, Max, 'Zum Briefwechsel zwischen Goethe und Zelter', *GJb* 27 (1906): 245f.

Blum, Lothar und Andreas Meier (eds), *Der Brief in Klassik und Romantik. Aktuelle Probleme der Briefedition* (Würzburg: Königshausen und Neumann, 1993).

Blumenthal, Marie Luise, 'Die Freundschaft zwischen Goethe und Zelter', *Die Sammlung* 12 (1957): 345–63.

Blumner, Martin, *Geschichte der Sing-Akademie zu Berlin* (Berlin: Horn & Raasch, 1891).

Bode, Wilhelm, *Die Tonkunst in Goethes Leben* (2 vols, Berlin: E.G. Mittler & Sohn, 1912).

—— *Goethes Schauspieler und Musiker* (Berlin: E.G. Mittler & Sohn, 1912).

Boerner, Peter, 'Goethes Briefwechsel mit Zelter', *Wissenschaftskolleg – Institute für Advanced Studies – zu Berlin* (1986/87): 27–9.

Böhme, Erdmann Werner, 'Zelter beschreibt Goethe Vorpommern, Rügen und eine Segelbootfahrt über die pommersche Ostsee', *Unser Pommerland* 17 (1932): 1–33.

Bohnenkamp, Anne, '…das Hauptgeschäft nicht außer Augen lassend'. Die Paralipomena zu Goethes 'Faust' (Frankfurt am Main and Leipzig: Insel Verlag, 1994).

Bohrer, Karl Heinz, Der Romantische Brief. Die Entstehung ästhetischer Subjektivität (Frankfurt am Main: Suhrkamp, 1989).

Bollert, Werner (ed.), Sing-Akakademie zu Berlin. Festschrift zum 175jährigen Bestehen (Berlin: Rembrandt Verlag, 1966).

Bollert, Werner, 'Die Händel-Pflege der Berliner Sing-Akademie unter Zelter und Rungenhagen' in Werner Bollert (ed.), *Sing-Akakademie zu Berlin. Festschrift zum 175jährigen Bestehen.* (Berlin: Rembrandt Verlag, 1966), pp. 69–79.

Bornemann, Wilhelm, Die Zeltersche Liedertafel in Berlin, ihre Entstehung, Stiftung und Fortgang (Berlin: Decker, 1851).

Brachvogel, Albert Emil, *Geschichte des Königlichen Theaters zu Berlin. Nach Archivalien des Königl. Geh. Staats-Archivs und des Königl. Theaters* (Berlin: O. Janke, 1877).

Brodtbeck, Felix, 'Carl Friedrich Zelter 1758–1832', *Tiroler Volkskultur* 34 (1982): 62f.

Bülow, Paul, 'Carl Friedrich Zelter', *Türmer* 34 (1932/33): 319f.

Büngel, Werner, Der Brief. Ein Kulturgeschichtliches Dokument (Berlin: Mann, 1938).

Bürck, August, 'Briefwechsel zwischen Goethe und Zelter in den Jahren 1796 bis 1832' in *Neue Leipziger Zeitschrift für Musik* 1 (1834), p. 2f; vol. 4, p. 13f; vol. 6, p. 21f; vol. 7, pp. 25–7; vol. 8, p. 29f; vol. 9, p. 39f; 2 (1835), vol. 29, p. 115f; vol. 30, p. 119f; vol. 32, p. 129f; vol. 33, p. 134f; vol. 34, p. 137f.

Bürgel, Peter, 'Der Privatbrief. Entwurf eines heuristischen Modells', *Deutsche Vierteljahresschrift* 50 (1976): 281–97.

Brusniak, Friedrich 'Ein unbekannter Brief Zelters an Schiller aus dem Jahre 1796', *JbDSG* 34 (1990): 20–23.

Dahlhaus, Carl, *Studien zur Musikgeschichte Berlins im frühen 19. Jahrhundert, Studien zur Musikgeschichte des 19. Jahrhunderts*, vol. 56 (Regensburg: Bosse, 1980).

Deetjen, Werner, 'Immermann über den Briefwechsel zwischen Goethe und Zelter', *GJb* 2 (1915): 246–9.

Eberle, Gottfried, 200 Jahre Sing-Akademie zu Berlin. 'Ein Kunstverein für die heilige Musik' (Berlin: Nicolai, 1991).

Eberwein, Karl, 'Goethes Hausmusik' in Wilhelm Bode, *Stunden mit Goethe* (Berlin: Mittler & Sohn, 1911): 70–290.

Ebrecht, Angelika, Regina Nörtemann und Herta Schwarz (eds), *Brieftheorie des 18 Jahrhunderts. Texte, Kommentare, Essays* (Stuttgart: Metier, 1990).

Eitner, Robert, 'Karl Friedrich Zelter', *ADB* 45 (1898): 46–52.

Elvers, Rudolf, 'Ein nicht abgesandter Brief Zelters an Haydn', *Musik und Verlag* (1968): 243–5.

—— 'Musikdrucker, Musikalienhändler und Musikverleger in Berlin 1750 bis 1850. Eine Übersicht' in Georg von Holschneider and Andreas Dadelsen (eds), *Festschrift Walter Gerstenberg zum 60.Geburtstag* (Wolfenbüttel, 1964).

Fairley, Barker, 'Inspiration and Letter Writing. A Note on Goethe's Beginnings as a Poet', *GR* 24 (1949):161–7.

—— 'Goethe's Last Letter' in *University of Toronto Quarterly* 27 (1957/58): 1–9.

Fischer, Lysander, 'Zwischen Beruf und Berufung. Ein Erinnerungsblatt für Carl Friedrich Zelter, den Mauer und Musiker, den Freund Goethes. Zu Zelters 200. Geburtstag', *Gewerbeschule* 49 (1958): 66–72 and 88–93.

Fischer-Dieskau, Dietrich, Carl Friedrich Zelter und das Berliner Musikleben seiner Zeit. Eine Biographie (Berlin: Nicolai, 1997).

Friedländer, Max, Gedichte von Goethe in Compositionen seiner Zeitgenossen, 2 vols *SchGG* 11 (1896) and *SchGG* 31 (1916).

—— *Das deutsche Lied im 18. Jahrhundert. Quellen und Studien*, 2 vols (Stuttgart and Berlin: Cotta, 1902; reprint, Hildesheim: Georg Olms Verlag, 1962).

—— 'Goethe und die Musik' in *GJb* 3 (1916): 275–340.

—— 'Musikerbriefe an Goethe', *GJb* 12 (1891).

Gappenach, Hans, 'Aus der Geschichte des Liedes "Es war einmal ein König in Thule"'. *Zum Gedenken an den 200. Geburtstag von Carl Friedrich Zelter, Der Chor* 10 (1958): 187f.

Geiger, Ludwig (ed.), 'Aus Berliner Briefen Augusts von Goethe (19–26 Mai 1819), Ein Brief der Ottilie (undatiert)', *GJb* 28 (1907): 26–56.

—— 'Einleitung' in *Der Briefwechsel zwischen Goethe und Zelter* (Leipzig: Reclam, o.J) vol.1, pp. 3–32.

Gerhard, Anselm, *Musik und Ästhetik im Berlin Moses Mendelssohns, Wolfenbütteler Studien zur Aufklärung*, vol. 25 (Tübingen: M. Niemeyer, 1999).

Gilow, Hermann, 'Zur ersten Aufführung von Goethes *Mahomet* in Berlin 1810', *GJb* 28 (1907): 218–24.

Goslich, Ilse, 'Zelter und seine Verleger', *JbSK* 8 (1929/30): 67–101.

Grupe, Walter, 'Neues über den Briefwechsel Goethe-Zelter', *Neue deutsche Literatur* 7 (1959): 152–4.

Guttmann, Oskar, *Johann Karl Friedrich Rellstab. Ein Beitrag zur Musikgeschichte Berlins* (Berlin: E. Ebering, 1910).

Hasselberg, Felix, 'Briefentwürfe Karl Friedrich Zelters. Ein kleiner Beitrag zu seinem Briefwechsel mit Goethe' in *Der Autographen-Sammler* 5 (1941), vol.9.

Hecker, Max (ed.), 'Die Briefe Johann Friedrich Reichardts an Goethe', *GJb* 11 (1925): 197–252.

—— 'Goetheverehrung der Goethezeit', *GJb* 21 (1935): 152–99.

—— 'Vater und Sohn. Briefe Carl Friedrich Zelters an seinen Stiefsohn Carl Flöricke', *Funde und Forschungen. Eine Festgabe für Julius Wahle* (Leipzig: 1921): 17–36.

—— 'Zelters Tod. Ungedrückte Briefe' *JbSK* 7 (1927/28), pp. 104–172.

Heinritz, Reinhard, 'Zur Theorie und Poetik des Briefwechsels im Umkreis von Klassik und Romantik, *Literatur im Wissenschaft und Unterricht* 20 (1987): 374–88.

Henzel, Christoph, 'Die Musikalien der Sing-Akademie zu Berlin und die Berliner Graun-Überlieferung', *Jahrbuch des Staatlichen Instituts für Musikforschung – Preußischer Kulturbesitz* (2002): 60–106.

Hermann, Rudolf, 'Goethes und Zelters Plan einer Reformationskantate' in *Zeitschrift für systematische Theologie* 18 (1941): 213–23.
—— Die Bedeutung der Bibel in Goethes Briefen an Zelter (Berlin, 1948).
Herzfeld, Friedrich, 'Sing-Akademischer Alltag' in Werner Bollert (ed.), *Sing-Akademie zu Berlin. Festschrift* (Berlin: Rembrandt Verlag, 1966), pp. 11–20.
Heuss, Alfred, 'Goethe-Zelters Lied "Um Mitternacht"', *Zeitschrift für Musik* 91 (1924): 685–92.
Hey'l, Bettina, Der Briefwechsel zwischen Goethe und Zelter. Lebenskunst und literarisches Projekt. (Tübingen: Niemeyer, 1996).
'Goethe und Zelters Reflexionen über die menschliche Stimme in *JbDSG* 40 (1996):181–209.
Hillebrand, Karl, 'Die Berliner Gesellschaft in den Jahren 1789 bis 1815' (1870) in Hermann Uhde-Bernays (ed.), *Unbekannte Essays* (Bern: Francke, 1955), pp. 11–81.
Holtzmann, Sigrid (ed.), *Zelters im Spiegel seines Briefwechsels mit Goethe* (Weimar: Gustav Kiepenheuer Verlag, 1957).
Jacobi, E.R., 'C.F. Zelters kritische Beleuchtung von J.N. Forkels Buch über J.S. Bach aufgrund neu aufgefundener Manuskripte', *International Musicological Society Congress Report* 11 (Kopenhagen: Hanson, 1972): 462–6.
Jappe, Georg, 'Vom Briefwechsel zum Schriftwechsel', *Merkur* 23 (1969): 351–62.
Kalischer, Alfred Christian,'Beethoven und Zelter' in *Beethoven und Berlin* (Leipzig: Schuster and Loeffler, 1908), pp. 211ff.
Kania, Hans, 'Ein neuentdecktes Zelter-Bild in Potsdam', *Potsdamer Männergesangsverein Monatliche Mitteilungen*, 5 Juni 1929, 77f.
Kettig, Konrad, 'Goetheverehrung in Berlin. Ein Besuch von August und Ottilie von Goethe in der preußischen Residenz 1819', *Schriften des Vereins für die Geschichte Berlins* 61 (1977): 87–132.
Knudsen, Jans, 'Goethes Werke auf den Berliner Bühnen' in Fritz Moser (ed.), *Goethe in Berlin* (Berlin: Wedding-Verlag, 1949): 95–127.
Koskenniemi, Heikki, *Studien zur Idee und Phraseologie des griechischen Briefes bis 400 n.Chr.* (Helsinki: Suomalaien Tiedeakatemie, 1956).
Kossmann, E.F., 'Der Chor in Zelters Auferstehungskantate', *Zeitschrift für Musikwissenschaft* 11 (1928/29).
Kräupl, Irmgard, 'Die Zelter-Bildnisse im Goethe-Museum Düsseldorf. Mit einem Verzeichnis aller übrigen nachweisbaren Porträts', *JbSK* 1 (1963): 70–100.
Kruse, Georg Richard, 'Goethe, Zelter und Otto Nicolai' in *GJb* 31 (1910): 163–68.
—— *Carl Friedrich Zelter* (Leipzig: Reclam, 1915).
Kuhlo, Hermann, Geschichte der Zelterschen Liedertafel von 1809 bis 1909 (Berlin: Horn und Raasch, 1909).
Kühne, Gustav, [Rez. Der Teile 4–6 des Goethe-Zelterschen Briefwechsels] in *Jahrbücher für wissenschaftliche Kritik* 1 (1835): 953–65; 969–72.

Kühnlenz, Fritz, 'Carl Friedrich Zelter' in Fritz Kühnlenz, *Weimarer Porträts. Bedeutende Frauen und Männer um Goethe und Schiller* (Rudolstadt: Greifenverlag, 1993), pp. 65–135.

Ledebur, Carl, *Tonkünstler-Lexikon Berlins von den Ältesten Zeiten bis auf die Gegenwart* (Berlin: L. Rauh, 1861).

Lichtenstein, Heinrich, *Zur Geschichte der* Sing-Akademie *in Berlin* (Berlin: Trautwein 1843).

Liebe, Anneliese, 'Carl Freidrich Zelter 1758–1832' in *Kulturelles Erbe. Lebensbilder aus sechs Jahrhunderten* (Bonn: Dümmler, 1985), vol. 2, p. 51f.

Lobe, Johann Christian, 'Gespräche mit Goethe und Zelter', *Fliegende Blätter für Musik* (1857).

—— 'Gespräche mit Goethe und Zelter' in Johann Christian Lobe, *Aus dem Leben eines Musikers* (Leipzig: J.J. Weber, 1859), pp. 81–141.

—— 'Gespräch mit Zelter' in Wilhelm Bode, *Stunden mit Goethe,* (Berlin: E.G. Mittler & Sohn, 1912), vol. 8, pp. 187–202.

Maack, Rudolf, 'Zelters Goethelied. Geschichte einer Freundschaft', *Der Kreis* 10 (1933): 21–32.

Mahling, Christoph Helmut, 'Zum Musikbetrieb Berlins und seinen Institutionen in der ersten Hälfte des 19. Jahrhunderts' in Carl Dahlhaus (ed.), *Studien zur Musikgeschichte Berlins im frühen 19. Jahrhundert* (Regensburg: Bosse, 1980), pp. 227–84.

Mann, Friedrich, 'Die Gunst des Augenblicks von Friedrich von Schiller; vierstimmig in Musik gesetzt von Carl Freidrich Zelter (Berlin, 1805)', *Berlinische Musikalische Zeitung* 1 (1805): 344–6.

—— 'Feierliche Versammlungen der Berlinischen Sing-Akademie im Jahr 1805', *Berlinische Musikalische Zeitung* 1 (1805), no. 19, column 73 and no. 27, columns 105–108.

Marggraf, Hermann, 'Goethe und die Mittwochgesellschaft' in *Blätter für literarische Unterhaltung* 34 (1858).

Meier, Andreas, 'Carl Freidrich Zelter: Ein literarischer Zeitgenosse' in Reinhold Kubrik und Andreas Meier (eds), *Zelter, Carl Friedrich. Lieder. Faksimile der wichtigsten gedruckten Sammlungen nebst Kritischem Bericht* (Munich: *Das Erbe deutscher Musik*, 1995), pp. xiii–xxii

Meyer, Christoph, 'Goethe in seinen Briefen', *Eckart* 28 (1959): 62–6.

Mies, Paul, 'Zu Musikauffassung und Stil der Klassik. Eine Studie aus dem Goethe-Zelter-Briefwechsel 1799–1832, *Zeitschrift für Musikwissenschaft* 13 (1930/31): 432–43.

Milltitz, Karl Borromäus [Rezension des Briefwechsels zwischen Goethe und Zelter], *Allgemeine Musikalische Zeitung* (1834), 9 Juli, column 458.

Milz, Friedemann, 'Zur Ästhetik der Berliner Sing-Akademie' in Werner Bollert (ed.), *Sing-Akademie zu Berlin. Festschrift* (Berlin: Rembrandt Verlag, 1966), pp. 50–60.

Morgenroth, Alfred, *Carl Friedrich Zelter: Eine Musikgeschichtliche Studie 1. Teil* (*Biographisches*) (Berlin: unpublished Doctoral Dissertation, Friedrich-Wilhelms-Universität, 1922).
—— 'Carl. Freidrich Zelter. Eine musikalische Studie' in Jahrbuch der Dissertationen der Philosophischen Fakultät der Friedrich-Wilhelms-Universität zu Berlin. Dekanatsjahr 1921–1922 (1926): 276–80.
Mosel, J.G.F. von, [Rezension des Briefwechsels zwischen Goethe und Zelter] in *Wiener Jahrbücher der Literatur* 74 (1836): 102–38.
Moser, Hans Joachim, 'Karl Friedrich Zelter und das Lied' in *Jahrbuch der Musikbibliothek Peters* 39 (1932).
—— 'Carl Friedrich Zelter und das Lied' in *Goethe und die Musik* (Leipzig: C.F. Peters, 1949), pp. 78–91.
Müller, Joachim, 'Drei Briefe Goethes an Zelter. Taedium vitae und fortdauerndes Leben. Eine Kommentierung im Kontext beider Briefwechsel', *Zeitschrift für Germanistik* 1 (1980): 166–82.
Müller. Wolfgang G., 'Der Brief als Spiegel der Seele. Zur Geschichte eines Topos der Epistolartheorie von der Antike bis zu Samuel Richardson' in *Antike und Abendland* 26 (1980):138–57.
Müller, Wolfgang, 'Der Brief' in Klaus Weißenberger, *Prosakunst ohne Erzählen*. (Tübingen: Max Niemeyer Verlag, 1985).
Müller, Fritz, 'Karl Friedrich Zelters Verdienste um die Wiedererweckung Bachscher Tonwerke', *Der Kirchenmusiker* 10 (1959).
Müller-Blattau, Joseph, 'Goethe und die Kantate' in *Jahrbücher der Musikbibliothek Peters* 38 (1931): 49–68.
—— 'Karl Friedrich Zelters Königsberger Briefe (1809)', *Altpreußische Forschungen* 12 (1935): 256–76.
—— 'Zelters Rede auf Friedrich den Großen', *Deutsche Musikkultur* 1 (1936/37).
—— 'Karl Friedrich Zelter, Mauermeister und Musiker' in *Deutsches Jahrbuch der Musikwissenschaft* 2 (1957).
Neumann, Wilhelm, 'Briefwechsel zwischen Goethe und Zelter in den Jahren 1796 bis 1832, ed. Dr. Friedrich Wilhelm Riemer, Großherzoglich Sächsischem Hofrathe und Bibliothekar. Erster bis dritter Theil. Berlin 1833', *Berliner Jahrbücher für Wissenschaft und Kritik*, 8 & 9 (1834) and in Wilhelm Neumann, *Schriften* 2 (1835):10–20.
Nickisch, Reinhard M.G., *Brief* (Stuttgart: Metzler, 1991).
Nitsche, Peter, 'Die Liedertafel in System der Zelterschen Gründung' in Carl Dahlhaus (ed.), *Studien zur Musikgeschichte Berlins im frühen 19 Jahrhundert* (Regensburg: Bosse, 1980), pp. 11–26.
Ottenberg, Hans-Günter, '"Möge Dich dieses Lied ... zu einer heitern Kompositionaufregen". Marginalien zu Zelters Vertonung eines Goethe-Gedichts' in Peter Bloch, (ed) *Denkmal Albrecht Thaers: Theodor Fontane, Johann Wolfgang von Goethe, Hugo Hagen, Christian Daniel Rauch, Karl Friedrich Zelter* (Berlin: Domäne Dahlem, 1992), pp. 109–12.

Petsch, 'Zelters Geburtsort und Geburtshaus', Brandenburgia, Monatsblatt der Gesellschaft für Heimatkunde der Provinz Brandenburg 5 (1896/97): 194.

Pfister, Werner, Vorwort in *Briefwechsel zwischen Goethe und Zelter* (Zurich: Artemis, 1987), pp. v–xxxi.

Pniower, Otto, 'Von Zelter bis Fontane. Berliner Briefe' in *Beiträge zur Literatur- und Theatergeschichte. Festschrift für Ludwig Geiger zum 70. Geburtstag* (Berlin: Behr, 1918), pp. 163–81.

Porter, Abbot H., 'Letters to the Self. The Clostered Writer in Nonretrospective Fiction', *PMLA* 95 (1980): 23–41.

Pröper, Rolf, Die Bühnenwerke Johann Friedrich Reichardts: 1752–1814 (Bonn: H. Bouvier, 1965).

Pulver, Jeffrey, 'Beethoven in the Goethe-Zelter Correspondence', *ML* 17 (1936): 124–30.

Rehberg, Karl, 'Ausstrahlungen der Sing-Akademie auf die Musikerziehung' in Werner Bollert (ed.) *Sing-Akademie zu Berlin. Festschrift* (Berlin: Rembrandt Verlag, 1966), pp. 106–16.

Reich, Willi (ed.), *Karl Friedrich Zelter. Selbstdarstellung* (Zürich: Manesse Verlag 1955).

Reichardt, Johann Friedrich, 'Die Berlinische Sing-Akademie', *Berlinische Musikalische Zeitung* 1 (1805): 29–31.

Rellstab, Ludwig [Rezension des Briefwechsels zwischen Goethe und Zelter] in *Vossische Zeitung* 299 (1833), 21. December.

Reuter, Hans-Heinrich, 'Die Weihe der Kraft. Ein Dialog zwischen Goethe und Zelter und seine Wiederaufnahme bei Fontane' in Wilhelm Heinse, Helmut Holtzhauer and Bernhard Zeller (eds), *Studien zur Goethezeit. Festschrift für Lieselotte Blumenthal* (Weimar: Böhlau, 1968) pp. 357–75.

Ribbeck, August Friedrich, 'Rede am 25jährigen Stiftungsfeste der Zelterschen Liedertafel, den 28 Jan. 1834' (Manuscript, DLA Marbach).

Richter, Thomas, 'Bibliotheca Zelteriana'. Rekonstruktion der Bibliothek Carl Friedrich Zelters. Alphabetischer Katalog (Stuttgart: Metzler Verlag, 1999).

—— Die Dialoge über Literatur im Briefwechsel zwischen Goethe und Zelter (Stuttgart: Metzler Verlag, 1999).

—— 'Doris Zelters Briefe nach Weimar, 1818–1834, Part 1, Die Briefe an Goethe', *GJb* 113 (1996): 291–307.

—— ' Doris Zelters Briefe nach Weimar, 1818–1834, Part 2, Die Briefe an Goethes Umkreis (1819–1832) *Goethe-Jahrbuch* 115 (1998): 245–80.

—— 'Ein Brief Doris Zelters über den Besuch mit ihrem Vater bei Goethe im Juli 1826', *GJb* 112 (1995): 365–73.

—— 'Projekt einer Edition von Carl Friedrich Zelters Gesammelter Korrspondenz. Als Ergänzung zu seinem Briefwechsel mit Goethe. Bericht und Suchanzeige', *Jahrbuch für Volksliedforschung* 40 (1995):135.

Riemer, Friedrich Wilhelm, Vorbericht des Herausgebers in *Briefwechsel zwischen Goethe und Zelter in den Jahren 1796 bis 1832* (6 vols, Berlin: Hermann Böhlau, 1833–34), vol. 1, pp. v–xxxviii.

Rintel, Wilhelm, 'Die erste Aufführung der Jahreszeiten von Haydn in Leipzig und Berlin und ein eigenhändiger Brief Haydns an Zelter nebst dessen Antwort', *Vossische Zeitung* 247/31 (1891): *Sonntagsbeilage* 22.

Rochlitz, Friedrich, *Für Freunde der Tonkunst* (4 vols, Leipzig: Carl Cnobloch, 1824–32).

—— 'Über Zeltern. 1832', *Allgemeine Musikalische Zeitung* 24 (1832), 13 and vi.

—— [Rezension des Briefwechsels zwischen Goethe und Zelter] in *Allgemeine Musikalische Zeitung* 37 (1835), 18 February, column 101ff.

Roentz, Wilhelm, 'C.F. Zelter und die Zeit seines akademischen Singkollegiums 1830–1832', *Deutsche Sängerbundeszeitung* 22/4 (1930), no.3, p. 3f.

Runze, Maximilian, 'Randglossen zu Breifen Zelters an Goethe. Auf Grund neu erschlossener Quellen', *Der Schatzgräber* 6 (1926/27):15–19.

Schaeffer, Albrecht, 'Goethes Zelter', *Kunst Welt Wissen* 1 (1931): 17. GSA 151/195.

Schleiermacher, Friedrich, 'Rede am Sarge Zelters' in Wilhelm Rintel, *Carl Friedrich Zelter. Eine Lebensbeschreibung* (Berlin: Janke Verlag, 1861), pp. 300–304 and in Blumner, Martin, *Geschichte der Sing-Akademie zu Berlin* (Berlin: Horn und Raasch, 1891), pp. 193–5.

Schmidt, Franz, 'Goethes letzter Brief', *GJb* 28 (1966): 284–8.

Schmidt, Jürgen, Goethes Briefstil in den Jahren 1805–1814. Beiträge zum Verständnis von Goethes Entwicklung un der Zwischenepoche nach Schillers Tod. (Hamburg, unpublished Doctoral Dissertation, 1957).

Schneider, Max, F., 'Eine Trauermusik der Sing-Akademie für Prinz Louis Ferdinand. Drei bisher unveröffentlichte Briefe der Mutter des Prinzen an Carl Friedrich Zelter' in Werner Bollert (ed.), *Sing-Akademie zu Berlin. Festschrift.* (Berlin: Rembrandt Verlag, 1966), pp. 90–96.

Schottländer, Johann-Wolfgang (ed.), *Carl Friedrich Zelters Darstellungen seines Lebens. Zum ersten Male vollständig nach den Handschriften* SchGG 44 (1931).

—— 'Die Reise nach Königsberg', *Vossische Zeitung* (1932) 6. August: Unterhaltungsblatt.

—— 'Einleitung' in *Carl Freidrich Zelters Darstellung seines Lebens* SchGG 44 (1931): xi–xxvii.

—— 'Zelters Beziehungen zu den Komponisten seiner Zeit', *JbSK* 8 (1929/30): 134–248.

—— 'Zelters Beziehungen zu Breitkopf und Härtel' in *Zeitschrift für Musikwissenschaft* 15 (1932): 97f.

—— 'Zelters "Johanna Sebus"', *JbSK* 9 (1931).

Schrenk, Oswald, Berlin und die Musik. 200 Jahre Musikleben einer Stadt. 1740–1940 (Berlin: Bote und Bock, 1940).

Schröder, Cornelia, (ed.), Carl Friedrich Zelter und die Akademie. Dokumente und Briefe zur Entstehung der Musik-Sektion in der Preußischen Akademie der Künste. (Berlin: Akademie der Künste Monographien und Biographien 3, 1959).

Schünemann, Georg, 'Die Bachpflege der Berliner Sing-Akademie, *Bach-Jahrbuch* 25 (1928): 138–71.
—— *Die Singakademie zu Berlin* (Regensburg: G. Bosse, 1941).
—— *Carl Friedrich Zelter, der Begründer der preußischen Musikpflege* (Berlin: Max Hesse, 1932).
—— *Carl Friedrich Zelter. Der Mensch und sein Werk* (Berlin: Berliner Bibliophilen-Abend, 1937).
—— Die Sing-Akademie zu Berlin 1791–1941 (Regensburg: G. Bosse, 1941).
Schwab, Heinrich W., *Sangbarkeit, Popularität und Kunstlied. Studien zu Lied und Liedästethetik der mittleren Goethezeit 1770–1814* (Regensburg: G. Bosse, 1965).
Schwartz, Rudolf, 'Zu Characteristik Zelters', *Jahrbuch der Musikbibliothek Peters*, 22 (1929/30).
Schwartz, Herta, 'Brieftheorie in der Romantik' in Herta Schwartz, Angelika Ebrecht And Regina Nörtemann (eds), *Brieftheorie des 18.Jahrhunderts* (Stuttgart: Metzler, 1990), pp. 225–38.
Sieber, Ludwig, *Karl Friedrich Zelter und der deutsche Männergesang* (Basel, 1862).
Taubert, Karl Heinz, *Carl Friedrich Zelter (1758–1832). Ein Leben durch das Handwerk für die Musik* (Berlin: Ries & Erler, 1958).
Unseld, Siegfried, 'Das Briefgespräch zwischen Goethe und Zelter in Siegfried Unseld, *Goethe und seine Verleger* (Frankfurt am Main/ Leipzig: Insel Verlag, 1991), pp. 600–615.
Valentin, Erich, 'C.F. Zelters Beziehungen zu Magdeburg. Ein Kapitel aus der Musikgeschichte Magdeburgs zu Beginn des 19. Jahrhunderts', *Montagsblatt. Wissenschaftliche Beilage der Magdeburgischen Zeitung* 74 (1932), 16 May.
—— 'Goethes einziger Duzfreund. Ein Wort für Carl Freidrich Zelter', *Neue Zeitschrift für Musik* 119 (1958).
——'Goethe-Jahre ist auch Zelter-Jahr' in *Lied und Chor* 74 (1982):103f.
Varnhagen von Ense, Karl August, *Goethe in den Zeugnißen der Mitlebenden. Erste Sammlung* (Berlin: Dümmler, 1823).
Vesper, Will, 'Vorwort' in Will Vesper (ed.), *Goethes Briefwechsel mit Zelter* (Berlin: Deutsche Bibliothek, o.J), pp. v–vii.
Victor, Walther, *Goethe in Berlin* (Berlin: Aufbau-Verlag, 1955).
—— 'Carl Friedrich Zelter. Über die Volksverbundenheit Goethes und eine Männerfreundschaft am Beginn des bürgerlichen Zeitalters' in Walther Victor, *Verachtet mir die Meister nicht. Reden und Schriften zu den Klassikern der deutschen Literatur und des Marxismus* (Weimar: Volksverlag, 1960), pp. 239–60.
—— *Carl Friedrich Zelter und seine Freundschaft mit Goethe* (Berlin: Das Neue Berlin, 1960).
Wachsmuth, Bruno, 'Goethes Verhältnis zu Berlin' in Fritz Moser (ed.) *Goethe in Berlin* (Berlin: Wedding-Verlag,1949), pp. 17–37.

Wahle, Julius, 'Drei Briefe Goethes an die Familie Mendelssohn-Bartholdy', *GJb* 19 (1898): 48–52.

Wätzold, Paul, *Carl Friedrich Zelter als Chordirigent* (Pritzwalk: Koch, 1932).

—— 'Zelters Lebensbild' in Nachrichtenblatt des Berliner Lehrer-Gesang-Vereins 9 (1932), 1, 2 & 5.

Wahl, Dora, 'Goethe und Zelter "damals in Wiesbaden"', *JbSK* 1 (1963): 101–38.

Weissmann, Adolf, *Berlin als Musikstadt. Geschichte der Oper und des Konzerts von 1740 bis 1911* (Berlin, Leipzig: Schuster und Loeffler, 1911).

Weizsäcker, Paul, 'Zelters Bild', *Goethe-Jahrbuch* 22 (1901): 107.

Wellek, Albert, 'Zur Phänomenologie des Briefes, Die Sammlung 15 (1960): 339–55 and in Albert Wellek, *Witz, Lyrik, Sprache. Beiträge zur Literatur- und Sprachtheorie mit einem Anhang über den Fortschritt der Wissenschaften* (Bern/Munich: Francke, 1970), pp. 43–67.

Welter, Friedrich, 'Die Musikbibliothek der Sing-Akademie zu Berlin. Versuch eines Nachweises ihrer früheren Bestände in Sing-Akademie zu Berlin'. *Festschrift*, (ed.) Werner Bollert (Berlin: Rembrandt Verlag, 1966), pp. 33–47.

Wigand, Otto, 'Zelter, der Berliner Mauermeister und Musikmeister' in *Jahrbücher für Wissenschaft und Kunst* 4 (1855): 2.

Wittmann, Gertraud, *Das klavierbegleitete Sololied Karl Friedrich Zelters* (Berlin: Triltsch & Huther, 1936).

Wulf, Berthold, 'Karl Friedrich Zelter, der Freund Goethes' in *Christengemeinschaft* 30 (1958):116–19.

Zehm, Edith, 'Briefwechsel mit Carl Friedrich Zelter' in Bernd Witte, Theo Buck, Hans-Dietrich Dahnke, Regine Otto and Peter Schmidt (eds), *Goethe-Handbuch* (4 vols, Stuttgart: Metzler Verlag 1997/98), vol. 4, pp. 484 and 496.

Zelter, Carl Friedrich, *Karl Friedrich Fasch* (Berlin: J.F. Unger, 1801).

# Index

The German definite article (der, die, das) is ignored in the alphabetical order.

First names in italics indicate names by which a person is usually known.

Abschatz, Hans Aßmann von (1646–1699) 45
Aeschylus
  *Eumenides* 51
  *Seven against Thebes* 51
  *Supplices* 51
Akademie der Künste 27, 125, 165, 245, 265, 404
Alfieri, Vittorio Graf (1749–1803)
  *Saul* 155
Allegri, Gregorio (1582–1652) 15
Almonde, Marianne Angelika von (1804–1866) 299, 300
Anatole, Auguste 202
Anatole, Constance Hippolyte 202
André, Johann Anton (1775–1842) 215
André, Johann Christian (1741–1799) 210
Arnim, Achim (Ludwig Joachim) von (1781–1831) 120, 145
  *Des Knaben Wunderhorn* 82, 138
Arnold, Ignaz Ferdinand, *Mozarts Geist* (1774–1812) 48, 52
Auber, Daniel François Esprit (1782–1871)
  *Fra Diavolo oder Das Gasthaus bei Terracina* 547
  *Der Gott und die Bajadere* 504, 546
  *La fiancée* (*Die Braut*) 451
  *La Muette de Portici* (*Die Stumme von Portici*) 420, 450
  *Die Liebestrank* 531
Aumur, Jean Pierre (1774/76–1833) 487
  *Aline, Königin von Golkonda* 291

Bach, Carl Philipp Emanuel (1714–1788) 14, 172, 205, 290, 530
  *Heilig* for double choir (Wq 217) 402
  *Sonata in A minor* 183

Bach, Johann Sebastian (1685–1750) 315
  *The Art of Fugue* 9
  Cantata (BWV 22) 39, 103, 110
  Cantata (BWV 39) 376
  Cantata (BWV 103) 376
  Cantata (BWV 110) 376
  Chorales 248
  *Das Wohltemperirte Clavier* (BWV 846–93) 248, 250, 252
  Mass in B minor (BWV 232) 26, 402, 459, 494
  Overture in D Major 13
  revival 13, 18, 34, 423, 525
  *St John Passion* 13, 371
  *St Matthew Passion* (BWV 244) 18, 22, 34, 309, 422, 423, 424, 426, 429, 463, 504, 525
  *Singet dem Herrn eine neues Lied, die Gemeine der Heiligen soll Ihn loben* (BWV 225) 521
Bach, Wilhelm *Friedemann* (1710–1784) 428, 429
Bacon, Francis (1561–1626) 416
Bader, Carl Adam (1789–1870) 392, 423, 426, 427, 465
Bagge, Charles Ernst von (1722–1791) 278–9, 431
Bavaria, Ludwig I of (1786–1868) 386, 410
Bavaria, *Therese* Charlotte Luise Friederkike Amalie of (1792–1854) 386
Beethoven, Ludwig van (1770–1827)
  *Christus am Ölberge* 159, 506–8
  Coriolan Overture, (op. 62) 402
  *Egmont* 69, 166, 167
  *Fidelio* 493, 504

Goethe on 156–7, 159
Mass in D Major (op. 123) 402
Symphony no. 3 in E flat major, the
Eroica Symphony (op. 55) 267
Symphony no. 5 in C minor (op. 67)
14, 402
Symphony no. 6 in F, the Pastoral
Symphony (op. 68) 267
*Wellington's Victory* (op. 91) 207–8,
267
Zelter on 259, 261–2
Bellini, Vincenzo (1801–1835)
*Der Pirat* 541
Benda, Franz (František) (1709–1786) 515
Benda, *Georg* Anton (Jirí Antonín)
(1722–1795)
*Ariadne auf Naxos* 147
*Medea* 147
Bendavid (Ben David), Lazarus (1762–1832) 428
Berger, Ludwig (1777–1839) 281, 319,
356, 411, 459, 477, 478
Berlin Hymnbook 460, 476
*Berliner Allgemeine Musikalische Zeitung*
(ed. A.B. Marx, 1824–1830) 339,
343
Berliner Künstlerverein 249, 251, 265, 340
*Berlinische Musikalische Zeitung* ed.
Reichardt 74, 312
Berlioz, Louis Hector (1803–1869)
*Huit Scènes de Faust* 23, 24, 430, 438,
446
*La Damnation de Faust* 24
Bertuch, Friedrich Justin, Journal des
Luxus und der Moden 7
Biedenfeld, Eugenie von (née Bonasegla)
(1788–1862) 320
Biedrzynski, Effi, Goethes Weimar 7
Birch-Pfeiffer, Charlotte (1799/1800–1868)
485
Blum, Karl Heinrich (c.1786–1844) 291,
449, 465
Bodenschatz, Erhard (c.1576–1636) 236
Bohn, Friedrich (1775–1872) 350
Boisserée, Johann Sulpiz (1783–1854) 216,
242, 461
Boucher, Alexandre Jean (1778–1861) 277,
278, 280, 281, 282, 284, 286

Boucher, Céleste (née Gallyot) (d.1841)
277, 278, 280, 281, 282
Brandt, Caroline (1794–1852) 220
Breßlau Friedrich Julius von (1776–1860)
201
Breidenstein, Heinrich Carl (1796–1876)
395
Breitkopf und Härtel, publishers 9, 98, 167,
205, 307, 347, 379, 395, 425, 505,
528
Brentano, Clemens (1778–1842) 120
*Des Knaben Wunderhorn* 82, 138
Brentano, Elizabeth *Bettine* (1785–1859) 145
Brizzi, Antonio Giovanni Maria (1770–
1854) 143, 150, 212
Brühl, *Carl* Friedrich Moritz Paul von
(1772–1837) 17, 180, 279, 283,
289, 333, 342, 427, 474
Buchholz, Carl August 231
Buchholz, Johann Simon 231
Burg Theatre, Vienna 256
Busolt, J.E. 423
Byron, Lord (1788–1824) 496

*Cäcelia, eine Zeitschrift für die
musikalische Welt* 320, 377
Calderón de la Barca, Pedro (1600–1681),
*Der standhafte Prinz, Don
Fernando von Portugal* 145
Campi, Antonia (née Miklaszewicz)
(1773–1822) 255, 284
Caracci, Annibale (1560–1609) 501
Carpani, Giuseppe Antonio (1751/52–1825)
*Le Haydine* 140, 255
*Le Rossiniane* 255
Catalani, Angelica (1780–1849) 201, 209,
213, 214, 215, 216, 234, 286, 372
Cellini, Benvenuto (1500–1571) 544
*Chaos* (Journal) 475, 477, 509–10, 531
Chélard, Hippolyte André Jean Baptiste
(1789–1861) 409
*Macbeth* 410, 454
Cherubini, Luigi (1760–1842) 121
Mass in A major for three-part choir
and orchestra 338
*Medea* 529
*Requiem* 258
*Der Wasserträger* 529

Chladni, Ernst Florens Friedrich (1756–1827) 42, 196, 199, 211, 326, 366, 372, 373, 434
  *Die Akustik* 9, 365
chronometer, *see* metronome
Cibbini, Katharina (1785–1858) 259, 260
Cimarosa, Domenico
  *Il matrimonio segreto* (*Die heimliche Ehe*) 218, 239, 302, 384, 481
Claudius, Matthias (1740–1815)
  'An die Freude' 138
  *Der Mensch lebt und bestehet* 74, 75
Coleridge, A.D., *Goethe's Letters to Zelter* 2
Corelli, Arcangelo (1653–1713) 515
Cotta, Elizabeth von (1789–1859) 413
Cotta, Johann Friedrich von (1764–1832) 92, 106
Couperin, François (1668–1733) 23, 373, 375
  *L'art de toucher le clavecin* 374
Cramer, Franz (1772–1848) 414
Crelinger, Sophie *Auguste* Friederike (née Düring) (1795–1865) 268, 270, 426, 427

Descartes, René (1596–1650) 416
Devrient, Philipp *Eduard* (1801–1877) 21, 418, 423, 465
Diderot, Denis
  *Essai sur la peinture*, Goethe's translation 8
  *Le Neveu de Rameau*, Goethe's translation 8, 296, 545
Drechsler, Joseph (1782–1852), *Der verlorne Sohn* 255
Dryden, John (1631–1700) 99, 102, 278, 369
Dürer, Albrecht (1471–1528) 400
Dussek, Johann Ludwig (1760–1812) 248

Eberwein, Franz *Carl* Adalbert (1786–1868) 106
  'Am Neujahrstage' 108–9
  *Der Graf von Gleichen* 108, 319
  'Ich denke dein' 109
Eberwein, Regina *Henriette* (née Haßler) (1790–1849) 104, 272

Eckermann, Johann Peter (1792–1854) 307, 472, 496, 497
Ehlers, Johann Wilhelm (1774–1845) 72, 102, 483
Elßler, Franziska (*Fanny*) (1810–1884) 485, 546
Elßler, Theresia (Therese) (1808–1884) 485
Emerson, Ralph Waldo (1803–1882) 15
Engel, Johann Jacob (1741–1802) 482
Eunike, *Katharina* Friederike Dorothea Bernadine (1804–1842) 320
Euripedes
  *Helena* 51
  *Iphigenie in Tauris* 51

Fasch, Carl Friedrich Christian (1736–1800) 34, 238, 294, 334, 404, 457
  *Missa a 16 voci in quarto Cori* 34, 521
  *Versetto a 5 Voci Soli* (*Meine Seele hanget Dir an*) 174
Fichte, Johann Gottlieb (1762–1814) 64, 84
Fichte, Maria Johanna (née Rahn (1755–1819) 64
Fischer-Schwarzböck, Beatrix 534
Fjodorowna, Maria, Empress of Russia (1759–1828) 245, 291, 434
Flemming, Friedrich Ferdinand (1778–1813) 173
Flöricke, Carl (1784–1812) 27, 47, 90, 159, 370, 425
Flöricke, Henriette (1780–1849) 89
Forkel, Johann Nikolaus (1749–1818) 243, 339–40, 370, 376
Förster, *Friedrich* Christoph (1791–1868), 'Die Campanelle' 475, 509
Frantzke, Thomas 6
Friedrich-Wilhelm University 27
Frisch, Johann Christoph (1738–1815) 86, 185
Froberger, Johann Jakob (1616–1667) 315
Fux, Johann Josef (1660–1741)
  *Gradus ad Parnassum* 9, 408
  *Singfundament* 406

Galilei, Galileo (1564–1642) 416
Gerber, Ernst *Ludwig* (1746–1819) 313

Gerbert, Martin
  *De Cantu* 112
Gerhardt, Paul (1607–1676) 45
Gern, Johann Georg (1757/59–1830) 460
Gesellschaft der Musikfreunde 396
Gherardini, Giovanni (1778–1861) 254
Gluck, Christoph Willibald (1714–1787)
  *Alceste* 484, 509
  *Armide* 191, 509
  *Iphigenie in Aulis* 130, 158
  *Iphigenie in Tauris* 479
Goethe, Christiane (née Vulpius) (1765–1816) 79, 195, 209
Goethe, Johann Wolfgang von (1749–1832)
  'Ach! Um deine feuchten Schwingen' 194, 263
  'Alle Menschen gross und klein' 269
  'Äolsharfe' ('Ich dacht ich habe keinen Schmerz') 295, 303
  on art, purpose of 9
  as *Augenmensch* 13
  'Aus wie vielen Elementen' 185, 251, 292, 412
  on Beethoven 156–7, 159
  on Beethoven's Fifth 14
  *Bei Allerhöchstet Anwesenheit Ihre Majestät der Kaiserin Mutter Maria Fjodorowna in Weimar Maskenzug* 247
  'Blumengruß' 336
  'Das Blümlein Wunderschön' 30, 32, 44, 461
  'Clärchens Lied' ('Freudvoll und Leidvoll') 69, 70
  *Clavigo* 201
  and contemporary music theory 11–12
  *Die Danaiden* 35
  'Derb und Tüchtig' 282
  *Dichtung und Wahrheit* 168, 217, 483, 511, 527
  'Donnerstag nach Belvedere' ('Die Lustigen von Weimar') 172
  'Dreistigkeit' 282, 292
  *Egmont* 69, 166
  *Eigentum* ('Ich weiß, daß mir nichts angehört') 169, 170
  'Ein Füllhorn von Blüten' 534
  'Elemente' 185, 268, 292, 412

*Elpenor* 96
'Ephiphaniasfest' ('Die heil'gen drei König') 157, 231, 289
*Epimenides* 177, 179, 180, 181, 182, 183, 186, 187, 189, 191, 197, 529
  performance 202
'Die Erinnerung' 30, 31, 45, 46
'Die erste Walpurgisnacht' 26, 30, 31, 40, 161, 162, 163, 527
'Es ist ein Schuß gefallen' 143
*Essai sur la peinture*, translation 8
'Euphrosyne' 131
*Farbenlehre* 11, 86, 92, 124, 357, 364
*Faust I* 18, 24, 96, 108, 117, 143, 144, 196, 199–201, 208, 253, 267–8, 269, 271, 446
*Faust II* 23, 24, 511, 523, 524
'Finnisches Lied' 144
'Flieh, Täubchen flieh' 229, 230
*Frühzeitiger Frühling* 35, 41
'Das Gastmahl' ('Offne Tafel') 172
'Gegenseitig' 229
'Die Geheimnisse' 150
'Generalbeichte' 102, 134, 138, 236, 349, 460, 477
'Genialisch Treiben' ('So wälz ich Unterlaß') 142
'Georgs Lied' 65, 66, 67
'Gleich und Gleich' 262
'Der Gott und die Bajadere' 194, 293, 369, 435, 461, 504, 546
'Das Göttliche' 490
*Götz von Berlichingen* 62, 63, 64, 65, 67
  performance 70–71, 524
on the Greek Chorus 51
'Herein, o du Guter' 230, 247
'Herr Ego' 204
'Hochzeitlied' 38, 39, 41, 42, 46
'In tausend Formen magst du dich verstecken' 269
'In te Domine speravi' (rhythmic setting) 170, 171, 172
*Iphigenie auf Tauris* 33, 60, 281
'Johanna Sebus' 124, 126, 143, 195, 196
'Der Junggesell und der Mühlbach' 30, 44
'Kennst du das Land'? 242, 315–6

'Klaggesang. Irisch' ('So singet laut den Pillalu') 249, 250, 251, 252
'Der König in Thule' 293, 461
'Kriegsglück'('Verwünschter weiß ich nichts im Krieg') 356, 358
'Künstlerlied' 231
'Künstlers Apotheose' 149
'Laßt fahren hin das Allzuflüchtige!' 337, 356, 418
*Leben des Benvenuto Cellini, Florentinischen Goldschmieds und Bildhauers, von ihm selbst geschrieben* 544
'Legende' 216, 461
*Die Leiden des jungen Werthers* 23, 161, 162, 198
on Leonardo's *Last Supper* 14
on lied/lieder 12, 15–16, 29, 30, 129, 134, 164, 235, 363
on listening to music 12–13
'Lustrum ist ein fremdes Wort' 236, 237, 243
on Lutheranism 222
'Mag der Grieche seinen Ton' 296
'Mailied' ('Wie herrlich leutet') 153, 525
on the minor tonality 110–11, 113–14
*Die Mitschuldigen* 321, 323, 516
'Der Müllerin Reue' 40, 41, 130
'Musen und Grazien in der Mark' 467
music theatre 6
music theory, engagement with 11–12
on music and visual arts 9
and musical modernity 3–4
musical reality, representation 13–15
musicality 15–16
musicological studies 8–11
mythologization 6–7
'Nachtgesang' 62, 64
'Nähe des Geliebten' 29, 109
*Die natürliche Tochter* 52, 54, 523
'Der neue Amadis' 41, 42
'Neue Liebe, Neues Leben' 153
*Neveu de Rameau*, translation 8
*Pandora* 117, 143, 144, 148, 276
*Prolog zu Eröffnung des Berliner Theaters im May, 1821* 281
*Die Propyläen* 94

*Prosperpina* 179, 185, 187, 188
'Das Publikum' 204
*Rameaus Neffe. Ein Dialog von Diderot aus dem Manuscript bersetzt und mit Anmerkungen begleitet von Goethe* 8, 75, 76, 196, 296, 545
'Rastlose Liebe' 25, 153, 525
'Rechenschaft' (aka 'Ächzlied' and 'Pflicht und Frohsinn') 132, 134
Reformation cantata, plan 220, 226
*Rinaldo* 152, 153, 154, 162, 430, 431, 437, 439
'Sagt es niemand, nur den Weisen' 268
'Sänge sind des Lebens Bild' 242, 243
'Der Sänger' 44, 461
'Sängers Ermutigung' ('Sänge sind des Lebens Bild', also 'Apotheose') 242
'Sankt Nepomuks Vorabend' ('Lichtlein schwimmen auf dem Strome') 274
'Schäfers Klagelied' 35, 41, 461
*Scherz, List und Rache* 176
'Schneidercourage' ('Es ist ein Schuß gefallen') 142, 143, 150
and Schubert 4–5
'Schweizerlied' 144
'Sehnsucht' ('Was zieht mir das Herz so'?) 44
'Sicilianlied' 144
'Soldatentrost' ('Nein! Hier hat es keine Not') 289
'Stirbt der Fuchs, so gilt der Balg' 95
'Das Sträußchen. Alt böhmisch' 295
*Tonlehre* 10–11, 13, 14, 357, 358, 364, 365, 366, 377, 381, 384, 385, 432–3, 436
'Totentanz' 216
'Trost in Tränen' 122
*Über die Nachteile der Stimmung* 9
*Über Kunst und Altertum* 194, 195, 210, 264, 296, 328, 355, 407, 426
'Um Mitternacht' 25, 240, 241, 242, 266
'Vanitas! Vanitatum vanitas!' 94, 95, 122
'Verschwiegenheit' 221

'Versus memorials' ('Invocavit') 157, 162
'Von Gott dem Vater stammt Natur' 354
*Die Wahlverwandtschaften* 159, 321
'Die wandelnde Glocke' 171
'Der Wanderer' 515, 518
'Wanderlied' 351, 353
'Die Weisen und die Leute' 178, 186, 276
'Weltseele' ('Herr Urian') 130, 346
'Wenn die Liebste zum Erwiedern' 221, 225
'Wer kauft Liebesgötter!' 40, 41, 195
'Wer nie sein Brot' 215
'Wiederfinden' 268, 466
*Wilhelm Meisters Lehrjahre* 44, 175, 215, 242, 436, 437, 523
'Worauf kommt es überall an' 282, 292
*Die Zauberflöte Zweiter Teil* 33, 35, 53, 169, 174
'Der Zauberlehrling' 30, 31, 40, 550
Zelter
    encounters, list of 555
    relationship 26–7
'Zu erfinden, zu beschließen' 230, 231
'Zum vierzehnten Mai 1824' 307, 316
Der Zwerg 46
'Zwischen Weizen und Korn' 142, 153
'Zwischengesang' 355, 356, 418
Goethe, Julius August von (1789–1830) 79, 240, 450, 464, 496–8
    death 498, 552
    travel diary 472, 498–9
Goethe, Ottilie von (1796–1872) 355, 475, 489, 496, 525
Goethe, Walther Wolfgang von (1818–1825) 240
Gotter, Friedrich Wilhelm (1746–1797)
    *Medea* 36
Graun, Carl Heinrich (1703/4–1759) 84
    *Die Auferstehung und Himmelfahrt Jesu* 138
    *Der Tod Jesu* 138, 181, 185, 206, 233, 235, 264, 279, 297, 309, 317, 326, 344, 463, 506, 508
    *Fetonte* 368
Greek Chorus, Goethe on 51

Grell, *August* Eduard (1800–1886) 172, 446, 473
Grétry, André Ernest Modeste (1741–1813) 529
Grillparzer, *Franz* Seraphicus (1791–1872) 263
Grünbaum, Therese (née Müller) (1791–1876) 141, 322
Grüner, Karl *Franz* (?1780–1845) 213

Haase, Johann Michael (d.1854) 444
Hackert, *Georg* Abraham (1755–1805) 261
Hackert, Jakob Phillipp (1837–1807) 261
*Hallische Allgemeine Literatur-Zeitung* 66
Handel, George Friedrich (1685–1759)
    *Alexanderfest* (*Alexander's Feast*) 99, 102, 228, 278, 287, 319, 369, 372, 411, 480, 488, 509
    *Judas Maccabeus* 394, 395, 457, 536, 538, 539
    *Messiah* 214, 222, 291, 297, 309, 312, 313, 316, 318, 373, 414, 417, 418, 419, 484, 491, 549
    *Samson* 414, 451
    *Te Deum* (HWV 283) 356, 489–90, 491
Hardenberg, Carl August von (1750–1822) 59, 231
Harmonichord 139, 140
Hartknoch, Karl Edward (1796–1834) 285
Hartmann, Tina, *Goethes Musiktheater* 6
Hasse, Faustina (née Bordoni) (1700–1781) 165
Hasse, Johann Adolph (1699–1793) 165, 395
    *Piramo e Tisbo* 499
    *Santa Elena al Calvario* 492, 495, 501
Hauser, Franz (1794–1870) 332
Haydn, Franz Joseph (1732–1809)
    *The Creation* 267, 344, 398, 465–7, 468, 514, 517, 541
    *The Seasons* (*Die Jahreszeiten*) 267, 398, 486, 487, 488, 494
Heaney, Seamus (b.1939) 3
Hegel, Georg Wilhelm Friedrich (1770–1831) 18, 283, 424
Heine, Heinrich (1797–1856) 18, 318
Heinefetter, Sabine (1809–1872) 475

Hellwig, Karl Friedrich *Ludwig* (1773–1838) 536
Henning, Karl Wilhelm (1784–1867) 320, 449
Hensel, Wilhelm (1794–1861) 300, 301–2, 441
Hentschel, Ernst Julius (1804–1875) 304
Herder, Johann Gottfried (1744–1803) 44, 45
  *Volkslieder* 46
Hérold, Louis Joseph Ferdinand (1791–1833), *Zampa oder die Marmorbraut* 543, 545
Herz, Henriette (1764–1847) 41, 528
Hessen-Darmstadt, Ludwig I von (1753–1830) 213, 244, 444
Heygendorff, Henriette *Caroline* (née Jagemann) (1777–1848) 81, 141
Hey'l, Bettina 2
Hientzsch, Johann Gottfried (1787–1856) 434
Himmel, Friedrich Heinrich (1765–1814) 107, 108, 137, 148, 149, 519
  *Die Sylphen* 89
Hirt, Aloys 241
Hoffmann, Ernst Theodor Amadeus (1776–1822) 271, 281
Hofmannsthal, Hugo von (1874–1927) 6
Holtbernd, Benedikt 6
Horace 73, 173, 341, 347, 380
Hufeland, Christoph Wilhelm (1762–1836) 64
Hufeland, Conradine Louise Wilhelmine (1776–1823) 35
Hufeland, Juliane Wilhelmine Friederike (née Amelung) (1771–1845) 64
Humboldt, Caroline Friederike von (née Dacheroeden) (1766–1829) 200
Humboldt, Friedrich *Wilhelm* von (1767–1835) 27, 127, 130, 352, 425, 538
Hummel, Johann Nepomuk (1778–1837) 5, 19, 279, 301, 345, 428, 494
  Concerto in E major 346
  Piano Concerto in A Major 399
  Rondo brillant (op. 98) 346
Huschka, Juliane (née Zelter) (1791–1862) 230

Iffland, August Wilhelm (1759–1814) 37, 48, 67
Institut für die Ausbildung von Organisten und Musiklehrern 26

Jacobi, Friedrich Heinrich (1743–1819) 76
Jagemann, *see* Heygendorff, Henriette *Caroline*
*Jenaische Allgemeine Literatur-Zeitung* 54, 55, 56, 58, 59, 66
John, Johann August Friedrich (1794–1854) 264, 454
Josephstödter Theater, Vienna 481
*Jüngere Liedertafel* 477–8, 480
Jungius, Joachim (1587–1657) 406, 409, 416

Kainz, *Marianne* Katharina Theresia (1800–1866) 284
Kanne, Friedrich August (1778–1833) 214
Kärnthnerthortheater 255, 256
Kaufmann, Johann *Friedrich* (1785–1866) 139
Kayser, Philipp Christoph (1755–1823) 176
Kerll, Kaspar (1627–1693) 315
Kestner, Georg *August* Christian (1777–1853) 495, 498
Kiesewetter, Johann Gottfried Karl Christian (1766–1819) 173, 174
Kirms, Franz (1750–1826) 69
Kirnberger, Johann Philipp (1721–1783) 253, 530
  *Die Kunst des reinen Satzes in der Musik* 9, 183
Kittel, Johann Christian (1732–1809) 205
Klein, *Bernhard* Joseph (1793–1832) 242, 281, 301, 319, 356, 411, 459, 477
  'Gott segne den König' 339
Klein, Elizabeth (Lili) (née Parthey) 301
Klingemann, Karl (1798–1862) 440
Klopstock, Friedrich Gottlieb (1724–1803), 'Die Auferstehung' 389
Knebel, Karl Ludwig von (1744–1834) 47, 236, 243
Königliche Bibliothek 387, 452, 468
Königliche Kapelle 291, 292, 298, 465, 516, 536, 550
Königliche Schauspiele 511

Königliches Institute für Kirchenmusik 525
Königliches Opernhaus 17, 130, 420
Königliches Orchester 458
Königliches Schauspielhaus 426, 485, 532, 544
Königliches Theater 415, 509
Königstädter Theater 326, 335, 481, 531
Königstädtisches Theater 320, 327, 449, 463, 516
Körner, Carl Theodor (1791–1813) 243, 510
  *Alfred der Große, König von England* 486, 487
Körner, Christian Gottfried (1796–1831) 293, 510
Kotzebue, August Friedrich Ferdinand von (1761–1819)
  *Die deutschen Kleinstädter* 321
  *Oktavia* 147

La Roche, Johann *Carl August* (1794–1884) 384
Lachner, Franz Paul (1803–1890), Serenade in G major for four cellos (op. 29) 540
Laffert, *Friedrich* von (1769–1841) 211
Langermann, Johann Gottfied (1768–1832) 156
Lauchery (1779–1853), Albert 56
Lauchstädt theatre 38, 50, 74
Lemm, Friedrich Wilhelm (1782–1837) 199, 203
Lessing, Gotthold Ephraim (1729–1781), *Emilia Galotti* 515
Levetzow, Theodore Ulrike Sophie von (1804–1899) 300, 302
Levin, Liepmann (1778–1832) (aka Ernst Friedrich Ludwig Robert, Robert-Tornow, Ludwig Robert) 68, 89
  *Die Tochter Jephthas* 155
Liebich, Johann Karl (1773–1816) 263
lied/lieder
  Eberwein's 266, 271
  Goethe on 12, 15–16, 29, 30, 129, 134, 135, 164, 170, 235, 363, 522
  Goethe's 535
  Nicolai's (*Otto*) 525
  Paer's 513

Reichardt's 62, 167, 397–8
Schubertian 3–5
Zelter on 24–5, 69, 109, 133, 138, 272, 350, 435
Zelter's 34, 36, 39, 40, 41, 42, 44, 50, 54, 62, 63–5, 72, 73, 95, 104, 150, 151, 174, 177, 194, 199, 207, 210, 215, 229, 237, 242, 263, 293, 295, 346, 369, 522
Lobe, Johann Elias Christian (1797–1881) 12, 273, 534
Loewe, Johann *Carl* Gottfried (1796–1869) 305, 328, 549
Lolli, Antonio (*c*.1730–1802) 515
Lortzing, Johann *Friedrich* (1782–1841) 280
Lotti, Antonio (1666–1740)
  *Crucifixus* 444
Ludwig, Johann Walter (1496–1570) 314
Ludwig, Robert, *Die Tochter Jephthas* 155

major triad 11, 110, 505; *see also* minor triad
major–minor tonalities debate 11, 110–12, 113–14, 432–3; *see also* major triad; minor triad
Mandelstam, Osip (1891–1938) 28
Mantius, Jakob Edward (1806–1874) 457, 546
Mara, Gertrud Elizabeth (née Schmeling) (1794–1833) 43, 46, 47, 48, 50, 54, 87–8, 214, 220, 292, 312, 349, 492, 493, 494, 495, 499–500, 508
Marinelli (Casperl) Theatre 254, 256
Marpurg, Friedrich Wilhelm (1718–1795) 248, 253
  *Abhandlung von der Fuge* 9, 530
Marschner, *Heinrich* August (1795–1861)
  *Der Templer und die Jüdin* 545
  *The Vampyr* 509
Marx, Adolph Bernhard (?1795–1866) 21, 343, 348, 402, 421
  *Berliner Allgemeine Musikalische Zeitung* (editor 1824–1830) 339, 343
  *Die Kunst des Gesanges, theoretisch-praktisch* 476

Mattheson, Johann (1681–1764)
  *Der vollkommene Capellmeister* 9, 248, 250, 318
Matthisson, Friedrich von (1761–1831) 105, 346
Mauer, August Wilhelm 231
May, Johann *Christoph* (1757–1828) 274
Mayr, Johann *Simon* (Giovanni Simone) (1763–1845)
  *Elena* 238, 239, 262
  *Ginevra* 150
Mecklenburg-Strelitz, *Carl* Friedrich August (1785–1837) 197, 199, 268, 270, 548
Mecklenburg-Strelitz, *Georg* Friedrich Karl Joseph (1779–1860) 200, 289, 548
Mecklenburg-Strelitz, *Marie Wilhelmine* Friederike von (1796–1880) 289
Meisl, Carl
  *Die Damenhüte im Theater* 254
  *Das Donnerwetter* 254
  *Der lustige Fritz. Ein Märchen aus neuer Zeit* 254
Mendelssohn, Abraham Ernst (1776–1835) 21, 55, 202, 204, 230, 288, 318, 328, 329, 332, 340, 422, 461, 464, 503, 519, 543, 548
Mendelssohn, Fanny (1805–1847) 24, 202, 441
  'Begräbnislied' 350
Mendelssohn, Felix (1809–1847) 297, 329, 382, 440, 461, 469–72, 480
  *Die beiden Neffen* (*Der Onkel aus Boston*) 20, 305
  *Die beiden Pädagogen* 283
  Concerto in A major for two pianos and orchestra 324
  Concerto in A minor for piano and string orchestra 290
  Dürer Cantata 402
  Gloria in E flat 290
  *Die Hochzeit des Camacho* 335, 368, 373
  *Das Mädchen aus Andros* 338, 364
  *Magnificat* in D minor 290
  *A Midsummer Night's Dream* (op. 21), overture 367, 422
  Octet in E flat major (op. 20) 20, 338
  Piano Quartet in B minor (op. 3) 22, 328
  Sextet in D for piano and strings (op. 110) 20
  *Soldatenliebschaft* 283
  String Quintet no. 1 in A major (op. 18) 349, 541
  Symphony no. 1 in C minor (op. 11) 422
  *Die wandernden Komödianten* 283, 290
Mendelssohn, Felizia Pauline *Lea* (née Salomon) (1777/78–1842) 5, 16–17, 19
Mendelssohn, Maria *Henriette* (1775–1831) 533
metronome (chronomètre) 18, 435, 510
Metternich, Klemens Wenzel, Prince von (1773–1859) 5, 286
Meyer, Ernst 9
Meyer, Johanna *Henriette* (née Schüler) (1772–1849) 48, 55
Meyerbeer, Giacomo (1791–1864)
  *Romilda e Costanza* 240
Mickiewicz, *Adam* Bernard (1798–1855) 438, 441
Milder-Hauptmann, (Pauline) Anna (1785–1838) 18, 158, 322, 418, 423, 465, 479, 484, 509, 510, 538
Milton, John
  *Paradise Lost* 397
  *Samson Agonistes* 451, 453
minor triad 107, 503
  Zelter on 110–11, 115–16, 504–5
  *see also* major triad
Mizler, Lorenz Christoph von Kolof (1711–1778) 408
Moeser, *Carl* Heinrich Ludwig Joachim Wilhelm (1774–1851) 19, 286, 336, 445, 448–9, 454, 506, 543
Moltke, Carl Melchior Jakob (1783–1831) 175, 211–12, 244
Morales, Cristóbal de (c.1500–1553) 15
Mortimer, Peter (1750–1828) 293–4
Moscheles, Ignaz (Isaac) (1794–1870) 19, 21, 322, 422

Mozart, Anna Maria Walpurga (née Pertl) (1720–1778) 425
Mozart, Johann Georg *Leopold* (1719–1787) 425
Mozart, Maria Anna ('Nannerl') (1749–1829) 425
Mozart, Wolfgang Amadeus (1756–1791)
  *Don Giovanni* (*Don Juan*) 302, 322, 352, 469, 479
  *Die Hochzeit des Figaro* 391, 463, 469
  *La Clemenza di Tito* 255, 284
  *Misericordias Domini. Offertorium de tempore* 222
  *Requiem* 18, 185, 187, 458, 543
    composition 378–80
  *Die Zauberflöte* 158, 352, 381, 392
Müller, August Eberhard (1767–1817) 52, 146, 236
Müller, Franz Ferdinand *Georg* (1808–1855) 426
Müller, Johannes von (1752–1809) 64, 94
Müller, Karl Friedrich (1797–1873) 427
Müller, Minna (née Gerson) (c.1804–1847) 426
Müller, Robert (c.1804–1855) 494, 501, 504
Müller, Wenzel (1767–1835) 141, 322
Müller, Wilhelm Christian (1752–1831) 506
Münchhofen, Adolf Lauer von (1795/96–1874), *Der Orakelspruch* 537

Nägeli, Hans Georg (1773–1836) 506
Naue, Johann Friedrich (1787–1858) 304, 439, 442
Naumann, Johann Gottlieb (1741–1801) 221, 391, 519
  'Die Ideale' 435, 482
  *I pellegrini al sepolcro di N.S. Gesù Christo* 325
Neureuther, *Eugen* Napoleon (1806–1849), lithographs 413, 461
Nicolai, Christoph *Friedrich* (1733–1811) 165, 482, 525
Nicolai, Karl *Otto* Ehrenfried (1810–1849) 525, 527
Niemeyer, August Hermann (1754–1828) 223

Nissen, Georg Nikolaus (1761–1826)
  *Biographie W.A. Mozarts nach Originalbriefen* 425

Oehlenschläger, Adam Gottlob (1799–1850) 120
  *Axel und Walburg* 234
Ordentliche Singschule 26
Ottenberg, Hans-Günter 2
Ottmer, Carl Theodor (1800–1843) 327, 334

Pachelbel, Johann (1653–1706) 306, 309, 314, 315
Paer, Ferdinando
  *Achilles* 143, 157
  *Der lustige Schuster oder die verwandelten Weiber* 141
  *Sargines oder der Triumph der Liebe* (*Sargines oder Der Zögling der Liebe*) 141, 322, 386, 513
Paginini, Niccolò (1782–1840) 429–30, 434, 436, 445, 446–7
  violin technique 431
Palestrina, Giovanni Pierluigi da (1525/26–1594) 408
Pavlovich, Alexander I of Russia, Aleksandr (1777–1825) 246
Perti, Giacomo Antonio (1661–1756)
  *Adoramus te Christe* 173
Pindar (Pindaros) 535, 536, 538
Pleyel, *Ignaz* Joseph (1757–1831) 385
Plotinus
  *Platoni, Platonicorum coryphaei, opera quae extant omnia* 79
  *Ennead* 79
Plutarch 451, 527
Pogwisch, *Ulrike* Henriette Adele Eleonore von (1798–1875) 288, 364, 397, 438, 444, 469
Poißl, Johann *Nepomuk* von (1783–1865)
  *Athalia* 232, 233
  *Die Prinzessin von Provence* 387
Poißl, *Maria* Walpurga von (1778–1826) 387
Pollet, Marie Nicole (née Simonin) (1787–1864) 152
Praun (Braun), *Sigismund* Otto von (1811–1830) 431

Printz, Wolfgang Caspar (1641–1717) 315
Prussia, *Elizabeth* Ludovike of (1801–1873) 316
Prussia, Frederick II of, 'the Great' (1712–1786) 34, 166, 187, 312, 313, 316, 543
Prussia, Friedrich Heinrich Ludwig of (1726–1802) 312
Prussia, Friedrich Wilhelm III of (1770–1840) 473, 516
Prussia, Friedrich Wilhelm IV of (1795–1861) 316, 366, 548
Prussia, *Maria* Luise Alexandrine of (1808–1877) 382, 458
Prussia, Maria Luise *Augusta* of (1811–1890) 458
Pulver, Jeffrey 2–3
Pythagoras 163

Radziwill, Antoni Heinrich (1775–1833), *Faust* 135, 197, 267–8, 272, 484, 502, 548, 550
Radziwill, Friederike Dorothea *Luise* Philippine (1770–1836) 199, 289
Radziwill, Friedrich Wilhelm Ferdinand August Heinrich Anton *Wladislaus* (1811–31) 199, 520
Rainer, *Rudolph* Johann Joseph (1788–1831) 262
Rameau, Jean-Philippe (1683–1764), *Samson* 154, 155
Ramler, Carl Wilhelm (1725–1798) 298, 508, 509
Raphael (1483–1520) 265, 273
Recke, Charlotte Elizabeth (Elisa), von der (née von Medem) (1756–1833) 106, 200
  'Wiegenlied für Mutter Naumann' 519
Redern, *Wilhelm* Friedrich von (1802–1883) 17, 461, 462, 511
Reichardt, Gustav (1797–1884),
  'Bundeslied' 478
Reichardt, Johann Friedrich (1752–1814)
  *Berlinische Musikalische Zeitung* 74
  'Clärchens Lied' ('Freudvoll und Leidvoll') 69, 70
  'Heidenröslein' 95, 461
  'Miltons Morgengesang' 283, 397

'Schneidercourage' ('Es ist ein Schuß gefallen' and 'Der junge Jäger') 142, 143, 150
'Der Taucher' 147
*Der Tod des Herkules* 36
  reception 37
'Der untreue Knabe' 95, 461
'Das Veilchen' 95
Rellstab, Heinrich Friedrich *Ludwig* (1799–1860) 280, 281, 319, 396, 411, 459, 487, 549
Rellstab, Johann Carl *Friedrich* (1759–1813) 280
Riemer, Friedrich Wilhelm (1774–1845) 1, 108, 142, 143, 151, 186, 490
Ries, Ferdinand (1784–1838) 538
  *Die Räuberbraut* 493
Ries, Hubert (1802–1886) 538, 545
Riese, Friedrich (d.1859) 539
Rietz, *Eduard* Theodor Ludwig (1802–1832) 423, 536, 541–2, 543
Righini, Vincenzo (1756–1812) 137, 158, 159
Ripienschule (Ripieno school) 27, 98, 115, 324
Robinson, Henry Crabb (1755–1867) 441, 452
Rochlitz, Johann *Friedrich* (1769–1842) 285, 306, 479
  *Für Freunde der Tonkunst* 414, 491, 492
Rosenmüller, Johann (c.1619–1684) 315
Rossini, Gioacchino Antonio (1792–1868) 462–3
  *Die Belagerung von Corinth* (*The Siege of Corinth*) 400, 455, 469
  *Das Fräulein am See* (*La donna del lago*) 531
  *Il barbiere di Siviglia* (*Der Barbier von Sevilla*) 284, 322, 323, 469
  *La Gazza Ladra* 254
  *Othello* 254, 463, 464, 469, 475
  *Semiramis/Semiramide* 469, 479
  *Tancredi* 235, 244, 323, 325, 400
  *William Tell* (*Guillaume Tell/Andreas Hofer*) 478, 479–80, 485
Zelter on 261

Rousseau, Jean-Jacques (1712–1778)
musical tastes 212
Royal Academy of Religious Music, Berlin 26
Rungenhagen, Carl Friedrich (1778–1851) 405, 411, 415, 490
Rupsch, Conrad (1475–1530) 314
Russia, Alexander I Pawlowitsch of (1777–1825) 245
Russia, Alexandra Fjodorowna of (1798–1860) 434

Sachsen-Weimar-Eisenach, Anna Amalie von (1739–1807) 59, 95, 96, 435, 502
Sachsen-Weimar-Eisenach, Maria Pawlowna von (1786–1859) 107, 245, 397
Salieri, Antonio (1750–1825) 158–9, 255, 458
*Missa capella* 259
Salieri, Therese, (née von Helfersdorfer) (1755–1807) 259
Salis-Seewis, Johann Gaudenz von (1762–1834) 105
Santini, Fortunato (1778–1861) 488
Sartori, Anton (1767–1821)
*Die Werber oder Die belohnt Treue* 254
Saxony, Friedrich August I, King of (1750–1827) 175, 415
Saxony, Marie *Amalie* Auguste, Queen of (1752–1828) 175
Scarlatti, Alessandro (1660–1725) 315
Schadow, Johann Gottfried (1764–1850) 197, 230, 241, 400
Schäfer, Sabine 2
Schale, Christian Friedrich (1713–1800) 505
Schätzel, Pauline von (1811–1882) 423, 455, 457, 486
Schechner, Nanette (1806–1860) 511
Scheidt, Samuel (1587–1654) 315
Schein, Johann Hermann (1586–1630) 315
Schick, Friedrich (1794–c.1858) 276
Schick, *Margarete* Luise (née Hamel) (1768/73–1809) 276
Schiller, Johann Christoph Friedrich (1759–1805)

'Der Alpenjäger' 61
'An die Freude' ('Liebe Freunde, es gab bess're Zeiten') 105, 138
'Berglied' 60, 62
'Die Braut von Messina' 48–9, 52
'Dithyrambe' ('Niemals erscheinen die Götter allein') 105
*Don Carlos* 160
'Die Gunst des Augenblicks' 72, 73, 129
'Hero und Leander' 44
'Die Ideale' 435
'Kabale und Liebe' 481
'Der Kampf mit dem Drachen' 36, 44
'Das Lied von der Glocke' ('Glocke') 26, 73, 77, 78, 80, 81, 82, 83, 85
*Macbeth* (translation) 130, 371
*Musenalmanach* (also *Almanach* and *Musen-Almanach*) 29, 30, 31, 36, 40, 194, 435, 436
'Die Piccolomini' 31, 482
'Punschlied. Im Norden zu singen' ('Auf der Berge freien Höhen') 37, 104, 129, 195
'Punschlied' ('Vier Elemente, innig gesellt') 37, 104, 129, 195
*Die Räuber* 481
'Reiterlied' 43, 46, 71
'Die Sänger der Vorwelt' 44
*Tafellieder* 37
'Der Taucher' 36, 435, 483
'Die Verschwörung des Fiesco zu Genua' 482
'Die vier Weltalter' 36
*Wallensteins Lager* 81, 482
*Wallensteins Tod* 482
*Wilhelm Tell* 58, 527
'Die Worte des Glaubens' 44
Schinkel, Karl Friedrich (1781–1841) 231, 232, 278, 280, 283
Schlegel, August Wilhelm 343
*Gesang und Kuss* 32
Schleiermacher, *Friedrich* Daniel Ernst (1755–1844) 18, 460
Schmidt, Johann Philipp Samuel (1779–1853) 91, 92, 460, 487
Schneider, Caroline (née Portmann) (1774/75–1850) 128

Schneider, Georg Abraham (1770–1839) 128, 401, 420, 449, 550
Schneider, Georg *Laurenz* (1766–1855) 389
Schöpke, Adalbert (1793–1844) 237, 238
Schröder, Antoine Luise Sophie (née Bürger) (1781–1868) 345
Schröder-Devrient, Wilhelmine 18, 493–4
Schubart, Christian Friedrich Daniel 483
Schubert, Franz (1797–1828)
  *Erlkönig* 16
  and Goethe 4–5
  *Gretchen am Spinnrade* 25
  *Lieder* (op. 19) 5
  *Wandrers Nachtlied* 25, 169, 175
Schultz, Christoph Ludwig Friedrich (1781–1834) 178, 184, 209, 234, 241
Schulz, Johann Abraham Peter (1747–1800) 36, 350
Schulze, Josephine (née Kilitzschky) (c.1790–1880) 325
Schütz, Heinrich (1585–1672) 315
Schütz, Henriette (née Schüler) (1772–1849) 147
Schütz, Johann *Heinrich Friedrich* (1779–1829) 12, 13, 205, 248, 252, 375
Schwendler, Friedrich Christian August von (c.1772–1844) 403, 542
Schwendler, *Henriette* August Sophie (née Mützschefahl) (1773–1853) 403
Seckendorff-Gudent Veit, Bernhard *Emil* von (1804–1890) 474
Seidel, Friedrich Ludwig (1765–1831) 449
Seidler, Caroline née Wranitzsky (1790/94–1872) 219
Senfl, Ludwig (1486–1542/3) 314
Sessi, Maria *Theresia* 234, 284
Shakespeare, William (1564–1616)
  *Macbeth* 130
  *Othello* 551
Sibbern, Frederik Christian (1785–1872) 151, 152, 167
Siboni, Giuseppe (1785–1839) 157
Silbermann, Andreas (1678–1734) 216, 218
Silbermann, Johann Andreas (1712–1783) 216
Simonin-Pollet, Marie Nicole 152

*Sing Collegium* 535, 539, 540, 551, 553
Sing-Akademie 18, 26–7, 34, 39, 40, 57, 58, 77, 84, 86, 91, 98, 99
Sistine Chapel 164, 488, 519
Socrates 537
song/songs, *see* lied/lieder
sonnet, Zelter on 31–2
Sontag, Gertrud Walpurgis *Henriette* (1806–1854) 18, 352, 353, 355, 358, 391, 392, 393, 463, 464, 465, 469, 481
Sophocles 36, 51
*Spenersche Zeitung* 322, 340
Spitzeder, Elizabeth (*Betty*) (née Vio) (1806/8–1872) 481
Spitzeder, Henriette (née Schüler) (1800–1828) 320
Spitzeder, Joseph (1795/96–1832) 320, 384
Spohr, Ludewig (Louis) (1784–1859)
  Double Quartet in D minor (op. 65) 540
  *Faust* 18, 448
  *Macbeth* 341
Spontini, Gaspare Luigi Pacifico (1774–1851)
  *Agnes von Hohenstaufen* 374, 420, 455
  *Alcidor* 330, 333, 335
  *Ferdinand Cortez* 145, 244, 274, 322
  'Lalla Rookh' 291
  *Les Athéniennes* 503, 537, 538, 539
  *Olympia* 270, 271, 283, 322, 401, 458
  *Die Vestalin* (*La Vestale*) 145, 270, 322, 388, 489
Stein zum Altstein, Carl von (1770–1840) 293, 460
Sterling, Charles (1804–1880) 496
Stieler, *Joseph* Karl (1791–1858) 472
Struve, *Carl* Ludwig (1785–1838) 343
Stümer, Anna Christina Henriette (née Weltz) 398
Stümer, Johann Daniel *Heinrich* (1789–1856) 398, 418, 423, 424
Süßmeyer, Franz Xaver 378, 379, 380
Sulzer, Johann Georg (1720–1779) 467
  *Allgemeiner Theorie der schönen Kunste*

Szymanowska, *Maria* Agata (née Wolowska) (1789–1831) 301, 304–5, 438, 439

Tartini, Giuseppe (1692–1770) 515
Taubert, Karl Gottfried Wilhelm (1811–1891), *Die Kirmes* 543
*Telemachus* 203
Telemann, Georg Philipp (1681–1767) 108, 315, 509
Teplitz 10, 137, 138, 139, 140, 142, 143, 148, 156, 167, 170, 171, 172, 181, 255, 276, 278, 411, 555
Teschner, Gustav Wilhelm (1800–1883) 512
*Teutschen Merkur* 474
Thaer, *Albrecht* Daniel (1752–1828) 307, 308, 318
Theater an der Wien 254, 256
Theile, Johann (1646–1724) 315
Thibaut, Anton Friedrich Justus (1772–1840) 195, 244
Thomson, John (1805–1841) 397–8, 441, 487
Tiedge, Christoph August (1752–1842) 105
'Hymnus an die Sonne' ('In flammen nähet Gott') 106, 134, 517
Tilly, Karoline *Auguste* (1800–1828) 224, 226, 228
Todd, Larry
*Mendelssohn's Musical Education* 20
Tralles, Johann Georg (1763–1822) 64
Türk, Daniel Gottlob (1750–1813) 223, 304, 365
Türrschmidt, Auguste (née Braun) (1800–1866) 423, 438, 457, 538

Unger, Friederike Helene (née Gothenburg) (1754?–1813) 12, 29
Unger, Johann Friedrich Gottlieb (1753–1804) 30, 33
Unzelmann, Wilhelmine (1802–1871) 69, 140–41

Valle, Pietro della (Il Pellegrino) (1586–1652) 407

Varnhagen von Ense, Antoine Friederike (Rahel) (née Rahel Levin) (1771–1833) 18, 68, 396
*Veni Creator Spiritus* 264, 271, 276, 277
Vetter, Daniel (1657/58–1721) 315
Viganó, Maria (?1756–1833) 546
Vivaldi, Antonio
Concerto in D minor for two violins and orchestra 428
*The Four Seasons* 488
Voß, Johann Heinrich (1779–1822) 73, 112
'Begräbnislied' (poem) 350
*Trommellied* 132, 134, 136, 138
Vogler, (Georg Joseph) Abbé (1749–1814) 176, 217
Voltaire (François Marie Arouet) (1694–1778)
*Samson* 154, 155
*Vossische Zeitung* 90, 118, 139, 147, 157, 158, 166, 181
Vulpius, Christian *August* (1762–1827) 255

Waldura, Markus 6
Weber, Bernhard Anselm 177, 180, 194, 197, 207, 270
Weber, Carl Maria von (1796–1826)
*Der Freischütz* 18, 283, 342
*Euryanthe* 319, 342, 389
'Lützows wilde Jagd' 243
*Oberon, Königin der Elfen* 400, 401, 405, 486
Weber, Friedrich *Dionys* (1766–1842) 506
Weber, Jacob *Gottfried* (1779–1839) 506
Weigl, Joseph (1766–1846)
*Die Schweizerfamilie* 141, 155, 158, 191, 194, 256, 322, 534
Weil, Simone, *Gravity and Grace* 3
Weitsch, *Friedrich* Georg (1758–1828) 265, 404
Wendt, Amadeus (1783–1836) 120, 216
Werneburg, Johann Friedrich Christian (1777–1851) 163, 165, 166
Werner, Zacharias (1768–1823) 181
Wessely, Carl Berhard (1768–1826)
Wieck, Johann Gottlob *Friedrich* (1785–1873) 528
Wieck, Josephine *Clara* (1819–1896) 528, 529

Wieland, Christoph *Martin* (1733–1813)
   *Oberon* 405
Wild, Franz (1792–1860) 219, 232
Winter, Peter von (1754–1825) 152, 430
   *Das Labyrinth, oder Der Kampf mit den Elementen* 53
   *Das unterbrochene Opferfest* 391, 392
   *Zaïra* 219
Wolf, Christian Wilhelm *Friedrich August* (1759–1824) 61, 74, 76, 79, 98, 129, 139, 140, 277
*Prolegomena ad Homerum* 241, 299, 317
Wolff, Anna *Amalie* (1780/3–1851) 147, 148, 179, 201, 205, 318, 427
Wolff, Pius Alexander (1782–1828) 56, 199, 201, 205, 213, 268, 270, 300, 318, 412, 547
Woltmann, Carl Ludwig (1770–1817) 64
Wolzogen, Baron Wilhelm Ernst Friedrich Franz August von (1762–1809) 47, 50, 52, 84
Wranitzky-Seidler, Caroline 322

Yeats, William Butler (1865–1939) 26

Zehm, Edith 2
*Zeitung für die elegante Welt* 466
Zelter, Adolph Raphael (1799–1816) 87, 90, 198, 370
Zelter, Carl Friedrich (1758–1832)
   'Alle Menschen gross und klein' 269
   'An die Freude' ('Liebe Freunde, es gab beßre Zeiten') 105, 138
   'Aus wie vielen Elementen 292
   on Beethoven 259, 261–2
   'Berglied' 60, 62, 195
   'Blumengruß' 336
   'Das Blümlein Wunderschön' 30, 32
   'Die Braut von Corinth' 30, 32, 343
   'Bundeslied' ('In allen guten Stunden') 30, 33, 138
   'Die Campanelle' 475, 509
   character, contradictions 16–17
   'Derb und Tüchtig' 282
   'Dithyrambe' ('Niemals erscheinen die Götter allein') 105
   'Dreistigkeit' 292
   'Eigentum' ('Ich weiß, daß mir nichts angehört') 169, 170
   'Elemente' 268, 412
   'Der Entfernte' ('Im Fernen') 229
   *Ephiphaniasfest* (*Ephiphanias*) 157, 231, 289, 350
   'Die Erinnerung' 30, 31, 45
   'Erschaffen und Beleben' 268
   'Frisch! der Wein soll reichlich fließen' 132, 134, 135
   *Der Fromme geht dahin* 85, 87
   'Frühlingsmusikanten' ('Es wollt einmal in Königreich') 319
   'Frühzeitiger Frühling' 35, 41
   'Das Gastmahl' 172
   'Die Geheimnisse' 150
   'Generalbeichte' ('Lasset heut im edeln Kreis') 102, 134, 138, 477
   'Genialisch Treiben' ('So wälz ich Unterlaß') ('Diogenes') 142
   'Georgs Lied' 65, 66, 67
   'Gleich und Gleich' 262
   *Gloria Für den Künstlerverein Saul und David am H. drei K. Feste 1817* 249
   Goethe
      encounters, list 555
      relationship 26–7
   'Der Gott und die Bajadere' 194, 293, 369
   'Die Gunst des Augenblicks' 134, 143
   'Die heiligen drei Könige' 157, 289
   'Das Herbstlied' 32
   'Hero und Leander' 44
   'Herr Urian', *see* 'Weltseele'
   'Hymnus an die Sonne' ('In flammen nähet Gott') 106, 134, 517
   'Ich denke Dein' 29, 109
   'In Flammen nähet Gott' 134
   'In tausend Formen magst du dich verstecken' 269
   on individualism 18–19
   'Invocavit' ('Versus memorials') 156, 157, 162
   'Johanna Sebus' 1, 9, 129, 131, 133, 135, 143, 146, 170, 266
   'Der Junggesell und der Mühlbach' 30, 32

'Der Kampf mit dem Drachen' 36, 43, 44
*Kirchenmusik zum Reformationsfeste für 4 Stimmen mit Orgel und Bleichinstrumenten* 232
'Klaggesang. Irisch' ('So singet laut den Pillalu') 249, 250, 251, 252, 381
'Der König in Thule' 293
'Kriegsglück' ('Verünschter weiß ich nichts im Krieg') 356, 358
'Laßt fahren hin das allzu Flüchtige!' 337, 418
on lied/lieder 24–5, 69, 109, 133, 138, 272, 350, 397, 435
'Die Lustigen von Weimar' 168, 172
'Lustrum ist ein fremdes Wort' 236, 237, 243
'Mädchens Held' ('Flieh, Täubchen flieh') 229
'Mailied' ('Wie herrlich leutet') 153
'Männerkreis' ('Mauerlied') ('Wenn die Liebste zum Erwiedern') 221, 225, 226
'Der Mensch lebt und besteht' 74, 75, 76, 454
on the minor triad 110–11, 115–16, 504–5
'Der Müllerin Reue' 40, 41, 130
musical achievements 26–7
'Der neue Amadis' 41, 42
'Neue Liebe, Neues Leben' 153
'Nur wer die Sehnsucht kennt' 245
'O Roma nobilis' 394
'Punschlied. Im Norden zu singen' ('Auf der Berge freien Höhlen') 37, 104
'Punschlied' ('Vier Elemente, innig gesellt') 104
'Rastlose Liebe' 25, 153
'Rechenschaft' (aka 'Ächzlied' & 'Pflicht und Frohsinn') 132, 134
Reformation Cantata 188, 226
*Reisebriefe aus Wien* 264
'Reiterlied' 43, 46
*Requiem* 74, 75, 76, 186, 265
*Ripienschule* (*Ripieno* school), foundation 27, 324
on Rossini 261
'Sagt es niemand, nur den Weisen' 268
'Der Sänger' 44, 461
'Die Sänger der Vorwelt' 44
'Sängers Ermutigung' ('Sänge sind des Lebens Bild') (aka 'Apotheose') 242, 243
'Sankt Nepomuks Vorabend' ('Lichtlein schwimmen auf dem Strome') 269, 274
'Schäfers Klagelied' 35, 41, 461
'Der Schneider' ('Es ist ein Schuß gefallen') 143
'Schneidercourage' ('Es ist ein Schuß gefallen') 142, 143, 150
'Der Schütze sang mit Freuden' 442
'Sehnsucht' ('Was zieht mir das Herz so'?) 44
'Selige Sehnsucht' 268
'So lang man nüchter[n] ist' 268
'So wälz' Ich Unterlaß' 142
'Soldatentrost' ('Nein! Hier hat es keine Not...') 289
on the sonnet 31–2
*Stabat Mater* 100, 105
'Das Sträußchen. Alt böhmisch'. 295
'Suleika' ('Ach! Um deine feuchten Schwingen') 263, 268
*Te Deum* 57
*Thekla* 31
'Der Totentanz' 174, 216, 461
travel diaries 491
'Um Mitternacht' 25, 242, 266
'Das Vaterland' 134
'Die wandelnde Glocke' 171
'Wanderers Nachtlied' ('Über allen Gipfeln ist Ruh') 25, 169, 175, 266, 522
'Weltseele' ('Herr Urian') 130, 134, 138, 346, 347
'Wer kauft Liebesgötter!' 40, 41
'Wer nie sein Brot' 215
'Wiederfinden' 268, 466
'Wiegenlied für Mutter Naumann' 519
'Willkommensgedicht'
'Worauf kommt es überall an' 292
'Der Zauberlehrling' 30, 31, 40
'Die Zauberlehrling' 343, 550

'Zu erfinden, zu beschließen' ('Dem edlen Künstler-Verein zu Berlin') 230, 231
'Der Zwerg' 46
'Zwischengesang' 355, 356, 418
Zelter, Clara Antigone (1800–1816) 218
Zelter, Dorothea (Doris) Auguste Cäcilie (1792–1852) 288, 300

Zelter, Georg (1723–1787) 159, 482
Zelter, Georg Friedrich (1789–1827) 90, 230, 370
Zelter, Juliane Karoline Auguste (1767–1806) 99, 300
Zinkgref, Julius Wilhelm (1591–1635) 45

For Product Safety Concerns and Information please contact our EU
representative  GPSR@taylorandfrancis.com
Taylor & Francis Verlag GmbH, Kaufingerstraße 24, 80331 München, Germany

www.ingramcontent.com/pod-product-compliance
Lightning Source LLC
Chambersburg PA
CBHW071358230426
43669CB00010B/1387